Microsoft® Windows® 8

Faithe Wempen
Lisa A. Bucki

Managing Editor: Christine Hurney
Developmental Editors: Brenda Owens, Spencer Cotkin
Production Editor: Lori Michelle Ryan
Cover Designer: Leslie Anderson
Design and Production Specialist: Julie Johnston
Copy Editor: Lianna Wlasiuk
Indexer: Ina Gravitz

Care has been taken to verify the accuracy of information presented in this book. However, the authors, editors, and publisher cannot accept responsibility for Web, e-mail, newsgroup, or chat room subject matter or content, or for consequences from application of the information in this book, and make no warranty, expressed or implied, with respect to its content.

Trademarks: Some of the product names and company names included in this book have been used for identification purposes only and may be trademarks or registered trade names of their respective manufacturers and sellers. The authors, editors, and publisher disclaim any affiliation, association, or connection with, or sponsorship or endorsement by, such owners.

We have made every effort to trace the ownership of all copyrighted material and to secure permission from copyright holders. In the event of any question arising as to the use of any material, we will be pleased to make the necessary corrections in future printings. Thanks are due to the aforementioned authors, publishers, and agents for permission to use the materials indicated.

ISBN 978-0-76384-797-5

Brief Contents

Contents

Preface

Windows 8 will help students learn how to operate a computer equipped with the powerful new Windows® 8 operating system. This text presents the essential conceptual information and procedures for students who want to learn how to manage files, secure and customize a computer, and more. Students can use the book without prior knowledge of computer operating systems and become proficient computer users. After successfully completing a course using this textbook, students will be able to:

- Start the system, and sign in and out
- Manage disks, folders, and files
- Use the new Start screen
- Run applications, including the new Windows 8 apps
- Add and remove hardware and software
- Customize the desktop and Start screen
- Browse the Web and use email
- Work with several media features
- Work with networking features
- Perform basic security and maintenance tasks

Microsoft® created several editions of the Windows 8 operating system. *Windows 8* covers the Windows 8 Pro edition, which offers the broadest feature set of all the editions. Users of any of the other Windows 8 editions can still work with this book, but their edition may not include all of the features covered.

Chapter Features: A Visual Walk-Through

Windows 8 was designed from the ground up to help novice students minimize frustration and maximize successful learning. The book presents concepts and skills in student-friendly language and provides clear steps for using the features of this new operating system from Microsoft.

Page Elements

Chapter pages are designed and formatted with special elements to make it easy for students to find specific types of information. These elements are highlighted below.

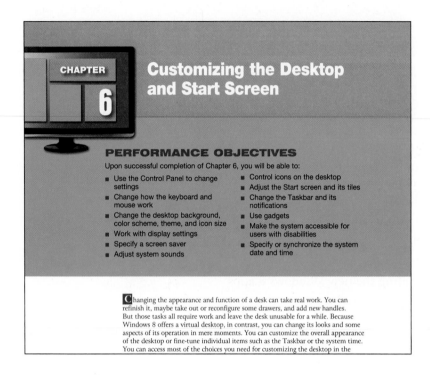

CHAPTER 6

Customizing the Desktop and Start Screen

PERFORMANCE OBJECTIVES

Upon successful completion of Chapter 6, you will be able to:

- Use the Control Panel to change settings
- Change how the keyboard and mouse work
- Change the desktop background, color scheme, theme, and icon size
- Work with display settings
- Specify a screen saver
- Adjust system sounds
- Control icons on the desktop
- Adjust the Start screen and its tiles
- Change the Taskbar and its notifications
- Use gadgets
- Make the system accessible for users with disabilities
- Specify or synchronize the system date and time

Changing the appearance and function of a desk can take real work. You can refinish it, maybe take out or reconfigure some drawers, and add new handles. But those tasks all require work and leave the desk unusable for a while. Because Windows 8 offers a virtual desktop, in contrast, you can change its looks and some aspects of its operation in mere moments. You can customize the overall appearance of the desktop or fine-tune individual items such as the Taskbar or the system time. You can access most of the choices you need for customizing the desktop in the

CHAPTER OPENERS present Performance Objectives that students should aim to achieve.

EXERCISES provide the opportunity for hands-on practice and instructor evaluation.

Exercise 3

Customizing the Desktop and Start Screen

1. Go to the desktop. Right-click the desktop, point to *View*, and then click *Show desktop icons*. Windows 8 hides the icons on the desktop.
2. Right-click the desktop, point to *View*, and then click *Show desktop icons* to redisplay the icons.
3. Drag the Recycle Bin icon to the right side of the desktop.
4. Right-click the desktop, point to *View*, and then click *Large icons*.
5. Capture a screen shot, and then save the file as **C06E03S05**.
6. Right-click the desktop, point to *View*, and then click *Medium icons*.
7. Right-click the desktop, point to *View*, and then click *Auto arrange icons*. The Recycle Bin should snap back to its default position.
8. Right-click the desktop, point to *View*, and then click *Auto arrange icons* to turn that feature off.
9. Select the Search charm.
10. Right-click Math Input Panel under *Windows Accessories* and then click *Pin to Start*.
11. Select the Start charm or press the Windows logo key ⊞ to display the Start screen.
12. Right-click the Calendar app tile.
13. With the tile commands on the screen, capture a screen shot, and then save the file as **C06E03S13**.
14. Right-click the Calendar tile again.
15. Right-click the Math Input Panel tile and then click *Unpin from Start*.
16. Submit your screen shots to your instructor.

refresh rate The rate at which the display redraws the image on the screen

resolution The dimensions of the current display size setting, expressed in pixels (dots) wide by pixels tall

DEFINITIONS call out key terms in the text.

To change window color and appearance in the Control Panel:

Here's How

1. Right-click the desktop and then click *Personalize*.
2. Click *Color* at the bottom of the window.
3. Click a color at the top of the Color and Appearance window.
4. Drag the *Color intensity* slider to make the color more or less intense, as desired.
5. To customize the color, click *Show color mixer*; drag the *Hue, Saturation,* and *Brightness* sliders that appear to adjust the color; and then click *Hide color mixer*.
6. Click Save changes to apply the new color settings.
7. Close the Control Panel window.

HERE'S HOW steps make it easy to find and review key procedures.

Quick Fix

Not Getting Expected Search Results
If you do not get the search results you expect, make sure you started in a high enough level location. To search across all drives at once, start at the Computer window.

QUICK FIX marginal notes identify common problems encountered by users and provide fast solutions.

Note: *To view the browsing history, choose View, Explorer Bars, History, or press Ctrl + Shift + H.*

NOTES and TIPS present details and shortcuts to enhance understanding and proficiency with Windows 8.

 TIP Because Windows Defender is only as good as its most recent list of definitions, it is important to allow Windows Update to download and install the latest Windows Defender updates.

Chapter Review Activities

Each chapter concludes with materials that review key concepts and reinforce newly learned skills.

CHAPTER SUMMARY

- The Control Panel provides a central location for accessing system settings.
- The Windows 8 PC settings app also enables you to change some system settings.
- Select the Settings charm from the desktop and then click *Control Panel* to open the Control Panel. Click a category icon or link to find lower-level categories of actions and then click the task to perform. You also can click a category or task in the list at the left side of the Control Panel.
- You can adjust such settings as the keyboard repeat rate, the mouse double-click speed, or the functions of the mouse buttons.
- Right-click the desktop and then click *Personalize* to find settings for customizing the desktop.

CHAPTER SUMMARY recaps vital concepts, commands, and tools presented in the chapter.

CONCEPTS CHECK

Completion: Answer the following questions in a Word document.

Part 1

Multiple Choice
1. To change system settings, use the _____ .
   a. Start screen
   b. Taskbar
   c. Control Panel
   d. desktop

2. Click the _____ command after choosing the Settings charm from the desktop to access system settings.
   a. Start menu
   b. Taskbar
   c. Control Panel
   d. desktop

CONCEPTS CHECK questions assess knowledge recall in both multiple choice and short answer formats.

SKILLS CHECK

Save all solution files to the default Documents folder or any alternate folder specified by your instructor.

Guided Check

Assessment 1

Slow Down the Mouse and Display Mouse Trails
1. Start the Control Panel.
   a. From the desktop, select the Settings charm.
   b. Click *Control Panel*.
2. Find Mouse Settings.
   a. Click *Hardware and Sound*.
   b. Click *Mouse* under Devices and Printers.
3. Slow down the mouse.
   a. Drag the *Speed* slider under Double-click Speed to the left until it is an increment or two to the left of the center point.
   b. Capture a screen shot of the desktop and then save it as **C06A01S03**.

SKILLS CHECK assessments test skill proficiency, prompting students to complete a variety of tasks using multiple Windows 8 features.

CHALLENGE PROJECT

As a special education teacher, you will be teaching a computer class to high-school students who have a variety of disabilities. You need to prepare specific computers in the computer lab for each student based on his or her unique capabilities.
1. Open WordPad and then create a new file named **Student Setup Needs**. Imagine that you have three students. Jane is blind. Tim has a disability that makes it difficult for him to use his hands. And Sam has both limited hearing and some trouble using his hands. Type each student's name into the WordPad file.
2. Open the Ease of Access Center and research settings you might change and other recommendations you might make to set up a system for each student.

The final activity, a chapter CHALLENGE PROJECT, invites students to apply their skills to complete a project based on a real-world computing scenario.

Student Resources

Internet Resource Center

For some exercises in *Windows 8*, students will need to download files. These Student Data Files can be accessed on the Internet Resource Center for this book, located at www.paradigmcollege.net/windows8.

eBook

For students who prefer studying with an eBook, *Windows 8* is available in an electronic form. The web-based, password-protected eBook features dynamic navigation tools, including bookmarking, a linked table of contents, and the ability to jump to a specific page. The eBook format also supports helpful study tools, such as highlighting and note taking.

Instructor Resources

Windows 8 offers a number of resources to help instructors enhance student learning, including an Instructor Resources CD with an **EXAM**VIEW® Assessment Suite, a password-protected Internet Resource Center and, for distance-learning or hybrid courses, Blackboard coursepaks.

Instructor Resources CD

This CD includes planning resources such as teaching hints and sample course syllabi; PowerPoint presentations; assessment resources, including an overview of assessment venues and PDF model answers for intrachapter projects and end-of-chapter exercises; and the **EXAM**VIEW® Assessment Suite with chapter item banks.

Internet Resource Center

Most of the content on the Instructor Resources CD is also available on the password-protected instructor side of the Internet Resource Center for this title at www.paradigmcollege.net/windows8.

Blackboard Course Content

Blackboard files provide course content, self-quizzes, and study aids, and facilitate communication among students and instructors via email and e-discussion.

System Requirements

This text is designed for the student to complete projects and assessments on a computer running a standard installation of Windows 8 Pro. To effectively run this operating system, your computer should be outfitted with the following:

- 1 gigahertz (GHz) 32-bit (×86) or 64-bit (×64) processor, with support for PAE, NX, and SSE2
- 1 gigabyte (GB) (32-bit) or 2 GB (64-bit) of system memory
- 16 GB available hard disk space (32-bit) or 20 GB (64-bit)
- Microsoft DirectX 9 graphics device with WDDM 1.0 or higher driver

In addition, the following are required to access certain features:

- Internet access (fees may apply)
- A Microsoft account for using features such as the Mail app
- A screen resolution of at least 1366 × 768 to use snap apps
- Depending on resolution, video playback may require additional memory and advanced graphics hardware
- HomeGroup networking requires a network with at least two computers running Windows 8
- DVD/CD authoring requires a compatible optical drive
- Music and sound require audio output

Note: *Screen captures in this book were created using a high resolution; your screens may look different if set to a higher or lower resolution.*

About the Authors

Faithe Wempen, M.A. (Purdue University, 1986), is a Microsoft Office Master Instructor, an adjunct instructor of Computer Technology at Indiana University/Purdue University at Indianapolis, and the author of more than 120 books on computer hardware and software, including *Computer and Internet Essentials: Preparing for IC³* (EMC Publishing). Her online courses in Office applications have educated more than a quarter-million students for corporate clients, and her articles about Microsoft Office have appeared in Microsoft Office PRO and Microsoft Office Solutions magazines. Wempen resides in rural Indiana in a 130-year-old house where in her spare time she runs a bed and breakfast.

Lisa A. Bucki (B.S., Summa Cum Laude, Public and Corporate Communications, Butler University) learned personal computers at an up-and-coming Indianapolis PR firm in the late 1980s. During those years she specialized in helping colleagues understand how to find their files in the brutal jungles of DOS, as well as showing clients how to create their own publications in PageMaker. After moving into the computer book and technical writing field, she edited or managed hundreds of titles on technology topics as diverse as PC basics, operating systems and utilities, memory management, desktop software, and desktop publishing. Also a contributing writer for Paradigm Publishing's *Guidelines for Microsoft Office 2010*, Bucki has written or collaborated on dozens of books and multimedia and online tutorials covering a variety of software and technology subjects, including Photoshop, FileMaker Pro and Keynote for the Mac, iPhoto, Fireworks and Flash from Macromedia, Windows, Microsoft Office applications, and digital photography. She has written software reviews and profiles of online retailers and products for popular online deals site Offers.com, as well as serving as that site's Money Monday blogger. In her consultant and trainer role, Bucki provides instruction in the use of Microsoft Project but also has conducted Word and Excel training courses. In her spare time, she dabbles in creating handmade tile and minds the dogs, the chickens, and the garden along with her husband, Steve, in the wilds of Western North Carolina.

Acknowledgements

The authors and Paradigm staff would like to thank Rob Neilly of Seneca College of Applied Arts and Technology, Toronto, Canada, for testing the exercises in this book and providing feedback on the text.

Microsoft® Windows® 8

Learning Windows 8 Basics

- Working with the Windows 8 Desktop

- Working with Disks and Other Removable Media

- Learning About Files, Folders, and Libraries

- Organizing and Protecting Information

- Using Windows 8 Programs

- Customizing the Desktop and Start Screen

CHAPTER 1

Working with the Windows 8 Desktop

PERFORMANCE OBJECTIVES

Upon successful completion of Chapter 1, you will be able to:

- Understand what an operating system does
- Learn some new gestures with a mouse or touchpad
- Start Windows 8, sign in to your user account, and connect to the cloud
- Work with essential Windows 8 tools, such as the Start screen, charms, Taskbar, and desktop icons
- Explore features such as Snap, Shake, Peek, and app switching
- Use menus, dialog boxes, and windows

- Start, snap, and close apps
- Create, edit, and remove Microsoft and local user accounts
- Pause a work session, and save power with sleep mode
- Protect information by locking the system when you are away
- Switch users without shutting down
- Restart or shut down the computer
- Browse and search for help or more information

Every time you start your computer, the Windows 8 Start screen will greet you. The Start screen and the desktop serve as gateways for accessing programs and files, viewing email or information on the Internet, accessing the cloud, and working on a network. Once you have started Windows 8, handy tools such as app tiles and folder windows make it easy to work with your programs and files. With Windows 8, you can create an account for each user of the computer to better organize and secure information, as well as to enable each person to customize the desktop to his or her own taste. You can take advantage of features that enable you to walk away from your computer and leave it in a secure and power-conserving state, and to restart and shut down the system as needed. Finally, Windows 8 Help is there when you need it.

Introducing Your Computer's Operating System: Windows 8 ■■■■■■■■■■■■■■■■■■■■■■■■■■■

hardware Physical computer parts

For most users, what goes on inside a computer system is a mystery. Although you might envision that your computer is stuffed with primitive switches or vacuum tubes or a Rube Goldberg-style system of hamster wheels and sprockets, what you would see inside the case is a relatively inert collection of circuit boards and silicon chips with tiny transistors. These physical parts within the computer case are called its **hardware**.

On its own, hardware cannot do much. It needs instructions and information to perform a task. Those instructions and information come in the form of *software*, or programs. Windows 8 refers to applications or programs operated by users as *apps*. Every computer has to have at least one type of program installed: the *operating system (OS)*. The operating system software runs the computer system overall and enables the hardware to work with apps that perform more specific tasks for end users, such as word processing.

The various versions of Windows operating systems run more computers than any other operating system today. This book teaches you how to use the latest version of the Windows operating system, Windows 8, to work with your desktop or mobile computer, such as a laptop, notebook, or netbook.

Learning New Mouse, Touchpad, and Touch Screen Skills

While you can accomplish some tasks using the keyboard and still others—like typing text—may require keyboard use, a mouse or touchpad provides the easiest, most natural way to accomplish tasks in Windows 8. Because Windows 8 also works with touch-enabled computers and mobile devices, it incorporates new actions called *gestures*. You also can perform every gesture with a mouse or touchpad. For consistency with the Windows 8 Help system, this book in some cases uses gesture terminology and assumes that you will be able to perform the equivalent steps with your system's mouse or touchpad.

A *mouse* is a plastic device that you roll on your desk using your hand. A ball housed in the bottom of a traditional mouse enables you to move the mouse smoothly and with precision. Using a mouse pad under the mouse helps the ball work more reliably than it would if rolled on a smooth surface. Alternate mouse types such as an optical mouse (wireless or wired) or trackball eliminate the need for a mouse pad. Further, a wireless mouse requires no cable connected to the computer.

As you move the mouse, a graphical on-screen *mouse pointer* moves in the corresponding direction and distance. When the pointer arrives over an object that you want to select or work with, you can use one of the buttons on the mouse to accomplish the action you want.

Mobile computers also typically include a pointing device called a *touchpad*. The touchpad appears as a rectangular inset below the keyboard. Dragging your finger across the touchpad moves the mouse pointer. When you have the pointer in position over an object, you can press a button below the touchpad or tap your finger on the touchpad to choose an action.

Windows 8 and programs running in Windows 8 typically enable the same type of mouse actions. The rest of this book assumes you can perform the following actions with a mouse or touchpad:

- **Point.** Drag the mouse or drag your finger on the touchpad until the mouse pointer is over the button, command, or other object you want to select or manipulate. Often when you point to an icon or button, a pop-up description of the item appears. (Some applications call these ScreenTips or ToolTips.)

- **Click.** After pointing to an on-screen item, press and release the left mouse or left touchpad button once, or tap once on the touchpad with your finger. You typically click to select a command from a menu or a choice in a dialog box. In some cases, you also click to select an on-screen object.

- **Double-click.** After pointing to an on-screen item, press and release the left mouse or touchpad button twice quickly. You also can tap twice on the touchpad or press and release the left touchpad button once. Double-clicking typically opens an item; for example, double-clicking an icon might start a program.
- **Right-click.** After pointing to an on-screen item, press and release the right mouse button or right touchpad button once. Some touchpads offer a special "hotspot" area, typically located in a corner, where you can tap to right-click. Right-clicking often displays a shortcut menu like the one that appears in Figure 1.1.

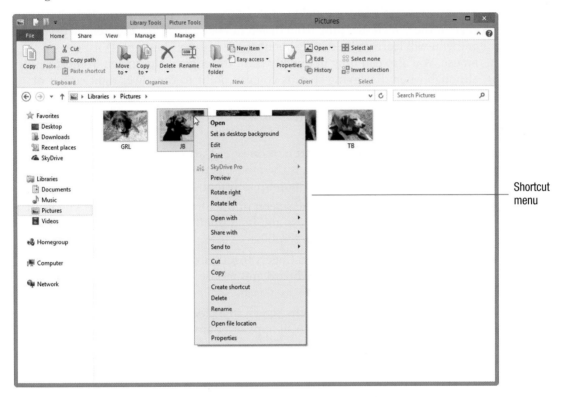

Figure 1.1 One of the mouse actions, right-clicking, displays a shortcut menu.

- **Drag.** You often drag to move or resize an on-screen item. With a mouse, point to the item, press and hold the left mouse button, move the mouse until the on-screen item reaches the desired destination or size, and then release the mouse button. A touchpad makes dragging a bit trickier. Typically, you point to the item, double-tap and hold your finger on the pad at the end of the second tap (tap-hold), drag your finger until the item reaches the desired destination, and then lift your finger off the touchpad.

Quick Fix

Touchpad Alternatives
If you do not like using the touchpad on a notebook computer, you can use a mouse instead.

- **Scroll.** Windows and lists often include scroll bars at the right and bottom to help you move additional window or list contents into view. Typically, you scroll by clicking the scroll arrows at either end of the scroll bar or by dragging the large scroll box in the middle area of the scroll bar. Some mouse models include a scroll wheel between the mouse buttons; with this type of mouse, you can scroll by pointing anywhere on the scroll bar (or sometimes anywhere in the window or list to be scrolled) and then rolling the wheel away from you to scroll up or toward you to scroll down. (You cannot use the wheel to scroll left and right.) Some touchpads enable you to scroll by pointing to the on-screen scroll bar and then dragging your finger along the right edge of the touchpad.

When you point to certain on-screen items or choose a particular tool, the mouse pointer may change shape. For example, the mouse pointer may change to a double-headed resizing pointer when over a window border or a crosshair (plus sign) after you have selected a drawing tool. The pointer changes shape in this way to indicate that Windows 8 or the program you are working with is ready for your next action.

A touch-enabled system is activated with some new gestures that make controlling the computer as easy as fingerpainting. These gestures each have mouse equivalents:

- **Swipe.** Slide your finger quickly in the direction indicated, usually from the edge of the screen. Swiping from different edges performs different actions, and you will learn more details about those in later chapters. With the mouse, you also can drag in quickly from the edge of the screen in most cases, although when displaying charms you can point to the lower right corner of the screen.

- **Tap.** Touch a button or on-screen area with your finger. Left-clicking is the mouse equivalent.

- **Press and hold.** Touch a button or on-screen area with your finger and hold it down briefly. Right-clicking is the mouse equivalent, although in some cases you can point to an object for pop-up information, as well.

- **Slide.** Move your finger on the screen in the direction indicated. If you want to move an on-screen item, press and hold briefly before dragging your finger. Mouse users can drag or use a scroll bar.

- **Pinch or stretch.** Moving two fingers together or apart on the screen generally changes the zoom. With a keyboard and mouse, press and hold the Ctrl key while moving the scroll wheel.

- **Rotate.** Move two fingers on the screen in a clockwise or counter-clockwise motion. Only a limited number of apps offer any mouse equivalent for this gesture.

Starting Windows 8 ■■■■■■■■■■■■■■■■■■■■■■■■■■■■■■

Windows 8 is the operating system (OS) for your computer. The operating system software enables you to give commands to both the system hardware and other software programs installed on the system. Without an operating system installed, a computer cannot operate.

Because a computer is a relatively expensive piece of equipment that can take up quite a bit of space, multiple users may share a single machine. For example, a number of students might share a computer in a school lab, family members might share a computer at home, or coworkers with different schedules might share a computer on the job.

Windows 8 enables you to create a ***user account*** for each person using a particular computer. When a user signs in to a user account, he or she can customize settings such as the desktop appearance without changing those settings for other users of the system. The user account settings also govern certain activities such as whether a user can edit certain files or install software.

When you start up your computer and Windows 8, you sign in with your user name. If your user name includes a password, you must enter it as well.

user account The user name, password, settings, permissions, and restrictions that govern how Windows 8 allows a particular user to work with the system

Note: *If your computer connects with a large corporate or campus network, Windows 8 might also prompt you to enter network domain information when you sign in. The network administrator can provide the proper domain sign-in information.*

Working in the Cloud versus Locally

We all live in a world in which we use an increasing number of computing devices in a variety of locations. Windows 8 consequently introduces more features for *cloud computing*, which means working with web-based services for email; for storing your files, contacts, and other data online; and more. If you read your email from your desktop computer at the office, on your mobile phone when you are traveling to see clients, or on a tablet device when you are working from home, accessing the information from a single online source ensures it is consistent and accurate. As you will learn later, you can access your apps and other cloud-based features from the new *Start screen*. The Start screen appears immediately after you sign in to the system.

To connect to the services and data storage features that Microsoft offers in the cloud, you must have a *Microsoft account*. When you sign in using a Microsoft account, you can interact immediately with your cloud-based apps and data to perform tasks such as:

- Store and share files and photos online via SkyDrive and other services.
- View your contacts and updates from a variety of social media services such as Facebook.
- Buy new apps from the Windows Store.
- Experience automatic syncing of your Windows 8 personal settings, such as themes, language, web browser favorites, and other app features.

Using a local account may be preferable for settings in which online connectivity is discouraged, such as a highly secured work environment. A *local account* is similar to user accounts in prior Windows versions. A local account does not prevent you from accessing the cloud, but the automatic connection and syncing features are not available because you are not signed in to Microsoft when using such an account.

Note: *You can associate your existing email address (with any provider) with a new Microsoft account. This enables Windows 8 to connect with your existing cloud resources and eliminates the need to create another email address and password. See the "Understanding User Accounts" section later in this chapter to learn more about creating user accounts.*

Note: *If you already have a Microsoft account (an existing Hotmail or Live account), you can create a Windows 8 user for it and use it to sign in to your computer. If not, your instructor will provide sign-in information to use until you create your own Microsoft account for exercises later in the chapter. Unless otherwise noted, the figures in this book show the use of a Microsoft account where applicable.*

Note: *When power-conserving features trigger, you generally have to sign back in to the system to reactivate it.*

Signing In with a Microsoft Account

The process for signing in begins with starting or restarting the computer system. Windows 8 displays an introductory screen that shows the date and time and a background image. From there, you navigate to the user accounts, select the appropriate Microsoft account name, and then enter your password to sign in.

cloud computing Working via various services and data storage locations online, so that you can access those tools and information from any Internet-connected computer or device

Start screen The Windows 8 screen that enables you to access your apps and cloud-based features; also the starting point for app and system activities in Windows 8

Microsoft account A type of Windows 8 user account that automatically connects to the cloud to take advantage of online storage, apps, and syncing features

local account A type of Windows 8 user account that does not connect automatically to the cloud or sync settings between the different systems you use

To sign in to a Microsoft account in Windows 8:

1. Power up the computer. (You also can restart it, if needed, as described later in this chapter.)
2. Press Enter or swipe up from the bottom of the screen. (With a mouse, drag rapidly with a short stroke up from the bottom of the screen.)
3. If needed, click the Switch user (left arrow) button to the left of the picture to display the pictures for all the accounts, and then click your Microsoft account.
4. Type your password in the *Password* text box.
5. Press Enter or click the blue Submit (right arrow) button to the right of the text box.

▼ **Quick Fix**

Passing a Bad Password
Passwords in Windows 8 are case-sensitive, meaning that you must type the password exactly as it was typed when originally created, including using capital letters for characters originally entered as capitals. If you type the wrong password or make a mistake when you type the password, Windows 8 notifies you of the incorrect password. Click OK and then retype your password or use the Reset password choice to finish signing in.

Signing In to a Local Account

The process for signing in to a local account is virtually identical to signing in to a Microsoft account. One difference is that a local account may not have a password assigned, although that is not the best practice for security purposes.

Here's How

To sign in to a Windows 8 local account:

1. Power up the computer. (You also can restart it, if needed, as described later in this chapter.)
2. Press Enter or swipe up from the bottom of the screen. (With a mouse, drag rapidly with a short stroke up from the bottom of the screen.)
3. If needed, click the Swich user (left arrow) button to the left of the picture to display the pictures for all the accounts, and then click your local account.
4. If applicable, type your password in the *Password* text box.
5. Press Enter or click the blue Submit (right arrow) button to the right of the text box.

Exercise 1

Signing In and Working On Screen

1. If you do not already have a user account set up on your system, ask your instructor what account name and password to use. Power on the system.
2. At the introductory screen with the date and time, swipe up or drag up with the mouse from the bottom of the screen, or press Enter.
3. If needed, click the Switch user (left arrow) button to the left of the picture to display the pictures for all the accounts, and then click your Microsoft account.
4. Type your password in the *Password* text box and then press Enter or click the blue Submit (right arrow) button to finish signing in. The Windows 8 Start screen appears.
5. Move the mouse around the desk, or drag your finger around on the touchpad. Notice how the default mouse pointer (an arrow) moves around on the screen in sync with the direction you move the mouse or your finger.

6.   Move your mouse pointer over the minus-sign icon at the lower right corner of the screen. Additional icons appear briefly along the right side of the screen. You will learn more about them shortly.

7.   Locate and move the mouse pointer over the tile that says *Desktop* and then click. The Windows 8 desktop, which you will learn more about shortly, appears.

8.   Locate and move the mouse pointer over the Recycle Bin icon. Note how a lighter highlight appears behind the icon.

9.   Right-click the Recycle Bin icon. A shortcut menu appears.

10. Move the mouse pointer away from the Recycle Bin icon and then click. The shortcut menu closes.

11. Point to the Recycle Bin icon, and drag it down and to the right. A picture of the icon appears behind the mouse pointer as you drag. (Remember, on a touchpad you have to double-tap and hold your finger on the touchpad at the end of the second tap to begin dragging.)

Quick Fix

Cannot Move Icon
If you cannot move the icon as described in Steps 11 and 12, right-click away from the icon, point to View in the shortcut menu, and then click Auto arrange icons to uncheck it. If Align icons to grid is checked, repeat the process to uncheck it, too.

12. Release the mouse button, and the Recycle Bin icon appears in its new position.

13. Drag the Recycle Bin icon back to its original location.

14. Press the Windows logo key ⊞ on the keyboard. The Start screen reappears.

Using the Windows 8 Interface ■■■■■■■■■■■■

Windows 8 performs as a bridge in some respects. It connects your local user experience with your cloud experience, as well as creates a more consistent feel whether you are using a desktop computer or a mobile device. It also initiates a transition to a new style of application. To accomplish these aims, Windows 8 introduces some big changes to the user interface. Even if you have used previous versions of Windows, you will need to familiarize yourself with how to get around in Windows 8.

Exploring the Start Screen

You have already seen the new Start screen that appears after you sign in to Windows 8. The Start screen is your starting point for Windows 8 app and system activities. From here, you can see and access your applications, including a new style of app called Windows 8 apps. **Windows 8 apps** establish a new design philosophy that emphasizes a cleaner look and feel, better ease of use on a touchscreen device, and greater integration with each other and the cloud. You start the new apps from the Windows 8 Start screen. Figure 1.2 shows the Windows 8 Start screen, the default Windows 8 apps at the left and other installed apps at the right. A square box or *tile* represents each of the apps. Some tiles are live, meaning that they display updated information from the cloud. For example, in Figure 1.2 the Calendar tile shows the date, and the Store tile shows a numeral 6 to indicate that app updates are available for download. You can open and switch between multiple apps, which you will learn more about later in this chapter.

Windows 8 apps Apps designed specifically for Windows 8, optimized for use on touchscreen devices and for a cleaner look and feel

tile The box representing an app on the Windows 8 Start screen

Figure 1.2 The Start screen enables you to access new Windows 8 apps.

Starting File Explorer on the Desktop

You saw in Exercise 1 how to go to the ***desktop*** from the Start screen: click the Desktop tile. All the file-management work you do in Windows 8 begins from the Windows 8 desktop. Just as you can have multiple file folders for in-process projects lying on your physical desktop, Windows 8 enables you to ***multitask*** and have multiple activities processing on your computer desktop. For example, you can have two programs open and switch back and forth between them, print from one of the programs, and view information from the Internet—all without needing to close any of the open programs. (Some applications still run on the desktop.) One of the more important activities you will handle on the desktop is managing your files. You do this with the File Explorer app. To start that app, click the File Explorer button on the Taskbar, as shown in Figure 1.3.

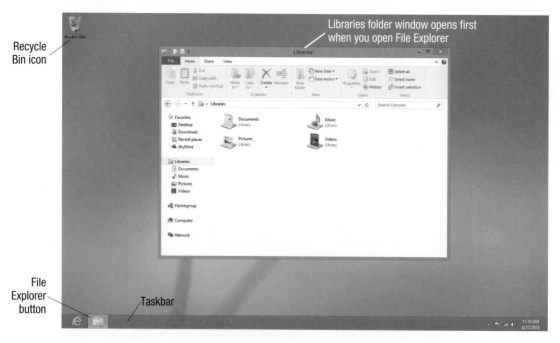

Figure 1.3   Work with files in Windows 8 from the File Explorer on the desktop.

Figure 1.3 shows the desktop, a File Explorer window, and the most important elements that appear there by default. Your desktop might look slightly different than the one pictured in Figure 1.3. For example, your system might have a different image displayed on the desktop, or you might have different icons resulting from a previous Windows installation. Despite such minor differences, the steps you use to work with the desktop and File Explorer remain consistent.

When you initially start File Explorer, it displays the Libraries window. The Libraries window (shown in Figure 1.3) holds your user *libraries*—Documents, Music, Pictures, and Videos—designated to manage *files* created or obtained by you only. You will learn more about working with the various libraries in later chapters.

Switching between the Start Screen and Desktop

The Start screen and desktop provide complementary working environments. Stay connected with live, updated information from the cloud on the Start screen while managing your local files and performing other activities from the desktop. There are multiple ways to switch between the desktop and the Start screen.

Here's How

To switch between the Start screen and Desktop:

If you have not yet displayed the desktop, click the Desktop tile on the Start screen and then click the File Explorer button on the Taskbar.

- Press the Windows logo key ⊞ on the keyboard to switch between the desktop and Start. (If an app launched from the Start screen is on the screen, pressing the Windows logo key ⊞ switches between the app and Start screen instead.)
- From the desktop, point to the lower left corner. When the Start tile appears, click it to return to Start. This method also works for returning to the desktop.
- From either Start or the desktop, point to the lower right corner. When the charms appear, click Start. This method works in either direction: desktop to Start or Start to desktop.

T I P You can pin a File Explorer tile to the Start screen. Clicking that tile then would go to the desktop and open the File Explorer to the Libraries window. See Chapter 6, "Customizing the Desktop and Start Screen," to learn how.

Using Charms

Windows 8 introduces a new feature that helps you access key system features. A *charm* is a hidden icon that enables you to use Search, start programs, change system settings, and more. You can display the charms from either the Start screen or desktop. Figure 1.4 shows the charms.

Figure 1.4 You can display the charms at the right side of the Start screen or desktop.

library A location for working with a particular type of file; each library may monitor a number of storage locations to identify and track a particular type of file such as a digital picture

file Digital information that you create and save with a name for later retrieval; a file may include programming instructions, an image, text, or any other type of content; also called a document

charm A new type of hidden icon that enables you to access Search, programs, system settings, and more

To display and use charms:

1. From either Start or the desktop, point to the lower right or upper right corner. Or swipe in from the right edge if you are using a touch screen.
2. Move the mouse pointer up below a charm to display its name, if needed.
3. Click or tap the desired charm.

To hide the charms, move the mouse pointer to the left, back over the main area of the Start screen or the desktop. You will learn more about using each charm throughout the book, but here is an overview of what each of the five charms does:

- **Search.** Enables you to search for information, both on your computer and the Internet, as well as to start apps.
- **Share.** Use this charm to send photos, links, and other information from your computer to contacts and social media sites.
- **Start.** As seen previously, use this charm to switch between Start and the desktop.
- **Devices.** Enables you to print to a printer, as well as to stream content such as video to network-enabled and compatible devices, such as TVs.
- **Settings.** Enables you to shut down the system, control speaker volume, turn notifications on and off, check network status, and access other system settings.

Starting a Program

Some programs have tiles pinned to the Start screen. Click the program's tile, and the program opens. The newer Windows 8 apps open to full-screen size. Apps that run on the desktop automatically display the desktop when they open. Similarly, if you click a program icon on the Taskbar on the desktop, the app will open.

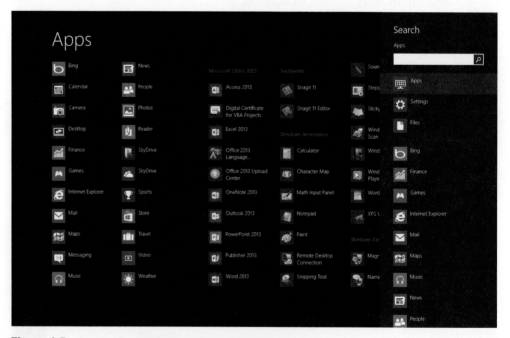

Figure 1.5   Use the Search charm to find and start programs.

Not all programs are pinned to the Start screen or the Taskbar. If a program does not appear on the Start screen or desktop Taskbar, you can use the Search charm to find it. After you click the Search charm, a list of all the programs installed on your computer appears, as shown in Figure 1.5. If you do not immediately see the program you want, start typing the program name, and Windows will display a list of matching programs, as shown in Figure 1.6. Click the program to start.

Figure 1.6 Type the name of the program to view a list of matching programs.

Here's How

To find and start a program:

1. Move the mouse pointer over the lower right or upper right corner of the Start screen or desktop or swipe in from the right edge if you are using a touch screen.
2. Click or tap the Search charm.
3. If needed, leave *Apps* selected in the list at the right and begin typing the name of the program. The screen lists matching programs.
4. Click the program name. The program opens.

Note that to search for other types of content, you can click *Settings* or *Files* in the list at the right after clicking the Search charm and then begin typing the name of the file or setting. In the list below the search text box, click the name of the desired match when it appears and then click the file or feature in the *Results* list at the left.

Note: *You will learn more details about exiting an open program in a later chapter. For now, if you need to close a program, press Alt + F4, or, from a Windows 8 app that opens from Start, drag from the top of the screen down to the bottom, or, when working on the desktop, click the Close (X) button in the upper right corner of the program window.*

Note: *Chapter 3 will teach you how to add a program tile to the Start screen or a program icon to the Taskbar.*

Capturing a Screen Picture to Complete an Assignment

This book includes exercises within the text and assessments at the end of each chapter. Your instructor may require you to demonstrate that you have successfully completed an exercise or assessment by capturing a picture of your Windows 8 screen and then emailing and/or printing the picture or providing it on a USB flash drive (also called a thumb drive). You may want to flag this page in the book with a sticky note so that you can refer to these steps whenever you need to provide a screen shot to your instructor.

Here's How

To capture, save, and print a picture of the computer screen:

1. Complete the steps required to come to the point in the exercise or assessment at which you need to shoot a picture of the screen.
2. Press the Print Screen key, which is commonly found to the right of the F12 key at the top of the keyboard. This key might have an abbreviated name, such as PrntScr. Some systems may require you to press the Shift key along with the Print Screen key (Shift + Print Screen). On some mobile computers, you may need to press a function (Fn) key along with the Print Screen key (Fn + Print Screen).
3. Select the Search charm.
4. Click Paint in the *Apps* list, under *Windows Accessories*. Scroll the screen to the right if you don't see the Paint tile.
5. Press Ctrl + V. This shortcut pastes the image into the Paint application.
6. Press Ctrl + S. The Save As dialog box opens.
7. Type the *file name* specified by the exercise or assessment. It will appear in the *File name* text box. Choose *PNG* or *JPEG* as the *Save as type* and then navigate to the folder location specified by your instructor.
8. Click Save. This saves the file. If your instructor wants you to submit the file by email, ask the instructor for instructions about how to do so.
9. If you instructor requires that you submit a printout of each screen shot, press Ctrl + P.
10. Click the printer to use (as indicated by your instructor) in the *Select Printer* area and then click Print. Label and submit the hard copy to your instructor.
11. Press Alt + F4 to exit Paint. Always exit Paint after saving and printing a screen shot unless instructed to do otherwise in the steps in this book. In the case of apps launched from the Start screen, you may also have to navigate back to your prior location in the app.

Quick Fix

Making Printouts a Single Page
If the Paint printout is more than one page, click the Paint File tab, point to Print, and click Page setup. Under Scaling, click the Fit to option button and then specify that the printout should be 1 by 1 page(s). Click OK and then reprint the document.

Note: *Windows 8 offers an easy keyboard combination for capturing and saving a screen shot: Press the Windows logo key* ⊞ *+ Print Screen. This technique creates a folder named Screenshots in the Pictures library. You can open that folder, rename each screen shot as instructed, and copy shots as needed from there. You can use this shortcut in place of the previous instructions if you are comfortable with it and your instructor approves of that technique.*

Using the Taskbar

Taskbar A bar at the bottom of the desktop that you use to manage active tasks

The *Taskbar* appears along the bottom of the desktop by default. You can use the tools on this bar (shown in Figure 1.7) to start tasks (programs and files) and manage active tasks.

Pinned items   Buttons for active tasks   Navigation area   Show desktop button

Figure 1.7 The Taskbar displays icons for launching programs and a button for each active task.

The tools that reside or appear on the Taskbar include the following:

- **Pinned items.** Two icons appear by default at the far left end of the Taskbar: Internet Explorer and File Explorer. Clicking an icon here starts the associated program. Clicking the File Explorer icon, which looks like a file folder, opens the Libraries window if it is not already open. You can pin and unpin other programs to the Taskbar, a process you will learn in Chapter 3.

- **Task buttons.** When you start a program or open a document, a task button for the program or document appears on the Taskbar. You can click the button to open its window. See the section "Moving between Windows" to learn more.

- **Show desktop button.** You can display a temporary preview of the desktop, temporarily hiding open windows. Click the Show desktop button at the right end of the Taskbar to hide open windows, and click the button again to redisplay them.

- **Notification area.** Also called the system tray, this area at the far right end of the Taskbar displays icons that show the status of certain system functions, such as a network connection or battery power, as well as icons used to manage certain programs and Windows 8 features, such as Action Center Alerts. To display hidden icons, click the Show hidden icons button at the left of the visible icons. Right-click any icon in the notification area to see a shortcut menu for working with that program or feature.

Note: *The Taskbar appears on the desktop by default. Chapter 6 explains how to hide the Taskbar.*

The *icons* for Windows 8 features often give the status of system functions, such as a network connection. To view the status of a function, point at the function's icon. A pop-up tip like the one shown in Figure 1.8 appears, giving the status information. Clicking an icon opens a larger window, as shown in Figure 1.9. This window displays the status information as well as one or more links that you can click to display and change settings for that icon's function.

icon A small picture that represents an item (object) or choice in Windows 8 and Windows programs

Show hidden icons button

Figure 1.8 Pointing to one of the icons in the notification area provides status information.

Note: *The icons that appear in the notification area vary depending on the software, hardware, and active Windows 8 features on your system, so the icons you see on your desktop may be different than those that appear in Figures 1.8 and 1.9.*

When you right-click an icon in the notification area, a shortcut menu displays choices for working with the program or feature. As shown at the left side of Figure 1.10, the shortcut menu for a program typically includes choices for opening the program in a window or exiting the program. As shown at the right side of Figure 1.10, the shortcut menu for a feature may include choices for changing program settings or choices for working with Windows features and hardware.

Status

Links

Figure 1.9 Clicking one of the icons in the notification area provides status information, plus one or more links that you can use to change settings.

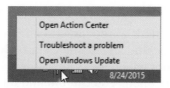

Figure 1.10 Right-clicking one of the icons in the notification area displays a shortcut menu.

Here's How

To work with a program or feature in the notification area:

1. Point to an icon to see a pop-up status window.
2. Click an icon to see a window that displays status information and links you can click to display and change settings for that function.
3. Right-click an icon in the notification area, or click the Show hidden icons button and then right-click an icon. Click a command in the shortcut menu that appears, such as *Exit* to exit a program or a command to change a feature setting or start a feature.

Quick Fix

Closing a Shortcut Menu
Press Esc to close a shortcut menu if you decide not to click a command on it.

---

notification A message that pops up in the notification area to warn you about a situation that may require action or a settings change

In addition to the icons that appear in the notification area, at times a ***notification*** like the one shown in Figure 1.11 will pop up. Click in the notification message to open a window where you can learn more or change settings related to the notification. These notifications deal with issues such as security settings; later chapters of the book teach you how to work with settings like these. As the right image in Figure 1.11 illustrates, in some cases, an icon's appearance will change to let you know that there is a problem. For example, a starburst appears on the icon for networking if network connections are available but you are not currently connected to a network.

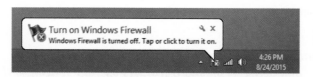

Figure 1.11 A notification may appear in a pop-up balloon in the notification area. Icon appearance also may change to communicate a problem.

Jump List A menu of frequently used documents and commands that you can access for a program via the Taskbar

Using a Jump List. Windows 8 includes a feature called Jump Lists. A ***Jump List*** for a program shows you documents that you have opened recently and, in some cases, common commands. The contents of a Jump List will vary depending on what you do with a program or what features the program offers. You can open a Jump List from either the Taskbar or Start screen. Right-click a Taskbar icon to see its Jump List. Once the Jump List is open, click a file to open it or a command to execute it. Figure 1.12 illustrates a Taskbar Jump List.

Figure 1.12 Jump Lists provide quick access to favorite files or commands.

Using Peek to Preview an Open Item. Peek also enables you to preview the contents of open folders or open documents for a program without closing the window that you are currently working in. To start, move the mouse pointer over the program's icon in the Taskbar. As shown in Figure 1.13, large thumbnails for the open items appear above the Taskbar icon. You can then move the mouse pointer over one of the thumbnails to preview it in its larger window, or click a thumbnail to switch to that document.

Figure 1.13 Hover the mouse over a Taskbar icon to take a peek at open windows.

Here's How

To preview an open document from the Taskbar:

1. Move the mouse pointer over the program icon on the Taskbar.
2. Move the mouse pointer over a thumbnail preview to preview the document's fully opened window.
3. Click a thumbnail to switch to that document, or move the mouse pointer off the thumbnail and then move it over the desktop or another document window to close the preview.

Selecting Icons, Buttons, and Other Items

The mouse provides the most quick and convenient way to make selections in Windows 8 and most programs that run in Windows 8. Whether you are working on the desktop, in a window, or in an application (both Windows 8 and desktop apps), selection techniques remain consistent:

- To select an icon, click it once with the mouse. A highlight appears around the icon, as shown in Figure 1.14. You also can drag over multiple icons to select them. On a touch screen, swiping over an on-screen item in the opposite direction as scrolling typically selects the item. In Windows 8 apps, you may click different graphic objects, such as picture thumbnails and links.

- To open a file or application, double-click its icon. Opening a file starts the application in which it was created and opens the file in that application.

- To select text in a document, web page, or Help window for copying or editing, drag over the text. A highlight appears behind the text, as shown in Figure 1.15.

toggle A command or feature that can remain in an "on" (toggled on) or "off" (toggled off) state

- To select a button on a ribbon or toolbar in File Explorer or in an application (more on ribbons and other tools later in the chapter), click the button. Note that some buttons **toggle** a feature, or turn the feature on and off. When you click the button to turn the feature on, it will take on a pressed in or colored appearance, as shown in Figure 1.16, to show you that the feature is active. Click the button again to toggle the feature off. You will learn more about ribbons and toolbars later in this chapter.

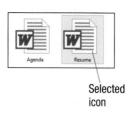

Selected icon

Figure 1.14
Click an icon to select it.

Selected text

Figure 1.15 Drag over text to select it.

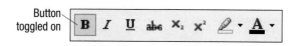

Button toggled on

Figure 1.16 Click a toolbar or ribbon button to select it.

Exercise 2

Using Charms, the Taskbar, and Apps

1. Power on the computer and sign in, if the system is not still on from the last exercise.
2. Point to the lower right corner of the screen until you see the charms and then click the top one, Search.
3. Use the Print Screen function as described previously to capture a screen shot. Use Paint as described previously to save the file as **C01E02S03**. Submit the file to your instructor via hard copy, email, or USB flash drive, and then close Paint. Consult your instructor if you have any questions about saving, printing, or emailing the file.
4. Select the Search charm again, scroll the list of programs to the right, and then, under *Windows Accessories*, click WordPad. The WordPad application starts on the desktop, displaying a blank document.
5. If the Libraries window is not open, click the File Explorer icon pinned to the desktop Taskbar.
6. Double-click the Documents icon in the Libraries window. A window holding your Documents library appears. There may or may not be folder and file icons in the Documents folder.
7. Select the Search charm, click *Settings* in the list at the right, and then type Firewall in the search text box.

8. Click *Check firewall status* in the *Results for* list.
9. Right-click the Taskbar and then click *Cascade windows*.
10. Use the Print Screen function to capture a screen shot. Use Paint to save the file as **C01E02S10**. Submit the file to your instructor via hard copy, email, or USB flash drive, and then close Paint.
11. Hover the mouse pointer over the File Explorer icon on the Taskbar to view the preview thumbnail.
12. Hover the mouse pointer off the icon.
13. Press the Windows logo key ⊞ on the keyboard.
14. Click the Games tile on the Start screen.
15. Use the Print Screen function to capture a screen shot and then drag down from the top of the screen to close the Games app. Use Paint to save the file as **C01E02S15**. Submit the file to your instructor via hard copy, email, or USB flash drive, and then close Paint.
16. If the Start screen does not already appear, press the Windows logo key ⊞ on the keyboard to display the Start screen and then click the Desktop tile to return to the desktop.
17. Right-click the Control Panel icon on the Taskbar (if you point to the icon, the thumbnail is named Windows Firewall for the system feature you opened in Step 8) and then click *Close window* in the Jump List.
18. Leave the Documents library and WordPad windows open for a later exercise.

Working with Other Menus

So far, you have seen and worked with both the shortcut menus and Jump Lists. In Windows 8 and in other applications, you will encounter other types of *menus*. Some menus open when you click a menu name on a menu bar. Others open when you click a button on a toolbar or ribbon tab or in the commands for Windows 8 apps.

Clicking a menu *command* tells Windows 8 or the application to perform that command. You can tell whether the command will be performed directly or whether you have to take further action based on the command's appearance on the menu:

- **Command name only.** When the command name appears by itself on the menu, clicking the command in the menu executes the command immediately.
- **Command with a right arrow beside it.** As shown in Figure 1.17, pointing to or clicking a command with a right arrow next to the command name displays a submenu. Click a command in the submenu to execute it.

menu A list of commands, usually appearing along the top of a window or as a list when you click a button or icon

command An action that you tell a program to perform

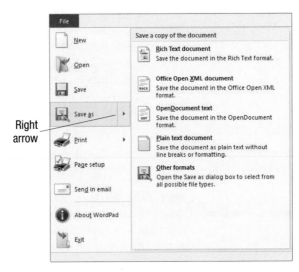

Right arrow

Figure 1.17 A right arrow beside a command indicates that a submenu or additional list of choices will appear when you click or point to the command.

- **Command with an ellipsis (…) beside it.** Figure 1.18 illustrates a Notepad menu with an ellipsis beside several of the commands. Clicking a command with an ellipsis opens a dialog box. Use the dialog box choices (described in the section "Working with Dialog Boxes") to provide more details about how Windows 8 or the program should complete the command.

- **Command with a check mark.** When a command has a check mark to the left of the command name, that command toggles on and off when you click it. Clicking the command when it is checked removes the check and toggles the command off, while clicking the command when it is unchecked rechecks it and toggles the command on. As shown in Figure 1.19, many commands that control window features toggle on and off.

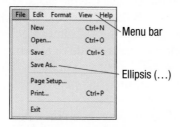

Figure 1.18 Clicking a command with an ellipsis opens a dialog box.

Figure 1.19 A check mark indicates that a command toggles on and off when you click it.

T I P Figure 1.18 shows that some commands have a keyboard combination, such as Ctrl + P beside the Print command. You can press that combination, often called a keyboard shortcut, to execute the command directly without using the menu. For example, pressing Ctrl + P opens the Print dialog box in many applications.

To choose a menu command:

1. Click the menu name, button on a menu bar, or ribbon tab. When working with the new Windows 8 apps launched from the Start screen, right-click to display the commands at the bottom of the screen.
2. Click the desired command, in the menu or for a Windows 8 app launched from the Start screen, at the bottom of the screen.
3. If a submenu appears or list of additional choices appears, click the desired command in the submenu. If a dialog box appears, make choices in the dialog box to refine the command's behavior as desired, and then click OK.

Working with a Ribbon

ribbon An enhanced tabbed toolbar in which each tab offers commands for a particular overall activity and groups commands for more specific activities

An increasing number of familiar applications—notably the WordPad, Paint, and File Explorer applications in Windows 8 and the applications in the recent version of the Microsoft Office suite—use a newer type of interface called a *ribbon*. The ribbon replaces the menu bar and organizes related commands on tabs. Each tab further collects related commands in various groups. Figure 1.20 shows the ribbon in WordPad. To display the commands on one of the tabs, click the tab. The far left tab is almost always a File tab, and clicking it opens commands for working with files. Note that the "commands" on each of the other tabs can take a variety of formats; in addition to buttons, there are other types of tools like those found in dialog boxes, which you will learn about next. Some buttons are even divided into two parts, where clicking the upper part gives the command, while clicking the lower part (usually labeled with a down arrow) opens a list or menu with additional choices. The lower right corner of some groups, notably in Office applications, also offers a small button called a *Dialog box launcher*. Clicking a Dialog box launcher opens a dialog box with more detailed settings for a particular activity. Finally, the Quick Access Toolbar above the ribbon offers buttons for the most commonly used commands, such as saving the file. In some instances, a *contextual tab* may appear when you select an object such as a graphic. A contextual tab offers additional commands for working with the selected item.

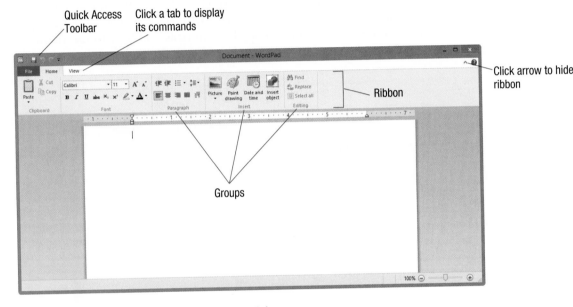

Figure 1.20 The ribbon presents commands on tabs.

T I P You can hide the ribbon to open up more space on the screen for working with the current file. To hide the ribbon in an application, press Ctrl + F1, or click the small up-pointing arrow in the upper right corner of the window. Press Ctrl + F1 again to redisplay it.

Here's How

To use the ribbon in a program:

1. Select any text or object on which you want to perform the command.
2. Click the tab or contextual tab that contains the settings to be changed, if needed.
3. In the group for the activity you want to perform, use a button or another control type to make a selection. Or, click the Dialog box launcher button at the lower right corner of the group to open a dialog box with more detailed settings.

Working with Dialog Boxes

control A type of
selection mecha-
nism in a dialog
box

Dialog boxes in Windows 8 and Windows 8 applications use fairly standardized *controls* to enable you to provide specific details about how a command should execute. For example, if you are working with text in a document and you have chosen a command for formatting that text, a Format dialog box might appear. That dialog box might have a list of fonts (letter styles) that you can apply; a list of styles, such as italics, that you can apply; a box for entering a new size for the text; other controls for applying special effects; or an area where you can choose a color for the text. A dialog box might arrange similar choices in a named group or might include tabs or sheets that group information.

After you make your choices in a dialog box, click the OK button to apply your changes. If you decide not to follow through with the changes, click Cancel. Here is a review of the most common dialog box controls and how to use them. Figure 1.21 shows how many of these controls look in a dialog box.

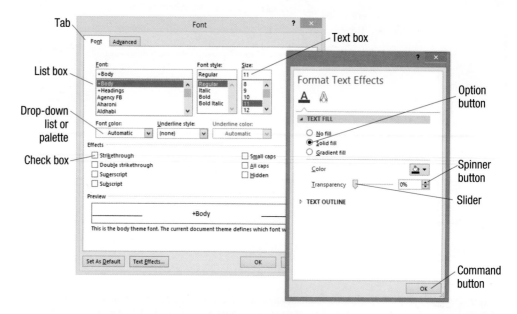

Figure 1.21 Dialog boxes include a variety of controls.

- **Tab.** Click a tab or sheet to display its group of controls in the dialog box.

- **Drop-down list or palette.** Click the drop-down list arrow (down arrow or right arrow) to open the list and then click a choice in the list. Rather than a drop-down arrow, the dialog box may offer a Palette button that you click. If the list is lengthy, it may include a scroll bar, and you can click the scroll arrows on the scroll bar to see additional choices. If clicking opens a drop-down palette of choices, such as color choices, click the desired choice in the palette.

- **Check box.** When a check mark appears in a check box, that control is active or selected. You can click any check box to check or uncheck (deselect) it as needed. When multiple check boxes appear in a dialog box, each one operates independently, and they can be checked or unchecked in any combination.

- **List box.** A list box includes a scroll bar at the right. Click the scroll arrows on the scroll bar to see additional choices and then click the desired choice. A list box (or a drop-down list) may include a text box where you can type in an entry rather than choosing from the list.

- **Text box.** You type a value or other entry such as a file name into a text box. If the text box contains a previous entry, drag over it to select it and then type a replacement entry. If the text box has an accompanying list, choosing one of the list items automatically fills in the text box.

- **Spinner buttons.** You can click the small up or down arrow button to change the value in the accompanying text box, also called a measurement box. If you prefer, you can instead drag over the value to select it and then type a new value to replace it.

- **Option buttons.** Option buttons are mutually exclusive. Only one option button in a group can be selected or active at a time. Click an option button to select it (make it active).

- **Command buttons.** Click a command button to confirm or cancel the other settings you have made in the dialog box. In many dialog boxes, for example, you must click an OK button to apply the changes you have made in the dialog box and close the dialog box.

- **Slider.** Some dialog boxes include a slider control that enables you to set a value or the intensity of a change. Drag the handle on the slider to change the value.

To use a dialog box:

1. If the dialog box contains tabs, click the tab that holds the settings to change, if needed.
2. Make changes to the desired control settings.
3. Repeat Steps 1 and 2 to make changes on other tabs.
4. Click OK to apply your choices. Or, click Cancel to close the dialog box without applying the command.

Here's How

Working with Windows

Windows in Windows 8 provide the capability to multitask desktop applications. You can have a letter open in a word processing program in one window, a digital photo open in an image editing program in another, and a web page open in a browser in another. You can switch between the windows at will, and you can adjust the size and position of any window as needed to enable you to work most efficiently. When you finish working with the contents of a window, you can close it to clear it off your desktop. Even the Windows 8 apps launched from the Start screen can be snapped so that you can see and work with multiple apps on screen at once, as described later in the chapter.

window An independent frame that holds a program, document, or folder contents

Minimizing and Redisplaying a Window

To *minimize* a window reduces it to a button on the Taskbar. The program in the minimized window continues to run, and any files open in the window remain active, too. Minimizing enables you to set a program or file aside temporarily while you work on other tasks. When you need to revisit the minimized program or file, you can open it more quickly from the Taskbar than opening it from scratch.

minimize To reduce a window to a Taskbar icon to temporarily clear it from the desktop

 T I P In some applications, you can open multiple files in the application and minimize each file within the application window as well.

You can use one of a variety of techniques to minimize a window from a traditional windowed application. One of the most common techniques is clicking the Minimize button at the right end of the ***title bar*** at the top of the window (shown in Figure 1.22). You also can use shortcut menus to both minimize and redisplay a window. Windows 8 also includes a feature called ***Shake*** that you can use to minimize all open windows except the one you want to focus on. Move the mouse pointer over the title bar of a window that you want to focus on and then drag back and forth quickly to simulate a shaking motion. Any other windows that are open will be minimized.

Figure 1.22 Click the Minimize button on the window title bar, or use a shortcut menu, to minimize a window.

To minimize a window:

- Click the Minimize button at the right end of the title bar.
  OR
- Right-click the window title bar and then click *Minimize*.
  OR
- Drag the title bar for a window that you want to leave open from side to side quickly, which minimizes all other open windows.

To redisplay a window:

1. Point to the Taskbar button for the minimized window. A ***Peek thumbnail*** appears so that you can preview the window contents to verify that you are redisplaying the correct window.
2. Click the Taskbar button to redisplay the window. Or, if multiple thumbnails appear, click the thumbnail for the window that you want to redisplay.

You learned previously about the Show desktop button at the far right end of the Taskbar. Showing the desktop temporarily minimizes all open windows to Taskbar buttons. Use this handy feature when you want to go directly to the desktop without the need to minimize open windows one by one.

Maximizing and Restoring a Window

When you need to focus on the contents of the file that you are working on in a windowed app, or when you need to see as much of a program or file on the screen as possible, *maximize* the window that contains that file or program. As the name suggests, maximizing increases the window to fill the full area available on the screen, as shown in Figure 1.23. When you want to return the window to a smaller size so that you can see other on-screen information in addition to the window, you can *restore* the window.

maximize To increase a window to full-screen size

restore To return a window to its size before it was maximized

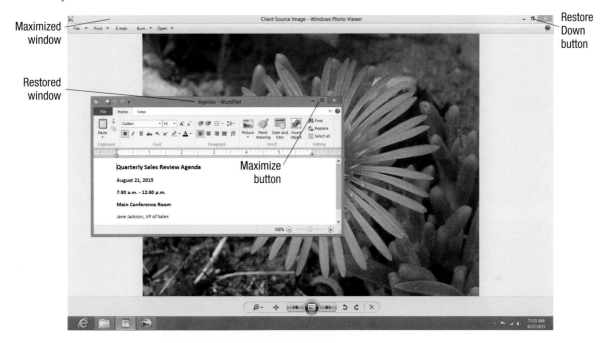

Figure 1.23   Maximize a window to have it fill the screen. Restore a window to return it to its prior (less-than-maximized) size.

Just as each window title bar includes a Minimize button, Maximize and Restore Down buttons appear as well so that you can perform those tasks on the window. You also can use shortcut menus to maximize and restore files. A feature called *Snap* enables you to maximize a window by dragging it toward the top of the desktop. Move the mouse pointer over the window's title bar, drag up until a preview outline of the full-sized window appears, and then release the mouse button.

Snap A feature that enables you to maximize or resize a window automatically by dragging the window to the edges of the screen

To maximize a window:

Here's How

- Click the Maximize button on the window title bar.
  OR
- Right-click the window title bar and then click *Maximize*. Or, point to the Taskbar button, right-click the window's preview thumbnail, and then click *Maximize*.
  OR
- Drag the window by its title bar to the top of the screen, and release the mouse button when the full-screen-sized preview outline appears.

TIP When a single document is open for an application, you can minimize and maximize its window by clicking its Taskbar button.

 Here's How

To restore a maximized window:

- Click the Restore Down button on the window title bar.
  OR
- Right-click the window title bar or the Taskbar button for the window and then click *Restore*.

TIP A maximized window has the Restore Down button on the title bar, and a restored window has the Maximize button on the title bar.

Resizing a Window

Windows 8 does not limit window sizing to the size that you see when you restore a window. You can resize any window that is not maximized by dragging the window border. When you move the mouse pointer over a window border, it changes to a resizing pointer (two-headed arrow). When you point to the left or right window border, the mouse pointer becomes a horizontal two-headed arrow, and you can drag left or right to resize the window. When you point to the bottom window border, the mouse pointer becomes a vertical two-headed arrow, and you can drag up or down to resize the window. When you point to a lower corner of the window, the mouse pointer becomes a diagonal two-headed arrow (Figure 1.24), and you can drag diagonally to resize the window width and height simultaneously.

Figure 1.24 Drag a window border to resize the window.

Note: *Figure 1.24 illustrates that the window border may take on a slightly different appearance depending on the application's design. Many applications have a narrower, plain border around the window rather than the one for the application shown in Figure 1.24. Regardless of the border's appearance, the edge of the window constitutes the window border.*

The Snap feature mentioned previously also enables you to resize windows so that they fit side-by-side on the screen. Drag the window by its title bar until it is about halfway off the left or right side of the screen. When a preview outline appears, as shown in Figure 1.25, release the mouse button, and the window will snap to the previewed size.

Preview outline

Figure 1.25 Drag a window halfway off the screen to snap it to a side-by-side size.

To resize a window:

- Point to the left or right window border, and drag horizontally.
  OR
- Point to the bottom window border, and drag vertically.
  OR
- Point to a lower corner of the window (typically the lower right corner), and drag horizontally.
  OR
- Drag the window to the left or right by its title bar until it is halfway off screen. When you see the preview outline, release the mouse button.

▼ Quick Fix

Cannot Resize a Window
If you are unable to resize a window, it may be maximized. Check to see if a Restore button appears on the title bar and then click it. You may then be able to resize the window.

Moving a Window

You can move any window that is not maximized to another position on your desktop. This is another technique that you can use to set up the desktop in any way that makes your current computing work more convenient. Moving the window is a simple matter of dragging.

Here's How

To move a window:

1. Point to the window title bar.
2. Drag the window to the desired location.

The desktop provides shortcuts for rearranging windows on the screen, as well. You can right-click a blank area of the Taskbar (that is, not on a Taskbar button) and then click *Cascade windows* to arrange the windows in a pile. Because this action sizes the windows at a less-than-full-screen size, you can see a bit of each window in the pile. If you right-click the Taskbar and then click *Show windows side by side*, Windows 8 arranges the open windows to fill the screen, so you see the maximum amount of each window. The shortcut menu also includes a *Show windows stacked* command, which maximizes all the windows and shows the most recently used one on top. You also can use the Show the desktop command on the shortcut menu to minimize all open windows.

Note: *The cascade and side-by-side arrangements work only on windows that are not minimized.*

Moving between Windows

active (current) window The working window on the screen, in which you can make selections and perform other actions

You can use an easy keyboard combination to get visual guidance when you want to switch to the file or program in another open window. Switching to another window makes it the *active (current) window*.

Here's How

To switch between open windows (program or document):

▼ **Quick Fix**

Sizing Situation
When you redisplay a window, it appears at its previous size. If the open windows were stacked or arranged in a particular way, your window may not appear to be selected at all. In such a case, maximize or resize the window as needed.

- Click the task's button on the Taskbar. If there are multiple windows open, move the mouse pointer over the Taskbar button and then click the thumbnail for the desired window.
  OR
- If you can see part of the window on the desktop, click the visible part of the window.
  OR
- Press and hold Alt + Tab. Press an arrow key or repeatedly press the Tab key to highlight the desired window in the task-switching window that appears and then release all keyboard keys.

Closing a Window

Closing a program window shuts down the program and file (if any) within the window, freeing up system resources and potentially space on the desktop. You should close program windows before shutting down your system, in particular because the application will prompt you to save any unsaved changes you have made to the file in the window. Every window includes a Close (X) button that you can click to close the window (Figure 1.26). You also can use the Taskbar to close a window. One way is to right-click the Taskbar icon and then click *Close window* in its Jump List. You also can move the mouse pointer over the Taskbar icon, move the mouse pointer over the thumbnail for the window to close, and then click the smaller Close (X) button that appears in the thumbnail.

Close
button

Figure 1.26 Click a button, close a window.

T I P The buttons on a title bar can help you tell the difference between a window and a dialog box. A dialog box typically lacks Minimize and Maximize buttons. A dialog box will have only the Close button, and perhaps an additional button you can click to get Help.

To close a window: Here's How

- Click the Close button on the window title bar.
  OR
- Right-click the window's Taskbar button, and click *Close window*.
  OR
- Move the mouse pointer over the Taskbar icon, move the mouse pointer over the thumbnail for the window to close, and then click the smaller Close (X) button that appears in the thumbnail.
  OR
- Press Alt + F4.

Finding Commands in Windows 8 Apps

The new Windows 8 apps do not work in the same type of windowed environment as the more traditional desktop style applications. For that reason, you will use different methods to issue commands and otherwise work with the Windows 8 apps. In Windows 8 apps, the commands appear in a bar at the bottom of the screen, although some apps such as the Windows 8 version of Internet Explorer may also display choices at the top of the screen. If you do not see commands initially, you can display them in a variety of ways.

To display and use commands in a Windows 8 app: Here's How

- Select an item that prompts the commands to appear.
  OR
- Right-click an open space in the app.
  OR
- Drag or swipe in from the top or bottom edge.

After you display the commands, you can use the buttons as you do on the desktop and in dialog boxes. Clicking a button may even open a menu, as shown in Figure 1.27.

Figure 1.27 Commands in Window 8 apps appear along the bottom of the screen, and clicking a button may open a menu like the one shown near the right.

Switching between Windows 8 Apps

Because you will not see a Taskbar when working with Windows 8 apps, the interface gives you a few other options for switching between applications when a Windows 8 app is open. These methods enable you to switch between running Windows 8 apps as well as desktop apps.

To switch between open Windows 8 apps:

- When working on the desktop, press Ctrl + Windows logo key ⊞ + Tab and then click the app to go to in the pane at the left. Or, press the key combination repeatedly to highlight the desired app tile or the Start tile and then release the keys and press Enter to display the selected item.
  OR
- Press and hold Alt + Tab. Press an arrow key or repeatedly press the Tab key to highlight the desired window in the task-switching window that appears and then release all keyboard keys.
  OR
- Point to the upper left corner of the screen to see the tile for the Windows 8 app you used most recently and then click the tile. This technique also works for switching between Windows 8 and desktop apps.

T I P If you press Ctrl + Windows logo key ⊞ + Tab from a Windows 8 app, one of the tiles that appears in the pane at the left may be for the desktop if you previously viewed it.

Snapping Apps

Snapping Windows 8 apps enables you to view and work with two apps side by side, as shown in Figure 1.28. With a Windows 8 app open, move the mouse pointer up to the top of the screen until you see the hand pointer and then drag to the left or right side of the screen until the app snaps to that side. Or swipe the app from the left edge of the screen to the position you want. Point to the upper left corner of the screen, then drag the tile for another app to the other open pane. Or click repeatedly until the desired app appears in the other pane of the screen. Note that you can place the desktop in the right pane, if it's open. Drag the vertical divider bar between the snapped apps to determine which one occupies the larger portion of the screen.

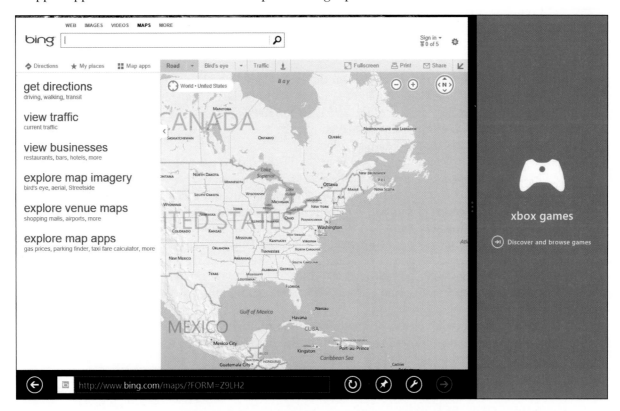

Figure 1.28 Snap Windows 8 apps to work with them side by side. This figure shows Internet Explorer at the left and Games at the right, with a divider bar in between.

Closing a Windows 8 App

Closing a Windows 8 app may not be intuitive, but it is easy. You can use either the mouse or the keyboard.

Here's How

To close a Windows 8 app:

- Move the mouse pointer up to the top of the screen until it changes to a hand and then drag down to the bottom of the screen.
  OR
- Swipe all the way from the top to the bottom of the screen.
  OR
- Press Alt + F4.

1. On the desktop, open File Explorer and then click the View tab on the ribbon of the Documents library window.
2. Click the Group by button in the Current view group. A submenu appears.
3. Move your mouse pointer over the *Authors* choice, but do not click it.
4. Use the Print Screen function to capture a screen shot. Use Paint to save the file as **C01E03S04**. Submit the file to your instructor via hard copy, email, or USB flash drive, and then close Paint. Consult your instructor if you have any questions about saving, printing, or emailing the file.
5. Switch to the WordPad window by clicking its Taskbar button (labeled Document-WordPad).
6. In the Insert group on the Home tab on the ribbon, click the Date and time button.
7. In the Date and Time dialog box that appears, click the *DD Month, YYYY* format (which shows the current date as in *15 July, 2015*) in the *Available formats* list and then click OK to insert the date at the top of the WordPad file.
8. Drag over the newly inserted date to select it.
9. Click the *Font size* drop-down list arrow in the Font group on the Home tab and then click *14* in the list to increase the text size.
10. Click the *Text color* drop-down list arrow in the Font group on the Home tab and then click *Vibrant blue* (the second from last swatch in the second column).
11. Press the right arrow key, press Enter, and then type your name.
12. Observe the ruler above the document text. Click the View tab on the ribbon and then click the *Ruler* check box in the Show or Hide Group. Observe how the ruler disappears. Click the *Ruler* check box again to redisplay the ruler.
13. Click the Home tab on the ribbon to redisplay its commands.
14. Drag over the two lines of text in the file.
15. In the Paragraph group on the Home tab on the ribbon, click the Center button.
16. Click the WordPad window Close button. In the message box that asks whether you want to save changes to the file, click Save.
17. Type **C01E03S17** into the *File name* text box to name the file. If needed, change the save location as indicated by your instructor. Click Save. Submit the file to your instructor via hard copy, email, or USB flash drive.
18. Maximize the Documents library window by dragging it up to the top of the screen.
19. Minimize the Documents library window using the method of your choice.
20. Maximize the Documents library window by moving the mouse pointer over its Taskbar button and then clicking the thumbnail.
21. Click the Restore Down button on the Documents library window to return the window to a smaller size.
22. Click the Internet Explorer button on the Taskbar and then resize the window to less-than-full-screen size using the method of your choice, if necessary.
23. Use the Snap feature (dragging the window partway off the side of the screen) to position the Internet Explorer window at the left and the Documents library window at the right.
24. Use the Print Screen function to capture a screen shot. Use Paint to save the file as **C01E03S24**. Submit the file to your instructor via hard copy, email, or USB flash drive, and then close Paint.
25. Press the Windows logo key ⊞ on the keyboard.
26. Click the Games tile on the Start screen.
27. Press Ctrl + Windows logo key ⊞ + Tab to open the pane for switching apps.

28. Use the Print Screen function to capture a screen shot. Use Paint to save the file as **C01E03S28**. Submit the file to your instructor via hard copy, email, or USB flash drive, and then close Paint.

29. Using the method of your choice, such as pressing Alt + F4 or clicking the window Close button, close each of the open windows and apps.

Understanding User Accounts

When you install and set up Windows 8 for the first time, it prompts you to enter the user name for the first user account. You can add more user accounts as needed to enable others to work with the system. In addition to enabling each user to customize his or her desktop, the user account controls the permissions and restrictions governing what the user can do when working with the system. As noted previously in the chapter, you also can choose between two user account types—a Microsoft account or a local account—to determine whether a user can interact with cloud-based content and services through Windows 8.

User accounts help enhance security and reliability. A user account can be set up to require the user to enter a password to sign in to Windows 8. In addition, user accounts work with the ***User Account Control (UAC)***, the Windows 8 feature that helps control changes to the desktop, including unauthorized changes made by a user or by malicious software.

User Account Control (UAC) The overall Windows 8 security component that works with user accounts to prevent unauthorized system changes

Note: *A User Account Control prompt may appear when you attempt to make changes to the system, such as adding a user account. In some cases, you must supply an administrator password to continue working.*

Further, Windows 8 creates a set of libraries for each user account, whether it is a Microsoft account or a local account. When you sign in to your account, you access and use only the files and folders for your account—not those of other users. This approach ensures that each user's data remains confidential and secure. Windows 8 also by default sets up different screen colors for each new user account added. A user can sign in and personalize his or her Windows settings as preferred.

Windows 8 differentiates between standard, administrator, and guest accounts. A standard user account enables the user to work with the software and hardware installed on the system, but the user is mostly prevented from making system changes that might affect other users, such as changing security settings. (However, standard account users can make some changes by supplying an administrator password when prompted.) An administrator user account enables the user to make changes to system hardware and software, settings that affect other users, and files not accessible to users with standard user accounts. By default, the first account established when Windows 8 is set up is an administrator account, and both Microsoft and local accounts can be designated as administrator or standard accounts. A guest account enables a user to work with some programs installed on the system, but the guest user may not make any system changes or access personal files.

Working with Microsoft Accounts and Local Accounts ■■■■■■■■■■■■■■■■■■■■■■■■

As a rule, most user accounts you create should be standard user accounts and will be by default. Ensuring that the system remains free from unstable or potentially damaging malicious software provides the best insurance for system reliability and safety. Because the standard user account prevents software installation (unless the user can provide an administrator password when prompted), this account type prevents the user from introducing potentially damaging software or making other changes that might have unwanted consequences.

Including a ***password*** as part of a user account setup also protects the security of that user's folders and files and is a requirement for Microsoft accounts. A standard user who wants to make changes to another user's folders and files must have the password to sign in to that user's account. No other standard account holder without the user's password can gain unauthorized access to his or her files.

You must be signed in as an administrator to add an account of any type.

Creating a Microsoft Account with Standard Access from the Start Screen

You can create user accounts from the Start screen if that is the location at which you are currently working. This saves you the trouble of switching to the desktop and provides a slightly different interface for completing the task. As you learned earlier in this chapter, a Microsoft user account is cloud-connected and enables you to synchronize data and settings between devices. By default, a Microsoft user account is set up with standard account access, but you can change it to an administrator account after its creation as described later in this chapter.

Here's How

To create a Microsoft Account with standard access:

1. Obtain an administrator account and password from an administrator of the computer system you use or from the IT (Information Technology) department in your organization if you do not have an administrator account. Sign in to Windows 8 using the administrator account sign-in information.
2. At the Start screen, select the Settings charm.
3. Click the Change PC settings link at the bottom of the Settings pane that appears at right.
4. Click *Users* in the PC settings pane that appears at left.
5. Click *Add a user* under *Other users* in the right pane.
6. Click the Sign up for a new email address link near the bottom of the screen that appears.
7. At the Sign up for a new email address screen, enter the preferred address using the *Email address* text box and then enter the other account information as prompted. Click Next.
8. At the next screen, enter *Mobile phone, Alternate email, Secret question,* and *Answer* security information. (If you prefer not to include your mobile

▼ Quick Fix

Established Account
If the user already has a Microsoft email address, you can enter it in Step 6 and click Next.

phone information, only two of the three items are required, so you can skip entering phone information.) Click Next.

9. At the next screen, specify the *Birth date* and *Gender*, and clear the check box about promotional offers. Click Next. Type the words shown in the *Enter these characters* CAPTCHA box. Click Next. Microsoft will verify whether the email address you specified in Step 7 is available for use.

10. At the Add a user screen that confirms the user will be able to sign in to the computer, click Finish.

11. Press the Windows logo key on the keyboard to return to Start.

Note: *If you want to create a user account based on your existing email address, instead of Step 6 above, enter the address to use in the Email address text box, click Next, and follow the remaining prompts.*

 To create what is known as a *strong password,* make it at least eight characters long and include a combination of uppercase and lowercase letters, numbers, and symbols, including spaces. Do not use complete words, but do use memorable acronyms or abbreviations, alternate spellings, or substitute numbers for entire words (2 to stand for *to*). Also avoid using any easily recognizable personal information such as your name, birth date, and so on. *P@yattenzion2Me* is a stronger password than *PayAttentionToMe.* As always, keep a written record of the password in a separate, but easy-to-access location such as a locked file cabinet.

Creating a Local Account from the Start Screen

Working from the Start screen, you can create a local account. This type of account enables the user to work with local files and programs and is set up with standard access by default.

To create a local account from Start:

Here's How

1. Obtain an administrator account and password from an administrator of the computer system you use or from the IT (Information Technology) department in your organization if you do not have an administrator account. Sign in to Windows 8 using the administrator account sign-in information.

2. At the Start screen, select the Settings charm.

3. Click the Change PC settings link at the bottom of the Settings pane that appears at right.

4. Click *Users* in the PC settings pane that appears at left.

5. Click *Add a user* under *Other users* in the right pane.

6. Click the Sign in without a Microsoft account link at the bottom of the screen that appears.

7. Click the Local account button.

8. At the next screen, enter *User name, Password, Reenter password,* and *Password hint* account information. Click Next.

9. At the final Add a user screen, click Finish.
10. Press the Windows logo key ⊞ on the keyboard to return to Start.

Changing between Microsoft and Local Account Types ■■■■■■■■■■■■■■■■■■■■■■■■■■■■■■■■

From the Start screen, you can change the currently signed-in account from a Microsoft account to a local account, and vice versa. You might want to do this, for example, if you started with a local account but realize you need to connect to the cloud. Or, if you started with a Microsoft account that you no longer want to connect to the cloud, you can change to a local account type to retain your libraries and your desktop settings. Changing an account from one type to the other eliminates the need to try to work with two different accounts depending on whether you want to work in the cloud.

Here's How → **To change between Microsoft and local accounts from Start:**

1. Sign in with the account to change.
2. At the Start screen, select the Settings charm.
3. Click the Change PC settings link at the bottom of the Settings pane that appears at right.
4. Click *Users* in the PC settings pane that appears at left.
5. Click *Switch to a local account* or *Switch to a Microsoft account* under *Your account* in the right pane.
6. Enter information as prompted, and then click Next.
7. Follow the process for entering account information for the appropriate account type as detailed previously.
8. Press the Windows logo key ⊞ on the keyboard to return to Start, if needed.

Adding a Standard User Account from the Desktop ■■■■■■■■■■■■■■■■■■■■■■■■■■■■■■

Control Panel The central location where you can change system preferences and settings

If you are working from the desktop, you can use the *Control Panel* in Windows 8 (Figure 1.29) to work with user accounts, among other settings. Creating a user account provides you a good first opportunity to work in Control Panel, although this process returns you to the PC settings screen you already worked with from the Start screen.

Figure 1.29 The Control Panel enables you to change settings in Windows 8.

Here's How

To add a user account from Control Panel:

1. Obtain an administrator account and password from an administrator of the computer system you use or from the IT (Information Technology) department in your organization if you do not have an administrator account. Sign-in to Windows 8 using the administrator account sign-in information.
2. Go to the desktop and select the Settings charm.
3. Click *Control Panel* in the *Settings* list that appears in the right pane.
4. Click the *User Accounts and Family Safety* category link.
5. Click the User Accounts link.
6. Click the Manage another account link.
7. Click the Add a new user in PC Settings link below the list of users.
8. In the PC Settings screen that appears, click *Add a user* under *Other users*, and follow the applicable previously described procedure to create either a Microsoft account or a local account.

Settings a Standard User Can Change

If you have a standard user account, you can make these changes to your account setup.

- Change your account password.
- Remove your account password.
- Create a PIN number as an alternate method for signing in to your account.
- Change your account picture.

You can accomplish each of these actions in the PC settings screen accessed from the Start screen. Note that users with an administrator account also can make these account changes, as well as changing other users accounts as described earlier.

T I P Users of touch-enabled devices also can use the Create a picture password to take advantage of another secure method to sign in.

Here's How

To change or remove a standard user account password:

1. Press the Windows logo key 🪟 on the keyboard to return to the Start screen, if needed.
2. Select the Settings charm.
3. Click the Change PC settings link at the bottom of the right pane.
4. Click *Users* in the PC settings pane at left.
5. Click *Change your password* under *Sign-in options*.
6. Type your current password into the *Current password* text box and then click Next. Or, if you are updating a Microsoft account, type the password in the *Old password* text box, enter your new password in both the *New password* and *Re-enter password* text boxes, click Next, and then click Finish.
7. Type the new password into the *New password* text box. Press Tab and then type the new password a second time in the *Reenter password* text box.
8. Type a hint that Windows 8 can display to help you remember the password in the *Password hint* text box.

9. Click Next.
10. At the Change your password screen that reminds you to use the new password the next time you sign in, click Finish.
11. Press the Windows logo key 🪟 on the keyboard to return to the Start screen, if needed.

To create a sign-in PIN for a standard user account:

1. Press the Windows logo key 🪟 on the keyboard to return to the Start screen, if needed.
2. Select the Settings charm.
3. Click the Change PC settings link at the bottom of the right pane.
4. Click *Users* in the PC settings pane at left.
5. Click *Create a PIN* under *Sign-in options*.
6. Type your current password into the *Password* text box, and click OK.
7. Type the new four-digit PIN in the *Enter PIN* text box, press Tab, and then type the new code a second time in the *Confirm PIN* text box.
8. Click Finish.

9. Press the Windows logo key on the keyboard to return to the Start screen, if needed. The next time you sign in to Windows, it will automatically prompt you to enter the new PIN. You can type it to sign in, or click *Sign-in options* and then click the Password button to sign in with your account password, instead.

TIP To manage a PIN, return to the Sign-in options for your account and then use Change PIN or Remove.

Your user account picture appears on the Start screen and sign-in screen once you add it. You can assign an account picture online for a Microsoft account, or you can do so from the Start screen for both Microsoft and local accounts. If you have recently started working with your computer and don't have many pictures on it, you will need to copy a few pictures to your Pictures library to have a selection to choose from.

To change a standard user account's picture:

Here's How

1. Press the Windows logo key on the keyboard to return to the Start screen, if needed.
2. Click your user name at the upper right corner of the screen.
3. Click *Change account picture* in the menu. The PC settings screen appears with *Personalize* selected in the list at the left.
4. Click *Browse* in the right pane.
5. If the Pictures library does not appear, click *Files* at the top of the screen. Then click *Pictures* to go to your Pictures library. (You can use one of the other choices to navigate to pictures stored elsewhere.)
6. Click the picture to select (navigate to a subfolder first, if needed) and then click Choose image.
7. Press the Windows logo key on the keyboard to return to the Start screen, if needed.

Quick Fix

No Image
If you do not have a digital image file to use for your user account, and a webcam is connected to your system, click the Camera button rather than the Browse button to snap a new profile photo.

Exercise 4

Creating Your Microsoft Account with Standard Access

1. Obtain the user name and password for your system's administrator account from your instructor for use with this exercise. You will use the account you create in this exercise for your activities throughout the rest of the book. Start Windows and then sign in to the administrator account.
2. Select the Settings charm.
3. Click the Change PC settings link at the bottom of the Start pane that appears at right.
4. Click *Users* in the PC settings pane that appears at left.
5. Click *Add a user* under *Other users* in the right pane.
6. Click the Sign up for a new email address link near the bottom of the screen that appears. (If you already have an email address that you want to use, enter it in the *Email address* text box instead, click Next, and then follow the on-screen prompts to finish creating the account.)

7. At the Sign up for a new email address screen, enter your preferred address using the *Email address* text box and drop-down, enter the other account information as prompted, and then click Next.

8. At the next screen, enter *Mobile phone, Alternate email, Secret question*, and *Answer* security information. (You can skip Mobile phone as desired; only two of the three are required.) Click Next.

9. At the next screen, specify your *Birth date and Gender*. Clear the check box about promotional offers and then click Next. Type the text shown in the *Enter these characters* CAPTCHA box and then click Next. Microsoft will verify whether the email address you specified in Step 7 is available.

10. At the Add a user screen that confirms you will be able to sign in to the computer, click Finish.

11. Press the Windows logo key ⊞ on the keyboard to return to Start.

12. Click the user name at the upper left and then click the name of your new user account.

13. Type the account password in the *Password* text box and then press Enter or click the blue Submit (right arrow) button.

14. Use the Print Screen function to capture a screen shot of the desktop with your new user account shown at upper right. Use Paint to save the file as **C01E04**. Submit the file to your instructor via hard copy, email, or USB flash drive, and then close Paint. Consult your instructor if you have any questions about saving, printing, or emailing the file.

Note: *If you want to create a user account based on your existing email address and your instructor approves of that method, instead of doing what's called for in Step 6 above, enter the address to use in the Email address text box, click Next, and follow the remaining prompts.*

Pausing or Finishing Your Work Session ▪▪▪▪▪▪

Most people do not spend hour after hour working nonstop on the computer. It is healthy to take frequent breaks. Most users work for shorter periods of time, with phone calls, meetings, and other types of distractions in between.

Windows 8 provides a variety of ways that you can put a work session on hold rather than shutting down your computer altogether. These features can provide security for your work, conserve power, or both.

Using Sleep or Hibernate

sleep A power-saving state that preserves your work in memory and on the hard disk so that you can resume working quickly

If you want to walk away from your computer for a while and save power without having to close all your files and shut down the system, you can take advantage of the *sleep* feature in Windows 8. When you choose to put the system to sleep, Windows 8 saves your files and information about which programs are open both in system memory and on the computer's hard disk (or system memory for a mobile computer); then it puts the computer in a lower-power state without shutting it down. When you wake the system up, your programs and files reappear on the desktop in a brief time, as little as several seconds.

The sleep state can save significant power. A desktop system will use about one tenth the power when asleep, and a mobile computer will consume only 1–2 percent of the power it consumes normally. Plus, sleep can give you peace of mind that your in-progress work remains secure. By default, if your account is password-protected, you must enter the password when you wake up the system, so that unauthorized users cannot wake up your computer and pry. You also can set up the system to go to sleep after a particular time frame so that if you leave the computer unattended, it will save and secure your work automatically, plus save power.

Note: *If you use Windows 8 on a mobile computer (or any type of mobile device), sleep has a few extra functions. If you leave the system in sleep mode so long that the battery power gets too low, sleep makes sure all your work is saved in system memory and then places the system in a low-power state. Also, by default, shutting the computer's lid puts the system to sleep. To wake it back up, press the hardware power button.*

Here's How

To put a computer to sleep and wake it up:

1. From either the Start screen or desktop, select the Settings charm.
2. Click Power and then click *Sleep*. The computer goes to sleep. The computer's power and disk lights may remain on, and the hardware power button might blink slowly or change colors.
3. To wake the computer back up, press the hardware power button quickly. On some systems, you may have to press and hold it for a moment before releasing the button, or you may be able to wiggle the mouse or press the space bar rather than pressing the power button.
4. Swipe up from the bottom of the screen or press the space bar, type your password in the *Password* text box, and then press Enter or click the blue Submit (right arrow) button to the right of the *Password* text box.

Some systems, particularly mobile computers, also offer a hibernate state. *Hibernate* saves the work session but shuts down the computer. Restarting opens your files and programs back on the desktop; however, this process works more slowly than the sleep state. To hibernate the system, select the Settings charm, click Power, and then click *Hibernate*. To resume work, restart the system by pressing the hardware power button.

Note: *Sleep and hibernate settings work with power plans in Windows 8. The BIOS (basic input/output system) for the computer must support sleep or hibernate for those modes to be available.*

Note: *Hibernate saves a lot of information to the hard disk, which is a problem if your system is low on disk space. Chapter 12 explains how to use Disk Cleanup to remove unneeded hibernate data and other files that may be clogging your system's hard disk.*

Locking the System

Locking the system hides the desktop, but does not shut the system down or conserve power. As with the sleep mode, if your user account is password-protected, you will need to enter the password to unlock the system and redisplay the desktop. You might lock the computer rather than putting it to sleep when you intend to be away from the system for a brief time only.

hibernate A more advanced shutdown state that saves your work and shuts the system down; your in-process work reappears on the desktop when you restart your system

lock A state that hides the desktop without shutting down the system or changing its power consumption

To lock and unlock the computer:

1. Press the Windows logo key ⊞ on the keyboard or select the Start charm to return to the Start screen, if needed.
2. Click your user name at the upper right and then click *Lock*. The Lock screen, which resembles the Windows 8 introductory sign-in screen with the date and time and a background image, appears.
3. To unlock the computer, swipe up from the bottom of the screen or press the space bar.
4. Type your password in the *Password* text box and then press Enter or click the blue Submit (right arrow) button to the right of the *Password* text box.

Step 2

Switching Users

If you are working in a hectic environment where many users need to sign in to and out of a system repeatedly throughout the day, shutting down and starting up the system or repeatedly signing in and out would take too much time. Instead, you can switch to your user account from the Start screen without forcing the current user to sign out or shut down.

This capability takes advantage of a Windows 8 feature known as *User Switching*. User Switching keeps each signed-in user's programs running and files open, so when a user switches back to his or her account, his or her files appear immediately on the desktop.

Note: *Because switching users does not automatically save your work, be sure to save any open files frequently to prevent losing data.*

User Switching
Changing between user accounts without shutting down files or programs for any signed-in user

To switch users:

1. Press the Windows logo key ⊞ on the keyboard or select the Start charm to return to the Start screen, if needed.
2. Click your user name at the upper right and then click the desired user account in the menu.
3. Type your password in the *Password* text box and then press Enter or click the blue Submit (right arrow) button to the right of the text box.

Signing Out

To *sign out* from the system shuts down your applications and open files, making more system resources available to other users signed in to the system. Signing out also provides added security because it prevents any other user from accessing your files when your system is connected to a network. It is a good practice to save and close your files before signing out to ensure that you do not lose any work.

sign out To exit your user account and desktop without shutting down the system

To sign out:

1. Press the Windows logo key ⊞ on the keyboard or select the Start charm to return to the Start screen, if needed.
2. Click your user name at the upper right and then click *Sign out*.
3. If you have any unsaved files open, a screen will prompt you to save changes and tell you which apps have unsaved work. Click Cancel, go to the specified app and save your work, and then return to Step 1. Alternately, you can click Sign out anyway to close open apps and discard the unsaved work. If you pause too long before completing this step, Windows 8 will display a black screen asking you to verify whether to log off. You can click Log Off Now to continue or Cancel to stop the log off.
4. To sign in to another account, swipe up from the bottom of the screen, click a user tile, type the account password in the *Password* text box, and then press Enter or click the blue Submit (right arrow) button to the right of the text box.

Restarting

You may need to restart the system after performing certain operations, such as installing new hardware or software. Sometimes, an install process displays a dialog box asking if you want to restart the system now, and restarting then becomes a simple matter of clicking Yes in that dialog box. In other cases, you may need to restart the system manually. To do so, you can again use a choice you access through the Settings charm.

To restart the system:

1. From either the Start screen or desktop, select the Settings charm.
2. Click Power and then click *Restart*.
3. If there are additional users signed in to the system, a message will warn you that they could lose unsaved work. Click Restart anyway to continue.
4. If you have any unsaved files open, a dialog box will prompt you to save changes. Click Yes or Save (depending on the program in which you are saving), and repeat the process for every prompt that appears.
5. At the Windows 8 introductory screen that appears after the system restarts, sign back in to the desired account.

Restarting When the Computer Hangs

While computers have dramatically increased in performance and reliability over the years, writing an operating system that works with thousands of possible internal and external hardware models remains a monumental task. For that reason, you still may encounter situations where the computer *hangs*—appears to stop working altogether, also known as being locked up—or has another problem, such as a display that appears differently. Situations like this force you to restart the system.

hang When the computer appears to freeze up and stop working during a particular operation

Restarting by using the Settings charm is called a **soft reboot** or **restart**. This process restarts the system without turning off its power, which is technically gentler on the internal and external components of the computer. However, if a computer is truly hung, it may not respond when you try to select the Settings charm.

In such a case, you can try a keyboard combination that will also perform a soft reboot, or you can try a **hard reboot** by powering the system all the way off and then back on.

Here's How

To restart a hung system:

- Press Ctrl + Alt + Delete. A screen with choices for locking the computer, switching users, and so on appears. Click the Shut down button at the lower right corner of this screen. If the mouse does not respond when you try to click the button, use the hard reboot technique described next.
  OR
- To hard reboot or restart the system, press any restart button on the system's case. (In some cases, the button will be a small, recessed button that you must press with a pen tip or other small object, such as the extended end of a paper clip.) If there is no restart button, press and hold the hardware power button until you hear the system beginning to shut down. When you hear the drives stop whirring and all the system lights go dark, press the power button again to restart the system as usual.

Shutting Down Completely

At the end of the workday, you should shut down your system. Saving your work and shutting down your system ensures that your work—even properly saved work—is much less likely to be damaged by power fluctuations or to be subject to improper viewing on a network.

Here's How

To shut down Windows 8 and your computer:

1. From either the Start screen or desktop, select the Settings charm.
2. Click Power and then click *Shut down*.
3. If you have any unsaved files open, a screen will show you which apps have unsaved changes. Click Cancel, save the work and close those apps, then return to Step 1 to initiate the shut down again.

1. Display the Start screen, click your user name at the upper right corner of the screen, and then click *Lock*.
2. Swipe up from the bottom of the initial screen or press the space bar, type your password in the *Password* text box, and then press Enter or click the blue Submit (right arrow) button.
3. Obtain the user name and password for an administrator account on the computer you are using from your instructor if you have not already done so. Display the Start screen, click your user name at the upper right corner, and then click the administrator account. Type the password in the *Password* text box and then press Enter or click the blue Submit (right arrow) button.
4. Use the Print Screen function to capture a screen shot of the Start screen while you are signed in to the administrator account. Use Paint to save the file as **C01E05**. Submit the file to your instructor via hard copy, email, or USB flash drive, and then close Paint. Consult your instructor if you have any questions about saving, printing, or emailing the file.
5. Display the Start screen, if needed, click your user name at the upper right, and then click *Sign out*.
6. Sign back in to your account.
7. Select the Settings charm, click Power, and then click *Restart*. At the message that reminds you that others are signed in to the computer, click Restart anyway to continue restarting.
8. Sign back in to your account when the system restarts.

Getting Help and Support ■■■■■■■■■■■■■■■■■■■

It took Microsoft programmers some years to develop and finalize the features in Windows 8. An end user would need a photographic memory to know about every feature available, how it works, and where to find its settings. The new Start screen interface in Windows 8 may even prompt questions from more experienced Windows users. Because people who have a photographic memory form a limited universe indeed, Windows 8 includes a built-in Windows Help and Support system supplemented by online help downloaded from the Microsoft website. Round out your skills now by learning how to find help when you have a problem using Windows 8.

Browsing in Windows Help and Support

Like previous Windows versions, Windows 8 includes a built-in Windows Help and Support system (Figure 1.30). This system combines help information that Windows installs on your computer system with help provided online by Microsoft. The online portion of the Help system ensures that the help you receive is the most timely and up-to-date help available. Online help typically downloads automatically as you browse or search.

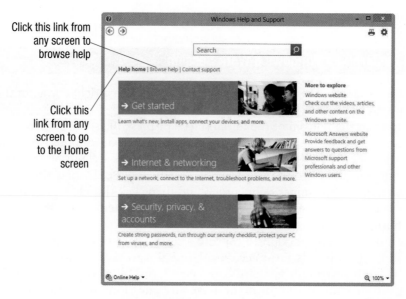

Click this link from any screen to browse help

Click this link from any screen to go to the Home screen

Figure 1.30 Access different forms of Help in the Windows Help and Support window.

To open the Windows Help and Support window, select the Search charm and then click *Help and Support* under *Windows System*. Pressing F1 from the desktop takes you to the Help screen with help that pertains to your current task.

Once you have opened the Windows Help and Support window, you can browse for help in three main ways:

■ Click the link to one of the main topics that appears.

■ Click the Browse help link near the top of the window. In the list that appears (Figure 1.31), click a link to an overall topic area and then click subsequent topics and links until you arrive at the help information you need. Click the Back and Forward buttons as needed to move between information in the window.

Back button

Forward button

Figure 1.31 To browse topics, click links that appear in the Windows Help and Support window.

- Type a topic to search for in the *Search* text box at the top of the Windows Help and Support window and then press Enter. You can then click a topic in the list of results to see help information about it.

Searching for Help on the Windows 8 Website

The Windows 8 website represents years of cumulative information about the Microsoft products. Even more than the Windows 8 Help system's online component, it provides detailed, up-to-date information about how to perform more advanced operations in Windows 8 and troubleshoot problems you may encounter. When you cannot find the information you need in the Windows Help and Support system, you can go to the Window 8 website.

To go to the Windows 8 website:

Here's How

1. Open the Windows Help and Support window by using the Search charm.
2. Click the Windows website link at the right under *More to explore*.
3. Scroll and review the available links on the site, and browse to the desired Help content.

Using Microsoft Answers

Like other functions in Windows, the Windows 8 Windows Help and Support system has become more robust and functional, making it an excellent resource for users both to explore and to learn more about working with Windows 8 and the computer. However, if you need more assistance than the Windows Help and Support window provides, you can tap into the expertise of the entire universe of Windows users through the interactive Microsoft Community website.

To go to the Microsoft Answers website:

Here's How

1. Open the Windows Help and Support window by using the Search charm.
2. Click the Microsoft Community website link at the right under *More to explore*.
3. Scroll to review the posted questions on the site, click a question to see more information, or click the Ask a question option button to start the process for posting a new question.

Browsing and Searching Windows Help and Support

1. From the Start screen, type Help, and then click *Help and Support*.
2. Click the *Get started* link. Scroll down in the window, if needed, and then click the *Touch: swipe, tap, and beyond* link.
3. To print this Help information, click the Print button (it has a printer on it) in the toolbar at the upper right corner of the Windows Help and Support window. Click a printer as indicated by your instructor and then click Print to send the topic to the printer. Label the printout as **C01E06S04**, and then submit it to your instructor.
4. Click the *Help home* link at the top of the window to return to the initial Help content.
5. Click the *Search* text box near the top of the window, type sign in, and press Enter.
6. Scroll down the list of results and then click one of the topics.
7. Click the Print button again. Select the printer indicated by your instructor and then click Print. Label this printout **C01E06S08** and then submit it to your instructor.
8. Click the Back button at the upper left corner of the window twice.
9. Click the *Help home* link.
10. Review the information and Help options on the page.
11. Click the Windows Help and Support window Close (X) button.
12. Use the Settings charm to shut down the computer.

CHAPTER SUMMARY

- Microsoft Windows 8 is an operating system for computers. The operating system enables you to tell the computer hardware and software what to do.

- You use a mouse or touchpad to interact with Windows 8, and on touch-enabled systems, you also can use gestures, such as swiping and tapping. Key mouse/touchpad skills include clicking, double-clicking, right-clicking, and dragging.

- Sign in with a Microsoft account when you want to connect to the cloud and have synchronized settings between multiple devices, or sign in to a local account to work offline.

- When you start Windows 8, power on the system, swipe up from the bottom of the screen or press the space bar, and then sign in to your user account by clicking the account tile. If the account is password-protected, type your password in the text box that appears and press Enter.

- The Start screen enables you to access the programs and cloud-enabled features that are part of Windows 8. Press the Windows logo key 🪟 on the keyboard or select the Start charm to open the Start screen. You can click a program tile to start a program or use the Search charm to find and start a program.

- The desktop enables you to organize your files using the File Explorer app, to run desktop applications, and to access system features.

- You can use the Windows logo key 🪟 and other methods to switch between the Start screen and the desktop.

- Charms enable you to search, share, start, use devices, and access settings. Point to the lower right corner of the screen to display the charms.

- The Taskbar along the bottom of the desktop provides icons for launching some programs.

- From the desktop, click an icon to select it or double-click an icon to open it. Drag over text to select it.

- Click a menu on a menu bar or command bar to open the menu, point to a command that displays a submenu, if needed, and then click the command to choose. An ellipsis (...) beside the command name means that clicking the command opens a dialog box.

- Dialog boxes contain controls such as text boxes and drop-down lists or palettes that are used to specify more detail about how a command should execute.

- A window is a frame that holds content such as a program, file, or folder on the desktop. You can open multiple windows and click the Taskbar button for a window to switch to that window.

- Click a Taskbar button to switch to that window. Or, if a program has multiple windows open, point to the Taskbar button, point to one of the preview thumbnails to temporarily display the window contents, and then click the preview thumbnail to open the window. The preview behavior is called Peek.

- When multiple programs are open, press Ctrl + Windows logo key ⊞ + Tab to display them in a pane at the left. Press Tab to cycle through the tiles and then press Enter to select the one to display. Or click the desired tile.

- Click the Show desktop button to minimize all open windows.

- Minimizing a window reduces it to a Taskbar icon. Maximizing a window expands it to fill the desktop. Restoring a window returns it to its prior non-maximized size.

- Use the Minimize, Restore, Maximize, and Close buttons at the upper right corner of a window to manipulate its size.

- Drag a window by its title bar to move it.

- The Shake feature enables you to minimize all windows except the one you are working on. Drag the desired window's title bar rapidly left and right, as if you are shaking it, to accomplish this.

- The Snap feature enables you to resize a window on the fly. Drag the window up to the top of the screen to maximize it. Drag a window halfway off the left or right side of the screen to size it for side-by-side viewing.

- Windows 8 enables you to create Microsoft and local accounts with standard access by default. You will learn in a later chapter how to change to an administrator account. Most user accounts are standard accounts.

- User accounts work with User Account Control, a security feature that prevents unwanted system changes. You must be signed in with an administrator account or have an administrator password to make changes that affect all users of the system.

- You can add a password to a user account, remove or change the password, change the account picture, or add a PIN.

- User Switching enables another user to sign in without forcing another user to close programs and sign out. On the Start screen, click your user name at upper right, click the desired user account in the menu, and enter the sign-in password to make the switch.

Working with the Windows 8 Desktop

- You can put the computer into the power-conserving sleep mode to save your files and program status when you need to leave the computer. Select the Settings charm, click the Power button, and then click *Sleep* to put the system to sleep. Pressing the hardware power button quickly wakes up the system.
- You can use the *Lock* command, found when you click your user name on the Start screen, to hide your desktop from other users. Swipe up, click your account tile, and then enter your password to unlock the system.
- Shutting down the system both signs out all users and powers down the computer. Select the Settings charm, click Power, and then click *Shut down*.
- You can use the Windows Help and Support window to browse for help, search for help, or go online to find more information. Select the Settings charm and then click *Help and Support* to open Help.

CONCEPTS CHECK

Completion: Answer the following questions in a Word document.

Part 1

Multiple Choice

1. To display the Start screen, press the _____.
   a. Open icon.
   b. Print Screen key.
   c. Windows logo key.
   d. Launch icon.

2. Select the _____ charm to find more programs from the Start screen.
   a. Search
   b. Share
   c. Devices
   d. Settings

3. The _____ appears along the bottom of the desktop by default.
   a. Taskbar
   b. command bar
   c. button bar
   d. sidebar

4. The _____ in a window holds commands.
   a. Taskbar
   b. ribbon
   c. menu bar
   d. Both b and c

5. The _____ organizes commands into tabs and groups.
   a. command bar
   b. menu bar
   c. ribbon
   d. Taskbar

6. A dialog box holds _____ that you use to give details about how a command should work.
   a. items
   b. choices
   c. markers
   d. controls

7. To close a program or window, press Alt +
   a. F1.
   b. F2.
   c. F3.
   d. F4.

8. Click the _____ button to reduce a window to a Taskbar button.
   a. Shrink
   b. Minimize
   c. Small window
   d. Reduce

9. Use the _____ command accessed via the Settings charm's Power button to put the system to sleep.
   a. Power
   b. Sleep
   c. Pause
   d. Blink

10. Clicking _____ in the menu that appears when you click your user name on the Start screen hides your desktop and requires you to sign in again.
    a. Change account picture
    b. Lock
    c. Sign out
    d. Both b and c

Part 2

Short Answer

11. How do you display the charms?

    _____

12. How do you find a program to start?

    _____

13. Why does Windows 8 require each system user to have a separate account?

    _____

14. What type of user account enables you to access the cloud?

    _____

15. Name the buttons you can use to resize windows.

    _____

16. What is the difference between a standard user account and an administrator account?

    _____

17. How do you put the system to sleep, and what happens when you do?

_____

18. How do you wake up the system?

_____

19. What command do you use to restart the system?

_____

20. Name two types of help you can get, or two ways to get help.

_____

SKILLS CHECK

Save all solution files to the default Documents folder or any alternate folder specified by your instructor.

Guided Check

Assessment 1

Starting Up and Opening Folders and Programs

1. Sign in to the system.
   a. Power on the system.
   b. Swipe up from the bottom of the screen or press the space bar.
   c. Click the tile for your user account.
   d. Type your password if your account has one and press Enter.
   e. Press Enter.
2. Start the Paint program.
   a. Select the Search charm.
   b. Click Paint under *Windows Accessories*.
3. Open the Documents library window.
   a. Click File Explorer on the Taskbar.
   b. Double-click *Documents*.
4. Display the Start screen and start Calculator.
   a. Press the Windows logo key ⊞ on the keyboard.
   b. Select the Search charm.
   c. Click Calculator under *Windows Accessories*.
5. Capture a screen shot, save it as **C01A01**, and then submit it to your instructor.

Assessment 2

Working with Open Windows

1. Minimize all windows to Taskbar buttons.
   • Click the Minimize button on each window.
   OR
   • Click the Show desktop button on the Taskbar.
2. Redisplay the Documents window.
   • Click the Documents library window Taskbar button.
   OR
   • Press Alt + Tab, hold down Alt and press the Tab key repeatedly until the Documents library window is previewed, and then release the keys.

3. Drag the Documents library window to the top of the screen to maximize it.
4. Maximize the Paint window from the Taskbar.
   a. Point to the Paint button on the Taskbar.
   b. Right-click the preview thumbnail.
   c. Click *Maximize*.
5. Click the Paint window's Restore Down button.
6. Capture a screen shot, save it as **C01A02**, and then submit it to your instructor.
7. Close the Documents library, Calculator, and Paint windows.
   a. Right-click each program's icon on the Taskbar.
   b. Click Close window in each program's Jump List.

Assessment 3

Sleeping and Waking the System

1. Put the system to sleep.
   a. Select the Settings charm.
   b. Click the Power button.
   c. Click *Sleep*.
2. Wake the system.
   a. Press the power button on the computer case quickly.
   b. Swipe up from the bottom of the screen or press the space bar and then click the tile for your user account.
   c. Type your password in the *Password* text box and then press Enter or click the blue Submit (right arrow) button to the right of the *Password* text box.

Assessment 4

Browsing Windows Help and Support

1. Start Windows Help and Support.
   a. Select the Search charm.
   b. Click *Help and Support* under *Windows System*.
2. Go to a topic.
   a. Click the *Browse help* link near the top of the window.
   b. Click the *Security, privacy, and accounts* category link.
   c. Click the *Security checklist for Windows* topic link.
3. Print a topic.
   a. Click the Print button near the upper right corner of the window.
   b. Select the printer indicated by your instructor and then click Print.
   c. Label this printout **C01A04** and then submit it to your instructor.
4. Click the Close (X) button for the Windows Help and Support window to close the window.

On Your Own

Assessment 5

Use Menus and Dialog Boxes

1. Restart the Paint program.
2. Use the Print Screen key to take a picture of your screen.
3. On the Home tab on the ribbon in Paint, click the Paste button in the Clipboard group.
4. On the Home tab, click the Resize button in the Image group. Type 75 in the *Horizontal* text box and press Tab. Type 75 in the *Vertical* text box if necessary. Click OK.

5. Click the Rotate button in the Image group and then click *Rotate left 90°*.
6. Maximize the Paint window.
7. Click the View tab on the ribbon.
8. In the Zoom group, click the Zoom Out button.
9. Click the Home tab on the ribbon to redisplay it.
10. Click the Save button on the Quick Access Toolbar, save the file as **C01A05**, and then submit it to your instructor.
11. Click the window Close (X) button to close Paint.

Assessment **6** **Working with Program Windows**

1. Open the following programs and windows in the order listed:
   Paint
   Internet Explorer (from the Start screen)
   WordPad
   Games (from the Start screen)
   File Explorer
2. Redisplay the Start screen and then press Ctrl + Windows logo key + Tab.
3. While the pane appears at the left showing the open programs, use the Print Screen key to take a picture of your screen.
4. Click the Desktop tile in the pane at the left.
5. Click the Paint button on the Taskbar.
6. Maximize the Paint window, if necessary. Paste in the screen shot, save it as **C01A06**, and then submit it to your instructor.
7. Close all the open program windows. (Remember to swipe down from the top of the screen to close Windows 8 apps.)

Assessment **7** **Pausing a Work Session**

1. Select the Settings charm, click Power, and then point to *Shut down*.
2. Capture a screen shot, paste it into Paint, save it as **C01A07**, and then submit it to your instructor.
3. Lock the system.
4. Sign in to the system again.
5. Sign out from your account.
6. Sign in to your account again.
7. Restart the system.

Assessment **8** **Group Activity: Searching the Windows Website**

Note that this assessment requires a working Internet connection.

1. As a group, agree on three help topics to search for.
2. Open the Windows Help and Support window.
3. Type the first topic to search for in the *Search* text box and then press Enter.
4. Click a topic in the *Search Results* list.
5. Click Print, select a printer in the dialog box, and then click the Print button.
6. Repeat Steps 3 through 5 to find and print information about your other two selected help topics.
7. Label the printouts with the name of all the members of your group and then submit the printouts to your instructor.

CHALLENGE PROJECT

Your company has bought a new computer with the Windows 8 operating system, and you have been asked to share the system with a coworker. Set up a password-protected account for the coworker and test it by signing in to it now.

1. From the Start screen, display PC settings, and create a new local user account with the following settings:
   - User name: Buddy
   - Password and Retype password: %Windows01*Challenge
   - Password hint: Chapter 1

Note: *Ask your instructor for an administrator password to complete this activity, if needed.*

2. Go back to the Start screen and then switch to the Buddy account.
3. Capture a screen shot of your Start screen, save it as **C01A09**, and then submit it to your instructor.
4. Sign out of the Buddy account and then sign in to your account.

Working with Disks and Other Removable Media

PERFORMANCE OBJECTIVES

Upon successful completion of Chapter 2, you will be able to:

- Understand and select storage
- Obtain information about computer disks
- Assign a volume label
- Work with USB flash drives and other flash media
- Copy files and folders to a flash drive
- Work with CD and DVD media
- Change the AutoPlay setting of a drive
- Copy files to a writable CD or DVD
- View disk usage information
- Turn on disk compression
- Check a disk for errors
- Check disk partitioning
- Work with an external hard disk

The files and folders you access from Windows are stored on disk drives. These disk drives form the basis of the storage system on a computer, and can include hard disk drives, CD drives, and USB flash drives. Windows enables you to check and protect disks, view usage statistics on a disk, assign volume labels to disks, and much more. Windows also includes built-in utilities for partitioning and formatting new disks to prepare them for use.

Understanding and Selecting Storage ■■■■■■■■

disk drive A mechanical device that reads and writes disks

Files can be stored on a variety of media types, including flash random access memory (RAM) devices, CDs/DVDs, and hard disks. As you save and manage data files, you must evaluate the available storage options on the computer you are using and select the best one for the job. Storage can be categorized according to several different criteria.

One popular type of storage device is a ***disk drive***. A disk drive is a mechanical device that reads and writes disks. It spins the disk platters past one or more read/write heads, which work with the operating system to retrieve and store files (shown in Figure 2.1). A wide variety of disk drives is available, including hard drives and CD drives.

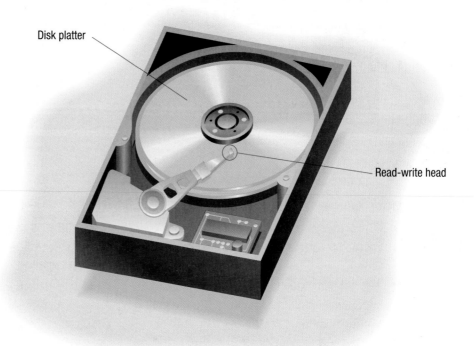

Disk platter

Read-write head

Figure 2.1 A disk drive stores data on spinning platters.

Some drives read and write data magnetically to disk; others read and write optically (with light). A *magnetic disk* stores data in patterns of positive and negative magnetic polarity in metallic particles on the surface of the disk platters, and a magnetic head in the drive changes the polarity on the disk surface to write data to it. Hard disks and floppy disks are magnetic. An *optical disc*, such as a CD-R or DVD-R, stores data in patterns of greater and lesser reflectivity on the shiny surface of a disc. A laser changes the surface reflectivity in certain spots to write the data.

Note: *For magnetic storage, the correct spelling is "disk"; for optical it is "disc."*

A *floppy disk* is a type of magnetic disk. It consists of a 3.5-inch thin plastic disk, encased in a flat square casing. It fits into a floppy drive in a computer. Floppy disks and drives are obsolete, but you still may encounter them in older computers. Their limited storage capacity (only 1.44 MB) and tendency toward developing errors make them less desirable to use than other media.

Flash RAM storage is becoming increasingly popular as an alternative to disk drives. *Flash RAM* is a type of static (*nonvolatile*) memory that retains its content even when the device is unpowered. The term "flash" comes from the way the data is updated—a "flash" of electricity erases and reprograms the data.

Some types of disks, such as CDs, DVDs, and floppies, can be removed from the drive. For those disk types, the terms "disk" and "drive" are separately defined: the drive is the read/write mechanism and the disk is the platter on which it reads and writes.

Hard disks, on the other hand, are stacks of disk platters permanently sealed inside a drive unit. As far as the end user is concerned, there is no hard disk separate from the hard drive, and vice-versa. Therefore the terms hard disk and hard drive are often combined as *hard disk drive*.

The most common type of flash RAM device is a **_USB flash drive_**, as shown in Figure 2.2 (also called a thumb drive or jump drive). The flash RAM is permanently embedded in the plastic casing and cannot be separated from the drive unit. USB flash drives are inexpensive and easy to carry, but if you want more capacity you must buy a whole new drive.

A **_solid state drive (SSD)_** is not a disk drive, despite the name; it is a high-capacity flash RAM device that substitutes for the mechanical hard disk drive in some systems. Solid state hard drives are more expensive than mechanical ones, but as their manufacturing costs decrease, they will replace mechanical hard disk drives in more systems.

A **_flash card reader_** (shown in Figure 2.3) is a drive that reads and writes data to flash RAM on removable plastic wafers, such as the flash memory cards from digital cameras and portable music players. Because a card reader is separate from the memory it reads, you can buy new flash memory cards at any time, or swap out one memory card for another as you would floppy disks. Card readers come built into many computers, and USB-based card readers also can be purchased separately. Some computers even have multiple card readers, each for a different type of card.

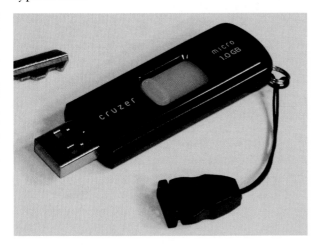

Figure 2.2 Flash RAM devices store data on nonvolatile memory chips.

Figure 2.3 A card reader reads and writes data on removable flash RAM cards.

Note: _There are many types of memory cards, and not all card readers are compatible. The major types include SmartMedia, CompactFlash, and Secure Digital. Make sure you buy the right type for the card reader you use._

Almost all storage media are portable. You can carry CD-Rs, DVD-Rs, USB flash drives, flash memory cards, and floppies from computer to computer freely, provided the other computer has an appropriate drive or port for it. Only internal hard disks are non-portable.

 TIP Hard disks can sometimes be portable too. An internal hard disk in the computer's case can be removed and transported to another computer, although it requires opening the case and disconnecting some cables. Also available are external hard disks that work via a USB, FireWire, or network port with any computer, and drive enclosures can be purchased that will convert an internal hard disk to an external USB model.

Working with Disks and Other Removable Media

Each time you need to save a data file, or transfer a file from one computer to another, you must evaluate the available storage media on the system and choose which is the most appropriate to use. Table 2.1 provides some pros and cons of the major storage types discussed in this chapter. Not all computers have all types of drives available, so your choice of storage medium depends on your system's capabilities.

Table 2.1   Storage Types

Storage Type	Attributes	Pros	Cons
Internal hard disk	Magnetic, internal, non-removable	High capacity, reliable, fast	Not easily portable
External hard disk	Magnetic, external, removable	High capacity, reliable, portable	Usually slower than internal, requires free USB or FireWire port, requires separate power source
Floppy drive and disks	Magnetic, portable	Compatible with older computers	Slow, low capacity, unreliable, newer computers do not have floppy drives
Writable CD or DVD drive and discs	Optical, portable	Most computers have a CD drive; CD blanks are inexpensive	Slow to write to compared with other media; CD-R blanks can be written only once; multi-write CD-RW and DVD-RW blanks are more expensive; reliability declines as they age; some types can start to degrade in as little as 18 months
USB flash drive	RAM-based, portable	Connects to a USB port, which most computers have, light-weight, compact to carry	Capacity is limited, more expensive per megabyte of storage than writable CDs or DVDs
Flash card reader and flash memory cards	RAM-based, portable	Connects to a USB port, lightweight, compact to carry, memory cards can be swapped out for additional storage	Capacity is limited, memory cards are expensive and easy to misplace
Solid state drive (SSD)	RAM-based, can be either internal or external	Reliable, fast, quiet	Expensive

Obtaining Information about Computer Disks ▪▪▪

Now that you know what types of storage are possible in a computer, the next step is to find out which storage types your computer supports. The easiest way to find this information is to look in File Explorer at the Computer window.

The Computer window shows the computer's built-in drives (hard drives, CD drive, and so on) plus any external drives that have been temporarily plugged in to USB ports or other ports (shown in Figure 2.4). To open the Computer window, open File Explorer (by clicking the File Explorer icon on the Taskbar) and then double-click Computer in the Navigation pane at the left.

If a drive is built in that is compatible with removable disks, the drive itself appears in the Computer window even if it does not currently contain a disk.

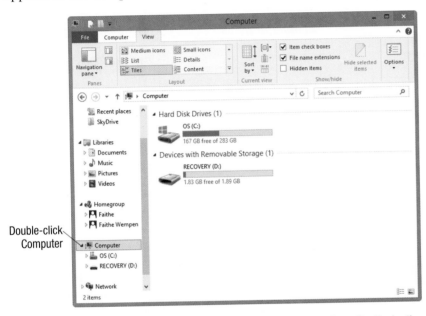

Figure 2.4   View the system's disks by choosing Computer from the Navigation pane.

Each drive has a unique letter identifier. Windows assigns these letters automatically based on the drive type, as follows:

- **A and B.** Floppy drives, if present
- **C.** Primary hard drive
- **D through Z.** Other drives

For each drive, the Computer window displays an icon that indicates the drive type. The name associated with the icon is either a generic label such as Local Disk, Floppy Disk, or a specific name (called a ***volume label)*** that has been assigned to it. For example, in Figure 2.4, the volume label for the C drive is OS, and the volume label for the D drive is RECOVERY. You will learn to change volume labels later in this chapter. The icon that represents the hard disk on which Windows is installed displays the Windows 8 logo. In Figure 2.4, you can see the Windows logo on the C drive's icon; this indicates that Windows is installed on that drive.

volume label A text description stored on the disk and displayed in the disk properties in Windows

When deciding which drive to use to store files, it is important to know how much space is left on the disk so you will know whether the files will fit on it. Knowing how much space remains on your hard disk(s) also can help you determine whether it is time to add another hard disk to your system or upgrade to a larger hard disk.

Data is stored on a computer in **binary** format—that is, in collections of 1s
and 0s. Each individual 1 or 0 is called a **bit**, which is short for binary digit. Even
the most complex data is broken down for storage into logical collections of bits.

A computer recognizes each group of eight bits as a **byte**. A byte represents
a single character of information; each number, letter, and symbol has its own
unique binary code. The capacity of a disk, the size of a file, and the amount
of memory installed in a computer are all described in terms of bytes. A single
file can consist of thousands or even millions of bytes, and a disk drive can hold
billions of bytes. Because it is common to work with bytes in large quantities,
names for various byte quantities are often used. These are described in Table 2.2.

Table 2.2   Terms for Groups of Bytes

Term	Number of Bytes	How Calculated
Kilobyte (KB)	1,024	2 to the 10th power bytes
Megabyte (MB)	1,048,576	A kilobyte of kilobytes
Gigabyte (GB)	1,073,741,824	A kilobyte of megabytes
Terabyte (TB)	1,099,511,627,776 (1,024 gigabytes)	A kilobyte of gigabytes
Petabyte (PB)	1,125,899,906,842,624 (1,024 terabytes)	A kilobyte of terabytes

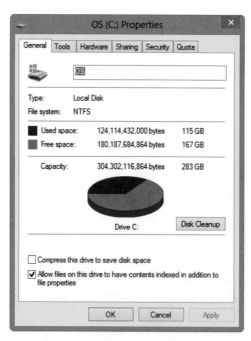

The space used on the drive appears
as a graphic showing the proportion of
the total space that has been used. A
rough estimate of the drive's space used
and space free also appears (rounded
to the nearest gigabyte for hard disks).
If you need to know the precise
amount of space used, you can get this
information from the Properties box for
the drive, as shown in Figure 2.5. To
view the Properties box, right-click the
drive's icon in the Computer window
and then click *Properties*.

Figure 2.5   More detailed capacity information
is available from the drive's
Properties box.

Assigning a Volume Label ■■■■■■■■■■■■■■■■■■■■

A volume label is a text description that you can optionally assign to a disk. If present, it appears in the disk properties in Windows. You can change the volume label only on a writable disk; for example, you cannot change a volume label on a CD-ROM. (A CD or DVD might have a volume label preassigned to it, however.) Volume labels can be up to 11 characters in length and can contain any numbers or uppercase letters, plus some symbols (but not any of these: * ? = + [ ] | \/).

If a hard disk or CD/DVD has a volume label, it appears in the Computer window along with the drive letter. In Figure 2.6, drive D has a volume label "RECOVERY." If no volume label is present, or if the drive does not contain a disk at the moment, a generic name appears that describes the general type of drive it is. In Figure 2.6, drive C has no volume label, so it appears as "Local Disk."

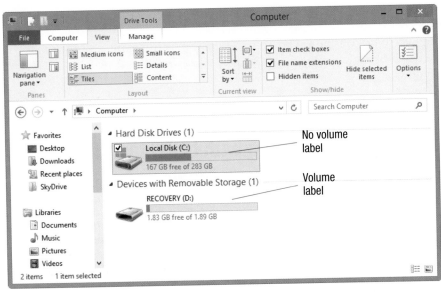

Figure 2.6   Volume labels appear in File Explorer.

Note: *Windows does not use the volume label internally to refer to the disk; the volume label is for human use only. Windows refers to disks only by their drive letters (and in some cases their internal serial numbers).*

Depending on the security settings on your computer, when you attempt to change the volume label for a drive, an Access Denied box may appear that reads "You will need to provide administrator permission to rename this drive." If you signed in to Windows with an Administrator-level user account, you can click Continue to move past this dialog box and complete the name change. If you are signed in with a Standard or Guest user account, you will need to sign in with an Administrator-level user name and password to complete this operation.

◀ **Here's How**

To set or change a disk's volume label:

1. Make sure you are signed in to Windows using an Administrator-level user account.
2. Click the File Explorer icon on the Taskbar and then click Computer.
3. In the Computer window, right-click the drive and then click Rename.
4. Type the new name and then press Enter.
5. If an Access Denied box appears, click Continue.

Working with Disks and Other Removable Media

Changing a Volume Label

1. Make sure you are signed in to Windows using an Administrator-level user account.
2. From the desktop, click the File Explorer icon on the Taskbar.
3. In the Navigation pane at the left, click Computer.
4. Write down the current volume label for drive C, as you will need it later.
5. Right-click the C drive and click *Rename*.
6. Type your last name and then press Enter.
7. If an Access Denied box appears, click Continue.
8. Capture a screen shot of the Computer window, save it as **C02E01**, and then submit it to your instructor.
9. Follow Steps 5-7 to rename the volume label to its original name. If drive C previously did not have a volume label (that is, it showed a generic label of Local Disk), after choosing Rename, press the Delete key on the keyboard to clear the existing name and then press Enter to leave the name blank.
10. Close all open windows.

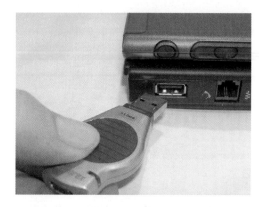

Figure 2.7 Connect a USB device to a USB port. Windows will automatically detect it.

Removable Disk (D:)

Choose what to do with removable drives.

 Speed up my system
Windows ReadyBoost

 Configure this drive for backup
File History

 Open folder to view files
File Explorer

 Take no action

Figure 2.8 An AutoPlay pop-up appears when Windows detects a new removable storage device and needs to know what you want to do with it.

Working with USB Flash Drives and Other Flash Media

A USB flash drive typically plugs into a USB port, as shown in Figure 2.7. Most computers have USB ports on the back or side (on notebooks), and some also have them on the front. USB connectors fit only one direction, so if the connector does not fit easily, try turning it over.

When you connect a USB flash drive, Windows might open an AutoPlay menu like the one shown in Figure 2.8. Click the choice that best suits the activity you want to do with the disk. In most cases, the correct choice is *Open folder to view files* (File Explorer). If this menu does not appear, right-click the drive icon and then choose *Open AutoPlay*.

Note: *Choosing the option* **Speed up my system Windows ReadyBoost,** *as shown in Figure 2.8, enables you to use flash RAM as a cache to speed up system performance. To use part or all of the drive's space as a cache, select the ReadyBoost tab that appears in the drive's Properties box.*

T I P You can suppress an AutoPlay pop-up by holding down the Shift key as you connect the drive or insert the disk. If the AutoPlay pop-up does not appear but you want it to, right-click the drive icon and click Open AutoPlay.

Copying a File or Folder to a Flash Drive

Flash drives, being removable, are useful for moving files from one computer to another. The files must be less than the drive's capacity in size, of course. USB flash drives are available in a wide variety of capacities between 512 MB and 256 GB, with drives as large as 1 terabyte coming in the near future.

You can do any of the following to copy files to a flash drive:

- Select the file or folder, copy it to the Clipboard (Ctrl + C), and then paste it into the destination (Ctrl + V).

- Right-click the file or folder, click *Send To*, and click the name of the flash drive.

- Open separate File Explorer windows for the source and the destination, and drag and drop between them, as shown in Figure 2.9. To open an additional File Explorer window from the desktop, hold down the Shift key and then click the File Explorer icon on the Taskbar.

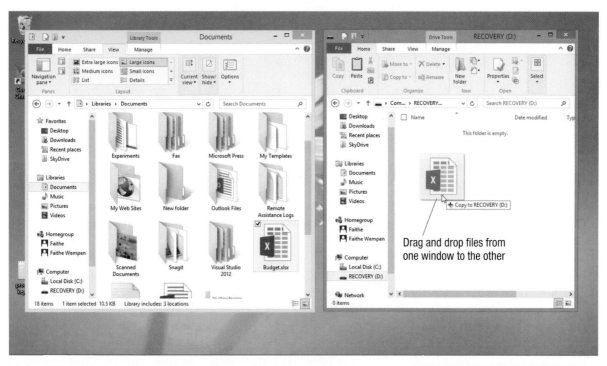

Figure 2.9   Copy a file or folder to a flash drive by dragging and dropping it into the destination.

Note: *The first time you connect a particular flash drive, Windows may need a few minutes to recognize the new device and install a driver for it. An icon appears in the notification area to indicate that this process is in progress. You are unable to use the drive until the process completes.*

To copy a file or folder to a flash drive (right-click method):

1. Connect a flash drive to the USB port on the computer.
2. From the desktop, click the File Explorer icon on the Taskbar.
3. Navigate to the location containing the file or folder to be copied.
4. Right-click the file or folder, point to *Send To,* and then click the flash drive name in the list.

◀ **Here's How**

To copy a file or folder to a flash drive (drag-and-drop method):

1. Connect a flash drive to the USB port on the computer.
2. From the desktop, click the File Explorer icon on the Taskbar.
3. Click Computer in the Navigation pane at the left.
4. Double-click the flash drive's icon in the pane at the right.
5. Hold down Shift and then click the File Explorer icon on the Taskbar.
6. Navigate to the location containing the file or folder to be copied.
7. Position the windows so you can see both at once.
8. Drag the file or folder to the window for the flash drive.

To copy a file or folder to a flash drive (copy-and-paste method):

1. Connect a USB flash drive to the computer.
2. From the desktop, click the File Explorer icon on the Taskbar.
3. Navigate to the location containing the file or folder to copy.
4. Select the file or folder to be copied and then press Ctrl + C to copy it to the Clipboard.
5. Click Computer in the Navigation pane at the left.
6. Double-click the flash drive's icon in the pane at the right to navigate to that location.
7. Press Ctrl + V to paste the copied file or folder.

Safely Removing Flash Media

When you are finished working with a removable storage device such as a USB flash drive or external hard disk, in most cases it is safe to simply disconnect it. Wait 30 seconds or so after the last usage to make sure all file operations have finished.

When data integrity is critical, however, you might want to take an extra safety precaution and use the Eject feature to stop the device before you unplug it. Windows waits for the device to finish any current operations and then stops it, so you are assured that it has no pending read or write operations before you disconnect it. To stop the device, right-click it in the Computer window and select *Eject*.

Figure 2.10 Click the Safely Remove Hardware and Eject Media icon in the notification area and then click the drive you want to eject.

Alternatively, click the Safely Remove Hardware and Eject Media icon in the notification area. A pop-up menu of the drives eligible for removal (any USB or other externally connected drives) appears. Click the drive you want to eject (shown in Figure 2.10).

Note: *Depending on the settings of your notification area, the File Explorer icon may not appear there. You may need to click the up-pointing arrow on the notification area to open a palette of additional icons to find it. For information about the notification area's settings, see Chapter 6.*

When you see the message shown in Figure 2.11, disconnect the flash drive from the computer.

Figure 2.11 When you see this message, it is safe to disconnect a removable storage device.

Here's How

To safely remove a USB or other removable storage device (Computer window method):

1. Right-click the removable drive's icon in the Computer window.
2. Click *Eject*.
3. Wait for the Safe to Remove Hardware message to appear in the notification area.
4. Disconnect the device.

To safely remove a USB or other removable storage device (notification area method):

1. Click the Safely Remove Hardware and Eject Media icon in the notification area. You may need to click the arrow to display hidden icons to see it.
2. Click the device you want to remove.
3. Wait for the Safe to Remove Hardware message to appear in the notification area.
4. Disconnect the device.

▼ **Quick Fix**

Getting Back In
To access the content of a flash drive after using the Eject feature, physically disconnect and reconnect it.

Exercise 2

Working with a Flash Drive

1. Connect the flash drive to an unused USB port on your computer.
2. If an AutoPlay pop-up appears, click *Open folder to view files (File Explorer)*. If AutoPlay does not appear, open File Explorer, click Computer to display a list of drives, and then double-click the icon for the USB flash drive.
   To open File Explorer from the desktop, click the File Explorer icon on the Taskbar.
3. Locate Student Data Files at www.paradigmcollege.net/windows8. If you have not already done so, download files to your computer or to your USB flash drive. Ask your instructor for assistance, if needed.
4. Navigate to the Chapter 2 folder and locate the file named **Estate**. Navigation to different file storage locations is explained in Chapter 3.
5. Right-click the file, point to *Send To*, and then click the name and letter of the USB flash device. Verify that the file you copied is on the flash drive. Then click the Close (X) button to close the File Explorer window.
6. In the notification area, click the Safely Remove Hardware and Eject Media icon.
7. Click the name of the flash drive.
8. Remove the flash drive from the computer and submit it to your instructor.
9. Close all open windows.

Working with CD and DVD Media ■■■■■■■■■■■■

Most computers have at least one optical drive, such as a CD or DVD drive. These discs store data in patterns of reflective and nonreflective areas on a shiny surface. A laser shines light on the surface of the disc, and a sensor measures the amount of light that bounces back.

Types of Optical Media

Optical media vary depending on the type (CD, DVD, or Blu-ray), the capacity per side (single layer or double layer), the number of readable sides (one or two), and, if writable, the number of times it can be written (once or multiple) and the type of writing standard it supports (for example, DVD+R or DVD-R). Later in the chapter you will learn the specifics of each of these variations. Both the discs and the drives that read them vary in these ways, although most modern drives support multiple types of discs.

Table 2.3 lists the capacities for basic non-writable discs. Later in this chapter you will learn about the specs for writable discs.

Table 2.3   Non-Writable Optical Media Types

Type	Capacity
CD-ROM	700 MB
DVD-ROM	4.7 GB
DVD-ROM Dual Layer	8.5 GB
Blu-ray	25 GB
Blu-ray Dual Layer	50 GB

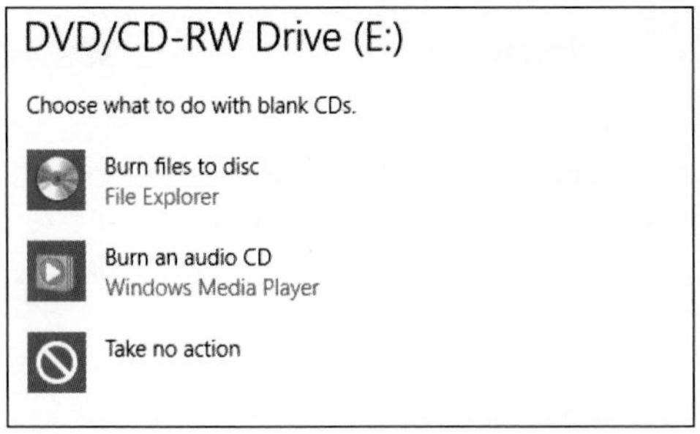

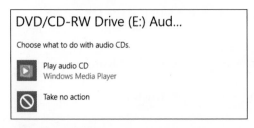

Figure 2.12   When a data CD is inserted, the AutoPlay choices pertain to working with data.

Figure 2.13   When an audio CD is inserted, the AutoPlay choices pertain to audio files.

Changing the AutoPlay Setting of a Drive

Optical drives automatically perform a specified action on a disc based on its content type (music, for example), provided you have specified a default action for that data type. If you do not specify a default action for a certain data type, the AutoPlay box opens every time you insert a CD or DVD of that type, asking what you want to do with the disc. The options differ depending on the type of content the disc contains. Figure 2.12 shows the options for a blank writable CD; Figure 2.13 shows the options for an audio CD. AutoPlay settings also are different for other types of discs, such as blank CDs, video DVDs, and software installation CDs and DVDs. If you have other programs installed for working with those content types, options for those programs might appear in the AutoPlay box, too. If you do not see an AutoPlay box when you insert a disk, right-click the drive's icon in File Explorer and then choose *Open AutoPlay*.

You can set defaults for the various types of content via the Control Panel. When a default is set, Windows automatically performs the action when a disc of that type is inserted. For example, by default Windows 8 plays audio CDs automatically rather than displaying the AutoPlay box (shown in Figure 2.13). Figure 2.14 shows the Control Panel interface for setting AutoPlay options.

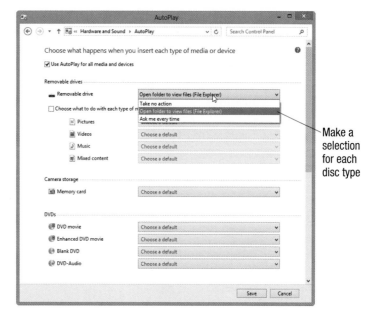

Make a selection for each disc type

Figure 2.14 Control the AutoPlay behavior for each type of disc.

To set the AutoPlay behavior for a disc type:

1. From the desktop, display the charms and then click Settings. To display the charms, move the mouse pointer to the lower right corner of the screen.
2. Click *Control Panel*.
3. Click *Hardware and Sound*.
4. Click *AutoPlay*.
5. Make sure *Use AutoPlay for all media and devices* is checked.
6. For each type of media, open the drop-down list and then select a default. Choose *Ask me every time* if you want the box to appear each time.
7. Click Save.

Here's How

Exercise 3

Setting the Default for a Type of Optical Media

1. From the desktop, display the charms and click Settings. To display the charms, move the mouse pointer to the lower right corner of the screen.
2. Click *Control Panel*.
3. Click *Hardware and Sound*.
4. Click *AutoPlay*.
5. Open the drop-down list for Audio CD and click *Play audio CD (Windows Media Player)*.
6. Capture a screen shot of this window, save it as **C02E03**, and then submit it to your instructor.
7. Return to the AutoPlay settings and then click Save.
8. (Optional) If you have an audio CD, insert it in the drive. It plays automatically.
9. Close all open windows.

Copying Files to Writable CD or DVD

Most computers include a writable **CD**, **DVD**, or **Blu-ray** drive that you can use to store files on writable discs. There are many types and variants of these discs, and it is important to match the type of blanks you buy with the write capabilities of the drive. Table 2.4 lists popular writable discs currently available in stores and their specifications.

Table 2.4   Writable Disc Types

Type	*Capacity*	*Writability*
CD-R	700 MB	Once
CD-RW	4.7 GB	Multiple
DVD-R	4.7 GB	Once
DVD-RW	4.7 GB	Multiple
DVD+R	4.7 GB	Once
DVD+RW	4.7 GB	Multiple
DVD+R Dual Layer	8.5 GB	Once
DVD-R Dual Layer	8.5 GB	Once
BD-R Blu-ray	25 GB	Once
BD-R Blu-ray Dual Layer	50 GB	Once
BD-RE Blu-ray	25 GB	Multiple
BD-RE Blu-ray Dual Layer	50 GB	Multiple

The main differentiating factors between blanks are:

- **CD, DVD, or Blu-ray?** CDs are the lowest capacity, DVDs are the mid-range, and Blu-ray is the highest capacity.

- **Recordable (R) or Rewritable (RW)?** Recordable discs can be written to only once, not erased and rewritten. Rewritable discs can be rewritten up to 1000 times and are more expensive. For Blu-ray discs, the abbreviations are BD-R for recordable and BD-RE for rewritable.

- **Plus or Minus?** There are two competing standards for DVD writing: +R (or +RW) and –R (or –RW). Many—but not all—drives support both. This is not a factor for CD or Blu-ray discs.

- **Single or dual layer?** A DVD can be either a single-layer disc (holding 4.7 GB of data) or a *dual-layer disc* (holding 8.5 GB of data). For each disc type there are again two competing standards: plus and minus. Dual layer drives are sometimes called DVDR9 drives (either +R9 or –R9). Blu-ray discs also can be either single layer or dual layer with 25 GB or 50 GB capacity, respectively.

When you insert a new blank disc, depending on your AutoPlay settings, the AutoPlay pop-up may open, providing a choice to burn a music CD or a data disc.

CD Stands for compact disc; a removable, optical disc that stores about 700 MB of data

DVD Stands for digital versatile disc (or digital video disc); a removable, optical disc that stores about 4.7 GB of data per layer

Blu-ray A high-capacity type of DVD that stores 25 GB of data per layer

dual-layer disc A type of DVD that stores data in two layers, enabling it to approximately double its capacity

If you choose *Burn files to disc* (File Explorer), Windows walks you through a Burn a Disc process in which you prepare the disc. You have a choice of two kinds of data disc, as shown in Figure 2.15.

Figure 2.15 Select the type of data disc you want to create.

■ **Like a USB Flash Drive.** Using the *Live File System* in Windows, you can treat the disk like a flash drive, freely writing, editing, and deleting files from it. Formerly available only for rewritable discs, this file system now allows even plain CD-R discs to be changed and erased, so you can write to a disc as if it were a USB flash drive. The drawback to this format is that older computer systems might not be able to read the disc. Some earlier versions of Windows do not support this technology, although on many older systems a third-party CD writing program added that capability.

Live File System A type of CD and DVD file system that enables discs to be written to multiple times

■ **With a CD/DVD Player.** This is the backward-compatible *Mastered* file system, enabling only single writes to a blank disc. You must write all the content to the disc in one pass, and that content cannot be edited later. However, such a disc is compatible with virtually every CD player and CD drive.

Mastered A type of CD and DVD file system that requires files to be written to the disc all at once

Note: *The Live File System format simulates multiple writing and erasing from a CD-R, but technically it is not erasing and rewriting—it is writing to a new section of the disc and creating a new table of contents that ignores the older version. Therefore, the more times you make a change to the content of a CD-R, the smaller the disc capacity becomes. For true rewriting capability, in which the disc capacity does not erode, use a CD-RW disc.*

If you choose the Live File System, Windows formats the disc. When it is finished, an AutoPlay dialog box appears, as if you had inserted a new USB flash drive. If you go with the Mastered data disc, no formatting takes place (because the disc will be formatted when it is eventually written to).

To write files to the disc, drag and drop files and folders into the Explorer window of the disc. With a Live File System disc, the files are immediately written to the disc as you place them in the window.

With a Mastered disc, the files and folders are not written to the disc right away, but instead they are placed in a holding area. When you are ready to write the files to disc, click the Manage tab and then click *Finish Burning*. A Burn to Disc window appears in which you specify a disc title and a recording speed (shown in Figure 2.16). Enter that information and click Next to complete the process. All files are then written to the disc.

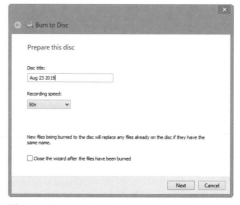

Figure 2.16 If writing a Mastered disc, you can specify a recording speed.

Note: *The default recording speed is the fastest speed that the drive can support. This may be a faster speed than the disc you are writing to can support. If the recording speed chosen is too fast for the disc, errors might occur, which will abort the entire process and render the disc unusable. Most discs list the maximum recording speed on the face of the disc.*

After writing files to a disc, you will probably want to label the disc to remember what is stored on it. Use only a soft-tipped marker, such as a Sharpie®, to label discs. Ball-point pens can damage the disc.

Here's How

To write files to a CD or DVD (Live File System):

1. Insert the blank disc. If the Burn a Disc dialog box opens, skip to step 3.
2. In the AutoPlay pop-up, click *Burn files to disc using File Explorer*.

   If the AutoPlay pop-up does not appear, open File Explorer, click Computer, and then right-click the drive icon and choose *Open AutoPlay*.
3. (Optional) Type a disc title.
4. Click Like a USB flash drive.
5. Click Next.
6. Wait for the disc to be formatted and then click OK.
7. If needed, reopen File Explorer, and drag and drop files to the disc window. The files are copied to the disc immediately.

To write files to a CD or DVD (Mastered):

1. Insert the blank disc. If the Burn a Disc dialog box appears, skip to step 3.
2. Click *Burn files to disc using File Explorer*.

   If the AutoPlay pop-up does not appear, open File Explorer, click Computer, and then right-click the drive icon and choose *Open AutoPlay*.
3. (Optional) Type a disc title.
4. Click With a CD/DVD Player.
5. Click Next.
6. Drag and drop files to the disc window. The files are copied into a holding area.
7. Click the Manage tab and click *Finish Burning*.
8. In the Burn to Disc window, type a disc title (optional) if you did not specify one in Step 3.
9. Select a Recording Speed.
10. (Optional) Mark the *Close the wizard after the files have been burned* check box.
11. Click Next.
12. Wait for the files to be transferred to the disc. A completion message appears when the burn process finishes.
13. Click Finish.
14. If you didn't choose to close File Explorer automatically in step 10, close it now.
15. Eject the disc if it did not eject automatically.

Backing Up Documents to a CD

1. Insert a blank CD-R or CD-RW disc into your writable CD or DVD drive. If the Burn a Disc dialog box appears automatically, skip to Step 3.
2. If the Burn a Disc dialog box does not appear automatically, complete the following steps to open it:
   a. Open File Explorer.
   b. Click Computer.
   c. Right-click the drive icon for the CD/DVD drive and choose *Open AutoPlay*.
   d. Click *Burn files to disc* (File Explorer).
3. In the *Disc title* text box, type **Backup**.
4. Click Like a USB flash drive, if it is not already selected.
5. Click Next.
6. Wait for the disc to be formatted. When the formatting finishes, the disc content opens in File Explorer. The disc is currently empty.
7. Hold down the Shift key and click the File Explorer icon on the Taskbar to open a second copy of File Explorer.
8. In the second copy of File Explorer, click Documents.
9. Click any file in the Documents library to select it. If you do not have any files in this location, ask your instructor what file and location you should use.
10. Make sure you can see both windows at the same time. Drag and drop the file from the Documents window to the CD's window.
11. Eject the disc and label it **File Backup Practice** with a soft-tipped marker. Submit the disc to your instructor.
12. If the Documents window is still open, close it now.

Working with Hard Disks ■■■■■■■■■■■■■■■■■■■■■

Although you will occasionally work with removable media such as flash drives and optical discs, the majority of your work in Windows will probably involve a hard disk. Hard disks are the most reliable form of storage, have the fastest access time, and provide the most capacity for the money.

Viewing Disk Usage Information

In File Explorer, blue bars appear to show the percentage of the space occupied on each hard disk, and beneath the bar the amount free and total space appears. In addition, when a drive is selected and the Details pane is displayed, the drive's information appears in the Details pane at the right of the drive icons, showing the same space information plus reporting the file system in use. In Figure 2.17, for example, the file system is NTFS. To hide or show the Details pane, click the View tab and then click Details pane.

Click here to display or hide the Details pane

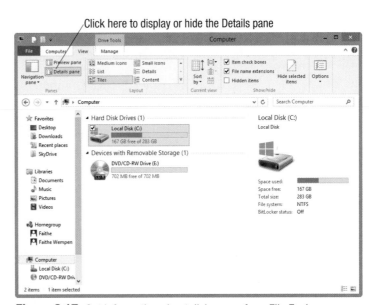

Figure 2.17 Get information about disk usage from File Explorer.

Note: *NTFS (New Technology File System) is the default file system in Windows versions XP and higher for hard disks. Windows 8 also recognizes older file systems such as FAT32 and FAT for backward compatibility. USB flash drives use FAT32. CDs and DVDs use CDFS, which stands for CD File System.*

For detailed information about the drive, such as the exact number of bytes of capacity and free space, display the Properties dialog box for the drive, as shown in Figure 2.18. To open the drive's Properties dialog box, right-click the drive icon and then click *Properties*.

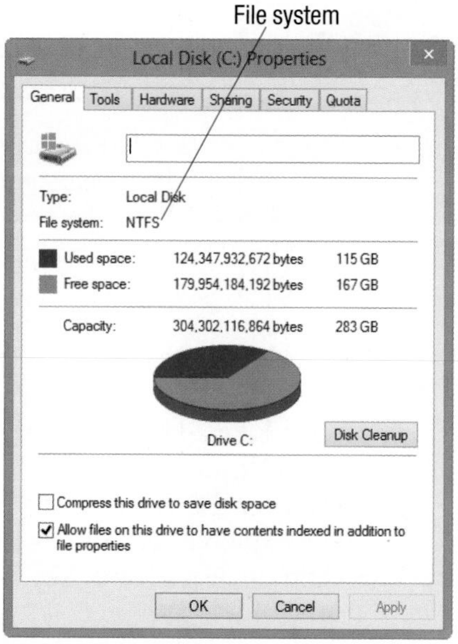

Turning on Disk Compression

If available disk space is in short supply, you might want to turn on disk compression for one or more hard disk drives. **Disk compression** enables the drive to store files so that they take up less space by running a simple compression algorithm on them. A **compression algorithm** is a mathematical formula used to remove wasted space in a file so that it takes up less space on the disk. For example, it might identify strings of a certain number, such as 00000000, and abbreviate them using fewer characters, like 0x8. It is available only on drives that use NTFS (the default file system).

Disk compression can be enabled for entire drives or for individual folders and can be enabled for the chosen location only or all subordinate folders under it. When you enable compression, a Confirm Attribute Change box appears asking whether the change should affect subfolders and files, too.

disk compression A means of decreasing the amount of space that files occupy on a disk by storing them more compactly

compression algorithm A mathematical formula used to remove wasted space in a file so that it takes up less space on the disk

File system

Figure 2.18 Get detailed information about disk usage from the Properties dialog box.

T I P Using disk compression causes a minor slowdown in disk access because of the extra step involved in compressing and decompressing data on the fly. Therefore, you should not enable it if you still have plenty of room left on your hard disk drive.

To enable or disable disk compression for a hard disk:

1. In File Explorer, click Computer to display a list of the drives on the system.
2. Right-click a hard drive and click *Properties*.
3. Mark or clear the *Compress this drive to save disk space* check box.

   If the check box is unavailable, the NTFS file system is not in use, and the drive cannot be compressed.
4. Click OK to display the Confirm Attribute Changes box.
5. Click the option to apply the changes either to the current location only or to all subfolders and files.
6. Click OK.
7. If a warning box appears that you need administrator permission, click Continue.

Checking a Disk for Errors

Over time, disks (especially hard disks) can develop errors in the storage system. These errors can be either physical, caused by bad spots on the surface, or logical, caused by improper shutdown or crashes in which files fail to be properly closed. Disk errors manifest themselves in problems reading or writing files or folders, or program crashes.

To check a disk for errors, use the **Check Disk** utility. To run it, open the drive's Properties box, click the Tools tab, and then click the Check button. Windows checks disks as you work, so it may have recently checked this disk for errors without your intervention. If a message appears notifying you that you do not need to scan this drive, click Cancel to close the dialog box, or click Scan drive to complete a check anyway.

Check Disk A Windows-based utility for finding and fixing physical and logical errors on a disk

Note: *Check Disk refers to areas on the disk surface as sectors. Sectors are numerically named areas of the surface that can be individually referenced by the drive controller. When there is an error within a sector, the entire sector is marked as "bad" and rendered unusable. Having a few bad sectors on a disk is normal.*

Here's How

To check a disk for errors:

1. Open File Explorer and then click *Computer*.
2. Right-click a hard drive and then click *Properties*.
3. Click the Tools tab and then click Check. If you see a message that you do not need to scan the drive, click Cancel, or proceed to the next step to scan anyway.
4. Click Scan drive.
5. Wait for the check to complete and then click OK.

Checking Disk Partitioning

A physical hard disk drive is divided into logical disk drives, each with its own drive letter assigned. Creating the organizational structure of the disk space is known as *partitioning*. Hard disks must be partitioned before they can be formatted, even if that partitioning simply consists of creating a single partition that occupies the entire physical disk.

Each physical disk must have at least one **primary partition**, which is a bootable partition. If there is only one partition on the drive, it is a primary one. Each primary partition can have only one logical drive on it, represented by one letter. In addition, a disk can have an **extended partition**. Extended partitions can have multiple logical drives, each with its own letter.

partition To logically divide the space on a physical hard disk into one or more logical drives

primary partition A bootable partition. A disk drive must have at least one primary partition

extended partition A secondary partition, in addition to the primary partition(s)

Note: *Your current hard disk is already correctly partitioned and formatted; otherwise, it would not be running Windows.*

To get information about the partitions of your drives, use the Disk Management utility, accessed from the Control Panel. Figure 2.19 shows an example in which there is one physical hard disk: Disk 0. Disk 0 has three partitions. However, only one of the partitions has a logical drive letter assigned to it (C). There is also a removable flash drive. The system's DVD drive is also listed (CD-ROM 0); it currently contains a disc that uses the CDFS file system. If this drive were empty, the drive information would appear at the left, but the space to the right would be blank.

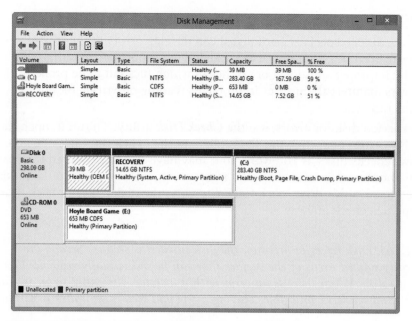

Figure 2.19 Examine partition information from the Disk Management utility.

Here's How **To examine the partition information for your system's disks:**

1. From the desktop, display the charms and click Settings.
2. Click *Control Panel*.
3. Click *System and Security*.
4. Under *Administrative Tools*, click *Create and format hard disk partitions*.
5. Examine the partition and drive information.

Working with an External Hard Disk

External hard disks have some things in common with internal ones and some things in common with removable devices, such as USB flash drives.

External hard disks are like regular hard disks in that they appear as hard disks in File Explorer, and they can be partitioned and formatted like any other hard disk. They are like USB flash drives in that they can be connected at any time, and an AutoPlay pop-up opens when you connect one unless you have set a default behavior for it. You can also use Eject to stop one before disconnecting it.

In addition to external hard disks that connect directly to a computer, there are also external hard disks that connect directly to a network, called *network attached storage (NAS)*.

network attached
storage (NAS) An
external hard disk
that is accessed
through a network
interface

1. Open File Explorer and then click Computer to see the drive icons.
2. Right-click the C drive icon and then choose *Properties*.
3. Click the General tab if not already active. Click *Compress this drive to save disk space* and then click Apply.
4. Click *Apply changes to drive C:\ only* and then click OK. If a message box appears warning that you need administrator permission, click Continue.
5. From the Desktop, display the charms and then click Settings.
6. Click *Control Panel* and then click *System and Security.*
7. Under *Administrative Tools*, click *Create and format hard disk partitions*.
8. Determine the number of partitions on each of your hard disks and the total space occupied by each one.
9. Capture a screen shot of this window, save it as **C02E05**, and then submit it to your instructor.
10. Close the Disk Management window and any other open windows.

CHAPTER SUMMARY

- File storage devices include CDs/DVDs, flash RAM devices, and hard drives.
- Magnetic disks, including hard drives and floppies, store data in patterns of magnetic polarity on the surface of one or more metal-coated platters. Optical discs store data in patterns of lesser and greater reflectivity on a smooth reflective platter.
- Flash RAM devices store data in nonvolatile RAM. The RAM in these devices can be built-in (as with a flash drive) or removable (as with a flash card reader). Solid state hard drives are flash RAM devices rather than disks.
- To examine the drives on your system, open File Explorer and then click *Computer*.
- Storage capacity is measured in bytes. A kilobyte is 1,024 bytes; a megabyte is 1,048,576 bytes. Hard disk capacity is measured in gigabytes (kilobytes of megabytes).
- A volume label is a text description stored on a disk and displayed in its properties. It can be assigned in the disk's Properties dialog box.
- To copy a file or folder to a removable storage location such as a USB drive, you can drag and drop it, copy and paste it, or right-click it and then choose *Send To.*
- Before removing a flash drive (or external hard drive) from the computer, use the Safely Remove Hardware and Eject Media utility (in the notification area) to stop the device and prevent data loss.
- Optical disc types can be broken down by type (CD/DVD), capacity, ability to be written to once or multiple times, and support for dual layers.
- Usage and capacity information for hard disks is available from File Explorer. You also can right-click the drive's icon and choose *Properties*.

- NTFS drives can use disk compression, which makes it possible to fit more files on the drive. To enable this option, mark the *Compress this drive to save space* check box in the properties for the drive.

- The Check Disk utility finds and fixes errors in the storage information for your drive. Use the Check button on the Tools tab of the drive's Properties box.

- To examine the partition information for each physical hard disk drive in your system, use the Disk Management tool. From the Control Panel, choose *System and Security, Administrative Tools, Create and format hard disk partitions*.

- External hard disks work like internal ones but can be connected and disconnected like flash RAM drives.

- Data CDs and DVDs can be burned in either of two formats: Live File Format or Mastered. Live File Format is more flexible, but Mastered is more backward-compatible.

CONCEPTS CHECK

Completion: Answer the following questions in a Word document.

Part 1

Multiple Choice

1. Which is an example of a magnetic disk?
   a. Flash RAM drive
   b. CD-ROM
   c. Hard disk
   d. All of the above

2. A group of eight bits is a _____ .
   a. kilobit
   b. byte
   c. megabit
   d. terabyte

3. How many bytes are in a megabyte?
   a. 1,024
   b. 1,048,576
   c. 1,073,741,824
   d. 1,099,511,627,776

4. A CD-ROM holds _____ of data.
   a. 700 MB
   b. 1 GB
   c. 1.44 MB
   d. 1 terabyte

5. Which of these symbols is not allowed in a volume label?
   a. @
   b. #
   c. %
   d. *

6. Which type of disc has a capacity of 8.5 GB?
   a. CD-R
   b. DVD-RW
   c. DVD-R Dual Layer
   d. CD-RW

7. What utility can you use to check your drives' partitioning and formatting?
   a. Disk Management
   b. Device Manager
   c. Partition Manager
   d. Services

8. What setting determines what happens when you insert a CD?
   a. Device Status
   b. AutoPlay
   c. Audio Manager
   d. None of the above

9. Which file system is most appropriate for a data CD you will be sharing with someone who uses some operating system other than Windows XP or higher?
   a. Live File System
   b. CDRW
   c. Mastered
   d. +R

10. One way to copy a file to a USB flash drive or floppy is to right-click the file and point to _____ on the menu that appears, then click the desired destination.
    a. Move
    b. Send To
    c. Transfer
    d. X-Copy

Part 2

Short Answer

11. What drive letter is assigned to the main (primary) hard drive?

    _____

12. Why would you want to use the Mastered file system on a CD rather than Live File System?

    _____

13. With which type of CD writing do you need to specify a recording speed?

    _____

14. What does the Check Disk utility check for?

    _____

15. What type of port does a flash drive usually connect to on a computer?

    _____

16. What does the Safely Remove Hardware and Eject Media command guard against?

_____

17. What file system needs to be in use in order to use disk compression in Windows?

_____

18. What are symptoms of disk errors that can be fixed by running Check Disk?

_____

19. How many partitions must a hard disk have, at minimum?

_____

20. How is an external hard disk similar to a flash drive, and how is it different?

_____

21. What is network addressable storage?

_____

SKILLS CHECK

Save all solution files to the default Documents folder or any alternate folder specified by your instructor.

Guided Check

Assessment 1

Copying a File to a Flash Drive
1. Connect a USB flash drive to the computer.
2. Copy the file named **sewing** from the Chapter 2 folder to the USB drive.
   a. From the desktop, click File Explorer.
   b. Click *Computer*.
   c. Double-click the C drive icon.
   d. Double-click the *EMCP* folder.
   e. Double-click the *Chapter 2* folder.
   f. Right-click *sewing*.
   g. Point to *Send To*.
   h. Click the USB flash drive.
   i. Wait for the file to be copied.
3. Use Eject to stop the flash drive.
   a. In the notification area, click the Safely Remove Hardware and Eject Media icon.
   b. Click the flash drive's name (varies depending on model).
   c. Wait for the message to appear that it is safe to remove the drive.
4. Submit the flash drive to your instructor.

Assessment 2

Setting Defaults for Media Types

1. Open the AutoPlay settings in the Control Panel.
   a. From the desktop, display the charms, and then click Settings.
   b. Click *Control Panel*.
   c. Click *Hardware and Sound*.
   d. Click *AutoPlay*.
2. For all the media types, open the drop-down list and then click *Ask me every time* so that Windows will prompt you each time one is connected. Do not mark the *Choose what to do with each type of media* checkbox, and do not specify an action for the media types listed beneath it.
3. Capture a screen shot of this window, save it as **C02A02**, and then submit it to your instructor.

> **TIP** See "Capturing a Screen Picture to Complete an Assignment" in Chapter 1 for help if needed.

4. Click Save.
5. Close all remaining open windows.

Assessment 3

Getting Information about Hard Disks

1. Display the Properties box for the C drive.
   a. From the desktop, open File Explorer.
   b. Click *Computer* in the Navigation pane.
   c. Right-click the *C drive* icon in the main (right) pane.
   d. Click *Properties*.
2. Capture a screen shot of this window and then save it as **C02A03S02**.
3. Check the C drive for errors.
   a. Click the Tools tab.
   b. Click Check.
   c. Click Scan drive. (Do this even if the message appears that you don't need to scan this drive.)
   d. While the check is occurring, capture a screen shot of the Error Checking window, save it as **C02A03S03**, and then submit it to your instructor.

On Your Own

Assessment 4

Using a Flash Drive to Copy Files between Computers

1. Connect a USB flash drive to the computer.
2. Copy the Chapter 2 folder containing student files for Chapter 2 to the flash drive.
3. Take the flash drive to another computer.
4. Copy the Chapter 2 folder from the flash drive to the other computer's hard drive (in the Documents library).
5. Submit your flash drive to your instructor.

Assessment 5

Group Activity: Shopping for Optical Discs

Note that this assessment requires a working Internet connection, or a trip to a store that sells discs, and a CD or DVD drive that can write to blank discs.

1. As a group, determine the type(s) of writable blank discs that will write to your computer.
2. Have each team member spend 15 minutes shopping for the best prices on each type of disc, either online or in a store.

Working with Disks and Other Removable Media

3. Prepare an informal written report summarizing your findings and reporting the best available prices for discs you could find and the website(s) where you found them. Save your report as **C02A05**, make sure all group member names are included, and then submit it to your instructor.

Assessment

6

Assessing Hard Disk Usage

1. Use Disk Management to view the system's current hard disk partitions. Note whether there is any unallocated space on any of the physical drives.
2. In File Explorer, examine the amount of free space available on each hard disk drive letter. Note how much space is available.
3. Assuming a disk should never get more than 85 percent full (except for a Recovery partition, if there is one), and assuming you were generating 200 MB of new data per week, at what point would you need to add another hard disk to this computer? Explain your answer and show how you calculated it.
4. Save an informal report with your findings as **C02A06** and then submit it to your instructor.

CHALLENGE PROJECT

A small insurance agency is going to buy three new computers for its clerical workers and set them up on a small local network. Recommend the types of drives or other storage devices that the computers should have, and look up prices on the Internet for computers with various configurations to determine how much each of the drives you recommend contributes to the overall cost. Write an informal report with your recommendations. Save the report as **C02A07** and then submit it to your instructor.

Learning about Files, Folders, and Libraries

PERFORMANCE OBJECTIVES

Upon successful completion of Chapter 3, you will be able to:

- Use the File Explorer interface to browse files and folders
- Work with libraries and user folders
- Select multiple files and folders
- Create and rename folders
- Move and copy files and folders
- Sort, filter, group, and arrange file listings

- Create a library and manage library settings
- Find files and folders
- Create shortcuts for easier file and folder access
- Delete items and retrieve them from the Recycle Bin
- Store files in the cloud with SkyDrive

Files are the basis of almost everything in computing. Whatever you do—whether it is running a program, typing a memo, or optimizing system performance—you are working with files. Most of the files on your system are there to run Windows 8 and your applications, but you also can create data files to store the work you do. You then can manipulate those data files in any way you like—rename them, copy them, organize them into folders, or even delete them altogether. When you need to access files from multiple locations using multiple devices, you can access your SkyDrive storage to save them in the cloud.

Using the File Explorer Interface ■■■■■■■■■■■■■

folder An organizing unit for storing related files together in groups, also called a location

File Explorer The file management interface in Windows 8

Disks can hold hundreds and even thousands of files, so some organizational structure is usually needed. *Folders* help organize a disk by creating logical groupings of files. In this section, you will learn how to use the File Explorer interface to browse the folders (also called locations) on your system and to display listings for different locations.

Understanding File Explorer

The window that you used in Chapter 2 to examine the disks on your system is part of a larger file-management interface called *File Explorer*. Each Explorer window (also called a *folder window*) displays the contents of a location you select. You can browse through a disk's content in a single window, or you can open multiple Explorer windows at once to compare the content of two locations or to move or copy between them.

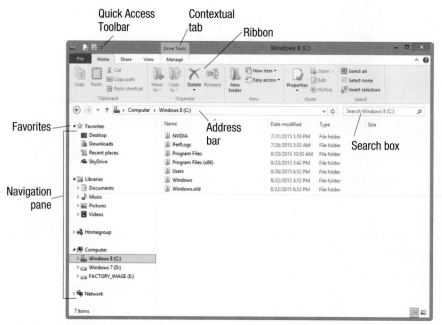

Figure 3.1 The File Explorer window provides several ways of accessing the files, folders, and disks on your computer.

Figure 3.1 shows an Explorer window, including the navigation and file-management features built into Windows 8. Later sections in the chapter will cover using these features in greater detail:

- **Quick Access Toolbar.** Provides buttons for common actions, such as checking file or folder properties and creating a new folder.

- **Ribbon.** Offers commands organized in groups on tabs. When you make a selection, such as selecting a network location or a disk as shown in Figure 3.1, the available tabs and commands may change or a contextual tab with settings pertaining to the selection may appear.

- **Address bar.** Shows the name of the folder (location) whose contents appear in the folder window, as well as the folder(s) holding that folder. You can use this bar, as well as the Back, Forward, and Up arrow buttons at the left of it, to navigate to other folders.

- **Search box.** Enables you to enter a file or folder name to tell Explorer to find that file or folder.

- **Navigation pane.** Enables you to move between locations, such as different disks and folders.

- **Favorites.** Provides shortcuts for jumping to frequently used folders and rerunning saved searches.

> **T I P** If you prefer to use the keyboard to navigate the ribbon, press Alt. To select a tab, press its KeyTip letter and then press the letter of the command to select.

Displaying Other Panes

When you are looking for a particular file or want to see how large a selected file or folder is, it can be useful to display the Preview pane or Details pane at the right side of the File Explorer window. Only one of these panes can be active at a time. Figure 3.2 shows each pane.

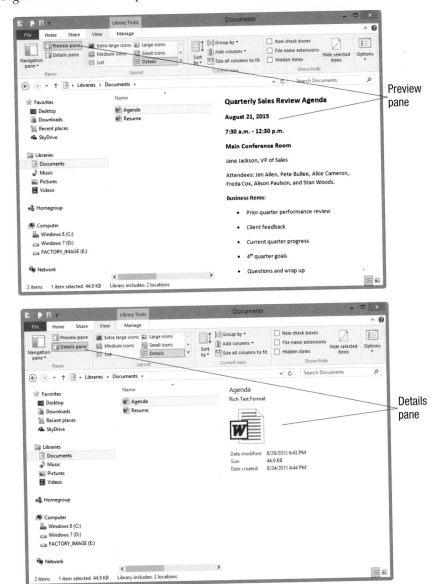

Figure 3.2   The Preview pane shows the selected file's contents, if available, and the Details pane provides information about the selected file(s).

Here's How

To display or hide the Preview or Details pane

1. If needed, click the File Explorer button on the desktop Taskbar to open a File Explorer window and then navigate to the folder that holds the files to view.
2. Click the View tab.
3. In the Panes group, click either the Preview pane or Details pane button.
4. To hide a pane, repeat Steps 2 and 3.

Learning about Files, Folders, and Libraries

Browsing Locations with the Folder List

The folder list displays the drives and folders for the computer in a hierarchical tree in the Navigation pane. It provides an alternative method of browsing and navigating between locations that is more visual than the Address bar (shown in Figure 3.3). Note that the *Favorites* and *Libraries* sections in the Navigation pane—as well as the *Homegroup* and *Network* sections, if present—also feature a similar list that works like the folder list.

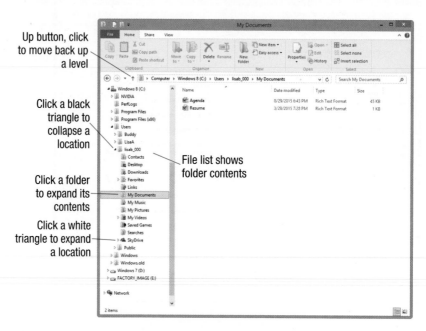

Figure 3.3   The folder list enables you to move between locations via a hierarchical tree.

file list The area in a folder or library window that shows the files and folders in the folder or library

To display the contents of a particular folder, click the folder's name in the Navigation pane. The contents of the folder appear in the *file list* area of the window. Using the folder list, you can quickly jump to any drive or folder on your system.

To collapse or expand a branch of the tree, double-click the drive or folder in the folder list. When the mouse pointer is in the Navigation pane, a triangle appears at the left of each folder in the folder list to indicate the location's status. A black triangle means the item is expanded; a white triangle means it is collapsed. Click the black and white triangles to collapse and expand locations, respectively.

Here's How

▼ **Quick Fix**

Navigation Pane Does Not Appear
If the Navigation pane does not appear, click the View tab. In the Panes group, click the Navigation pane button and then click *Navigation pane* in the menu.

To select a location from the folder list:

1. If needed, double-click *Computer* in the Navigation pane to display the available disks.
2. Expand the desired drive by double-clicking it or clicking the white triangle beside it.
3. Expand/collapse folder levels as needed.
   a. Click a white triangle to expand a branch.
   b. Click a black triangle to collapse a branch.
4. Click the folder whose contents you want to view.
5. To move up one level at any time, click the Up button at the left of the address bar. From there, you can use the Back and Forward buttons to navigate, as well.

When you move the mouse pointer over a triangle, a highlight appears on the triangle to show you what drive or folder will be expanded or collapsed when you click.

Note: *You may notice in Figure 3.3 that the user name, lisab_000, seems nonsensical. That is because the user name is for a Microsoft account and is a truncated version of the sign-in email address for that account.*

Viewing a Disk's Root

When you click a drive in the Navigation pane, a list of files and folders appears at its top level of organization—its *root directory*. Figure 3.1 shows the root directory on the C drive of a computer. It contains these items:

- **Program Files and in some cases Program Files (x86).** The folder(s) that stores the installed applications; on a system with the 64-bit version of Windows 8 installed, the Program Files folder holds 64-bit applications, while the Program Files (x86) folder holds 32-bit programs. A system with the 32-bit version of Windows 8 installed will have only the Program Files folder, which in that case holds 32-bit applications.
- **Users.** The folder that stores information and settings for each local user.
- **Windows.** The folder that stores the files Windows 8 itself needs to operate.

  Other items the root directory might contain include:

- **Windows.old.** A folder created if a previous version of Windows was installed on the system or if a custom Windows 8 installation was performed.
- **PerfLogs.** Holds the data files that are generated by a Windows 8 program called the Windows Reliability and Performance monitor. Often used by IT professionals planning for new technology, this advanced program monitors various system activities and identifies those that have a negative impact on how the system operates.
- **Other Driver and System Software Folders.** The root may contain folders holding files related to special software that helps a piece of hardware, such as the display, run. Software like this is typically provided by the manufacturer of a particular system component, and you or the computer system's manufacturer installs it in Windows 8.

When you are working at the root directory, clicking the Up button displays drive icons in the file list. Double-clicking a drive icon displays its root directory. Note that the ScreenTip showing the full name of the Up button changes to reflect the location that you would move to if you clicked the button.

Note: *Directory is synonymous with folder on a computer. Folders were called directories in MS-DOS, the original operating system for the IBM Personal Computer, in the 1980s. The term was changed to folder in Windows because a folder is a more fitting metaphor.*

Browsing a Folder

To browse the contents of one of the folders in the file list, double-click the folder. For example, if you double-click the Users folder in the root directory of C, the folders that have been set up for each individual user on the computer appear. In Figure 3.4, there are four user folders: Buddy, LisaA, lisab_000, and Public. Notice that the Address bar shows the *path* taken to the current location: first Computer, then the local disk (called Windows 8 (C) in this case) and then Users. The location immediately above or preceding a location is called its **_parent_**. For example, the C drive is the parent of the Users folder.

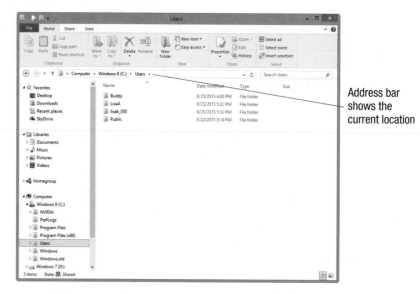

Address bar shows the current location

Figure 3.4 To browse folders within folders, double-click the desired folder in the file list.

Note: **The name that appears for the hard disk (Windows 8 in this chapter's examples) is called its volume label. You can change the volume label if desired. Chapter 2 provides more information about volume labels.**

Windows 8 shows paths in the Address bar as links with arrows between them (shown in Figure 3.4). The traditional description of a path is the disk letter, a colon, backslash (\), and then the folder names separated by backslashes:

C:\Users\Public

In the Address bar, each level of the path is a clickable link; you can jump to that location by clicking its name in the Address bar. You can reach other locations at any level of the path by clicking the arrow at the right of a link in the Address bar and then clicking the desired folder in the menu that appears.

If you want to see the path of the current location displayed in its original format, click any blank area of the Address bar box to temporarily change the path to the old-style notation. Click in the file list to return the Address bar to its normal notation.

Here are some tips for moving to other locations:

■ **To jump to a location** listed in the _Favorites_ section of the Navigation pane, click it.

■ **To return to the previously viewed location,** click the Back button. To go back several locations, click the Back button repeatedly, or click the Recent locations button (the down arrow to the right of the Back and Forward buttons) and select a previously viewed location from the menu that aappears (shown in Figure 3.5).

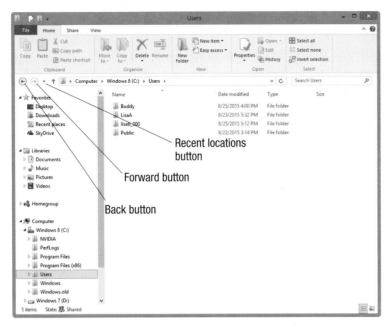

Figure 3.5 The Back button goes back one location at a time, and the Recent locations button opens a menu of previous locations.

- **To go forward again** after going back, click the Forward button.
- **To jump to one of the higher-level folders in the current location's path,** click that folder's name in the Address bar. For example, in Figure 3.5, you could click Windows 8 (C) to return to the root directory.
- **To jump to a different folder at a certain level,** click the arrow to the right of its link in the Address bar and select from the list. For example, in Figure 3.6, to jump to a different top-level folder on the C disk, click the arrow to the right of Windows 8 (C) and then click a different folder.

Figure 3.6 To jump to a different folder, click the arrow to the right of its link and select it from the list.

Learning about Files, Folders, and Libraries

To browse a location:

1. Click *Computer* in the Navigation pane, or click a folder under one of the other sections in the Navigation pane. If you do the latter, skip to Step 3.
2. Double-click the disk containing the folder in the file list.
3. If the folder is within another folder, double-click the folder that contains the desired folder in the file list.
4. Keep double-clicking folders until you arrive at the folder containing the desired file.

Browsing a Different Disk

You can display the content of a different disk in File Explorer in several ways:

- Click Computer in the Address bar to return to the Computer window, which displays icons for all the available disk drives, and then double-click the desired disk.

- In the Address bar, click the arrow button at the right of *Computer* to display a drop-down list of disks and then click the desired disk (shown in Figure 3.7).

- Click the desired disk in the folder list under *Computer* in the Navigation pane. Double-click *Computer* first if the disks do not appear.

- Select the Search charm and then click *Computer* under *Windows System*.

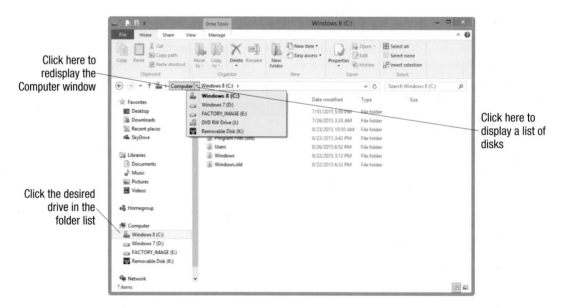

Click here to redisplay the Computer window

Click here to display a list of disks

Click the desired drive in the folder list

Figure 3.7 To jump to a different disk, select from the folder list or use the Address bar.

Browsing Locations

1. Display the desktop. Click the File Explorer button on the Taskbar and then click *Computer* in the Navigation pane. The Computer window appears.
2. Double-click the *C* drive in the file list. (There will likely be a volume label along with the drive letter.) Its folders and files appear.
3. Double-click the *Users* folder. Its folders and files appear.
4. Double-click your user name folder, the *Favorites* folder, and then the *Favorites Bar* folder.
5. Capture a screen shot of your desktop, save it as **C03E01S05**, and then submit it to your instructor.
6. Click your user name in the Address bar to jump back your user name folder.
7. Click *Users* in the Address bar to jump back to the Users folder.
8. Click the Back button to return to your user name folder.
9. Click the Back button again to return to the Favorites Bar folder.
10. Click the arrow at the right of your user name in the Address bar to display a menu of folders within that folder.
11. Click *My Documents*. Its folders and files appear.
12. If the folder list does not appear under *Computer* in the Navigation pane, double-click *Computer* there and then double-click the *C* drive to display the folder list.
13. Click the white triangle beside *Users* in the folder list.
14. Click *Public* in the folder list.
15. Capture a screen shot of your desktop, save it as **C03E01S15**, and then submit it to your instructor.
16. Collapse all the expanded levels beneath *Computer* in the folder list in the Navigation pane by clicking the black triangle next to *Computer.* You may need to scroll up in the pane to find the *Computer* section.
17. Close the Explorer window.

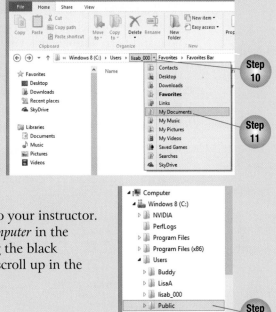

Using Your Windows 8 Personal Folder

You learned in Chapter 1 that if more than one person uses a computer, you can create different user accounts to keep each user's data and gaming files separate. For each user added on the system, Windows 8 creates special folders. Each user's account folders are contained in a ***personal folder***, which has the same name as the account name.

personal folder
The parent folder holding folders for a user's account

Each folder within the personal folder is designed for a specific type of content:

- **Contacts.** For stored contact information used by email and some other programs.
- **Desktop.** Holds files and folders you have created or saved on your desktop.
- **Downloads.** Holds files you have downloaded from the Internet.

Learning about Files, Folders, and Libraries

- **Favorites**. Holds items that you have identified as favorite places in the Internet Explorer web browser.
- **Links**. Holds the shortcuts that you have added to the *Favorites* section in the Navigation pane.
- **My Documents**. For data files from information-based business and productivity applications such as word processing, spreadsheet, and presentation programs.
- **My Music**. For digital music clips and audio books.
- **My Videos**. For video clips transferred to your system and video projects you create.
- **Saved Games**. For the games that come with Windows 8, as well as games you install yourself.
- **Searches**. For searches you have created and saved.
- **SkyDrive**. Appears when you install the SkyDrive client app as noted later in the chapter. Holds local copies of your files that will be synced with the copies on your SkyDrive.

To access any of these folders from the desktop, click the File Explorer button on the Taskbar, click the Up to "Desktop" button at the left of the Address bar box, and then double-click the system folder that displays your user name in the file list. This opens a folder window for your personal folder, displaying all the subfolders it contains (shown in Figure 3.8). Note that installing additional Windows programs and features may add folders within your personal folder or any of the folders it contains, and you may also have an Account Pictures folder holding any picture you have assigned to your account from your computer.

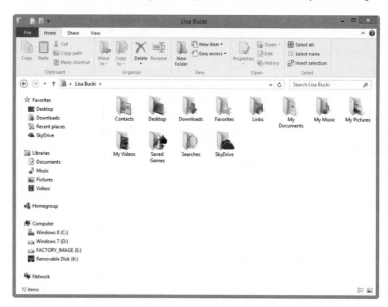

Figure 3.8   For quick access to any of the default folders that Windows creates for your data, select your user name from the Desktop folder.

You can navigate to any of the personal subfolders using the Navigation pane or Address bar. To try this for yourself, navigate to the following path in any folder window: Computer > C: > Users > (your user name or the abbreviated version of your Microsoft account email address). All the folders listed in this location are for your own data, for example Computer > C: > Users > (your user name) > My Documents.

Note: *This chapter uses Windows 8 Address-bar-style notation to indicate paths, with arrows between the locations: C: > Users. In other chapters, on the Web, and in other books, you might see DOS-style notation, with slashes separating the locations: C:\Users.*

Note: *When you use the File Explorer window to navigate to different folders, you cannot open the personal folder of another user.*

To open your personal folder:

Here's How

- Click the File Explorer button on the Taskbar, click the Up to "Desktop" button at the left of the Address bar box, and then double-click the system folder with your user name in the file list.
  OR
- Navigate to Computer > C: > Users > (your user name) using the Address bar or folder list in the Navigation pane in a folder window.

Understanding Libraries

As a reminder, a library is a place for working with a particular type of file. Windows 8 sets up Documents, Music, Pictures, and Video libraries by default, each for managing the type of file that its name suggests. A library does not store any files itself. Instead, it shows you all the contents of specified folders so that you can view and work with the files in those folders at the same time. For example, say you are a commercial photographer who has taken digital photos of a number of products for a client. On your computer's hard disk, you have organized the photos of each product in a separate folder named for the product. This aids you in finding the digital photos of a particular product when the client needs the images or wants you to edit an image. However, there may be other instances in which you want to see all the digital photo files at once, such as if you need to burn a selection of photos of multiple products to a CD or DVD. In such a case, it would be easier to have the contents of all the individual product photo folders shown in a single library window so that you can easily select images from a variety of locations and burn them to a disc.

The default libraries are each set up to monitor two locations holding the same file type: the one in your personal folder and the one in the Public folder. For example, the Documents library shows the contents of both C: > Users > Lisa > My Documents and C: > Users > Public > Public Documents. Likewise, the Music library is set up to show you the music files from both the personal and public locations on your system, and so on for the Pictures and Videos folders.

You can select a library in the *Libraries* section of the Navigation pane in any File Explorer window to open a library. Another way to open a library is via the Libraries window, as shown in Figure 3.9. To open your Libraries window, showing the available libraries, click the File Explorer button on the Taskbar, or use the Search charm and click *File Explorer* under *Windows system*. Then double-click the icon for the library that you want to open.

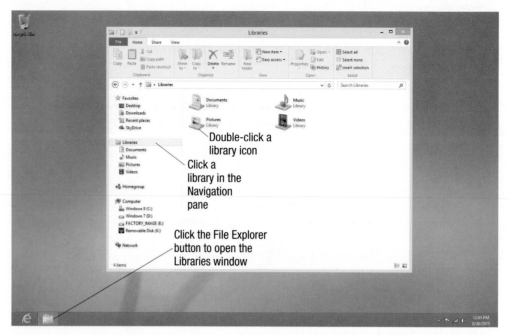

Figure 3.9 You can access your libraries in a variety of ways.

Here's How **To open a library:**

- Click the desired library in the *Libraries* section of the Navigation pane in any folder window. (Double-click *Libraries* if you do not see the individual libraries listed below it.)
  OR
- Open the Libraries window (click the File Explorer button on the Taskbar, or select the Search charm and click File Explorer under Windows System) and then double-click the icon for the desired library. If another folder window is already open on the screen, then right-click the File Explorer button and click *File Explorer* in the Jump List.

 To open a second library window, right-click the File Explorer icon on the Taskbar and then click File Explorer.

A library window looks and works much like any other folder window. One key way to tell the difference between a folder window and a library is that the status bar at the bottom of the window will tell you how many locations it is monitoring, as will the folder list if you expand the library folder, as shown in Figure 3.10. You can work with the files and folders in a library just as you would work with them in the folder where they are actually stored. You can cut, copy, paste, and so on as described in this and other chapters. The "interface" between the library and a particular file's location will require no special actions on your part. Windows 8 does not limit you to working with the default libraries and their settings. You can customize one of the existing libraries to monitor additional locations, and you can create and customize your own libraries. You will learn how to do so later in this chapter.

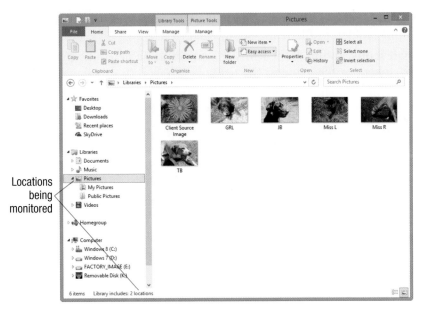

Locations being monitored

Figure 3.10 A library looks like a regular folder but monitors multiple locations.

> **T I P** To quickly go to the location where a particular file in a library is stored, right-click the file and then click *Open file location* in the shortcut menu that appears.

Opening Additional Folder Windows

To view two or more locations simultaneously, you may want to open more windows. You can do this by right-clicking the File Explorer button on the Taskbar and then clicking either File Explorer or one of the locations listed under Frequent on the Jump List, or by opening one of the default data or library folders from the Navigation pane as described previously. You also can click the File tab on the ribbon and then click *Open new window*. Size and arrange the windows so that all are visible at once. As you learned in Chapter 1, you can use Snap to arrange windows side by side; use the Taskbar shortcut menu to choose various window arrangements; or resize and position windows manually.

Changing How Folders and Files Appear

Changing the view in a folder window enables you to control how the window presents files and folders. The various views present more or less information, and use smaller or larger thumbnails or icons. Smaller generic icons might be appropriate, for example, if a folder holds many files and you want to see as many of them as possible in the folder window. In another case, seeing more information about a file or folder might help if you are looking for a file you last worked with on a particular date. Here are the views available to apply to any folder or library window:

- **Extra Large Icons.** This view shows items as large thumbnails with the disk, folder, or file name below. This view can be useful for looking at previews of pictures, for example. (Windows 8 is sometimes able to display a preview thumbnail of a data file rather than a generic icon, depending on the file type.)

- **Large Icons.** This view shows thumbnails that are slightly smaller than the Extra Large Icons view, with the disk, folder, or file name below.

- **Medium Icons.** This view reduces the thumbnail size even further and lists the disk, folder, or file name below each icon.
- **Small Icons.** In this view, icons appear the same height as the text, with the disk, folder, or file name to the *right* of each icon (not below it).
- **List.** This view shows the same information as the Small Icons view, but arranges the items in multiple columns.
- **Details.** This view retains the Small Icons approach, but lists several columns of additional information to the right of each item's icon and name. The columns that appear by default will vary depending on the type of files being viewed, but may include such columns as Date or Date modified, Tags, Size, or Contributing artists. To change the width of a column, drag the divider between that column and the one to its right.

Note: *Some of these properties, such as Type, are assigned when you create the file in a program such as a word processor.*

- **Tiles.** This view shows disk icons of the same size as Medium Icons, but shows the file name and some additional information about the file below. The information that appears depends on the type of icon. For drives, disk usage information appears. For document files, the file type and file size appears.
- **Content.** This view shows larger icons with larger names for easier reading.

To select a view, click the View tab in the folder window, scroll down the list of views in the Layout group, and then click the desired view as shown in Figure 3.11. Or, you can right-click in the folder window, point to View, and then click the desired view. Or, to change to Details view or Large Icons view without using the View tab, click the applicable view button in the lower right corner of the folder window, as shown in Figure 3.11.

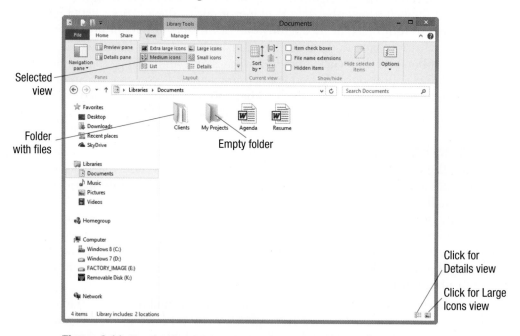

Figure 3.11 Use the View tab Layout group to change the view for the current folder.

Note in Figure 3.11 that when folders display at larger thumbnail sizes, you can tell via the thumbnail whether the folder is empty or contains files or other folders. The thumbnail will include a folder and file within the folder if the folder has contents, or the thumbnail will show an empty folder when the folder is empty.

To toggle between Details and Large Icons views:

- Click the applicable view button in the lower right corner of the folder window.

To select a view from the View tab:

1. Click the View tab on the ribbon.
2. Scroll the list in the Layout group, if needed, and then click the desired view.

Note: *If you want to apply the same icon size to all folders of the same type (for example, folders that hold document files versus folders that hold pictures), click the Options button down arrow on the View tab of the folder window, and then click* Change folder and search options. *Click the View tab, click Apply to Folders, and then click OK.*

T I P To specify additional viewing options, open the Folder Options dialog box by clicking Options on the View tab, click the View tab, and then select one or more items from the Advanced Settings list. For example, you can turn the Status bar on or off or choose whether to show or hide important system files.

In a library window, you can reset the window to its default view. To do so, right-click a blank area of the file list, point to Arrange by, and click *Clear changes.*

Exercise 2

Viewing Personal Folders and Libraries

1. At the desktop, click the File Explorer button to open the Libraries window, if needed. Click the Up to "Desktop" button at the left of the Address bar, and then double-click your user name system folder in the file list. A window for your personal folder appears.
2. Click each of the view buttons in the lower right corner of the window to toggle between views.
3. Click the View tab and then click Extra large icons in the Layout group. The view changes to display the larger icons.
4. Capture a screen shot of your desktop, save it as **C03E02S04**, and then submit it to your instructor.
5. In the Layout group, click Small icons.
6. Click List in the Layout group on the View tab.
7. Right-click the File Explorer button on the Taskbar and then click *File Explorer* in the Jump List.

8. Capture a screen shot of your desktop, save it as **C03E02S08**, and then submit it to your instructor.

9. In the window you opened in Step 7, double-click the Documents icon.

10. Click the View tab, scroll down the list in the Layout group, and then click *Tiles*.

11. In the Music window, right-click the file list, point to *Arrange by*, and then click *Clear changes*. Close the window.

12. In your personal folder window, click the Options button down arrow on the View tab and then click *Change folder and search options*. Click the View tab in the Folder Options dialog box, click the Reset Folders button in the *Folder views* section of the dialog box, and then click Yes in the Folder Views dialog box to confirm resetting the folder and others of its type. Click OK and then close the personal folder window.

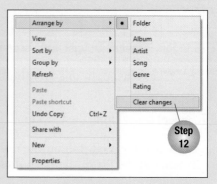

Managing Files and Folders ▪▪▪▪▪▪▪▪▪▪▪▪▪▪▪▪▪

Now that you know how to control the File Explorer interface and how to navigate to various locations, this section describes what you can do when you get to a location. In this section you will learn how to select, rename, move, and copy files and folders.

Selecting Files and Folders

Before you can perform an action on a folder or file, such as deleting or renaming it, you must select it. Any commands you issue affect the selected item(s). Some commands can be performed on multiple items at once, such as moving or copying; other commands work only on individual items, such as renaming.

A selected file or folder appears with a blue or gray selection highlight over it, and information about it appears in the Details pane, if displayed. When multiple items are selected, they all appear with the same selection highlight, and the status bar reports the total number of items selected and summary information for them, such as the total aggregate file size.

A group of selected files and/or folders can be either contiguous (all together) or noncontiguous. It makes no difference except in the technique used to select them. To select a contiguous block of items, hold down Shift as you click the first and last file in the group to select; to select a noncontiguous block, hold down Ctrl as you click each file you

Selected files and folder →

Figure 3.12 Select noncontiguous items by holding down Ctrl as you click each one.

want. Figure 3.12 shows a noncontiguous selection. To remove a selection, click a blank area in the folder list.

The Select group on the Home tab also includes some tools for selecting or deselecting items more quickly. Click the Select all button to select everything in a folder, click the Select none button to clear the current selection, or click the Invert selection button to reverse which items are selected or deselected in the file list.

> **T I P** You can force files to be contiguous with one another by sorting, filtering, or grouping them according to the property they have in common. For example, to select all WordPad documents, sort the list by *Type*, using the *Sort by* drop-down list in the Current view group on the View tab, so they are all together on the list.

Here's How

To select a single item:

- Click the item.

To select multiple contiguous items:

1. Click the first item.
2. Hold down the Shift key and click the last item.

To select multiple noncontiguous items:

1. Click the first item.
2. Hold down the Ctrl key and click the next item.
3. Repeat Step 2 for additional items.

To select all the items in the current location:

- Press Ctrl + A.
  OR
- Click the Select all button in the Select group on the Home tab.

To cancel (deselect) a selection:

- Click away from the selection.
  OR
- Click the Select none button in the Select group on the Home tab.

Creating a New Folder

As you begin creating data files in various applications and for various purposes, you will probably want to create new folders to organize your work. You can create folders on a hard disk, on removable media, such as USB flash drives, on an external hard disk, or in a library. You also can create folders on any shared network location to which you have access. Once you have created a folder, you can save a document you have created from another program or copy or move files into the folder.

Some people choose to create their data folders as subfolders within the Documents library, so that they can easily access their folders from the Navigation pane. The Documents library is also the default storage location for most applications, and some applications will automatically create folders there; however, you are free to create folders nearly anywhere you like. A library is not an actual location but instead is like a mirror that reflects the contents of other physical folder locations on the hard disk, so any folder or file you create or save in a library will be stored in a specified folder location. You will learn more about designating the save folder for a library later in the chapter.

Note: *If you are signed in as a standard user, you may be prevented from creating folders in certain locations or need to supply an administrator password. All users will be prompted to confirm the operation when creating a folder in certain locations, such as the Windows folder. These restrictions are part of the Windows 8 User Account Control security scheme.*

For example, say you work as a salesperson and want to use folders to organize your files for faster access. You might create a folder on your office computer called *Clients.* Within that Clients folder, you could then create a specific folder to hold the files you create for each client account, such as Smith Electronics, Argyle Aggregates, or Kelly Appliances. Then, when you needed to work on a file you created for a particular client, you would know exactly which folder to open.

Here's How

To create a folder:

1. Open the Libraries window using the File Explorer button on the desktop Taskbar.
2. Display the location (folder or library) in which you want to create the folder.
3. Right-click a blank area of the file list, point to *New*, and then click *Folder.*
   OR
   On the ribbon, click New folder in the New group on the Home tab.
   OR
   On the Quick Access Toolbar, click the New folder button.
4. Type a name for the new folder.
5. Press Enter.

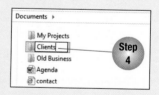

Renaming a File or Folder

If you made a typo when creating a folder or file name or need to update its name, you can do so at any time in a folder window, either by using the Rename button in the Organize group on the Home tab or by right-clicking the file or folder. File and folder names can contain up to 255 characters and can include spaces and most punctuation marks (but not any of the following: / \ * ? " | < >). Every file name includes a file name extension, added automatically when the file is saved. (Chapter 5 covers saving files.) The *file name extension* consists of a period and additional letters added at the end of the file name and identifies the type of file and program used to create it. If the file name extension is visible when you rename the file, be sure not to delete or change it. Otherwise, you will no longer be able to open the file by double-clicking it, and the program in which you created the file may no longer recognize the file.

Note: *Do not rename folders that Windows 8 or your applications create, such as Windows, Program Files, or Users, or Windows will not work correctly. It is safe only to rename user-created folders and files.*

To rename a file or folder:

1. Open the Libraries window using the File Explorer button on the desktop Taskbar and then navigate to the folder or file to be renamed.
2. Select the item to rename by clicking it.
3. Right-click the folder or file and then click *Rename*.
   OR
   On the ribbon, click the Home tab and then click the Rename button in the Organize group.
   OR
   Press F2.
4. Type a new name or edit the existing name.
5. Press Enter.

 T I P   To undo a Rename operation, press Ctrl + Z immediately after making changes.

Copying or Moving a File or Folder

Copying a file or folder makes a duplicate of it and places that duplicate in a new destination. For example, you might have a flash memory card from your digital camera that has some recent pictures. When you place that card in the appropriate removable media disk drive connected to your computer, you can copy the image files to a folder on the hard disk. The original images remain on the flash card until you decide to remove them.

You can copy files or folders in three ways: with the Windows Clipboard (via the Cut, Copy, and Paste commands), with tools in the Organize group on the Home tab, or via drag-and-drop.

Copying or Moving with the Cut, Copy, and Paste Commands

The Windows Clipboard is a temporary internal storage area in Windows 8. You can place files and folders into that storage by selecting them and issuing either the Cut or Copy command. Cut removes the original; Copy leaves the original in place. You then can navigate to the new location and issue the Paste command to insert the Clipboard's content. Figure 3.13 illustrates how the Clipboard works.

One advantage of the Clipboard method of copying and moving is that multiple pastes are possible. After you have cut or copied something, you can then paste it into multiple locations without having to recut or recopy it. Another advantage is that you do not have to see both the original and the destination locations at the same time. You can perform the cut or copy operation, and then open the destination location at your leisure.

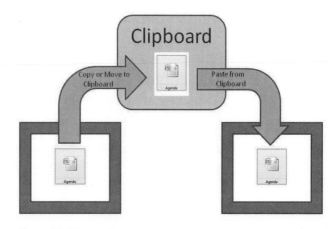

Figure 3.13 The Clipboard enables you to copy and move from one location to another.

T I P The Clipboard does much more than copy and move files. You can use the Clipboard within most Windows applications to copy and move content between data files. For example, you could use the Clipboard to copy a drawing from a graphics program and paste it into a word processing document.

There are many ways to issue the Cut, Copy, and Paste commands, including mouse methods, keyboard methods, and menu methods.

 Here's How

To copy a file, folder, or group (cut-and-paste method):

1. Select the files(s) and/or folder(s) to copy.
2. Issue the Copy command in any of these ways:
    *   Press Ctrl + C.
    *   Right-click the selection and choose *Copy*.
    *   Click the Copy button in the Clipboard group on the Home tab.
    *   Press Alt, H, C, and then O.
3. Display the destination location.
4. Issue the Paste command in any of these ways:
    *   Press Ctrl + V.
    *   Right-click an empty area of the destination location and choose *Paste*.
    *   Click the Paste button in the Clipboard group on the Home tab.
    *   Press Alt, H, and then V.

To move a file, folder, or group (cut-and-paste method):

1. Select the files(s) or folder(s) to move.
2. Issue the Cut command in any of these ways:
    *   Press Ctrl + X.
    *   Right-click the selection and then choose *Cut*.
    *   Click the Cut button in the Clipboard group on the Home tab.
    *   Press Alt, H, and then T.
3. Display the destination location.
4. Issue the Paste command in any of these ways:
    *   Press Ctrl + V.
    *   Right-click an empty area of the destination location and choose *Paste*.
    *   Click the Paste button in the Clipboard group on the Home tab.
    *   Press Alt, H, and then V.

Copying or Moving with the Organize Tools

The Organize group on the Home tab includes additional tools you can use to copy or move files without having to navigate in the folder window to an alternate location. The Move to and Copy to buttons enable you to copy or move a file to a location on the applicable drop-down menu or use the Choose location choice to select the file's destination from a dialog box.

To copy a file or folder with the Copy to button:

1. Select either the files(s) or folder(s).
2. Click the Copy to button in the Organize group on the Home tab.
3. If the destination location appears in the drop-down list, click it. Otherwise, click *Choose location.*
4. In the Copy Items dialog box, select the destination location.
5. Click Copy.

To move a file or folder with the Move to button:

1. Select either the files(s) or folder(s).
2. Click the Move to button in the Organize group on the Home tab.
3. If the destination location appears in the drop-down list, click it. Otherwise, click *Choose location.*
4. In the Move Items dialog box, select the destination location.
5. Click Move.

Here's How

Quick Fix

Need a New Folder
When using this method to move or copy a file, you can use the Make New Folder button in either dialog box to create a new destination.

Copying or Moving with the Drag-and-Drop Method

This method requires having both the source and the destination locations visible at the same time. The locations can be in two separate File Explorer windows, or the destination location can be a folder or location icon (such as for a disk or library folder) in the Navigation pane.

What happens when you drag and drop: Does it move, or does it copy? That depends on the relationship between the source and destination locations. If the source and destination are on the same disk, drag-and-drop actions move the material. If the source and destination material are on different disks, drag-and-drop actions copy the material. To override this default behavior, hold down the Ctrl key if you want to copy, or hold down the Shift key if you want to move.

To copy a file, folder, or group (drag-and-drop method):

1. Select the file(s) and/or folder(s).
2. If the destination is on the same disk as the source, hold down the Ctrl key.
3. Drag the selection to the new location and drop it.

To move a file, folder, or group (drag-and-drop method):

1. Select the file(s) and/or folder(s).
2. If the destination is on the same disk as the source, hold down the Shift key.
3. Drag the selection to the new location and drop it.

Here's How

Quick Fix

Accurate Dropping
If you are dragging a selection into a folder in the *Favorites* section or the folder list in the Navigation pane, make sure you position the mouse accurately over the folder before releasing the mouse button. When the mouse pointer is in the correct spot for dropping on that location, a large icon appears over the location with a Move To indicator under it, as shown in the example to the left.

Learning about Files, Folders, and Libraries

Creating and Managing Folders and Files

1. Click the File Explorer button on the desktop Taskbar and then double-click the Documents icon. The Documents library opens.
2. Create a new folder named **Practice**. One possible method:
   a. Click New folder in the New group on the Home tab on the ribbon.
   b. Type **Practice**.
   c. Press Enter.
3. Rename the folder **Transport**. One possible method:
   a. Right-click the new folder.
   b. Click *Rename.*
   c. Type **Transport**.
   d. Press Enter.
4. Right-click the File Explorer button on the Taskbar and then click *File Explorer.* The Libraries window opens.
5. Arrange the two windows so both are visible.
6. Locate Student Data Files at www.paradigmcollege.net/windows8. If you have not already done so, download files to your computer or to your USB flash drive. Ask your instructor for assistance, if needed.
7. In the second Explorer window that you opened, navigate to the folder for Chapter 3 and then select the **Airline** file.
8. Copy the **Airline** file to the Documents library. One possible method:
   a. Hold down the Ctrl key.
   b. Drag the file to the Documents library.
9. Close the folder window for the student data files.
10. Capture a screen shot of your desktop, save it as **C03E03S10**, and then submit it to your instructor.
11. In the Documents library window, rename the copied file:
    a. Right-click the **Airline** file.
    b. Click *Rename* in the shortcut menu.
    c. Type **Railroad**.
    d. Press Enter.
12. Move **Railroad** to the *Transport* folder. One possible method:
    a. Select **Railroad** and then press Ctrl + X to cut it.
    b. Double-click the *Transport* folder to open it.
    c. Press Ctrl + V to paste **Railroad** into the *Transport* folder.
13. Double-click the *Transport* folder to open it, if needed. Remove the properties and personal information from the Railroad file, which creates a copy of the file:
    a. Right-click **Railroad** and then choose *Properties.*
    b. On the Details tab, click the Remove Properties and Personal Information link.
    c. In the Remove Properties dialog box, click OK.
    d. Click OK to close the Properties dialog box.
    e. Capture a screen shot of your desktop, save it as **C03E03S13**, and then submit it to your instructor.
    f. Click OK.
14. Close the Transport folder window.

Organizing Files and Folders ■■■■■■■■■■■■■■

When a location contains many files, it can be difficult to make a meaningful evaluation of what is there. How many different file types are present? Were any files recently modified? Which files occupy the most disk space?

These important questions and more can be answered by applying ***sorting***, ***grouping***, ***filtering***, or ***arranging*** to the display of files. Each of these techniques is useful for answering different questions about the data or browsing it in a different way.

Sorting the File and Folder Listing

Sorting arranges the items in a folder or library window according to a file property, such as alphabetically by name or in ascending order by size. When you have changed to the Details view in a folder or library window, some common sort criteria appear in a column headings bar immediately above the file listing: *Name*, *Date modified*, *Type*, and *Size* (shown in Figure 3.14). These represent the columns that appear when viewing the file list in Details view, but the column headings remain visible even in some other views. Click any of those column headings to sort by that criterion. Click the same column heading again to toggle between ascending and descending sort order.

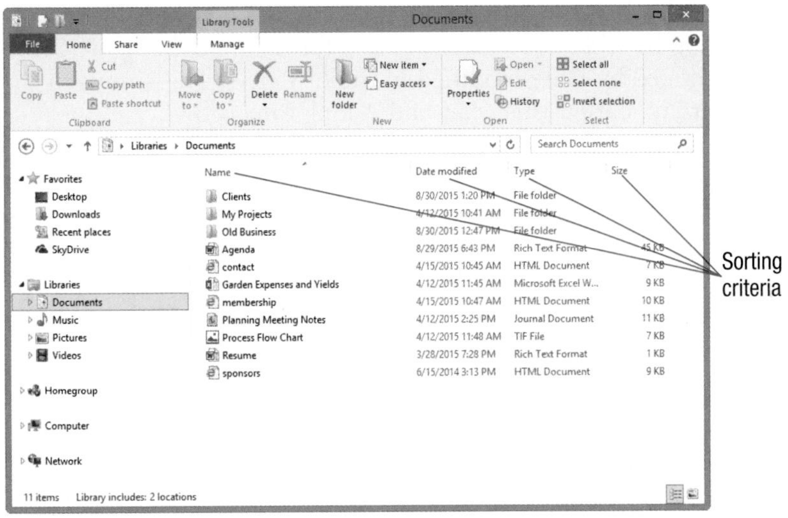

Figure 3.14 To sort a file and folder listing, click the column heading that describes the criterion by which to sort.

To sort by a property other than the column headings listed, you can add the desired property as a column heading in the File Explorer window. To add a column, right-click any column heading and then click *More*. In the Choose Details dialog box, mark or clear check boxes to indicate which properties should be column headings and then click OK.

> **T I P** You also can use the Add columns button in the Current view group on the View tab to add or hide columns to the view.

sorting Arranging items in a particular order based on a property

grouping Arranging items into grouped sections of a list based on a property

filtering Displaying only certain items based on a property

arranging Summarizing the items in a library into stacks based on a property

Here's How

To sort by a column heading's criterion:

1. Display the Details view, if needed.
2. Click a column heading. Click it a second time to reverse the order.
   OR
   Click the Sort by button in the Current view group on the View tab and then click the name of a column heading.

To sort by a property not shown as a column heading:

1. Display the Details view, if needed.
2. Right-click any visible column heading.
3. Click *More*.
4. Mark the check box for the property by which you want to sort.
5. Click OK.
6. Click the column heading. Click it a second time to reverse the order.

Grouping Files and Folders

Grouping is like sorting except the items are divided into separate sections of the window based on their membership in one group or another. The groups depend on the criterion by which you are grouping; for example, in Figure 3.15, the files are shown grouped by Date modified in the List view. The groups in the figure are Today, Yesterday, Earlier this year, and A long time ago.

Figure 3.15 This grouped listing shows files and folders placed in different sections based on their Date modified.

 TIP In the Details view, you can expand and collapse groups in the file list using the triangles to the left of the group name or by right-clicking a group name and choosing *Expand all groups* or *Collapse all groups* in the shortcut menu.

To group by a column heading's criterion:

1. Right-click the file list and point to *Group by*.
   OR
   Click the Group by button in the Current view group on the View tab.
2. Click the criterion to group by from the choices at the top of the menu.

To group by a property not shown as a column heading:

1. Right-click the file list, point to *Group by*, and then click *More*.
   OR

   Click the Group by button in the Current view group on the View tab and then click *Choose columns.*
2. Mark the check box for the property by which you want to group.
3. Click OK.
4. Right-click the file list.
5. Point to *Group by.*
6. Click the property (criterion) you selected in Step 2.

To remove grouping:

- Right-click the file list, point to *Group by*, and then click *None*.
  OR
- Click the Group by button in the Current view group on the View tab and then click (*None*).

Filtering to Show Only Certain Files or Folders

Filtering displays only files that match particular criteria, such as a particular file type. To filter, switch to the Details view and then move the mouse pointer over one of the column headings above the folder and file icons. Click the drop-down list arrow that appears, click the check boxes for one or more criteria in the drop-down menu, and then press Enter or click outside the menu to close the drop-down box. Figure 3.16 shows *A long time ago* chosen from the Date modified list, showing only

the files created during the current week. To remove the filtering, open the drop-down list again, clear the check boxes, and then close the list.

A filter creates a ***virtual folder***, which is a temporary means of grouping files. Notice in Figure 3.16 that the Address bar indicates that you are in the folder called *A long time ago*. That folder does not exist even though it was created by the filter. When you remove the filter, the virtual folder will go away. If you want to save a filter specification, create a reusable virtual folder (see "Saving a Search" and "Using Saved Searches" later in this chapter).

virtual folder A temporary logical grouping of files, such as the files resulting from filtering or searching

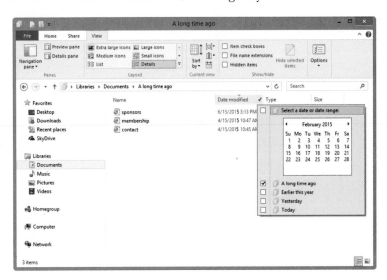

Figure 3.16 To filter the file list, open the menu for one of the column headings and mark a checkbox that represents the filter to apply.

To filter the file list in Details view:

1. Point to a column heading and then click its down arrow to open its menu.
2. Mark the check box for the desired filter criteria. Check multiple criteria if desired.
3. If needed, click the file list to close the menu.
4. Repeat Steps 1–3 to specify additional filtering for additional columns.

To remove a filter in Details view:

1. Point to the column heading for the filtered column (it will have a check mark at the right of its name) and then click the check mark to open its menu.
2. For each filter to remove, click its check box to clear the check mark.
3. Click the file list to close the menu.
4. Repeat Steps 1–3 to remove filtering from additional columns.

Arranging Items in a Library

A library window provides the ability to arrange items, hiding the individual items and instead showing icons or folders that represent various categories of the items. Arrange the items by right-clicking the file list, pointing to *Arrange by*, and then clicking the desired category. The categories depend on which library you are working in. For example, in Figure 3.17, items in the Documents library are stacked by *Type*. In the Music library, you can arrange items by other categories such as *Artist*. The arranged items might appear as stacks, as shown in Figure 3.17, or they may appear as icons. To view the contents of an arranged stack or icon, double-click it. Each stack is a virtual folder (a temporary folder). To go back to all of the stacks or icons, click the Back button. To remove an arrangement, open the Arrange by menu and click *Folder*.

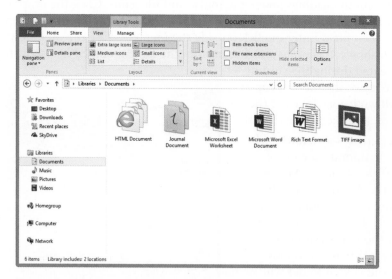

Figure 3.17 Arranging creates a series of virtual folders and displays them instead of the individual items.

To arrange a library:
1. Right-click the file list and then point to *Arrange by*.
2. Click the desired category.

To remove the arrange setting:
1. Right-click the file list and then point to *Arrange by*.
2. Click *Folder*.

Working with Libraries ▪▪▪▪▪▪▪▪▪▪▪▪▪▪▪▪▪▪▪▪▪▪

You have already had an introduction to how each of the default libraries in Windows 8 keeps track of a particular type of file and folders stored in designated locations. The Documents library collects your data-oriented work, the Music library collects digital songs, the Pictures library presents digital images, and the Videos library is for movie clips and projects. As with folders, Windows 8 provides the option of creating additional libraries to meet your file-management needs and to customize a number of aspects of how any library—including any of the default libraries—operates.

Making or Deleting a Library

You can add a new library to create a central location for files pertaining to, say, a particular topic or client. Windows 8 enables you to add and remove libraries on an as-needed basis. Once you have created a new library, you need to set it up to monitor particular folders and choose other settings controlling how it behaves. After that point, you can copy and move files and folders into your custom library just as you would one of the default libraries. You need to be working in the Libraries window, which shows the default libraries, to create a new library. There, you can use the New item button in the New group on the Home tab to get the job done.

 T I P After you create and configure your own library, you can add a shortcut for it to the Windows 8 desktop so that you can open the library more quickly. To do so, right-click the library, point to *Send to*, and then click *Desktop (create shortcut)*.

To create a library:

1. If no windows are open, click the File Explorer button on the Taskbar. Or, in an open folder window, click *Libraries* in the Navigation pane.
2. Click the New item button in the New group on the Home tab on the ribbon and then click *Library*.
3. Type a name for the new library.
4. Press the Enter key.

To delete a library:

1. If no windows are open, click the File Explorer button on the Taskbar. Or, in an open folder window, click *Libraries* in the Navigation pane.
2. Right-click the library to delete and then click *Delete* in the shortcut menu. You also can click the Library icon and press the Delete key.

Controlling Which Folders a Library Monitors

save location The
folder where a
library will physi-
cally store any file
or folder created
or copied to the
library

Each of the default libraries initially monitors and displays a pair of folders. For example, the Documents library shows the contents of the My Documents folder in your personal folder and the Public Documents folder in the Public folder. Each of the other default libraries monitors the pair of personal and public folders corresponding to the library's name. One of the folders set up for each library is designated as the *save location*. A library functions as a virtual folder and does not store the files or folders you create or copy in it. Instead, those files or folders are physically created in another folder on a disk, the save location.

Initially, a new library you create monitors no folders. You must include one or more folders in the list of locations that the library shows. If you try to open a library for which no folders have been included, Windows 8 will prompt you to include a folder, as shown in Figure 3.18. Click the Include a folder button, browse to and select the desired folder in the dialog box that appears, and then click the Include folder button. The first folder you include for a library becomes the save location by default. If you remove the save location folder from the library, Windows 8 designates the next folder as the save location. You can add as many folders as desired and change the save location for any library, including the default libraries, at any time in the Properties dialog box for the library. To open the Properties dialog box, right-click the library's icon in a file list or its name in the Navigation pane, and then click *Properties*. Or, at the Libraries window, click the icon for a library, click the Library Tools Manage tab on the ribbon, and then click the Manage library button. This opens a Library Locations dialog box for the library, which you can use to add and delete folders.

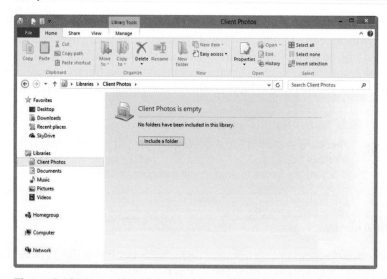

Figure 3.18 You must include one or more folders in a new library.

Windows 8 places a few restrictions on which folders you can include in a library. Of course you can include the folders on your computer and its internal hard disk(s). You cannot include a folder from optical media (readable and writable CDs and DVDs) or any other type of removable media, such as a USB flash drive. You can include folders from an external hard drive, as long as the drive is connected to the system, powered on, and fully recognized. If your computer can connect to folders elsewhere on a network, the network folder must be made available offline so it will be added to your computer's index to be included in the library. (You will learn about working with offline folders in Chapter 16.)

To include a folder in a library:

Here's How

- If the library is new and has no folders, open the library and then click Include a folder. Navigate to and select a folder in the Include Folder dialog box that appears and then click Include folder.
  OR
1. In the Libraries window, double-click the library.
2. On the Library Tools Manage tab of the ribbon, click the Manage Library button in the Manage group.
3. In the Library Locations dialog box, click the Add button.
4. In the Include Folder dialog box that appears, navigate to and select the desired folder.
5. Click the Include folder button.
6. Click OK.
  OR
1. In the Libraries window, right-click the library and then click *Properties*. Or, in an open folder window, right-click the library in the Navigation pane and then click *Properties*.
2. Under *Library locations*, click the Include a folder button.
3. In the Include Folder dialog box that appears, navigate to and select the desired folder.
4. Click the Include folder button.
5. Click OK.

To change the save location in a library:

1. In the Libraries window, double-click the library.
2. On the Library Tools Manage tab on the ribbon, click the Set save location button in the Manage group.
3. Click the folder to set as the save location in the menu.
  OR
1. In the Libraries window, right-click the library and then click *Properties*. Or, in an open folder window, right-click the library in the Navigation pane and then click *Properties*.
2. Under *Library locations*, click the folder that you want to set as the save location. (It will not have an icon beside it.)
3. Click the Set save location button.
4. Click OK.

To remove a location from a library:

1. In the Libraries window, right-click the library and then click *Properties*. Or, in an open folder window, right-click the library in the Navigation pane and then click *Properties*.
2. Under *Library locations*, click the folder that you want to remove.
3. Click the Remove button.
4. Click OK.
    OR
1. In the Libraries window, double-click the library and then click the Manage Library button in the Manage group on the Library Tools Manage tab on the ribbon.
2. In the Library Locations dialog box, click the folder to remove in the Library locations list.
3. Click the Remove button.
4. Click OK.

Changing Other Library Settings

Two other important library settings need to be specified for new libraries and can be changed for existing libraries. First, a library needs to be optimized for the types of files being managed by the library. The default optimization setting, General Items, groups files by folder location in the file list by default and shows items in the Details view. A better arrangement for photos is the Large Icons view; if you optimize a library for Pictures, it will use the Large Icons view by default. Other library optimization choices are Documents, Music, and Videos. The second setting you may wish to control is whether a custom library appears in the Navigation pane. If you have added a shortcut for a library to the desktop or often work in the File Explorer window that shows all your libraries, you may decide that having a library appear in the Navigation pane (the default setting) is overkill. You can work with both of these settings in the Properties dialog box for the library or using the Library Tools Manage tab.

To optimize a library and control its Navigation pane display:

1. In the Libraries window, right-click a library and then click Properties. Or, in an open folder window, right-click the library in the Navigation pane and then click *Properties*.
2. Click the *Optimize this library for* drop-down list and then click the desired optimization.
3. Beside Attributes, click the *Shown in Navigation pane* check box, if necessary. Marking the check box specifies that the library will appear, while clearing it removes the library from the Navigation pane.
4. Click OK.
    OR
1. In the Libraries window, double-click a library.
2. Click the Library Tools Manage tab, click the Optimize this library for button in the Manage group, and then click the desired optimization in the drop-down list.
3. On the same tab, click the Shown in Navigation pane button. Toggling the button on specifies that the library will appear, while toggling it off removes the library from the Navigation pane.

Finding Files and Folders ▰▰▰▰▰▰▰▰▰▰▰▰▰

As you use Windows 8 features and applications, you will likely create many data files such as reports, spreadsheets, photos, video clips, and so on. As the number of folders and files grows, the difficulty increases in remembering where you saved a particular file or in which location you created a particular folder. In this section you will learn some ways of locating a file or folder on your system.

Note: *The search features of Windows 8 find more than just files and folders; they also find information within an Outlook data file, including emails, contacts, calendar items, and tasks on to-do lists. This chapter focuses on files and folders, but as you perform searches, some of the results you get will likely be Outlook data items.*

▼ **Quick Fix**

Not Getting Expected Search Results
If you do not get the search results you expect, make sure you started in a high enough level location. To search across all drives at once, start at the Computer window.

Performing a Quick Search by Name, Content, or Keyword

The search box in the top right corner of a folder or library window enables you to perform quick searches on a word or phrase you enter. Navigate to the drive or folder from which you want to start the search and type the criteria for your search, such as part of the file name or a keyword, into the search box. The search will be performed on that location and all its subordinate locations.

In Figure 3.19, for example, the word *client* was used as the search term, and Windows 8 found files and folders that contain *client* in their names or contents. If any files had a file type of client, they would appear in the search results, too.

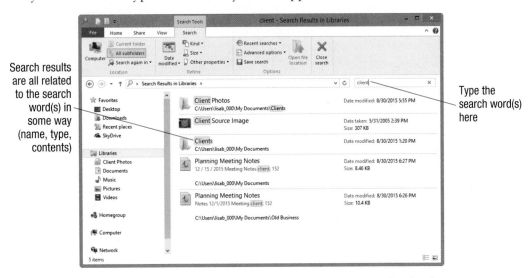

Figure 3.19 A search filters all files and folders to find items related to the word(s) you search for.

Search results begin appearing immediately; the view in the current window is filtered to show the files and folders that match the text you have typed so far. It may take a few seconds or even a few minutes to see the full results if the search scope encompasses many locations, such as the entire contents of a large hard disk.

T I P You can speed up searches of locations that you frequently search by indexing them. Indexing a location creates an internal lookup table that the Search tools in Windows 8 can use to search the location more efficiently. Indexing is covered later in this chapter.

To perform a search:

1. Click in the search box in a folder or library window.
2. Type a file name, type, date, key words, or other criterion.
3. When you have typed as much of the search term as needed, press Enter.

To clear the search results:

- Click the Close Search button at the right end of the Search Tools Search tab on the ribbon.
  OR
- Click Back to return to the previous window contents.
  OR
- Press Esc.

The Search charm also enables you to perform a file and folder search. Select the Search charm from the desktop or Start screen, click *Files* in the right pane, type the search term in the box at the top, and then click the search (magnifying glass) icon at the right end of the text box. In Figure 3.20, the matching file names appear immediately in the left pane. Click a match in the results list to open it in its application.

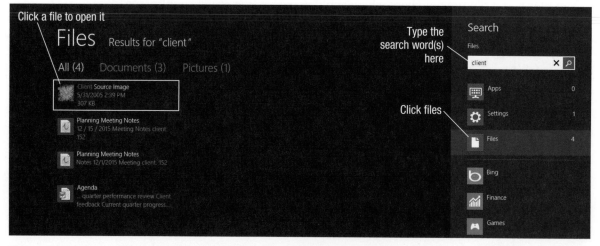

Figure 3.20 You can use the Search charm to search for files Windows 8 style.

 You can use wildcards (? and *) and comparison operators (< and >) with a search in a search box. For example, entering ??bb returns files that have any character as the first two characters and bb as the third and fourth characters. Entering *.htm returns files of the .htm file type (file extension). Entering <7/20/09 returns all files created before 7/20/09.

Repeating a Search

The Search Tools Search tab tracks terms that you have searched for over time. After you have performed a search, click the Recent searches button in the Options group on that tab, and a drop-down list with the previous searches appears. Click one of those searches to run it again.

To repeat a search:

1. Click in the search box in a folder window, and then click the icon at the far right, if necessary, to display the Search Tools Search tab on the ribbon.
2. Click the Recent searches button in the Options group.
3. Click one of the previous searches that appears.

T I P If the list of prior searches becomes too cluttered for practical use, you can clear the list. Click the Recent Searches button on the Search Tools Search tab and then click *Clear search history.*

When you perform a search, you have the option of repeating the same search in another location. In Figure 3.19, the Search Tools Search tab displays a Search again in button in the Location group. To expand the search to one of those larger locations, click the button and then click the location to search. For example, click Libraries to rerun the search in all the libraries, or click Internet to expand the search to the Web.

To repeat a search in more locations:

1. Click in the search box in a folder window.
2. Type the file name, type, date, key words, or other criterion and then press Enter.
3. Click the Search again in button in the Location group on the Search Tools Search tab.
4. Click the location to search.

Using Search Filters

As you type an entry in the search box at the top of a folder or library window, the Search Tools Search tab that appears also includes filter categories in the Refine group that you can use to make the search more specific (shown in Figure 3.21). You can either use a filter alone, or use it in conjunction with a search term that you enter. To apply one of the filters, click its button and then click one of the criteria that appear. For example, say you want to search for document files that include the word *client*. You could click the search box, type ***client,*** press Enter, click the Kind button, and then click *Document*. To change a filter criterion, click it in the search box and then delete the blue filter text, which will read something like *kind:=document*.

Note: *Windows 8 determines a file's type by its extension. An extension is a code that follows the file name, separated from it by a period—for example, myfile.docx or yourfile.txt. Windows 8 maintains a list of common file extensions and the types of files they represent, and uses this information to perform searches by general category of file such as music or pictures.*

Filters

Figure 3.21
You can include a filter with a search.

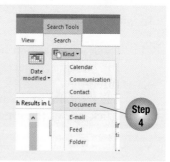

Here's How → **To use a filter in a search:**

1. Click in the search box in the folder or library window.
2. Type the search term(s) and then press Enter.
3. Click a filter button in the Refine group on the Search Tools Search tab.
4. Click the desired criterion.

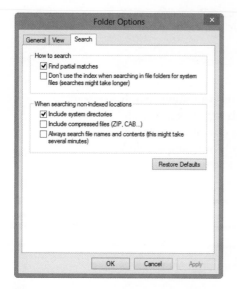

Figure 3.22 Click the Search tab of the Folder Options dialog box to set options for how the search will behave.

TIP After using one or more filter criteria, if you type the search term again, the search box displays a drop-down list of the past matching searches. Click one of the choices to run the search again.

Setting Search Options

The search box makes certain assumptions about what you want. In particular, it assumes that you want to include partial matches and search system directories. These choices slow down the search results considerably but provide the most thorough results. You can change those settings and more in the Search tab of the Folder Options dialog box (shown in Figure 3.22). You can change to searching both file names and contents in nonindexed locations and turn on/off other options for indexing and search methods here.

Here's How → **To set search options:**

1. Click the View tab on the ribbon of a folder window and then click the Options button down arrow.
2. Click *Change folder and search options*.
3. Click the Search tab of the dialog box.
4. Mark or clear check boxes for the options as desired.
5. Click OK.

You also can set some search options from the Search Tools Search tab on the ribbon using the Advanced options drop-down. For example, you can choose whether search results include partial matches, specify what to search in nonindexed locations, and use the *Change indexed locations* command to work with indexes as described next.

Indexing a Location for Faster Searching

As you are performing some searches, you might notice that the search progress bar across the Address bar moves slowly, because the location being searched is not indexed. To avoid this, you can index the locations that you search most frequently.

Indexing creates a table of contents of the location that includes all the properties of all the files and folders within it. So when you search that location later, Windows 8 can refer to that table of contents rather than the actual file properties and the search can take place much more quickly. Indexing occurs automatically behind the scenes when it is enabled for a location. All user folders and libraries and some special folders like those that store Internet browsing history information are indexed by default, but you will need to enable indexing for other locations where you may store many files, such as a storage folder on a second hard disk installed on your system.

Here's How

indexing A process that creates an index, an internal information set about a location, used to enable faster searching

To enable or disable indexing for a location:

1. In any folder window, type a letter in the search box to display the Search Tools Search tab on the ribbon.
2. In the Options group, click the Advanced options button and then click *Change indexed locations*.
3. In the Indexing Options dialog box, click *Modify*.
4. In the Indexed Locations dialog box, click the Show all locations button and then click Continue in the User Account Control dialog box if you are not using an administrator account.
5. Click to mark or clear the check mark next to a location.
   OR
   Click the triangle next to a location to expand it and then mark or clear check boxes for individual folders within that location.
6. Click OK.
7. Close the other open dialog boxes and windows, clearing the search in the Control Panel window before closing it.

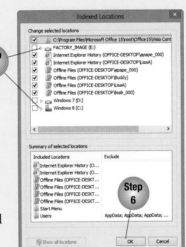

 TIP You also can open the Control Panel window, search for *index*, and then click *Indexing Options* to work with index settings. You will learn about the Control Panel in later chapters in the book.

TIP Click the Advanced button in the Indexing Options dialog box to work with even more settings, such as whether to index encrypted files or what file types to index.

When an indexed location is searched, the actual content of the location is ignored by default, and the search uses only the index as a reference. Therefore, if the index is out-of-date, the search results will not be accurate. Windows 8 attempts to keep the index current by indexing in the background as you work, but it sometimes requires an hour or more to index a complex location initially. If you must have accurate results at all times and do not mind that the search speed is slower because of it, you have two options:

Learning about Files, Folders, and Libraries

- Turn off indexing for the location. This prevents Windows 8 from continuing to index this location, so if you turn indexing back on, it might take a while to update.

- In the Folder Options dialog box's Search tab (shown in Figure 3.22), check the *Always search file names and contents* check box (this might take several minutes). This leaves indexing enabled but forces the search to look at the actual files, not just the index.

Saving a Search

After creating a search, you might wish to save it so you can rerun the same search again without having to set it up manually.

To save a search, run the search and then click the Save search button in the Options group on the Search Tools Search tab on the ribbon. Specify a name for the saved search in the Save As dialog box and click Save. Do not change the save location. Saving the search to the default folder will make it easier to use, as described next. After you do that, the search is available in the saved searches list (accessible in the Searches folder in your personal folder).

Using Saved Searches

Your personal folder includes a Searches folder, where you can select from the saved searches you have created to find files. Each of these searches is a virtual folder. A virtual folder is like a query; every time you open it, you get the most recent results based on its search specifications.

Searches that you save will be added to the Searches folder, unless you specify another save location, which is best to avoid. Click the File Explorer button on the Taskbar to open the Libraries folder, click the Up to "Desktop" button at the left of the Address bar box, double-click your user name system folder, and then double-click the Searches folder to display a list of saved searches, as shown in Figure 3.23. Double-click any of the saved searches to run it and display the results. Windows 8 also adds saved searches to the *Favorites* section of the Navigation pane in a folder or library window. Click a search there to display the search results in the file list.

Figure 3.23 Saved searches appear in the Searches folder, ready for use.

Note: *The path to the Searches folder is in your personal folder within Users. Each user has his or her own separate set of Searches. This is advantageous because you can create your own custom saved searches that only you can access.*

Creating Libraries and Searches

1. Click the File Explorer button on the Taskbar.
2. Click the New item button on the Home tab and then click *Library*.
3. Type **Assignments** and then press Enter.
4. Right-click the Assignments library icon and then click *Properties*.
5. Click the Add button. Navigate to and then click the *Public Documents* folder. ***Hint: Find the personal folders for the Public user***. Click Include folder.
6. Choose *Documents* from the *Optimize this library for* drop-down list and then click OK to close the library's Properties dialog box.
7. Capture a screen shot of your desktop with the open Libraries window, save it as **C03E04S07**, and then submit it to your instructor.
8. In the Libraries window, click in the search box at the upper right corner of the window.
9. Click the Date modified: button in the Refine group on the Search Tools Search tab.
10. Click *Today* in the menu that appears.
11. Group the search results by file type (extension):
    a. Right-click the file list.
    b. Point to *Group by* in the shortcut menu.
    c. Click *Type*.
12. Capture a screen shot of your desktop, save it as **C03E04S12**, and then submit it to your instructor.
13. Click the Save search button in the Options group on the Search Tools Search tab.
14. Enter **Current Files** in the *File name* text box and then click Save.
15. Close the current window.
16. Click the File Explorer button on the Taskbar, click *Desktop* in the Navigation pane, and then double-click your user name folder.
17. Double-click the *Searches* folder.
18. Double-click the *Current Files* search to rerun it.
19. Close the File Explorer window.

> ▼ **Quick Fix**
>
> **No Matching Files Appear**
> If no matching files appear, clear the current search and then reapply the search filter using the *This week* menu item.

Creating Shortcuts for Easier File and Folder Access ▪▪▪▪▪▪ ▪▪▪▪▪▪▪▪▪▪▪ ▪▪▪▪

Now you know how to find any file or folder on your system, but you probably do not want to go through all that trouble every time you want a particular item. If there are files and folders you use frequently, you might find that you can save time by creating a shortcut for that file or folder.

A shortcut provides you with an alternative way to navigate to a folder or library or open a file. For example, if you create a shortcut to your My Documents folder on the desktop, you do not have to open the Libraries window first every time you want to access it. Double-clicking a shortcut opens the disk, folder, library, or file that it represents.

A shortcut is not the original file; it is a pathway to it. Shortcuts can be distinguished from the original files in several ways:

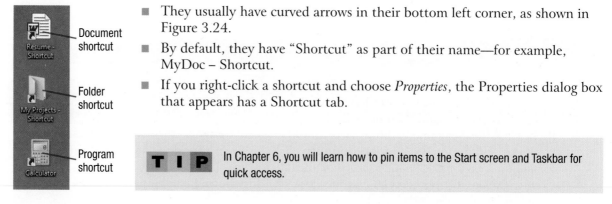

- They usually have curved arrows in their bottom left corner, as shown in Figure 3.24.
- By default, they have "Shortcut" as part of their name—for example, MyDoc – Shortcut.
- If you right-click a shortcut and choose *Properties*, the Properties dialog box that appears has a Shortcut tab.

T I P In Chapter 6, you will learn how to pin items to the Start screen and Taskbar for quick access.

Figure 3.24
A shortcut icon usually has an arrow on it, and may also have the word "shortcut" in its name.

Creating a Desktop Shortcut to a File, Folder, or Library

You can create shortcuts in any folder, but the most common and convenient location for shortcut icons is the desktop. You can have as many shortcuts as you like on the desktop (although it might start to seem cluttered at some point). The easiest way to create a shortcut on the desktop is with drag-and-drop; hold down the Alt key as you drag any file or folder to the desktop to create a shortcut for it there.

Arrange desktop shortcuts any way you like by dragging them where you want them. By default, icons automatically snap to an invisible grid on the desktop so that they do not overlap each other sloppily. You can turn that feature on or off by right-clicking the desktop and choosing *View, Align icons to grid*.

You also can have Windows 8 automatically arrange the desktop icons in orderly columns along the left side of the desktop. To enable this feature, right-click the desktop and choose *View, Auto arrange icons*.

Here's How

To create a desktop shortcut (drag-and-drop method):

1. Open the Libraries window by clicking the File Explorer icon on the desktop. Click the Restore Down button so the window does not fill the screen.
2. Navigate to the folder holding the item for which you want to create a shortcut, if needed.
3. Select the item for which you want to create a shortcut.
4. Hold down the Alt key.
5. Drag the item to the desktop.

To create a desktop shortcut (copy-and-paste method):

1. Open the Libraries window by clicking the File Explorer icon on the desktop.
2. Navigate to the folder holding the item for which you want to create a shortcut, if needed.
3. Select the item for which you want to create a shortcut.
4. Copy the item to the Clipboard in any of these ways:
   - Press Ctrl + C.
   - Right-click the selection and then choose *Copy*.
   - Click Copy in the Clipboard group on the Home tab.
   - Press Alt, H, and then CO.
5. Right-click the desktop.
6. Choose *Paste shortcut*.

Adding a Shortcut to the *Favorites* Section

As you saw at the beginning of this chapter, the Navigation pane in any File Explorer window contains a *Favorites* section at the top, containing shortcuts to frequently used locations. You can define what locations appear here by adding and removing shortcuts from the list.

To add a location to the *Favorites* section, drag it from any file list or from any other location (such as the desktop) and drop it onto the *Favorites* section name. The only restriction is that it must be a folder, library, or a drive, not an individual file.

To add a shortcut to the *Favorites* section:

1. Select the icon representing the drive, folder, or library.
2. Drag the icon to the *Favorites* section in the Navigation pane and then drop it.

To remove a shortcut from the *Favorites* section:

1. Right-click the shortcut.
2. Click *Remove*.

Here's How

Deleting and Retrieving Files and Folders ■■■■■■

How many times have you thrown something into a trash can, only to realize that you needed it again? Although digging through a trash can is no fun, it sure beats the alternative of losing your valuable item. Windows 8 has its own trash can you can dig through—the Recycle Bin. When you delete files and folders in Windows 8, they are not destroyed right away; instead they are moved to a hidden folder. The Recycle Bin icon on the desktop is a shortcut to that folder. From it, you can retrieve files and folders that were accidentally or ill-advisedly deleted, or you can purge the Recycle Bin contents so that others cannot see what you have been deleting.

Note: *Only files and folders deleted from a hard disk are placed in the Recycle Bin. The Recycle Bin cannot hold or restore the files from removable media or a network disk.*

Deleting a File or Folder

Deleting a file or folder moves it to the Recycle Bin. You can delete individual files, individual folders, or groups. (Select multiple items before issuing the command to delete.) Deleting a folder deletes everything within the folder.

 You can control whether you need to click OK at a confirmation box each time you delete something. Open a File Explorer window, click the Delete button down arrow in the Organize group, and then check (enable) or uncheck (disable) Show recycle confirmation.

Here's How ▶

To delete a file or folder:

1. Open File Explorer and then select the file(s) and/or folder(s) to be deleted.
2. Do any of the following:
   - Right-click the selection and choose *Delete*.
   - Press the Delete key on the keyboard.
   - Click the Delete button in the Organize group on the Home tab.
   - Press Alt, H, and then D.
3. If a confirmation box appears, click OK. Or, if the Delete button menu appears, click Recycle to send the file to the Recycle Bin or Permanently delete to remove the file.

To delete a file or folder permanently (bypassing the Recycle Bin):

1. Select the file(s) and/or folder(s) to be deleted.
2. Hold down the Shift key.
3. Press the Delete key on the keyboard.
4. At the confirmation box, click OK.
   OR
   - Click the Delete button down arrow in the Organize group on the Home tab and then click *Permanently delete*.

▼ **Quick Fix**

Cannot Delete a File
If a file or folder cannot be deleted for some reason (for example, perhaps its Read-Only attribute is turned on, or perhaps it is in use by an application), an error message appears. Make sure all applications are closed that might be using the file, and check the file's properties to make sure *Read-only* is not set for it.

Restoring a File or Folder

The Recycle Bin icon on the desktop changes to include wadded-up paper once you have deleted one or more items. This shows you that the Recycle Bin holds some items that are available for retrieval. As with a real-life trash can, you can "reach in" the Recycle Bin to take out (*restore*) any item that is in there. When you restore a file or folder from the Recycle Bin, Windows 8 places the item in its original folder location.

To view the contents of the Recycle Bin, double-click its icon on the desktop. Figure 3.25 shows a Recycle Bin with a few items in it. It resembles a regular File Explorer window, but it has different buttons on the command bar.

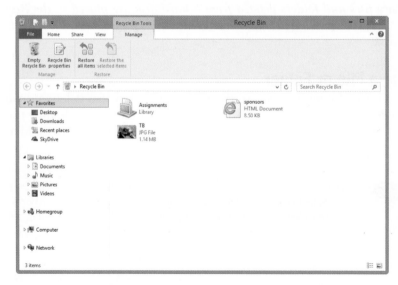

Figure 3.25 View and restore deleted items in the Recycle Bin window.

To open the Recycle Bin:

- Double-click the Recycle Bin icon on the desktop.

To view information about a deleted item:

1. Select the item in the Recycle Bin.
2. Click the Details pane in the Panes group on the View tab on the ribbon.
   OR
1. Double-click the item.
2. View the information in its Properties dialog box.
3. Click OK.

To restore an item to its original location:

1. Select the item in the Recycle Bin.
2. Click Restore the selected items in the Restore group on the Recycle Bin Tools Manage tab on the ribbon.
   OR
1. Right-click the item in the Recycle Bin.
2. Choose *Restore*.
   OR
1. Double-click the item in the Recycle Bin.
2. In its Properties box, click Restore.
   OR
- Click Restore all items in the Restore group on the Recycle Bin Tools Manage tab on the ribbon and then click Yes. If a Destination Folder Access Denied message appears, click Continue.

To restore an item to another location:

1. Select the item in the Recycle Bin.
2. Drag and drop the item to another location (desktop or a folder window).

Permanently Deleting the Recycle Bin Contents

You can really "take out the trash" by emptying the Recycle Bin. Just as emptying a trash can and putting the trash on the curb for the garbage collector means you will not ever be able to get that trash back, emptying the Windows Recycle Bin permanently deletes its files and folders, making them unrecoverable. You can permanently delete a single item, selected items, or everything at once.

If you want to delete everything at once from the Recycle Bin, you do not need to open its window; you can do it by right-clicking the icon and choosing Empty Recycle Bin. If you want to be selective about what gets purged, you must open the Recycle Bin window and delete files from it as you would delete files from any other location. The difference is that rather than going to the Recycle Bin as normal files would, these files are destroyed.

To permanently delete a single item, or selected items:

1. Select the item(s) to delete permanently.
2. Do any of the following:
   - Press the Delete key.
   - Right-click the selection and then choose *Delete*.
3. At the confirmation box, click Yes.

To empty the Recycle Bin (Recycle Bin window open):

- Click Empty Recycle Bin in the Manage group on the Recycle Bin Tools Manage tab.
  OR
1. Right-click any blank area of the Recycle Bin window.
2. Click Empty Recycle Bin.
3. Click Yes in the Delete Multiple Items dialog box.

To empty the Recycle Bin (Recycle Bin window closed):

1. Right-click the Recycle Bin icon on the desktop.
2. Click Empty Recycle Bin.
3. Click Yes in the Delete Multiple Items dialog box.

Configuring the Recycle Bin

The Recycle Bin will store deleted files until the space is needed or until the maximum Recycle Bin size has been reached; then it will start deleting files, starting with the ones that have been there the longest. You can control the maximum size of the Recycle Bin through its Properties dialog box, and you also can choose to turn the Recycle Bin off completely, so files are deleted immediately.

To access the Recycle Bin's properties, right-click its icon and choose *Properties* or, in the Recycle Bin window, click Recycle Bin Properties in the Manage group on the Recycle Bin Tools Manage tab. A list of locations appears for which the Recycle Bin is active. Unless any disk quotas have been set for the system, all locations have the same amount of space available (shown in Figure 3.26).

To change the maximum size allocated to the Recycle Bin, enter a different number in the *Maximum size (MB)* text box. Or, to turn off the Recycle Bin completely, select *Don't move files to the Recycle Bin*.

To suppress the delete confirmation dialog box that appears each time you delete a file, clear the *Display delete confirmation dialog* check box.

Figure 3.26 Configure how the Recycle Bin works from its Properties box. You can suppress the delete confirmation, set its maximum size, and even turn it off completely.

To turn off the Recycle Bin completely:

1. Right-click the Recycle Bin and then click *Properties*, or, in the Recycle Bin window, click *Recycle Bin Properties* in the Manage group on the Recycle Bin Tools Manage tab.
2. Click the disk for which you want to turn off the Recycle Bin in the list at the top.
3. Click Don't move files to the Recycle Bin.
4. Click OK.

To change the maximum size of the Recycle Bin:

1. Right-click the Recycle Bin and then click *Properties*, or, in the Recycle Bin window, click Recycle Bin Properties in the Manage group on the Recycle Bin Tools Manage tab.
2. Click the disk for which you want to change the Recycle Bin's size in the list at the top.
3. Change the value in the *Maximum size (MB)* text box.
4. Click OK.

To enable or suppress the delete confirmation message when deleting:

1. Right-click the Recycle Bin and then click *Properties*, or, in the Recycle Bin window, click Recycle Bin Properties in the Manage group on the Recycle Bin Tools Manage tab.
2. Mark or clear the *Display delete confirmation dialog* check box.
3. Click OK.

Exercise 5

Creating Shortcuts and Using the Recycle Bin to Delete and Restore

1. Open the Libraries window. (Click the File Explorer button on the Taskbar.)
2. Drag the icon for the Assignments library you created in Exercise 4 to the *Favorites* section in the Navigation pane.
3. Capture a screen shot of your desktop, save it as **C03E05S03**, and then submit it to your instructor.
4. Remove the shortcut from the Favorites section:
   a. Right-click *Assignments* under *Favorites*.
   b. Click *Remove*.
5. Place a shortcut to the Assignments library on the desktop:
   a. Hold down the Alt key.
   b. Drag the Assignments library icon to the desktop.
   c. Drag the new shortcut icon to the top right corner of the desktop.
6. Capture a screen shot of your desktop, save it as **C03E05S06**, and then submit it to your instructor.
7. Remove the shortcut from the desktop:
   a. Right-click the shortcut for the Assignments library.
   b. Click *Delete*.
8. Navigate to your personal folder using the method of your choice.
9. Double-click the Searches folder to open it.

10. Move the Current Files search to the Recycle Bin:
    a. Select the icon.
    b. Press the Delete key to delete it.
    c. Click *Yes* in the dialog box that asks you to confirm moving the folder to the Recycle Bin.
    d. Close the window.
11. Restore the Current Files search to the Searches folder:
    a. On the desktop, double-click the Recycle Bin icon.
    b. Capture a screen shot of your desktop, save it as **C03E05S11**, and then submit it to your instructor.
    c. Click the Current Files icon.
    d. Click Restore the selected items in the Restore group on the Recycle Bin Tools Manage tab on the ribbon.
12. Select the Assignments library shortcut icon.
13. Click Restore the selected items in the Restore group on the Recycle Bin Tools Manage tab on the ribbon.
14. Close the Recycle Bin window.
15. Repeat Steps 4 and 7–10 to delete the items again. Also remove Current Files under Favorites in the Navigation pane, and then close all windows.
16. Empty the Recycle Bin:
    a. Right-click the Recycle Bin icon on the desktop.
    b. Click Empty Recycle Bin.
    c. Click Yes in the Delete Multiple Items dialog box.
17. Close any other open windows.

Accessing Your SkyDrive ▪▪▪▪▪▪▪▪▪▪▪▪▪▪▪▪▪▪▪▪

SkyDrive is a free online file-storage service that enables you to securely store up to 7 GB of files (though you can secure more space by paying an annual fee) in a Microsoft-sponsored cloud. A cloud is an Internet-accessible storage system. Your SkyDrive is your personal storage area within the cloud, that is, tied to your Microsoft account. Signing in to Windows 8 with a Microsoft account gives you seamless access to any files that you have stored on your SkyDrive.

Note: *This section assumes that you are signed into Windows with a Microsoft account; otherwise, you will be unable to use the SkyDrive feature. See "Understanding User Accounts" in Chapter 1 if you need help setting up a Microsoft user account.*

You can work with your SkyDrive in three ways:
- Through File Explorer, after downloading and installing a free SkyDrive app for File Explorer.
- Through the Windows 8 SkyDrive app on the Start screen.
- Via your web browser at Skydrive.com.

You also can save and open files in Microsoft Office applications to or from your SkyDrive.

Understanding Folder Sharing Permissions

SkyDrive keeps your files organized by enabling you to store them in folders. Each folder has one of three permission levels:

- **Everyone Can view.** Anyone can access its contents.

- **People with a link.** Anyone can access its contents as long as they have the correct hyperlink; you can send the hyperlink to email recipients or publish it on social networking sites.

- **Just me or Not shared.** Only you can access its contents.

By placing the files you upload in a folder with the appropriate permissions, you can control the access to files without having to manually set the permission on each file individually.

Note: *You cannot view or change a folder's sharing permissions via the Start screen SkyDrive app, but you can do so via the Web.*

Using SkyDrive in File Explorer

You may have noticed SkyDrive icons in a few screenshots of File Explorer earlier in the chapter. You can download a free SkyDrive app that enables you to connect directly to SkyDrive from File Explorer on your computer. Go to http://windows.microsoft.com/en-US/skydrive/download-skydrive and then click the Download SkyDrive for Windows button to begin the download and install process.

After you complete the SkyDrive install process, SkyDrive icons appear as one of your personal folder subfolders and under Favorites in the Navigation pane of any File Explorer window. If you click SkyDrive under Favorites, the local counterparts of your online SkyDrive folders appear in the file list, as shown in Figure 3.27.

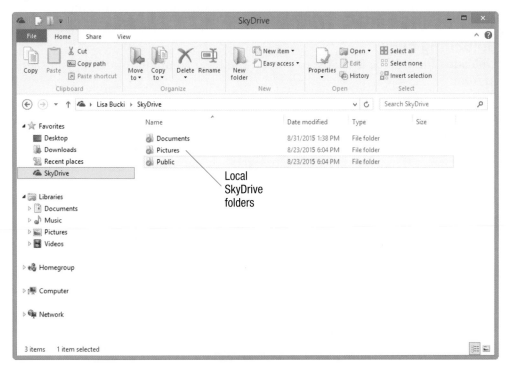

Figure 3.27 Download and install the free SkyDrive app to connect File Explorer to your SkyDrive and create syncing local folders.

As long as you are signed in with your Microsoft account, the contents of the local SkyDrive folders automatically sync with your online SkyDrive. For example, you can right-click the File Explorer icon on the desktop Taskbar, click File Explorer to open another window, navigate to a file to copy in that window, and then select the file. Press Ctrl + C to copy the file, double-click the Documents folder in the SkyDrive window, and then press Ctrl + V to paste the file. Windows automatically syncs the local folder with the Documents folder on your online SkyDrive, uploading the file.

Similarly, when you add a file or folder to your online SkyDrive, the next time you sign in to Windows, the local SkyDrive folders automatically sync, downloading a local copy of the new online file or folder.

Once you have the SkyDrive app installed for File Explorer, work with the local folders as you normally would in File Explorer. Of the three default folders—Documents, Pictures, and Public—keep in mind that only the Public folder is initially shared, although you will have to inform other users by providing or posting a link to the shared folder. The Documents and Pictures folders are not shared by default.

Using SkyDrive from the Start Screen or Web Browser

Using SkyDrive from the Start screen or your web browser requires just a bit more know-how. This section introduces you to both of these methods for working in the cloud.

To start the Windows 8 style SkyDrive app, display the Start screen and then click the SkyDrive tile. The SkyDrive app opens, listing your folders as blue rectangular tiles. The number on each tile represents the number of documents stored in that folder.

To access your SkyDrive via the Web, open Internet Explorer and go to https://skydrive.live.com. Sign in with your Microsoft account if prompted.

Uploading Files

Uploaded files will be available to you on whatever computer or device you sign in from.

The first step for uploading a file depends on how you access your SkyDrive. In the SkyDrive Start screen app, click the folder into which you want to upload a file. Right-click to open the toolbar at the bottom of the screen, and then click the Upload button, select a file, and click Add to SkyDrive. When the item finishes uploading, it will appear in the folder, as shown in Figure 3.28. Via the web interface, click the tile for the destination folder, click Upload, select a file in the Choose File to Upload dialog box, and click Open.

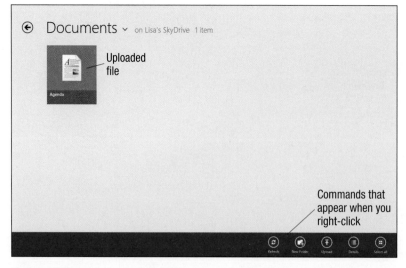

Figure 3.28 Upload a file via the SkyDrive app on the Windows 8 Start screen.

If you do not select a folder into which to upload a file, it will be placed in the main SkyDrive folder. Otherwise, choose one of the three default folders: Documents, Pictures, and Public. In both the SkyDrive app and the Web, folders appear as tiles, as shown in Figures 3.29 and 3.30. In the app, you can navigate to different locations by clicking the arrow beside SkyDrive, by clicking a tile, or by using the left arrow (back) button that appears at the left when you are displaying a folder's contents. In the web interface, click a folder tile to open it and then click the browser's Back button to back up.

Figure 3.29 The default folders in the SkyDrive app.

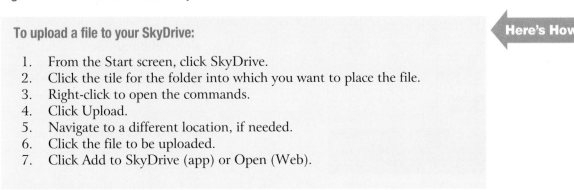

Figure 3.30 The default folders in SkyDrive on the Web.

Here's How

To upload a file to your SkyDrive:

1. From the Start screen, click SkyDrive.
2. Click the tile for the folder into which you want to place the file.
3. Right-click to open the commands.
4. Click Upload.
5. Navigate to a different location, if needed.
6. Click the file to be uploaded.
7. Click Add to SkyDrive (app) or Open (Web).

Opening a File Stored on Your SkyDrive

To open a file stored on your SkyDrive from the SkyDrive app, navigate to and click the file. If it is a file for which Microsoft Live has an application available, such as an Office app, the file opens in that application. Or, if you have the app installed on your computer, such as Word, the app will launch and the document will appear. If a document opens in a web app, you can click Edit in Browser to edit the document in the Web version of the app (such as Word), or click Open in Word (or the applicable command) to open the full version of Word or the applicable app installed on your computer.

If it is a file for which your computer does not have an application, a prompt appears offering to help you install an appropriate application or download the file to your hard disk for later viewing.

To access a file on your SkyDrive:

1. Open the SkyDrive Windows 8 app, if it is not already open.
2. If the file to open is stored in a folder, click the folder tile.
3. Click the tile for the file to open.
   OR
1. In SkyDrive on the web browser, click the folder tile for the folder that holds the file.
2. Click the file tile.
3. In the message box at the bottom of the screen, click a button to specify whether to Open or Save the file. If you click Save, you can then click a button to open the file or click Open folder to view the downloaded file in Explorer.

Creating Folders

You can create your own folders to further organize your SkyDrive contents. You can do this from either the SkyDrive app or the web interface.

To create a folder in the app, navigate to the folder in which you want to create the folder. Right-click to display the tools and then click New Folder. In the pop-up box that appears (shown in Figure 3.31), type a folder name and then click Create folder. After a moment, the new folder appears onscreen.

To create a folder from the web-based interface, click Create on the SkyDrive command bar and then click Folder in the menu. Type the new folder name, as shown in Figure 3.32, and then press Enter.

By default a new folder is shared with nobody; only you can access it. To share the folder from the Web, click the folder tile and then click Share folder in the command bar. A pop-up box appears with three tabs at the left side:

Type folder name

Figure 3.31 Creating and naming a folder in the Windows 8 SkyDrive app.

- **Send email.** Sends a link to the new folder to an email recipient. Only people who receive the link to the folder can access it.

- **Post to.** Posts the link to a social networking site, such as Facebook.

- **Get a link.** Creates one of three types of hyperlinks to the file: View only, View and edit, or Make it public. If you choose one of the first two options, the folder is shared only with those who use the link you create to access it. If you choose Make it public, the folder is set for public sharing (shown in Figure 3.33).

Figure 3.32 Create a new folder in the web interface.

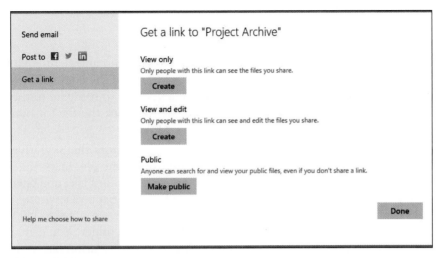

Figure 3.33 Choose the type of sharing you want.

Here's How

To create a new private folder:

1. From the SkyDrive web interface, click Create and then click *Folder*.
2. Type the new folder's name and press Enter.

To create a new shared folder:

1. In your SkyDrive on the Web, click the folder tile and then click the Share folder in the command bar.
2. Click the Get a link tab.
3. Click Create under the *View only* or *View* and edit heading.
4. Select the link and then press Ctrl + C to copy it.
5. Click the Send email link at the left.
6. Enter a recipient's email address in the *To:* text box, click in the message text box, press Ctrl + V to paste the link, and then click Share.

To create a new public folder:

1. In your SkyDrive on the Web, create a new private folder, if needed, and then select the folder to make public.
2. Click the folder tile and then click Share folder on the command bar.
3. Click the Get a link tab.
4. Click *Make public* under the Public heading.
5. Select the link and then press Ctrl + C to copy it.
6. Click the Send email link at the left.
7. Enter a recipient's email address in the *To:* text box, click in the message text box, press Ctrl + V to paste the link, and then click Share.

Note: *At the time of writing of this book, Microsoft was making numerous changes to SkyDrive and other online features. Some procedures for working with SkyDrive may have changed.*

Saving Local Copies of Files

Files on your web-based SkyDrive can be transferred to any local drive, so you can access them without having to connect to SkyDrive. By transferring files to the SkyDrive from one computer or device and then downloading those files from the SkyDrive to another computer or device, you can transfer files between computers.

Download command

Figure 3.34 Download a file from the SkyDrive web interface.

In the Windows 8 Start screen app, find and right-click the tile for the file to open. Click Download in the commands that appear at the bottom, use the Files screen to navigate to the folder where you want to store the file, click the tile for that folder, and then click Choose this folder.

To save a file to your local computer from the SkyDrive web interface, open the folder that holds the file, mark the checkbox in the upper right corner of the file's tile, and then click Download in the command bar at the top (shown in Figure 3.34). In the bar at the bottom of the browser window, click Save. The file is saved to your Downloads folder. You can access that folder from the *Favorites* list in the Navigation bar in the File Explorer window.

Exercise 6

Working with Your SkyDrive from the Start Screen

1. From the Start screen, click the SkyDrive tile to open the SkyDrive app.
2. Click the *Documents* folder to open that folder.
3. Right-click and then click the Upload button.
4. Navigate to the folder that contains the data files for this chapter.
5. Click the *Agenda* file.
6. Click Add to SkyDrive.
7. Press the Windows logo key and then click the Desktop tile to display the desktop.
8. Click the Internet Explorer icon on the Taskbar and then navigate to https://skydrive.live.com. Sign in to your account if prompted.
9. Click the Documents folder tile.
10. Mark the checkmark in the **Agenda** file tile.
11. Capture a screen shot of this window, save it as **C03E06**, and then submit it to your instructor.
12. In the SkyDrive web interface, click Manage on the command bar and then click *Delete*.
13. Close the Internet Explorer window.

CHAPTER SUMMARY

- Key navigational tools in an Explorer window include the Address bar, the search box, the ribbon, and the Navigation pane.
- To display KeyTips for the ribbon in a folder or library window, press Alt.
- Windows 8 includes four default libraries for each user's own files: Documents, Pictures, Music, and Videos. These are all accessed by clicking the File Explorer button on the Taskbar, among other methods.

- Navigating to the user name in a folder window opens the personal folder, which holds a number of subfolders for organizing various types of files and information.
- To select multiple contiguous files or folders, hold down Shift as you click; for a noncontiguous selection, hold down Ctrl.
- To create a new folder, right-click, point to *New*, and then click *Folder.*
- To rename a file or folder, right-click it, click *Rename*, and then type the new name.
- To move or copy, use the drag-and-drop method. Hold down Shift to move or Ctrl to copy.
- You also can move or copy with the Clipboard (Ctrl + X to cut, Ctrl + C to copy, and Ctrl + V to paste) or the tools in the Clipboard group on the Home tab.
- Grouping and filtering are methods in Windows 8 for organizing file listings. Use the drop-down menu for a column heading to enable any of them.
- You can arrange items in a library using the *Arrange by* choice on the shortcut menu that appears when you right-click a blank area of the file list.
- Add a library by clicking *New item* and then *Library* in the New group on the Home tab of the Libraries window.
- Control which folders the library monitors and manage other library settings in the Properties dialog box for the library.
- You can save a search to rerun it later.
- The search box in the upper right corner of any Explorer or library window performs quick searches based on the word(s) you enter. You also can search for files by selecting the Search charm, clicking *Files*, and then typing the search word(s).
- You can use one of the filters that appears when you click the search box to build the search criteria.
- Indexing a location makes searching it go faster.
- To create a shortcut, press Alt and drag the original to the desired location.
- Deleting a file or folder (by selecting it and pressing Delete) sends it to the Recycle Bin. You can restore items from the Recycle Bin to their original locations.
- To empty the Recycle Bin, right-click its icon on the desktop and then choose Empty Recycle Bin.
- SkyDrive enables you to create folders and store files that are online using a Microsoft-sponsored cloud service.
- Sign in to Windows with a Microsoft account to access SkyDrive.
- Download a free SkyDrive app to integrate SkyDrive into File Explorer. Click SkyDrive under Favorites in the Navigation bar and then copy files to the default folders that appear to sync those files to your online SkyDrive.
- You also can use the SkyDrive Windows 8 style app from the Start screen or a web browser to access SkyDrive.

CONCEPTS CHECK

Completion: Answer the following questions in a Word document.

Part 1

Multiple Choice

1. To display other panes in an Explorer window, use the _____ tab.
    a. Home
    b. Share
    c. View
    d. Library Tools Manage

2. To copy a file from one location to another on the same disk with drag-and-drop, hold down the _____ key as you drag.
    a. Ctrl
    b. Alt
    c. Shift
    d. Insert

3. Which pane can you display to show the contents or appearance of a selected file?
    a. Navigation
    b. Preview
    c. Details
    d. Window

4. To select multiple noncontiguous files, hold down the _____ key as you click each one.
    a. Ctrl
    b. Alt
    c. Shift
    d. Insert

5. To copy the selected files to the Clipboard, press Ctrl + _____ .
    a. V
    b. D
    c. C
    d. X

6. A(n) _____ monitors the contents of multiple locations, making it easier to find and work with files of a particular type.
    a. Explorer window
    b. Recycle Bin
    c. Personal Folder
    d. Library

7. _____ arranges a list of files into sections, with each individual file shown.
    a. Sorting
    b. Grouping
    c. Filtering
    d. Stacking

8. _____ shows only the files matching one or more specified criteria.
   a. Sorting
   b. Grouping
   c. Filtering
   d. Stacking

9. To permanently delete a file, bypassing the Recycle Bin, hold down _____ as you press Delete.
   a. Ctrl
   b. Alt
   c. Shift
   d. Insert

10. Which of these folder permissions is available on SkyDrive?
    a. Everyone Can view
    b. People with a link
    c. Just me or Not shared
    d. All of the above

Part 2

Short Answer

11. What is your personal folder?

    _____

12. What is the benefit of indexing a location?

    _____

13. List three of the four default libraries in Windows 8.

    _____

14. List six of the eight available views in File Explorer.

    _____

15. Name two locations where you can place shortcuts to a folder.

    _____

16. What does the *Arrange by* choice on the submenu in a library window do?

    _____

17. What is a parent folder?

    _____

18. How can you sort items in a folder or library?

    _____

19. How do you find and rerun your saved searches?

    _____

20. Is it possible to restore files deleted from removable media, and why/why not?

    _____

SKILLS CHECK

Save all solution files to the default Documents folder or any alternate folder specified by your instructor.

Guided Check

Assessment 1

Deleting and Restoring a File

1. Open the Chapter 3 Student Data Files folder.
2. Move the **Recycle** file into the Recycle Bin.
   a. Click the *Recycle* file.
   b. Press Delete.
3. Minimize the folder window by clicking its Minimize button.
4. Double-click the Recycle Bin icon.
5. Capture a screen shot of your desktop, save it as **C03A01**, and then submit it to your instructor.
6. Restore the **Recycle** file from the Recycle Bin window.
   a. Click the *Recycle* file.
   b. Click Restore the selected item in the Restore group on the Recycle Bin Tools Manage tab.
7. Close the Recycle Bin window by clicking its Close (X) button.
8. Open the Chapter 3 folder by clicking the File Explorer button on the Taskbar.
9. Verify that the **Recycle** file again appears in the window.
10. Close the window.

Assessment 2

Creating Folders and Copying Files

1. Open the Documents window.
   - Right-click File Explorer on the Taskbar, click File Explorer in the Jump List, and then click *Documents* in the Navigation pane.
2. In the Documents library, create a new folder called Construction and then open it.
   a. Click New folder in the New group on the Home tab on the ribbon.
   b. Type Construction.
   c. Press Enter.
   d. Double-click the Construction folder icon to open it.
3. Open the Chapter 3 Student Data Files folder in a separate window.
4. Copy the file **Townsend** into the Construction folder.
   a. In the data files folder window, click *Townsend*.
   b. Hold down the Ctrl key and drag **Townsend** into the Construction folder.
   c. Close the chapter's data files folder window, leaving the Construction folder open.
5. Capture a screen shot of your desktop, save it as **C03A02**, and then submit it to your instructor.
6. Copy the Construction folder onto a USB flash drive.
   a. In the Address bar for the Construction folder window, click Documents.
   b. Select the Construction folder's icon.
   c. Press Ctrl + C to copy it to the Clipboard.
   d. In the Navigation pane, click *Computer* to display a list of drives.
   e. Insert a USB flash drive.

    f. Double-click the icon for the flash drive in the file list.

    g. Press Ctrl + V to paste the copied folder from the Clipboard.

  7. Submit the USB flash drive to your instructor.

  8. Close all open windows.

Assessment 3   **Finding Files**

  1. Run a search that shows only documents.

    a. Click the File Explorer button on the Taskbar.

    b. Click the search box and then click the Kind button in the Refine group on the Search Tools Search tab.

    c. Click *Document* in the menu.

    d. Look in the status pane for the number of items found.

  2. Create and save a custom search that finds files containing "Town."

    a. Click the x in the search box to clear the previous search.

    b. Type Town in the search box.

    c. Capture a screen shot of your desktop, save it as **C03A03**, and then submit it to your instructor.

    d. Click Save search in the Options group on the Search Tools Search tab.

    e. Type Town Search.

    f. Click Save.

  3. Copy the saved search you created to a USB flash drive.

    a. Insert a USB flash drive.

    b. Click Searches in the Address bar.

    c. Double-click Searches.

    d. Click ***Town Search*** and then press Ctrl + C to copy it.

    e. In the Navigation pane, under *Computer*, click the USB drive.

    f. Press Ctrl + V to paste the search file.

    g. Close the open windows.

  4. Use a saved search.

    a. In the open folder window, click *Desktop* under *Favorites* in the Navigation pane and then double-click your user name folder.

    b. Double-click Searches.

    c. Double-click ***Town Search***.

    d. Close the window.

  5. Submit the USB flash drive containing the search file from Step 2 to your instructor.

Assessment 4   **Exploring Your SkyDrive**

  1. Press the Windows logo key ⊞ on the keyboard to display the Start screen.

  2. Click the SkyDrive tile.

  3. If needed, click the left arrow button to return to the main screen.

  4. Click the Documents tile.

  5. Upload the **Recycle** file.

    a. Right-click and then click *Upload* in the commands that appear.

    b. Use the *Files* drop-down list and the Go up links to navigate to the Chapter 3 data files.

    c. Click the ***Recycle*** file.

    d. Click Add to SkyDrive.

    e. After the file uploads, capture a screen shot of your desktop, save it as **C03A04**, and then submit it to your instructor.

6. Drag from the top of the screen to the bottom to close the SkyDrive app.
7. Click the Desktop tile to return to the desktop.

On Your Own

Assessment 5 Moving, Copying, and Renaming Files and Folders

1. Insert a USB flash drive.
2. Open two Explorer windows. Navigate to the USB drive in one and the Chapter 3 data files in the other.
3. Copy all the graphics files (JPG extension) from the Chapter 3 data folder (in the data files for this book) to the USB drive.
4. Make a copy of **Estate**, and rename the copy **MyEstate**.
5. Move the file **MyEstate** onto the USB drive.
6. On the USB drive, make a copy of **MyEstate**, and rename the copy **Backup**.
7. Copy **Backup** to the Chapter 3 folder.
8. Submit your USB flash drive to your instructor and close all open windows.

Assessment 6 Creating A Filtered Search

1. Open the Libraries window, create a new custom search that finds only files in which the Date created is later than 01/01/12, and then save the search as **2012 and Newer**. *Hint: First set the Date modified: filter to today's date and then, in the search box, edit the text after the colon to use the greater than symbol plus the desired date.*
2. Return to the Libraries window and then create a new custom search that finds all files with the Medium Size: filter.
3. Filter the results of the Medium Files search to show only Picture files.
4. Save the search as **Medium Pictures**.
5. Submit the saved searches to your instructor.

Assessment 7 Creating Desktop Shortcuts

1. Open the folder containing the Chapter 3 files for this book.
2. Create shortcuts on the desktop to the following files:
   Blue Square
   Purple Squiggle
   Red Circle
3. Close any open folders.
4. Arrange the shortcut icons neatly on your desktop.
5. Capture a screen shot of your desktop, save it as **C03A07**, and then submit it to your instructor.
6. Double-click the *Red Circle* shortcut.
7. Drag from the top of the window to the bottom to close the preview of the file.
8. Click the Desktop tile to return to the desktop.
9. Delete the desktop shortcuts you created in Step 2.
10. Empty the Recycle Bin.

Finding a "Lost" File and Final Clean-up

1. Open the Chapter 3 Student Data Files folder.
2. Make a copy of the file **Bowl.jpg**, but keep the name of the file secret. You can use any combination of letters and numbers, but do not change the file extension (.jpg).
3. Place that copy in any folder on your hard disk.
4. Make a note of the file's size and date modified and then write that information on a blank piece of paper.
5. Trade computers with someone else in your class and then trade your pieces of paper.
6. Find your partner's missing file based on the information you know about it (its size, type, and date modified).
7. Copy the missing file to a USB flash drive and then submit it to your instructor.
8. Delete any saved searches listed in the *Favorites* section of the Navigation pane.
9. Delete the saved searches themselves. ***Hint: Click a saved search under* Favorites *in the Navigation pane and then click Searches in the Address bar to find the searches and delete them.***
10. Delete the Assignments library you created in Exercise 4, if you have not already done so, as well as any folders you have created in the Documents library and their contents.
11. Empty the Recycle Bin.
12. Close all open windows.

CHALLENGE PROJECT

As part of your company's marketing campaign, you have been asked to catalog all the high-resolution graphics files you have available on your computer. Use the Search feature in Windows 8 to find every JPEG and TIFF graphic file at least 1 MB in size.

1. Gather the following information, using any combination of the searching, filtering, sorting, and other techniques you learned in this chapter:
    • How many files are there of each file type (based on the extension)?
    • What is the largest file size, and what are the dimensions (in pixels) of that picture?
    • How much space would it require on a disc to copy all those files to it?
2. Burn a CD containing the pictures you found or copy them to a USB flash drive, and submit it to your instructor. If you found more than 700 MB of pictures, choose as many pictures as will fit on a single CD.

CHAPTER 4

Organizing and Protecting Information

PERFORMANCE OBJECTIVES

Upon successful completion of Chapter 4, you will be able to:

- Change the File Explorer window layout
- Customize how File Explorer displays information
- Add and edit file properties
- Remove file properties and personal information
- Work with file and folder versions
- Set file and folder permissions

The Windows 8 file-management interface, File Explorer, is customizable. You can set it up to function in whatever way works best to match your working style. File Explorer enables you to define properties and set or clear personal information for files and folders, recall previous versions of files, and control who can access files.

Changing the File Explorer Window Layout ■■■■■

The File Explorer window can be set up to display or hide several types of listings and information. For example, you can show or hide the Preview and Details panes, and you can choose what appears in the Navigation pane.

Displaying the Preview or Details Pane

On the right side of a File Explorer window, you can optionally display either of two panes:

- **Details pane.** This pane provides information about the selected file(s), folder(s), or drive(s). For a file, this information includes Date Created, Date Modified, and Size. For some types of files, such as Microsoft Office documents, many more details appear as well, such as author names, total editing time, and tags or keywords.

- **Preview pane.** This pane shows a preview of certain types of data files when they are selected. If the selected item cannot be previewed, a *No preview available* message appears here instead.

In Windows 8, these two panes are mutually exclusive; you can show either or neither of them, but not both at once. To display or hide one of these panes, click the View tab and then click the Preview pane or Details pane button (shown in Figure 4.1).

Preview pane button

Details pane button

Details pane

Figure 4.1 On the View tab, choose to display the Preview or Details pane, if desired.

Here's How

To display or hide the Preview pane:

1. Click the View tab on the ribbon.
2. Click Preview pane in the Panes group.

To display or hide the Details pane:

1. Click the View tab on the ribbon.
2. Click Details pane in the Panes group.

Customizing the Navigation Pane

The Navigation pane appears at the left side of the File Explorer window, providing shortcuts in such sections as *Favorites, Libraries*, and so on. As you learned in Chapter 3, you can use the Navigation pane to quickly jump to a variety of locations. On the View tab, click the Navigation pane button for access to the following menu of on/off toggles:

- **Navigation pane.** Shows or hides the Navigation pane.

- **Expand to open folder.** Ensures that the Navigation pane always shows the complete folder hierarchy expanded down to the level of the currently displayed folder. (It may do this anyway, depending on how you navigated there.)

- **Show all folders.** Displays the sections of the Navigation pane (other than *Favorites*) as a single hierarchical list organized under the *Desktop* section. When this option is off, the Navigation pane displays as multiple sections such as *Libraries, Homegroup, Computer,* and *Network*. Figure 4.2 compares the two views. One benefit to enabling Show all folders is that it makes a link to the Control Panel appear in the Navigation pane.

- **Show favorites.** Shows or hides the *Favorites* section of the Navigation pane.

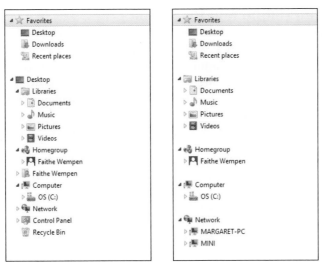

Figure 4.2 At the left, the Show all folders option is toggled on; at the right, the option is toggled off.

TIP Click the arrow at the left of the *Favorites* section on the Navigation pane to collapse the section down to its heading only.

To change Navigation pane display options:

1. Click the View tab.
2. Click Navigation pane.
3. Click the option to toggle on or off.

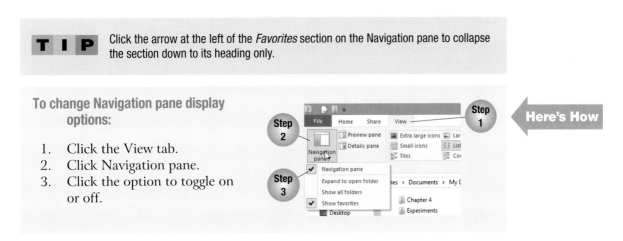

Resizing Panes

Several of the panes in File Explorer can be resized. Because resizing a pane does not change the overall size of the window, space added to one pane subtracts space from the adjacent one. Resizing panes can be useful when you need to see more of one pane's content than is currently displayed and you do not mind if the adjacent pane's content has less room. If you need to see a larger portion of both panes, you must resize the entire window instead.

To resize a pane, drag the divider between two panes. The mouse pointer turns into a double-headed arrow. Once the double-headed arrow appears, hold down the mouse button and drag. Release the mouse button when the pane reaches the size you want.

Customizing How File Explorer Displays Files and Folders ■■■■■■■■■■■■■■■■■■■■■■■■■■■■

In addition to modifying the look of File Explorer itself, you also can modify how the file and folder listings appear within that window. The following sections explain some of the modifications you can make.

Showing and Hiding File Extensions

By default, Windows 8 hides file extensions for known file types. As you learned in Chapter 3, an extension is a code that follows the file name, separated from it by a period. Windows 8 determines a file's type by its extension. For example, the file Memo.docx is a Word file because it uses the .docx extension. However, in a default File Explorer window, that file would appear as Memo, not as Memo.docx. The file's type could be deduced by looking at its icon and noticing the "W" on it for "Word," but if you do not recognize the icons for all the applications you have on your system, that might not be useful. Instead, you might prefer to turn on the display of file extensions for all files.

Note: *Another benefit of turning on file extensions is that they make it more noticeable when a file has a double extension, such as graphic.gif.vbs. An executable extension on the end like that (.vbs is a Visual Basic script) often indicates a virus-carrying file.*

Windows 8 provides an easy way to change the setting. On the View tab, mark or clear the *File name extensions* check box (shown in Figure 4.3). Setting the display of file extensions is a global setting for all locations.

Figure 4.3 Mark the *File name extensions* check box to see file extensions.

Here's How

To display or hide extensions for known file types:

1. Click the View tab.
2. Mark or clear the *File name extensions* check box in the Show/Hide group.

Revealing Hidden Files and Folders

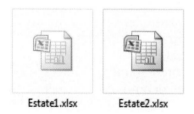

Estate1.xlsx   Estate2.xlsx

Figure 4.4 A hidden file (left) appears dimmed compared to an unhidden one (right).

As you will learn in "Changing File Attributes" later in this chapter, one of the attributes you can apply to a file or folder is Hidden. When the Hidden attribute is turned on for a file or folder, that file or folder does not appear in the File Explorer window—that is, unless you have specified that hidden files and folders be visible there. When you choose to turn on the display of hidden files, folders, and drives, hidden items appear with their icons slightly faded to distinguish them from unhidden ones, as shown in Figure 4.4.

From the View tab, mark the *Hidden items* check box to display hidden files and folders, or clear the check box to hide them (shown in Figure 4.3).

You will probably want to leave the hidden files hidden most of the time because otherwise there is not much point in having hidden files and folders. Files and folders are hidden to prevent others from knowing they exist. However, whenever you need to work with a hidden file or folder, you must temporarily turn on its display so that you can access it. There are also occasionally situations where you may need to browse a hidden folder to make a system change. For example, if you want to work with Microsoft Office templates, you must have access to a folder called AppData in your user folders, which by default is hidden.

Here's How

To reveal or hide hidden files and folders:

1. Click the View tab.
2. Mark or clear the *Hidden items* check box in the Show/Hide group.

Showing and Hiding Operating System Files

The *operating system files* that Windows 8 requires to function are hidden by default from standard File Explorer listings so that they are not accidentally moved or deleted. At some point, you might need to see these files. For example, you might need to check a date on a file as you are troubleshooting a problem. To make this change, click the View tab and then click the Options button. The Folder Options dialog box appears. Click the View tab in the dialog box and then clear the *Hide protected operating system files (Recommended)* check box.

operating system files Files that the operating system (Windows 8) needs to start the system and keep it running

Here's How

To display or hide protected operating system files:

1. Click the View tab.
2. Click the *Options* button.
3. Click the View tab in the dialog box.
4. Mark or clear *Hide protected operating system files (Recommended)*.
5. Click Yes to confirm.
6. Click OK.

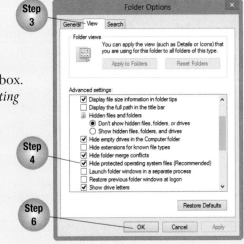

Customizing a Folder Icon's Appearance

By default, for most folders, the folder's icon includes a preview of the folder's content. Not all types of content are necessarily previewed there, though; the type of content previewed depends on the type you have set for the folder.

The default type for most folders is General Items, which causes Windows 8 to use previews appropriate for each data type—text files for documents, pictures for graphics, and so on. The exact appearance of the icon depends on the number of files in the folder, their types, and whether there are subfolders. Figure 4.5 shows several examples of folders that use the General Items type.

Courses   Dell Webcam Center   Downloads   July09Reading   LDW

Figure 4.5   Several examples of folder icons when the type is set to General Items.

Alternate types include Documents, Music, Videos, and Pictures. When you change to one of those folder types, files of the specified types are used for the previews on the folder's icon.

To set a folder type for a folder, start on the Customize tab of the folder's Properties dialog box (shown in Figure 4.6) and choose one of the predefined templates that Windows 8 provides from the Optimize this folder for drop-down list.

TIP In Windows 8, you cannot customize the folder appearance for folders in a library. The folders in libraries take on the type for which the library is optimized. See Chapter 3 for more information about how a library is optimized for a certain data type.

Figure 4.6 Use the Customize tab of the folder's Properties box to set up its icon's appearance.

The *Folder pictures* section of the Customize tab enables you to specify one of the files to function as the preview for the folder. If you choose a file from here, only that file's preview will appear, even if the folder contains other files as well.

The Restore Default button resets the folder's icon back to its default. This is useful to reverse the effect of having chosen a specific file.

If you want the folder's icon to be a fixed icon rather than a preview, click the Change Icon button and then select an icon file. System icons come, by default, from a file called SHELL32.DLL, but other files also can contain icons you can use. When you specify a fixed icon, the folder's preview capabilities are disabled until you click Restore Default to put the folder back to using previews.

Here's How

To customize the folder icon's appearance:

1. Right-click the folder in a File Explorer window and then choose *Properties*.
2. Click the Customize tab. If there is no Customize tab, this folder cannot have its icon appearance changed.
3. Open the *Optimize this folder for* list and then click a template type.
4. (Optional) Do any of the following:
   - Click Choose File, select an image file to be previewed on the icon, and then click OK.
   - Click the *Also apply this template to all subfolders* check box.
   - Click Restore Default to return the folder to its default setting.
   - Click Change Icon, select an icon to use instead of a folder preview, and click OK.
5. Click OK.

Quick Fix

No Customize Tab
If there is no Customize tab, you are probably trying to access the folder from within a Library. Try accessing it from its actual location, outside the Library.

Customizing the File Explorer Interface

1. Open File Explorer.
2. Make notes about the current settings for the Navigation pane, Preview pane, and Details pane. Make the following settings changes to the File Explorer window:
   - Turn on the Preview pane.
   - Set the Navigation pane to be displayed, to Show all folders, and to Show favorites.
3. Make the following changes to the way Windows 8 displays files and folders:
   - Display file extensions for known file types.
   - Show hidden files and folders.
4. Display the properties of the folder containing the data files for this chapter on your USB flash drive. Ask your instructor for help, if needed, in locating the folder.
5. Display the EMCP folder. The Chapter 4 folder appears as an icon.
6. Capture a screen shot of this window, save it as **C04E01**, and then submit it to your instructor.
7. Check with your instructor, and, if needed, return all settings for File Explorer and for the affected folders to their original settings.

Working with File Properties ■■■■■■■■■■■■■■■

A *file property* is information about a file or attached to a file. Properties include two types of information:

- **Metadata.** Information attached to a file that states something about that file, such as its author name and keywords. Metadata is most often associated with data files, such as Word documents.

- **Attributes.** On/off flags set for a file that determine such things as whether the file is read-only, indexed, hidden, modified since being backed up, compressed, and/or encrypted. All files have attributes, not just data files.

file property Information about a file or information attached to a file

metadata Information attached to a file that provides descriptive data such as the author's name

attributes On/off flags set for a file, such as read-only

Adding and Editing Metadata

Depending on the file type, a Details tab might be available in the file's Properties box. On the Details tab, you can define values for various metadata properties.

Some of the metadata for a file is not editable, such as Date created, Size, Program name, and so on. If you click in the Value column for one of these, the entire row is highlighted and there is no insertion point. For other items, however, you can click to move the insertion point into the text box and then type a new value, as shown in Figure 4.7.

Figure 4.7 Examine a file's metadata in its Properties box, and change any details as needed.

To view and change metadata for a file:

1. Right-click the file and then choose *Properties*.
2. Click the Details tab.
3. Click in the Value column of the property you want to set and then type a new value.
4. Repeat Step 3, as needed, and then click OK.

Changing File Attributes

A file's attributes define basic yes/no facts about it. Depending on the file system the drive is using, you might have access to some or all of these attributes:

- **Read-only.** The file cannot be deleted or modified.

- **Hidden.** The file does not appear in File Explorer file listings (unless hidden files are set to be shown, as you learned how to do previously in this chapter).

- **Archive (File is ready for archiving).** The file has changed since it was backed up with a backup program that sets the archive flag to off.

- **Indexed (Allow this file to have contents indexed in addition to file properties).** The content of the file is included in the Windows 8 index of the disk's contents, so any searches for words it contains will find the file.

- **Compressed (Compress contents to save disk space).** The file has been compressed with NTFS compression. This is available only on drives that use the NTFS file system. When you apply this to a folder, rather than a file, you are prompted to choose whether to apply the change to the selected folder only or all its subfolders and files as well.

- **Encrypted (Encrypt contents to secure data).** This file has been encrypted with NTFS encryption. This is available only on drives that use the NTFS file system. Read-only and Hidden attributes can be turned on or off from the General tab of the file's Properties box. For other properties, you must click the Advanced button on the General tab to open the Advanced Attributes dialog box (shown in Figure 4.8).

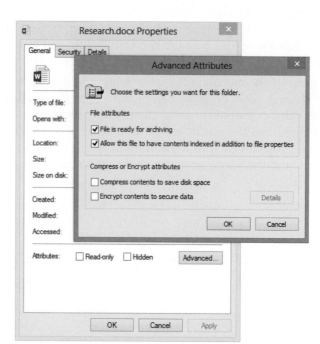

Figure 4.8 Set the attributes for the file from the General tab of its Properties box and from the Advanced Attributes dialog box.

To set or clear the Read-only and/or Hidden attributes:

1. Right-click the file and then choose *Properties*.
2. On the General tab, mark or clear the *Read-only* check box.
3. Mark or clear the *Hidden* check box.
4. Click OK.

To set or clear the Archive, Indexed, Compressed, or Encrypted attributes:

1. Right-click the file and then choose *Properties*.
2. On the General tab, click Advanced.
3. Mark or clear the *File is ready for archiving* check box.
4. Mark or clear the *Allow this file to have contents indexed in addition to file properties* check box.
5. Mark or clear the *Compress contents to save disk space* check box.
6. Click OK.
7. Click OK.
   If you changed the *Compress contents to save disk space* check box's status for a folder, complete the following steps:
8. Click Apply changes to this folder only, or click Apply changes to this folder, subfolders and files.
9. Click OK.

Removing File Properties and Personal Information

Before you share files with others, you may want to remove any personally identifiable information from its metadata, such as the author's name or keywords you have added. Windows 8 provides an easy way to remove this metadata.

To remove all the metadata that might in any way identify you, click Select All, or choose individual properties to remove, as shown in Figure 4.9. Alternatively, you can choose to create a copy that lacks the properties, leaving the original intact.

Figure 4.9 Select properties to remove from the file before distributing it.

To remove file properties and personal information from a file:

1. Right-click the file and then choose *Properties*.
2. Click the Details tab.
3. Click *Remove Properties and Personal Information*.
4. Click *Create a copy with all possible properties removed*.
   OR
   Click *Remove the following properties from this file*.
5. Either mark the check boxes for the properties to remove or click Select All.
6. Click OK.

Exercise 2

Working with File Metadata and Attributes

1. If you have not already done so, download the student data files to your computer or to your USB flash drive from www.paradigmcollege.net/windows8. Ask your instructor for assistance, if needed.
2. Open the Chapter 4 folder. Copy the file **Townsend.doc** and name the copy **C04E02.docx**.
3. Display the Properties box for **C04E02.docx**.
4. Display its Details tab and then set the following metatags:
   Title: Townsend
   Authors: *delete the existing author and then type your own full name*
5. Click Apply.
6. On the General tab, click *Read-only*.
7. Click OK.
8. Copy the file to a USB flash drive and then submit it to your instructor.

Working with File and Folder Versions ▬■■■■■■■■

Windows 8 includes a File History feature that enables you to restore a file or folder to a previous version. For example, if you have made and saved changes to a file, you may decide you no longer want those changes. The application you used to change the file may not enable you to retrieve the previous versions. However, Windows 8 tracks the changes you have made to the file and enables you to select a previous version to reinstate.

TIP File History is available for most file types, but it is useful to the end user primarily for data files. You would not typically restore a previous version of a system file, for example, because it was probably updated for a reason, such as Windows Update activity.

Enabling File History

In Windows 8, the File History feature is turned off by default; you must enable the feature before Windows will save previous versions of files.

To enable File History, open the Control Panel, and under *System and Security*, click Save backup copies of your files with File History. Click the Turn On button to start saving file versions. If the Turn On button is unavailable, click Select drive to set up a backup location. Windows 8 requires you to choose an external drive or a network location to which it saves previous versions (shown in Figure 4.10). (This is a change from Windows 7, which saved previous versions to the same hard disk.) Choose a drive or location that is available all the time, not one that you temporarily have connected.

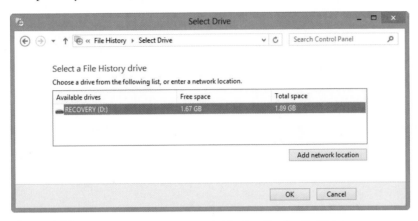

Figure 4.10 Select a network or external drive location for file history.

File History saves copies of files that are in your libraries, contacts, favorites, and files on your desktop. It does not save versions of files stored elsewhere unless you add that storage location to a library. See "Controlling Which Folders a Library Monitors" in Chapter 3 to add a folder to a library. It may take several hours after you turn on File History for all the backup copies to be made. You will not be able to restore a file from backup until that process has completed.

Here's How

To enable File History saved to an external drive:

1. Select the Settings charm.
2. Click *Control Panel*.
3. Under *System and Security*, click *Save backup copies of your files with File History*.
4. Make sure an external drive is connected.
5. Click Turn on.
6. If a prompt recommends this drive to other members of your homegroup, click No.
7. Close the File History window.

To enable File History saved to a network location:

1. Select the Settings charm.
2. Click *Control Panel*.
3. Under *System and Security*, click *Save backup copies of your files with File History*.
4. Click Change drive.
5. Click Add network location.
6. Browse and select a folder on a network drive.
7. Click Select Folder.
8. Click Turn on.
9. If a prompt recommends this drive to other members of your homegroup, click No.
10. Close the File History window.

Restoring a Previous Version of a File

After you have enabled File History, as explained in the previous section, Windows saves versions of the files that change. You can return to any of these saved previous versions as needed. (You cannot revert to a version of a file that you saved before enabling File History.)

To examine the available previous versions of a file or folder, from the File History window in the Control Panel, click Restore personal files and then navigate to and select the file you want to restore. The File History window shows a preview of the most recent previous version of the file. Click the Previous version (left-pointing) arrow at the bottom of the dialog box to check out older versions. When you see the version you want to restore, click the Restore to original location button (shown in Figure 4.11).

When you restore a previous version, if the original location already contains a file with the same name, you are prompted to either replace it or skip the file.

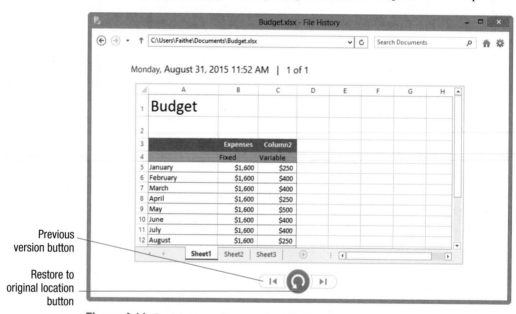

Previous version button

Restore to original location button

Figure 4.11 Restore a previous version of a file.

Here's How

To restore a previous version:

1. View the desired version to restore in File History.
2. Click the Restore to original location button.
3. If prompted, click Replace the file in the destination folder.

Setting File or Folder Permissions ▪▪▪▪▪▪▪▪▪▪

local file permission The permission to access a file belonging to another user on the same computer

network sharing permission The permission to access a file stored on a different computer

You can assign two types of permissions to files and folders:

- **Local file permission.** Permission for users on the same local computer to access each other's files. The user is determined by the user name used when signing into Windows 8. Local file permissions are covered in the following sections.

- **Network sharing permission.** Permission to access a file that is stored on a computer other than the one you are working with.

Understanding Groups and Users

In addition to any network account, each computer has one or more local user accounts. When a particular user is logged on, that user automatically has permission to access all files and folders that he or she has created. The user can, if desired, restrict access of other individuals or groups by changing the permissions on the file or folder.

A *group* provides a convenient way of assigning the same permissions to multiple users at once. If you define a group and set up a list of users to be part of it, then you can assign permissions to the group rather than to the individuals. Individual users can be part of multiple groups and also can have individual permissions assigned in addition to any inherited from the group(s).

group A named set of individual users to which the same permissions are assigned

Note: *Local permissions can be set only on drives that use the NTFS file system. You cannot apply local permissions to USB flash drives or CD or DVD drives, for example.*

There may already be multiple users set up on your system, and several predefined groups exist by default:

- **Everyone.** A group that includes all users. Assign permissions to this group to affect every user, including guests.
- **Administrators.** A group that includes all users who have Administrator rights.
- **Users.** A group that includes all users who have User rights, which are less powerful than Administrator rights.

Note: *Microsoft recommends that you operate Windows 8 from a Standard-level account on a day-to-day basis, and switch to an Administrator-level account only to make changes such as installing new software or updating device drivers. Therefore, a single person may have more than one user account on the computer.*

▼ **Quick Fix**

No Security Tab
If there is no Security tab, the drive does not use the NTFS file system, and you will not be able to set local permissions for files and folders on that drive.

Viewing Local Permissions for a File or Folder

To view the permissions for a file or folder, click the Security tab of its Properties box. Click a group or user name at the top of the dialog box, and the permissions appear in the bottom section (shown in Figure 4.12). Check marks that appear in gray represent permissions inherited from higher levels in the folder structure; black check marks represent permissions set for the specific folder or file.

Adding or Removing a Permission

You can set permissions at the file level, but it is better to set them at a folder level. Then whatever you put into that folder inherits its permissions. That way you have fewer permissions to keep track of and you do not have to reset the permissions for files individually.

Note: *In most cases, to allow or not allow a permission, you should mark or clear the Allow check box for an item. The absence of the Allow setting is in effect a denial. Use the Deny check box only rarely to specifically override an inherited permission for a particular individual or group. Troubleshooting problems caused by forgotten Deny settings can be difficult.*

Figure 4.12 View the local user and group permissions for a folder or file.

To add or remove a permission for a file or folder:

1. Right-click the file or folder and then choose *Properties*.
2. Click the Security tab.
3. Click Edit. The Permissions dialog box opens.
4. Click the desired group or user name.
5. In the *Permissions for* section, mark or clear the *Allow* check boxes for each permission, as needed.
6. Click OK.
7. Click OK.

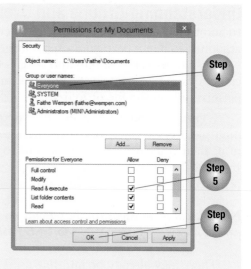

Exercise 3

Working with Permissions

1. Open the Computer window and then navigate to the folder containing the data files for this chapter.
2. Copy the Chapter 4 folder to your hard drive and then rename the copied folder **C04E03S02**.
3. Grant full control of the folder to the Authenticated Users group.
4. Capture a screen shot of the C04E03S02 Properties window, save the file as **C04E03S04**, and then submit it to your instructor.
5. Delete the C04E03S02 folder from your hard drive.

CHAPTER SUMMARY

- The customizable parts of a File Explorer window include the Details pane, Preview pane, and Navigation pane. To turn these on or off, use the controls on the View tab.

- To resize the panes within a File Explorer window, drag the dividers between panes. The overall window size does not change.

- To customize how files and folders appear, such as hiding extensions for known file types, hiding operating system files, and showing hidden files and folders, mark or clear the checkboxes on the View tab, or click Options on the View tab and then set the options on the View tab of the Folder Options dialog box.

- To customize the appearance of a folder's icon, right-click the folder and then choose *Properties.* On the Customize tab, choose a template, and, if desired, customize the settings for the template by selecting a specific icon or picture.

- Files have two types of properties: metadata and attributes. Metadata is assigned mostly to data files; it includes text descriptions of properties such as Author. Attributes are on/off switches for qualities such as Read-only.

- To remove personally identifiable information from a file, right-click it and then choose *Properties*. On the Details tab, click *Remove Properties and Personal Information*, choose what to remove, and then click OK.

- To retrieve previous versions of a file or folder, use the File History feature in Windows 8.

- You can grant two kinds of access to content on your hard disk: network and local. Local permissions can be assigned only to files and folders on NTFS volumes.

- For ease of administration, it is often preferable to assign permissions to a group of users rather than to individual ones. It is also easier to assign permissions to entire folders rather than individual files.

- To assign local permissions, right-click the file or folder, choose *Properties*, and then set up the permissions on the Security tab.

CONCEPTS CHECK

Completion: Answer the following questions in a Word document.

Part 1

Multiple Choice

1. If the *Favorites* section does not appear in the Navigation pane in File Explorer, click the _____ tab, click Navigation pane, and then click *Show Favorites*.
   a. Home
   b. View
   c. Share
   d. Manage

2. Where in the File Explorer window does the Preview pane appear, if it is not hidden?
   a. Left
   b. Right
   c. Top
   d. Bottom

3. When you drag the divider between two panes in the File Explorer window, how is the overall size of the window affected?
   a. It does not change.
   b. It changes vertically but not horizontally.
   c. It changes horizontally but not vertically.
   d. It changes both horizontally and vertically.

4. To reveal hidden files and folders, click the View tab and then click the _____ check box.
   a. Image file names
   b. File name extensions
   c. Hidden items
   d. Display all

5. To set a folder's type, and thereby affect the folder's icon appearance, right-click the folder, choose _____ , and then click the _____ tab.
   a. *Customize,* Folder
   b. *Properties,* Customize
   c. *Change,* Icon
   d. *Setup,* Image

6. Which of these is an example of file metadata?
   a. Compressed
   b. Read-only
   c. Author
   d. Hidden

7. Compression and encryption are available only if _____ .
   a. you are using Windows 8, not a previous version of Windows
   b. the drive uses the NTFS file system
   c. you are signed in as a user named Guest
   d. the drive uses the FAT32 file system

8. To view a file's history and restore a previous version, view the desired version to restore in File History, and then click _____ .
   a. Undo
   b. Version
   c. Restore to original location
   d. Revert to stored history

9. What does it mean when a file has the *File is ready for archiving* check box marked?
   a. File has been changed since backed up with a backup utility.
   b. File has *not* been changed since backed up with a backup utility.
   c. File's creation date was more than six months ago.
   d. File has not been accessed in more than six months.

10. Which two attributes are available directly on the General tab of a file's Properties box?
    a. Hidden and System
    b. Archive and Encrypt
    c. Read-only and Hidden
    d. Indexed and Read-only

Part 2

Short Answer

11. In a File Explorer window, which two panes are mutually exclusive, allowing only one of them to appear at a time?

_____

12. How can you display file extensions for known file types in File Explorer windows?

_____

13. Why might you want to display hidden files and folders?

_____

14. List four ways to customize the File Explorer window interface (*not* the display of the files within the window).

_____

15. What is the difference between metadata and attributes for a file?

_____

16. From which tab of a file's Properties dialog box can you remove properties and personal information?

_____

17. What is the difference between local file permission and network sharing?

_____

18. What are the advantages of assigning local file permissions to folders rather than to files?

_____

19. If no Security tab appears in a folder's Properties box, what can you assume about the drive's file system?

_____

20. Why should you avoid marking the *Deny* check box to remove permissions from a file or folder?

_____

SKILLS CHECK

Save all solution files to the default Documents folder or any alternate folder specified by your instructor.

Guided Check

Assessment

1

Change the File Explorer Window Layout
1. In File Explorer, in the Navigation pane, click *Computer*.
2. Turn off the Preview pane and the Details pane if either are currently displayed.
   a. Click the *View* tab.
   b. If the Preview pane button is selected, click it to turn it off.
   c. If the Details pane button is selected, click it to turn it off.
3. Set the Navigation pane's view to Show All Folders.
   a. Click the View tab.
   b. Click Navigation pane.
   c. If the *Show all folders* check box is not marked, click it.
4. Capture a screen shot of this window, save it as **C04A01**, and then submit it to your instructor.

Customizing How File Explorer Displays Files and Folders

1. Check to see whether file extensions are hidden; if not, hide them.
   a. Open File Explorer and then click the View tab.
   b. If the *File name extensions* check box is not marked, click it.
2. Check to see whether hidden files are visible; if not, make them visible.
   a. Click the View tab.
   b. If the *Hidden items* check box is not marked, click it.
3. Display the contents of the Users folder on your primary hard drive.
   a. In the Navigation pane, click *Computer*.
   b. Double-click the *C* drive (or the drive that contains Windows).
   c. Double-click the *Users* folder.
4. Make sure the Default folder (a hidden folder) is showing in the File list. If it is not, recheck your work in Step 2.
5. Capture a screen shot of this window, save it as **C04A02**, and then submit it to your instructor.
6. Turn off the display of file name extensions and hidden items by clearing the checkboxes you marked in Steps 1 and 2.
7. Close all remaining open windows.

Assigning Metadata to a file

1. Open the folder containing the data files for this chapter. Ask your instructor for help in locating the folder, if needed.
2. Copy the file **Budget.xlsx** and name the copy **C04A03.xlsx**.
   a. Select Budget.xlsx.
   b. Press Ctrl + C to copy.
   c. Press Ctrl + V to paste.
   d. Right-click the copy and then click *Rename*.
   e. Type C04A03 and then press Enter.

   > Note: *If file extensions are hidden, do not type .xlsx on the end; if file extensions are visible, then do type that extension.*

3. Open the Properties for **C04A03.xlsx**.
   a. Right-click *C04A03.xlsx*.
   b. Click *Properties*.
4. On the Details tab, enter a title of Budget, a subject of Business Budget, a tag of Financial, and a comment of Preliminary Draft.
   a. Click the Details tab.
   b. Point to the area at the right of Title, so that the placeholder Add a Title appears, click, and then type Budget.
   c. Point to the area at the right of Subject, click, and then type Business Budget.
   d. Point to the area at the right of Tags, click, and then type Financial.
   e. Point to the area at the right of Comments, click, and then type Preliminary Draft.
5. Change the Authors entry to your name.
   a. Next to Authors, select the current name and then press Delete.
   b. Type your full name.
6. Capture a screen shot of this window, save it as **C04A03**, and then submit it to your instructor.
7. Click OK.
8. Close all remaining open windows.

Assessment

4

Removing personal information from a file

1. Open the Chapter 4 Student Data Files folder.
2. Open the properties for **Budget.xlsx**.
   a. Right-click **Budget.xlsx**.
   b. Click *Properties*.
3. Create a copy of the file that contains no personal metadata.
   a. Click the Details tab.
   b. Click *Remove Properties and Personal Information*.
   c. If it is not already selected, click *Create a copy with all possible properties removed*.
   d. Click OK.
   e. Click OK.
4. The copy is currently named **Budget - copy.xlsx**. Rename the copy **C04A04.xlsx** and then submit it to your instructor.

Assessment

5

Assigning permissions to a folder

1. Create a new folder with your last name as its name in the root directory of your C drive.
   a. Open File Explorer.
   b. Click *Computer*.
   c. Double-click the *C* drive.
   d. Click *New folder* in the Quick Access toolbar (at the left end of the window's title bar).
   e. Type your last name.
   f. Press Enter.
2. Set the permissions on that folder so that the Users group has full control of it.
   a. Right-click the folder you created in Step 1.
   b. Click *Properties*.
   c. Click the Security tab.
   d. Click Edit.
   e. Click Users.
   f. Mark the *Allow* check box for Full Control.
   g. Click OK.
3. Click the Users group so that the Users group permissions check boxes are marked in the *Permissions for Users* section of the dialog box.
4. Capture a screen shot of the Security tab in the Properties dialog box, save it as **C04A05**, and then submit it to your instructor.
5. Click OK to close the Properties box.
6. Delete the folder you created.
   a. Click the folder.
   b. Press the Delete key. If you see a Delete Folder confirmation pop-up box, click Yes.

On Your Own

Assessment

6

Turning on all optional File Explorer window elements

1. Open File Explorer.
2. On the View tab, click Navigation pane and then make a note of which options are enabled.
3. Turn on every available option for the Navigation pane.
4. Turn on the Details pane.
5. Turn on the display of File name extensions and Hidden items if they are not already on.

6. Capture a screen shot of the File Explorer window, save it as **C04A06**, and then submit it to your instructor.
7. Return the window to its original condition using the notes you made in Step 2.

Assessment 7

Displaying operating system files

1. Open the Folder Options dialog box on the View tab (View, Options), make sure that the *Hide protected operating system files (Recommended)* check box is marked, and then close the Folder Options dialog box.
2. Display the top level of the C drive and then count the number of files and folders.
3. Return to the Folder Options dialog box and then clear the *Hide protected operating system files (Recommended)* check box.
4. Display the top level of the C drive again and then count the number of files and folders.
5. Record the counts from Steps 2 and 4 and the names of at least four files that appeared only when operating system files were not hidden, save the file as **C03A07**, and then submit it to your instructor.

Assessment 8

Customizing the appearance of a folder

1. In the Chapter 4 folder, create the following five new folders: General Items, Documents, Pictures, Music, and Videos.
2. Configure each of the folders with the folder template that matches its name.
3. Copy each of the following files from the Chapter 4 folder into each of the new folders: **Distance.wma, bowl.jpg, Estate.xlsx, Townsend.doc.**
4. Submit an informal written report that describes the differences in the way the folder icons appear.

Assessment 9

Experimenting with Attributes

1. In the Chapter 4 folder, select and copy the file **Register.txt** to the Clipboard and then paste it to a USB flash drive.
2. On the flash drive, open the properties for **Register.txt** and clear the *File is ready for archiving* check box.
3. Open **Register.txt** in Notepad and make a minor change to the file. Save and close the file.
4. Examine the attributes for **Register.txt**, and note that the archive attribute has been enabled.
5. Write a paragraph explaining how this attribute might be useful to a computer user.

CHALLENGE PROJECT

Suppose you want to give a copy of all of the data files for this chapter to an acquaintance, but you first want to remove as much personal information as possible. Not all of the files used for this chapter's exercises and assignments store personal information, however. Some of them include only details that are fixed, such as file size or on/off attributes such as archive.

Create a copy of the data files for this chapter. Remove the personal information from as many of them as possible, copy the files to a USB flash drive, and then submit it to your instructor.

CHAPTER

5

Using Windows 8 Programs

PERFORMANCE OBJECTIVES

Upon successful completion of Chapter 5, you will be able to:

- Find a program with the Search charm
- Start and exit a desktop app
- Create and save a new file
- Open and resave an existing file
- Print a regular or OpenXPS file
- Create unformatted and formatted documents with Notepad and WordPad
- Track your notes with Windows Journal

- Use the Math Input Panel
- Create a graphic picture in Paint
- Use the Snipping Tool
- Copy content from one application to another
- Launch an application from the command prompt
- Launch and exit Windows 8 apps
- Find commands in Windows 8 apps
- Switch between open programs and apps

As your computing workspace, the Windows desktop offers a number of application tools or programs geared to help you accomplish specific computing tasks. For example, you can use the Calculator to crunch numbers and use WordPad to create documents like letters and reports. Applications enable you to create, save, and print files and, in some cases, to perform special activities like faxing a file. The Start screen offers a new style of app called Windows 8 apps; as you will learn in Chapter 13, you can download more apps as needed. You can start and close applications and have multiple programs open on the desktop to work with them as needed, and you can switch between open desktop and Windows 8 apps to use the precise tool that you need at any time.

Performing Basic Application Activities ■■■■■■■

application or program A set of instructions for performing a particular task or set of tasks, such as word processing or drawing a picture

The Windows 8 operating system enables you to install and use numerous types of *applications* or *programs*, each developed to handle a special type of activity. An application consists of a fixed set of instructions that the computer can execute, so, for the most part, each application or program stands alone and is used individually. In addition to enabling you to install applications that you need, Windows 8 includes a number of its own applications, some of which you will learn about later in the chapter. Windows 8 includes applications you use from the desktop, which you will learn about first, and Windows 8 apps you access from the Start screen. You will read more about the Windows 8 apps later in the chapter.

Learning to use a variety of programs is easier than ever because the majority of programs have some operations in common and even use similar commands and navigational tools.

Finding, Starting, and Exiting a Desktop Program

Starting a program loads its instructions into the computer's *RAM* (random access memory), the "working memory" that contains instructions for running programs and unsaved file information. By default, the Windows 8 desktop Taskbar has icons you can click to start two programs: Internet Explorer and File Explorer. To find and start other available programs, use the Search charm. After you click the Search charm, you can use either the Search pane that appears at the right side of the screen to find an app, or scroll to the right to close the Search pane and see the apps that are installed on your system, as shown in Figure 5.1. The Windows 8 apps are listed at the left, and the desktop apps are listed at the right. Click any listed app to start it. A new program you install may appear either with the Windows 8 apps or elsewhere on the screen, depending on the type of app it is and how its installer is set up.

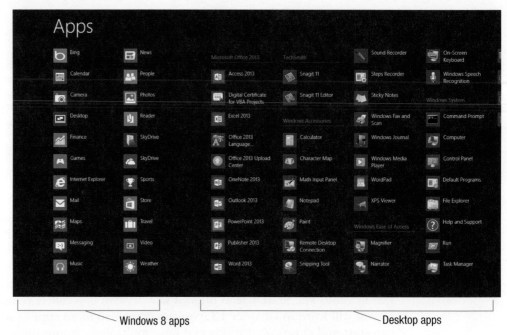

Windows 8 apps   Desktop apps

Figure 5.1   Find the apps installed on your system via the Search charm.

Here's How

To find and start a program:

1. Move the mouse pointer over the lower right corner of the Start screen or desktop, or swipe in from the right edge if you are using touch.
2. Click or tap the Search charm, which is the top charm.
3. If needed, leave Apps selected in the Search pane at the right, and begin typing the name of the program. The screen lists matching programs.
   OR
   Use the scroll bar at the bottom to scroll the screen to the right, which closes the Search pane.
4. Click the program tile. The program opens on the desktop.

Step 2

Search

Note: *If you know where a program's startup command is located on your hard disk, double-click the command icon in a File Explorer window to start the program.*

Exiting or *shutting down* a program removes it from the screen and from RAM. Shutting down a program not only frees up RAM for use by other programs and processes, but it also secures your work so that no unwanted viewer can see your work in a particular program. You typically can use one of a few different methods to shut down a program.

To shut down a desktop program and any open files in the program:

1. Click the File tab or menu.
2. Click the *Exit* or *Quit* or *Close* command.
   OR
   Click the program window Close (X) button.
   OR
   Press Alt + F4.
3. If a dialog box asks whether to save your changes to the current file, click Yes or Save to save, or click No or Don't Save to close without saving.

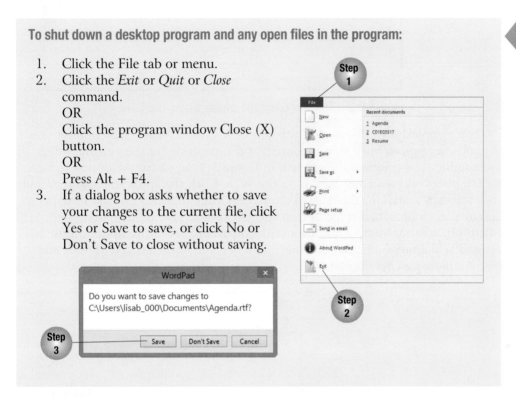

Here's How

Note: *Rather than the File menu, recent versions of Microsoft Office applications and Windows 8 desktop applications have a File tab at the far left of the ribbon that you click to open the menu or screen with commands for working with files.*

Making a Blank File

In many cases, starting an application automatically creates a new, blank file in the program. For example, when you start the Notepad application, it opens with a new, blank document file. However, if you have already added information to the current file or are working in a file that you previously saved and reopened, then you will need to take action to open a new file if you need one.

To open a new, blank file, click the File tab or menu, and then click *New* (shown in Figure 5.2), or press Ctrl + N. In many of the applications that are part of Windows 8, a blank file appears immediately.

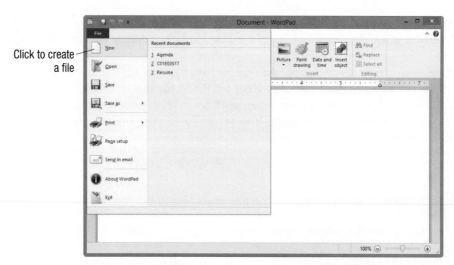

Click to create a file

Figure 5.2 The New command creates a new, blank file.

Some applications, like recent versions of Microsoft Word, may prompt you to choose a **template** with starter content and formatting for the new file when you use the New command. As shown in Figure 5.3, you have the option to look for templates on your computer or on the Web. Click the applicable category and then select or search for the desired template. Other applications may prompt you to select a document type or to name and save the file immediately (like Microsoft Access). Many applications, like the Microsoft Office applications, assign a temporary numbered file name to a new file until you save the file and give it a more descriptive name.

Templates

Figure 5.3 Some applications give you the option to use a template or choose a document type when you create a new file.

Note: Pressing Ctrl + N typically creates a blank file without asking you to choose a template. In older versions of some applications, clicking the New button on the toolbar creates a blank file without prompting you to choose a template.

Saving a New File and Closing

Once you have created the blank file, you can begin adding content into it, as needed. Of course, the type of content you create will vary depending on the nature of the application. In word processing programs such as Windows 8 NotePad or WordPad, you type the text for your document. In a spreadsheet program, you enter values and formulas. In a graphics program such as Windows 8 Paint, you create an image using program tools.

As you are working, the information you are creating exists only in RAM. To retain the ability to later open and work with the content you have already created, you have to *save* the file to disk.

During the process of saving a new file, you also assign a name to the file. Note that the application will also append a period plus a three- to five-letter file name extension that identifies the file format. Typically, each program creates files in a unique default format, such as .txt for Notepad and .rtf for WordPad, but many programs can create and read files in a variety of formats. For example, Word can save documents in its own format, plus .html (web page) format and others.

TIP Try to make your file names unique and descriptive to make it easier to find the file you need at a later time. For example, *Letter* is too generic, while *Benson Engine Sales Letter* gives you more information about the file's contents. Including a date in the file name helps distinguish between files that you may update from time to time, as in *Resume 05-01-2015* and *Resume 09-01-2015*.

Here's How

To save a new file in a desktop application:

1. Click the File tab or menu and then click *Save*; or press Ctrl + S. If the program has a toolbar with a Save button, click that button, instead.
2. If you want to save in a location other than your default Documents library and you do not see a Navigation or other pane at the left side of the Save As dialog box, click the Browse Folders button. This expands the Save As dialog box to include a pane at the left.
3. As in a File Explorer window (see Chapter 3), navigate to and select the folder where you want to store the saved file in the Navigation pane. If there is no Navigation or left pane, the dialog box will offer other methods for selecting a folder.
4. Click the *File name* text box and then type the desired file name.
5. Click Save.

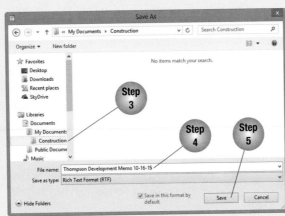

Note: *Some apps, such as Office 2013 applications, may show a screen with save locations after the previous Step 1. There, choose whether to save to your SkyDrive or computer, and then click a folder or the Browse button to open the Save As dialog box.*

When you finish working in a file, you typically will no longer want it open in the program window, nor taking up usable RAM capacity. In such a case, you can *close* the file. In most programs, each file exists in its own program window, so you can close the file by closing the program window. To do so, click the Close (X) button for the file window, which typically appears below the program's Close button and is sometimes called the Window Close button. Many programs also include a Close command on the File tab or menu. In other programs, you click the Close (X) button for the program window itself to perform the close. As when you exit a program, if you have any unsaved work in the file being closed, the program prompts you to save your changes.

Opening an Existing File

If you have already saved a file in a folder on your system's hard disk, you can *open* the file in the program in which you created it to resume working with the file, to print it, to copy information from it, and more. Opening the file loads the saved information into the system's working memory. To open the existing file, you must know the disk and folder location where it was saved.

To open an existing file:

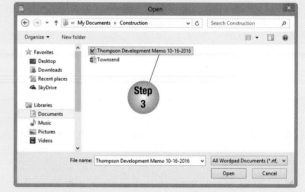

1. Click the File tab or menu, and then click *Open*; or press Ctrl + O. If the program has a toolbar with an Open button, click that button instead.
2. If you saved the file in a location other than your default Documents library or one of its subfolders, navigate to the save location in the pane at the left or by other means available in the Open dialog box for the program that you are using, and then select the location (folder).
3. Double-click the file icon. Or, click it once and then click the Open button.

Note: *Some apps, such as Office 2013 applications, may show a screen with storage locations after the previous Step 1. There, select your SkyDrive or your computer depending on where the file to open is located, and then click a folder or the Browse button to open the Open dialog box.*

TIP Double-click a file's icon in any folder or library window to both start the application used to create the file and open the file itself.

Saving Changes Made to an Existing File

Even though you will see a prompt to save file changes when you close the file or exit the program, you should still save your work periodically. If some type of power surge or other problem causes your system to stop working, you will have preserved at least some of your most recent work. Get in the habit of saving every 10 minutes or so.

To save your work in an existing file, click the File tab or menu, and then click *Save*. If the menu includes both Save and Save As commands, click the *Save* command. Most applications also enable you to press Ctrl + S to save your work.

 You can use the Save As command to save a copy of a document under a new name or in a new format. For example, if you choose File and then Save As in WordPad, one of the format choices is Office Open XML document, which is the format used by recent versions of Word.

Note: *Some programs include an automatic saving feature that saves your file automatically at an interval you specify, such as every five or 10 minutes. However, this type of feature can sometimes cause the program to "pause" while the save takes place, slightly interrupting your work.*

Printing a File

Printing a file creates a paper or hard copy version of the file's contents so that you can mail or otherwise give the document to someone who needs it. Most organizations preserve documents in hard-copy format for record-keeping purposes. The emergence of inexpensive, high-quality color printers in the last several years enables not only more attractive, eye-catching business document printouts, but also the ability for users to print their own digital photos and create other personal projects that were previously unattainable.

Another type of printout does not involve paper at all. When you ***print to a file***, Windows 8 essentially converts the file contents to another format, typically one that can be read or printed by more programs or even a specialized ***viewer application***. You will learn about this type of printout shortly.

print to a file A method of converting a file to a more easily shared format

viewer application An application that can read files printed or converted to a particular type of file format

printer driver The printer control file that interprets print information from an application

Regular File Formats Because different printer models require different printing instructions, installing a printer under Windows 8 installs a ***printer driver*** file. The printer driver translates the information about a file format from a particular application in such a way that the printer can print the file correctly. When you send a printout or print job to the printer, the printer driver handles the file information and passes it along to the printer. If you have multiple printers installed on a system, then the print process includes selecting the desired printer (and therefore its printer driver) for the current print job.

Note: *Printing requires that a printer be installed to work with Windows 8 and that it be connected to your system or network, be powered on, and have a supply of paper. After connecting and powering on a printer, from the desktop select the Settings charm, and under Settings click Control Panel. Under the* Hardware and Sound *category, click the Add a device link, which will start a scan of your system to find a printer to install. You also can change printer settings in the Devices and Printers window, accessed by clicking View devices and printers under* Hardware and Sound. *Chapter 13 provides more information about adding and removing a printer.*

Printing also includes choosing other settings for the specific print job, such as the number of copies you would like to print and which pages in the file you would like to print. Some applications and printers enable you to choose other settings, such as whether to collate the printed pages.

Some applications also include a Print Preview command that enables you to see how your file will look when printed. Check the File tab or menu, the *Print* submenu, or the application toolbar to see if it offers a Print Preview command or button. Choose the command or button to open the preview. If the preview needs no changes, you can typically click a Print button at the top of the view to open the Print dialog box (see Step 2). If the document needs further changes, click the Close or Close preview button to return to the regular view and make changes before printing.

Here's How

To print a file:

1. Open the file to print in the application used to create it.
2. Click the File tab or menu and then click *Print*; or press Ctrl + P. A Print dialog box or screen with printing options appears. The available settings typically vary depending on the application and printer being used.
3. Select the printer to use in the *Select Printer* section, printer *Name* drop-down list, or the applicable list of printer choices.
4. If you want to change settings for the selected printer, click the Preferences or Properties button. The dialog box that appears offers more detailed settings pertaining to the

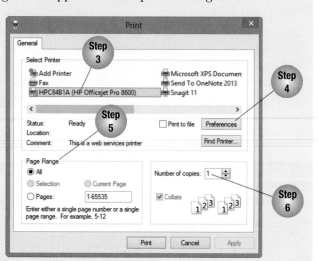

selected printer. For example, for a color inkjet printer, the dialog box may offer the choice of whether to print in black and white or color, and what type of paper (such as photo paper) to use for the printout. The dialog box may offer multiple tabs of options and may also include an Advanced button that you can click to see even more settings. Click OK after making your changes to close the open printer settings or properties dialog boxes.
5. Select the settings for the pages or area to print in the section or control named *Page Range* or something similar. Typically, if you choose to print a selection of pages, you type in the page numbers separated by a hyphen (for continuous pages) or a comma (for noncontiguous pages).
6. Change the *Number of copies* value to print more copies, if desired. You can select the initial entry and type a new value or click the up spinner button.
7. Change any other settings, as desired. Again, the available settings may vary depending on your program and printer.
8. Click Print or OK. The Print dialog box or screen closes, and the program sends the printer job to the printer.

▼ Quick Fix

File Does Not Print
If you see a message that the print job has failed and you do not see a paper jam, check the other obvious issues first. Make sure that the printer is turned on, has ink, toner, and paper, and is connected to the system. You also can shut down and restart the printer, which will usually resume the print job automatically.

Understanding OpenXPS Documents XPS stands for XML Paper Specification, a type of document format intended to be portable—that is, easily viewed by a variety of users and providing a consistent appearance when viewed on the screen or printed. The **OpenXPS** standard expands the portability aspects of XPS. Windows 8 includes the built-in Microsoft XPS Document Writer printer driver. When you select Microsoft XPS Document Writer as the printer for a print job from any program, the printed result is a file with the .oxps file name extension (an OpenXPS file or document) rather than a hard copy printout. Once you create the .oxps file, you can share it with others, make it available for download from a web page, and so on.

To convert the current file you are working on in any application to an OpenXPS file, click File and then click *Print*, or press Ctrl + P. In the Print dialog box or screen, select *Microsoft XPS Document Writer* as the printer to use from the *Select Printer* list, printer *Name* drop-down list, or the applicable list of printer choices, as shown in Figure 5.4. Choose other print settings as desired and then click Print or OK. In the Save the file as dialog box that appears, specify the file name and location to save to, as you would for any other file, and then click Save. The XPS printer driver generates the file and automatically assigns the .oxps file name extension.

To view an OpenXPS document, double-click the document icon in any folder or library window. The document opens in the Windows 8 Reader app, which also enables you to view PDF files. You also can open Reader or the desktop XPS Viewer application using the Search charm.

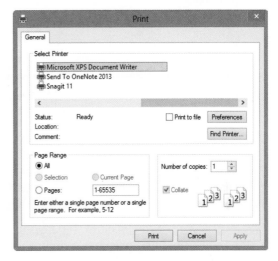

Figure 5.4 Selecting Microsoft XPS Document Writer "prints" an OpenXPS file.

Note: *Once you have opened an OpenXPS file in the Reader application, you can use its commands to work with the file and perform advanced operations, such as finding text or viewing file permissions.*

Faxing a File

One method for faxing works much like generating an OpenXPS file. To fax, you "print" a file to the fax printer driver (Microsoft Windows Fax and Scan) built in to Windows 8 by choosing *Fax* from the *Select Printer* list, printer *Name* drop-down list, or the applicable list of printer choices in the Print dialog box or screen. When you then click Print or OK, the fax driver generates the electronic fax document and opens the New Fax window, where the document being faxed appears as an attachment in the *Attach* text box.

To start a fax from scratch rather than initiating it from the Print dialog box, use the Search charm to open the Windows Fax and Scan desktop application. In the Windows Fax and Scan window that opens, click New Fax on the toolbar below the menu bar.

Type the recipient's fax number in the *To* text box, as shown in Figure 5.5, and then enter the fax topic in the *Subject* text box. Type and format additional text in the message body area and then click Send. Enter information such as your area code and line access number if the Location Information dialog box appears, and then click OK twice. The Microsoft Windows Fax and Scan application dials the system's fax modem and sends the fax.

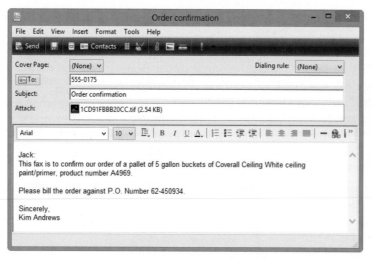

Note: *The first time you fax a document, a Fax Setup dialog box appears. Click the Connect to a fax modem or Connect to a fax server on my network choice, as applicable, and then respond to the additional dialog boxes that appear to specify fax settings. These steps assume that the fax modem hardware has been properly installed in the system and is connected to a phone line, if needed.*

Figure 5.5 Print to the FAX driver to fax a document, or use the Windows Fax and Scan application to create a fax from scratch.

Exercise 1

Using WordPad to Create, Save, and Print a Letter

1. Select the Search charm, type wo in the search box, and then click *WordPad*.
2. Click the Line spacing button in the Paragraph group on the Home tab and then click *1.0* in the drop-down list.
3. Click the Line spacing button in the Paragraph group on the Home tab again and then click *Add 10pt space after paragraphs* in the drop-down list to clear the check box beside it. Note that this selection may already have been selected.
4. Type today's date and then press Enter four times.
5. Type the following addressee information and then press Enter four times:

Accounts Payable Department
Allen Products
222 E. 82nd St.
Indianapolis, IN 46222

6. Type the following salutation, body, and closing text, pressing Enter twice after the salutation and body text and four times after the closing:

Dear Jack:

Enclosed find our check number 1162 in the amount of $1,296.42, payment in full for your invoice 3232.

Sincerely,

7. Type your name.
8. Click the File tab and then click *Save*. Enter C05E01 as the file name and then click Save to save the file in the default Documents library.

   Note: *If your instructor asks you to save your file in another location, save it there instead of the Documents folder.*

9. Click the File tab and then click *Exit* to exit WordPad.
10. Restart WordPad.

11. Click the File tab and then the *C05E01* file in the Recent documents list at the right to reopen the file. (If the file does not appear in the Recent documents list, click *Open*, navigate to the location where you saved the file, and then double-click the file in the file list of the Open dialog box.)

12. Click the File tab, click the right-pointing arrow beside *Print* in the menu, and then click *Print preview*. The Print preview view of the file appears. Click the Close print preview button in the Close group on the Print preview tab on the ribbon to return to the regular view of the file.

13. Click the File tab and then click *Print*. Select the printer specified by your instructor, click Print to print the file, and then submit it to your instructor.

14. Close WordPad and the file.

Using Calculator ■■■■■■■■■■■■■■■■■■■■■■■■■■■■■

Calculator is a small, special-purpose application that has been a part of all released versions of Windows. Like a separate hand-held calculator, the Calculator in Windows 8 can perform calculations such as addition, subtraction, multiplication, and division, as well as more advanced scientific calculations.

Start Calculator with the Search charm, as you would any other application. Select the Search charm and then click Calculator under *Windows Accessories* in the desktop apps (scroll right first, if needed).

Calculator's default view enables you to perform math computations in what is called its Standard mode. However, if you click the View menu, you can click one of three additional views or modes for performing more complex calculations. For example, if you click *Scientific*, the Calculator expands to display buttons for more complex calculations, as shown in Figure 5.6. Click View and then *Standard* to change back to the regular view for Calculator.

Figure 5.6 The Standard (left) and Scientific (right) modes of Calculator.

T I P To open a second window of a program like Calculator or Internet Explorer, right-click its Taskbar button and then click the program name.

To use the on-screen keys for the Calculator, click with the mouse. Most users can work faster with Calculator using the keyboard. As long as the NUM LOCK key is active, pressing the numbered keys above the letters on the keyboard enters the number in Calculator, and the period key enters a decimal place. Use the following keys for mathematical operators, pressing Shift as needed:

Parentheses to group values	( )
Addition	+
Subtraction	−
Multiplication	*
Division	/
Equals	Enter

For example, to enter the equation (6 * 5) + (2 * 8) = into Calculator, type **(6*5)+(2*8)** and then press Enter for the equal sign. Calculator displays the subtotal *30* after you type the first close parenthesis, but continue entering the equation to arrive at the total.

The following are useful techniques to know when you use Calculator:

- To clear the most recent calculated total, click the C button.

- To store a number in Calculator's memory, click the MS button.

- To recall a stored number, click the MR button. For example, you can add 10 numbers together and then press MS to store the total. You then could multiply two numbers, press +, click MR, and then press Enter to add the stored total to the multiplied numbers.

- MC clears the stored value from memory.

- To add a newly calculated value to the stored total in memory, click the M + button and then MR, to see the new stored total.

- To copy the number currently displayed in Calculator and paste it into another application, press Ctrl + C (Edit, *Copy*) to copy the value and then press Ctrl + V (Edit, *Paste*) to paste it in the destination application.

The Windows 8 version of Calculator has been upgraded to include Programmer and Statistics modes, as shown in Figure 5.7, that are also accessible from the View menu. Programmer mode offers the ability to perform calculations as well as choose the number format and data type, common needs in the programming field. Use the top group of option buttons at the left to change the number format: hexadecimal (*Hex*), decimal (*Dec*), octal (*Oct*), and binary (*Bin*). Use the second set of option buttons to change the data type: QWORD (*Qword*), DWORD (*Dword*), WORD (*Word*), and BYTE (*Byte*). This mode also displays integers only, discarding decimals. Similarly, Statistics mode includes added function buttons that are useful to any professional who needs to perform statistical calculations, such as summing, averaging, and finding the standard deviation in a group of values. For example, if you want to calculate an average, you would enter each value and then click the Add button to add it to the dataset. You then would click the button for the statistical operation to perform.

Calculator offers even more benefits. You can choose either *Unit conversion* or *Date calculation* from the View menu to expand the calculator window. You can perform a variety of unit conversions, such as converting

Figure 5.7 The Programmer (left) and Statistics (right) modes of Calculator.

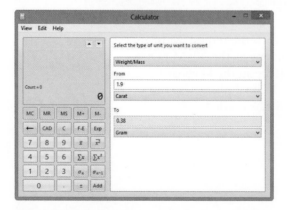

Figure 5.8 Using Calculator to convert a weight.

between various weight units or between various other types of measure like power, length, date, and more. For example, as Figure 5.8 shows, a jeweler could convert a weight in carats to the equivalent weight in grams. Available date calculations include finding the difference between two dates or adding and subtracting days to a date you specify.

Lastly, Calculator includes four worksheets—Mortgage, Vehicle lease, Fuel economy (mpg), and Fuel economy (L/100 km)—available from the *Worksheets* submenu of the View menu. Use each worksheet to calculate the type of data suggested by its name, such as calculating a mortgage payment. After displaying a worksheet, enter data in the worksheet fields and then click the Calculate button to display the result in the box at lower right.

To hide a converter or worksheet and return to the default for the current Calculator mode, click View and then click *Basic*. Click the Calculator window's Close (X) button to close Calculator.

Creating a Plain Text File with Notepad ▪▪▪▪▪▪▪

Like Calculator, Notepad has been part of every Windows version. Use Notepad to create document files in ***plain text (.txt)*** format. This format creates the most basic and compact type of document. Although you can change the type of lettering used for on-screen text in Notepad, the file saves only the text content, removing any special formatting.

plain text (.txt) A file format for document files that does not allow for or save any text formatting information

You need to know about using Notepad to create and work with plain text files because the plain text file type is used in a variety of ways with computers. For example, some programs use tracking-log files or startup-settings files that have various file name extensions but are in fact plain text files that you can open and edit in Notepad. Similarly, because the language used to create Web pages depends on special text codes or tags like <head> and </table>, you actually can create and edit basic Web pages using Notepad. Finally, because Notepad files are small, you may prefer to use Notepad to create documents when file size or storage space is an issue.

Start Notepad by selecting the Search charm, scrolling right, if needed, and then clicking Notepad under *Windows Accessories* in the desktop apps. From there, the same File commands discussed so far in this chapter—New, Open, Save, Print, and Exit—work the same in Notepad as in other applications. Type the text that you want, pressing Enter or Tab and using capital letters to set off or highlight information, as needed. Figure 5.9 shows the Notepad window with a file open in it. Note that you need to click Format and then click *Word Wrap* to have lines of text wrap (move to the next line) within the current window size.

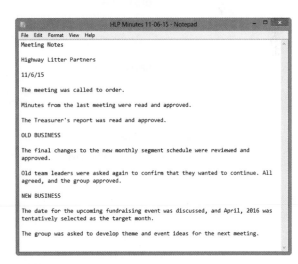

Figure 5.9 Create compact, plain text files in Notepad.

T I P The plain text (.txt) file format is portable in a way that OpenXPS files are not. Most programs can open and save files stored in the .txt format, making a plain text file an ideal medium for transferring data (but not formatting) from one application to another. The Open and Save As dialog boxes for most applications include a drop-down list that enables you to select the file format, such as *Text Documents (*.txt)*, of the file to open or save.

Creating a Text File with Formatting in WordPad ▪■■■■■■■■■■■■■■■■■■■■■■■■■■

font A typeface—a style of lettering—appearing either on the screen or in print

Rich Text Format (.rtf) A basic document file format that preserves some text formatting

WordPad represents a step up from Notepad in that it enables you to apply, save, and print basic text formatting. WordPad enables you to not only change the text *font* (type of lettering), but also a variety of other settings that apply to text and paragraphs.

As you saw earlier in the chapter, select the Start charm and then click WordPad to start WordPad. Use commands as for other applications to create and manage files. By default, saving a WordPad file saves it in ***Rich Text Format (.rtf)***, a format name that indicates that file formatting will be preserved.

After you drag over text to select it for formatting, WordPad enables you to work with these formatting settings, some of which are shown in Figure 5.10.

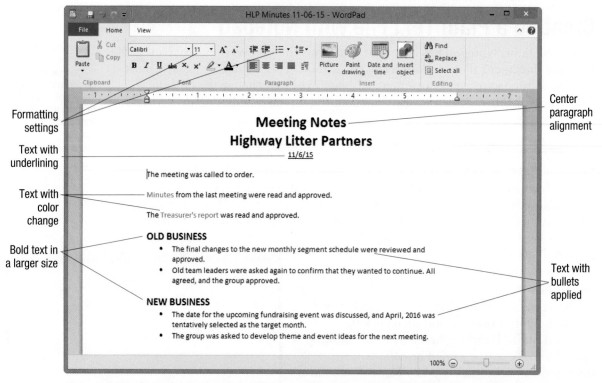

Figure 5.10 This is the same text as the Notepad document in Figure 5.9, but this example in WordPad has formatting applied, starting with a different font.

- **Font.** Use the buttons and lists in the Font group on the Home tab on the ribbon to change the text font family, font size, style (Bold, Italic, and so on), size, effects (Strikethrough, Underline, and so on), and other settings such as text color.

- **Bullets.** The Start a List drop-down list in the Paragraph group, by default, turns bullets on or off for the paragraph holding the insertion point, or the selected paragraphs. Use the drop-down arrow for this button to change to another list style, such as a numbered list.

- **Alignment.** The Paragraph group on the Home tab on the ribbon enables you to add or remove indents for paragraphs, set line spacing, and choose a paragraph alignment (Align text left, Align text right, Center, or Justify).

- **Other.** Click a ruler location to create a custom tab stop, or use the tools in the Insert group on the Home tab on the ribbon to incorporate elements such as the date and time and graphics in the document.

Note: *The ruler appears above the document text and shows measurements in 1/8-inch increments.*

Creating a Meeting Flyer in WordPad and Converting with Calculator

1. Select the Search charm, scroll right, if needed, and then click WordPad under *Windows Accessories* to launch the WordPad application.
2. Click the Line spacing button in the Paragraph group on the Home tab and then click *1.0* in the drop-down list.
3. Click the Line spacing button in the Paragraph group on the Home tab again and then click *Add 10pt space after paragraphs* in the drop-down list to clear the check box beside it.
4. Type the following information, pressing Enter twice after each line and pressing Tab after each colon, and type your name where indicated by *Student Name* in the last line:
   Highway Litter Partners
   New Team Member Meeting
   When: 7 p.m. November 4
   Where: Regent Community Center
   Contact: Student Name, 555-0606
5. Press Enter one more time and then type the following text:
   Highway Litter Partners is a volunteer organization dedicated to keeping roadsides clean in our community. If you can spare two hours a month to join a cleanup team, we need you! Last year, volunteers removed 10.5 tons of roadside waste.
6. Press Enter twice and then type the following two lines, pressing Enter after each line:
   Cleaner communities
   A better world
7. Select the Search charm, scroll right, if needed, and then click Calculator under *Windows Accessories*.
8. Click View and then click *Unit conversion*.
9. Select *Weight/Mass* from the *Select the type of unit you want to convert* drop-down list.
10. Enter 10.5 in the *From* text box, select *Short ton* from the accompanying drop-down list, and then select *Pound* from the *To* drop-down list.
11. Drag over the result in the *To* text box and then press Ctrl + C to copy it.
12. Click View and then click *Basic* to hide the converter. Close Calculator by clicking its Close (X) button.
13. Use the Taskbar to redisplay the WordPad document, if needed.
14. Paste the copied value:
    a. Select *10.5 tons* in the body text.
    b. Press Ctrl + V to paste the value and replace the selection.
    c. Type a space and pounds.
    d. Add a comma in the pasted value.
15. Click the File tab and then click *Save,* or click the Save button on the Quick Access Toolbar. Enter C05E02 as the file name and then click Save, to save the file in the default Documents library.

   Note: *If your instructor asks you to save your file in another location, save it there instead of the Documents folder.*

16. Drag over all text in the document, or press Ctrl + A. This selects all of the text. Open the *Font family* drop-down list in the Font group on the Home tab on the ribbon, scroll down, and then click *Georgia*. Open the *Font size* drop-down list and then click *14*.

17. Drag over the first two lines in the document. Use the tools in the Font group on the Home tab on the ribbon to change the Font family to *Arial* and the Font size to *20*. Also, click the Center alignment button in the Paragraph group to center the text.

18. Format the words *When:*, *Where:*, and *Contact:* in boldface by dragging over each selection and then clicking the Bold (B) button in the Font group.

19. Drag over the When:, Where:, and Contact: paragraphs to select them. Click the 1.5-inch mark on the ruler above the document text. The text at the right of the new tab stop shifts to the right based on the new tab.

20. Click anywhere in the paragraph of text that starts with *Highway Litter Partners* and then click the Increase indent button in the Paragraph group on the Home tab. All lines of the paragraph are indented at the left.

21. Drag over the last two lines of text to select them and then click the Start a list button in the Paragraph group on the Home tab on the ribbon. The paragraphs change to a bulleted list.

22. Press Ctrl + S to save your changes to the file.

23. Click the File tab, click the right-pointing arrow next to *Print*, and then click *Print preview*. The Print preview view of the file appears. Click the Close print preview button in the Close group on the Print preview tab to return to the regular view of the file.

24. Click the File tab and then click *Print*. Select the printer specified by your instructor, click Print to print the file, and then submit it to your instructor.

25. Close WordPad.

Using Windows Journal ■■■■■■■■■■■■■■■■■■■■■

tablet PC A type of laptop computer on which you can select commands and give other user input using a stylus (tablet pen) or sometimes a finger

graphics tablet An external input device that generally connects to the computer via a USB port and with which you can select commands, give user input, and draw images using a stylus (pen)

Windows Journal is a new note-taking feature in Windows 8. If you have a *tablet PC* or have a *graphics tablet* connected to your computer (either with or instead of a mouse), Windows 8 can recognize handwritten content that you create in Journal. Write text in your natural handwriting, as shown in Figure 5.11. To convert the handwriting to text, choose Edit, *Select All* (Ctrl + A), and then Actions, *Convert Handwriting to Text*. As shown in Figure 5.12, the Text Correction dialog box appears and gives you the opportunity to fix any words that are not recognized correctly. Double-click a word, click the desired correction in the *Alternative* list, and then click Change. After you finish your corrections, click OK. Next, choose Copy to the Clipboard or Insert in the same journal note, and then click Finish.

Edit, save, and print your notes as for any other file. Even better, your notes can include sketches and diagrams that you could not otherwise create easily in Notepad or WordPad.

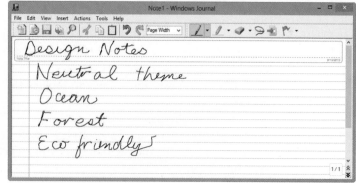

Figure 5.11 Use Journal to jot notes in your natural handwriting if you are a slow typist.

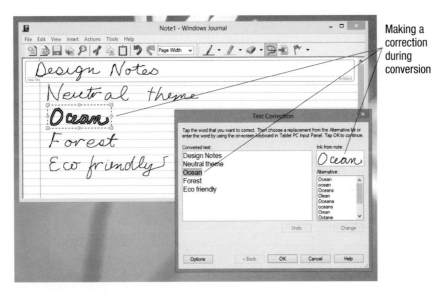

Making a correction during conversion

Figure 5.12 Convert Journal notes to editable text.

Using the Math Input Panel

The Math Input Panel works well with a tablet PC or graphics tablet. The Math Input Panel recognizes and converts the symbols and equations you draw into a nicely formatted digital equation that you can insert into documents you create, as shown in Figure 5.13. The Math Input Panel recognizes symbols and equation types commonly used in high school- and college-level math topics, such as calculus, functions, algebra, geometry, sets, and more. Students and professionals in a variety of fields, or anyone else who needs to create technical documents that include complex math, can benefit by attaching a graphics tablet to their computer and using the Math Input Panel.

Preview area

Buttons for working with the expression

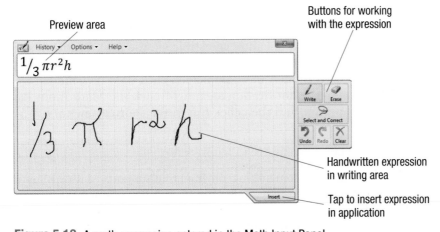

Handwritten expression in writing area

Tap to insert expression in application

Figure 5.13 A math expression entered in the Math Input Panel.

After you enter an expression in the Math Input Panel and Windows 8 digitizes the expression, you then can insert the converted expression into a document in another program. The target program must support a standard called **MathML** (Mathematical Markup Language), an XML-based language for creating and sharing mathematical expressions between programs. MathML was originally developed to facilitate the presentation of complex math on web pages, and it is now supported by a host of programs designed for editing and using math in documents, as well as OpenOffice, an open source software suite. (A list of supported programs is available via the W3C website: www.w3.org/Math.) Support for MathML was

MathML An XML-based standard for describing mathematical expressions in programs, published by the W3C Math Working Group (www.w3.org/Math)

incorporated into Microsoft Office Word 2007, and although Word uses its own similar XML-based standard for mathematical expressions, the transition between the two standards is seamless when you use the Math Input Panel and Word 2007, 2010, or 2013. Figure 5.14 shows an expression that has been inserted into a Word document from the Math Input Panel. You can edit and format the expression in Word and even use the Equation Tools Design tab on the ribbon to change the expression, as shown in Figure 5.14. The expression disappears from the Math Input Panel after being inserted, but you can reopen it there using the History menu.

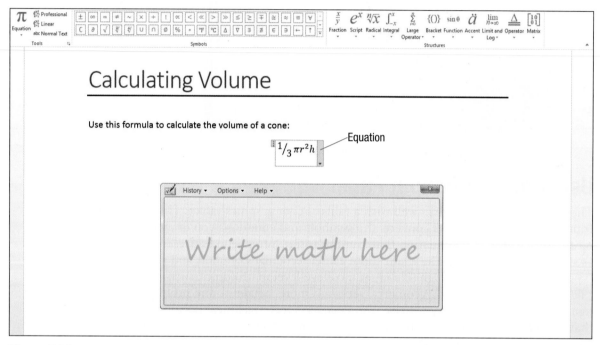

Figure 5.14 A math expression inserted into a Word document.

After you finish using the Math Input Panel and click its window Close (X) button, it remains an active application accessible via the notification area. This allows you to reuse any equation that is in the History for the current work session. To exit the Math Input Panel completely, click the Show hidden icons button at the left end of the notification area, right-click the Math Input Panel icon in the list that appears, and then click *Exit* in the shortcut menu.

Here's How ▶ **To create a math expression and insert it into a document:**

1. Open or create the document (in a program that supports MathML) into which you want to insert a math expression and then position the insertion point at the location where you would like the expression to appear.
2. Select the Search charm, scroll right, if needed, and then click Math Input Panel under *Windows Accessories*.
3. Using the pen or stylus, start writing in the writing area, which initially displays the message *Write math here*.
4. Tap the Undo button at the right to undo any stroke or character or the Redo button to redo actions.
5. Tap the Insert button at the lower right to insert the equation into the document.
6. Click the Math Input Panel window Close (X) button to hide the application.

▼ **Quick Fix**

No Graphics Tablet
You can use the Math Input Panel with a mouse if you lack a graphics tablet, but doing so is much more challenging. Changing a mouse setting such as the pointer speed might help you have greater success in drawing equations. Chapter 6 describes how to change mouse settings.

To edit an expression in the Math Input Panel:

1. Reopen the Math Input Panel by clicking the Show hidden icons button at the left side of the notification area and then click the *Math Input Panel* icon in the list that appears.
2. If needed, select the equation to edit from the History menu.
3. Tap the Select and Correct button at the right.

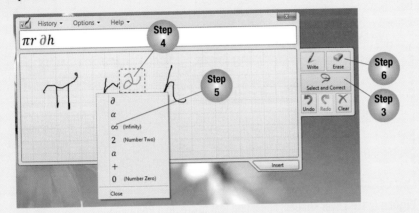

▼ **Quick Fix**

Wrong Interpretation
If the Math Input Panel interprets your input incorrectly, you can correct an individual symbol or character. Or, you can tap the Clear button at the right to clear the writing area and start all over again. Drawing separate strokes, such as a downward stroke and then a cross stroke for a t, can sometimes enhance recognition.

4. Drag with the pen to draw a circle around the symbol or character that you would like to correct. When the symbol or character turns red, it is selected for correction.
5. When you release the mouse button, a list of possible corrections appears. You can either tap one of the suggestions in the list, or draw a replacement character within the selection marquee.
6. To remove extraneous content, tap the Erase button at the right, and then drag over the content to erase in the writing area.
7. Click Write to resume adding more to the expression.

Note: *Some web browser programs cannot display MathML correctly. For example, Internet Explorer typically needs an added plug in (mini program) such as MathPlayer to add the needed support.*

Creating a Basic Picture with Paint ■■■■■■■■■■■■

The Paint app enables you to create basic graphics and save them in a variety of file formats, such as PNG (Portable Network Graphics, the default format) or JPEG (.jpeg or .jpg) file format. Because *compression* in these file formats makes the files fairly compact, many files on web pages are created or converted as PNG or JPEG files. The compression used in PNG files is lossless, meaning all the original data is contained in the compressed file, while the JPEG compression is lossy, meaning it can make smaller files by discarding some of the original data. Other file formats Paint can save, such as TIFF (Tagged Image File Format), use no compression at all.

> **compression** Using an algorithm that reduces file size

The Paint program includes several groups of tools on the Home tab on the ribbon that you can use to create lines, shapes, and text to build an image, as shown in Figure 5.15. The Home tab also includes selection tools, an eraser, a fill tool, a color picker, and a magnifier.

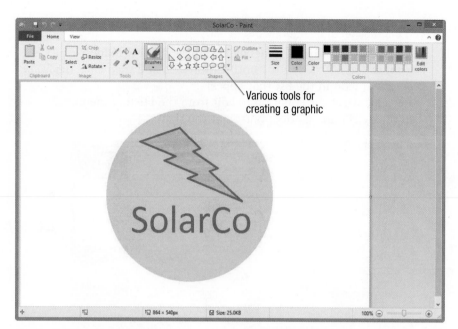

Figure 5.15 Layer shapes, lines, and text to create a Paint image.

Note: *Depending on the size of the Paint window, the Shapes choices appear as either a button or as a scrolling list that previews the shapes as shown above.*

Like most of the other applications discussed in this chapter, Paint is in the *Windows Accessories* section of applications. Select the Search charm, scroll right, if needed, and then click Paint under *Windows Accessories* to start Paint. Paint opens with a new, blank file, and you also can click the *New* command on the File tab to create a file.

One of the first things to do for each Paint file you create is to specify its size. Click the File tab and then click *Properties* to open the Image Properties dialog box, where you can specify the Width and Height for the file in units of *Inches*, *Centimeters*, or *Pixels*. You also can specify whether the image should be *Black and white* or *Color*. Click OK to finish establishing the image size.

Once you have created the image, you can use these techniques to add and work with its contents:

▼ **Quick Fix**

Undoing a Change
Because any change you make either removes or paints over existing pixels, press Ctrl + Z immediately to undo any unwanted change.

- **Add a line or shape.** Click the down-pointing arrow of the Shapes button in the Shapes group and then click the line or desired shape in the palette that appears. Use the Shape outline and Shape fill drop-downs to select the shape outline and fill type and the Size drop-down list to choose a line or outline width. Click the Color 1 button in the Colors group and then click the desired color for the line or shape outline. To select the color for the specified shape fill, click the Color 2 button in the Colors group, and then click the desired color for the line or shape fill. To create the shape or line, drag diagonally on the image. (Note that the Polygon and Curve tools require some extra techniques you can learn about in Help.) To make freeform lines, use the Pencil tool in the Tools group.

- **Add text.** Click the Text button in the Tools group. Click the Color 1 button in the Colors group, and then click the desired text color. Drag diagonally on the image to specify the area where you want the text to appear. Choose a font, font size, and attributes on the Text Tools Text tab on the ribbon, and then type the desired text.

- **Make and change a selection.** Click the down-pointing arrow of the Select button in the Image group and then click the type of selection you want to make. Drag on the image to make the selection. Drag the selection to move it, press Delete to delete it, or use another Image group choice such as Rotate or flip to make a change.
- **Erase and fill.** Click the Eraser tool, click the Size down-pointing arrow, select an eraser size, and then drag on the area to erase. Or, select a Color 2 color, click the Fill with color tool in the Tools group, and then click the area to fill. Note that the area to fill must be a continuous area of the same color.

  Remember to save your changes to any Paint file you create.

▼ **Quick Fix**

Deselecting
To deselect an object you have created, click another tool. Otherwise, you may inadvertently apply changes such as color changes to your new object.

Note: *Graphics programs that paint work differently from those that draw. Paint programs change individual dots or pixels of color in the image file, while draw programs create shapes based on easily changed shape outlines. Paint programs are also called raster programs, and draw programs are also called vector programs.*

Using the Snipping Tool

The Snipping Tool app enables you to capture an image of all or part of what is on the desktop (but not the Start screen). You can paste what you have snipped into another program or save it as a PNG, JPEG, GIF (another graphic format), or MHT (single-file web page) file. The Snipping Tool is a great way to share content between applications when doing so might otherwise not be possible, such as when copying and pasting directly between applications does not work. Images you create and save with the Snipping Tool can be inserted into a document or email message, for example, if you want to show a colleague how to complete an action in an application. The Snipping Tool is fairly easy and straightforward to use.

To capture a screen shot with the Snipping Tool:

◀ Here's How

1. Make sure that the information you want to capture appears on the desktop.
2. Select the Search charm, scroll right if needed, and then click Snipping Tool under *Windows Accessories* to open the Snipping Tool window.
3. To change the snip type from the default *Rectangular* type, click the New button down-arrow, and then click *Free-form Snip*, *Window snip*, or *Full-screen Snip*.

4. A full-screen snip will be taken immediately. For a window snip, click the window to snip. For the other snips, drag on the screen to select the area to snip.

5. When you release the mouse button, the snip appears in the Snipping Tool window. Use the tools there to save, copy, email, or annotate the snip. Click the New button to create a new snip.
6. Click the window Close (X) button to close the Snipping Tool. If prompted to save the snip, choose the appropriate option.

Exercise 3

Creating a Logo Using Math Input Panel, Snipping Tool, and Paint

1. Select the Search charm, scroll right, if needed, and then click Math Input Panel under *Windows Accessories* to open the Math Input Panel.
2. In the writing area, write the calculation for the area of a circle: πr^2. Correct the expression as needed.
3. Select the Search charm, scroll right if needed, and then click Snipping Tool under *Windows Accessories* to open the Snipping Tool.
4. If necessary, move the Math Input Panel down so you can see the Snipping Tool window. With the default (*Rectangular snip*) snip type selected, drag to select the expression in the preview area of the Math Input Panel.
5. Close the Math Input Panel by clicking its window Close (X) button. Click Show hidden icons in the notification area, right-click the Math Input Panel icon, and then click *Exit*.
6. Select the Search charm, scroll right, if needed, and then click Paint under *Windows Accessories* to launch the Paint application.
7. Click the File tab and then click *Properties*. Leave the Units set to Pixels, and enter 240 in both the *Width* and *Height* text boxes. Also, leave the *Color* option selected. Click OK.
8. Use the Taskbar to switch back to the Snipping Tool window, click its Copy button on the toolbar, and then click the window Close (X) button. Click No if prompted whether to save the snip.
9. Back in Paint, click the Paste button to paste the math expression snip. Drag the lower right handle of the pasted item's selection box to increase its size slightly. Move the mouse inside the selection, and when you see the four-arrow mouse pointer, drag the selection to center it about one-third of the way from the top of the picture file.
10. Add more text:
    a. Click the Text tool in the Tools group on the Home tab on the ribbon.
    b. Make sure that black is selected for the Color 1 box in the Colors group.
    c. Click below the pasted expression. Select *Times New Roman* from the font family list in the Font group on the Text Tools Text tab on the ribbon, and also change the font size to *28*.
    d. Type Media.
    e. Size and drag the selection box for the text so that the text is centered below the pasted expression. Do not worry if the position of the text is not perfect.
    f. Click outside the text to deselect it.

11. Add a circle shape:
    a. Click the Color 1 box and then click the Purple color (far right of the top row) in the Colors group.
    b. In the Shapes group, click the down-pointing arrow at the bottom of the Shapes button and then click the *Oval* shape. Or click the oval shape if the selection of shapes is visible in the Shapes group.
    c. Click Shape fill and then make sure that *No fill* is selected.
    d. Drag to draw a circle around all the logo text (Media), pressing and holding the Shift key as you drag to create a perfect circle.
    e. Resize and reposition the finished circle as needed and then click away from it.
12. Fill the circle:
    a. Click the Color 1 box and then click the light turquoise color (third from right of the middle row) in the Colors group.
    b. Click the Fill with color tool in the Tools group.
    c. Click inside the indigo circle to fill it. Also click in the background rectangle of the pasted math expression and the open parts of the *e*, *D*, and *a* to fill them. ***Hint: Zooming in helps make this process easier.***
13. Click the File tab and then click *Save*. Enter C05E03 as the file name, leave PNG (*.png) selected as the *Save as type*, and then click Save to save the file in the default Documents library.

    Note: *If your instructor asks you to save your file in another location, save it there instead of the Documents folder.*

14. Click the File tab and then click *Print*. Select the printer specified by your instructor, click Print to print the file, and then submit it to your instructor.
15. Close Paint and the file.

Copying Data between Files and Applications ▪▪▪

As you learned in Chapter 3, Windows 8 manages a special storage location in your system's memory called the *Clipboard*. In that chapter, you saw how you could cut or copy a file from a folder to the Clipboard and then paste the file into a new location from the Clipboard.

Just as you can use the Clipboard to copy or move files between folders, you can use the Clipboard to copy or move information from *within* a file to a location within another file—even a file within another program in many instances. For example, Figure 5.16 shows a graphic from Paint pasted into a document in WordPad. You can use one of two methods to accomplish this.

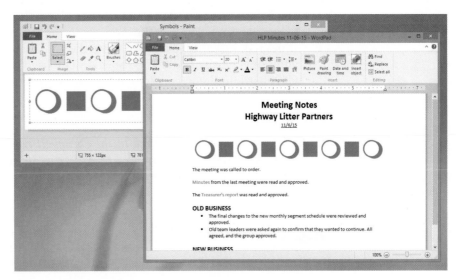

Figure 5.16 The selected graphic in Paint has been pasted into WordPad (right).

Using the Clipboard

Cutting and pasting information moves it from one location to another, removing the original selection and placing it in a new destination. Copying and pasting copies information, leaving the original selection in place and inserting a copy of that information in the destination that you specify.

Start the move or copy by selecting some text or cells (typically by dragging over them) or by clicking an object to select it. Use the *Cut*, *Copy*, and *Paste* commands in the Clipboard group on the ribbon or on the Edit menu to perform the move or copy. Cut or copy the selection, choose the destination for the cut or copied information, and then paste. While some applications offer toolbar buttons that provide shortcuts for copying and pasting, the following keyboard shortcuts work in almost all Windows-based applications, including those in Windows 8 itself:

- Cut   Ctrl + X
- Copy   Ctrl + C
- Paste   Ctrl + V

Here's How

To copy or move a selection with commands:

1. Open the file that holds the information to copy or move.
2. Select the information to copy or move by dragging over it (text and cells) or clicking it (graphics and other objects).
3. In a program that uses the ribbon, click the Copy or Cut button in the Clipboard group on the Home tab. Or, in a program that uses menus, click Edit and then click *Copy* to copy the selection or *Cut* to cut the selection. You also can press Ctrl + C to copy, press Ctrl + X to cut, or click any Copy or Cut button available on a toolbar.
4. Open or switch to the file where you want to place the copied or moved information. Or, if you are copying or moving within the same file, scroll to or display the location where you would like to place the copied or cut information.
5. Click to position the insertion point in the location, often called the destination location, where you want to insert the pasted information.
6. In a program that uses the ribbon, click the Paste button in the Clipboard group on the Home tab. Or, click Edit and then click *Paste* or press Ctrl + V. The selection appears in the destination location.
7. If desired, repeat Steps 4–6 to paste the Clipboard contents into additional destinations. The copied or cut selection remains on the Clipboard until you copy or cut another selection or shut down the system.

Note: *Be careful to examine the area in the document where you have cut or pasted a selection. In some cases, you may need to add extra spaces or lines so that the document looks good and reads correctly.*

T I P   Most Microsoft Office applications have their own special Clipboard called the Office Clipboard. The Office Clipboard can hold up to 24 different copied items, and you can select which item to paste into a destination document.

Using the Drag-and-Drop Method

Just as you can drag and drop a selected file between folder or library windows, you can drag and drop a selected text or object between documents. Use this technique if you prefer using the mouse to copy or move selections.

To copy or move a selection with the drag-and-drop method:

1. Open the file that holds the information to copy or move.
2. If you are copying or moving information to another file, open that file.
3. Size and position the open file (or application) windows on the desktop so that both windows are at least partially visible.
4. Return to the window of the file that contains the information to copy or move and select the information by dragging over it (text and cells) or clicking it (graphics and other objects).
5. Drag the selection from the source file over to the window of the destination file; when the destination file window becomes active, drag up and down as needed to position the insertion point at the specific location where you want to place the copied or cut information. Note that you have to press and hold the Ctrl key when you drag to copy. If you do so, the mouse pointer includes a plus sign for the copy; if not, the mouse pointer includes only a selection box.
6. Release the mouse button. The moved or copied information appears in the destination location.

Step 5

> **Quick Fix**
>
> **Dragging and Dropping within a Document**
> Drag-and-drop does not work as well if you need to move or copy information to different pages within a particular document. Often, the document will appear not to scroll as you are dragging and then jumps beyond the location where you wanted to stop. If this is the case, use the Edit menu commands or shortcuts, instead, to perform the copy or move.

Exercise 4

Using a Picture and Calculated Values in a Memo

1. Select the Search charm, scroll right, if needed, and then click WordPad under *Windows Accessories* to launch the WordPad application.
2. Type Memorandum and then press Enter.
3. Insert the date:
   a. Type Date.
   b. Press the Tab key.
   c. Click Date and time in the Insert group on the Home tab on the ribbon.
   d. In the *Available formats* list of the Date and Time dialog box, click the format that resembles *August 21, 2015*. (The formats reflect the current date.) Click OK.
   e. Press Enter.
4. Click Line spacing in the Paragraph group, and then click Add 10pt space after each paragraph to remove the check mark. Type the following text, pressing Enter twice after each line except the last one, adding your name in the place of *Student Name*, and pressing Tab after each colon:
   To: Al Smith, Pi R-Squared Media
   From: Student Name
   Re: New Logo
   The new logo is complete and appears below. At our hourly design rate of $45, the total fee comes to
5. Click the WordPad menu button and then click *Save*. Enter C05E04 as the file name and then click Save to save the file in the default Documents folder.

   Note: *If your instructor asks you to save your file in another location, save it there instead of the Documents folder.*

6. Select the Search charm, scroll right, if needed, and then click Paint under *Windows Accessories* to launch the Paint application.
7. Open the **C05E03** file you created in Exercise 3.
8. Click the bottom portion of the Select button (with the arrow) in the Image group on the Home tab on the ribbon, and then click *Select all* or press Ctrl + A. Paint selects the whole logo image.
9. Click the Copy button in the Clipboard group, or press Ctrl + C. This copies the selection to the Clipboard.
10. Click the File tab and then click *Exit,* or press Alt + F4 to close Paint. The copied information remains on the Clipboard.
11. Click at the end of the **C05E04** memo file, if needed, and press Enter twice.
12. Click the Paste button in the Clipboard group on the Home tab on the ribbon, or press Ctrl + V. The logo appears.
13. Select the Search charm, scroll right, if needed, and then click Calculator under *Windows Accessories* to launch the Calculator application.
14. Use the keyboard or click Calculator keys to multiply 2.5 x 45.
15. Press Ctrl + C, or choose Edit, *Copy* to copy the calculated amount to the Clipboard.
16. Click the window Close (X) button to close Calculator. The copied information remains on the Clipboard.
17. Click to position the insertion point at the end of the last line of the memo. Press the spacebar to add a space, if needed, and then click the Paste button on the ribbon.
18. Add a dollar sign at the left of the pasted value and a zero and period after.
19. Press Ctrl + S to save your changes to the memo file.
20. Click the File tab and then click *Print.* Select the printer specified by your instructor, click Print to print the file, and then submit it to your instructor.
21. Close WordPad and the file.

Using the Command Prompt ■■■■■■■■■■■■■■■■■■■

command prompt A line of text displayed by an operating system to indicate that it is prepared for you to type in commands

switch A forward slash and a letter or phrase code that specify a further aspect of how a command line command should run

The most prevalent operating system before Windows, called DOS, required the user to enter all commands at a ***command prompt***, which initially looked like **C:\>** on most systems. The user had to enter all commands as typed codes or words, some of which could be rather obscure, like *chkdsk*. As you might imagine, this command prompt or command line interface made computers daunting to use for many people who did not have the time to learn to navigate to folders from a prompt or to remember lists of commands.

The Windows operating system has done away with the command prompt—almost. In some instances, you may need to work from the command prompt, especially to perform certain system maintenance and troubleshooting tasks. For example, if your system is having trouble connecting to your school or company network, the Help Desk staff member might ask you to run the *ipconfig* command to gather some diagnostic information.

To use the command prompt, you open a command prompt window in Windows 8. Once that window is open, you type the desired command, along with any ***switches*** to specify another detail about how the command should run. A switch usually consists of a forward slash plus a letter, word, or phrase, all typed after the command on the command line. To see the available switches for a particular name, type the command name at the prompt, press spacebar, type /?, and then press Enter. For example, Figure 5.17 shows the information about switches that appears when you type **ipconfig** /? at the command prompt and then press Enter.

Figure 5.17 View the available switches for ipconfig by typing *ipconfig /?* and then pressing Enter.

By default, the command line shows the path to your user folder. To navigate to other folders and view files, you can use these commands at the command line:

- **cd** *directory name* Changes to a subfolder within the current folder.
- **mkdir** *directory name* Makes a new subfolder within the current folder.
- **cd.** Moves up a directory level.
- **dir** Lists the files and folders in the current folder.

If you include the /p switch, the listing pauses at each full window, so you can review the list and then press spacebar to continue.

If you include the /w switch, the command lists the files in a wide, multi-column format. You also can include both /p and /w.

You can run a variety of other commands from the command prompt, including but not limited to:

- **copy** *old file name new file path and name* Copies a file. To copy within the same folder, omit the path from the new file name, but do use a different file name.
- **del** *file name* Deletes the specified file. You can use wildcards with this command to delete multiple files.
- **help | more** (the center symbol is the pipe symbol, or the Shifted Backslash) Lists the available commands and pauses at a full window listing. Press spacebar to continue.

Note: *When you enter a file name at the command prompt, you must include the period and file name extension.*

Using Windows 8 Programs

In addition to running commands with a limited scope from the command prompt, you also must start certain full programs from the command prompt. For example, you type *mmc* at the command line to start the Microsoft Management Console, including the path and name of a snap-in module, if required. Typing *msinfo32* starts a System Information application, while *secpol.msc* starts the Local Security Policy application.

Here's How → **To open a command prompt window and use a command or start a program:**

1. Select the Search charm, scroll right, and then, under *Windows System,* click Command Prompt to open a command prompt window.
2. Type the command or program name, including any required switches and parameters (such as a file name).
3. Press Enter. The command executes or the program starts.
4. Enter additional commands, if required.
5. Click the command prompt window Close (X) button, or type exit and then press Enter to close the window when you finish.

Note: *It is possible to elevate a command prompt session to the administrator level, if needed. To do so, select the Search charm, scroll right, and then right-click Command Prompt. Click Run as administrator in the commands at the bottom of the screen and then click Yes in the User Account Control dialog box that appears.*

Exercise 5

Getting Help in the Command Prompt Window

1. Select the Search charm, scroll right, and then click Command Prompt under *Windows System.* The command prompt window opens.
2. Type help | more and then press Enter. (You can include spaces before and after the pipe symbol or leave them out. The command will run either way.)
3. Capture a screen shot and then save the file as **C05E05**.
4. Press the spacebar and then review the next screen of commands.
5. Press the spacebar as many times as needed to scroll to the end of the list.
6. Type exit and then press Enter to close the command prompt window.
7. Submit the file to your instructor.

Working with the New Windows 8 Apps ▪▪▪▪▪▪▪▪

You learned in Chapter 1 that the new style of Windows 8 apps do not follow the same windowed model as the desktop applications. Each Windows 8 app fills the screen when displayed, and the commands typically remain hidden until you need them. To contrast with what you have learned so far in the chapter, take another look at how the new apps work. In some instances, you will have a choice between nearly identical Windows 8 apps and desktop apps. For example, Windows 8 includes an Internet Explorer app in the new style as well as the Internet Explorer desktop app you can launch from the Taskbar. You can choose the version of the app that feels most comfortable for you to use or is most accessible from your current location—the Start screen or the desktop.

You can customize both the Start screen and Taskbar to show the apps that you want. You will learn to do this in Chapter 6.

Starting and Exiting the App

You saw in Chapter 1 that you can click the tile for an app on the Start screen to launch the app. However, as you install an increasing number of apps, you may have more than you can reasonably show on your Start screen. In such a case, you can use the Search charm to find and start a Windows 8 app, just as for desktop apps.

Here's How

To start and exit a Windows 8 app:

1. Move the mouse pointer over the lower right corner of the Start screen or desktop, or swipe in from the right edge if you are using touch.
2. Click or tap the Search charm.
3. Leave Apps selected in the Search pane at the right and then begin typing the name of the program. The screen lists matching programs, so you can click the one you want.
   OR
   Click the app in the Search pane, scrolling down first if needed.
   OR
   Click the program name under Apps at the left side of the screen. The program opens on the desktop.
4. Swipe or drag down from the top to the bottom of the screen to exit the app.

Finding the App Commands

You learned in Chapter 1 that there are three methods for displaying the commands in the new Windows 8 apps:

- Select an item to make the commands appear at the bottom.
- Right-click an open space in the app.
- Drag or swipe in from the top or bottom edge of the screen.

The bar with commands that appears is called the ***app bar***. As you explore more apps, you will learn that each has its own unique commands and capabilities. Unlike the consistent menu or ribbon structure built into desktop applications, the new apps put the content front and center. Having the commands remain hidden is intended to encourage the user to interact more directly with the content on the screen.

In some cases, clicking on the screen brings up additional choices or navigational aids not found on the app bar. For example, in the Photos app, clicking an opened photo displays an arrow button at the upper left so that you can move back to the picture thumbnails.

To dismiss the app bar, right-click again on the screen.

app bar The bar that displays available command choices at the top or bottom of an app when you display commands

Viewing All Open Apps ■■■■■■■■■■■■■■■■■■■■■■ ■■ ■

The fact that the new apps occupy the entire screen does not mean that you can run only one app at a time in Windows 8. In fact, you can run multiple Windows 8 apps and multiple desktop apps at any given time. Switching between your desktop and open apps is easy.

When working in an app or on the desktop, press Ctrl + Windows logo key ⊞ + Tab, point to the left side of the screen with the mouse, or swipe in from the left. Thumbnails of the open apps and desktop apps appear at the left, as shown in Figure 5.18. The desktop appears as one of the tiles in the pane; you can click it to return to the desktop and your open apps there, click a tile for any other app that appears to switch back to that app, or click the Start tile at the bottom to go back to the Start screen. You also can press Ctrl + Windows logo key ⊞ + Tab repeatedly to highlight the desired app tile or the Start tile, release the keys, and then press Enter to display the selected item.

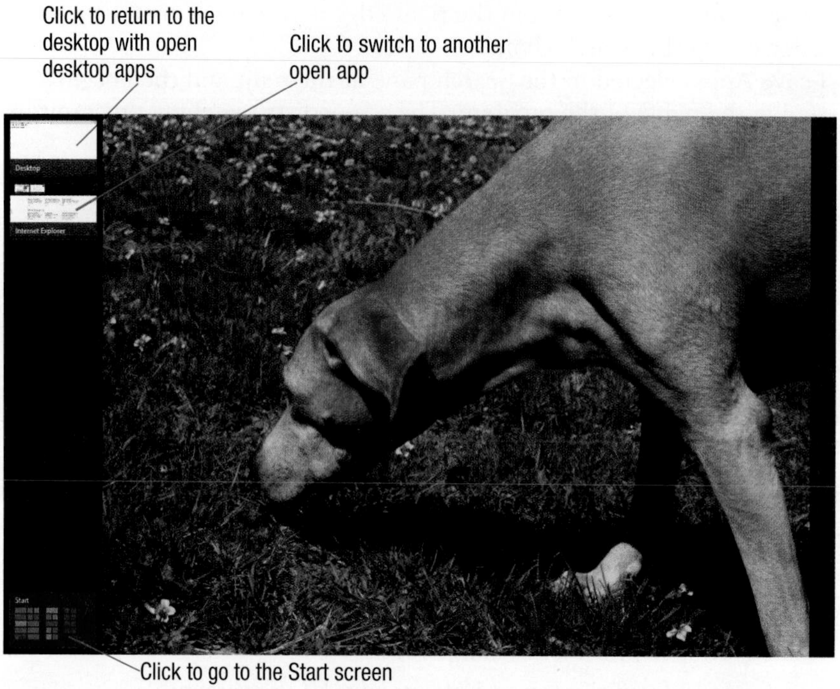

Click to return to the desktop with open desktop apps

Click to switch to another open app

Click to go to the Start screen

Figure 5.18 Switch from a new Windows 8 app back to the desktop, and vice versa.

T I P You can right-click an app at the left and then click *Close* to shut it down.

The Alt + Tab keyboard combination enables you to switch between open applications, as in previous Windows versions, and also cycles through open apps in Windows 8. Press and hold Alt + Tab. Press an arrow key or repeatedly press the Tab key to highlight the desired window in the task-switching window that appears (shown in Figure 5.19) and then release all keyboard keys.

Open desktop apps

Desktop

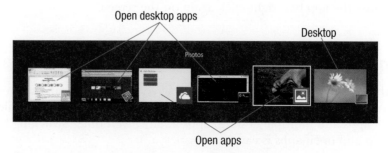

Open apps

Figure 5.19 Alt + Tab enables you to switch between open apps.

The final way to cycle between open Windows apps and the desktop is to move your mouse pointer over the upper left corner of the screen, whether you are working on the desktop or in a Windows 8 app. An app tile appears there, as shown in Figure 5.20. Click repeatedly until the app you want or the desktop appears on the screen. Drag down to tile all of the open apps.

Figure 5.20 Cycle between apps by clicking at the upper left corner of the screen.

Exercise 6

Opening Windows 8 Apps, and App Switching

1. From the desktop, select the Search charm and then click Store in the listing of the new Windows 8 apps at the left.
2. Select the Search charm and then, in the Search pane at the right, click the Internet Explorer app. Press Esc to close the Search pane, if needed.
3. Press Ctrl + Windows logo key 🪟 + Tab.
4. Capture a screen shot and then save the file as **C05E06S04**. Return to the Internet Explorer screen and then redisplay the app tiles or thumbnails at the left.
5. Click the Store tile in the pane.
6. Point at the upper left corner of the screen to display the tile for the Internet Explorer app.
7. Capture a screen shot and then save the file as **C05E06S07**. Return to the Store screen, point at the upper left corner again, and then drag down to display the tiles for all the open apps.
8. Click the Internet Explorer app.
9. Close the Internet Explorer app.
10. Point at the upper left corner of the Start screen and then click once to return to Store.
11. Close the Store app.
12. Click the Desktop tile on the Start screen to return to the desktop.
13. Submit your screen shots to your instructor.

CHAPTER SUMMARY

- Use the Windows 8 Search charm to find and start a program.
- Use the New command (Ctrl + N) on the File tab or menu at the left end of the ribbon to start a new file. If prompted, select a file type or template.
- Use the Save command (Ctrl + S) on the File tab or menu at the left end of the ribbon to save and name a file. Use the Save As command when you want to save an existing file under a new name, and press Ctrl + S to save ongoing work to an existing file.
- Click the window Close (X) button to close the file, program, or folder window.
- Use the Print Preview command on the File tab or menu to review a document before printing.

- Choose the Print command (Ctrl + P) on the File tab or menu to start a print job, choose a printer and other settings such as the number of copies in the Print dialog box, and then click Print or OK.
- Print to the Microsoft XPS Document Writer printer (driver) to create an OpenXPS file.
- Print to the FAX printer (driver) or start Windows Fax and Scan application to send a fax.
- Use Calculator to calculate mathematical and scientific values. Input values and operators with the keyboard or its 10-key keypad, if available.
- Calculator offers new Programmer and Statistics modes with conversion and calculation functions.
- Calculator also includes new converters and worksheets for performing common activities like calculating a mortgage payment.
- Use Notepad to create plain text (.txt) documents.
- Use WordPad to create Rich Text Format (.rtf) documents, which save text and paragraph formatting.
- Use Windows Journal to capture handwritten notes from a tablet or graphics tablet and convert those notes to digital text that you can copy and paste to other applications.
- The Math Input Panel works with a tablet PC or graphics tablet and converts math expressions you write into digital versions that you can paste into other applications.
- Use the Paint program to create simple graphics files saved by default in the PNG (.png) format.
- Tools on the ribbon in WordPad and Paint enable you to format text and objects.
- The Snipping Tool enables you to capture a screen shot of all or part of what is on the screen and to save that content for use in other documents.
- To make a selection in a document, drag over text or cells, or click the item to select.
- To move or copy with the Clipboard: Ctrl + X to cut, Ctrl + C to copy, and Ctrl + V to paste, switching to the destination window and clicking to position the insertion point before pasting.
- To move or copy using drag-and-drop: hold down the Ctrl key to copy.
- Open the command prompt window to enter operating system commands and start programs at the command prompt.
- When using the command prompt, type the desired command along with any switches or parameters and then press Enter.
- Including the /? switch with a command at the command prompt displays information about using the command, including switches you can use with it.
- Use the Search charm to start the new Windows 8 apps. Drag or swipe from the top of the screen down to exit the app.
- Right-click a blank area in an app to display or hide its commands.
- Press Ctrl + Windows logo key ⊞ + Tab and then click an app tile at the left to switch to that app or the desktop. Alt + Tab also cycles through both types of apps, and pointing to the upper left corner of the screen and clicking also cycles between apps.

CONCEPTS CHECK

Completion: Answer the following questions in a Word document.

Part 1

Multiple Choice

1. To start a program, use the _____ charm.
   a. Search
   b. Share
   c. Start
   d. Devices

2. To create a file, choose the _____ command.
   a. Open
   b. New
   c. Save
   d. Print

3. To save a file, choose the _____ command.
   a. Open
   b. New
   c. Save
   d. Print

4. To work with a file you have previously saved and closed, choose the _____ command.
   a. Open
   b. New
   c. Save
   d. Print

5. Use _____ to see how a file will look when printed.
   a. Print Review
   b. Print Overview
   c. Print Preview
   d. Print Purview

6. To select a printer and create a print job, choose the _____ command.
   a. Open
   b. New
   c. Save
   d. Print

7. To copy the selected text or object to the Clipboard, press Ctrl + _____.
   a. X
   b. C
   c. D
   d. V

8. To copy a selection from one location to another with drag-and-drop, hold down the _____ key as you drag.
   a. Ctrl
   b. Alt
   c. Shift
   d. Insert

9. Which program do you use to create a plain text (.txt) file?
   a. WordPad
   b. TextPad
   c. Notepad
   d. PlainPad

10. Which program do you use to add numbers?
    a. PlusPad
    b. Add
    c. Command Prompt
    d. Calculator

Part 2

Short Answer

11. Why start a program?

12. What happens in some programs when you select the New command?

13. When do you assign a name and location for a stored file?

14. How do you display a worksheet in Calculator?

15. Explain the difference between a plain text (.txt) and RTF (.rtf) file, and name the programs used to create each.

16. Name one of the primary tabs that appears in most applications with the ribbon.

17. Describe the difference between copying and moving a selection.

18. How do you create an expression in the Math Input Panel?

19. Explain how to open the command prompt window.

20. Name one way to switch between open apps.

SKILLS CHECK

Save all solution files to the default Documents folder or any alternative folder specified by your instructor.

Guided Check

Assessment 1

Starting and Exiting Programs

1. Start Windows Journal.
   a. Select the Search charm.
   b. Scroll right.
   c. Click Windows Journal under *Windows Accessories*.
2. Start WordPad.
   a. Select the Search charm.
   b. Scroll right.
   c. Click WordPad under *Windows Accessories*.
3. Start Notepad.
   a. Select the Search charm.
   b. Type no.
   c. Click *Notepad* in the Apps list.
4. Start Calculator.
   a. Select the Search charm.
   b. Type calc.
   c. Press Enter.
5. Cascade the open windows.
   a. Right-click the Taskbar.
   b. Click *Cascade windows*.
   c. Capture a screen shot, save the file as **C05A01**, and then submit it to your instructor.
6. Close the Windows Journal window.
   a. Click the Taskbar button for the window.
   b. Click the window Close (X) button.
7. Close the Calculator window.
   a. Click the Taskbar button for the window.
   b. Click the window Close (X) button.
8. Close the Notepad window.
   a. Click the Taskbar button for the window.
   b. Click the File menu.
   c. Click *Exit*.
9. Close the WordPad window.
   a. Click the File tab.
   b. Click *Exit*.

Assessment 2

Creating and Saving a File

1. Start WordPad.
   a. Select the Search charm.
   b. Type wordpad.
   c. Press Enter.

2. Type the following text into the document, pressing Enter once after the first two paragraphs and twice at the end of the last line:
Saving a File
Saving a file enables you to specify both a file name and disk and folder in which to save the file. Use the Save command or press Ctrl + S to start the save.
Use the Open command or press Ctrl + O to open the dialog box you can use to choose a file to reopen.
3. Select the first line in the file, and then apply formatting.
   a. Open the *Font family* drop-down list in the Font group on the Home tab on the ribbon and then click *Arial Black*.
   b. Open the *Font size* drop-down list in the Font group and then click *20*.
4. Apply bold to the selected words in the body paragraphs, as shown below:
Saving a file enables you to specify both a file name and disk and folder in which to save the file. Use the <u>Save</u> command or press <u>Ctrl + S</u> to start the save.
Use the <u>Open</u> command or press <u>Ctrl + O</u> to open the dialog box you can use to choose a file to reopen.
5. Save the file as **Saving**.
   a. Click the File tab.
   b. Click *Save*.
   c. Type Saving.
   d. Navigate to the library or folder to save to, if required.
   e. Click Save.
6. Click the File tab and then click *Exit* to close WordPad.
7. Submit the file to your instructor.

 Assessment 3 Opening, Editing, and Printing a File
1. Start WordPad.
   a. Select the Search charm.
   b. Type wordpad.
   c. Press Enter.
2. Open the Chapter 5 Student Data Files folder. Ask your instructor for assistance, if needed. Open the **WordPad Document Formats** file.
   a. Click the File tab.
   b. Click *Open*.
   c. Navigate to the folder with the student data files for this book.
   d. Double-click the *WordPad Document Formats* file.
3. Copy the text in the file.
   a. Press Ctrl + A to select all the text in the document.
   b. Press Ctrl + C.
4. Open the **Saving** file.
   a. Click the File tab.
   b. Click *Open*.
   c. Navigate to the folder where you saved the file in Assessment 2.
   d. Double-click the *Saving* file. (Do not save the **WordPad Document Formats file,** if prompted.)
5. Add text to the end of the document.
   a. Press Ctrl + End to move the insertion point to the end of the document.
   b. Press Backspace to remove the extra paragraph.
   c. Type WordPad can open and resave documents in other formats.
   d. Press Enter.
6. Paste the copied text into the **Saving** file by pressing Ctrl + V.

7. Reformat the paragraph text.
   a. Drag over all paragraph text, including the pasted text, to select it. (Do not select the first title line.)
   b. Open the *Line spacing* drop-down list in the Paragraph group on the Home tab on the ribbon and then click *1.0*.
   c. Click outside of the text to deselect it.
8. Save the edited file with a new name.
   a. Click the File tab.
   b. Click *Save As*.
   c. Type Saving 2.
   d. Navigate to the folder to save to, if required.
   e. Click Save.
9. Preview the printout.
   a. Click the File tab.
   b. Click the right-pointing arrow beside *Print*.
   c. Click *Print Preview*.
   d. After reviewing the preview, click Close print preview on the Print preview tab on the ribbon.
10. Print the file.
    a. Click the File tab.
    b. Click *Print*.
    c. Choose the printer specified by your instructor.
    d. Click Print to send the printout to the printer and then submit it to your instructor.
11. Click the File tab and then click *Exit* to close WordPad.

Assessment 4

Creating an OpenXPS Document

1. Start WordPad.
   a. Select the Search charm.
   b. Scroll right.
   c. Under *Windows Accessories*, click WordPad.
2. Open the **Saving 2** file.
   a. Click the File tab.
   b. Click *Open*.
   c. Navigate to the folder where you saved the file in Assessment 3.
   d. Double-click the ***Saving 2*** file.
3. Print the file as an OpenXPS document.
   a. Click the File tab.
   b. Click *Print*.
   c. Click *Microsoft XPS Document Writer* in the *Select Printer* list.
   d. Click Print to send the printout to the printer.
   e. Type Saving 3.
   f. Navigate to the folder to save to, if required.
   g. Click Save.
4. To view the OpenXPS document, immediately click or tap the pop-up message that appears in the upper right corner. (If you do not see the message, open the Windows Reader app using the Search charm, right-click, and then click *Open* to navigate to and open the file.)
5. Drag down from the top of the Windows Reader screen to close the file.
6. Click the Desktop tile on the Start screen to return to the desktop.
7. Click the File tab and then click *Exit* to close WordPad.
8. Submit the file to your instructor.

On Your Own

Assessment

5

Calculating and Pasting Values

1. Start Notepad.
2. Start Calculator.
3. Perform the following calculation, using the appropriate keyboard keys for the math operators:

   $(197+202) \div (1+2.45) =$
4. Copy the result, paste it into the first line of the Notepad file, and then press Enter.
5. Switch back to Calculator and clear the previous total.
6. Find the square root of 236.
7. Copy the result, paste it into the next line of the Notepad file, and then press Enter.
8. Switch back to Calculator and clear the previous total.
9. Select *Scientific* from the View menu.
10. Find 11^3 (11 to the 3rd power or 11 cubed).
11. Copy the result and then close Calculator.
12. Paste the result into the next line of the Notepad file.
13. Save the file as **Calculations**.
14. Submit the file to your instructor.

Assessment

6

Snipping and Editing a Graphic

1. Open the File Explorer on the desktop.
2. Open the folder that holds the student data files for this chapter.
3. Right-click the Waterfall file, point to *Open with* in the shortcut menu, and then click *Paint* to open it in Windows Paint.
4. Resize the Paint window to see more of the image, if needed.
5. Start the Snipping Tool application.
6. Snip a rectangular area at least 2 inches in height and width from the picture.
7. Click the Copy button on the Snipping Tool toolbar.
8. Switch back to Paint.
9. Create a new file, and do not save changes to the sample image, if prompted.
10. Click the Paste button in the Clipboard group on the Home tab.
11. Click the Text button in the Tools group on the Home tab, and change the Color 1 color to one that will stand out on the image background.
12. Click the image, type Snip!, and then size and position the text as desired.
13. Save the file as **Snipped Image** in the PNG format, in the folder or library specified by your instructor.
14. Submit the file to your instructor.
15. Close the open applications and windows. Do not save the Snipping Tool content if prompted.

Assessment

7

Using the Command Prompt and Windows 8 Apps

1. Select the Search charm, scroll right, and then click Command Prompt under *Windows System*.
2. Type secpol.msc and then press Enter. Click *Continue* in the User Account Control dialog box, if it appears. (If the command doesn't initially work, type cd.. and press Enter twice to move to the root directory.)
3. Select the Search charm and then click Weather. If a message appears asking to use your location, click Block and then Cancel.
4. Press Ctrl + Windows logo key ⊞ + Tab.

5. Capture a screen shot of the desktop, save it as **C05A07**, and then submit it to your instructor.
6. Close Paint, point at the upper left corner of the screen, and then click the tile that appears to return to the Weather app.
7. Press Alt + Tab to return to the desktop.
8. Press Alt + Tab again to return to Weather.
9. Close the Weather app.
10. Click the Desktop tile on the Start screen to return to the desktop.
11. Close the Local Security Policy window.
12. Type exit and then press Enter to close the command prompt window (You may have to click the window first to activate it.).

Assessment 8

Partner Activity: Writing and Printing a Report

1. Find a partner and pick a topic about which you would like to write a brief report. Pick a topic for which a Paint graphic would be appropriate.
2. Decide which of you will enter the text and which will create the graphic.
3. Open WordPad and then create the text. Decide on the contents together while the designated typist enters the information. Save the file as **Assessment 8 Report**.
4. Now switch users, and share ideas on how to create the illustration for the report in Paint. Only the designated "artist" should create the Paint graphic. Save the file as **Assessment 8 Graphic**.
5. Press Ctrl + A and then Ctrl + C to copy the graphic in Paint.
6. Switch back to the WordPad document, click to position the insertion point at the destination location, and then press Ctrl + V.
7. Add both of your names at the bottom of the document and then apply any text and paragraph formatting desired.
8. Save the file.
9. Print a copy of the file and then submit it to your instructor.

CHALLENGE PROJECT

As a member of the sales team of your company, you have been asked to develop a proposed schedule and agenda for an upcoming meeting with a client and to send a memo to the sales team members to gather feedback and move the plan along.

1. Open Paint and then create a picture of the product (or service) that you will be presenting to the client. For example, you can combine shapes to create a car, cell phone, or coffee cup. (Do not worry about creating a perfect drawing. Developing advanced drawing skills can take months or years.)
2. Open WordPad and then create a memo document with the proposed agenda, including your name on the *From* line. Copy the product image from Paint and then paste it into the memo document.
3. Save the document as **Challenge Client Meeting Agenda**.
4. Imagine that you need to post the document to the Web for the clients involved, so "print" it as an OpenXPS file. Because some of the sales people in your company's group will not have access to a hard copy or the Web, start the process for faxing the file to see how it works. (Note that you probably will be unable to send a fax, so close the window after reviewing how the fax would look.)
5. Submit the files to your instructor.

CHAPTER 6

Customizing the Desktop and Start Screen

PERFORMANCE OBJECTIVES

Upon successful completion of Chapter 6, you will be able to:

- Use the Control Panel to change settings
- Change how the keyboard and mouse work
- Change the desktop background, color scheme, theme, and icon size
- Work with display settings
- Specify a screen saver
- Adjust system sounds
- Control icons on the desktop
- Adjust the Start screen and its tiles
- Change the Taskbar and its notifications
- Use gadgets
- Make the system accessible for users with disabilities
- Specify or synchronize the system date and time

Changing the appearance and function of a desk can take real work. You can refinish it, maybe take out or reconfigure some drawers, and add new handles. But those tasks all require work and leave the desk unusable for a while. Because Windows 8 offers a virtual desktop, in contrast, you can change its looks and some aspects of its operation in mere moments. You can customize the overall appearance of the desktop or fine-tune individual items such as the Taskbar or the system time. You can access most of the choices you need for customizing the desktop in the Control Panel or on the desktop itself. You also can customize the Start screen to determine which programs you can access there and how the tiles function.

Understanding the Control Panel ▪▪▪▪▪▪▪▪▪▪▪▪▪▪▪

The Windows 8 Control Panel provides a central location where you can access and change system settings. You use the Control Panel to perform system operations, from adding users to adjusting the desktop's appearance to adding and removing hardware. Many of the tasks you will learn about later in this chapter and throughout the book require that you can move around and find desired settings in the Control Panel.

Opening the Control Panel

There are two ways to open the Control Panel. From the Start screen or desktop: you can use the Search charm, scroll right, and then, under Windows System, click Control Panel; or, from the desktop, select the Settings charm and then click Control Panel under Settings, as shown in Figure 6.1. The Control Panel window opens.

Figure 6.1 Use the Settings charm to open the Control Panel.

The Control Panel organizes its settings into categories to make them easier to find. Figure 6.2 shows the Control Panel home screen, which shows categories by default. You will find an icon and accompanying link for each of these categories:

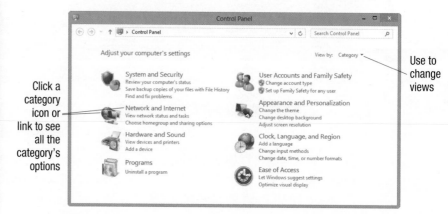

Figure 6.2 The Control Panel initially shows categories of options.

- **System and Security.** This category offers choices for viewing system performance, viewing hardware information and working with hardware, making backups, and viewing and adjusting system performance-related settings, among other settings. It also includes the Action Center for protecting, updating, troubleshooting, and recovering the system, as well as other tools for maintaining the system, such as Windows Update and administrative tools.

- **Network and Internet.** Go here to access the Network and Sharing Center, where you can view and set up your network, as well as handle tasks like working with a network homegroup and changing Internet browser settings.

- **Hardware and Sound.** Change system sounds and work with hardware such as the mouse, keyboard, scanners, cameras, sound, and the display using settings from this category, as well as working with some specialized settings such as power settings, pen or touchpad settings, tablet PC settings, and location settings.

- **Programs.** In this category, find the choices for installing and uninstalling programs and Windows 8 features, and specifying default programs.

- **User Accounts and Family Safety.** As you learned in Chapter 1, this category in the Control Panel provides the settings for working with user accounts. It also offers parental control settings, among other choices.

- **Appearance and Personalization.** The choices here enable you to make the desktop your own—choose from fun stuff like specifying your own background and adding fonts. Make the system friendlier by customizing the Taskbar, Start menu, and folder settings.

- **Clock, Language, and Region.** Look in this category when you need to make sure the system is set to the proper date, time, and time zone, or even to work with language settings for Windows 8 and the keyboard.

- **Ease of Access.** Use the settings found in this category to customize the system for a user with special needs. For example, you can replace sounds with visual cues or turn on speech recognition.

Some settings appear in multiple categories. For example, Power Options choices appear in both the *System and Security* and *Hardware and Sound* categories. This enables you to find the desired settings via any of the categories to which they are relevant. Other options are also duplicated via the Start screen's PC settings app. You will get familiar with some of these options in the section "Customizing the Start Screen."

Many Control Panel settings, such as the *Appearance and Personalization* settings, apply to the currently signed-in user only. This enables each user to set up the desktop to work exactly as he or she prefers.

You cannot access all of the Control Panel options via the Category view. To find these options, open the *View by* list and then click either *Large icons* or *Small icons*. (Choosing *Category* redisplays the categories.) Other Control Panel settings are accessed most easily by right-clicking the desktop. This book will use the easiest method for selecting the particular Control Panel settings under discussion.

Working with the Control Panel Window

The Control Panel home window (shown in Figure 6.2) enables you to move quickly to the system task that you want to perform. Clicking a category icon displays all of the available subcategories and tasks in the category. However, if the task you want to perform appears on the Control Panel home window below a category name, you can click the task link to begin the task immediately.

After you click a category icon, the Control Panel displays lower-level categories and the tasks within each of them. For example, Figure 6.3 shows how the Control Panel appears when you click the *Appearance and Personalization* category icon. You can click a task link under any category to start performing that task. To back up to the Control Panel home window, either click the Back (left arrow) button as you would for any Explorer window, click the *Control Panel Home* link at the top of the list at the left side of the window, or click the Up to "*Control Panel*" button to the left of the Address bar. Pressing Alt + Up Arrow on the keyboard also works. If the task you want does not appear in the selected category, click another category in the list at the left side of the window.

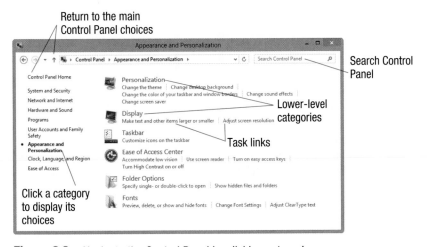

Figure 6.3   Navigate the Control Panel by clicking categories and tasks.

When you finish your work with the Control Panel, click the window's Close (X) button to close it.

Changing Keyboard and Mouse Settings ■■■■■■

As *user input devices*, the mouse and keyboard enable you to give commands to and enter information into your computer. Using these devices effectively requires manual dexterity in the hands and wrists. Because dexterity levels vary from user to user and are affected by other factors such as whether one is left-handed or right-handed, Windows 8 provides settings for adjusting how the mouse and keyboard respond to user actions.

In the Keyboard Properties dialog box (shown in Figure 6.4), you can adjust the *Repeat delay* slider (the length of time that you can press and hold a key before the computer starts repeating the character on the screen) and the *Repeat rate* slider (how quickly a character repeats when you press and hold a key) for the keyboard. Increasing the keyboard repeat delay and reducing the repeat rate can reduce repeated characters for any user with stiffness in the hands and fingers. You also can drag the *Cursor blink rate* slider to the left to slow down the flashing speed of the vertical insertion point, making it easier to see. Note that touch-enabled systems do let you display and use an on-screen keyboard.

The Mouse Properties dialog box (shown in Figure 6.5) offers four tabs of settings that may be active (the fifth tab is for the driver), depending on the type of mouse (or touchpad or trackball) installed with the system. Depending on the mouse or other input device you have installed and whether it includes its own software, you may even see additional tabs in the Mouse Properties dialog box. Some setting names also might vary.

Figure 6.4 You can change the repeat delay and repeat rate for the keyboard, as well as the cursor blink rate.

Figure 6.5 You can set up the mouse for a left-handed user, choose new pointers, and more.

The default tabs and the settings they offer include:

■ **Buttons.** You can check the *Switch primary and secondary buttons* check box to flip the functions of the left and right mouse buttons, making the right mouse button the primary button for clicking and double-clicking. This makes the mouse easier for a left-handed person to use. You also can drag the *Speed* slider to change how fast a user must perform a double-click for the system to recognize it; slower speeds work better for users with stiff fingers. Marking the *Turn on ClickLock* check box enables you to make selections or drag by briefly pressing and holding the mouse. You can then reposition the mouse and click to finish the drag or select. Use the Settings button to control how long you must press and hold the mouse to activate ClickLock.

■ **Pointers.** On this tab, you can choose different mouse pointers, either for functional or fun reasons. In Windows, the mouse pointer's appearance changes to cue you about the current activity going on, such as when the mouse is in the right position to resize a window. Use the *Scheme* drop-down list to choose new pointers overall. For example, you can choose one of the schemes with (Large) in its name to make the pointers easier to see on the screen. To change any individual pointer, click the pointer in the *Customize* list and then click the Browse button. Use the Browse dialog box that appears to find and select a new pointer and then click Open. Clicking Use Default returns a pointer to its original appearance. If you have changed several pointers, you can use the Save As button in the Scheme area to save your own scheme. Activating (marking) *Enable pointer shadow* places a shadow under the pointer, making it easier to see on the screen.

■ **Pointer Options.** The options on this tab control the mouse pointer's Motion, Snap To behavior, and on-screen Visibility. Drag the *Select a pointer speed* slider under Motion to make the pointer move faster or slower relative to how quickly you drag the mouse. Choose a slower speed for users who have trouble using the mouse. If you have the pointer speed set to a fast speed, leave *Enhance pointer precision* checked so that the mouse will move less quickly when you move the mouse more slowly or stop it. To save work, click *Automatically move pointer to the default button in a dialog box*; this enables a feature that snaps the mouse to the button. To make the pointer easier for those with vision difficulties to see, click *Display pointer trails* to enable this feature, and *Hide pointer while typing* to disable it. To enable a way to highlight a lost pointer on the screen, click the *Show location of pointer when I press the CTRL key* check box.

■ **Wheel.** This final tab of settings applies only when a wheel mouse or touchpad that mimics wheel behaviors is installed on the system. To change the Vertical Scrolling speed for the scroll wheel button when you move it, either change the specified number of lines under *The following number of lines at a time* or click the *One screen at a time* option to select it, instead. If the wheel also has Horizontal Scrolling capability, you can change the setting under *Tilt the wheel to scroll the following number of characters at a time*, as desired.

Here's How

To work with keyboard and mouse settings in the Control Panel:

1. Select the Search charm, scroll right, and then, under *Windows System*, click *Control Panel*.
2. In the search box, type keyboard.
3. Click the *Keyboard* link or icon.
4. Change settings on the Speed tab of the Keyboard Properties dialog box (shown in Figure 6.4) as desired and then click OK.
5. In the Control Panel window, click the Back button.
6. Click the *Hardware and Sound* category icon or link.
7. Under *Devices and Printers*, click the *Mouse* link.
8. Change the settings on various tabs of the Mouse Properties dialog box (shown in Figure 6.5) as desired and then click OK.
9. Close the Control Panel window.

Note: When you have a graphics tablet attached to the system or the system is a tablet PC, the Hardware and Sound *category in the Control Panel offers the lower-level* Pen and Touch *and* Tablet PC Settings *categories that you can use to adjust how user input works for those devices. For example, under* Pen and Touch, *you can choose what pen actions will represent right-clicking and double-clicking. Under* Tablet PC Settings, *you can calibrate the screen and adjust where menus appear on the screen for right-handed or left-handed pen usage.*

Exercise 1

Using the Control Panel to Slow Down the Keyboard and Mouse

1. Start Windows, click the Desktop tile, select the Settings charm, and then click *Control Panel* to open the Control Panel home window.
2. In the search box, type keyboard.
3. Click the Keyboard icon to open the Keyboard Properties dialog box.
4. Drag the *Repeat delay, Repeat rate*, and *Cursor blink rate* sliders all the way to the left.
5. Capture a screen shot and then save the file as **C06E01S05**.
6. Click Cancel to close the dialog box without applying those changes.
7. Click the Back button to return to the Control Panel home window.
8. Click the *Hardware and Sound* link or icon.
9. Click the *Mouse* link under *Devices and Printers* to open the Mouse Properties dialog box.
10. Drag the *Speed* (or Double-Click Speed) slider on the Buttons tab all the way to the left and then click the *Turn on ClickLock* check box to check it.
11. Capture a screen shot and then save the file as **C06E01S11**.
12. Click the Pointer Options tab, drag the *Select a pointer speed* slider all the way to the left, and then click the *Display pointer trails* check box. (Note that the mouse pointer movement will be extremely slow until after Step 14.)
13. Capture a screen shot and then save the file as **C06E01S13**.
14. Click Cancel to close the dialog box without applying those changes.
15. Close the Control Panel window.
16. Submit your screen shots to your instructor.

Changing Display Settings ■■■■■■■■■■■■■■■■■■■■

Any time you look at the computer screen for a long period of time, its contents can have an impact on both your mood and your eyesight. You can change a variety of appearance-oriented settings for the desktop, such as the background color or picture used and the default color for windows and the Taskbar. You also can change settings that affect the viewing quality and function of the display, such as the resolution, screen saver, and text size. The Control Panel enables you to work with these Appearance and Personalization settings, and more.

To display the Appearance and Personalization settings in the Control Panel, you can use one of two methods:

■ From the desktop, select the Settings charm and then click *Control Panel* under Settings. In the Control Panel home window, click the Appearance and Personalization icon and then click *Personalization*.

■ Right-click the Windows 8 desktop and click *Personalize* in the shortcut menu.

The Personalization settings for the desktop appear in the Control Panel, as shown in Figure 6.6.

Changing the Background

Windows 8 displays the desktop background specified by the theme set up when Windows 8 was installed. You can change the selected background at any time to use one of the other available pictures or to use your own picture. You also can choose a solid color to use as the background, which can make icons on the desktop easier to see. Note that changing the desktop picture may also change the color of window borders and the Taskbar.

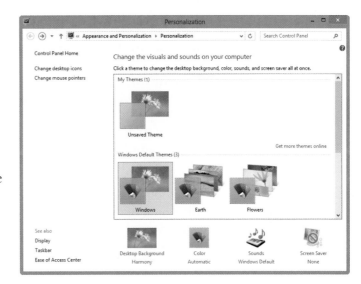

Figure 6.6 Use the Personalization choices to specify your desktop appearance.

Here's How

To change the desktop background in the Control Panel:

1. Right-click the desktop and then click *Personalize*.
2. Click *Desktop Background* at the bottom of the window.
3. Click the *Picture location* drop-down list and then click the desired type of background to apply.
4. Choose the background to use. The method you choose will vary depending on the choice you made in Step 3.

- **Windows Desktop Backgrounds.** This choice lists all the desktop background wallpaper images included with Windows 8. Scroll through the available wallpapers and click the one to use.

- **Pictures Library.** This choice lists the images in the Pictures library. Scroll through the available pictures and then click the picture to use.

- **Top Rated Photos.** This choice displays the Pictures library photos with the highest ratings assigned. (If you have not yet rated any photos, see the note after these steps to learn how.)

- **Solid Colors.** This choice displays thumbnails of solid colors that you can apply to the desktop as a background. Scroll down and click the desired thumbnail, or click More to open the Color dialog box, where you can select a custom color.

> **▼ Quick Fix**
>
> **Gaps in the Background**
> Some of the Windows Wallpaper choices are sized for wide-format displays. Choose one of those background choices if you see black gaps at the left and right of the screen after applying another image as the background.

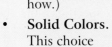

- **Browse.** If you clicked one of the first four choices in the list but did not find the desired picture, you can click the Browse button beside the *Picture location* drop-down list to navigate to another folder and then find a picture to use.

5. If you chose a picture as the desktop background, click one of the options in the *Picture position* drop-down list. *Fill* increases the image's width until the image can fill the screen vertically. *Fit* increases the image's width to match the horizontal dimension of the screen. *Stretch* changes the image proportions as needed and sizes the image to fill the screen. *Tile* repeats a small image as many times as needed to fill the desktop. And the *Center* option places the image in its original size in the center of the desktop.

6. Click Save changes to apply the new desktop background.

7. Close the Control Panel window.

Note: *To assign a rating to a picture in the Pictures library, right-click the picture, click* **Properties***, and then click the Details tab. Click the desired number of stars beside Rating and then click OK. You also can display the details pane for the library window and use it to set the rating.*

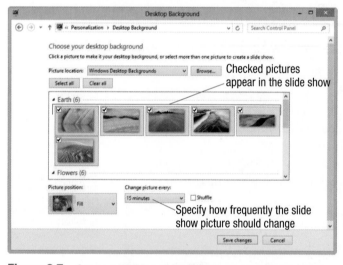

Figure 6.7   Set up a desktop slide show.

Playing a Desktop Slide Show

If a static desktop background fails to offer the interest that you are seeking, you can play a series of selected desktop backgrounds or pictures as a desktop slide show. Select the type of background image you want to apply from the *Picture location* drop-down list in Desktop Background settings in the Control Panel. Use the Select all or Clear all button to select or deselect all the picture thumbnails and then click individual thumbnails as needed to refine your selection (shown in Figure 6.7). Only checked pictures will appear in the slide show. Make a choice from the *Change picture every* drop-down list to specify how long each picture should appear on the screen, use the Shuffle check box to determine whether the images display in random order, and then click Save changes to start the show. Close the Control Panel window if you are finished working with settings.

Changing the Window Color and Appearance

Windows 8 applies a specific color to window borders and the Taskbar. You can choose another color for these items. Windows 8 also applies specific colors and settings to every other element on the screen.

The default colors for fully Windows 8-compatible systems (that is, systems with advanced display adapters or graphics cards) is the Automatic setting. (Themes using the Automatic color have a color fan on them to indicate that the color may vary depending on other personalization settings and application behaviors.) No matter what colors your system uses, you can change the color applied to window borders and the Taskbar.

To change window color and appearance in the Control Panel:

1. Right-click the desktop and then click *Personalize*.
2. Click *Color* at the bottom of the window.
3. Click a color at the top of the Color and Appearance window.
4. Drag the *Color intensity* slider to make the color more or less intense, as desired.
5. To customize the color, click *Show color mixer*; drag the *Hue*, *Saturation*, and *Brightness* sliders that appear to adjust the color; and then click *Hide color mixer*.
6. Click Save changes to apply the new color settings.
7. Close the Control Panel window.

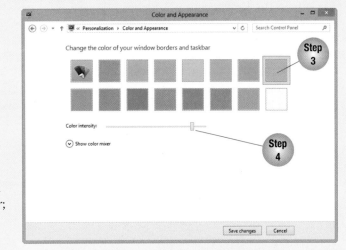

Changing the Display Resolution, Refresh Rate, and Other Settings

Display or monitor settings can have a big impact on comfort when you are viewing the screen. If on-screen items are too large or small, you can have difficulty reading and finding information. If the monitor uses a *refresh rate* that is too low, you may see an unpleasant screen flicker. You also may have to change resolution and refresh rate settings if you need to connect the computer to an external projector. For example, the projector may work only with lower resolution or refresh rate settings or may not display a readable on-screen image unless you choose a low resolution. *Resolution* is expressed as a measurement of width by height, in pixels. Pixel is a short version of "picture element," referring to each dot of color that the monitor displays. So, a monitor set to display at 1440 x 900 is showing an image 1,440 pixels wide by 900 pixels tall. A 1024 x 768 display is 1,024 pixels wide by 768 pixels tall. The available settings vary depending on the capabilities of the system's installed display adapter card and the attached monitor.

refresh rate The rate at which the display redraws the image on the screen

resolution The dimensions of the current display size setting, expressed in pixels (dots) wide by pixels tall

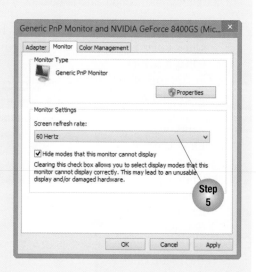

Here's How

To change display settings in the Control Panel:

1. Right-click the desktop and then click *Screen resolution*.
2. Open the *Resolution* drop-down list and then click the desired resolution.
3. Click *Advanced settings*.
4. Click the *Monitor* tab.
5. Open the *Screen refresh rate* drop-down list, click the desired rate, and then click OK to close the dialog box.
6. Click OK to apply the new display settings.
7. Close the Control Panel window.

Choosing a Screen Saver and Delay

A screen saver appears on the screen when your computer has been idle for a designated period of time. Screen savers serve important privacy and security functions, as well as helping prevent images from "burning in" on some newer flat-panel monitors. Having a screen saver come on when you step away from your computer hides the contents of sensitive documents or private emails. You can set up the screen saver to prompt the user to sign in to stop the screen saver, providing the security that only you can sign in to the system.

In choosing a screen saver, you specify how long the system must be idle before the screen saver starts, and whether the sign-in screen appears when a user attempts to resume the system. You also can choose settings for some screen savers, and preview the selected screen saver at full-screen size.

Note: *Windows 8 comes with several preinstalled screen savers available via the Screen Saver drop-down list in the Screen Saver Settings dialog box. The Photos choice displays the picture files in the Pictures library.*

Here's How

To choose a screen saver in the Control Panel:

1. Right-click the desktop and then click *Personalize*.
2. Click *Screen Saver* to open the Screen Saver Settings dialog box.
3. Click the *Screen saver* drop-down list and then click the desired screen saver.
4. Click the Settings button, choose the desired settings in the Settings dialog box that appears, and then click OK. For example, for the 3D Text screen saver, you can enter custom text, work with size and rotation settings, adjust the surface style, and more. If the screen saver has no options, click OK in the No options message box that appears.

5. To preview the screen saver at full-screen size, click the Preview button. Wiggle the mouse or tap the touchpad to return to the Screen Saver Settings dialog box.
6. Change the *Wait (x) minutes* text box entry, as needed, to specify how many minutes the system must be idle before the screen saver displays. Drag over the existing entry and type a new entry, or click the spinner arrow buttons to change the entry.
7. To require a user to sign in after resuming the screen saver, click the *On resume, display logon screen* check box to check it.
8. Click OK to apply the new screen saver settings.
9. Close the Control Panel window.

When you need to resume using your system after the screen saver has kicked in, wiggle the mouse, tap the touchpad, or press a key. If you specified that the screen saver should require you sign in, display the icon for your user account if needed, and click it. If your account is password-protected, type your password in the *Password* text box and then press Enter, or click the Submit right-pointing arrow at the right of the *Password* text box.

Note: *If your system's power settings are configured to let the system sleep or hibernate, this feature works separately from the screen saver.*

theme A named collection of appearance settings you can apply to the Windows 8 desktop

Choosing a Theme

A *theme* specifies a variety of appearance settings for the desktop, including the desktop picture or background, icons, window appearance, and so on. Choosing a theme applies all the settings stored in that theme to the Windows 8 desktop. In this way, a theme makes it easy for you to change the desktop appearance in a snap.

To apply another theme using the Control Panel, right-click the desktop and then click *Personalize*. Scroll down the list of available themes and then click the theme you want to apply (shown in Figure 6.8). It appears on the desktop immediately, so all you have to do next is close the Control Panel Personalization window.

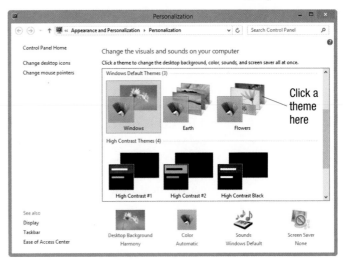

Figure 6.8 The Personalization window enables you to select a theme.

Customizing the Desktop and Start Screen

If you have changed a variety of desktop appearance settings, such as the background and window color, you can save those changes as your own theme that you can reapply at any time. To do so, click *Save theme* in the My Themes section of the list of themes in the Personalization window, type a name for the theme in the *Theme Name* text box of the Save Theme As dialog box that appears, and then click Save. You can then select the theme from the *Personalization* settings in the Control Panel, as you would any other theme. To find more themes, click the *Get more themes online* link under My Themes.

Changing Text and Icon Size

By default, text in Windows 8 displays at 96 pixels per inch (ppi). If you change the display resolution for the system and text looks too small at its default size, you can change the text size to an enlarged size of Medium – 125% (120 ppi) or Larger – 150% (144 ppi). The larger sizes make icons, menus, and dialog boxes look larger, too.

To change the font size (in DPI), select the Settings charm from the desktop and then click *Control Panel*. Click *Appearance and Personalization* and then, under *Display,* click *Make text and other items larger or smaller.* The Control Panel settings shown in Figure 6.9 appear.

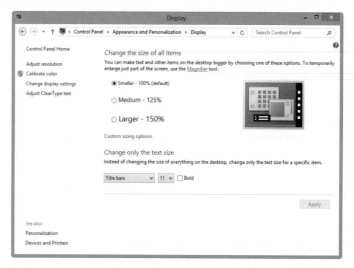

Figure 6.9 Choose an existing text size or use the *Custom sizing options* link to specify your own.

Click one of the size settings to choose it. Or, click the *Custom sizing options* link, enter a new scale percentage in the *Scale to this percentage of normal size* text box or use its drop-down list to click a preset percentage, and then click OK. You also can use the drop-down lists under *Change only the text size* to change the size of the text for items such as window title bars, message boxes, and icons. In the Control Panel window, click Apply to apply your changes. A message box appears to inform you that you must sign out of your computer to apply these changes. Click Sign out now to do so immediately, or Sign out later to have the new font size take effect the next time you shut down and start up or restart the system.

Customizing Sound Settings ■ ■ ■ ■ ■ ■

In addition to the mouse pointer changing to give you visual cues about your actions in Windows 8, the operating system plays sounds to alert you when certain events occur, such as to warn you when battery power is getting low on a mobile computer or to alert you when you have received an email message. You can change the sound for any individual program event and turn the Windows 8 startup sound on and off via the Control Panel.

Right-click the desktop and then click *Personalize*. Click *Sounds* at the bottom of the window. On the Sounds tab of the Sound dialog box, click an event in the *Program Events* list. As shown in Figure 6.10, the *Sounds* list at the bottom of the dialog box becomes active. Click the *Sounds* list to open it and then click another sound to use; you also can click the Browse button and use the Browse for New Event Name Sound dialog box that appears to navigate to and double-click a .wav sound file to assign to the event. Click the Test button to test the new sound. Turn off or reenable the sound that plays when you start up the system, click the *Play Windows Startup sound* check box to clear or check it, as desired. Click OK to apply the sound changes and then close the Control Panel window.

Figure 6.10 You can change the sound played for a program event.

Note: *As with a theme, you can save the set of sounds you have assigned to the various program events as your own custom sound scheme using the Save As button on the Sounds tab of the Sound dialog box.*

Exercise 2

Changing the Window Color, Desktop Background, and Sounds

1. Right-click the desktop and then click *Personalize*.
2. Click *Color* at the bottom of the window. Write down the current color settings so that you can refer to them later.
3. Click the Color 7 (orange) color, drag the *Color intensity* slider all the way to the right, and then click Save changes.
4. Back in the Personalization settings in the Control Panel, click *Desktop Background*. Write down the current color settings so that you can refer to them later.
5. Select *Windows Desktop Backgrounds* from the *Picture location* drop-down list, if needed, and then click one of the images in the *Earth* section. Click Save changes, which returns you to the Personalization settings.
6. Capture a screen shot and then save the file as **C06E02S06**.
7. Click *Sounds* in the Personalization settings in the Control Panel.
8. Click *Close Program* in the *Program Events, Windows* list, open the *Sounds* drop-down list, and then click *tada*. Click the Test button to test the sound playback.
9. Capture a screen shot and then save the file as **C06E02S09**.
10. Click Cancel to close the Sound dialog box without applying the sound change.
11. Use the *Window Color* and *Desktop Background* choices to return to the default window color and the previous desktop background. Click Save changes before completing the next step.
12. Close the Control Panel window.
13. Submit your screen shots to your instructor.

Working with Desktop Icons ■■■■■■■■■■■■■■■

Desktop shortcut icons are meant to provide you with an easy and convenient way to launch files and open programs. However, if the icons overlap or you cannot find the one you want, then you do not experience the convenience you were seeking by creating the icons in the first place. You can take steps to control the display and arrangement of icons on the desktop to set them up for maximum convenience.

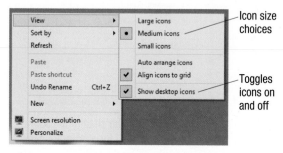

Icon size choices

Toggles icons on and off

Figure 6.11 Right-click the desktop and point to *View* for sizing and display choices.

Setting Icon Display

Icons are visible on the desktop by default, but you can hide the desktop icons temporarily, when needed. For example, if you want to hide the icons so that others do not see that you are using a particular program or file, you can do so. You also can change the icon size for desktop icons.

To make either of these changes to the desktop icons, start by right-clicking the desktop. To work with icon size and visibility, point to the *View* command to display the submenu, as shown in Figure 6.11. Click one of the three icon sizes above the top divider line on the View submenu to set a new icon size. To hide or redisplay desktop icons, click *Show desktop icons* to uncheck it (hide icons) or check it (display icons).

 TIP If you right-click the desktop and then click Personalize, you can click *Change desktop icons* in the list of tasks at the left to open a dialog box that enables you to specify which system icons appear on the desktop by default and even to change the picture used by a system desktop icon.

Arranging Icons

Align icons to grid A feature that snaps an icon into alignment with a desktop grid when you move the icon

Auto arrange icons A feature that arranges desktop icons to fill the desktop grid slots in order

You can move a desktop icon to any position by dragging it with the mouse. By default, the icon will align or snap to an invisible grid, which helps keep the desktop neat and prevents one icon from overlapping and hiding another. If you prefer, you can turn off the **Align icons to grid** feature to give you total control of where icons appear. You also can turn an **Auto arrange icons** feature on and off. This feature automatically arranges icons to fill the desktop grid positions in order, and it places each new icon in the next available grid position.

To turn the Align icons to grid and Auto arrange icons features on and off, right-click the desktop, point to the *View* command, and then click either *Auto arrange icons* or *Align icons to grid*, as needed. If a check appears beside either of these choices on the submenu, the feature is already enabled.

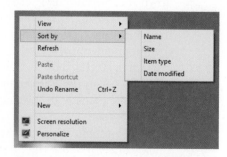

Figure 6.12 When you click one of the sort order choices on this submenu, Windows 8 immediately places the desktop icons in the new order specified.

You also can sort the icons on the desktop just as you can sort the icons in an Explorer window. In the case of desktop icons, you can sort by *Name, Size, Item type,* and *Date modified.* To sort the desktop icons, right-click the desktop, point to *Sort by,* and then click one of the sort order choices, as shown in Figure 6.12.

Customizing the Start Screen ■■■■■■■■■■■■■■■

As you begin to add your favorite apps to your Windows 8 system and work increasingly from the Start screen, you may want to modify that screen's appearance as well. Many of the modifications you can make to the Start screen are similar to those you have already learned to make to the desktop or will learn about later in the chapter.

Changing Start Screen Settings

The Start screen has two specific settings that you can use that pertain to it alone: you can determine whether icons for administrative features appear on the screen, as shown in Figure 6.13, and you can clear personal information stored in the tiles.

Figure 6.13 You can display tiles for administrative features on the Start screen.

Windows 8 administrative features

To change Start screen settings:

▶ **Here's How**

1. Select the Start charm or press the Windows logo key ⊞ to display the Start screen, if needed.
2. Select the Settings charm and then click *Tiles* under Settings.

3. To determine whether to display or hide tiles for administrative features, slide the Show administrative tools slider all the way to the left for No or all the way to the right for Yes.

4. Click Clear if you want to clear personal tracking information from Start screen tiles.

5. Click a blank area of the Start screen to close the pane.

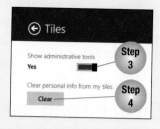

After displaying administrative tools, your Start screen may be more than full and a scroll bar will appear at the bottom. Click the minus button at the far right (point to the lower right corner of the screen if you do not see it) to zoom out so you can see all the tiles. Click a blank area of the Start screen to return the tiles to normal zoom.

Figure 6.14 Choose your Lock screen picture.

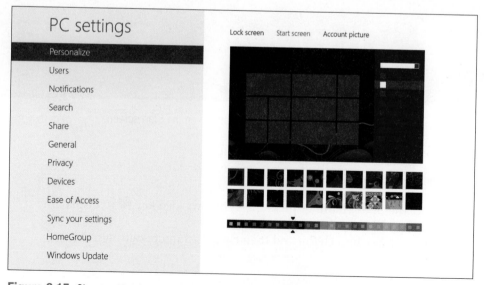

Figure 6.15 Choose a background tattoo and color for the Start screen.

Personalizing the Start Screen

You can personalize three aspects of the start screen: the picture for the *Lock screen* that appears when you lock your system, wake it from sleep or hibernate modes, or have installed apps that show status on the Lock screen (shown in Figure 6.14); the Start screen tattoo (background image) and color (shown in Figure 6.15); and your account picture. Use the Settings charm from the Start screen to make these changes.

Lock screen The screen that appears when you lock your system or wake it from sleep or hibernate

To personalize the Lock screen, Start screen background, and account picture:

Here's How

1. Select the Start charm or press the Windows logo key ⊞ to display the Start screen, if needed.
2. Select the Settings charm and then click *Change PC settings* at the lower right corner of the pane.
3. If necessary, click Personalize in the left pane of the PC settings app (shown in Figure 6.14).
4. Click the Lock screen link at the top of the right pane, if needed.
5. Click one of the available Lock screen pictures to select it (shown in Figure 6.14), or click the Browse button, select a picture from your Pictures library, and then click Choose picture.
6. To add a background app to include on the Lock screen, click one of the plus buttons under Lock screen apps and then click an app in the pop-up menu that appears.
7. At the top of the pane, click Start screen.
8. Below the Start screen preview (shown in Figure 6.15), click the background tattoo you want.
9. Drag the color slider below the tattoos to change the background appearance as desired.
10. At the top of the pane, click Account picture.
11. Click Browse, click Go up, and then click Pictures. Select a picture from your Pictures library and then click Choose image. Alternately, from the Account picture screen (see Step 10), if you have previously used another image and it appears below the current account picture, you can click its thumbnail to reselect it. You also can click Camera to launch the camera app and create a new account picture.
12. Drag from the top of the PC settings app to the bottom of the screen to save your settings and close the app.

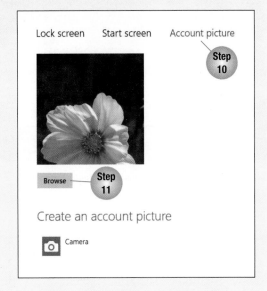

Pinning a Shortcut to the Start Screen

The Start screen contains many shortcuts; all its program tiles are shortcuts to those programs. When you install most apps, a tile for the newly installed app appears automatically on the Start screen.

You also can add, or *pin*, your own shortcuts to the Start screen. The shortcuts you pin to the Start screen can be either Windows 8 modern or desktop apps. As shown in Figure 6.16, pinning an app to the Start screen places a tile for it there and enables you to start it directly from the Start screen rather than using the Search charm. You can pin an app to the Start screen via the Search charm or within a File Explorer window.

Figure 6.16 Pinning an app to the Start screen gives you faster access.

Here's How

To pin an app to the Start screen:

1. Select the Search charm and then either scroll or search for the app to pin, if needed.
2. Right-click the app.
3. Click *Pin to Start* in the app commands that appear at the bottom of the screen.

4. Select the Start charm or press the Windows logo key ⊞ to display the Start screen.

OR

1. Go to the desktop and then open a File Explorer window.
2. Navigate to the location holding the startup command for the app. For many apps, the startup command can be found in subfolders of the Program Files and Program Files (x86) on drive C (the Windows 8 startup drive). However, startup commands for other apps might be found in subfolders of your user folder, in locations such as C:\Users\ *user*\AppData\Roaming or C:\Users*user*\AppData\Local.

3. Right-click the startup command and then click *Pin to Start*.
4. Select the Start charm or press the Windows logo key to display the Start screen.

 You also can pin any disk or folder location to the Start screen from a File Explorer window. To pin a location from the Navigation pane, right-click it and then click Pin to Start.

T I P If you have a location pinned to the Start screen, you can right-click it and then click Open file location in the commands that appear at the bottom of the screen.

Here's How

To unpin an app from the Start screen:

1. Select the Start charm, or press the Windows logo key to display the Start screen.
2. Right-click the app tile.
3. Click *Unpin from Start* in the app commands that appear at the bottom of the screen.

Changing Tile Settings

As you learned in Chapter 1, the ability to sign in to Windows 8 with a Microsoft account keeps your system connected to the cloud. When you are signed in with your Microsoft account, some Windows 8 apps can pull data from the cloud and display it in real time on the Start screen. For example, the Calendar app updates to show the current date, as well as reminders for upcoming appointments. Other apps might pull and display live information from your system. For example, the Photos app can display the digital pictures from your Pictures library.

You can determine whether a tile is live (displays live data), as well as specify the tile size in some cases.

Here's How

To change tile settings on the Start screen:

1. Select the Start charm, or press the Windows logo key to display the Start screen.
2. Right-click the app tile.
3. Click the desired command in the app commands at the bottom of the screen. Click either Turn live tile off or Turn live tile on to control the tile functionality, and click either Smaller or Larger to control the tile size.

Step 2

Step 3

Controlling App Notifications

Part of the live functionality of Start screen tiles includes notifications that appear to alert you of new information. For example, the Store tile displays a number in its lower right corner when updates are available for your apps. You can turn this notification feature on or off, overall, and for some individual apps. You make these changes via the PC settings *Notifications* choices (shown in Figure 6.17).

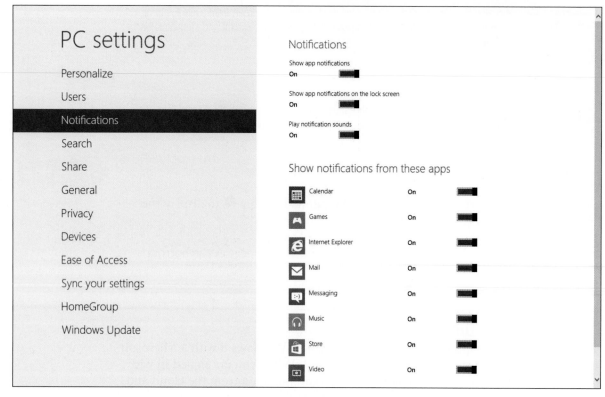

Figure 6.17 Control whether Start screen tiles display notifications.

Here's How To change notification settings on the Start screen:

1. Select the Start charm or press the Windows logo key ⊞ to display the Start screen.
2. Select the Settings charm and then click *Change PC settings* at the bottom of the pane.
3. Click Notifications under PC settings.
4. Drag the sliders to turn notifications on or off as needed (shown in Figure 6.17). The Show app notifications option controls overall Start screen notifications; the Show app notifications on the lock screen option determines whether the Lock screen also includes notifications. The Play notification sounds option turns notifications sound effects on or off. Under *Show notifications from these apps*, you can turn notifications for individual apps on and off.
5. Drag from the top of the screen down to the bottom to apply your changes and close the PC settings app.

Customizing the Desktop and Start Screen

1. Go to the desktop. Right-click the desktop, point to *View*, and then click *Show desktop icons*. Windows 8 hides the icons on the desktop.
2. Right-click the desktop, point to *View*, and then click *Show desktop icons* to redisplay the icons.
3. Drag the Recycle Bin icon to the right side of the desktop.
4. Right-click the desktop, point to *View*, and then click *Large icons*.
5. Capture a screen shot and then save the file as **C06E03S05**.
6. Right-click the desktop, point to *View*, and then click *Medium icons*.
7. Right-click the desktop, point to *View*, and then click *Auto arrange icons*. The Recycle Bin should snap back to its default position.
8. Right-click the desktop, point to *View*, and then click *Auto arrange icons* to turn that feature off.
9. Select the Search charm.
10. Right-click Math Input Panel under *Windows Accessories* and then click *Pin to Start*.
11. Select the Start charm or press the Windows logo key ⊞ to display the Start screen.
12. Right-click the Calendar app tile.
13. With the tile commands on the screen, capture a screen shot and then save the file as **C06E03S13**.
14. Right-click the Calendar tile again.
15. Right-click the Math Input Panel tile and then click *Unpin from Start*.
16. Submit your screen shots to your instructor.

Customizing the Taskbar and Notifications Area ▪▪▪▪▪▪▪▪▪▪▪▪▪▪▪▪▪▪▪▪▪▪▪▪▪▪▪▪▪▪▪▪▪▪

The Taskbar provides you with a variety of ways to launch and work with programs and Windows 8 features. By default, the Taskbar displays icons (for Internet Explorer and File Explorer) at the left and the notification area (also called the system tray) at the right. You can customize the icons that appear in either location as well as hide and display other desktop toolbars.

Pinning a Program to the Taskbar

Adding an icon for a program to the Taskbar is called pinning the program to the Taskbar. This enables you to open that program via the Taskbar and to open its documents via a Jump List even if the program is not running. For example, Figure 6.18 shows WordPad pinned to the Taskbar; you can see the command for unpinning it in the displayed Jump List. You can unpin any program you have added to the Taskbar.

To pin a program to the Taskbar, you can use one of two methods, depending on whether the program is running. Unpinning a program is easy, as well.

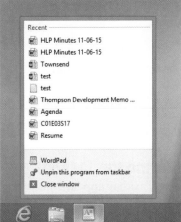

Figure 6.18 Pin an application to the Taskbar so that its icon always appears.

To pin a program to the Taskbar:

- If the program is running, right-click its Taskbar icon and then click *Pin this program to taskbar*.
  OR
- Open a folder window, navigate to the folder holding the executable (startup) file for the program, right-click it, and then click *Pin to taskbar*.
  OR
  Right-click the program's tile on the Start screen or Apps screen displayed from the Search charm, and click *Pin to taskbar* in the app commands that appear at the bottom of the screen.

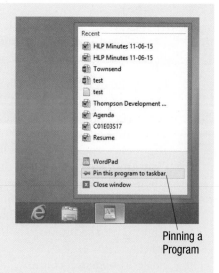

Pinning a Program

To unpin a program from the Taskbar:

- Right-click the program's Taskbar icon and then click *Unpin this program from taskbar*.

To pin a file to a pinned program's Jump List, drag the file's icon over the pinned program's icon on the Taskbar, and then, when you see the Pin to (*program name*) pop-up tip, release the mouse button. To unpin the file, right-click the program's icon on the Taskbar to open its Jump List, right-click the file in the Pinned section at the top of the Jump List, and then click *Unpin from this list*.

Adding a Toolbar to the Taskbar

You can display one of several other default toolbars on the Taskbar: Address (Address bar), Links, Touch Keyboard, and Desktop. In most cases, these "toolbars" appear as an additional text box or a menu button that you can click. For example, Figure 6.19 shows how the Address toolbar looks when added to the Taskbar. You can enter a web page address in the Address toolbar text box and then press Enter to open that page in your system's browser.

Figure 6.19 Display another toolbar on the Taskbar to add functionality, such as the ability to type in a web page address.

To display or hide any Taskbar toolbar, right-click the Taskbar, point to Toolbars in the menu that appears, and then click the name of the desired toolbar. A checkmark appears beside the name of any displayed toolbar in the submenu.

Moving the Taskbar

The Taskbar appears along the bottom of the desktop by default, but your preference for the Taskbar location might be different. For example, if you are a left-handed user and you have already flipped the functions of the mouse buttons, you might find it more natural to make selections when the Taskbar is positioned along the left side of the screen, as shown in Figure 6.20. Notice that when you move the Taskbar, Windows 8 shifts the desktop icons out of the way automatically and reorients the pinned icons and notification area contents to reflect the new Taskbar position.

Figure 6.20 Moving the Taskbar to another position on the screen may make it easier for you to use.

You can use one of two methods to move the Taskbar: drag it to the desired location on the screen, or right-click the Taskbar and then click *Properties.* Choose the desired Taskbar location from the *Taskbar location on screen* drop-down list on the Taskbar tab of the Taskbar Properties dialog box and then click OK.

> **T I P** You can drag the dotted dividers that appear when the Taskbar is unlocked to resize the toolbars displayed on the Taskbar.

auto-hide A feature that hides the Taskbar unless the mouse pointer is over the Taskbar location

Auto-hiding the Taskbar

When enabled, the ***auto-hide*** feature tells Windows 8 not to display the Taskbar unless you move the mouse pointer over the location where the Taskbar should normally appear. Enabling auto-hide provides a bit more room on the screen for you to work with the files and applications you are using.

To auto-hide the Taskbar, right-click the Taskbar and then click *Properties.* Click the *Auto-hide the taskbar* check box to check it, as shown in Figure 6.21, and then click OK. To redisplay the Taskbar at any time, move the mouse pointer over the location where you have set up the Taskbar to appear. To turn off the auto-hide feature, click the check box again on the Taskbar tab of the Taskbar Properties dialog box.

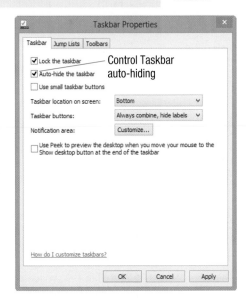

Figure 6.21 Click the *Auto-hide the taskbar* check box to turn auto-hiding on and off.

Setting Up Icon Display in the Notification Area

You can control how the icons work in the notification area. You can set up all or some of the icons to display all of the time, not at all, or only when in use. You can specify whether notification icons for the Action Center, Network, Volume, Windows Explorer, and other apps appear. You can turn off the display of the Clock, Volume, Network, Power, and Action Center icons, or turn their display back on altogether.

Here's How

To customize the notification area icons:

1. Right-click the Taskbar and then click *Properties*.
2. On the Taskbar tab of the Taskbar Properties dialog box, click the Customize button beside *Notification area*.
3. For each icon listed, choose one of the following Behaviors from its drop-down list: *Show icon and notifications*, *Hide icon and notifications*, or *Only show notifications*.

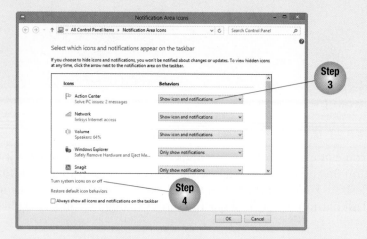

4. Click *Turn system icons on or off*.

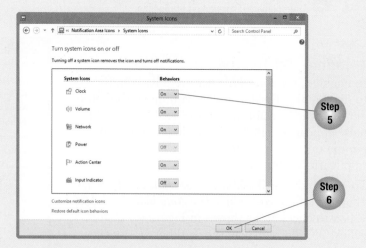

5. For each icon listed, choose *On* or *Off* from the Behaviors drop-down list.
6. Click OK twice to close the Control Panel windows.
7. Click OK to close the Taskbar Properties dialog box.

Choosing Other Taskbar Properties

There are a few remaining settings on the Taskbar tab of the Taskbar Properties dialog box (shown in Figure 6.21) that you should be aware of in case you want to turn them off to suit your working style. Right-click the Taskbar and then click *Properties*. Modify the following settings on the Taskbar tab, as needed, and then click OK to apply your changes:

■ **Use small Taskbar icons.** Displays Taskbar icons in a smaller size, so the Taskbar itself displays at a smaller size.

■ **Taskbar buttons.** If you often have many files open, you can choose an option here to specify whether Windows 8 should consolidate all the open files from a program onto a single Taskbar button.

■ **Use Peek to preview the desktop.** When this option is enabled, moving the mouse over the Show desktop button hides open windows so that you can see the desktop.

Exercise 4

Updating the Taskbar

1. Select the Search charm.
2. Right-click Calculator under *Windows Accessories*, and then click *Pin to taskbar* in the app commands at the bottom of the screen.
3. Press Esc to return to the desktop and then click the Calculator button on the Taskbar to start Calculator.
4. Close the Calculator window.
5. Right-click the Taskbar and then click *Lock the taskbar*.
6. Drag the Taskbar to the right side of the desktop.
7. Capture a screen shot and then save the file as **C06E04S07**.
8. Drag the Taskbar back to its default position at the bottom of the screen.
9. Right-click the Taskbar and then click *Lock the taskbar*.
10. Right-click the Calculator button on the Taskbar and then click *Unpin this program from taskbar*.
11. Right-click the Taskbar and then click *Properties*. Click *Auto-hide the taskbar* to check it and then click OK.
12. Move the mouse pointer over and away from the Taskbar area at the bottom of the screen a few times to see how auto-hide works. Finish by moving the mouse pointer off the Taskbar area so that the Taskbar auto-hides.
13. Capture a screen shot and then save the file as **C06E04S13**.
14. Move the mouse pointer over the bottom of the screen so that the Taskbar appears, right-click the Taskbar, and then click *Properties*. Click *Auto-hide the taskbar* to uncheck it and then click OK. This turns auto-hide off. The desktop should now look as it did when you started the exercise.
15. Submit your screen shots to your instructor.

Using the Ease of Access Settings ▪▪▪▪▪▪▪▪▪▪▪▪▪

The Ease of Access Center in Windows 8 Control Panel enables you to set up a system for use by someone with visual impairments and other special challenges. For example, the system can be optimized for use without a display at all, where the Narrator reads on-screen information aloud. The system can be optimized to make the screen easier to see, or it can be set up for a form of input other than the mouse or keyboard—Speech Recognition or an On-Screen Keyboard. You also can change settings to make the mouse and keyboard easier to use, as you learned earlier in the chapter.

Starting the Ease of Access Center turns on a Narrator and offers initial settings that you can use to begin to set up the system for a user with special needs. From there, you can choose different pages of information to perform different optimizations. As Figure 6.22 shows, the *Quick access to common tools* section at the top of the Ease of Access Center gives the option of starting four common accessibility features.

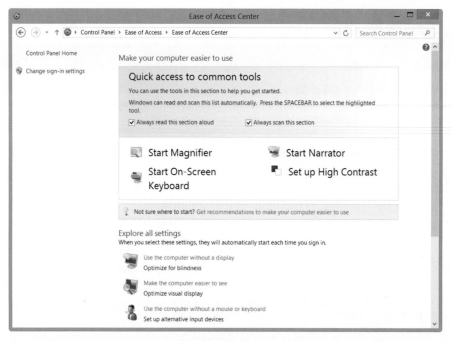

Figure 6.22 The Ease of Access Center Narrator makes some initial suggestions about accessibility settings but also offers a variety of additional settings.

▪ **Magnifier.** A pane that shows an enlarged version of the screen area around the mouse. This feature can help those who have trouble seeing.

▪ **On-Screen Keyboard.** A keyboard that appears on the screen so that you can "type" by clicking or tapping letters rather than using a keyboard for input. This feature can help users who find it difficult or painful to use the keyboard.

▪ **Narrator.** Turns on the Narrator feature, which reads on-screen content to the user. This feature helps users unable to see a display.

▪ **High Contrast.** Sets up the screen to make it easier to read by making colors more distinct. This is another feature that can help anyone who has difficulty reading the screen.

Below the *Quick access to common tools* section, the *Explore all settings* area (shown in Figure 6.22) in the Ease of Access Center offers additional categories of accessibility settings that you can use to set up the computer as desired, including settings for working with the Narrator, Speech Recognition, and more.

Note: *To use audio features such as the Narrator and Speech Recognition, the computer must be equipped with speakers and a microphone.*

To open and start using the Ease of Access Center: Here's How

1. From the desktop, select the Settings charm and then click *Control Panel*.
2. Click the *Ease of Access* category icon.
3. Click the Ease of Access Center icon. (Note that you can work with Speech Recognition settings from this point, instead.)
4. Use the arrow keys to select the various Quick access to common tools options and listen as the Narrator reads the choices. To select one of the choices, press the spacebar after the Narrator reads its name. Or, click the desired choice with the mouse.
5. Scroll down, if needed, and click any of the icons in the Explore all settings area.
6. Use the settings that appear to adjust system accessibility. For example, if you clicked *Make the mouse easier to use* in Step 5, the Ease of Access Center displays options such as *Change the color and size of mouse pointers*.
7. Click the Back button to return to the Ease of Access Center.
8. Repeat Steps 5–7 to choose additional settings, as desired.
9. Close the Ease of Access Center (Control Panel) window.

You also can adjust some of the Ease of Access settings in the Windows 8 Start screen's PC settings app, as shown in Figure 6.23. This method provides faster access to some of the more common Ease of Access settings.

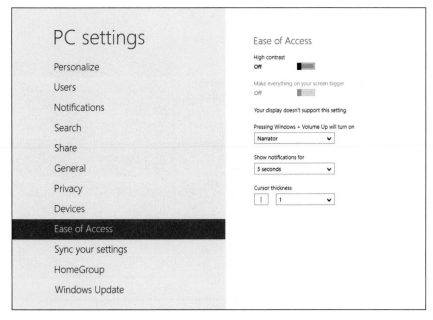

Figure 6.23 Change Ease of Access settings in PC settings.

To choose Ease of Access settings in PC settings:

1. From either the desktop or Start screen, select the Settings charm and then click *Change PC settings* at the bottom.
2. Click the *Ease of Access* choice.
3. Turn the following features on and off using the sliders: High contrast, and Make everything on your screen bigger (shown in Figure 6.23).
4. Use the drop-down lists for the other three options to choose what pressing the Windows logo key ⊞ + Volume up does, to control how long notifications appear, and to set the cursor (insertion point) thickness.
5. Drag from the top to the bottom of the screen to apply the changes and close PC settings.

Working with the System Date and Time ■■■■■■

Because your computer applies a date and time "stamp" to every file and email you create, it is a good practice to make sure that the computer is set to the right date, time, and time zone. Further, if you rely on calendar software to track and remind you of your appointments, you want the time to be accurate so that you will arrive at your appointments on time.

Windows 8 installation may prompt the user to set up the date, time, and time zone for the system. If you need to change that information, such as if the system fails to update for a daylight saving time change, you can change the date, time, or time zone yourself at any time

Changing the Date, Time, or Time Zone

You can set the date and time via the Control Panel by clicking *Clock, Language, and Region* in the Control Panel home window and then clicking one of the tasks under *Date and Time* in the Control Panel window that appears. You also can change the date, time, and time zone directly from the clock display in the notification area.

To change the system date, time, and time zone:

1. Right-click the clock (time) in the notification area at the right end of the Taskbar on the desktop and then click *Adjust date/time*.
2. Click Change date and time on the Date and Time tab of the Date and Time dialog box. If a User Account Control dialog box appears, enter an administrator password and click Yes.
3. Click another date on the calendar, if needed. To change months, click the arrows beside the month and year or click the month and year itself and then click another month in the zoomed view of the calendar that appears.

4. To set each segment of the time (hour, minute, second, a.m./p.m.), click in that segment and then click the spinner arrow buttons, as needed, to change the time.
5. Click OK to apply the time change and return to the Date and Time dialog box.
6. Click Change time zone on the Date and Time tab of the Date and Time dialog box.
7. Choose the desired time zone from the *Time zone* drop-down list in the Time Zone Settings dialog box and then click OK.
8. Click OK to close the Date and Time dialog box and apply the changes.

 If you need to track the time in multiple time zones for business purposes, such as if you work on the East Coast but serve clients on the West Coast, use the Additional Clocks tab in the Date and Time dialog box to display up to two additional clocks set to different time zones.

 You can change the time zone and automatic daylight saving time behavior by starting PC settings, choosing General, and then using the settings under *Time* at the right.

Synchronizing to an Internet Time Server

Like other timepieces, the system clock within your computer may not always keep perfect time. If you have an always-on Internet connection, you can ensure that the system is always set to an accurate time by synchronizing it with an ***Internet time server***.

Internet time server
A website that provides highly precise times

Windows 8 by default uses this feature, synchronizing the system time to the Windows Internet time server: <u>time.windows.com</u>. If you prefer to use another server, Windows 8 lists some additional government time servers such as <u>time.nist.gov</u>. Or, you can turn off Internet time synchronization if you do not have an always-on Internet connection or want to set the time yourself.

To work with Internet time settings, right-click the clock (time) in the notification area at the right end of the Taskbar and then click *Adjust date/time*. Click the Internet Time tab in the Date and Time dialog box and then click the Change settings button. If a User Account Control dialog box appears, enter an administrator password and then click Yes. If you want to leave time synchronization on but use another server, choose the alternate server from the *Server* drop-down list and then click Update now. To turn off Internet time synchronization, click the *Synchronize with an Internet time server* check box to clear it. Click OK twice to close the dialog boxes and apply your changes.

Changing Date and Time Settings

1. Display the desktop, if needed, and look at the clock in the notification area. Write down the current time and the current date.
2. Right-click the clock (time) in the notification area at the right end of the Taskbar and then click *Adjust date/time*.
3. Click *Change date and time* on the Date and Time tab of the Date and Time dialog box. If a User Account Control dialog box appears, enter an administrator password and then click Yes. (Your instructor can provide an administrator password to use.)
4. Click the current month and year at the top of the calendar. Click *June* in the zoomed calendar to display the calendar for June of the current year. Click *21* to set the date to June 21.
5. Click the hour in the text box at the right and then click the spinner arrow buttons as needed to change it to *12*.
6. Click OK twice to close the dialog boxes and apply the new settings.
7. View the new date and time settings in the notification area as in Step 1. Compare the current date and time with the values you recorded earlier.
8. Reset the date and time by synchronizing to an Internet time server. Right-click the clock (time) in the notification area at the right end of the Taskbar and then click *Adjust date/time*.
9. Click the *Internet Time* tab and then click *Change settings*. If a User Account Control dialog box appears, enter an administrator password and then click Yes.
10. Make sure that the *Synchronize with an Internet time server* check box is checked and then click *Update now*.
11. After the Internet Time Settings dialog box informs you that the synchronization has finished, click OK twice to close the dialog boxes and apply the time change.
12. View the new date and time settings in the notification area as in Step 1. Compare the current date and time with the values you recorded earlier.

CHAPTER SUMMARY

- The Control Panel provides a central location for accessing system settings.
- The Windows 8 PC settings app also enables you to change some system settings.
- Select the Settings charm from the desktop and then click *Control Panel* to open the Control Panel. Click a category icon or link to find lower-level categories of actions and then click the task to perform. You also can click a category or task in the list at the left side of the Control Panel.
- You can adjust such settings as the keyboard repeat rate, the mouse double-click speed, or the functions of the mouse buttons.
- Right-click the desktop and then click *Personalize* to find settings for customizing the desktop.
- You can change window colors, the picture or background on the desktop, screen saver, theme, and system sounds. You also can choose the correct resolution and refresh rate for the display (monitor).
- You can change the sounds Windows 8 plays for system events, such as when you shut down the system.

- Right-click the desktop and use the *View* and *Sort By* submenu choices to choose icon size, alignment settings, and sort order.
- From the Start screen, select the Settings charm and then click *Tiles* to display the settings for customizing the Start screen.
- You can personalize the Start screen in PC settings by changing the Lock screen, Start screen, and account pictures, as well as choosing which apps show status on the Lock screen. To display PC settings, select the *Settings* charm and then click *Change PC settings*.
- You can pin applications and locations to the Start screen to create tiles for them there as well as customize tile size and whether some tiles are live.
- You can control whether live app tiles on the Start screen display notifications and other updates.
- On the desktop, right-click the Taskbar and then click *Properties* to display the settings for customizing the Taskbar.
- You can pin a program to the Taskbar to add a button for the program there.
- Display and hide various toolbars on the Taskbar, or unlock the Taskbar to move it to a new position. You also can set up the Taskbar to remain hidden (auto-hide) unless you point to it with the mouse.
- The icons in the notification area can be set up to be hidden when inactive.
- The Ease of Access Center in the Control Panel offers settings for customizing the system for users with special needs.
- When you open the Ease of Access Center, the Narrator starts and prompts you to enable one of the four most common accessibility features. You also can scroll down and choose individual features as desired.
- You can change Ease of Access settings in PC settings.
- Right-click the time in the notification area and then click *Adjust date/time* to open the Date and Time dialog box where you can choose a new date, time, or time zone.
- The Date and Time dialog box also offers a tab to synchronize the system with an Internet time server.

CONCEPTS CHECK

Completion: Answer the following questions in a Word document.

Part 1

Multiple Choice
1. To change system settings, use the _____ .
   a. Start screen
   b. Taskbar
   c. Control Panel
   d. desktop

2. Click the _____ command after choosing the Settings charm from the desktop to access system settings.
   a. Start menu
   b. Taskbar
   c. Control Panel
   d. desktop

3. To make the mouse easier to use, you can _____ .
   a. slow the double-click speed
   b. flip mouse buttons
   c. slow the pointer speed
   d. Any of the above

4. The _____ feature snaps an icon you are moving to the nearest available slot in the invisible desktop grid.
   a. Align icons to grid
   b. Auto arrange icons
   c. Show desktop icons
   d. Line up icons

5. The _____ feature moves icons to fill available slots in the invisible desktop grid.
   a. Align icons to grid
   b. Auto arrange icons
   c. Show desktop icons
   d. Show desktop

6. When customizing the Start screen, _____ an app or location to be able to access it directly from the Start screen.
   a. Tile
   b. Add
   c. Pin
   d. Link

7. The _____ feature removes the Taskbar from view until you point to its location.
   a. Auto-hide
   b. Minimize
   c. Peek
   d. Cloaking

8. A tile is _____ when it shows user data or information from the cloud.
   a. floated
   b. pinned
   c. live
   d. always on top

9. How many extra clocks can you display on the Taskbar?
   a. Zero
   b. One
   c. Two
   d. Three

10. Synchronizing to an _____ keeps the system date and time accurate.
    a. online dating site
    b. alternate time zone
    c. Internet time location
    d. Internet time server

Part 2

Short Answer

11. Name one of the two primary keyboard settings you can change.

_____

12. Name at least two types of backgrounds that you can apply to the desktop.

   _____

13. Describe what a screen saver is and why you might use one.

   _____

14. Describe what a theme is.

   _____

15. Explain how to hide the icons on the desktop.

   _____

16. Name at least two of the toolbars you can display on the Taskbar.

   _____

17. Describe a situation in which you need to unlock the Taskbar.

   _____

18. Describe how to pin a program to the Taskbar.

   _____

19. Name the Windows 8 app that you can use to customize some Start screen settings and some overall system settings.

   _____

20. Explain what the Ease of Access Center is and how to use it.

   _____

SKILLS CHECK

Save all solution files to the default Documents folder or any alternate folder specified by your instructor.

Guided Check

Assessment 1

Slow Down the Mouse and Display Mouse Trails
   1. Start the Control Panel.
      a. From the desktop, select the Settings charm.
      b. Click *Control Panel*.
   2. Find Mouse Settings.
      a. Click *Hardware and Sound*.
      b. Click *Mouse* under Devices and Printers.
   3. Slow down the mouse.
      a. Drag the *Speed* slider under Double-click Speed to the left until it is an increment or two to the left of the center point.
      b. Capture a screen shot of the desktop and then save it as **C06A01S03**.

4. Turn on pointer trails.
   a. Click the Pointer Options tab in the Mouse Properties dialog box.
   b. Click the *Display pointer trails* check box to check it.
   c. Drag the slider to the desired setting for the pointer trails length.
   d. Capture a screen shot of the desktop and then save it as **C06A01S04**.
5. Click OK to apply the changes.
6. Drag the mouse on the screen to see how it behaves.
7. Repeat Steps 2–5 to undo the settings changes you made.
8. Close the Control Panel window.
9. Submit the screen shots to your instructor.

Assessment 2

Change the Screen Resolution and Colors

1. Find screen resolution settings.
   a. Right-click the desktop.
   b. Click *Screen resolution*.
2. Change display resolution.
   a. Click the *Resolution* drop-down list. Make a note of the current setting.
   b. Drag the resolution slider to the highest or lowest available setting, as you prefer.
   c. Click OK in the Screen Resolution window.
   d. Click Keep changes when asked whether to keep the new display settings.
3. Find personalization settings.
   a. Right-click the desktop.
   b. Click *Personalize*.
4. Change window colors.
   a. Click *Color*. Make a note of the current color.
   b. Click *Color 8*.
   c. Click Save changes.
   d. Scroll down the list of themes to display the High Contrast themes.
5. Capture a screen shot of the desktop and then save it as **C06A02**.
6. Close the Control Panel window and then repeat Steps 1–4 to undo the settings changes you made.
7. Close the Control Panel window.
8. Submit the screen shot to your instructor.

Assessment 3

Hide and Redisplay Desktop Icons and the Taskbar

1. Hide desktop icons.
   a. Right-click the desktop.
   b. Point to *View*.
   c. Click *Show desktop icons*.
2. Turn on auto-hide for the Taskbar.
   a. Right-click the Taskbar.
   b. Click *Properties*.
   c. Click the *Auto-hide the taskbar* check box to check it.
   d. Click OK.
3. Capture a screen shot of the empty desktop and then save it as **C06A03**.
4. Repeat Steps 1–2 to undo the settings changes you made.
5. Submit the screen shot to your instructor.

Assessment 4

Unlock and Move the Taskbar

1. Unlock the Taskbar.
   a. Right-click the Taskbar.
   b. Click *Lock the taskbar*.
2. Drag the Taskbar to the top of the screen.

3. Right-click the moved Taskbar.
4. With the shortcut menu open, capture a screen shot of the desktop and then save it as **C06A04**.
5. Close the shortcut menu, if needed, by clicking a blank area of the desktop.
6. Drag the Taskbar back to the default location at the bottom of the screen.
7. Lock the Taskbar.
   a. Right-click the Taskbar.
   b. Click *Lock the taskbar*.
8. Submit the screen shot to your instructor.

On Your Own

Assessment
5

Pin Calculator and Computer as Start Screen Tiles
1. Select the Search charm.
2. Right-click Calculator under *Windows Accessories*.
3. Click the *Pin to Start* choice in the app commands at the bottom of the screen.
4. Press Esc, click the Desktop tile, if needed, to go to the desktop, and then open the Libraries window. If you are already at the desktop, click the File Explorer button on the Taskbar.
5. Scroll down the Navigation pane, if needed, right-click Computer, and then click *Pin to Start*. Close the window.
6. Select the Start charm or press the Windows Logo key ⊞ to display the Start screen.
7. Capture a screen shot of the Start screen and then save it as **C06A05**.
8. On the Start screen, remove the Calculator and Computer tiles by right-clicking each one and then clicking *Unpin from Start*.
9. Submit the screen shots to your instructor.

Assessment
6

Draw a Picture and Display on Desktop
1. Start Paint.
2. Use the File tab, *Properties* command to set the image size to 100 x 100 pixels.
3. Draw some shapes or lines in the graphic. You are free to be as creative as you want.
4. Save the file as **Background**, as a JPG image, in your default Pictures library and then close Paint.
5. Right-click the desktop, click *Personalize*, and then click *Desktop Background*.
6. Apply the picture you created and then saved in the Pictures folder as the new desktop background, using the *Tile* option to repeat it on the desktop.
7. Close the Control Panel.
8. Capture a screen shot of the new desktop and then save it as **C06A06**.
9. Return to the prior desktop background, as desired.
10. Submit the screen shot to your instructor.

Assessment
7

Group Activity: Customization Assessment
1. Divide into teams of four. Imagine that you are computer consultants hired to set up a number of new Windows 8 systems for a company.
2. Create a WordPad document and save it as **Recommendations**.
3. Type the following categories into the document:
   Mouse and Keyboard:
   Desktop Background:
   Screen Saver:
   Start screen:

4. As a group, share ideas on how to set up the systems with regard to each of the listed categories.
5. Type in your setup ideas beside or below each category.
6. Save your changes to the document.
7. Submit the file to your instructor.

CHALLENGE PROJECT

As a special education teacher, you will be teaching a computer class to high-school students who have a variety of disabilities. You need to prepare specific computers in the computer lab for each student based on his or her unique capabilities.

1. Open WordPad and then create a new file named **Student Setup Needs**. Imagine that you have three students. Jane is blind. Tim has a disability that makes it difficult for him to use his hands. And Sam has both limited hearing and some trouble using his hands. Type each student's name into the WordPad file.
2. Open the Ease of Access Center and research settings you might change and other recommendations you might make to set up a system for each student.
3. Type your system setup suggestions as a bulleted list under each student's name in the WordPad file. Include the general steps or process for implementing each setup suggestion.
4. Save your document and then submit it to your instructor.

Microsoft®

Windows® 8

Using the Internet and Multimedia with Windows 8

- Browsing with Internet Explorer

- Ensuring Your Safety and Privacy on the Internet

- Using Mail and Social Features

- Working with Digital Photographs and Music

Browsing with Internet Explorer

PERFORMANCE OBJECTIVES

Upon successful completion of Chapter 7, you will be able to:

- Start and exit Internet Explorer on the desktop
- Understand what a URL is
- Display a web page
- Browse web pages
- Use tabs to open multiple web pages
- Search for a topic

- Use accelerators
- View content when not connected
- Deal with the Notification bar
- Set up and read an RSS feed
- Start, exit, and use the Internet Explorer app from the Start screen

---

$\mathbf{W}$ith Windows 8 and an Internet connection, a nearly unlimited store of information and content becomes available. You can read the news, learn how to manage your money, find reviews about the new TV that you want to buy, shop for nearly anything you want, sell stuff that you want to get rid of—the World Wide Web offers it all. This chapter shows you how to use Internet Explorer, the built-in web browser for Windows 8. Windows 8 includes desktop and Windows 8 versions of Internet Explorer.

Starting and Exiting Internet Explorer on the Desktop ▪▪▪▪▪▪▪▪▪▪▪▪▪▪▪▪▪▪▪▪▪▪▪▪▪▪▪▪▪▪▪▪

web browser A program that enables you to view and retrieve information from the World Wide Web

World Wide Web A structure of linked documents stored on Web server computers connected to the Internet

Windows 8 includes the Internet Explorer 10 *web browser* program that you can use to view and retrieve information from the *World Wide Web*. Web server computers connected to the Internet store and deliver the linked documents that make up the Web.

The documents on the Web are primarily based on a language called HTML: HyperText Markup Language. HTML is called a markup language because it uses tags to "describe" the contents of a document, identifying titles, lists, tables, and so on. Internet Explorer can read the tag information and display each document correctly on the screen.

To start Internet Explorer, also called IE, click the Internet Explorer button at the left end of the Taskbar, by default, as shown in Figure 7.1.

Figure 7.1
Start Internet Explorer from the desktop Taskbar.

When you start Internet Explorer, it connects to the Internet and displays the designated home page, the page set up to display first. By default, this page is the MSN website, but on your system it may be another page set up by the computer's maker or your school.

Note: *The first time IE is started on a system, a second tab with the Bing search service may appear. Click Check it out to try Bing or No thanks and then click the tab's Close (X) button to close the tab. Similarly, a notification bar may appear below the tabs to prompt you to make MSN your home page. That is already the default setting, so you can click the Close (X) button to close the message.*

Note: *If your computer uses a dial-up Internet connection, you may see a dialog box prompting you to start the connection process. Click the Connect button to do so.*

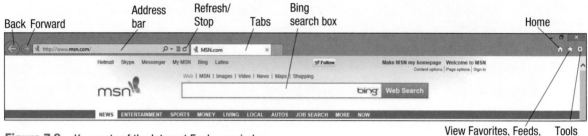

Figure 7.2 Key parts of the Internet Explorer window.

▼ Quick Fix

Loading a Finicky Web Page
The 64-bit version of Windows 8 has both 64-bit and 32-bit versions of Internet Explorer installed, with the 64-bit version pinned to the Taskbar. The 32-bit version of IE supports only 32-bit ActiveX controls (an ActiveX control is like a mini program that performs a specific function such as displaying video) and objects, while the 64-bit version supports only 64-bit ActiveX controls and objects. If a web page fails to open correctly in the 64-bit version of IE, start the 32-bit version by double-clicking iexplore in the C:\Program Files (x86)\Internet Explorer folder of the hard disk and then reload the page.

The Internet Explorer window has a number of features that you use to find and display web documents and information (shown in Figure 7.2).

- **Address bar.** Make an entry to go directly to a web location.
- **Back and Forward buttons.** Become active after you begin browsing. These buttons give you another way to move around.
- **Refresh/Stop button.** Reloads the current web location. While a page is loading the button changes to an x, and clicking it stops the loading.
- **Bing search box.** Enables you to search for information online. If you do not see the Bing search box, you can click in the Address bar, type search terms, and then click the Search (magnifying glass) button to search.
- **Home button.** Returns to your default Home page.
- **View favorites, feeds, and history button.** Displays or hides the Favorites Center, which enables you to mark and list your favorite web locations and more.
- **Tools.** Offers commands for printing and saving pages and controlling how IE works.
- **Tabs.** Each tab holds a single web location, but you can use multiple tabs to open more than one location at a time.

When it is open, Internet Explorer behaves like any other desktop program, meaning you can minimize, restore, resize, and maximize its window. To close the program when you finish working, click the window Close (X) button, or press Alt + F4.

 T I P If you want to access IE commands using a menu bar or command bar, right-click at the left of the Home button and then click either *Menu bar* or *Command bar.*

Understanding URLs ■■■■■■■■■■■■■■■■■■■■■■■■

You learned in Chapter 3 how each computer document exists as a separate named file stored in a specific folder, and the "directions" to that location are known as the file's path. Similarly, each web document or **web page** you view is a separate file stored in a particular location on the Web. To open the document, you have to specify its address and file name, known as its **URL (Uniform Resource Locator)**.

Each URL has distinctive parts that communicate information about the location and nature of the web page it represents, as shown in Figure 7.3.

web page An HTML file (web document) stored in a particular location

URL (Uniform Resource Locator) The address of a web page

Figure 7.3 Key parts of a URL.

- **Protocol.** Represents the communication standards used by the location identified. Web page URLs use HTTP (HyperText Transfer Protocol) or HTTPS (Hypertext Transfer Protocol Secure). The *https://* protocol indicates extra security features and is verified as trusted via a certificate and certificate authority; a secure website typically requires you to sign in for security.
- **Domain.** This part of the URL identifies the overall website that holds the specific web page being referenced. In Figure 7.3, *www.treasury.gov* is the website of the United States Department of the Treasury. The *.gov* suffix at the end of the domain is the top-level domain (TLD) name, which identifies the type of organization that operates the domain. Table 7.1 lists common top-level domains. If you exclude the path and file name in the URL, the home page of the domain loads by default. Other top-level domains represent countries, such as the .au domain for Australia or .ca for Canada.
- **Path.** The folder path to the web page file.
- **File name.** The file name of the web page. The file name may have a file name extension of .htm, .html, or some variation such as .shtml, or it may have an extension such as .asp or .php if it is an active type of web page created with a framework or scripting language that works with HTML.

Table 7.1 Common Top-Level Domains (TLDs)

Name	Type
.biz	business
.com	business or information
.edu	school or other educational institution
.gov	government

Table 7.1   Common Top-Level Domains (TLDs)—*continued*

.info	informational
.mil	military (U.S. Department of Defense)
.name	individual person or family
.net	business or ISP
.org	nonprofit organization
.us	federal agency (U.S.)

Note: *Some URLs include additional information, such as a port and query, to request more specific information from the web server.*

Because URLs cannot include spaces, you may see the underscore (_) character used to separate words. Make sure that you type the URL as specified, including any underscore characters. If the page does not load and you see an error message in the browser window, you may have mistyped the URL. Select the Address bar contents, retype the URL entry, and then press Enter to try again.

Going to a Web Page

To go directly to a web page—that is, to open or load the web page directly in the Internet Explorer web browser—you use the Address bar at the top of the IE window. Note that when you type in a URL, IE lets you leave off the *http://* protocol portion; for example, you can type *www.msn.com* instead of *http://www.msn. com.* In some cases, you can leave off the *www.* portion of the domain, and enter *msn.com* rather than *www.msn.com.*

history An IE feature that tracks websites and pages you have visited within a recent time period—by default, the previous 20 days

Windows 8 includes what Microsoft calls a smarter Address bar. When you start typing an Address bar entry, the Address bar reviews sites you have previously visited, called the *history* or browsing history, your favorites, and RSS feeds (which you will learn about later in this chapter) and suggests possible matches. As shown in Figure 7.4, you can either click one of the suggested matches or press the keyboard shortcut, when present, to jump to that page. The list shows you both the site or page name in addition to its URL, making it easier to select the desired destination. If you want to see additional matches in the list, click the *Turn on suggestions (send keystrokes to Bing)* link.

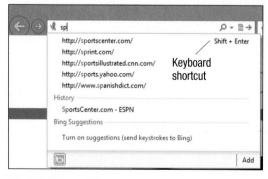

Note: *When you load a web page, the Status bar displays the URL and a progress bar as the page loads. In place of the domain, you may see an IP (Internet Protocol) address such as http://192.168.1.1.*

Figure 7.4   The smarter Address bar suggests matching sites.

Note: In some instances, when you open a web page for the first time, the Microsoft SmartScreen filter displays a blocking web page. This indicates that the website has been found on a list of sites known to have content that can infect and damage your computer. You have the option of going to your home page or proceeding to the blocked page. You will learn more about the SmartScreen filter, what it does, and how to change its settings in the next chapter.

Here's How

To go to a web page:

1. Select the URL currently in the Address bar. In some cases, clicking the URL once selects it. If that does not work, either drag over the URL or right-click the Address bar and then click *Select All*.

2. Type a different URL in the Address bar. If one of the matches that appears is the page you want to visit, click it. Otherwise, continue to Step 3.

3. Press Enter, and the page loads.

Exercise 1

Going to a Web Page

1. Display the desktop and then click the Internet Explorer button on the Taskbar.
2. If needed, click or drag over the URL in the Address bar to select it.
3. Type finance.yahoo.com and then press Enter. The Yahoo! Finance page appears.
4. Click or drag over the contents of the Address bar again.
5. Type www.smithsonian.org and then press Enter. The Smithsonian Institution's website appears.
6. Click or drag over the contents of the Address bar again.
7. Type http://en.wikipedia.org/wiki/Jackson_Pollock and then press Enter. The Jackson Pollock article on the Wikipedia website opens.
8. Click the Tools button at far right, point to *Print*, and then click *Print*. In the *Page Range* area, click Pages, leave 1 entered, and then click Print to print a copy of the first page of web page information. Write your name on the printout and then submit it to your instructor.
9. Click the window Close (X) button to close the website and browser.

Browsing Pages

browse Displaying and reading web pages in whatever order suits you

Imagine if all the billions of pages on the Web were crammed onto a single page that you had to review from top to bottom, like a long scroll of paper. It would take forever to find any information you needed! That is why the contents of the Web were engineered as discreet pages that you can "flip" to as needed, in a nonlinear fashion, more like the pages in a magazine. When a topic catches your eye, you can *browse* to the page that covers that topic by following a link.

Following a Link

hypertext A document format or system in which the document contains links to other content

hyperlink An item on a web page that you click to display another web page or to download information

The term *hypertext*, referred to in the HTML file-type acronym and http:// protocol, means that a web page document contains links, called hyperlinks, to other pages and files. Clicking a *hyperlink* (also called a link) displays the destination web page or, in some cases, begins a file download.

Hyperlinks originally appeared as specially formatted text on a web page, but today's web pages also include links in the form of graphics (pictures), buttons, navigation bars or tabs, drop-down lists, buttons for expanding lists of links, and even online advertisements. Traditionally, hyperlinked text was blue and underlined, but web page designers no longer adhere to that style. Hyperlinks may be any color, may be bold, and may lack an underline. How can you identify hyperlinked text if you are not certain how the web page designer has formatted it? You can typically point to the text or on-screen object with your mouse. If the text or object is a hyperlink, it may change color or appearance, and the mouse pointer will change from an arrow to a hand, as shown in Figure 7.5. A pop-up message displays the URL to the linked destination page, in case you want to check it to verify where the link will take you before you follow it.

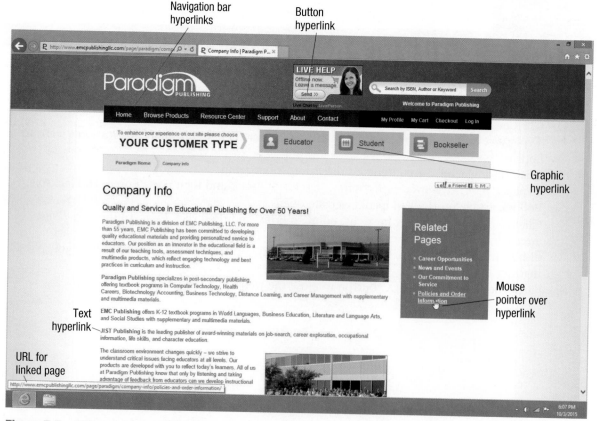

Figure 7.5 Different types of hyperlinks.

To follow any hyperlink, click it with the mouse. The contents of the destination page will download and appear in IE. After you follow a text hyperlink, it typically changes to another color or style; the default is generally for hyperlinks to start out blue and turn purple when followed.

Note: *A link that starts a download opens a prompt message at the bottom of the screen. Click the Save button to save directly to your Downloads folder in your personal folders, or click the Save down arrow, click* Save As, *specify the save location in the Save As dialog box, and then click Save to download the file.*

Backing Up or Going Forward

When you initially start Internet Explorer, the Back and Forward buttons in the upper left corner are disabled or grayed out. That is because you have not done any browsing yet. Once you move to the first page beyond your IE home page on the current tab, the Back button becomes active, and you can click it to back up to the previously viewed page.

After you click Back at least once from the current tab, the Forward button becomes active, and you can click it to move forward to the page from which you have backed up. As you back up or move forward, the Back and Forward buttons track the pages you have visited. Click and hold either button to open a menu of previously visited pages (shown in Figure 7.6) and then click one of the listed pages to redisplay it. The drop-down list saves you from having to click the Back or Forward button numerous times.

Figure 7.6   Open the menu of recent pages by clicking and holding the Back or Forward button to redisplay a previously visited page.

Note: *The History command that appears at the bottom of the menu of recent pages opens the Favorites Center pane with the History tab selected at the left side of Internet Explorer. Use that pane to go back to pages visited on previous days (shown in Figure 7.7). Click a day to list the pages you viewed and then click the page to redisplay. Click the pane's Close (X) button to close the pane.*

Going to Your Home Page

You can redisplay the Internet Explorer home page at any time. To do so, click the Home button at upper right or press Alt + Home.

To change the home page or add a new home page, first browse to the page that you want to use as a home page. Right-click the Home button and then click *Add or Change Home Page.* Click one of the options for adding the home page in the Add or Change Home Page dialog box that appears (shown in Figure 7.8) and then click Yes. Note that some web pages include a link for setting the displayed page as the IE home page. If you add a web page as an additional home page tab, each home page appears on a separate tab when you start IE. Likewise, clicking the Home button displays each of the specified home pages on a separate tab.

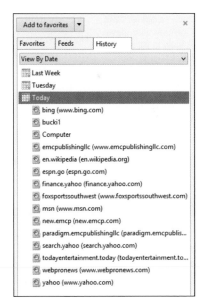

Figure 7.7   View pages from a previous day in the Favorites History tab.

Note: *To remove any previously marked home page, click the Tools button, and then click* Internet options. *In the* Home page *section on the General tab, drag over the URL of the home page to remove, right-click and click Delete, and then click OK.*

Figure 7.8 You can change the home page or add the current page as an additional home page.

Refreshing or Stopping a Page

If a page has problems loading correctly, the Refresh/Stop button at the far right end of the Address bar (shown in Figure 7.9) comes in handy. If a page does not load completely, some or all of its text may not appear, or you may see a box with a red *x* inside a frame where a graphic did not load. In such a situation, clicking the Refresh button to reload the page can help the missing information appear. While a page is loading, the Refresh button changes to the Stop button. If a page loads too slowly or you realize you have clicked the wrong link, click the Stop button to stop the page load. You can then browse to another location or click Refresh to try reloading it.

▼ **Quick Fix**

Using the Refresh Button
Click the Refresh button if you load a page and it displays information from a prior day. Or, if you are viewing a web page that updates frequently, such as a page with stock quotes, clicking Refresh ensures that the page will display the latest available data.

Figure 7.9 The Compatibility View button appears to the left of the Refresh (center)/Stop (right) button at the far right end of the Address bar.

Using Compatibility View

Compatibility View
A view in Internet Explorer that enables it to better display sites and pages designed for older browser versions

A third button, shown at the left in Figure 7.9, becomes active when you visit some web pages. The **Compatibility View** button appears whenever IE identifies a site that was designed for an older browser version. Because website programming methods and standards change over time, a site created for a set of standards supported by older browsers may not display correctly in the latest IE browser. If menus, images, or text appear out of place on the web page, click the Compatibility View button. Doing so enables IE to display the page more accurately. You need not click the Compatibility View button if a page appears to be loading and displaying correctly.

Exercise 2

Browsing the Yahoo! Website

1. Go to the desktop, if needed. Click the Internet Explorer button on the Taskbar.
2. If needed, click or drag over the URL in the Address bar to select it.
3. Type www.yahoo.com and then press Enter. The home web page of the Yahoo! site appears.
4. Click the *Jobs* link in the *Yahoo! Sites* list at the left.
5. Capture a screen shot and then save the file as **C07E02S05**.
6. Click one of the category links (such as *Career Tools*) at the top of the page.
7. Click the Back button.
8. Click the Forward button.
9. Click and hold either the Back or Forward button, and then click *Yahoo!* to return to the Yahoo! website.
10. Click the *News* link and then browse to any news topic of interest using the World tab.
11. Click the Compatibility View button.

12. Capture a screen shot and then save the file as **C07E02S12**.
13. Click the Home button to return to the home page.
14. Close Internet Explorer.
15. Submit your screen shots to your instructor.

Working with Tabs ■■■■■■■■■■■■■■■■■■■

Web page tabs is a feature that has made the latest versions of Internet Explorer, and many other browsers, much more flexible to use and more magazine-like. The tabs feature enables you to display multiple web pages at once within the IE window, rather than having to open a separate IE window for each web page you would like to view. The tabs feature can be helpful when you are performing research, for example, or when you need to compare prices for an item from two different websites.

Adding a Tab for a URL

Web page tabs appear at the top of the IE window, on the same row as the command bar and directly below the Address bar. The rightmost tab, called the New Tab button, is always blank and ready for you to use to display another web page.

Here's How

To open a web page in a new tab:

1. Click the New tab button at the right of the active web page tab(s) at the top of Internet Explorer or press Ctrl + T. The tab activates and displays thumbnails of frequently used tabs.
2a. Type a URL in the Address bar and then press Enter.

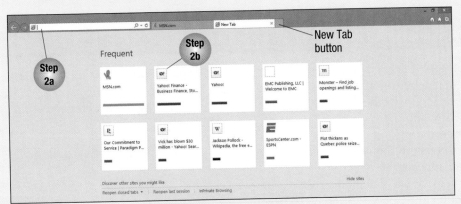

OR

2b. Click one of the page thumbnails under *Frequent*.
The page loads, and the page content appears on the new tab.

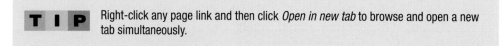

T I P Right-click any page link and then click *Open in new tab* to browse and open a new tab simultaneously.

Switching and Closing Tabs

As with a tab in a dialog box, you click an Internet Explorer web page tab to bring that tab to the forefront and display its content. As you open more tabs, however, the row of tabs may become crowded, and the more condensed tabs may not be able to show you enough of the tab name to make navigation easy. To fix this, display tabs on a separate row, as shown in Figure 7.10. Right-click any tab and then click *Show tabs on a separate row*. Repeat the process to redisplay tabs at the right of the address box.

Moved
tabs

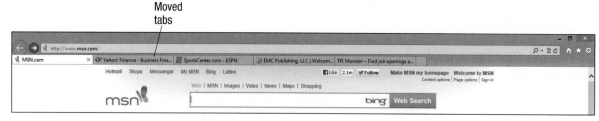

Figure 7.10 Displaying tabs on a separate row makes it easier to work with many open tabs.

To close any individual tab, click the Close (X) button that appears on the tab itself when the tab is active. If you have multiple tabs running when you exit Internet Explorer, the program prompts you to confirm that you want to close all tabs. Click Close all tabs to do so.

Exercise 3

Using Tabs to View Multiple Web Pages

1. Go to the desktop, if needed, and then click the Internet Explorer button on the Taskbar.
2. Click the New Tab button at the right of the tab for the home page.
3. Type whitehouse.gov in the Address bar and then press Enter. The main web page of the White House site appears.
4. Click the New Tab button at the right of the tab for the White House page.
5. Type wikipedia.org in the Address bar and then press Enter. The main web page of the Wikipedia site appears.
6. Click the home page tab. The home page becomes the active web page.
7. Click the White House page tab. That tab becomes active.
8. Click the New Tab button at the right of the open tabs.
9. Capture a screen shot and then save the file as **C07E03**.
10. Click the tab for the Wikipedia website.
11. Click the tab Close (X) button to close the Wikipedia tab.
12. Click the tab Close (X) button to close the White House tab.
13. Click the tab Close (X) button to close the New Tab tab.
14. Leave IE open for the next exercise.
15. Submit your screen shot to your instructor.

Searching the Web ■■■■□■□□□□□■■□□□□□■■■■■■□■□□

Internet Explorer's Address bar combines its navigational capabilities with a built-in search feature. The Address bar in IE provides a direct, convenient way to search for information on the Web. In this case, the search feature, by default, uses the **Bing** Internet *search engine* operated by Microsoft to search the Web for the word or phrase you specify.

To search the Web:

1. Click in the Address Bar of the IE window.
2. Type the word, words, or phrase you want to search for.
3a. Press the Enter key or click the Search (magnifying glass) button to display the search results in the current tab.
    OR
3b. Press Alt + Enter or click the Go To (right-pointing arrow button at the far right end of the address bar) to display the search results in a new tab.

Here's How

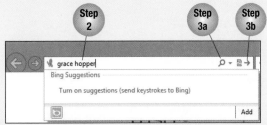

> **T I P** To start a search within the contents of the displayed web page, press Ctrl + F. Type the search term in the *Find* text box and then press Enter.

Bing lists the search results links and includes a brief description of each. For example, Figure 7.11 shows the results that appear after a search for *grace hopper*. When there are numerous results, you can scroll down to the bottom of the page and then click a number link to display another page listing additional results. The Navigation bar above the search results list actually enables you to find different types of information about the search term. For example, you could click the *Images* link to see pictures of the word or phrase you searched for. Bing also includes links to Related Searches at the right. Click any link in the list of search results or in the lists at the left to display information about the search subject.

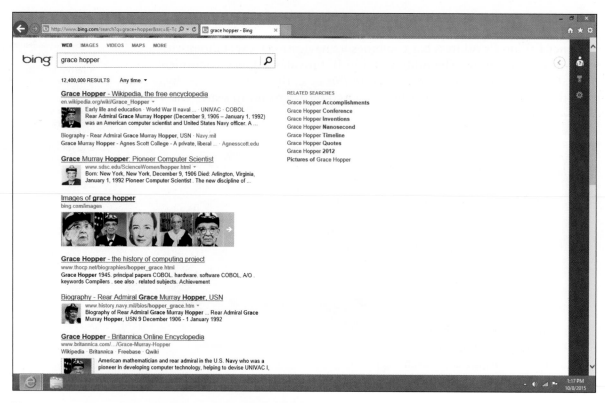

Figure 7.11 The results listed after a search for *grace hopper*.

Note: *Internet Explorer can be customized to use another search engine such as Google, Yahoo, Ask.com, or dogpile.com. Your school may have customized its computers to use another search tool, in which case you can use the search engine that appears. Most search engines work in the same way.*

Note: *Other search engines may present search results differently. For example, some search engines rank results or give you estimates about how well a result matches the search text you entered.*

Because of the vast volume of information now available on the Web, searching for a one-word, generic term yields such a long list of results that you may never find the particular bit of information that you need. For example, searching for *flower* on the day this chapter was written yielded 601,000,000 matching results! Bing and other search engines enable you to use a number of techniques to make your search more specific so that you see a more targeted (better matching) list of search results.

For starters, use more specific words and phrases, and include the search phrase in quotation marks. The search box can accept entries up to 150 characters long. If you include quotation marks around the term, the search engine looks for the exact phrase you specify. For example, a search for *yellow ladyslipper* returns more than 134,000 matches, while adding the quotes to search for *"yellow ladyslipper"* reduces the matches to about 31,600. In either case, those results are more narrow than the 601 + million matches returned for *flower.*

Most search engines, including Bing, enable you to use operators to specify whether the results should match any or all of the words entered in cases where you leave out the quotation marks. Table 7.2 lists the basic operators. You must enter the operators in all capital letters.

Table 7.2   Web Search Operators

Operator	Use	Example	Alternatives in Other Search Engines
AND	Results must match all words; typically assumed if omitted.	knicks AND pistons	and, and sometimes + (plus)
OR	Results may match any of the words.	knicks OR pistons	or, and sometimes | (pipe)
NOT	Results include the first word but not the second word (the word preceded by the operator).	knicks NOT pistons	- (minus)

 Most search engines ignore other common words such as *the* or *in*. Use the most descriptive words that you can when performing a search. Most search engines also ignore capitalization. Many websites include a search box for searching the site's contents. In many instances, you also can use quotation marks and operators for more specific searches using a site-based search box.

You can include keywords or meta words with a search term when using some search engines. The keywords make the search more specific, enabling you to search by location or file type. Table 7.3 lists often-used search keywords; most search engines support the same or similar keywords. (Most search engine pages have a Help link that you can click to learn about techniques such as using keywords.)

Table 7.3   Common Search Keywords

Keyword	Use	Example
contains:	Specifies that matching sites must have links to the specified file type.	"yellow ladyslipper" contains:jpg
site:	Finds all documents on a domain (website) and its subdomains.	"yellow ladyslipper" site: www.fs.fed.us
intitle: or inbody:	Finds all documents that have the search text in the document title (intitle:) or body text (inbody:).	inbody:"yellow ladyslipper"
url:	Searches to check whether a specific domain or file is indexed by the search engine.	url:www.purdue.edu

Using Bing Suggestions

Bing suggestions A feature that enables Bing to suggest searches that are more specific based on the search term you enter

The Address box provides a form of built-in assistance called **Bing suggestions**. When you type a search word or phrase in the search box, the search suggestions pane appears below the box. The pane lists suggestions that further refine the search term(s) you typed and help you narrow your search, as shown in Figure 7.12. Click one of the suggestions in the list to perform that search.

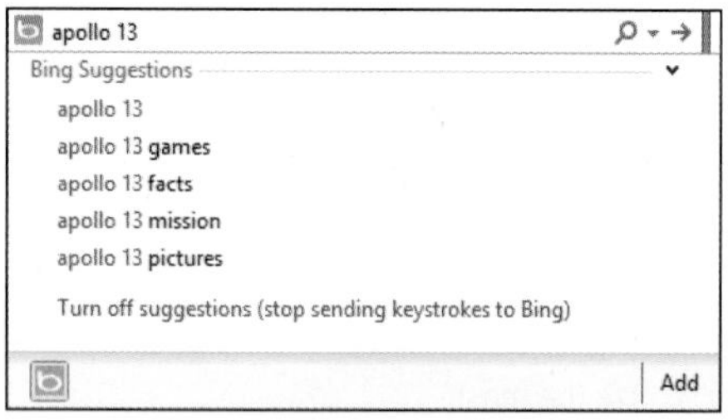

You can turn Bing suggestions off and back on. Start typing a search term in the Address bar and then click the *Turn on suggestions (send keystrokes to Bing)* link in the menu. To turn suggestions off, repeat the process but click *Turn off suggestions (stop sending keystrokes to Bing)*.

Figure 7.12 Turn Bing suggestions on and off using the choice at the bottom of the menu.

Adding a Regular or Visual Search Provider

For even more robust searches, you can set up a visual search provider. Doing so enables the search suggestions list to include **visual suggestions**, images and information about a potential search match, so you can go directly to a result that best answers your question or provides the information you need. Once you have installed one or more visual search providers, you can display and select from visual suggestions in the search suggestions list.

visual suggestions Enhanced search functionality provided by a search partner that enables the search suggestions list to include images and information

You use the same process to add a regular search provider to supplement the results provided by Bing. While major search engines such as Google and Yahoo! work much the same as Bing, other search providers perform more specialized searches; examples include weather search providers, company search providers, and search providers offered by particular media outlets or even Facebook.

Here's How

To add a regular or visual search provider in IE:

1. Click in the Address bar and then start typing a search term.
2. Click *Add* in the lower right corner of the menu. IE opens the Internet Explorer Gallery page in a new tab.
3. Scroll through the search provider thumbnails that appear to find the one you want. A search provider that offers visual search includes *Visual Search* in its name at the bottom of its thumbnail. Click the thumbnail of the desired search provider. 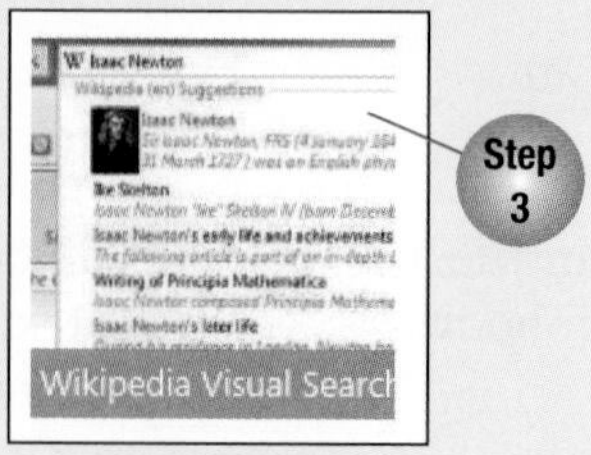
4. Click the Add to Internet Explorer button for the desired search partner. The Add Search Provider dialog box appears.
5. In the Add Search Provider dialog box, click Add.
6. Close the Internet Explorer Gallery tab.

Step 3

To perform a visual search:

1. Type the search term(s) in the Address bar. If suggested keystrokes are turned off, click *Turn on suggestions (send keystrokes to Bing)* to turn them on.
2. At the bottom of the search suggestions pane, click the icon for the visual search provider, if that provider is not already selected. The visual search suggestions appear. (Click the Bing icon to switch back to normal search suggestions when desired.)
3. Click the desired visual suggestion.

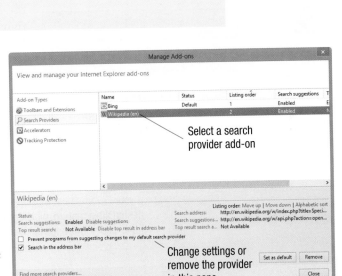

Manage search providers and their settings in the Internet Options dialog box. Click the Tools button and then click *Internet options* in the menu. Click the Programs tab and then, under *Manage add-ons*, click the Manage add-ons button. In the Manage Add-ons window that appears, click *Search Providers* in the *Add-on Types* list at the left. In the list that appears, click the add-on to manage. As shown in Figure 7.13, you can then make such changes as disabling and enabling suggestions or removing the search provider add-on. Click Close to close the Manage Add-ons window after making your changes and then click OK to close the Internet Options dialog box.

Figure 7.13 Change search provider settings or remove a search provider.

Exercise 4

Searching for a Topic Online

1. With IE open from the last exercise, select the text in the Address bar.
2. Type **thomas edison phonograph** and then press Enter.
3. Capture a screen shot and then save the file as **C07E04S03**.
4. Click Images on the Bing Navigation bar above the search results.
5. Capture a screen shot and then save the file as **C07E04S05**.
6. Click the text in the Address bar to select the text.
7. Type **th** and then click *Turn on suggestions (send keystrokes to Bing)*. If keystrokes are already turned on, click the link to turn them off, and click it again to turn them on.
8. Type **omas edison** to finish the name and then click one of the search suggestions. (If at any point you are prompted to turn on AutoComplete, at the bottom of the screen, click No.)
9. Capture a screen shot and then save the file as **C07E04S09**.
10. Click one of the results links.
11. Click the Back button.
12. Submit your screen shots to your instructor.

Working with Favorites ■■■■■■ ■■■■■■■■ ■ ■ ■■ ■

favorite page A frequently visited website or page that is saved in the list in the Favorites Center for easy access

You have already seen that Internet Explorer enables you to set up multiple home pages. Because most users quickly develop a list of sites they visit frequently to perform research, get news and entertainment, handle finances or shop online, and so on, IE offers an even better way to record and even organize sites you visit often. You can mark a frequently visited site as a ***favorite page***. You can use a listed favorite to return to the corresponding page or site without having to remember its name.

Displaying and Using the Favorites Bar

For fastest access to your favorites, you can display a Favorites bar below the page tabs and add your favorites to it, although you should reserve this technique for the sites you use frequently. To display or hide the *Favorites bar*, right-click a blank area at the right of the New Tab button and then click *Favorites bar*. Browse to the page that you want to add to the Favorites bar and then click the Add to Favorites bar button on the Favorites bar (shown in Figure 7.14). To remove a favorite from the Favorites bar, right-click it and then click *Delete*.

Add to Favorites bar button

Button for a favorite

Figure 7.14 You can populate the Favorites bar with buttons for jumping to favorite pages.

> **T I P** If your Favorites bar includes the Suggested Sites button, click it to turn on the suggested sites feature, which gives you ideas about sites you can check out that might have similar offerings to sites you have visited.

Marking a Favorite Page

The upper right corner of Internet Explorer includes the View favorites, feeds, and history button, which looks like a star. You use this button to open the Favorites Center, which you can use to mark a web page as a favorite on the Favorites Center list.

Here's How

To add a web page to the Favorites list:

1. Jump or browse to the page that you want to mark as a favorite.
2. Click the View favorites, feeds, and history button near the upper right corner of IE or press Alt + C.
3. Click the Favorites tab in the pane.
4. Click the Add to favorites button. The Add a Favorite dialog box opens.

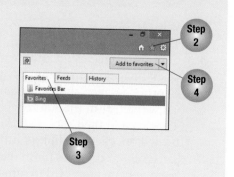

5. Edit the favorite name listed in the *Name* text box, if needed.

6. If you want to store the favorite in an existing folder, choose the desired folder from the *Create in* drop-down list. To place the favorite in a new folder, click New folder, make an entry in the *Folder Name* text box of the Create a Folder dialog box, make a choice from the *Create in* drop-down list to designate the new folder as a subfolder, and then click Create.

7. Click Add to close the Add a Favorite dialog box and finish creating the favorite.

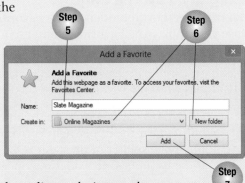

 Ctrl + D is the keyboard shortcut for opening the Add a Favorite dialog box to mark a favorite page.

Organizing Favorites

You can think of a favorite (and even a folder for favorites) as a temporary setting, because you can make changes to your favorites at any time. You can delete, rename, and move favorites and folders to suit your changing needs.

To handle these tasks, open the favorites by clicking the View favorites, feeds, and history button or by pressing Alt + C and then clicking the Favorites tab. Click the Add to favorites button drop-down arrow and then click *Organize favorites* in the menu that appears. The Organize Favorites dialog box appears. If the favorite you want to work with is in a folder, click the folder and then click the item to change. (To select a folder, click it.) As shown in Figure 7.15, use the buttons at the bottom to make the following changes:

Figure 7.15 Manage favorites in the Organize Favorites dialog box.

- **Create a new folder.** Click the New Folder button, type a folder name, and then press Enter.

- **Move the favorite or folder.** Click the Move button, select or create the folder where you would like to place the selected item in the Browse for Folder dialog box that appears, and then click OK.

- **Rename the favorite or folder.** Click the Rename button, type the new name, and then press Enter.

- **Delete the favorite or folder.** Click the Delete button and then click Yes in the Delete File or Delete Folder confirmation dialog box that appears.

When you finish making your changes to favorites, click the Close (X) button in the Organize Favorites dialog box.

▼ **Quick Fix**

Backing Up Your Favorites
Windows 8 stores your favorites in the Favorites subfolder of your personal folder, and if you periodically create a backup of that folder, it can help you find and retrieve a lost favorite. Display the contents of the backup Favorites folder in a File Explorer window, navigate to the favorite you want to restore, and then double-click its shortcut. When the page opens in IE, re-mark it as a favorite.

Going to a Favorite Page

The favorites remain hidden in the Favorites Center until you need to use them. Once you display the Favorites Center, you can open a folder and then click the favorite page that you want to display.

Here's How

To display a favorite web page:

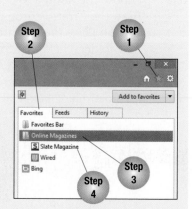

1. Click the View favorites, feeds, and history button near the upper right corner of Internet Explorer or press Alt + C.
2. If the list of favorites does not appear in the pane that opens, click the Favorites tab.
3. If the favorite you wish to view is in a folder, click the folder that holds the favorite to display. If needed, click additional subfolders.
4. Click the desired favorite. The Favorites Center pane closes, and the favorite page opens in Internet Explorer.

Exercise 5

Marking and Using a Favorite

1. Click the Home button to return to the home page.
2. If needed, click or drag over the URL in the Address bar to select it.
3. Type www.refdesk.com and then press Enter. The Refdesk.com website offers links to dozens of research, writing, news, and information sites, making it a great resource for students, writers, researchers, and anyone else with a healthy dose of curiosity.
4. Click the View favorites, feeds, and history button near the upper right corner of IE, click the Favorites tab if needed, and then click *Add to favorites*.
5. Edit the *Name* text box entry to read **Refdesk.com...Reference, Facts, News**.
6. Click the New folder button.
7. Type Research Resources in the *Folder Name* text box of the Create a Folder dialog box that appears. Make sure that *Favorites* is selected as the *Create in* drop-down list choice, and then click Create.
8. Back in the Add a Favorite dialog box, click Add to finish adding the new favorite.
9. Click Home on the command bar to redisplay the home page.
10. Click the View favorites, feeds, and history button and then click the Favorites tab, if needed.
11. Click the *Research Resources* folder to display the Refdesk.com favorite.
12. Capture a screen shot and then save the file as **C07E05**.
13. Click the Home button to close the View favorites, feeds, and history pane and return to the home page.
14. Click the View favorites, feeds, and history button to redisplay the Favorites Center pane and then click the Favorites tab, if needed. Click the *Research Resources* folder, if needed, to display the Refdesk.com favorite and then click the favorite. The Refdesk.com website appears.
15. Exit IE.
16. Submit your screen shot to your instructor.

Using Accelerators

As fast as researching any topic on the Web has become, IE 10 includes a way to make it even faster: *accelerators*. You can select text on a web page, right-click, and then click one of the accelerators that appears at the bottom of the shortcut menu. The accelerators enabled, by default, include Email, Map with Bing, Search with Bing, and Translate with Bing. For example, in Figure 7.16, a geographical location is selected on the web page. To view a map of the location, right-click the selection and then point to *Map with Bing* to display a pop-up map. Clicking *Map with Bing* opens a separate tab with more map information. Pointing to *All Accelerators* displays a submenu with choices including a choice to find more accelerators.

accelerators A feature in IE that enables you to perform tasks with selected content, such as mapping a selected location or performing a search for a selected term

Right-click the selection on the web page

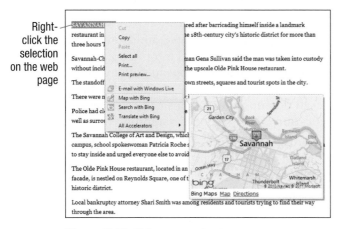

Figure 7.16 Using an accelerator.

Pinning a Site to the Taskbar

Internet Explorer now enables you to pin selected websites to the Taskbar. This places an icon for the site directly on the desktop Taskbar so that you can click the icon to both start IE and to jump to the pinned site. To pin a site, navigate to its page and then drag its browser tab down to the Taskbar, as shown in Figure 7.17. When you release the mouse button, an icon for the page appears. To remove a pinned web page, right-click its icon and then click *Unpin this program from taskbar*.

Already pinned web page   Web page being pinned

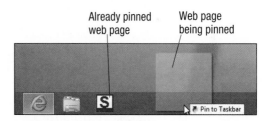

Figure 7.17 Pin a web page to the Taskbar for easier access.

Note: *If you need to limit your time online, such as when using a mobile hotspot, you can go offline after you have opened the page or pages that you want to read. Press the Alt key, click File to open the File menu, and then click* Work Offline. *Repeat the command sequence when you are ready to go back online.*

Responding to the Notification Bar

Internet Explorer, by default, is set up to protect your system by taking a cautious approach toward any type of active content or controls. *Active content* typically refers to interactive or animated elements on a web page, including such items as pop-ups and self-playing movies. Receiving and using or displaying this type of content often requires the transfer of software add-ins, such as Adobe Flash Player or other executable code. Because they make web pages livelier, you may welcome

active content On-line content that is interactive or ani-mated; also loosely refers to pop-ups and certain down-loads that may be required to run such content

some of this content and the accompanying code or programs, such as an ActiveX control or Flash Player, but you need to keep in mind that these seemingly harmless transfers may be hiding malicious code intended to damage your system. (More about this in Chapter 8.)

When a web page wants to download or display some type of active content on a page, the Notification bar pops up at the bottom of the screen, as shown in Figure 7.18.

Figure 7.18 The Notification bar appears at the bottom of the screen.

The choices for dealing with the Notification bar message will vary depending on the nature of the notification. For example, in Figure 7.18, one type of notification asks if IE should save password information, and you can click Yes or No as desired. The Notification bar also appears for any file download, giving you the option of saving the file or in some cases running the file. Other notifications alert you about blocked pop-ups and add-ons and other active content. Use the buttons in the Notification bar to respond as appropriate.

If you prefer to dismiss the Notification bar without performing any action, click the Close (X) button at the far right end of the bar.

Note: *The Notification bar cannot be turned on or off. However, it automatically fades away if you ignore it.*

Note: *In some cases, in addition to the Notification bar, a dialog box appears asking you whether to install software needed by the website. Make sure the software is from a trusted source before doing so.*

Working with RSS Feeds ■■■■■■■■■■■■■■■■■■■■■■

RSS (Really Simple Syndication) feed Regularly updated website information, such as news or pictures, which a user can visit or subscribe to; also called XML feeds, syndicated content, and web feeds

When you find favorite websites that are useful and informative, you might get into a routine of visiting those sites on a regular basis. But even then you have to browse through the site to find the relevant content that you want to read. Internet Explorer solves this problem by enabling you to subscribe to RSS feeds. An *RSS feed* delivers specially designated content on a website.

While you can certainly browse to and read RSS content, you save even more time by subscribing to have the content delivered to Internet Explorer. Having the latest content delivered directly to your system saves time, as you might imagine. You do not have to visit a site and review its contents to see if you have read the latest.

Adding a Feed

The Internet Explorer command bar provides an automatic alert when you browse to a website that offers an RSS feed. The View feeds on this page button becomes active, and you can use it to subscribe to the feed.

To subscribe to an RSS Feed:

1. Right-click at the right of the New Tab button and then click *Command bar* to display the command bar.
2. Navigate to the page that has the RSS feed you want to follow.
3. Click the down-pointing arrow next to the View feeds on this page button on the IE command bar when it becomes active (turns orange). If there is only one feed on the page, click the button itself and then skip to Step 5.
4. Click the feed that you want to view.
5. Click the *Subscribe to this feed* link on the page, or click the View favorites, feeds, and history button on the Favorites bar, and then click the Subscribe to this feed button.
6. Edit the *Name* text box entry, if desired, and optionally make a new subfolder in the Feeds folder to hold the feed.
7. Click Subscribe. The feed subscription is added.

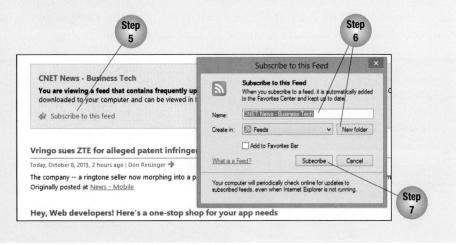

Note: *You also can click an orange RSS feed icon on a web page to start the process of subscribing to the feed.*

Reading a Feed

The Favorites Center where you list your favorite web pages for easier access also is the location where you select and view RSS feeds.

 You can use a keyword search to find websites with feeds about a topic of interest. For example, search for *rss feeds: stocks* to find feeds about stocks and the stock market. Many websites display an RSS icon, like the one in the IE command bar, next to any link that leads to an RSS feed. Click the link and then click *Subscribe to this feed*, if desired, on the page that appears.

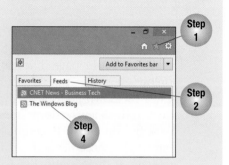
To display a subscribed feed:

1. Click the View favorites, feeds, and history button or press Alt + C.
2. Click the Feeds tab.
3. If needed, click the folder that holds the feed to display any subfolders.
4. Click the desired feed. The Favorites Center pane closes, and the feed page opens in Internet Explorer.

Using the New Internet Explorer App from the Start Screen

If you want a more streamlined approach to web browsing in which you can see more of each page online and do not have to bother so much with settings and controls, try the new Windows 8 Internet Explorer app, accessed from the Windows 8 Start screen.

To get started, open the Start screen and then click the Internet Explorer app tile. As shown in Figure 7.19, the screen that appears has no navigation controls, leaving more screen real estate available for viewing your information.

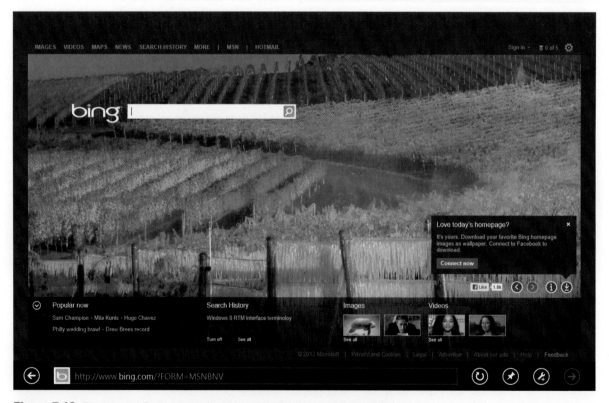

Figure 7.19 The Internet Explorer app displays streamlined on-screen controls.

To quit this version of IE, drag down from the top of the screen as for any other app.

Navigating

If you do not see IE's navigation controls and commands, right-click on the screen. As shown in Figure 7.20, the Address bar appears at the bottom of the screen, the Back button at left, a Refresh button at right, and tabs along the top. To go to a page, type its URL in the Address bar and then press Enter. To open a new tab, click the New Tab (plus) button to the right of the tabs along the top of the screen, enter the URL in the Address bar, and then press Enter. Click tab tiles along the top to move between tabs. Clicking the X button in the upper right corner of a tab tile closes the tab. Navigating on the page is the same as the desktop version of IE; however, some active content may not work correctly in the new IE. While you are working in IE, right-click as needed to toggle the commands and tab tiles on and off the screen.

T I P As you type an address in the Address bar, tiles for previously viewed pages appear. Click a tile to display that web page.

T I P The IE app includes a new feature called Flip ahead for faster browsing on touch-enabled devices. To turn this feature on, select the Settings charm from the IE app. Click Internet Options, and in the pane that appears, drag the Turn on flip ahead slider to the right. Press Esc to close the pane.

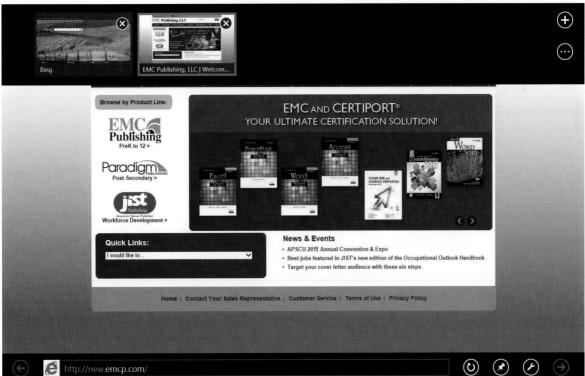

Figure 7.20 Right-click the screen to display navigation controls and commands in the Internet Explorer app.

Figure 7.21 A tile for Slate online magazine's home page is added to the desktop (right).

Pinning a Page to the Start Screen

One of the command buttons available in the IE app is the Pin site button, which is at the right of the Refresh button and has a pushpin icon. Click it and then click *Pin to Start* in the menu. Click *Pin to Start* again in the pop-up that appears to add a tile for the active web page to your Start screen (shown in Figure 7.21).

Exercise 6

Using the Internet Explorer App from the Start Screen

1. Display the Windows 8 Start screen.
2. Click the Internet Explorer tile.
3. If needed, right-click to display the Address bar and commands at the bottom and then click or drag over the URL in the Address bar to select it.
4. Type money.cnn.com and then press Enter. The CNNMoney.com website offers information about financial markets and personal finance.
5. Right-click in a blank area of the active screen so that you see the tabs at the top and then click the New Tab button.
6. Type si.edu in the Address bar and then press Enter.
7. Right-click the screen to display both the Address bar and the tab tiles.
8. Capture a screen shot and then save the file as **C07E06**.
9. Go back to IE, if necessary, display the page tabs if needed, and then click the CNNMoney tab to return to that tab.
10. Submit your screen shot to your instructor.
11. Close the Internet Explorer app by dragging down from the top of the screen.

CHAPTER SUMMARY

- The World Wide Web consists of HTML-formatted documents that can be viewed using a web browser program connected to the Internet.
- The Internet Explorer web browser is included as part of Windows 8. Start IE using the button on the desktop Taskbar. Close the IE window to close the program.
- The Internet Explorer window includes an Address bar for navigating, as well as other features for navigating and browsing.
- A website's URL identifies its location on the Internet, including domain (website), folder, file name, and the communications protocol used to retrieve it.
- To go directly to a web page, type its URL in the Address bar and then press Enter.
- Click links or hyperlinks to browse between web pages. Use the Back and Forward buttons to visit pages previously viewed during the current IE work session. Click the Home button on the command bar to redisplay the home page.
- Change to Compatibility View to display web pages designed for earlier browsers if text, menus, or other objects appear out of place.

- The tabs feature enables you to have multiple web pages open at once. Click the blank New tab button, type a URL in the Address bar, and then press Enter to activate a new tab.
- Click a tab to view its contents.
- To search for information on the Web, type the search term(s) in the Address bar and then press Enter.
- Include quotation marks to search for an exact phrase, or use operators or keywords to make a search more specific.
- Turn on search suggestions, and as you type a search term, search suggestions appear. Click a search suggestion to select a more detailed search.
- Set up a visual search provider to enable the search suggestions list to display images and information as search suggestions.
- Right-click at the right of the New Tab button and then click a submenu choice to display and hide the Favorites bar, command bar, and more.
- If you view a web page often, you can add it to the Favorites bar or mark it as a favorite, which lists it in the Favorites Center. To view a favorite, click it on the Favorites bar or open the Favorites Center, click the Favorites tab, and then click the favorite.
- Select content on a web page, right-click, and then point to or click an accelerator choice to perform a task using that data.
- To pin a web page to the Taskbar, drag its page tab to the Taskbar.
- The Notification bar pops up at the bottom of the screen to alert you when a web page wants to download active content to your system, to ask you whether to save password information, to notify you about blocked pop-ups, and more. Use the buttons in the Notification bar to respond as desired.
- An RSS feed delivers specially formatted content to which frequent readers can subscribe.
- Use the *View feeds on this page* button on the Favorites bar, when it becomes active, to choose a feed. Click the *Subscribe to this feed* link to begin the subscription process.
- To view a feed to which you have previously subscribed, open the Favorites Center, click the Feeds tab, and then click the feed.
- Use the Windows 8 Internet Explorer app from the Start screen for a less cluttered browsing experience.
- Right-click the IE app to display its Address bar, tabs, and other controls.

CONCEPTS CHECK

Completion: Answer the following questions in a Word document.

Part 1

Multiple Choice
1. The Web organizes information into _____ of information.
   a. blocks
   b. pages
   c. categories
   d. libraries

2. To start Internet Explorer on the desktop, use the _____ .
   a. Search charm
   b. Taskbar
   c. Navigation pane
   d. Both a and c

3. URL stands for _____ .
   a. Uniform Resource Label
   b. Unisource Reform Location
   c. Uniform Resource Locator
   d. Under Radar Level

4. To go directly to a web page, type its URL in the _____ and then press Enter.
   a. Address bar
   b. URL box
   c. Navigation bar
   d. browse bar

5. A hyperlink on a web page can be _____ .
   a. linked text
   b. a linked graphic
   c. a linked button
   d. Any item from a through c

6. Click the _____ and _____ buttons to view a web page already viewed during the current Internet Explorer work session.
   a. Browse, Return
   b. Back, Forward
   c. Reverse, Continue
   d. Up, Down

7. The _____ feature enables you to open multiple web pages in Internet Explorer.
   a. Pages
   b. Snap
   c. Tabs
   d. Reveal

8. A _____ enables you to find information on the Web.
   a. Find bar
   b. Navigation bar
   c. search monitor
   d. search engine

9. Use the _____ to return to a favorite web page.
   a. Favorites Center
   b. Favorites Menu
   c. Favorites Tab
   d. Favorites Dialog Box

10. RSS stands for _____ .
    a. Random Statistic Service
    b. Really Simple Syndication
    c. Relative Service System
    d. Retrieving Statistics Service

Part 2

Short Answer

11. What does HTML stand for?

_____

12. What are hyperlinks in a hypertext document?

_____

13. Describe how to open a web page in a new tab in both versions of IE.

_____

14. Explain how to switch between open tabs in both versions of IE.

_____

15. What is a search suggestion?

_____

16. Explain why you would mark a page as a favorite.

_____

17. What is an accelerator?

_____

18. What is the purpose of the Notification bar?

_____

19. Explain what an RSS feed is.

_____

20. How do you pin a page in both versions of IE?

_____

SKILLS CHECK

Save all solution files to the default Documents folder or any alternate folder specified by your instructor.

Note: *If the Notification bar appears at any point during these exercises, click the Close (X) button at the far right end of the bar to close it. Also, skip any online ads that appear.*

Guided Check

Assessment 1

Display a Web Page in Desktop IE

1. Go to the Windows desktop and then click the Internet Explorer button on the Taskbar.

2. Display another web page.
   a. Click in the Address bar. (Drag over the text to select it if IE does not select the entire entry for you.)
   b. Type www.cnn.com.
   c. Press Enter.
   d. Capture a screen shot of the desktop and then save it as **C07A01S02**.
3. Display another web page.
   a. Click in the Address bar. (Drag over the text to select it if IE does not select the entire entry for you.)
   b. Type senate.gov.
   c. Press Enter.
   d. Click the Compatibility View button.
   e. Capture a screen shot of the desktop and then save it as **C07A01S03**.
4. Redisplay the home page by clicking the Home button near the upper right corner of the IE window.
5. Click the window Close (X) button to close Internet Explorer.
6. Submit the screen shots to your instructor.

Assessment
2

Browsing the Web
1. Click the Internet Explorer button on the Taskbar if the desktop version of IE is not already open.
2. Display another web page.
   a. Click in the Address bar. (Drag over the text to select it if IE does not select the entire entry for you.)
   b. Type www.wsj.com.
   c. Press Enter.
3. Browse the page.
   a. Click the MarketWatch button link near the top.
   b. Click the *Personal Finance* link, which is the fifth choice on the Navigation bar at the top of the page that appears.
   c. Capture a screen shot of the desktop and then save it as **C07A02**.
   d. Back in Internet Explorer, click the Back button.
   e. Click the Forward button.
   f. Click the link for the lead story on the page.
4. Redisplay the home page. (Click the Home button near the upper right corner of the IE window.)
5. Submit the screen shot to your instructor.

Assessment
3

Using Web Page Tabs
1. With IE still open, display another web page.
   a. Click in the Address bar. (Drag over the text to select it if IE does not select the entire entry for you.)
   b. Type www.moma.org.
   c. Press Enter.
2. Activate another tab and display a page in it.
   a. Click the New Tab button at the right of the active tab.
   b. Type www.guggenheim.org.
   c. Capture a screen shot of IE with the multiple tabs open and then save it as **C07A03S02**.
3. Switch tabs.
   a. Click the tab of the MoMA page. The page becomes active.
   b. Click the Compatibility View button.
   c. Capture a screen shot of IE with the MoMA tab active and then save it as **C07A03S03**.

4. Close a tab.
   a. Back in Internet Explorer, click the New York (Guggenheim Museum) tab.
   b. Click the tab's Close (X) button to close the tab.
5. Redisplay the home page by clicking the Home button.
6. Submit the screen shots to your instructor.

Assessment 4 Searching the Web
1. With IE still open, perform a broad search.
   a. Click in the Address bar.
   b. Type T Rex.
   c. Press Enter.
   d. Capture a screen shot of the search results and then save it as **C07A04S01**.
2. Perform a more narrow search using an operator.
   a. Drag over the contents of the Address bar.
   b. Type "T Rex" NOT dinosaur AND band. This tells the search engine to exclude the word *dinosaur* from the results but to ensure that matches do have the word *band*.
   c. Press Enter.
   d. Capture a screen shot of the search results and then save it as **C07A04S02**.
3. Search for a particular type of content using a keyword.
   a. Drag over the contents of the Address bar.
   b. Type "T Rex" AND band contains: MP3. This tells the search engine to find results that include the word *band* and music files in the MP3 file format.
   c. Press Enter.
   d. Capture a screen shot of the search results and then save it as **C07A04S03**.
4. Redisplay the home page by clicking the Home button.
5. Submit the screen shots to your instructor.

On Your Own

Assessment 5 Browsing and Using Tabs in the Internet Explorer App from the Start Screen
1. Display the Start screen and then click the Internet Explorer tile.
2. Go to www.nasa.gov.
3. Click the NASA in Your Life button.
4. Capture a screen shot of the web page and then save it as **C07A05S04**.
5. Return to the IE app, right-click to display the commands, if needed, and then click the Back button.
6. Right-click the Solar System button and then click *Open link in new tab*. Right-click and then click the tile for the new tab if it does not activate on its own.
7. Right-click to display the tabs at the top of the screen.
8. Capture a screen shot of the web page and then save it as **C07A05S08**.
9. Return to the IE app and then close the second tab.
10. Go to investing.money.msn.com/investments/stock-price.
11. Type MSFT in the *Enter a name or symbol* text box and then click Get Quote.

12. Wait at least five minutes and then click the Refresh button to update the stock quote.
13. Close the IE app and then return to the desktop version of IE, which should still be open from the last assessment.
14. Submit the screen shots to your instructor.

Assessment 6 Marking and Using Favorite Sites

1. Go to cnet.com. (In some cases you can skip typing the *www.* part of a URL.)
2. Save the site as a favorite in the Favorites Center, naming it CNET and placing it in a new folder named Computers that you create.
3. Go to zdnet.com.
4. Save the site as a favorite in the Favorites Center, naming it ZDNET and placing it in the Computers folder.
5. Drag the zdnet.com tab to the Taskbar to pin it there. Maximize the IE window, if needed.
6. Open the Favorites Center, click the Favorites tab, and then click the Computers folder.
7. Capture a screen shot with the Favorites Center open and then save it as **C07A06**.
8. Use the Favorites Center to go to the CNET favorite page.
9. Use the Favorites Center to go to the ZDNET favorite page.
10. Redisplay the home page.
11. Unpin the zdnet.com icon from the Taskbar.
12. Submit the screen shot to your instructor.

Assessment 7 Subscribing to and Viewing a Feed

1. Use the Favorites Center to go to the ZDNET favorite you created in Assessment 6.
2. Click the All Writers choice on the top row of the Navigation bar.
3. Browse the blogs and then click the blog titled *All About Microsoft*.
4. On the page, click the orange RSS Feed button beside Follow via:.
5. Click the *Subscribe to this feed* link, leave the blog name as suggested in the *Name* box, leave the Feeds folder selected, and then click Subscribe.
6. Redisplay the home page.
7. Open the Favorites Center and then click the Feeds tab.
8. Capture a screen shot with the Favorites Center open and then save it as **C07A08**.
9. Use the Favorites Center to go to the feed you subscribed to in Step 5.
10. Redisplay the home page.
11. Submit the screen shot to your instructor and then delete the subscribed feed.

Assessment 8 Group Activity: Researching a Topic

1. Pair off with another student to complete this project.
2. Select a topic that you want to research from another class or your job. For example, research a particular leader discussed in a history or political science class, or a particular plant species covered in a botany class.
3. Use Internet Explorer to find and print at least five web pages covering the selected topic.
4. Write a paragraph or two summarizing the key points in the pages you found and then print your summary.
5. Label all the printouts with your names and then submit them to your instructor.

CHALLENGE PROJECT

You are the IT manager for a small company, and you need to purchase new notebook computers that use the Windows 8 operating system. Use Internet Explorer to find an online computer retailer and then select a notebook model to purchase. Capture a screen shot of the web page with the model and price of the system, and then save it as **C07A09S01**. Find three other sites that offer the same model, or one with comparable features, capture screen shots of the web pages displaying those systems and prices, and then save the files as **C07A09S02**, **C07A09S03**, and **C07A09S04**. Submit the screen shots to your instructor.

Ensuring Your Safety and Privacy on the Internet

PERFORMANCE OBJECTIVES

Upon successful completion of Chapter 8, you will be able to:

- Adjust Internet Explorer security settings
- Manage website credentials
- Configure privacy preferences
- Protect the system with Windows Firewall
- Protect against viruses and other malware with Windows Defender

The Internet is a wonderful resource, but it also poses some hazards. Hackers can take control of your system, your data can be destroyed or stolen, and your Computer can be damaged by malicious programs such as viruses and malware. Windows 8 protects you from these hazards via several built-in utility programs.

Evaluating Your System's Overall Security Status

Throughout this chapter you will learn about the various security measures Windows 8 provides for your protection. The Action Center offers an overview of the statuses of each of these utilities and provides easy-to-use buttons for enabling any of them that are not currently operational.

To view the Action Center, first open the Control Panel. (Display the charms from the desktop, click *Settings*, and then click *Control Panel*.) In the *System and Security* category, click *Review your computer's status*. There are two categories in the Action Center: *Security* and *Maintenance*. Any unresolved issues appear beneath a category heading. For now, postpone making any fixes because the rest of the chapter details how you can not only enable but also fine-tune the settings of the various utilities.

Click the Expand button (down-pointing arrow) for a category to reveal the settings and what the statuses of the various utilities are. For example, in Figure 8.1, the *Maintenance* category is expanded to reveal, among other things, that Check for solutions to problem reports is turned on.

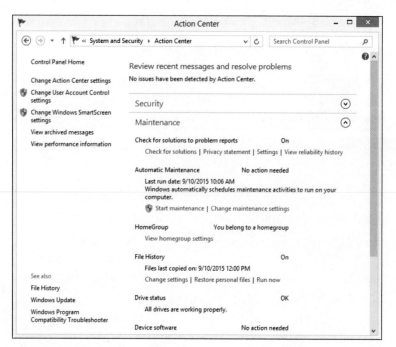

Figure 8.1 Examine the system's overall security status in the Action Center.

Adjusting Internet Explorer Security Settings ▣▣▣

Internet Explorer (IE) requires security because some web pages run applications that can potentially harm your computer, make unwanted changes to its settings, or compromise your data. The security settings in Internet Explorer help minimize those risks by specifying what types of programs web pages can run and under what circumstances.

Configuring Internet Security Zones

Internet Explorer classifies all websites (and HTML-based local content, such as a web page stored on a local area network) in one of four zones. Each zone can be separately configured for security:

- ▪ **Internet.** The standard setting, used unless otherwise specified.
- ▪ **Local intranet.** Pages on your local *intranet*.
- ▪ **Trusted sites.** Sites you have designated as safe, to be granted extra permissions.
- ▪ **Restricted sites.** Sites you have designated as unsafe, to receive extra restrictions.

For each zone, there is a slider you can adjust to set a security level, as shown in Figure 8.2. The settings available on the slider depend on the zone. For example, the lowest level of the Internet zone is *Medium* because untested and untrusted sites are at that level. In contrast, the Trusted Sites zone can be set to any of several levels from *High* to *Low*. For each zone you also can click the Custom level button to fine-tune the settings for the chosen level.

For each zone except Internet, you can click the Sites button to specify which sites—or which types of sites—will be included. You can optionally restrict the list (or not) to only *secure sites*—that is, sites that begin with https:// rather than http://. The rationale is that only secure sites can be trusted to be what they appear to be, and, therefore, only secure sites should be subject to loosened security. However, if you need a specific nonsecure site to have looser security to work properly, you may want to override that limitation.

---

intranet A private network, usually within a company or organization, that uses the same types of content and the same protocols as the Internet

secure site A website that uses a secure protocol, https://, rather than the usual http:// to ensure that the communication is not intercepted or hacked

▼ **Quick Fix**

Slider Does Not Appear
The security level slider does not appear when custom settings have been defined for that level. Click the Default level button to reset the custom settings and to display the slider.

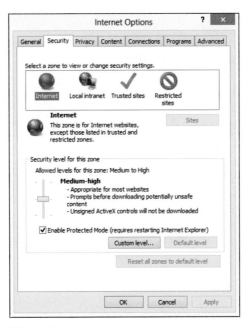

Figure 8.2 Set a security level for each of the four security zones.

All procedures in this section are from within Internet Explorer.

To adjust the basic security level for a zone:

1. From Internet Explorer, click Tools and then click *Internet options*.
2. Click the Security tab.
3. Click the icon for the zone to configure.
4. Drag the security level slider up or down.
5. (Optional) Repeat Steps 3–4 for other zones.
6. Click OK.

To customize the security level for a zone:

1. From Internet Explorer, click Tools and then click *Internet options*.
2. Click the Security tab.
3. Click the icon for the zone to configure.
4. Click the Custom level button.
5. Change any settings desired in the Security Settings dialog box.
6. Click OK.
7. (Optional) Repeat Steps 3–6 for other zones.
8. Click OK.

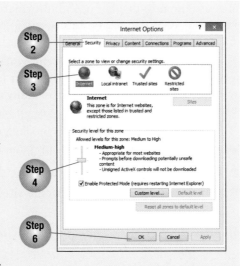

Here's How

▼ **Quick Fix**

Two Tool Sets
The upper right corner of Internet Explorer includes a Tools (button), which looks like a cog. You also can access a Tools menu by pressing the Alt key and then clicking *Tools*. The button and the menu each provide different commands, but both have the *Internet options* menu item needed for this procedure. In this chapter when it is important to click one or the other, instructions will differentiate the path by identifying either the Tools (button) or the Tools menu.

To specify sites to be included in a zone:

1. From Internet Explorer, click Tools and then click *Internet options*.
2. Click the Security tab.
3. Click the icon for the zone to configure (*Local intranet*, *Trusted sites*, or *Restricted sites*).
4. Click the Sites button.
5. If you chose *Local intranet* in Step 3, click Advanced. This step is not necessary if you chose *Trusted sites* or *Restricted sites*.
6. Type the site's address in the *Add this website to the zone* text box.
7. Click Add.
8. Repeat Steps 6–7 for additional sites, if needed.
9. Click Close.

▼ Quick Fix

Server Verification

If the *Require server verification (https:) for all sites in this zone* check box is marked (available for Trusted Sites or Local intranet only), the URL you enter in Step 6 must begin with https://, not http://. The *s* indicates that it is a secure site.

Configuring the Pop-Up Blocker

pop-up An extra window that appears automatically as a result of a certain web page being displayed

A ***pop-up*** is an extra window that automatically opens as a result of a certain web page being displayed. The use of pop-ups in web design is controversial. Some sites use them to display useful information, but they are mostly used to display unwanted advertisements. Internet Explorer includes a built-in pop-up blocker that prevents most pop-ups from appearing.

When the pop-up blocker is on, you can temporarily allow pop-ups on a specific page by holding down the Shift key as you click the link that triggers the pop-up to appear. To permanently allow a certain site to use pop-ups, you can add it to the Exceptions list for the pop-up blocker.

After turning on the pop-up blocker, you can set a filter level:

■ **High.** Blocks all pop-ups; hold down Ctrl + Alt to override.

■ **Medium.** Blocks most pop-ups (the default).

■ **Low.** Allows pop-ups from secure sites.

All procedures in this section are from within Internet Explorer.

To enable or disable the pop-up blocker (menu method):

• Press Alt, click Tools (menu), click *Pop-up Blocker*, and then click *Turn on Pop-up Blocker*.
  OR
• Press Alt, click Tools (menu), click *Pop-up Blocker*, and then click *Turn off Pop-up Blocker*.

To enable or disable the pop-up blocker (dialog box method):

1. Click Tools and then click *Internet options*.
2. Click the Privacy tab.
3. Mark or clear the *Turn on Pop-up Blocker* check box.
4. Click OK.

To configure the filtering level for the pop-up blocker:

1. Press Alt, click Tools (menu), click *Pop-up Blocker*, and then click *Pop-up Blocker Settings*.
2. Open the *Blocking level* list and then choose a level of blocking (*Low*, *Medium*, or *High*).
3. Click Close.

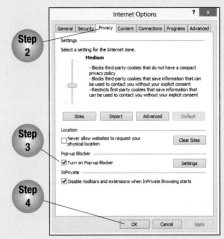

To allow pop-ups from a certain site:

1. Press Alt, click Tools (menu), click *Pop-up Blocker*, and then click *Pop-up Blocker Settings*.
2. Type the address of the site in the *Address of website to allow* text box.
3. Click Add.
4. Repeat Steps 2–3 for other sites, if needed.
5. Click Close.

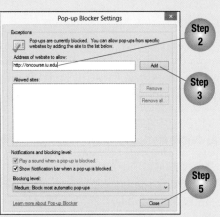

To turn off automatic tracking protection:

1. Click Tools (button), click *Safety*, and then click *Tracking Protection*.
2. Click OK.

To turn on automatic screening:

1. Click Tools (button), click *Safety*, and then click *Turn on SmartScreen Filter*.
2. Click OK.

To check a website (if automatic screening is off):

1. Click Tools (button), click *Safety*, and then click *Check this website*.
2. If a confirmation appears, click OK.
3. When the results appear, click OK.

To completely disable the SmartScreen filter:

1. Choose Tools and then click *Internet options*.
2. Click the Advanced tab.
3. In the *Settings* section, scroll down to the *Security* section.
4. Clear the *Enable SmartScreen Filter* check box.
5. Click OK.

Managing Your Stored Credentials

When you enter sign-in information (credentials) at a website, Internet Explorer asks if you want it to remember that information. Then, when you revisit the same website, it fills in your user name and password automatically, saving you time.

The Credential Manager in Windows 8 enables you to modify or delete those stored credentials to prevent others who might be using your computer from gaining access to those secure websites. The Credential Manager is available from the Control Panel, in the *User Accounts and Family Safety* category. From the Credential Manager, you can manage individual saved credentials, or back up or restore all of your credentials at once. You can manage your Windows credentials or your web credentials by clicking the corresponding icon at the top of the dialog box.

TIP To easily move all of your credentials from one computer to another, back it up to a USB flash drive, take it to the other computer, and then restore it using the Credential Manager.

As you learned previously, you can display the Control Panel by opening the charms from the desktop, clicking *Settings*, and then clicking *Control Panel*. You also can access the Control Panel from the bottom of the Navigation pane in File Explorer if Show All Folders is enabled for the navigation pane.

To delete stored Windows or Web sign-in information:

1. Display the Control Panel.
2. Click the *User Accounts and Family Safety* category.
3. Click *Manage Windows Credentials*.
4. Click *Windows Credentials* or *Web Credentials*.
5. Click the stored credential to delete. Its listing expands.
6. Click *Remove*.
7. Click Yes.

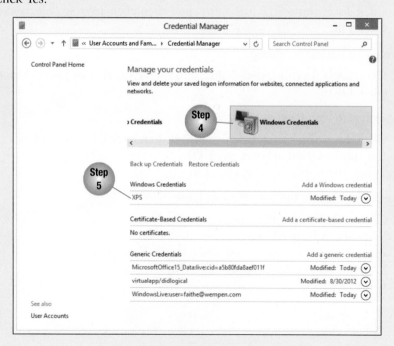

To edit stored Windows sign-in information:

1. Display the Control Panel.
2. Click the *User Accounts and Family Safety* category.
3. Click *Manage Windows Credentials*.
4. Click the stored credential to edit. Its listing expands.
5. Click *Edit*.
6. Retype the user name and password.
7. Click Save.

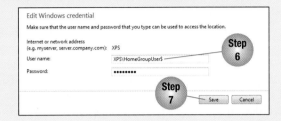

▼ **Quick Fix**

No Credentials
If you do not have any stored Windows credentials, you can use one of your web credentials to practice editing credential information.

To back up all stored Windows sign-in information:

1. Display the Control Panel.
2. Click the *User Accounts and Family Safety* category.
3. Click *Manage Windows Credentials*.
4. Click *Back up Credentials*.
5. Click the Browse button and then select a storage location.
6. Type a file name in the *File name* text box and then click Save.
7. Click Next.
8. Press Ctrl + Alt + Delete.
9. Type and retype a password for the backup.
10. Click Next.
11. Click Finish.

To restore backed-up Windows sign-in information:

1. Open the Control Panel.
2. Click the *User Accounts and Family Safety* category.
3. Click *Manage Windows Credentials*.
4. Click *Restore Credentials*.
5. Click the Browse button, select the file containing the backup, and then click Open.
6. Click Next.
7. Press Ctrl + Alt + Delete.
8. Type the password for the backup.
9. Click Next.
10. Click Finish.

Exercise 1

Configuring Internet Explorer Security

1. Open a Word document and then save the file as **C08E01**.
2. Display the Action Center, evaluate your computer's current security status, and then record any issues you find in your Word document. Close the Action Center window when you are finished.

3. Set the security settings for the Internet zone to Medium-High:
    a. Start or switch to Internet Explorer, click Tools, and then click *Internet options*.
    b. Click the Security tab.
    c. Click *Internet*.
    d. Drag the slider to *Medium-High*, if not already at that setting.
    e. Click OK.
4. Turn off the pop-up blocker in Internet Explorer. Press Alt, click Tools (menu), click *Pop-up Blocker*, and then click *Turn off Pop-up Blocker*. If the Pop-up Blocker warning dialog box appears, click Yes.
5. Navigate to a website that uses pop-ups. For example, go to www.popuptest.com and then click one of the pop-up test hyperlinks.
6. In your Word document, record the URL of the website you tested and whether the pop-up(s) were blocked.
7. Close the pop-up window(s), if any are open, but keep the original pop-up test window open.
8. Turn on the pop-up blocker in Internet Explorer.
9. Reload the page by pressing F5 and then click a pop-up link to retest. Observe whether the pop-up window reappears.
10. Record whether the pop-up(s) were blocked.
11. Visit a known phishing site. You can find a list of recently identified phishing sites at www.phishtank.com.
12. Click Tools (button), click *Safety*, click *Check this website*, and then click OK.
13. In your Word document, record the URL and whether Internet Explorer identified it as a phishing site.
14. If a message appears that the site is not a reported phishing site, do the following:
    a. Click OK.
    b. Choose Tools (button), click *Safety*, and then click *Report unsafe website*.
    c. Mark the *I think this is a phishing website* check box.
    d. Type the characters shown in the picture.
    e. Click Submit.
    f. Close the browser window.
15. Submit the Word document to your instructor.

Configuring Privacy Preferences ▪▪▪▪▪▪▪▪▪▪▪▪▪▪

Whereas security settings help protect your computer and data from harm, privacy settings keep your data safe from anyone who might want to snoop. This is especially useful on a computer that multiple people share.

Note: *When you sign in to the local computer with a different user name, Internet Explorer's history, cookies, and AutoComplete settings are all stored separately, so it is not necessary to take privacy precautions to prevent one user from accessing another user's Internet usage information. You may find it easier to sign in as a different user instead of clearing all of the settings described here.*

Configuring Tracking Protection

Some of the content, images, and ads that you see on websites you visit are provided by outside or third-party websites. These third-party websites sometimes track your behavior across multiple sites. Tracking Protection provides you an added level of control and choice about the information that third-party websites can potentially use to track your browsing activity.

With Tracking Protection Lists (TPLs), you can choose which third-party sites can receive your information and track you online. When you install a TPL, Internet Explorer prevents your information from being sent by limiting data requests to the third-party websites on the list. For each list that you add, the setting applies across all pages and sites you visit. And each time you begin a new browsing session, the blocking stays on until you decide to turn it off.

You can create your own custom TPL, but you may find it much more convenient to download and install a list that an individual or organization creates and maintains. To view and add TPLs from Microsoft, visit www.iegallery.com and then click *Tracking Protection Lists*. When you click Add to add a TPL, it is automatically set up on your computer and automatically enabled.

To get a Tracking Protection List:

Here's How

1. Open Internet Explorer and then navigate to www.iegallery.com.
2. Click *Tracking Protection Lists*.
3. Click the Add button for the list you want to install.

4. Click Add List.

To enable or disable a list:

1. In Internet Explorer, click Tools (button), click *Safety*, and then click *Tracking Protection*.
2. Click the desired list.
3. Click Disable or Enable.
4. Click close.

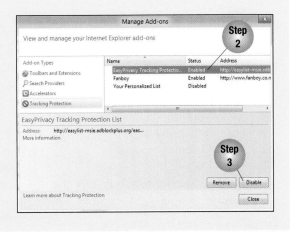

Blocking and Allowing Cookies

A *cookie* is a small, plain text file stored on your hard disk to keep track of your settings for a specific website. For example, when you shop for items at an online store, the information about the items in your shopping cart are stored in a cookie until you are ready to check out. Websites that use cookies create them automatically for you as needed. A cookie can be either a session cookie or a persistent one. A *session cookie*, also called a *temporary cookie,* is deleted when you close the browser window; a *persistent cookie*, also called a *saved cookie,* remains on your hard disk indefinitely and usually stores sign-in information to help a website identify a return visitor.

cookie A small, plain text file that stores your settings for a specific website

session cookie A cookie that is automatically deleted when the browser window is closed; also called a temporary cookie

persistent cookie A cookie that remains on your hard disk indefinitely; also called a saved cookie

A cookie can be read only by the website that created it, so there is little risk of anyone gathering any information about you remotely by browsing your cookies online. However, other local users on the computer can potentially browse cookies simply by opening the cookie files in Notepad. (Cookie files have .txt extensions.)

Note: *Internet Explorer can operate without cookies, but many websites will not display correctly, especially those that involve buying and selling.*

Cookies can be either first-party or third-party. A ***first-party cookie*** is one that has been created by the website you are viewing. A ***third-party cookie*** is one created by an advertisement on the website you are viewing, owned by some other company and used to track your Web usage for marketing purposes. Third-party cookies are less likely to be useful to you.

Anyone with access to your computer can look inside cookie files to gather information you have entered at various websites, such as your user name and password. You can prevent this by deleting the cookie files and then preventing cookies from being saved in the future. However, you will not automatically be signed into those websites anymore when visiting them if the cookies no longer exist, and some websites will not work if you do not allow cookies.

You can optionally choose to retain the cookies for websites that are on your Favorites list, while deleting all other cookies. This enables you to retain data for sites you use often while still preserving your privacy for other sites.

Here's How

To delete existing cookies:

1. From Internet Explorer, click Tools and then click *Internet options*.
2. Click the General tab.
3. Under *Browsing history*, click Delete.
4. (Optional) Mark the *Preserve Favorites website data* check box.
5. Make sure the *Cookies and website data* check box is marked.
6. Click Delete.
7. Click OK.
8. If a browser message box appears, close it.

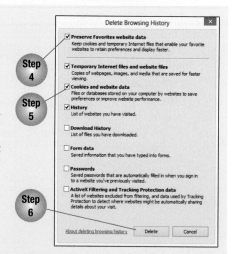

To specify a cookie-handling policy:

1. From Internet Explorer, click Tools and then click *Internet options*.
2. Click the Privacy tab.
3. In the *Settings* section, drag the slider up or down.
4. (Optional) To override default cookie handling:
   a. Click the Advanced button.
   b. Mark the *Override automatic cookie handling* check box.
   c. In the *First-party Cookies* section, click a setting.
   d. In the *Third-party Cookies* section, click a setting.

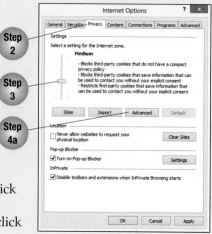

e. Mark or clear the *Always allow session cookies* check box.

f. Click OK.

5. (Optional) To block or allow cookies from a certain website:

    a. On the Privacy tab, click the Sites button.

    b. Type the address of the site.

    c. Click Block, or click Allow.

    d. Repeat Steps 5b–c for another site, if needed.

    e. Click OK.

6. Click OK.

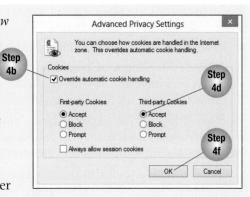

Using InPrivate Browsing

InPrivate browsing is a mode in Internet Explorer that enables you to browse websites anonymously. When using this mode, Internet Explorer does not retain any information about the browsing in cookies, history, or temporary Internet files, so someone snooping on your computer for information about your browsing habits would not find anything.

When you activate InPrivate browsing, a new IE window opens for the private session. The Address bar shows an InPrivate indicator (shown in Figure 8.3) to remind you of the mode you are using. A message about InPrivate browsing also appears.

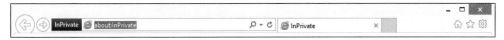

Figure 8.3 A new InPrivate browsing window.

Here's How

To open an InPrivate Browsing Window:

1. From Internet Explorer, click Tools (button), click *Safety*, and then click *InPrivate Browsing*.
OR
Press Alt, click Tools (menu), and then click *InPrivate Browsing*.

2. Enter the address of the page you want to display in the Address bar and then press Enter.

3. Close the InPrivate Browsing window after you have viewed the page.

Clearing the History and Other Personal Information

To make it easier to use the Web, Internet Explorer stores a variety of personal information on your hard disk:

- **Temporary Internet files.** Copies of web pages, images, and media that are cached from previous viewing for quicker reloading of pages.

- **Cookies.** Text files containing settings specific to a website, covered earlier in this chapter.

- **History.** A list of the pages you have visited, so you can return to a page even if you have forgotten its address as long as you remember what day you accessed it.

- **Form data.** Information you have typed into web-based forms, accessible via drop-down lists in form fields.
- **Passwords.** Passwords you have stored for accessing secure sites.
- **ActiveX filtering and tracking protection data.** Information about which advertisers have ads at sites you have visited, used to determine Tracking Protection settings (covered previously in this chapter).

If you like, you can exclude data from websites that are on your Favorites list from deletion. This step enables you to clear the data for most sites but still retain the passwords and quick-loading capabilities for sites you use most often.

You can clear any of this information at any time so that others who use your computer will not be able to access it. You also can tell Internet Explorer how many days of history it should store. The default is 20 days.

Note: *To view the browsing history, choose View, Explorer Bars, History, or press Ctrl + Shift + H.*

Here's How

To clear personal information:

1. From Internet Explorer, click Tools (button), click *Safety*, and then click *Delete Browsing History*; or press Ctrl + Shift + Delete.
2. (Optional) If you want to preserve stored data for sites on your Favorites list, mark the *Preserve Favorites website data* check box.
3. Mark each check box for the types of content you want to delete.
4. Click Delete.
5. Close the InPrivate Browsing window after you have viewed the page.

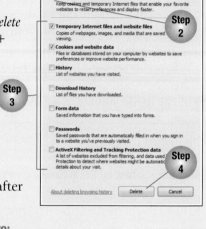

To specify the number of days of history to store:

1. From Internet Explorer, click Tools and then click *Internet options*.
2. Click the General tab.
3. In the *Browsing history* section, click Settings.
4. Click the History tab.
5. Enter the number of days in the *Days to keep pages in history* measurement box.
6. Click OK.
7. Click OK.

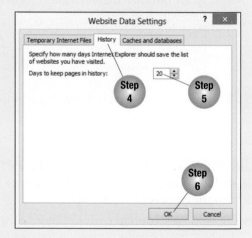

Temporary Internet files can take up a substantial amount of space on the hard disk, but they can make pages that you have previously accessed load faster. You can control the amount of caching that is done and how often Internet Explorer checks for a new version of the pages by clicking the Settings button on the General tab of the Internet options dialog box to display the Website Data Settings dialog box, as shown in Figure 8.4. You also can change the location where such pages are stored (by default it is in C:\Users*username*\AppData\Local\Microsoft\Windows\Temporary Internet Files), and you can view the files and other objects that are stored.

Figure 8.4   You can specify the amount of caching for temporary Internet files.

Here's How

To specify caching settings for temporary Internet files:

1. From Internet Explorer, click Tools and then click *Internet options*.
2. Click the General tab.
3. In the *Browsing history* section, click *Settings*.
4. Choose an option in the *Check for newer versions of stored pages* section.
5. In the *Disk space to use* measurement box, type the maximum amount of disk space to use for cached pages.
6. (Optional) To change the location where pages are cached:
   a. Click the Move folder button.
   b. In the *Browse for Folder* box, click the new location.
   c. Click OK.
7. Click OK.
8. Click OK.

Exercise 2

Configuring Internet Explorer Privacy

1. In Internet Explorer, override the default cookie handling to prompt for both first-party and third-party cookies:
   a. Click Tools and then click *Internet options*.
   b. Click the Privacy tab.

Ensuring Your Safety and Privacy on the Internet

    c.   Click the Advanced button.

    d.   Mark the *Override automatic cookie handling* check box, if not already marked.

    e.   In the *First-party Cookies* section, click *Prompt*.

    f.   In the *Third-party Cookies* section, click *Prompt*.

    g.   Click OK.

    h.   Click OK.

2.   Navigate to a site that uses cookies. Use a site designated by your instructor, or use www.msn.com.

3.   When the Privacy Alert window opens, capture a screen shot of the window, save it as **C08E02**, and then submit it to your instructor. Click Allow Cookie as many times as prompted to do so.

4.   Change the cookie handling settings so that automatic cookie handling is no longer overridden:

    a.   Click Tools and then click *Internet options*.

    b.   Click the Privacy tab.

    c.   Click the Advanced button.

    d.   Clear the *Override automatic cookie handling* check box.

    e.   Click OK.

5.   Delete all of the temporary Internet files and cookies from your browser:

    a.   Click the General tab.

    b.   Click Delete.

    c.   Make sure the *Temporary Internet files and website files* check box is marked.

    d.   Click Delete.

    e.   Click OK.

    f.   If a confirmation information bar appears, close it.

> **▼ Quick Fix**
>
> **Allowing Cookies**
> If the Privacy Alert window reappears, mark the *Apply my decision to all cookies from this website* check box and then click Allow Cookie.

Protecting the System with Windows Firewall ▪▪▪▪

port A numbered software channel that directs network input and output

firewall Software or hardware that prevents unauthorized access to ports

Have you ever wondered how your computer's Internet connection can deliver various types of content without getting confused? It always sends your email to your email program, web pages to your browser, and so on. This works because each application—and in some cases each function within an application—uses a different port. A ***port*** is a numbered software channel that directs network input and output. For example, email typically goes out on port 25 and comes in on port 110.

When a port is unused, any application can use it, and therein lies the security problem. Malicious programs can use unsecured ports to send commands to your system that compromise it. A ***firewall*** can prevent this from happening. Firewall software blocks port access requested by unknown programs, allowing only the programs you specify to get through. There are also hardware-based firewalls, especially in larger corporate networks.

The Windows Firewall is enabled by default, but on some systems it is turned off because it is not needed. This might be the case, for example, on a system with a third-party firewall program installed, or on a system

Figure 8.5   Check the status of the Windows Firewall via the Control Panel.

connected to a network that has a hardware firewall solution installed. To check the firewall's status, click the *Windows Firewall* link from the Control Panel under the *System and Security* category. In Figure 8.5, for example, the firewall is turned on. You can turn it off by clicking *Turn Windows Firewall on or off* in the left pane.

As shown in Figure 8.5, you can have separate firewall on/off settings for public versus private networks. In most cases you will probably want the firewall to remain on for both. A ***public network*** is one in which you do not know or trust all of the other computer users, such as a public café. A ***private network*** is one in which you do trust the others, such as in a home office network.

Here's How

To check the status of the Windows Firewall:

1. Open the Control Panel.
2. Click the *System and Security* category.
3. In the Windows Firewall section, click *Check Firewall Status*.

To turn the Windows Firewall on or off:

Note: *If you are using a third-party firewall program on your computer, you may be unable to complete these steps.*

1. Open the Control Panel.
2. Click the *System and Security* category.
3. Click *Windows Firewall*.
4. Click *Turn Windows Firewall on or off*.
5. In the *Private network settings* section, click *Turn on Windows Firewall* or *Turn off Windows Firewall (not recommended)*.
6. In the *Public network settings* section, click *Turn on Windows Firewall* or *Turn off Windows Firewall (not recommended)*.
7. Click OK.

The Windows Firewall blocks incoming requests from connecting to your system except for programs that are specifically set up as exceptions. Windows sets up some programs as exceptions for you and you can fine-tune these settings on your own for more control. For each program or service, you can choose whether it should be allowed through the firewall for public and/or private networking. You also can add other programs to the list and specify settings for them too.

To allow a program through the firewall:

1. Open the Control Panel.
2. Click the *System and Security* category.
3. Under *Windows Firewall*, click *Allow an app through Windows Firewall*.
4. Click the Change Settings button if the button is available. If the button is not available, changes are already allowed.w
5. Find the desired program in the list.
6. Mark or clear the *Private* check box.
7. Mark or clear the *Public* check box.

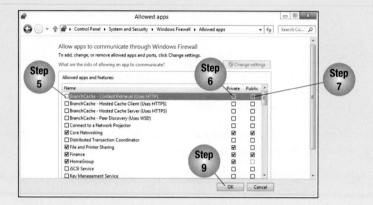

8. If the program does not appear on the list, do the following:
   a. Click *Allow Another App*.
   b. Click the desired program name.
   c. Click *Network types*.
   d. Mark or clear the *Private* or *Public* check boxes as needed and then click OK.
   e. Click Add. The program now appears in the list.
9. Click OK.
10. Close the Control Panel.

To prevent all incoming connections:

1. Display the Control Panel.
2. Click the *System and Security* category.
3. Click *Windows Firewall*.
4. Click *Turn Windows Firewall on or off*.
5. For both Private and Public networks, click *Block all incoming connections, including those in the list of allowed apps*.
6. Click OK.
7. Close the Control Panel.

▼ **Quick Fix**

Blocking All Incoming Connections
If the firewall is set to *Off*, the *Block all incoming connections* check box is not available. Click *On* to enable it.

malware A generic term for software that is designed to harm your computer

spyware A type of malware that spies on your computer usage malware A generic term for software that is designed to harm your computer

Protecting against Viruses and Other Malware with Windows Defender ■■■■■■■■■■■■■■■■■■■■■■

Windows Defender is a utility that protects your system against malware. *Malware* is short for "malicious software," which is designed to harm your computer. Malware includes both spyware and adware. *Spyware* is software that secretly spies on your usage habits and collects information about you, sometimes including your passwords and credit card information, and sends it back to its owner. *Adware* is software that pops up ads or redirects your web browser.

Windows Defender operates by comparing the installed programs, drivers, and other helper files against a list of known threats (definitions). It then removes or prompts you to confirm removal of any items it finds that could potentially cause your system harm.

> Because Windows Defender is only as good as its most recent list of definitions, it is important to allow Windows Update to download and install the latest Windows Defender updates.

Windows Defender offers two types of protection:

- **Scans.** Windows Defender can be set for automatic system scans on a scheduled basis, and you also can manually initiate extra scans at any time.
- **Real-time protection.** Windows Defender monitors the system and alerts you when potentially unwanted software attempts to install itself or run, or when a program attempts to change an important Windows 8 setting.

Malware also includes viruses. A *virus* is a self-replicating, self-spreading, malicious program that moves from one executable file to another. A related threat, called a *worm*, is similar but moves from computer to computer, infecting the computer itself rather than any individual file. Both can cause your system to behave strangely, to slow down, to delete files, and even to stop working altogether. In previous Windows versions, there was no virus protection, so users needed to install third-party antivirus software to be safe. However, Windows 8 includes basic antivirus functionality via Windows Defender. Therefore, if you have Windows 8, you do not need a separate antivirus application.

Windows Defender is available from the Control Panel but is not assigned to any of the categories you see in Categories view. To find it, you must switch to the Large Icons or Small Icons view of the Control Panel, or search for it using the Search box in the upper right corner of the Control Panel.

Here's How

To open Windows Defender (Control Panel method):

1. Open the Control Panel
2. In the upper right corner, click *Category* to open the menu of views and then click *Large Icons*.
3. Click *Windows Defender*.

To open Windows Defender (Start screen method):

1. Display the Start screen.
2. Right-click and then click *All apps*.
3. Click *Windows Defender*.

Performing a Windows Defender Scan

Windows Defender automatically scans your system according to a schedule you set up (covered later in this chapter), but you also can initiate an additional scan any time that you suspect a problem. You can choose to run any of these three types of scans:

- **Quick scan.** Scans only the locations on your hard disk that spyware is most likely to affect. Use this scan type on a routine basis.
- **Full scan.** Scans all files on your hard disk and all currently running programs, but might make your computer run more slowly as it scans. Use this scan type when you suspect a problem.
- **Custom scan.** Scans only certain drives and folders.

Here's How ➤

To perform a quick or full scan:

1. Open Windows Defender, if it is not already open.
2. On the Home tab, click *Quick* or *Full* in the *Scan options* section.
3. Click the Scan now button.

To perform a custom scan:

1. Open Windows Defender, if it is not already open.
2. On the Home tab, click *Custom*.
3. Click the Scan now button.
4. Mark the check boxes of the locations to check. Click the plus sign next to a location to expand it, if needed.
5. Click OK.

Dealing with Threats Found by Windows Defender

When Windows Defender finds a potential threat, it classifies the threat in one of the alert levels listed in Table 8.1. Different levels of threat are subject to different default actions.

Table 8.1   Windows Defender Alert Levels

Alert Level	Explanation	What to Do
Severe	A harmful program that will damage your computer or compromise your security.	Remove this software immediately.
High	A program that might cause a system problem by changing a setting in Windows 8 or collecting your personal information.	Remove this software immediately.

Medium	A program that might make changes or compromise your privacy, but not necessarily.	Review the alert details to see where the software came from and why it is running. Then block or remove, it if needed.
Low	A program that may collect information about you or change system settings, but only in agreement with the licensing terms it displayed when you installed it.	If you intended to install this software, it is probably benign. Check the alert details to make sure you recognize the program's name and publisher.
Not yet classified	Programs that are typically harmless unless they were installed without your knowledge.	If you recognize the software and trust its publisher, allow it to run.

Windows Defender warns you when a malware attack is occurring. You can choose to Remove All, Review, or Ignore.

If you click Review, information about the item appears. From there you can Remove All or Apply Actions. The latter refers to the action selected in the Action column in the upper part of the window.

When Windows Defender finds an unclassified threat, a message about it appears in the Windows Defender window. Click Review and take action to get information about it.

To review and respond to a threat from Windows Defender: **Here's How**

1. Click Review and take action.
2. Read the information about the threat.
3. In the Action column, open the drop-down list and then choose *Deny* or *Permit*.
4. Click Apply Actions.
5. Close the Windows Defender window.

Exercise 3

Protecting Your Computer with Windows Firewall and Windows Defender

1. Open the Windows Firewall Settings dialog box:
   a. Open the Control Panel.
   b. If not already in Category view, set *View by* to *Category*.
   c. Click the *System and Security* category.
   d. Click *Check firewall status*.
2. Make sure the Windows Firewall is turned on. If it is not:
   a. Click *Turn Windows Firewall on or off*.
   b. Click *Turn on Windows Firewall* in the *Private network settings* and the *Public network settings* sections.
   c. Click OK.

3. Click *Allow an app or feature through Windows Firewall*.
4. Click Change Settings (if command is available).
5. Mark the check box in the Public column for *Windows Media Player*.
6. Add Notepad to the Exceptions list:
   a. Scroll down to the bottom of the Allowed Apps dialog box and then click Allow another app.
   b. Click Notepad.
   c. Click Add.
7. Capture a screen shot that shows Notepad on the list and then save it as **C08E03S07**.
8. Open Windows Defender and then do a quick scan:
   a. Open the Control Panel, type Defender in the Search box, and then click the shortcut for Windows Defender.
   b. Click *Quick* and then click the Scan now button. While the scan runs, capture a screen shot and then save it as **C08E03S08**.
9. Submit your screen shots to your instructor.

CHAPTER SUMMARY

- To display the Action Center, open the Control Panel and then, in the *System and Security* section category, click *Review your computer's status*.

- There are four security zones in Internet Explorer: Internet, Local intranet, Trusted sites, and Restricted sites. From Internet Explorer, click Tools, click *Internet options,* and then click the Security tab to configure the security zones.

- To enable or disable the pop-up blocker in Internet Explorer, click Tools (menu), click *Pop-up Blocker*, and then click *Turn on (off) Pop-up Blocker*. You can allow pop-ups from certain sites (Tools, *Pop-up Blocker*, *Pop-up Blocker Settings*).

- A phishing site pretends to be a legitimate website to steal personal information. To check a website for phishing, click Tools (button), click *Safety*, and then click *Check this website*.

- Manage your stored sign-in information for various websites with the Credential Manager. Access it from the *User Accounts and Family Safety* category in the Control panel.

- Tracking Protection prevents bulk advertisers from receiving information about your browsing habits. To turn it on or off, choose Tools (button), click *Safety*, and then click *Tracking Protection*. You need to download one or more Tracking Protection Lists (TPLs) if you have not already done so. Click *Tracking Protection Lists* from www.iegallery.com.

- Cookies are small, plain text files stored on your hard disk to keep track of your settings for certain websites. They are necessary for some pages to operate properly. Session (temporary) cookies last only as long as the browser window is open. Persistent (saved) cookies carry over between sessions. First-party cookies are created by the website being viewed. Third-party cookies are created by ads on the page.

- To delete existing cookies from IE, click Tools and then click *Internet options*. On the General tab, under *Browsing history*, click *Delete*, mark the *Cookies* check box, and then click Delete.

- To specify a cookie-handling policy, click Tools and then click Internet options. On the Privacy tab drag the slider up or down in the *Settings* section

- An InPrivate browsing session retains no information about your browsing habits. To open one, click Tools (button), click *Safety*, and then click *InPrivate Browsing,* or press Ctrl + Shift + P.

- To clear personal information from Internet Explorer, choose *Tools* and then click *Internet options*. On the General tab, in the *Browsing history* section, click Delete, mark the *History* check box and any other check boxes desired, and then click Delete.

- A firewall blocks port access requested by unknown programs to keep hackers out of your system. The Windows Firewall is enabled by default. To check its status, open the Control Panel, click the *System and Security* category, and then click *Windows Firewall*.

- Windows Defender protects your system against viruses and other malware. It scans for existing threats and provides real-time protection.

- To run a Windows Defender scan, open Windows Defender, either from the Control Panel (Large Icons or Small Icons view) or from the Start screen's *All Apps* list. Click the Home tab, click *Full* in the *Scan options* section, and then click the Scan now button.

CONCEPTS CHECK

Completion: Answer the following questions in a Word document.

Part 1

Multiple Choice
1. What does the Action Center do in Windows 8?
    a. Suggests system maintenance actions you can take to improve your system.
    b. Reports spyware and adware alerts.
    c. Reports viruses detected.
    d. All of the above.

2. What does it mean if there is no slider shown on the Security tab in the Internet options dialog box?
    a. Custom settings have been specified for the chosen zone.
    b. Cookies have been disabled.
    c. There are no current security threats.
    d. You are signed in as a Standard user and therefore cannot make security changes.

3. A secure website is one that begins with _____ rather than http://.
    a. ftp://
    b. smtp://
    c. https://
    d. shttp://

4. If a website creates its own cookie, such as a shopping cart cookie, on your hard disk, it is considered a _____ cookie.
   a. first-party
   b. provisional
   c. third-party
   d. residual

5. From which tab of the Internet options dialog box do you delete cookies?
   a. General
   b. Security
   c. Privacy
   d. Advanced

6. From which tab of the Internet options dialog box do you specify a cookie-handling policy?
   a. General
   b. Security
   c. Privacy
   d. Advanced

7. What does Windows Defender protect your system from?
   a. Port hacking
   b. Malware
   c. Spam
   d. UAC

8. Windows Defender is able to protect your system against the latest threats because Windows Update regularly downloads the latest _____ .
   a. definitions
   b. kernels
   c. INIT files
   d. backups

9. What does a full scan do in Windows Defender that a quick scan does not?
   a. Scans each location more rigorously.
   b. Scans more locations.
   c. Connects to the Internet to get the latest scan information.
   d. All of the above.

10. Which of these is a good reason to turn off Windows Firewall?
    a. You already have a third-party firewall app.
    b. Your system is infected with a virus.
    c. The firewall slows down your system.
    d. You cannot check your email when the firewall is active.

Part 2

Short Answer

11. What are the two categories in the Action Center?

    _____

12. What are the four security zones for Internet Explorer?

    _____

13. What is phishing, and how can it be harmful to a user?

_____

14. What is the difference between a session cookie and a saved cookie?

_____

15. What are the pros and cons of regularly deleting temporary Internet files from your hard disk?

_____

16. What kind of danger does a firewall protect your computer from?

_____

17. Why is it important to use Windows Update regularly to get updates for Windows Defender?

_____

18. What is the difference between spyware and adware?

_____

19. What is a virus?

_____

20. What is the purpose of InPrivate browsing?

_____

SKILLS CHECK

Save all solution files to the default Documents folder or any alternative folder specified by your instructor.

Guided Check

Assessment

1

Experimenting with Cookies
1. Open a Word document and then save the file as **C08A01**.
2. Delete all cookies and temporary Internet files.
   a. Choose Tools, *Internet options*.
   b. Click the General tab.
   c. Click Delete.
   d. Mark the *Temporary Internet files and website files* and *Cookies and website data* check boxes. Mark or clear any other check boxes as desired.
   e. Click Delete.
   f. Click OK.
   g. If a confirmation message box appears, close it.
3. Block any future cookies from being stored on your computer.
   a. Choose Tools, *Internet options*.
   b. Click the Privacy tab.
   c. Click Advanced.

> d. Click *Override automatic cookie handling*.
> e. Set both first-party and third-party cookies to *Block*.
> f. Click OK.
> g. Click OK.

4. Visit www.weather.com to test Internet Explorer's cookie acceptance. In your Word document, record the message that appeared (if any) and whether the page loaded fully.

5. Set first-party and third-party cookies to *Prompt*:
   a. Choose Tools, *Internet options*.
   b. Click the Privacy tab.
   c. Click Advanced.
   d. Set first-party and third-party cookies to *Prompt*.
   e. Click OK.
   f. Click OK.

6. Visit www.weather.com to test Internet Explorer's cookie acceptance, and then click Allow Cookie as many times as needed to allow each cookie.

7. When a Privacy Alert prompt appears, record the message and then click Allow Cookie. If the prompt repeats, click Apply my decision to all cookies from this website and then click Allow Cookie to accept all other cookies.

8. Locate a cookie on your hard disk that was saved by the cookie test you previously performed.
   a. From a File Explorer window, click the Options button on the View tab.
   b. Click the View tab in the Folder Options dialog box.
   c. Click *Show hidden files, folders, and drives*.
   d. Clear the *Hide protected operating system files (Recommended)* check box, and then click Yes at the Warning prompt.
   e. Click OK to close the dialog box, and then click Yes at the Warning prompt.
   f. Navigate to C:\users*username*\AppData\Roaming\Microsoft\Windows\Cookies\Low where *username* is your Windows user name.
   g. Double-click one of the cookie files to open it in Notepad.

9. Record the contents of that file. If it is a long string of text, record only the first 12 characters or so and then close the file.

10. Close the File Explorer window and return Internet Explorer to its default cookie-handling setting.
    a. Choose Tools, *Internet options*.
    b. Click the Privacy tab.
    c. Click Advanced.
    d. Clear the *Override automatic cookie handling* check box.
    e. Click OK.
    f. Click OK.

11. Submit your Word document to your instructor.

Assessment
2

Clearing and Viewing Internet Explorer History

1. In Internet Explorer, delete your browsing history.
   a. Choose Tools (button), *Safety*, *Delete browsing history*.
   b. Mark the *History* check box and then click Delete.
   c. If a confirmation message box appears, close it.

2. Visit at least five different websites of your choice.

3. View the browser history (Ctrl + Shift + H) and then click *Today*.

4. Capture a screen shot of the history list showing only the sites you visited in Step 2 and then save the file as **C08A02**. Submit it to your instructor.

5. Delete the browsing history again, as in Step 1.

Assessment 3   **Experimenting with Pop-Up Blocker Settings**

1. In Internet Explorer, set the pop-up blocker filtering level to *Low*.
   a. Click Tools (menu), *Pop-up Blocker, Pop-up Blocker settings*.
   b. Click the *Blocking level* list and then choose *Low*.
   c. Click Close.
2. Go to www.popuptest.com, click Multi-PopUp Test, and then count the number of pop-ups that get through the pop-up blocker. Record the answer in a Word document saved as **C08A03**.
3. Set pop-up blocker filtering to *Medium* (see Step 1).
4. Repeat Step 2, again counting the number of pop-ups. Record your answer.
5. Set the pop-up blocker filtering to *High*.
6. Repeat Step 2, again counting the number of pop-ups. Record your answer.
7. Hold down Ctrl + Alt and then repeat Step 2, again counting the number of pop-ups (if any). Record your answer.
8. Turn off the pop-up blocker.
   a. Click Tools, *Internet options*.
   b. Click the Privacy tab.
   c. Clear the *Turn on Pop-up Blocker* check box.
   d. Click OK.
9. Repeat Step 2, again counting the number of pop-ups. Record your answer.
10. Write a short paragraph summarizing what you learned about pop-up blocking, and then submit your Word document to your instructor.
11. Repeat Step 8, but this time mark the *Turn on Pop-up Blocker* check box.

Assessment 4   **Performing a Scan with Windows Defender**

1. Start Windows Defender.
   • From the Start screen, right-click, choose *All apps*, and then click *Windows Defender*.
2. Perform a custom scan that scans only your main hard disk (C).
   a. On the Home tab, click *Custom*.
   b. Click *Scan now*.
   c. Mark the check box for the C drive.
   d. Click OK.
3. While the scan is running, search the Web for a product called Winfixer. What is this product? Is it spyware? What do experts recommend you do if it is on your system? Record your answers in a Word document saved as **C08A04**.
4. Describe the results of the Windows Defender scan. Did it find any threats? If so, how did you respond to them? (If Defender is still scanning, minimize the window. When the scan is complete, return to this step to complete it.)
5. Submit your Word document to your instructor.

On Your Own

Assessment 5   **Letting an Application through the Firewall**

1. Identify a program installed on your system that accesses the Internet.

Note: *Your instructor may tell you what program to use for this exercise. If not, choose any email, web, or FTP program, or any program that automatically updates itself over the Internet, such as an antivirus program.*

2. Determine whether this program is set up as an exception, able to bypass the Windows Firewall.
3. If the program is not yet set up as an exception, make it so.
4. Capture a screen shot of the Allowed Apps screen with that program's check box marked. Save it as **C08A05** and then submit it to your instructor.

Assessment 6

Configuring the Trusted Sites Zone

1. For the Trusted sites zone in Internet Explorer, customize the following settings:
   - Allow Scriptlets: *Prompt*
   - Download unsigned ActiveX controls: Prompt
   - Logon: Prompt for user name and password.

2. Identify a secure website that you trust.

   Note: *You can use any secure site—that is, one with a URL that begins with https://. It can be an online store, a school site, or some other site. Your instructor may tell you which site to use. If you cannot find a secure site to use, use an unsecure site and clear the* Require server verification *check box so that Internet Explorer will allow it.*

3. Add that site to the Trusted Sites zone.
4. Capture a screen shot of the Trusted Sites dialog box with the added URL visible. Save it as **C08A06** and then submit it to your instructor.

Assessment 7

Tracking a Person's Internet Usage (Partner Activity)

1. Delete all browsing history information from Internet Explorer (all categories).
2. Visit at least five popular websites. At least one of the sites you visit should use cookies.
3. Switch computers with a classmate.
4. Using the History, Cookies, and Temporary Internet Files on the computer, determine as much information as possible about the other person's browsing history.
5. Write a brief report summarizing the information you gathered in Step 4. Save the file as **C08A07** and then submit it to your instructor.

Assessment 8

Exploring Other Malware Protection Programs

Windows Defender is one of several antimalware programs you can use to combat adware and spyware. Others include Spybot Search & Destroy and Ad-Aware.

Using the Web, research the two above-mentioned programs for the following information:
- The program's cost (if not free).
- Whether there are multiple versions available (for example, a free version and a pay version).
- Whether it works with Windows 8.

CHALLENGE PROJECT

Your supervisor has asked you to determine the most cost-effective virus protection solution for your company, which consists of 20 employees, each with their own Windows 8 computer. The supervisor is looking for a more full-featured antivirus program than Windows Defender, with the ability to schedule automatic scans to run at certain dates and times.

Gather information about two or more brands of Windows 8-compatible virus protection programs. Write a one- or two-page report summarizing your findings, including what features it offers that Windows Defender lacks. Save the report as **C08A09** and then submit it to your instructor.

Using Mail and Social Features

PERFORMANCE OBJECTIVES

Upon successful completion of Chapter 9, you will be able to:

- Start and exit the Mail app
- Add an email account
- Create and send a message
- Format a message and add attachments
- Receive, read, and respond to a message

- Share to Mail with the Share charm
- Manage messages
- Handle junk mail
- Add, manage, and email a contact
- Track events with the Calendar app

W indows 8 enables you to take advantage of one of the most significant capabilities that the Internet has made widely available: email. You can pound out an electronic message on your keyboard, send it, and within minutes, it can travel across the room, country, or globe to its recipient. This chapter shows you how to use the Mail email app to send, receive, read, respond to, and organize messages. You also will learn how to work with junk mail, contacts (People), and Calendar.

Starting and Exiting the Mail App ▪▪▪▪▪▪▪▪▪▪▪▪

email Short for electronic mail; provides the ability to send and receive digital messages via a wired or wireless network, or more broadly, the Internet

snail mail Slang term for postal mail; derived from the fact that postal mail is slow relative to email

The ability to send *email* messages over a network of computers emerged sometime during the mid-1960s. At that point, networks typically enabled communications within the organization's limited environment. When the Internet emerged as a widely available communications system during the 1990s, users could suddenly email people other than colleagues on the company network. Customers could email questions to businesses, friends could email friends, partners from different companies could discuss a project, and so on. Because email messages typically arrive in a matter of minutes rather than the days or weeks required for postal mail (or *snail mail*, as it is now often called), email, for the first time, made it possible for colleagues in different physical locations to work together in near-real time, and for friends and family members to share information across the miles.

Sending email today requires an Internet connection via an organization network or Internet service provider (ISP). You also need to have an email account with an ISP if one is not provided by another organization, such as your school or employer.

web mail A service that enables you to access your email through a web browser rather than a standalone email program

Many email account providers enable access to email via the Web and a web browser, called *web mail.* Web mail is convenient because it provides the ability to access email from any computer with an Internet connection and browser, such as when using a computer at a library. The downsides to web mail are that you must be connected to the Internet to read the mail, which also slows the process; features offered by the web mail site may be limited; and the provider may limit the amount of online storage provided with the account, meaning that you have to pay more to store more email online. For these reasons, most accounts—even ones thought of as web mail accounts such as Hotmail and Gmail—give you the option of retrieving and storing your email on your system via an email program. An email program also provides the added benefit of enabling you to retrieve and store messages from multiple email accounts in a single location.

Previous versions of the Windows operating system included the Outlook Express email program, until Windows Vista migrated to a new program called Windows Mail. Subsequently, Windows 7 enabled users to download a free email program called Mail from download.live.com. Windows 8 goes a step further and includes the new Mail app that you can access from the Start screen. If you created your Microsoft account with an @live.com or @hotmail.com email address to sign in to Windows 8, then your account is set up automatically in the Mail app. With this account, Microsoft is essentially your email ISP and you can use the Mail app to send and retrieve messages. (You also can sign in to your account at home.live.com to send and retrieve email.) In addition to your Live or Hotmail account, the Mail app also supports other email accounts when you set up the account using the required server information and other details. These other email accounts include Gmail (Google), MSN, AOL, and Yahoo!; Outlook accounts, including Office 365, Outlook.com, and Microsoft Exchange; and accounts from other ISPs such as Earthlink.

The Mail app enables you to compose, send, and receive messages; reply to and forward messages; and file and manage messages. It also works with the People app that enables you to store and retrieve recipient information.

Start the Mail app by clicking the Mail tile (shown in Figure 9.1) on the Start screen. You also can select the Search charm and then click Mail under Apps if you are at the desktop. As shown in Figure 9.2, the Mail app starts and shows any new messages waiting in your Inbox. For a new Microsoft or Outlook.com account, the account may contain a welcome message or two. Existing accounts, by default, download and show messages received in the Inbox within the last two weeks.

Figure 9.1 Start the Mail app by clicking the Mail tile.

Note: *The first time you start the Mail app, you may be prompted to choose an account type (Exchange, IMAP, or POP). Select the appropriate account type, and follow the prompts to provide the requested information. In other cases, you may simply be prompted to specify your email address and password. If you need to supply more information (such as incoming and outgoing server information supplied by your ISP), click* Show more details. *After entering your account information, click* Connect *to start using Mail.*

Each time you start the Mail app, it automatically connects to the Internet and downloads any new messages to the Inbox folder.

Note: *If your computer uses a dial-up Internet connection, you may see a dialog box prompting you to start the connection process when you start Mail. Click the Connect button to do so.*

Figure 9.2 shows the key features of the Mail app screen:

■ **Accounts and folders pane.** Shows the email accounts that are set up to work with Mail as well as the folders for each account.

■ **Message list pane.** The center pane displays the Message list, which shows the messages contained in the folder that is selected in the Accounts and folders pane at the left.

■ **Reading pane.** The Reading pane shows a preview of the contents of the message selected in the Message list pane.

■ **Command buttons.** Buttons in the upper right corner of the Mail app represent the currently available commands. For example, when a message is selected in the Inbox, as shown in Figure 9.2, New, Respond, and Delete buttons appear in the upper right corner.

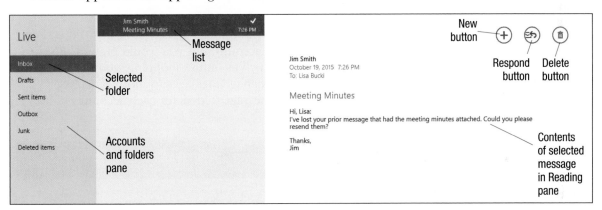

Figure 9.2 Key parts of the Mail app screen.

You can switch between the Mail app and other apps, as for any Windows 8 app. To close the program, drag or swipe down from the top to the bottom of the screen. By default, the Mail tile on the Start screen is live; it displays and updates the number of new messages in your Inbox, so you can start the Mail app and read them.

If you signed in to Windows with a local account, when you start the Mail app, you are prompted to enter an email address and password to sign in with a Microsoft account, as shown in Figure 9.3. To access the Mail app and other social and scheduling apps, enter the required information and then click the Save button. The Mail app will remember the sign-in information the next time you start the app. Click the *Sign up for a Microsoft account* link if you need to create your account. Chapter 1 covers local accounts versus Microsoft accounts and how to sign up for a Microsoft account.

Figure 9.3 Mail prompts you to sign in with a Microsoft account, if needed.

Adding an Email Account

As you just learned, signing in to Windows with your Microsoft account automatically connects you with the associated Hotmail or other email account. To enable the Mail app to interact with other accounts on a Live, Hotmail, Gmail (Google), Outlook, or Exchange *mail server*, or one of the other previously mentioned email account types, you must provide both your sign-in information and server information. The Mail app is designed to enable you to work easily with multiple *email accounts.* Each account you set up in Mail stores the proper sign-in information that enables Mail to interact with the applicable mail servers to send and receive email messages. Before you start the process of setting up another email account, ensure you have the *email address* and password. To use an account that is not one of the popular web mail services, you will also need the incoming and outgoing server information, which your ISP can provide.

Exchange accounts additionally require a server address, domain, and user name. The Information Technology (IT) department at your organization can provide this information.

Note: *If you use Windows 8 on your employer's or school's network, chances are that the organization's IT department has configured your Mail email account for you.*

The Mail app enables you to set up multiple email accounts, as needed. For example, if you currently use one email account, but you would prefer to use another account for a special purpose, such as online shopping, you can set up each email account in the Mail app to manage messages for both accounts. The setup process creates a separate set of message folders for each account.

Here's How

To set up an email account in the Mail app:

1. With the Mail app open, select the Settings charm.
2. Click *Accounts* under *Settings*.
3. Click the *Add an account* link and then click either *Hotmail, Google,* or one of the other account types.
4. In the prompt to add your account, type the email address of the account in the *Email address* text box.
5. Type the account password in the *Password* text box. (For Outlook and ISP accounts, you would then click the *Show more details* link and then enter the server addresses, domain, and user name in the applicable text boxes.)
6. Click the Connect button.
7. Mail connects to the account, adds the account to the list in the Accounts and folders pane, and displays a number beside the Inbox folder if the account has any new messages. Click the Inbox folder to view the messages, if it doesn't open automatically.

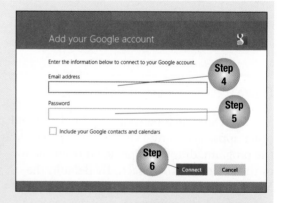

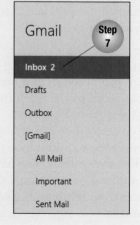

Note: *To complete the exercises in this chapter, you must have an email account set up on the computer system you are using for the purposes of this course, whether your own system or one in a computer lab. If you need information about which email account to use or how to set up an email account for the exercises in this chapter, consult your instructor.*

Note: *During the writing of this book, Microsoft was changing the branding and functions for web-based email accounts using the live.com and hotmail.com domains. These accounts, as well as other types of email accounts such as those for other webmail services and ISPs, have been rebranded as Outlook accounts when accessed by signing in at* home.live.com *or* Outlook.com. *If the account rebranding continues in the future, your screens with account information may differ from those in this book.*

Creating an Email Message ■■■■■■■■■■■■■■■■■■□□

You compose an email message in the Mail app and then send that message to one or more *recipients*. The message you create can include text and other digital content, and you can send as many messages as needed. No matter what the content or purpose of the message, you follow the same process to create the message.

Opening a New Message

You compose a message in the *message screen*. As shown in Figure 9.4, the message screen is divided into two panes. In the left pane, you enter the recipients to whom you want to send the message. In the right pane, you specify the message topic (subject) and message content (body). The recipients, subject, date sent, and sender collectively form the *message header*, which identifies your message in each recipient's Inbox.

recipient A person to whom you are sending an email message

message screen The area where you compose and address an email message in the Windows 8 Mail app; also called a composition screen

message header The key message information, including date sent, sender, recipient(s), and subject; also called the email header

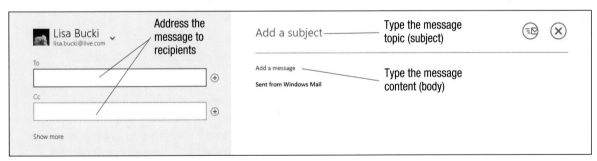

Figure 9.4   Creating a new message.

To open the new message screen in the Mail app: ◀ **Here's How**

1. Start the Mail app and then, in the Accounts and folders pane at the left, select the account from which you want to send the message.
2. Click the New button in the upper right corner of the screen.

Note: *At low screen resolution settings, the main Mail app screen changes so that two columns appear instead of one. If you do not see the Accounts and folders information at left, as indicated in Step 1 above, and instead see a message list for a folder, click the circled left arrow button adjacent to the account name at the top of the pane. Then click an account or folder in the Accounts and folders pane as needed.*

Using Mail and Social Features

Specifying Recipients, Priority, and Subject

You need to supply the email address of each recipient who will receive an electronic copy of the message. The left pane of the new message screen initially lists two text boxes for entering recipient information:

- **To.** Enter the email address(es) for the primary recipient(s).

- **Cc.** Enter the email address(es) for any secondary recipient(s) to whom you want to send a reference copy of the message. (Cc is considered a carbon copy in traditional business terminology.)

Click the Show more link at the bottom of the pane to display Bcc and Priority choices. Bcc is considered a blind carbon copy; any recipient you add to this text box receives a copy of the message, but his or her contact information is not visible to the To and Cc recipients.

To address the message, click in the *To* text box and then type each recipient's email address, separating the addresses with a semicolon or comma. As shown in Figure 9.5, Mail deletes the punctuation and formats each complete email address with a blue background. To send a copy of the message to other recipients, click in the *Cc* or *Bcc* text box and then enter additional email addresses as you did in the *To* text box.

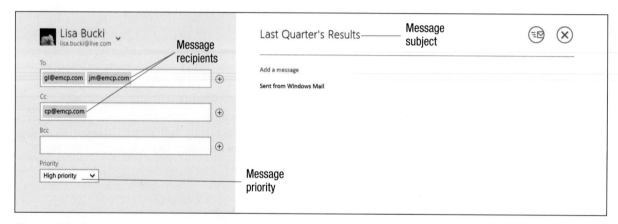

Figure 9.5   Enter information into the text boxes in the left pane to address the message, set priority, and add attachments; specify a subject in the right pane.

If you are entering the email address for a recipient who is one of your contacts (See the "Working with People (Contacts)" section later in this chapter to learn about creating contacts.), the Mail feature for automatically completing email addresses displays a drop-down list with suggested matching recipient names, as shown in Figure 9.6. To complete your entry, click one of the listed email addresses to save yourself some typing.

Figure 9.6   If the Mail app displays one or more recipient names, you can click the name to use.

To address a message to one of your contacts in the People app, click the Add people from your contact list button (circle with a plus in it) beside the *To*, *Cc*, or *Bcc* text box. In the People app, click each contact to add and then click the Add button (shown in Figure 9.7). The recipients appear in the *To*, *Cc*, or *Bcc* text box, according to the circled plus buttons you initially clicked. When you add recipients via People, the contact names appear in the recipient text boxes rather than the email addresses, as shown in Figure 9.8.

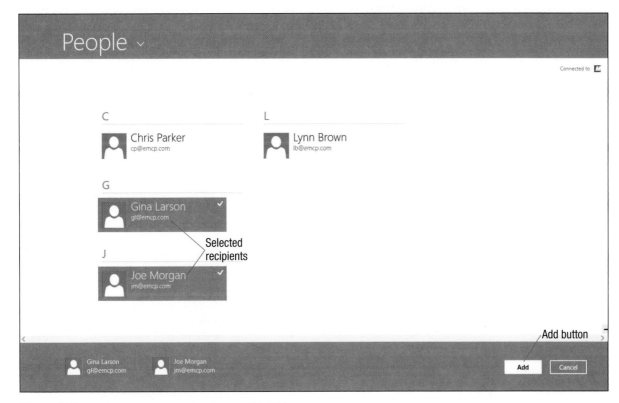

Figure 9.7 Click recipients to add and then click Add.

In addition to specifying recipients, you can assign a priority setting to tell the message recipients whether imminent or delayed action is required. By default, all messages are set to Normal priority. To change the message to High or Low priority in the message screen, click the *Show more* link, if you have not already done so. Click the down-pointing arrow at the right end of the *Priority* box (shown in Figure 9.5) and then click a priority in the pop-up menu that appears.

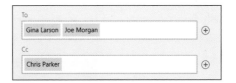

Figure 9.8 When you address a message via People, the contact names appear, not the email addresses.

When you apply either High or Low Priority to an outgoing message, an icon and message appear that identify the priority in your recipient's Inbox. The icon corresponds to the priority setting: a red exclamation point for a High Priority message, and a blue down-pointing arrow for a Low Priority message. The "Reading and Responding to Messages" section later in this chapter shows the appearance of each message priority icon in the Mail Inbox.

Finally, click *Add a subject* at the top of the right pane and then type a subject for the message. The subject text replaces *Add a subject* in the right pane of the message.

Adding and Formatting Text

The text you add to the message is called the ***message body***. When email emerged, all messages contained only plain, unformatted text because that was the only type of text that email servers and software supported. This limitation actually provided an advantage during earlier days when network and Internet transfer capacities were smaller. Plain text messages are smaller and, therefore, did not exceed network capacity.

> **message body**
> The text of an email message, entered or viewed in the message screen

Today, many servers and email programs support Rich Text (HTML) formatted messages, which can include different fonts, attributes like bold and colored text, and even automatic bulleted and numbered lists. By default, the Mail app supports text formatting in any message and provides several commands to do so.

Here's How

To enter and format text in a message:

1. In the right pane of the message screen, click Add a subject. Type a subject line, such as Last Quarter's Results.
2. Type the message text.
3. To apply formatting to any text, drag over the text to select it. The formatting commands appear on the app bar at the bottom of the screen.

Quick Fix

Using Proper Email Etiquette
Most people use the email medium to communicate for both personal and business purposes, so it is important to be mindful of the recipients and the purpose of your message and set the appropriate tone. For example, a serious business message should not include emoticons or abbreviations. Also, typing in ALL CAPS is considered impolite; it is the equivalent of screaming in all forms of electronic communication.

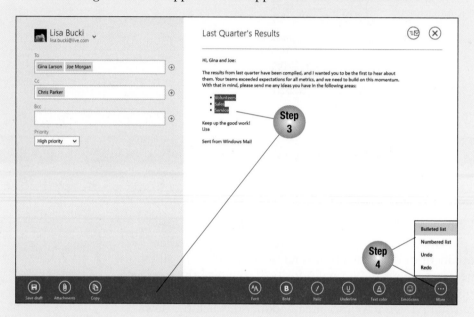

4. Click the desired tool to use it. For example, click the Font command and then select the desired font or size from the drop-down lists in the pop-up that appears. You can select a list of items, click the More command, and then click one of the list choices to format the items as a numbered list or bulleted list.

T I P You can copy and paste information in the body of an email message. You can even select and copy information from a web page, such as a URL, and paste it in the message. After copying the information from its source, return to the Mail message, click to position the insertion point where you want the pasted material to appear, right-click, and then click the Paste command at the left end of the app bar.

Note: *The "Sent from Windows Mail" text that appears by default at the bottom of the message body is the email signature. You can personalize the signature by selecting the Settings charm in Mail, clicking Accounts in the Settings pane, clicking the account, and editing the contents of the Use an email signature text box. Press Esc to close the pane.*

Adding Emoticons

Face-to-face conversations provide a more rich communication experience because of nonverbal elements including facial expressions, gestures, and other body language. Written forms, like email, can seem lacking in comparison and may even be subject to misinterpretation by recipients. For example, it might be difficult for the reader to understand when a written comment is intended to be sarcastic. In plain text email, you can make that more clear by typing ;-) (to indicate a smile and a wink) after the sarcastic comment. The Mail app enables you to insert small graphical *emoticons* to clarify the emotional context of a statement or to emphasize a point. Mail offers several categories of emoticons available to suit a variety of situations.

emoticon A small graphic inserted into a message to convey tone or emotion, such as a smiley face icon

Note: *Although online communication has become more casual and personal over time, some business communications still require a formality that makes emoticons inappropriate. For example, avoid using emoticons when submitting your resume to a potential employer.*

To insert an emoticon in a message:

Here's How

1. In the right pane of the message screen, click in the message body where you want to insert the emoticon.
2. Right-click the same location to display the commands at the bottom of the screen.
3. Click the Emoticons command.
4. Click the icon of an emoticon category at the top of the left pane. From left to right, the categories are: Recently Used, People and faces, Activities, Food and things, Travel, Nature, and Symbols.
5. Click the emoticon you want to insert. It immediately appears in the message body at the insertion point.

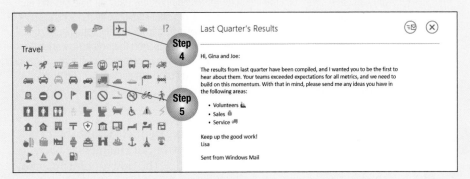

6. Press Esc to close the pane of emoticons.

To delete an emoticon from a message:

1. In the right pane of the message screen, click at the right of the emoticon.
2. Press the Delete key.

TIP Rather than formatting lists using default bullets, you can insert emoticons from the *Symbols* category to set off paragraphs.

Attaching One or More Files

When a file such as a word processing document or spreadsheet includes extensive information and you do not want to or cannot re-create the information in the body of an email message, then you can send the file as a *file attachment* with the email message. The attachment travels along with the message to the recipients, who can then view the message and save its attachment to their systems' hard disks, if needed.

Adding an attachment to an email message takes only a moment or two, but keep these considerations in mind with regard to file attachments:

- While there is no official limit on the size of the files that you attach to an email message, be mindful of Internet connection speeds (yours and the recipient's) and the size of the recipient's email storage. Large files take too long to transmit over slow dial-up connections. Some ISPs limit the size of individual messages to 5MB to 10MB, so any message that exceeds the limit is rejected.

- In most cases (with notable exceptions being common graphic file formats, which can be opened by a variety of programs), the recipient must have the software used to create the attached file installed on his or her computer to open the file. Make sure any file attachment you send is in a format that the recipient's computer can open.

- Some email programs and/or corporate mail servers screen for executable files (with .exe, .bat, and .inf file name extensions) and other types of files, such as images, and prevent the user from opening or receiving attached files in those formats. Computer viruses and other malicious software can be transmitted in executable files, so you may need to use another means, such as sharing online via your SkyDrive, to transmit this type of file to a recipient.

> **T I P** If you have a large file or group of files that you must send as an email attachment, you can often compress the file(s). Compressing not only can combine several files into a single file or folder for easier sending, but also significantly reduces the size of the included file(s). In a File Explorer window in Windows 8, select the files to compress, right-click, click *Send to* in the shortcut menu, and then click *Compressed (zipped) folder* in the submenu. Type a name for the new folder when it appears and then press Enter. You also can use a third-party program such as WinZip or WinRAR to compress files.

To attach a file to an email message, right click and then click *Attachments* in the commands at the bottom of the message screen. In the Files app screen that appears, click the down-pointing arrow beside Files, and then click the personal folder in which the file to attach is stored (shown in Figure 9.9). Click folder tiles to navigate to the folder that holds the file(s) to attach. Once you are in the correct folder, click each file to attach and then click the Attach button at lower right, as shown in Figure 9.10. An icon and the name and size of the attached file appear at the top of the message body in the right pane of the message in the Mail app.

Figure 9.9 Use the Files app to navigate to the folder holding the file to attach.

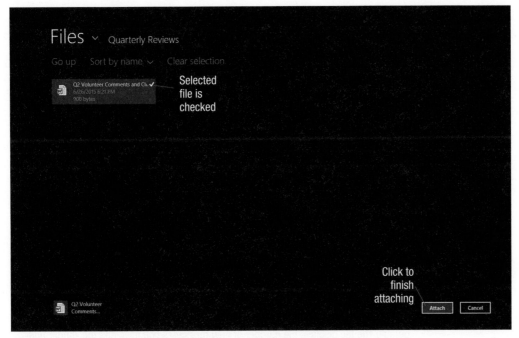

Figure 9.10 Select the file(s) to send with your message and then click *Attach*.

Sending and Receiving Messages ▪▪▪▪▪▪▪▪▪▪▪▪

When your message is complete, click the Send button in the upper right corner of the right pane of the message screen, as shown in Figure 9.11. Sending an email message initially places the message in the *Outbox* folder in the account that you are using in Mail. At that point, you can either wait until Mail automatically syncs messages and sends the outgoing message, or you can manually sync to send and receive messages and ensure that your outgoing mail leaves the Outbox promptly.

Outbox The Mail account folder that holds email messages that you have composed but not sent

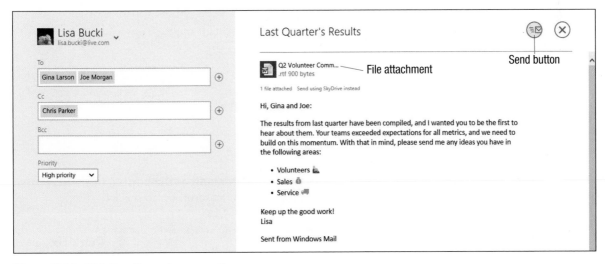

Figure 9.11 Click *Send* to send your email.

Using Mail and Social Features

To sync to send an email message and check for incoming messages:

1. Click the Send button in the message screen.
2. Back at the Mail screen, right-click to display the app bar.
3. Click Sync. Received messages are placed in the Inbox folder of your email account in the Accounts and folders pane.

The email server for your account stores email messages addressed to you until you start the Mail app or later sync to receive the messages. By default, receiving messages in Mail by clicking the Sync command downloads them from the email server to your computer. (If you have multiple accounts set up, click the account to use in the Accounts and folders pane before using the Sync command.) Click the Inbox folder under your email account name in the Accounts and folders pane. The Message list in the middle pane shows a row of header information for each received message.

T I P Mail syncs even when it is not open, and the Mail tile on the Start screen is live by default. The tile displays the number of new messages you have and the sender and subject for each.

Exercise 1

Sending a Message

1. On the Start screen, click the Mail tile.
2. Select the account to send from in the Accounts and folders pane and then click the New button in the upper right corner of the Mail screen's right pane.
3. Type your instructor's email address in the *To* text box.
4. Click *Add a subject* at the top of the right pane and then type Chapter 09 Exercise 01.
5. Click below the border under the message subject.
6. Type the following message:

   So far in this chapter, I have learned how to:
   Start and exit the Mail app
   Set up an email account
   Compose a message
   Sync to send and receive messages

7. Drag over the entire message and then click the Font command at the bottom of the screen.
8. Select *14* from the *font size* drop-down list (you may have to scroll up to see 14).
9. Drag over the list of items in the message body, click the More command, and then click *Numbered list* to apply numbering to the list.
10. Click at the end of item 4 in the list and then press spacebar.
11. Right-click and then click the Emoticons command.
12. Click the Symbols category icon (located at the far right of the category icons in the pane of emoticons).
13. Click the Curly loop symbol emoticon (located in the third row, sixth symbol from the left).
14. Press Esc to close the pane with emoticons.
15. Click the Send button in the upper right corner of the right pane.

 Quick Fix

Jumping Emoticons
If the emoticon appears in the wrong location, drag over it to select it. Press Ctrl + X to cut it. Click at the correct location, and then press Ctrl + V to paste it.

16. Right-click the Mail screen and then click the Sync button on the app bar.

17. Swipe or drag down from the top to the bottom of the screen to close the Mail app.

Reading and Responding to Messages

When you click the Sync command in the Mail app, Mail signs in to the selected email account, checks for messages, and then downloads any new messages to your **Inbox**. This is also called *checking* your email. If you do not see your messages in the **Message list pane**, as shown in Figure 9.12, click the Inbox folder under your email account.

If a message has a priority other than Normal, an icon for the priority appears at the right of the sender's name. To read a message, click it in the Message list. The message content appears in the Reading pane at the right side of Mail. After you click it, the selected message header changes from bold to regular text in the Message list pane to indicate that you have read the message. If necessary, a scroll bar appears in the Reading pane so that you can scroll down to view the rest of the message content.

If a message includes attached or embedded pictures, they, by default, do not download for security reasons. If you trust the source of the message, click Download under the image thumbnail in the Reading pane to download and view the picture in the message (shown in Figure 9.13). If the message with pictures is not from a trusted source, you can delete the message without reading it instead.

Inbox The Mail account folder that holds email messages you have received

Message list pane The pane that lists the email messages in the currently selected folder in the Accounts and folders pane

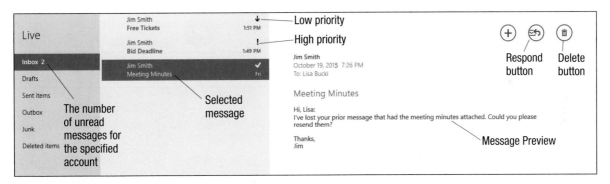

Figure 9.12 Use the Message list pane to preview and open messages in the Inbox.

When you want to respond to the selected message, click the Respond button at upper right to open a drop-down menu with three choices:

- **Reply.** Opens a reply message addressed to the message sender only. Includes Re: before the message subject.

- **Reply all.** Opens a reply message addressed to the message sender and anyone else who received a copy of the message to which you are responding. Includes Re: before the message subject.

- **Forward.** Opens a reply message not addressed to anyone. Includes Fw: before the message subject.

 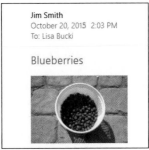

Figure 9.13 Click the picture thumbnail (left) to download and view the picture (right).

Using Mail and Social Features

Whether you are replying to or forwarding information, add or change the *To* and *Cc* recipient information as needed, type response text in the message body area above the quoted text from any prior message(s), and then send the message as described previously in this chapter.

Here's How

To read and respond to an email message::

1. After syncing, if the messages do not appear in the message list, click the account in the left pane and then click Inbox if needed.
2. Click the message you want to read in the Message list pane.
3. Click Download under any picture thumbnails to view pictures as desired.
4. Click the Respond button.
5. Click the desired response type in the menu that appears.
6. Type your response above the quoted (received) message, edit recipient information, and then add attachments as desired.

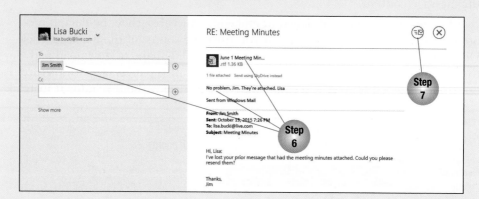

7. Click the Send button.

Exercise 2

Receiving and Responding to a Message

1. On the Start screen, click the Mail tile.
2. Select the account to send from in the Accounts and folders pane and then click the New button in the upper right corner of the Mail screen's right pane.
3. Type your own email address in the *To* text box. If your email address appears in your contact list in People, your contact name appears in the *To* text box.
4. Click *Add a subject* at the top of the right pane and then type Chapter 09 Exercise 02.
5. Click below the border under the message subject.
6. Type the following message:

   I can respond to an email message in one of three ways:
   Reply

   Reply all

7. Select the second and third lines by dragging over them.

8. Click the More command on the app bar and then click *Bulleted list*.
9. Click the Send button in the upper right corner of the right pane.
10. Wait a few moments, and if the message does not appear, right-click the Mail screen and then click the Sync command on the app bar. The message should arrive in your Inbox.
11. Click the Inbox folder in the appropriate email account in the Accounts and folders pane, if needed, and then click the received *Chapter 09 Exercise 02* message in the Message list pane. When you read the text in the Reading pane, notice that you have left out one of the three message response types.
12. Click the Respond button in the upper right corner of the right pane and then click *Reply*.
13. Click in the *Cc* text box in the left pane and then type your instructor's email address.
14. Click above the quoted text in the right pane and then type the following:

    I also can Forward the message.

15. Click the Send button in the message screen to send the message to both you and your instructor.

Sharing Mail with the Share Charm ▪▪▪▪▪▪▪▪▪▪▪

The new Windows 8 style apps use a method called a contract to define how they interact with one another. Apps can be enabled to participate in the **Share contract**, which enables them to share content. The Mail app works with the Share contract, meaning that other apps that also participate in the Share contract can share content to it. Notably, the new Internet Explorer app can share information to the Mail app. Use the Share charm to facilitate the sharing between apps. To find out if a particular app can share to other apps, display the content you want to share and then select the Share charm. Windows then shows you which apps the current app can share to. To proceed with the share, click the desired app in the list that appears.

Share contract The Windows 8 app contract that enables apps to share (exchange) information

To share content from the Internet Explorer app to the Mail app:

Here's How

1. From the Start screen, open the Internet Explorer app and then navigate to the content to share.
2. Select the Share charm by pointing to the lower right corner of the screen to display the charms and then clicking Share.
3. In the Share list in the right pane, click *Mail*. A new message opens in the left pane and a preview of the shared content loads.
4. Type the recipient's email address in the text box, or start typing a contact name and then click the contact in the drop-down menu that appears.
5. Click below the subject and type your message.
6. Click the Send button in the upper right corner of the pane. Windows 8 sends the message with a link to the shared content to the specified recipient(s).

Managing Messages ■■■■■■■■■■■■■■■■■■■■■■■■■

A busy person's email Inbox might receive dozens of incoming messages per day. Just as incoming "stuff" can quickly clog the workspace on the desk in your office, incoming messages can clutter up your Inbox and make it tougher to find the messages you need. Mail works with your online web mail account to offer features that enable you to organize the messages that hit your Inbox.

Filing and Viewing Messages

Outlook (live.com), Hotmail, and Gmail accounts enable you to create new folders in your online accounts when you sign in, as do most mail services.. (Gmail calls them labels rather than folders.) In Hotmail, you click the New folder link under *Folders* in the Accounts and folders pane, type a folder name, and then press Enter. In Outlook, click New folder under Folders, type the folder name, and press Enter. In Gmail, click the More down-pointing arrow in the list at the left and then click the Create new label link. In the pop-up box that appears, type the new label name in the top text box. If you want to nest the folder as a subfolder within an existing label, click the *Nest label under* check box, open the *Please select a parent* drop-down list, click the parent label, such as Work, and then click Create. Other mail services offer similar methods for creating folders. The next time you sync the Mail app with the account in which you created a new folder (or label), the folder appears in Mail under that account.

Folders help you organize email messages, in particular, received messages. Say you work for an advertising firm and you are managing three client accounts. To help you keep better track of the messages, you could create a folder for each client and move the messages pertaining to each client to the respective client folder.

After you create the desired folder, you can move messages to it and view its messages at any time.

> **Here's How** ▶

To file a received message in another folder and view the messages in a folder:

1. Select the account to work with in Mail and then sync it, if needed, to ensure that any folders you have recently created online show up.
2. To move (file) a message to a folder other than the Inbox, click the message in the Message list pane.
3. Right-click a blank area of Mail to display the commands and then click Move. The screen becomes partially gray.
4. In the Accounts and folders pane, click the folder to which you want to move the message.
5. To view the message in the folder, click the folder in the Accounts and folders pane. The message you moved to the folder appears in the Message list pane. Select any message in the list to view its contents in the Reading pane at the right.

The bold number that appears at the right of a folder name in the Accounts and folders pane identifies the number of unread messages in that folder. If you sync your email account and such a number appears at the right of a subfolder that you have created, click the subfolder to view the new messages.

Saving a Message Attachment

When you receive a message that has a file attached, a paper clip icon appears at the right of the sender name in the Message list pane. To save the attached file to your computer's hard disk, click the message in the Message list pane. In the Reading pane, click Download under the file's icon to load the rest of the file's information to verify that you want to save it. Right-click the file's icon and then click *Save*, as shown in Figure 9.14. In the Files app that appears (shown in Figure 9.15), click the down-pointing arrow beside Files and then click a folder/location name or *SkyDrive*. If additional subfolders appear, click the tile for the one in which you want to save the file. Edit the file name shown at the bottom of the Files screen, if desired, and then click Save.

Figure 9.14 To open or save an email attachment, right-click its name or icon in the message body.

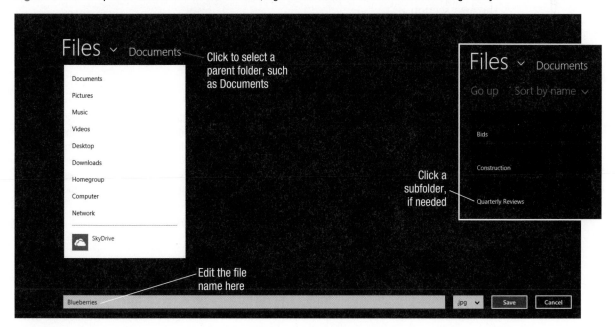

Figure 9.15 The Files app opens so that you can finish saving the attachment.

Using Mail and Social Features

junk email Like paper junk mail, these are commercial email messages sent to you without request; also called spam

junk email filter A Hotmail and Gmail feature that automatically moves likely junk email messages to the Junk email folder

Dealing with Junk Mail

One particular type of email calls for special handling. ***Junk email*** or spam messages can clog up your Inbox and distract your attention from more important incoming email messages. In some cases, commercial or sales-oriented messages might be legitimate messages from websites for which you have signed up to receive email messages about sales and new items or even newsletters. In other cases, the messages come from entities that send unsolicited messages to large groups of users without prior request or agreement by the user.

Even benign spam messages can clog up your Inbox. More troubling is that some spam messages contain content that many users find questionable or objectionable, and a certain percentage of junk emails are outright scam attempts to solicit money, or to dupe you into providing personal information that can lead to identity theft, or to deliver messages intended to infect your computer with a virus or other malware. By default, Outlook (Live) and Hotmail accounts enable a ***junk email filter***, also known as Microsoft SmartScreen, to provide a low level of protection, which tells Outlook or Hotmail to place obvious incoming spam messages directly into the Junk email folder. When you sync your Outlook or Hotmail online account in the Mail app, the junk messages appear in the Junk folder in the Accounts and folders pane rather than the Inbox. Similarly, your Gmail online account flags some messages as spam and moves them to the Spam folder; when you select and sync your Gmail account in the Mail app, any messages marked by Gmail as spam appear in the Spam folder in the Accounts and folders pane. Other mail services have similar junk filtering features.

Tip Top Tailors June 27, 2012 10:15 PM
This message is marked as junk mail.
All links, images, and attachments have been disabled to help protect you. If you trust the sender, mo...
Sportswear Up to 50% Off: Also Polos + Shorts from $19.99
To: 1X1PROMOTIONS@gmail.com

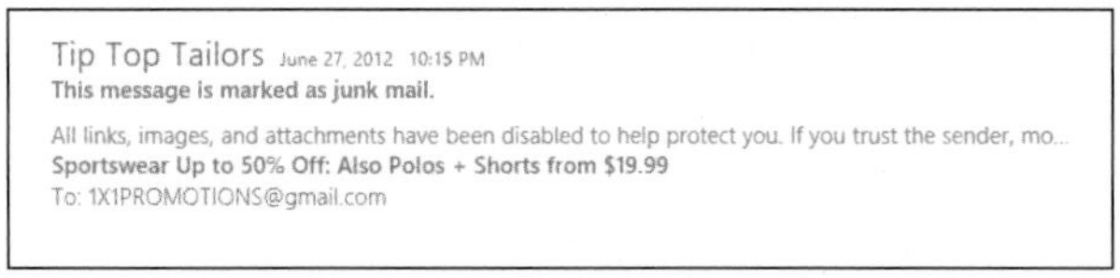

Figure 9.16 Moving a message to the account's Junk folder marks the message as junk mail.

If you want to manually mark a message as junk mail for a Live (Outlook), Hotmail, or Gmail account, click the message in the Message list pane and then move it to the Junk folder using the procedure presented previously. You can then click the message in the Junk folder to see that it has been marked as junk, as shown in Figure 9.16. (If you consider a message junk email, you can delete it manually as described in the next section.)

It is a good practice to click your Junk email folder (or Spam for a Gmail account) from time to time to check for messages that are not junk. If you find a message that is not junk, move the message back to your Inbox.

TIP To change spam settings in Hotmail, open your web browser and then sign in to your Hotmail account on home.live.com. Click the down-pointing arrow at the right of your profile name in the upper right corner and then click *Options*. Click the Mail choice at the left and then use the links under *Preventing junk email* to work with *Filters and reporting* and *Safe and blocked senders*. For Outlook, the process is similar, but once signed in, click the Options icon (it looks like a sprocket) to the left of your user name, and then click More mail settings.

Deleting Messages

Even if you do a good job of managing your incoming email messages with filing, messages may stack up to an unruly number quickly. You can delete a message from the Inbox or any other folder when you no longer need the message. Select the account and folder that holds the unwanted message, click the message in the Message list pane, and then click the Delete button at upper right. Mail moves the message from the current folder to the Deleted items folder. If you mistakenly move a message there, select the message and move it back to the Inbox or another folder by right-clicking, clicking the Move command, and then clicking the folder.

To delete messages permanently, you have to delete them from the Deleted items folder.

To delete a message:

1. Select the account and the folder that holds the message.
2. Click the message in the Message list pane.
3. Click the Delete button in the upper right corner.

Here's How

Step 3

To permanently delete messages from the Deleted items folder:

1. Select the account and then click the Deleted items folder in the Accounts and folders pane.
2. Click the message to delete in the Message list pane. To delete multiple messages, click the message and then use Shift + click to select contiguous messages or Ctrl + click to select non-contiguous messages.
3. Click the Delete button in the upper right corner.

T I P To see settings that you can change, such as when new messages (content) automatically download, select the Settings charm from Mail, click *Accounts,* and then click an account.

Printing a Message

In the new Windows 8 apps, you use the Devices charm to print information. From Mail, select the account and folder and then select the message you want to print in the Message list pane. Display the charms and then select the Devices charm. Click an installed printer in the pane at the right, specify settings to set up the printout, and then click Print. The print settings vary depending on the printer's capabilities.

To print a message:

1. Select the account and the folder that holds the message.
2. Click the message in the Message list pane.
3. Select the Devices charm.
4. Click a printer in the list that appears in the right pane. (Printers must be powered on to appear.)
5. Choose printout settings.
6. Click Print.

Here's How

Step 3

Step 5

Step 6

1. From the desktop, open Internet Explorer, navigate to home.live.com, and then sign in to your account, if necessary. Click Hotmail at the top of the screen. For an Outlook account, the email screen should automatically appear. If not, click the down arrow adjacent to Outlook, and then click the Mail tile.
2. At the left side of the screen, click the *New folder* link. Type Chapter 09 Exercises and then press Enter.
3. Leave Internet Explorer open, go to the Start screen, and then click the Mail tile.
4. Select your Live or Hotmail account, if necessary. If you do not see the new folder, right-click the screen and then click the Sync command on the app bar.
5. Click the *Inbox* folder, if needed.
6. In the Message list pane, click the message that you sent in Exercise 2 of this chapter (subject: *Chapter 09 Exercise 02*), and then hold down the Ctrl key and click the received response message (subject: *Re: Chapter 09 Exercise 02*).
7. On the app bar, click Move and then click the *Chapter 09 Exercises* folder in the Accounts and folders pane.
8. Click the *Chapter 09 Exercises* folder again.
9. Capture a screen shot and then save the file as **C09E03S09**. Return to the Mail app.
10. Click each message in the *Chapter 09 Exercises* folder and then click the Delete button.
11. Return to your Hotmail or Outlook account in Internet Explorer. *Hint: Press Alt + Tab*. Right-click the *Chapter 09 Exercises* folder in the list of folders and then click *Delete*. Click OK to confirm the deletion.
12. Return to the Mail app and then select your Live or Hotmail account, if necessary. If the deleted folder still appears, right-click the screen and then click the Sync command.
13. Click the *Deleted items* folder in the Accounts and folders pane.
14. Capture a screen shot and then save the file as **C09E03S14**. Return to the Mail app.
15. Shift-click the second item to select all the messages in the folder and then click the Delete button at upper right.
16. Submit the screen shots to your instructor. Return to Internet Explorer, sign out of your email account, and then close the browser.

---

contact A listing including the email address and other contact information of a person entered in the People app

Working with People (Contacts)

Windows 8 includes the People app for managing *contacts*—people whom you email or phone often. Use People to track mailing, phone, fax, email, and job title information, and personal details, notes, and tracking ID information for anyone with whom you interact. Once you add a contact in People, you can select that contact when addressing an email message, as described previously. This is another example of how contracts enable the new apps to share information seamlessly. Building a list of contacts not only serves as a handy reference list when you need to make a call or send a letter, but also enables you to address emails more quickly. Contacts sync automatically with your online Hotmail (Live) account.

Figure 9.17 Click this tile on the Start screen to launch the People app for managing contacts.

To start working with contacts in the People app, go to the Start screen and then click the People tile, as shown in Figure 9.17.

Adding a Contact

When you add a contact, you can specify as few or as many details as you want. To set up a contact to whom you want to send email, at a minimum, you should enter the contact's name and email address.

Here's How

To add a new contact:

1. On the Start screen, click the People tile.
2. Right-click the People app and then click the New command on the app bar at the bottom of the screen.
3. In the New Contact screen, enter information in the text boxes (fields) as desired, pressing Tab to move between the boxes.
4. To open a field that is hidden, such as for the Work Email, click the applicable circled plus button and then click the name of the field to display.
5. When you finish adding the desired contact information, click the Save command on the app bar. The new contact appears in the list on the People screen.

New contact

Account

Live

Name
First name
Robert

Step 3

Last name
Tate

Company
EMCP

⊕ Name

Email
Work
Other

⊕ Email

Phone
Mobile ∨

Step 4

⊕ Phone

Address
⊕ Address

Other info
⊕ Other info

Note: *The contacts in People initially exist separately from the contacts you can create in the Contacts folder found in your personal folder in Windows 8. Use the New Contact button on the command bar in the Contacts folder window to add a contact.*

Adding Social Media Contacts

Anyone who uses social media accounts like Facebook, LinkedIn, and Twitter already has a number of contacts established within those services. From the People app, you can connect to one or more of your social media accounts, as well as to your Outlook contacts, to share contacts and other information. This not only saves you the trouble of entering contacts, but also ensures that whenever a contact updates his or her information on the social service, People receives the updates as well.

Connecting to one of your social media accounts automatically adds all your "friends" or contacts from that account to your contact list in People. To connect to a social media account, click the account at the left side of the People screen, as shown in Figure 9.18. When prompted to confirm the connection, as when connecting to Facebook, click Connect. When prompted for your email address or username and password, enter the information and then click Log In or Connect. (The process varies depending on what service you sign in to.)

▼ **Quick Fix**

No social account list? If you do not see the list of social accounts in the People app, select the Settings charm, click Accounts in the right pane, and then click Add an account. Click one of the choices that appears to start adding that type of account.

Figure 9.18 Click the social media service to which you want to connect.

The upper right corner of the People screen displays an icon for each of the social services to which it is currently connected. Figure 9.19 shows icons for the Microsoft, Hotmail, and Google (Gmail) services, from left to right. If you want to disconnect from one of the services, select the Settings charm from People, and then click Accounts. Click the account you want to remove in the right pane and then click the Remove account button.

Figure 9.19 In this example, People is connected to the Microsoft, Hotmail, and Google services.

Viewing, Changing, or Deleting a Contact

You can view and edit the profile for a contact at any time to ensure you are using the most up-to-date information possible and prevent returned emails. To view a contact's profile, click the contact in the list in People and then click View profile, as shown in Figure 9.20. You can click the Back (left-pointing arrow) button beside the contact's name to return to the full list.

If you see information you need to change, right-click the People screen and then click the Edit command. (You also can select the Edit command from the initial contact screen.) If a menu with accounts pops up, click the account that holds the contact. Make the changes as needed in the Edit contact info screen and then click the Save command.

You may need to delete a contact, for example, if you entered a contact manually and the contact was also added when you connected to social media, as shown in Figure 9.21. Deleting a contact deletes the contact permanently, so verify that you want to delete the contact. To delete the contact, click it in the People list, right-click the next screen, and then click the Delete command. In the message box asking you to confirm the deletion, click Delete. The contact is permanently deleted.

Figure 9.20 Click View profile to see the details you entered for a contact.

Figure 9.21 Duplicate contacts may result when you connect People with a social media account.

Emailing a Contact

The Mail and People apps work together to enable you to address email messages more quickly. In fact, you can create a new message to a contact from the People app rather than going back to Mail.

Click the contact in contact list, and then click Send email (shown in Figure 9.20). The new message opens in Mail where you can add a subject, body, and attachments and then send it as described previously in the chapter.

Note: *The Messaging app also connects with your People app contacts and social media accounts. After clicking the Messaging tile, right-click, click Invite, and click Add a new friend. Follow the prompts to add Messenger friends. Then, in the future, you can use the New message button to start an on-screen chat.*

Exercise 4

Adding and Deleting a Contact

1. Go to the Start screen and then click the People tile.
2. Right-click the People app screen and then click the New command.
3. Click in the *First name* text box, if needed, and then type My.
4. Press Tab to move to the *Last name* text box and then type Instructor.
5. Click the circled plus button under Email and then click *Work*.
6. Type instructor@school.edu.
7. Click the Save command and then, if needed, click the Back button beside My Instructor to return to the contact list in People.
8. Under M, click the *My Instructor* contact.
9. Capture a screen shot and then save the file as **C09E04**. Return to the People app.
10. Right-click the app screen.
11. Click the Delete command.
12. At the message prompting you to confirm the deletion, click Delete.
13. Drag or swipe down from the top of the screen to close People.
14. Submit your screen shot to your instructor.

Managing Your Time with the Calendar App ▪▪▪▪

Use the Calendar app to manage your appointments and events. Calendar can help a typical person organize his or her home, student, or professional life. To display the Calendar, go to the Start screen and then click the Calendar tile. The Calendar app opens showing the current date, as shown in Figure 9.22.

Calendar automatically creates a separate calendar for each email account you set up in the Mail app. The appointments for each calendar are color-coded with the color you specify when you create the calendar. Color coding makes it easier to see at a glance which activities pertain to a particular calendar.

Select the Settings charm from the Calendar app, click Accounts, and then click Add an account to create a calendar for the account.

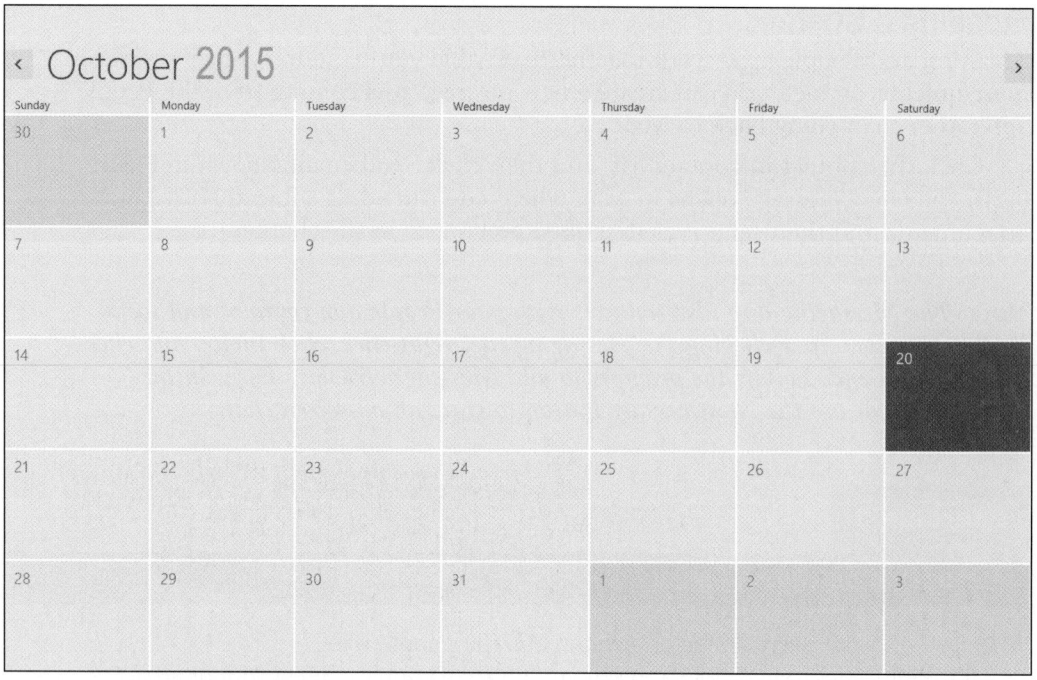

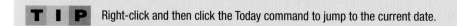

October 2015

Sunday	Monday	Tuesday	Wednesday	Thursday	Friday	Saturday
30	1	2	3	4	5	6
7	8	9	10	11	12	13
14	15	16	17	18	19	20
21	22	23	24	25	26	27
28	29	30	31	1	2	3

Figure 9.22 Track appointments using the Calendar app.

Displaying a Date

With any luck, you will use Calendar to plan your activities well in advance of when you need to attend an appointment. Accordingly, you need to be able to display the future date on which an appointment occurs to schedule that date in Calendar. Use the arrows that appear beside the month, week, or day information at the top of the app to display a particular date for scheduling.

If the date on which you need to schedule an appointment occurs during the month currently displayed, click the desired date on the calendar. If the calendar shows the wrong month, use the arrows at the left and right of the month and year to scroll to another month.

Here's How

To display another month:

- Click the left- or right-pointing arrow beside the month and year at the top of the Calendar app.
  OR
  Scroll until you see the desired month.
- Click the desired date. The Details for that date appear.

T I P Right-click and then click the Today command to jump to the current date.

Changing the View

When you are trying to keep on track for a particular day, viewing the calendar in the default Month view does not provide the needed level of detail. To change the view of your calendar to see a single day or week (shown in Figure 9.23), right-click and then click the desired view command: Day, Week, or Month.

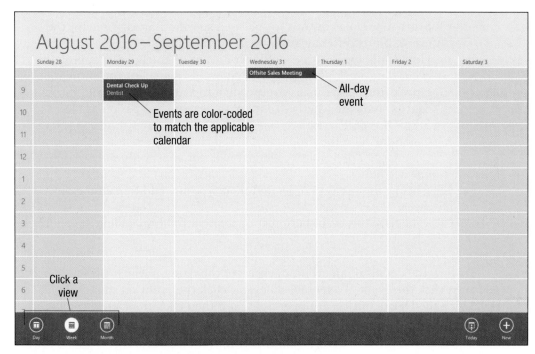

August 2016–September 2016

| | Sunday 28 | Monday 29 | Tuesday 30 | Wednesday 31 | Thursday 1 | Friday 2 | Saturday 3 |

Offsite Sales Meeting

All-day event

9 — **Dental Check Up** / Dentist

Events are color-coded to match the applicable calendar

10

11

12

1

2

3

4

5

6 — Click a view

Day   Week   Month   Today   New

Figure 9.23 Change to view the Day, Week (shown here), or Month.

Adding an Event

An *event* is a period of time identified in the Calendar during which you are scheduled for a specified activity in a certain location. You schedule events in the Calendar so that you can see your commitments and avoid making overlapping commitments.

The Day and Week views show each event's name and location and graphically identify the time schedule for the event. Each event is color-coded to match the calendar to which it belongs and is marked as an all-day event, if applicable.

event A time pe-riod for which you have scheduled a particular activity in Calendar

To create an event:

▶ Here's How

1. Select Day or Week view and then navigate so that you can see the day on which you want to add the event.
2. Click the time for the event in the day's schedule. (Make sure you click in the column for the desired day when working in Week view.) The Details screen opens.
3. Type the event's name at the insertion point at the top of the screen.
4. Enter additional event information as applicable in the Details pane at the left (click Show more to display all the details).
   - **Where**. Type the location for the appointment.
   - **When**. Change the date, if needed.

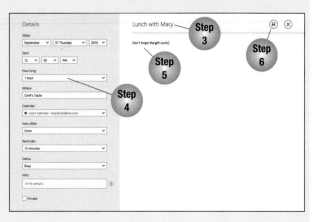

Using Mail and Social Features

- **Start.** Use time controls to specify a specific starting time for the event, if it is different from the time you clicked.
- **How long.** Open this drop-down list and then click the appropriate event duration. *All day* specifies an event that spans the entire day.
- **How often.** Use this list to specify a repeat interval for the event.
- **Status.** Indicate whether to mark the event time period as *Free*, *Busy*, *Out of Office*, or *Working elsewhere*.
- **Calendar.** Use the drop-down list to choose another account calendar, if applicable. (Calendar will not appear if you have only one account.)
5. Click below the subject border and then type any additional notes or messages.
6. Click the Save this event button at upper right to finish adding the event.

To view the details of an event, navigate to the date on which the event occurs and then click the event. To remove an event, click the event on the schedule, right-click the Delete button at upper right, and then click the Delete command on the app bar.

The Calendar automatically syncs with your online account. Any event you add to your Microsoft account in the Calendar app, for example, is automatically added to Hotmail calendar, and vice versa. Once you sign in to your Hotmail calendar and select a time zone, it automatically adds U.S. holidays, which are then synced with and appear in the Calendar app.

 After you open an event by clicking it, you can invite one or more recipients to attend. Click the *Invite people to* text box under *Who*, type the recipients' addresses, and then click the Send invite button that appears in the upper right corner of the screen.

Exercise 5

Setting Up an Event in the Calendar App

1. Go to the Start screen and then click the Calendar tile. Switch to Month view, if necessary.
2. Point at the top of the Calendar screen and then click the right-pointing arrow button as many times as needed to display September of next year.
3. Right-click and then click the Week command on the app bar.
4. Point at the top of the screen and then click the right-pointing arrow until you see the second full week of September.
5. Click the box for 2 p.m. in the Tuesday column.
6. In the screen that appears, type Staff Meeting as the subject.
7. Click in the *Where* text box under *Details* and then type Conference Room C.
8. Use the *How Long* drop-down list to select *90 minutes*.
9. Click the Save this event button at upper right.
10. Capture a screen shot and then save the file as **C09E05**.
11. Close Calendar by dragging or swiping down from the top to the bottom of the screen.
12. Submit your screen shot to your instructor.

CHAPTER SUMMARY

- Windows 8 includes the Mail app to send and receive email messages.
- Click the Mail tile on the Start screen to start Mail.
- When you sign in to Windows using a Microsoft account, Mail, by default, sets up an email account using that sign-in information.
- You can add additional Hotmail, Outlook (Live), Gmail (Google), and Yahoo! accounts in Mail, as well as accounts for other ISPs such as Earthlink. Select the Settings charm in Mail, click *Accounts*, and then click *Add an account*.
- Select the account you want to work with in the Accounts and folders pane of Mail and the folders for that account appear.
- Click the New button in the upper right corner of Mail to open a new message.
- Address the email message by entering recipient email addresses in the *To* text box. Include a comma or semicolon after each address when typing multiple email addresses into the text box. Add additional recipients in the *Cc* text box. Click the Show more link to display the *Bcc* text box to add blind carbon copy recipients.
- If you have entered the email address of a recipient into the People app as a contact, you can click the name in the list that appears as you type in the *To*, *Cc*, or *Bcc* box. Or, click the Add people from your contact list (circled plus) button beside any of the addressing text boxes to select contacts from People.
- After you click More details, use the *Priority* drop-down list to set a message to High priority or Low priority to inform a message recipient of the message's relative importance.
- Click *Add a subject* in the right pane, type the message subject and then click below the border and type the message.
- Select message text and then use the commands on the app bar to change the text formatting.
- Attach one or more files to send along with the message by right-clicking and clicking the Attachments command.
- Click Send in the upper right corner to send the message to your Outbox.
- Right-click and then click the Sync command to send outgoing messages and receive incoming messages for the currently selected account.
- Select an account in the Accounts and folders pane and then click the Inbox folder, if needed. Click a message in the Message list (middle) pane to preview its contents in the Reading (right) pane.
- Use the Respond command at upper right to respond to a message.
- To create a new folder, sign in to your Hotmail, Outlook (Live), Gmail, or other mail account via your web browser and then create the folder. Return to Mail and then use the Sync command for the account to display the new folder.
- Select an account and folder in the Accounts and folders pane, click a message in the Message list pane, right click, and then click the Move command. Click the desired folder in the Accounts and folders pane to move the selected message to that folder.
- To save the attachments for a selected message, click the attachment icon to verify that you want to download its contents. Right-click the attachment icon or file name in the Reading pane and then click *Save*. You can use this same method and click *Open* to open an attachment.
- Junk mail or spam email messages are commercial messages sent to you without request.

- Because junk mail messages clog your Inbox and may include malicious software, your web-based Hotmail or Outlook (Live) account, by default, uses its junk email filter to move suspect messages to the Junk email folder. They also appear in that folder in the Mail app when you sync.
- Select a message in the Message list pane and then click the Delete button at upper right to move the message to the Deleted items folder. To delete messages permanently, select the Deleted items folder in the Accounts and folders pane, select one or more messages to delete in the Message list pane, and then click the Delete button.
- Use the Share charm from another app, such as the Internet Explorer app from the Start screen, to share content to the Mail app.
- To print the selected message in Mail, select the Devices charm. Click a printer in the list that appears, specify print settings, and then click Print.
- Click the People tile on the Start screen to open the People app, which you can use to manage information about your contacts, people whom you communicate with often, particularly via email.
- Contacts sync automatically with your online account(s).
- Right-click the People screen and then click the New command to display the New contact screen. Enter the desired information and then click the Save command to add a new contact.
- To add contacts from your social media accounts, click the account type at left or use the Settings charm, click Accounts, and then click Add an account. Follow the prompts to provide your sign-in information to connect to the account. Your account contacts appear in People once the connection is complete.
- Click a contact and then click View profile to see detailed contact information. Right-click from the profile screen or the previous screen, click the Edit command, and then click the account, if prompted. Edit contact information as desired and then click Save. Use the left-pointing arrow button beside the contact name to return to the contact list.
- To delete a contact, click the contact, right-click, and then click the Delete command. In the message box that prompts you to confirm the deletion, click Delete.
- To email a contact, click the contact in the contact list, and then click Send email.
- To track upcoming events, click the Calendar tile on the Start screen. Point at the top of the screen and then use the left- and right-pointing arrow buttons to move to later or earlier dates. Use the Day, Week, or Month commands to select a view. Click the desired date and time to open the Details screen. Enter event schedule information and then click Save.

CONCEPTS CHECK

Completion: Answer the following questions in a Word document.

Part 1

Multiple Choice

1. Email is short for _____.
   a. effective mail
   b. event mail
   c. electronic mail
   d. effortless mail

2. Windows 8 includes the _____ app for sending, receiving, and reading email.
   a. Calendar
   b. Messaging
   c. People
   d. Mail

3. A person to whom an email message is addressed is called a _____.
   a. receiver
   b. recipient
   c. postal resident
   d. box owner

4. Bcc: stands for _____.
   a. blind carbon copy
   b. backup carbon copy
   c. backward carbon collection
   d. beneficial cyber communication

5. Before a message is sent by Mail, the message goes to the _____ folder.
   a. Send
   b. Hold
   c. Outbox
   d. Forward

6. A received email message is placed in the _____ folder in Mail.
   a. Receive
   b. Inbox
   c. To Read
   d. Incoming

7. _____ a file to send it along with an email message.
   a. Insert
   b. File
   c. Pin
   d. Attach

8. Create a _____ in your online account and then sync the account in Mail so you can see it to move messages into it.
   a. folder
   b. folio
   c. dropbox
   d. message center

9. The _____ app helps you manage the names and email addresses of people you email frequently.
   a. Calendar
   b. Messaging
   c. People
   d. Mail

10. You can connect and sync contacts with this social media service: _____.
    a. Twitter
    b. Facebook
    c. LinkedIn
    d. All of the above

Part 2

Short Answer

11. How do you start Mail?

_____

12. How do you create a new email message?

_____

13. When addressing a message, how do you use an email address that is one of your contacts?

_____

14. How do you send and receive messages?

_____

15. How do you read a received message?

_____

16. After clicking Respond, which choice do you click to send a response to all original recipients of the message?

_____

17. After clicking Respond, which choice do you click to send a message to someone who was not one of the original message recipients?

_____

18. Name at least one reason why junk email might be a problem.

_____

19. How do you create a new contact?

_____

20. How do you create an event in the Calendar app?

_____

Save all solution files to the default Documents folder or any alternative folder specified by your instructor.

Guided Check

Assessment 1

Start Mail and Send a Message

1. Trade email addresses with another student, and use your partner's email address to complete this assessment. He or she should use your email address to complete the assessment.
2. Start the Mail app.
   a. Display the Start screen.
   b. Click the Mail tile.
3. Create and address a new message.
   a. Make sure your account is selected in the Accounts and Folders pane.
   b. Click the New button.
   c. Click in the *To* text box.
   d. Type your partner's email address.
   e. Click in the *Cc* text box.
   f. Type your instructor's email address.
4. Enter a subject.
   a. Click *Add a subject* in the right pane.
   b. Type Chapter 09 Assessment 01.
5. Enter the message body.
   a. Click below the border in the message area.
   b. Type Thank you for receiving my practice message.
   c. Press Enter twice.
   d. Type your name.
6. Format the message text.
   a. Drag over all the text in the message body.
   b. Click the Font command, open the *font size* drop-down list, scroll up, and then click *18*.
   c. Click the Text color command and then click *Blue* (the third color in the first column).
   d. Click at the end of your name to deselect the text.
   e. Capture a screen shot and then save it as **C09A01**. Switch back to the Mail app.
7. Send the message.
   a. Click the Send button in the upper right corner of the message.
   b. Right-click the Mail screen and then click the Sync command on the app bar.
8. Submit the screen shot to your instructor.

Assessment 2

Send a Message with File Attachments

1. Create another message to your student partner. With your account selected in Mail, click the New button.
2. Address the message.
   a. Click in the *To* text box.
   b. Type your partner's email address.
   c. Click in the *Cc* text box.
   d. Type your instructor's email address.

3. Enter a subject.
   a. Click *Add a subject* in the right pane.
   b. Type Chapter 09 Assessment 02.
4. Attach the files.
   a. Right-click and then click the Attachments command.
   b. Open the Chapter 9 Student Data Files folder by clicking the down-pointing arrow beside files, clicking a parent folder or location, and then clicking subfolders as needed to drill down to the data files folder.
   c. Click the **Mail Accounts** JPEG file in the Files app screen.
   d. Click the **Mail** text file in the Files app screen.
   e. Click the Attach button.
5. Add a message.
   a. Click below *2 files attached* in the message body.
   b. Type See attached files to learn about Mail accounts.
   c. Capture a screen shot and then save it as **C09A02**. Switch back to the Mail app.
6. Send the message.
   a. Click the Send button in the upper right corner of the message.
   b. Right-click the Mail screen and then click the Sync command on the app bar.
7. Submit the screen shot to your instructor.

Assessment 3 **Receive a Message and Save a File Attachment**
1. In the Mail app, right-click and then click Sync to receive messages. The message(s) from your class partner should arrive.
2. Read a message.
   a. Select your account and then click the Inbox folder in the Accounts and folders pane, if needed.
   b. Click the **Chapter 09 Assessment 01** message in the Message list pane.
   c. View the message contents in the Reading pane.
   d. Capture a screen shot and then save it as **C09A03**. Switch back to the Mail app.
3. Save message attachments.
   a. Click the Chapter **09 Assessment 02** message in the Message list pane.
   b. Click Download under the first file attachment icon in the Reading pane. After the image appears, right-click it and then click *Save*.
   c. Use the Files app to navigate to the folder specified by your instructor.
   d. Click Save.
4. Repeat Step 3 to save the second attachment.
5. Drag or swipe down from the top of the screen to the bottom to close the Mail app.
6. Submit the screen shot to your instructor.

Assessment 4 **Add a Contact in People**
1. Go to the Start screen and then click the People tile.
2. Create a contact.
   a. Right-click a blank area of the app and then click the New command.
   b. Enter Taylor in the *First name* text box and Diaz in the *Last name* text box.
   c. Click the circled plus button under Email and then click *Work* in the menu.
   d. Type td@emcp.com in the *Work* text box.
   e. Capture a screen shot and then save it as **C09A04**. Switch back to the People app.
   f. Click the Save command.

3. Drag or swipe down from the top of the screen to the bottom to close the People app.
4. Submit the screen shot to your instructor.

On Your Own

Assessment 5 **Create a Folder in Your Hotmail or Live (Outlook) Account and Sync It in Mail**
1. Go to the Windows desktop and click the Internet Explorer button on the Taskbar to start Explorer.
2. Navigate to home.live.com and sign in to your account, if necessary.
3. Click Hotmail at the top of the screen. In Outlook, the mail tools should appear, but if not, click the down arrow adjacent to Outlook and then click the Mail tile.
4. In the Inbox list at the left under Folders, click New folder. In Outlook, click New folder under Folders.
5. Type Chapter 09 Assessments as the folder name and then press Enter.
6. Switch to or open the Mail app and make sure that your account is selected.
7. Right-click a blank area of the Mail screen and then click the Sync command.
8. After the account syncs and the folder appears, capture a screen shot and then save it as **C09A05**. Switch back to the Mail app.
9. Submit the screen shot to your instructor.

Assessment 6 **File and Delete Your Class Messages**
1. In the Mail app, click the Inbox folder in the Accounts and folders pane.
2. Select the two messages you received during these assessments in the Message list pane and then click the Move command.
3. Click the *Chapter 09 Assessments* folder in the Accounts and folders pane to move the selected files there.
4. Click the *Chapter 09 Assessments* folder again to display its contents. Capture a screen shot and then save it as **C09A06S04**. Switch back to the Mail app.
5. In the Message list pane of the Chapter 09 Assessments folder, select both messages and then click Delete.
6. Capture a screen shot and then save it as **C09A06S06**.
7. Select the Deleted items folder and then delete the messages from there to make the deletion permanent.
8. Submit the screen shots to your instructor.
9. Switch back to your Hotmail account in Internet Explorer. Sign out and close the Internet Explorer window.

Assessment 7 **Add an Event to Your Calendar**
1. Go to the Start screen and then click the Calendar tile.
2. Change to the Month view, if needed.
3. Display and click the date May 24, 2016. Add an all-day event for that date with Last Day of School as the title and Campus as the *Location*.
4. Click the Save this event button at upper right.
5. Reopen the message by clicking it in the Calendar.
6. Click the *Invite people* text box under Who, and then type your instructor's email address.
7. Click the Send invite button to finish the event and then send the email.
8. Close the Calendar app and then return to Mail.
9. Sync mail to make sure that the message sends.
10. Close the Mail app and any other open applications.

Class Activity: Create an Email Emoticon and Shortcut Collection

To start this project, your instructor creates a Notepad file that lists the email address for each student in the class. The instructor saves the file as **Emoticons and Abbreviations** and then sends an email message to the first student on the list with **Emoticons and Abbreviations** attached as a file.

The student who receives the file first saves the **Emoticons and Abbreviations** file to the system hard disk. He or she then opens the file, types in an emoticon or common messaging abbreviation (such as LOL for Laugh Out Loud), and then deletes his or her own email address from the file. He or she should then note the email address for the next student on the list, save and close the file, and then email the file to the next student on the list.

In this way, the **Emoticons and Abbreviations** file is forwarded to each student in the class, so he or she can save the attachment, add an emoticon or shortcut (that has not already been added by another student), delete his or her own email address, and then email the updated file to the next student on the list.

The final student emails the file back to the instructor after adding the last emoticon or shortcut and then deleting his or her own name.

Note that you are allowed to research emoticons and abbreviations on the Web, so feel free to do so.

CHALLENGE PROJECT

You are self-employed and recently started using the Windows 8 operating system, but you have been using the Facebook social media service to connect with friends and colleagues for some time. In the People app, connect with your Facebook account. After the account connects and syncs with People, capture a screen shot that shows the contacts that have been added, save the file as C09A09, and then submit it to your instructor. Use the Settings charm to remove the account.

Working with Digital Photographs and Music

PERFORMANCE OBJECTIVES

Upon successful completion of Chapter 10, you will be able to:

- Import pictures from a digital camera
- Use the Pictures library and preview a picture
- Play pictures on the screen as a slide show
- Zip images to a single file
- Import images to Photo Gallery
- Organize, tag, and adjust images in Photo Gallery

- Print and email images
- Connect to your online image photo albums in the Photos app
- Build a music library in Media Player
- Rip songs from an audio CD
- Build and play a playlist
- Sync to a portable music player
- Burn a playlist to a CD-R
- Stream music

The Web and more powerful computers have paved the way for more rich and interactive electronic communications. Even everyday business communications, such as a letter, might contain a picture; other communications, such as email, might include sounds. Media capabilities also make your computer more personal and pleasing to use: display on your desktop or an app tile a digital picture you took, for example, or play some favorite music while you work. Business communications increasingly include more media, as well, from newsletter emails that include product information and photos to presentations with audio and video. This chapter shows you how to use the digital media management capabilities featured in Windows 8, including the new Photos app.

digital picture An image or picture saved in digital format for use in computer documents and web pages

digital camera A device that captures pictures and stores them on digital storage media

Importing Pictures from a Digital Camera or Removable Media to Windows 8 ■■■■■■■■■

Documents that integrate pictures, as well as text, have become more of the norm rather than an exception in business and personal communications. Most commercial web pages include at least one *digital picture*. Windows 8, like its predecessor Windows versions, enables you to transfer digital images from a *digital camera* and store and organize those images on your computer's hard disk for use in your business and personal documents.

A digital camera works in a way that is similar to a traditional film camera. Light comes through the lens and an opening called the aperture when you press a button to take the picture (open the shutter). Rather than striking film to create the image, in a digital camera the light strikes an optical sensor that then enables the camera to digitize the image and store it on digital storage media within the camera.

Three factors have contributed to the fast rise in popularity of digital cameras. First, there is immediacy. You do not have to wait for film to be developed to see your pictures. With digital cameras and camera phones, you can view a picture immediately on the LCD screen on the back of the camera or front of the phone. Second, storing images on removable media, a hard disk, or a CD-R or DVD-R is extremely cheap compared with the costs of film and film development. And third, digital images are more easily shared and used than prints from a photo camera. You can email your images, post them online, include them in documents, combine them in a collage, and manipulate them in any number of ways depending on the software you have available.

Most digital cameras connect to the computer via a USB port. Generally speaking, if your camera model is supported by Windows 8, all you do is make the connection, and Windows 8 enables you to transfer the images to your system's hard disk. If you prefer to remove the Secure Digital (SD), Compact Flash (CF), or other removable flash memory card from the camera and insert it in a card reader, Windows 8 also recognizes the images. Windows 8 can transfer images from CD or DVD, as well. Many notebook and desktop computer models have built-in flash media card readers.

In Windows 8, the new Photos app handles the photo import process. Whether you start the import from the Start screen or the desktop, Photos launches automatically.

Here's How

To transfer digital photos from a digital camera or storage card:

1. Connect the camera to the computer via the camera's USB cable, or connect the digital card reader to the system via its cable. If your digital card reader is integrated into the system, as on some newer "media center" or mobile computers, you need not connect it.
2. Power the camera on and put it in its Playback or Transfer mode. If you are working with a digital card reader, insert the card in the reader or slot.
3. The first time you connect a camera or flash memory card, a prompt appears in the upper right corner of the screen asking you to choose an action for the device. Click or tap the prompt to open the list of choices and then click *Import photos and videos*. *Photos* appears below that choice to indicate that the Photos app will launch.

Step 3

Canon EOS DIGITAL REBEL...

Choose what to do with this device.

Import photos and videos
Photos

Open device to view files
File Explorer

Take no action

4. Photos reads your camera's contents, tells you how many photos you have, and automatically selects them all. To select a more limited number of photos, click Clear selection at upper right and then click the thumbnails for the photos you want to import. *Hint: Move the mouse pointer above the commands at the bottom of the screen to display a scroll bar so that you can scroll right to see more photo thumbnails.*

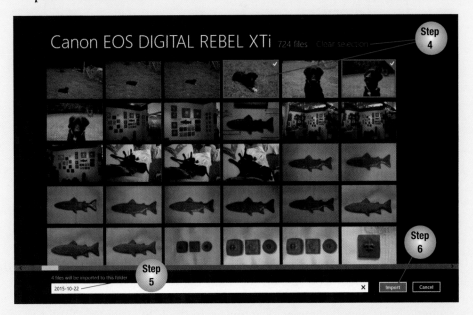

5. At the bottom of the window, the text box, by default, shows the date the first photo was taken. The entry becomes the name of the subfolder in your Photos library in which Photos will place the imported digital photos. Edit the entry as desired.
6. Click Import.
7. After the import finishes, which may take several minutes depending on the number of images stored in your camera, Photos displays a Done! message. Click the Open folder button to open the new photo album in Photos. Power off and disconnect the camera.

Note: *Rather than importing pictures from a camera, you can copy and paste them like any other file. To do so, go to the desktop and then open a File Explorer window. Under* Computer *in the Navigation pane, click the camera or storage card and then navigate to the folder that holds the images to copy. Select and copy image files and then paste them to any folder on your system, just as you would for any other file.*

Viewing Pictures in the Pictures Library

By default, images that have been transferred to your system are placed in a subfolder of the My Pictures folder in your personal folder, meaning they also appear in the Pictures library by default. To open the Pictures library, go to the desktop, click the File Explorer button on the Taskbar, and then double-click the Pictures icon.

Each time you use Windows 8 to import images automatically, the import process creates a folder with the name you specified, as shown in Figure 10.1. To view the pictures in any folder, double-click the folder icon.

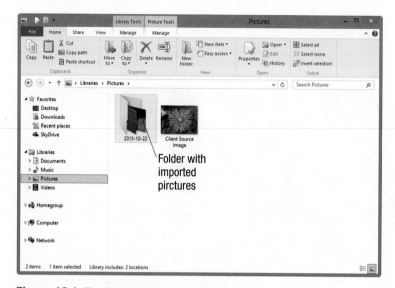

Figure 10.1 The folder holding imported pictures uses the name you specified during the import.

As shown in Figure 10.2, the icon of each imported picture is a preview of the picture. Choose a larger icon size on the View tab to preview the pictures more easily in the Pictures library. The imported files use the file names assigned by the camera. Most digital cameras save images in the JPEG (.jpg) or TIFF (.tif) file format automatically.

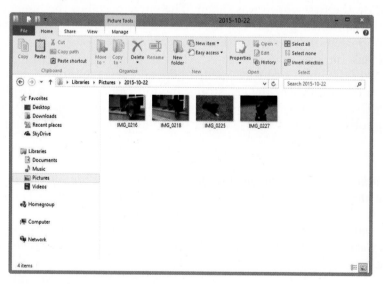

Figure 10.2 Each imported picture uses the file name assigned by the camera.

To select a photo, click it. To preview a digital photo at a larger size, double-click it in the Pictures library. By default, the picture opens in the Photos app. If instead you want to view it in another application, select the picture, click the Open drop-down arrow in the Open group on the Home tab on the ribbon, and then click the name of the application in which you want to open the picture.

TIP Right-click any image in a Pictures library or a subfolder and then click *Set as desktop background* to place the image on the desktop.

Exercise 1

Transferring Digital Camera Images

1. Take at least 10 pictures with your digital camera or a digital camera being made available for this class by your instructor. (Ideally, you will not have any other images stored on the camera when you start.)
2. Connect the camera or a card reader to the system via its cable.
3. Power the camera on and then put it in its playback or transfer position. Or, remove the storage card from the camera and then place it in the card reader or slot on the computer.
4. Click *Import photos and videos* in the AutoPlay dialog box.
5. Click the Clear selection choice at upper right and then click at least three photo thumbnails to select those photos for import.
6. Type **Chapter 10 Exercise 01 Import** in the text box at the bottom of the screen.
7. Click Import.
8. When the import finishes, click Open folder.
9. Power down and disconnect the camera, or safely remove the storage card from the card reader.
10. Close the Photos app.
11. Display the desktop, open a File Explorer window, and then double-click the Pictures icon.
12. Double-click the folder icon of the Chapter 10 Exercise 01 folder that holds the pictures you imported. (Your view may vary.)
13. Capture a screen shot and then save the file as **C10E01**.
14. Close the Pictures library window.
15. Submit the screen shot to your instructor.

Showing a Slide Show of the Pictures in a Folder

Although you can personalize your Windows 8 desktop background with a digital picture you have taken, why settle for one image? Instead, play back the images stored in any subfolder of your Pictures library as an on-screen *slide show*.

Not only does a slide show make a nice decorative statement on the desktop, but you also can use a slide show to present pictures of a subject or topic during a presentation if you lack a true presentation graphics program.

slide show A feature that automatically displays on the screen each picture from a folder in sequence

Note: *Even if a folder holds picture files of the same file formats typically used by digital cameras (JPEG or TIFF), you cannot play the folder's contents as a slide show unless the folder is properly customized. Windows 8 recognizes only subfolders of the My Pictures folder (in your user folder) and the Pictures library as pictures windows, by default. To optimize a folder stored outside your libraries for picture features, navigate to the folder in a File Explorer window, right-click the folder name or icon, and then click* Properties *in the shortcut menu. On the Customize tab of the Properties dialog box, open the* Optimize this folder for *drop-down list, click* Pictures, *and then click OK. Some folders, such as system folders, cannot be customized in this way.*

To rotate a photo to the correct position before running the slide show, use the Rotate left and Rotate right buttons in the Rotate group on the Picture Tools Manage tab on the ribbon.

Figure 10.3 Right-click a slide show to open a menu of options for controlling its playback.

To start a slide show, open the Pictures library (click the File Explorer button on the desktop Taskbar and then double-click *Pictures*) and then navigate to and open the folder that holds the picture files to play. Click the Picture Tools Manage tab on the ribbon and then click Slide show in the View group. The slide show begins playing immediately.

To control the slide show, right-click any slide. As shown in Figure 10.3, a shortcut menu of options for controlling the show appears.

- **Pause.** Click to stop the slide show, freezing it at the current image. To resume the slide show, right-click the screen and then click *Play*.
- **Next and Back.** Jump ahead to the next image or go back to a previously displayed image.
- **Shuffle or Loop.** Click one of these options to determine whether the slide show displays images in random order (Shuffle) or each in order, repeating the sequence after all images have been displayed (Loop).
- **Slide Show Speed—Slow, Slide Show Speed—Medium, or Slide Show Speed—Fast.** Click one of these choices to specify how quickly Windows 8 moves from one image to the next in the slide show.
- **Exit.** Click to exit the slide show.

In addition to using the Exit command on the shortcut menu to end the slide show, you can press Esc on the keyboard.

Note: *To set up the contents of your Pictures library as a screen saver, right-click the desktop and click Personalize. In the Personalization window, click Screen Saver at bottom right. Open the Screen saver drop-down list in the Screen Saver settings dialog box, click Photos, and then click OK.*

Zipping Pictures in the Pictures Library

The previous chapter included a tip about zipping files before emailing them so that you can attach a single file to a message rather than multiple files. If you are an avid photographer, chances are you like to send your pictures to friends and family via email. When you want to send a group of pictures, it makes sense to first zip them together. Use the Zip choice in the Send group on the Share tab on the ribbon in the Pictures library to do the job. The zip process creates what is called a compressed (zipped) folder.

Here's How

To zip selected picture files:

1. In the Pictures library, navigate to and open the folder with the digital image files to zip.
2. Select the desired image files.
3. Click the Share tab on the ribbon and then click Zip in the Send group.
4. A new folder displaying the zip icon appears with the temporary name selected so that you can replace it. Type the desired folder name and then press Enter.

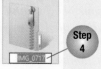

Step 4

Email the compressed folder as a file attachment using the Mail app, as described in Chapter 9. If you have a separate legacy client email application installed to work with the desktop, such as Microsoft Outlook or Mozilla Thunderbird, or the free Windows Mail program (downloadable from windows.microsoft.com/en-US/windows-live/essentials-home), the Email button in the Share group of the File Explorer window becomes active. Select one or more files to email and then click that button to launch a new message window in your email client with the file(s) attached. Address the message, add any message text, and then send.

Note: *You also can select and burn image files to a CD-R or DVD-R using the same method as for other files. To review that process, see the section "Copying Files to Writable CD or DVD" in Chapter 2.*

Exercise 2

Viewing Your Pictures Library and Playing a Slide Show

1. Go to the desktop, click the File Explorer button on the Taskbar, and then double-click Pictures.
2. Double-click the **Chapter 10 Exercise 01 Import** folder you created in Exercise 1.
3. On the Picture Tools Manage tab, click Slide show in the View group.
4. Right-click the slide show. With the shortcut menu open, capture a screen shot and then save it as **C10E02S04**. Click Exit to leave the slide show. (You cannot work in applications with the slide show running.)
5. Go back to the Chapter 10 Exercise 01 Import folder window.
6. Click the Slide show button in the View group to run the show again.
7. Press Esc to exit the slide show.
8. Back in the Chapter 10 Exercise 01 Import folder in the Pictures library, select all your downloaded photos. *Hint: Press Ctrl + A.*
9. Click the Share tab on the ribbon and then click the Zip button in the Send group.
10. Type C10E02S10 as the file name and then press Enter.
11. Close the Pictures library window.
12. Submit the screen shot and compressed (zipped) file to your instructor.

Playing Images to a TV

Newer smart TVs connect wirelessly to your network so that you can share images and more from your computer to your TV. The Pictures library lets you take advantage of this capability. You can play back any folder of images to a capable TV on your network. You can do this for entertainment purposes or for a business reason, such as to give a presentation of product images to a group of customers. The TV must be connected to the network—wirelessly for newer models or via a wired connection for older models. Appropriate device driver software must be installed on the computer, if required. Chapter 11 explains how to connect to a network, and Chapter 13 explains how to add devices to a system in Windows 8.

To view a folder of pictures on your TV:

1. Make sure your TV is on and both it and the computer are connected to the network.
2. In the Pictures library, navigate to and click the icon of the folder with the digital image files to play to the TV.
3. Click the Picture Tools Manage tab. In the View group on the ribbon, click *Play to* and then click the name or model of your TV in the drop-down list that appears. At this point, you may need to use the TV's remote to respond to a prompt asking you to accept the connection. Do so, if needed, and change any other settings as needed (such as changing the video source to the TV), and then continue.
4. Click the Play/Pause button as needed to pause and restart the image playback.
5. Click the window Close (X) button to finish the show.

Using Photo Gallery ■■■■■■■■■■■■■■■■■■■■■■■■■■■■

Photo Gallery provides a centralized location where you can view and organize digital images. It offers all of the features that the Pictures library does, plus some additional features like the ability to fix a photo or add additional information such as a caption or more tags. Download Photo Gallery (part of the Windows Essentials programs) for free at <u>windows.microsoft.com/en-US/windows-live/essentials-home</u>.

Note: *The free download includes Movie Maker, a program you can use to create your own movies from your video clips, digital photos, and music.*

Starting and Exiting Photo Gallery

To start Photo Gallery, as shown in Figure 10.4, select the Start charm and then click Photo Gallery under *Apps*. The install process also adds a tile for Photo Gallery on the Start screen. You can go to the Start screen and then click the app tile there.

If the Sign in with your email address dialog box opens, enter your email address and password and then click Sign in, or click Cancel to bypass the dialog box. Signing in with a Microsoft account or other email address enables you to take advantage of additional features such as automatically publishing your photos online. By default, the photos are grouped by date taken. To turn off grouping, as shown in Figure 10.4, right-click in the list of files, point to *Group by*, and then click *None*.

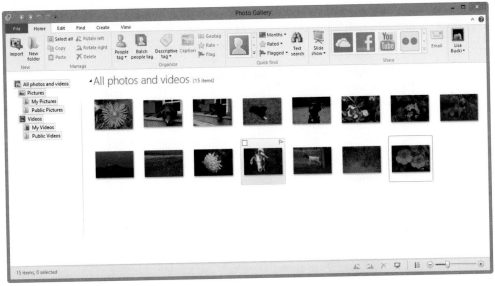

Figure 10.4 Use Photo Gallery to work with and organize the images you have imported.

To exit Photo Gallery, click the File tab on the ribbon and then click *Exit*, click its window Close (X) button, or press Alt + F4.

Importing Images to the Photo Gallery

By default, Photo Gallery shows all of the pictures in your My Pictures folder as well as those in the Public Pictures folder, just as the Pictures library does. (It also shows all of the videos stored in the corresponding folders for videos.) Photo Gallery enables you to import images from a digital camera, flash memory card, CD, or DVD to a new folder in the Pictures library.

Start by connecting the digital camera or card reader and then power on the device. In the case of a camera, also put it in Playback or Transfer mode. Insert the flash card in the appropriate slot. (If the Photos app launches, you can close it and switch back to Photo Gallery on the desktop.) In Photo Gallery, click the Home tab and then click the Import button in the New group.

Note: *After you install Photo Gallery and connect a digital camera or insert a flash media card with pictures, a message appears letting you know you have new choices for the device. Tap or click it, and the pop-up that appears includes an Import pictures and videos (with Photo Gallery under it) choice that you can then click. This option launches Photo Gallery automatically each time you connect the camera or insert a card with pictures.*

In the Import Photos and Videos dialog box that appears (shown in Figure 10.5), click the camera or device from which you want to import and then click the Import button. When importing from a camera or card reader, Photo Gallery indicates the number of items found for import. You can leave the *Review, organize, and group items to import* option selected and then click Next. In the expanded dialog box that appears (shown in Figure 10.6), check and uncheck groups to import, click an *Enter a name* prompt and type a name for a group, or click an *Add tags* prompt and type additional descriptive tags to help with organizing and finding images. Click Import when you finish making your choices. Or, if you click *Import*

Figure 10.5 Select the device from which you want to import.

Working with Digital Photographs and Music

all new items now in the Import Photos and Videos dialog box, type a name and add tags directly and then click Import to import all images under the specified name and tags. When the import finishes, power down and disconnect the device, if desired.

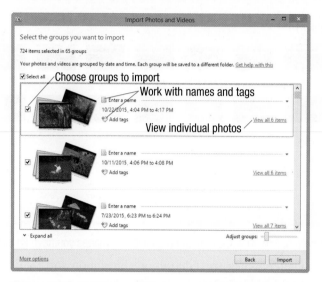

Figure 10.6 Choosing which groups and images to import.

Note: *Graphic images from existing sources, such as magazines, or online sites, such as Flickr, are typically protected by copyright law. Make sure you understand fair use laws and different forms of licenses such as Creative Commons before you download and use an image for any commercial purpose.*

Adding a Folder of Images

If images have already been stored elsewhere on your system network, or SkyDrive (assuming you have the SkyDrive app installed so that you can access your SkyDrive from File Explorer), you can add that folder to the folders tracked by the Pictures library through Photo Gallery. No matter where an image is actually stored, adding it to the library means that you can work with it just like an image that you have imported directly.

Here's How

To add or remove a Pictures library folder:

1. Click the File tab on the ribbon and then click Include folder. The Pictures Library Locations dialog box appears.
2. Click Add. (To remove a folder tracked by the Pictures library, you would click a folder in the existing list, click Remove, and then go to Step 5.)
3. In the Include Folder in Pictures dialog box that appears, navigate to and then select the folder that holds the images to add.
4. Click Include folder.
5. Click OK to close the Pictures Library Locations dialog box.

Viewing Images and Organizing in Photo Gallery

As noted previously, Photo Gallery, by default, groups images according to the date the photos were taken.

You can instead group photos by a number of other criteria, such as the Tag, Rating, Camera used, or other date information. To change the grouping, use the choices in the Arrange list group on the View tab. For a more extensive list of choices, right-click a blank area in the list of photos, point to *Group by*, and then click the desired grouping criterion. For example, Figure 10.7 shows images grouped by tag.

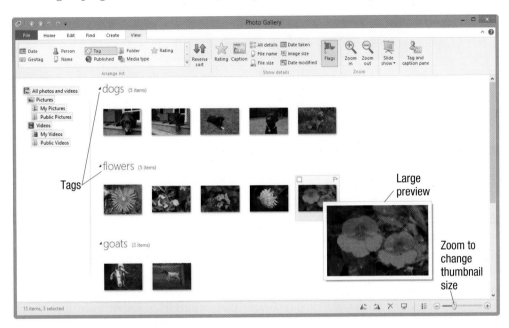

Figure 10.7 Images grouped by tag.

To select an image, click its thumbnail. If you want to see a larger preview of any image, move the mouse pointer over its thumbnail. Figure 10.7 shows an example of this type of preview. You also can drag the slider in the lower right corner of the window to resize all of the thumbnails.

You can use the folder tree that appears under *All photos and videos* to create folders in which you might want to further organize your photos. Right-click any folder or subfolder there, click *Create new folder*, type a folder name, and then press Enter. To copy or move a photo to any folder that you have created, first go to the location or choose the display method that shows the desired picture in the list of thumbnails. In the pane at the left, navigate to the folder into which you want to copy the photo using the arrows at the left of the folder icons. (If you click the folder itself, the gallery list of images changes.) Drag an image thumbnail from the list to the destination folder, as shown in Figure 10.8. If the folder is on the same disk, it is moved rather than copied.

To delete an image from any location via Photo Gallery, click its thumbnail and then press the Delete key. Click Yes to confirm the deletion in the Delete File dialog box. Remember, if you imported an image from a location other than your computer, such as a network location, deleting an image deletes it permanently. Deleting an image stored on your system's hard disk moves the image to the Recycle Bin.

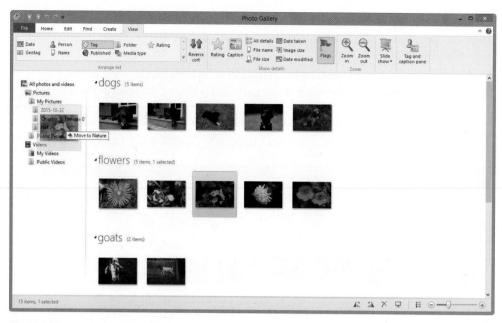

Figure 10.8 Drag an image to a folder to move or copy the image there.

Applying Photo Fixes

Both the Pictures library and Photo Gallery enable you to correct a photo's orientation. You might need to do this, for example, if you rotate the camera to shoot a picture using a portrait (tall) orientation to fit in a subject that is vertically oriented. The imported photo, however, displays in landscape orientation in the Pictures library or Photo Gallery. To correct this situation in either location, right-click the photo and then click either *Rotate right* or *Rotate left*. The photo immediately snaps to the corrected orientation and keeps that orientation until you rotate it again. The Manage group on the Edit tab on the ribbon in Photo Gallery also includes Rotate left and Rotate right commands.

Photo Gallery offers the advantage of enabling you to make additional corrections to a selected photo. You can adjust exposure (apparent brightness and contrast), color, cropping, or fix red-eye (when the subject's eyes glow red or green in a photo). Note that correction options are not available for all graphic file formats.

Here's How

To correct a photo:

1. Select the folder that holds the photo to edit in the pane at the left.
2. Double-click the thumbnail of the photo to fix in the list. The photo opens for editing with the Edit tab selected.
3. Use the choices on the Edit tab to fix the photo as desired. You can use one or any combination of the fixes. If you plan to make multiple changes, Microsoft recommends that you click Fine tune in the Adjustments group and then apply the fixes in the order in which the Fine tune pane lists them. To collapse an option, click the option name again. Favorite fixes you might make are:

    • **Auto adjust.** Click the Auto adjust button in the Adjustments group on the Edit tab to have Photo Gallery fix exposure and color for you.

- **Adjust exposure.** Click the Exposure arrow in the Adjustments group on the Edit tab and then click either the choice under *Auto adjust exposure* or one of the presets under *Choose exposure adjustment*. If working in the Fine tune pane, click *Adjust exposure* and then drag the *Brightness*, *Contrast*, *Shadows*, and/or *Highlights* sliders until the image looks as desired.

- **Adjust color.** Click the Color arrow in the Adjustments group and then click either the choice under *Auto adjust color* or one of the presets under *Choose color adjustment*. If working in the Fine tune pane, click Adjust color, and then drag the *Color temperature*, *Tint*, and/or *Saturation* sliders until the image looks as desired.

- **Straighten photo.** Click Straighten in the Adjustments group to automatically correct the image angle. If working in the Fine tune pane, click Straighten photo and then drag the slider until the image looks as desired.

- **Crop photo.** Click Crop in the Adjustments group and then drag the handles on the crop frame until it identifies the portion of the image that you want to keep. Click the Crop button again to apply the crop.

- **Adjust detail.** Click Adjust detail in the Fine tune pane and then drag the *Sharpen* slider. Clicking the Analyze button provides a suggested *Reduce Noise* setting.

- **Red eye.** Click Red eye in the Adjustments group and then drag over the eye to fix in the image.

- **Effects.** Open the gallery in the Effects group and then click one of the thumbnails to colorize the image accordingly.

4. To undo and redo changes as you make them, click Undo or Redo on the Quick Access Toolbar. You also can use the Revert to Original button on the Edit tab to undo multiple changes.

5. When the image looks the way you want, click Close file at the right end of the Edit tab. Photo Gallery automatically saves the changes you made to your image. Click OK if a dialog box notifies you that you can revert the changes.

Sharing Images

Like the Pictures library, Photo Gallery enables you to email the currently selected photos if you have an email client such as Mail or Outlook installed. Click the Email choice in the Share group on the Home tab to open a new message window for your email client with the file(s) already added as attachments. Address the message, add text, and then send it.

You also can use the choices in the Share gallery in the Share group to share an image or folder of images as an album to your SkyDrive account, Facebook, YouTube, Flickr, Vimeo, or Windows Live Groups. Select the image(s) or folder to share and then select the desired service from the Share gallery. Follow the on-screen prompts to sign in to your account, if needed, create an album, if required, and then upload the image(s).

rating Assigning a certain number of stars to a file to identify how much you like it or how important it is

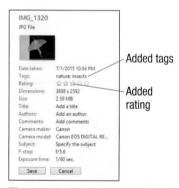
Added tags
Added rating

Figure 10.9 Apply tags and a rating to a photo in the Details pane of the Pictures library window.

Figure 10.10 The Properties dialog box may display additional details about the image and the camera settings used to take it.

Applying Tags, Ratings, and Other Info ■ ■

As with rotating a photo, you can work with some photo information (properties) in either the Pictures library or Photo Gallery.

In the Pictures library, click the View tab and then click Details pane in the Panes group to display the Details pane. Click an image and add a tag or a *rating* using the Tags or Rating choices in the Details pane at the right side of the window. Click at the right of Tags so that you see *Add a tag,* type the new tag, and then press Enter or click Save. If you start typing a tag name that exists, a drop-down list appears. Click to place a check mark beside the desired tag and then click Save.

To add a rating, point to the number of stars you want to add beside Rating in the Details pane. When the correct number of stars is highlighted, as shown in Figure 10.9, click the star under the mouse pointer and then click the Save button. To close the Details pane, click Details pane in the Panes group again.

You can work with tags, ratings, and other file information in the Properties dialog box for an image file, as for any other file, which you learned about in Chapter 4. Right-click the image file in the folder and then click *Properties.* Click the Details tab, change settings as desired, and then click OK to apply the changes. For several of the fields, click at the right of the field name to display a text box, and then type the desired entry. Special settings you may want to pay attention to include adding a photo *Title, Subject,* and *Authors* to help better identify the photo if it will be distributed for use by other parties. In such a scenario, adding a *Copyright* field entry is also a good idea to put others on notice that permission is required for reusing the image. Note that if you scroll down the Details tab, you can see information about the image size, the camera and settings used to create the image (shown in Figure 10.10), and more.

And, as with any other file, you can rename a picture file in a folder window by right-clicking the file, clicking *Rename,* typing the new name, and then pressing Enter.

In Photo Gallery, you also can change a variety of settings, but you use the Tag and caption pane. Click the photo for which you want to change settings in the gallery list, click the View tab, and then click Tag and caption pane at far right. The Tag and caption pane appears at the right side of the window, as shown in Figure 10.11.

Figure 10.11 Use the Tag and caption pane in Photo Gallery to change image settings.

Changing settings in the Tag and caption pane primarily consists of clicking and typing. Click the *Filename*, *Date taken*, *Add descriptive tags*, or *Add caption*; type the desired new entry or changes; and then press Enter. You also can add people tags and geotags as desired. To assign a rating, click the desired number of stars at the right of Rating. When you finish updating the image information in Photo Gallery, click the Tag and caption pane button again to close the pane.

Exercise 3

Fixing and Tagging an Image

1. With your instructor's permission, download and install the Photo Gallery app from windows.microsoft.com/en-US/windows-live/essentials-home.
2. Select the Search charm and then click Photo Gallery under *Apps*.
3. Click the File tab on the ribbon and then click *Include folder*. The Pictures Library Locations dialog box appears.
4. Click Add. In the Include Folder in Pictures dialog box, select the folder that holds the student data files for Exercise 3 in this chapter and then click Include folder. Click OK to close the Pictures Library Locations dialog box.
5. Double-click the **Yellow Rose** file thumbnail.
6. Click the Exposure down-pointing arrow in the Adjustments group of the Edit tab.
7. Under *Choose exposure adjustment*, click the bottom middle preset, *High brightness, original shadows, medium-low highlights*.
8. In the Adjustments group, click the Color down-pointing arrow.
9. Under *Choose color adjustment*, click the far right preset in the second row, *High temperature, original tint*.
10. Click Close file at the far right end of the Edit tab to save the file with your changes. Click OK at the dialog box that notifies you that you can revert the changes.
11. With the image still selected, click the View tab and then click the Tag and caption pane button.
12. Click to apply a rating of four stars under *Information*.
13. Click *Add descriptive tags* higher up in the pane, type flowers, and then press Enter.
14. Capture a screen shot and then save the file as **C10E03**.
15. Submit the screen shot to your instructor. Leave Photo Gallery open for the next exercise.

Printing an Image ■■■■■■■■■■■■■■■■■■■■■■■■■■

You can print the selected image from either the Pictures library window or Photo Gallery. In the Pictures library, use the Print choice in the Send group on the Share tab. In Photo Gallery, click the File tab, point to *Print*, and then click *Print*. In either case, Windows 8 displays the Print Pictures dialog box, which offers special settings for photo prints. For example, you can print an image at standard photo sizes such as 4 x 6 inches, 5 x 7 inches, and wallet size.

Here's How

To print a photo:

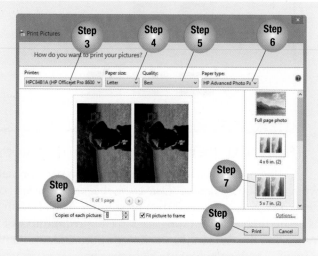

1. Select one or more photos to print in the Pictures library or Photo Gallery.

2. In the Pictures library, click Print in the Send group on the Share tab. In Photo Gallery, click the File tab, point to *Print,* and then click *Print*. The Print Pictures dialog box opens.

3. Click the *Printer* drop-down list and then click the printer to use.

4. Click the *Paper size* drop-down list and then click the paper to use.

5. Click the *Quality* drop-down list and then click the quality setting to use.

6. Click the *Paper type* drop-down list and then click the paper to use. This setting is available only if the selected printer is an inkjet printer or another type of printer that changes ink or toner usage based on paper type.

7. Scroll down the list of available print layouts at the right and then click the layout of your choice.

8. If you selected a single photo in Step 1 and the selected layout has a position for more than one image, increase the *Copies of each picture* text box entry to a number that matches the number of photo positions on the layout. This repeats the image to fill all of the spots on the layout.

9. Click Print. The Print Pictures dialog box sends the picture(s) to the printer.

Photo Gallery offers an additional print feature. If you click Order prints in the Share group on the Create tab, the Order Prints dialog box appears with a list of online printing companies. Select a company and send digital pictures to it to have prints made, which typically requires that you set up an account and provide credit card payment information. This can be a good option when you want high-quality prints or even specialty items like a mug from a digital photo.

Printing an Image and Removing Folders

1. In Photo Gallery, click **Chapter 10 Exercise 01 Import** under My Pictures in the Navigation pane. This displays the photos you imported in Exercise 1 of this chapter.
2. Click the thumbnail for any of the images.
3. Click the File tab, point to *Print*, and then click *Print*.
4. Select a printer from the *Printer* list, if needed. Leave *Letter* selected in the *Paper size* drop-down list.
5. Scroll down the layouts and then click *3.5 × 5 in. (4)*.
6. Increase the *Copies of each picture* value to *4*.
7. Click Print.
8. Label the printout as **C10E04** and then submit it to your instructor.
9. Click the File tab and then click Include folder. The Pictures Library Locations dialog box appears.
10. Click the *Exercise 03* folder, click Remove, and then click OK.
11. Click the *Chapter 10 Exercise 01 Import* folder under My Pictures in the Navigation pane.
12. If needed, right-click the list of thumbnails, point to *Group by*, and then click *None*.
13. Close the Photo Gallery window.

Viewing Images in the Photos App ■■■■■■■■■

Windows 8 features a new app called Photos. With Photos, you can view all of the images in your Photo library in a larger, full-screen format. Photos also enables you to connect to your photo albums on SkyDrive, Facebook, and Flickr, as well as photos stored on compatible devices. To start Photos, display the Start screen and then click its app tile. As shown in Figure 10.12, if you already imported photos to the Pictures library, the app's live tile displays the library files as a mini slide show on the tile. As with any other app, drag down from the top of the screen to the bottom to close the app.

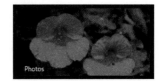

Figure 10.12 The Photos app live tile shows a mini slide show of the images in the Pictures library on the Start screen.

You learned in the previous section "Importing Pictures from a Digital Camera or Removable Media to Windows 8" that Windows 8, by default, uses the Photos app to import pictures when you connect a digital camera or removable media that stores picture files. If you connect your device or insert your flash media card and the import process does not start automatically, right-click the initial Photos screen, click the Import command in the app bar at the bottom, and then click the device name in the list to start the import. Continue with the import as described previously in the chapter.

Viewing Images in a Folder

The initial Photos screen includes a tile for the Pictures library at bottom left. Click that tile to display a screen with tiles of the top-level folders, as shown in Figure 10.13. Moving the mouse pointer over the tile opens a scroll bar at the bottom so that you can scroll right to view additional folder tiles and scroll left to go back. Click a tile to view the contents of its folder. If needed, click the tile(s) of additional subfolders to navigate to the subfolder that holds the images you want to view.

Click to go back

Pictures library 4 folders, 2 files

2015-10-22   Nature   Outdoors   Luna Moth

Figure 10.13 The Photos app shows each folder as a tile after you click the Pictures library tile.

Once you are in the desired folder, move the mouse pointer over the current image to open the scroll bar at the bottom and then scroll to view additional images. Click the plus and minus icons at lower right to zoom in (plus) and zoom out (minus). To view the images as a slide show, right-click and then click the Slide show command.

To select all of the images in the folder, right-click and then click the Select all command. To select an individual image, make sure the app bar is closed by pressing Esc, if needed, and then click the image tile. Click the right-pointing arrow button at the right side of the screen to display and select subsequent images in the folder. To deselect the image, press Esc. To back up from any of the folder screens, click the circled left-pointing arrow button at the left of the folder name.

Choosing the App Tile or Lock Screen Image

If you prefer that the Photos app tile display a single image, rather than a slide show, you can specify the image to use in the Photos app. Likewise, you can specify an image in your Pictures library or your online albums (if connected) to use as the lock screen image.

Here's How

To set a photo to display on the app tile or lock screen:

1. Start the Photos app by clicking the Photos tile on the Start screen.
2. Click the Pictures library tile or the tile of an online social media service (see the next section), if available.
3. Click folder/album tiles to navigate to the location that holds the photo you want.
4. If necessary, scroll to display the tile for the desired photo and then click it.
5. Right-click and then click the Set as command.
6. Click either *App tile* or *Lock screen* as desired.
7. Press Esc to close the selected picture and then back up as needed in the Photos app.

▼ Quick Fix

Get the Slide Show Back
Use a different method to return the Photos tile to displaying a slide show. In Photos, select the Settings charm and click Options. Drag the Shuffle photos on the app tile slider to the right to set it to On, then press Esc to close the pane.

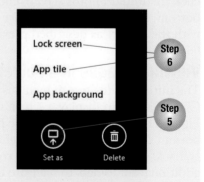

Lock screen — Step 6

App tile

App background

Step 5

Set as   Delete

Viewing Your Albums on SkyDrive or Other Social Media Services

As shown in Figure 10.14, the initial Photos screen includes a tile for the Pictures library, along with tiles for connecting to your albums on SkyDrive, Facebook, and Flickr. Click the tile of the desired service. If you are currently signed in with a local user account, you are prompted to sign in with a Microsoft account. Click Connect. Enter your sign-in information when prompted—usually your email address and password—and then click Log in. A Request for Permission screen may appear prompting you to verify what information the Microsoft service can access from the other service. Click Allow to continue and then click Done at the You're ready to go screen.

Continue by clicking the tile of the online service. Each album appears as a tile, and you can click the album tile to view the photos it contains.

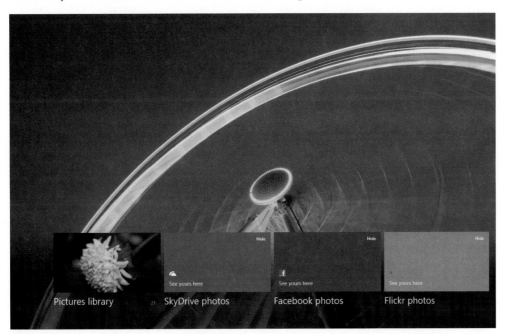

Figure 10.14 Add albums from your online accounts to Photos from the initial app screen.

Using Windows Media Player ■■■■■■■■■■■■■■■■

After working with digital photos moved into the spotlight as a primary use of computers, the next wave—digital music—hit. The built-in Windows Media Player application in Windows 8 enables you to listen to digital music and view digital video. On the music side, you can do much more than listen. You can convert songs from your audio CDs to digital music, build a list of songs from different artists for playback, and even burn your own music CDs.

Note: *The new Music app enables you to sign in to a Microsoft account and then listen to music through the Xbox Music service. (You will be prompted to create an Xbox LIVE account, which starts a free 30-Day Music Pass trial. After that, you can choose to pay a monthly or annual fee to renew your pass.) Click the Music app on the Start screen, sign in, if prompted, click tiles to navigate to releases from an artist you like, and then click a song. Click Play to play the song. Right-click to see commands for adding a song to a playlist, pausing song playback, and more.*

Starting and Exiting Media Player

To start Windows Media Player, select the Search charm and then click Windows Media Player under *Windows Accessories*.

Note: *The first time you start Windows Media Player, it asks you to choose initial settings, such as making Media Player the default music and video player. You can click Recommended settings and then click Finish to continue working.*

To exit Windows Media Player, press Alt to open a menu, point to *File*, and then click *Exit*; click its window Close (X) button; or press Alt + F4.

Adding Files to the Player Library

Media Player tracks all of your digital music and other media in various libraries. For example, its Music library, by default, tracks the same folders as the File Explorer Music library. It also tracks the Pictures and Videos libraries, as well as has two additional libraries for Recorded TV and Other media. Once a song is in the Music library (either via the Music library in Explorer or Windows Media Player), you can play it, add a rating, add it to a list of songs for playback, and so on. To display the Music library and its folders (shown in Figure 10.15), double-click *Music* in the Navigation pane at the left side of the Media Player window. Note that it also lists the libraries for the other types of content: Videos, Pictures, Recorded TV, and so on. Media Player also adds any file you play from another location on your computer or network to the library. And, when you add songs from a CD or buy them from an online music service, they become part of the library. Windows Media Player supports music files in the ***Windows Media Audio (WMA)***, MP3, and WAV formats.

Windows Media Audio (WMA) The default file format to which Windows Media Player converts and saves song files

Figure 10.15 Windows Media Player enables you to organize your digital songs.

In most instances, then, you do not have to take any action to add songs to the library. To add or remove a folder that Media Player monitors, click Organize on the command bar, point to *Manage libraries*, and then click *Music* in the submenu. In the Music Library Locations dialog box, click the Add button to open the Include Folder in Music dialog box, select the folder to add, and then click Include folder. When you finish adding folders, click the OK button in the Music Library Locations dialog box to close the dialog box. To remove a folder, click the folder in the Music Library Locations dialog box and then click the Remove button.

 T I P When you play music, the tracks automatically appear in the Play tab at the right to give you information about what is playing.

Browsing and Rating Songs

To perform different activities in Media Player, you use the Navigation pane choices and the tabs at the top to move between functions. Click *Music* in the Navigation pane to return to your Music library.

Use the Music library choices in the Navigation pane at the left to choose how the library lists music and to find songs. For example, to view music by artist, click *Artist*. You can then double-click any artist to see the songs by that artist. To view music by type, click *Genre* and then double-click any category to see the songs in that category.

After you have browsed to a particular list of songs, you can click a song to select it, or double-click a song to play it. You can click the Back button in the upper left corner, which looks and works like the Back button in an Explorer window, to back up from the location to which you browsed. Or, to return to viewing a list of songs, click *Music* in the Navigation pane.

As with pictures, you can apply or change the star rating for a song. To do so, browse to the song in the library. Move the mouse pointer over the desired number of stars in the Rating column (shown in Figure 10.16) and then click.

1	P Good	3:42	☆☆☆☆☆	Bob Moog Foundation	Menage
2	Until I see Stars Again	2:57	☆☆☆☆☆	Bob Moog Foundation	The Greenfields
3	Now You Know	5:24	☆☆☆☆☆	Bob Moog Foundation	Yo Mama's Big Fat Boot...
▸4	Me Have Fun	4:21	☆☆☆☆☆	Bob Moog Foundation	Ruby Slippers
5	My Heart Trembles	4:59	☆☆☆☆☆	Bob Moog Foundation	The Broomstars
6	Willow	3:19	☆☆☆☆☆	Bob Moog Foundation	Chris Tanfield
7	Funk in your Knock	3:45	☆☆☆☆☆	Bob Moog Foundation	Agent 23

Figure 10.16 Click the rating to apply to the song.

Ripping a CD

Although more and more people are transitioning to purchasing their music via digital services, such as eMusic, or using streaming services, such as Xbox Music, Pandora, and Rhapsody, music (audio) CDs continue to be a medium for distributing music. Purchasing used CDs and converting them to digital format can be an affordable way to build a sizeable music collection. Swapping CDs in and out of the computer to play them gets a bit tiresome, and if you are traveling with your mobile computer, you do not want to add the weight of a pile of CDs.

Quick Fix

Hide the List
If Media Player is displaying the Play, Burn, or Sync pane at the right and you want to close it, click Organize, point to *Layout*, and then click *Show list* to uncheck it. Or, click the tab that is displayed to hide the list.

Use Windows Media Player to *rip* music from a CD and store the music in digital format in the library. By default, Media Player saves each ripped song file in the Windows Media Audio file format. The songs ripped from each CD are placed in a separate subfolder of your My Music folder, which is monitored by the Music library, by default. Windows Media Player creates a folder for each artist and then, within that folder, a folder for each CD (album).

Note that you use this process only for audio CDs published by a music company. If you have a CD with songs that you own that have already been converted to MP3 format, for example, you should copy them to your system's hard disk in a subfolder of your Music folder. Be sure to observe all copyright laws; do not share your songs with others illegally.

Here's How

To rip songs from an audio CD:

1. Make sure that your system has a live Internet connection so that Windows Media Player can assign accurate song information to each song file.

2. Insert the audio CD in the system's CD or DVD drive. Windows Media Player downloads information about the artist, album, and songs and starts playing the CD. If the AutoPlay dialog message box appears asking how to handle the CD after you insert the CD to rip it, close it or ignore it.

3. Click the Rip CD button on the command bar. Windows Media Player displays progress information about the song being ripped.

4. When the ripping operation finishes, all of the songs show Ripped to library in the *Rip status* column, and the Stop rip button changes back to Rip CD, which is disabled because the disc in the drive is already ripped. Click the Stop playback control button, if you started playing the CD before ripping it, eject the CD (right-click the CD name in the Navigation pane and then click *Eject*), and then rip additional CDs, if desired.

Quick Fix

No Rip CD Button
If you cannot see the Rip CD button, be sure that the list pane at the right is closed. Click the List options button in the upper-right corner of the list pane and then click *Hide list* to hide the pane.

Quick Fix

Format Changes
To rip a CD to a format other than WMA, click the Rip settings button, point to *Format* in the menu that appears, and click the desired format before starting the rip. You also can use the *Audio Quality* submenu to choose a different quality setting.

Note: *Windows Media Player does not rip inserted CDs automatically. If you want to set it up to do so, click Organize on the command bar and then click Options. Click the Rip Music tab, click the* Rip CD automatically *check box to mark it, and then click OK.*

Creating a Playlist

Using Windows Media Player as your digital jukebox breaks through some of the limitations of traditional audio CD players. Even though some models can play multiple CDs and use a special mode to play songs in a random order, they sometimes take a while to switch between discs, and the song order may not suit you.

In Windows Media Player, you create a *playlist* to set the order in which a group of songs plays. A playlist offers a number of advantages, including allowing you to combine songs from different artists and albums and make the playlist as long or short as you like. For example, if your company is sponsoring a party and you want music at the event, you can create a playlist that runs for a few hours, so there is no need for someone to change CDs during the event.

playlist A list that specifies a group of songs for Media Player to play and the order in which to play them

Here's How

To build a playlist in Media Player:

1. Click the Play tab and then click *Clear list* if the List pane shows previously played songs.
2. In the Music library, navigate to a song to add.
3. Drag the song from the library to the desired position in the List pane.

4. Repeat Steps 2 and 3 to add additional songs to the list.
5. After you add all of the songs, drag them to reorder them as desired.
6. Click Save list.
7. Type a name for the list and then press Enter.
8. Click the Stop playback button to stop the playlist, if desired.
9. Click the Play tab again to hide the pane.

Playing a Playlist

To play any individual song in the library, double-click it. To play a playlist, double-click *Playlists* in the Navigation pane to open that folder and then double-click the name of the playlist to play. The music begins playing immediately. Note that if you try to play a song that was licensed from another source and your system does not have the correct permissions or logon installed, playback stops and a Media Usage Rights Acquisition error message appears.

If you are working in a File Explorer window, double-clicking an audio file opens and plays it in the app, not Windows Media Player.

 Click the Switch to Now Playing button in the lower right corner of the Windows Media Player window to switch to Now Playing mode, which has a smaller window. Move the mouse pointer over that window and then click the Switch to Library button to redisplay the Player Library.

Exercise 5

Ripping a CD and Making a Playlist

1. Select the Search charm and then click Windows Media Player under *Windows Accessories*. Make sure the system is connected to the Internet.
2. Insert an audio CD (one of your own or one provided by your instructor) in the system's drive.
3. If the rip process does not start automatically, click Rip CD.
4. When the rip process finishes, capture a screen shot and then save the file as **C10E05S04**.
5. Click the Stop button to stop playback, if necessary.
6. Right-click the CD name in the Navigation pane and then click *Eject*.
7. Click the Play tab.
8. Navigate to the songs of the CD you ripped, starting by clicking Music in the Navigation pane.
9. Drag at least three songs to the playlist in the List pane.
10. Click Save list above the new list.
11. Type Chapter 10 Exercise 05 List and then press Enter to name the playlist.
12. Capture a screen shot and then save the file as **C10E05S12**.
13. Submit the screen shots to your instructor.
14. Click the Stop button to stop the playlist, and leave Windows Media Player open for the next exercise.

Syncing to a Portable Device

The ability to play back songs or audio information on a portable device such as a digital music player is more than just a luxury. If you can play back vital information, such as an audio book file, during a long commute, you can make good use of time that would otherwise have been wasted. Given that many schools are starting to distribute lectures and other class materials via audio files, you might even have need to sync study materials to a device for listening on the go.

Windows Media Player supports a wide variety of portable devices to which you can transfer your music and other audio files. Connect the device, power it on, start Media Player, and then click the Sync tab to get ready to *sync*. The first time you connect, Media Player checks your device and selects the best sync method based on its capabilities and storage capacity. Devices with more than 4 GB of capacity are set up to sync automatically, meaning that all content in the library syncs, so you can just click the Start sync button on the Sync tab at the right.

For a device that you or Media Player set up to sync manually, you choose which items (songs and other forms of audio content) and playlists to add.

To set up a device to sync manually:

1. Click the Sync options button on the Sync tab, point to the device name, and then click Select settings.
2. Click the device on the Devices tab and then click Properties to open the device's properties.
3. Click the Start sync when this device connects check box, if available.

Here's How

After you click the Sync tab, drag items and playlists from the library to the List pane (shown in Figure 10.17). If more than one device is connected, click the applicable device in the Navigation pane, before you choose songs, other audio, and playlists. If your device is low on capacity, make sure to check at the top of the tab to verify that you have enough space remaining before you add additional items. Click Start sync to sync the music and/or other audio.

Note: *Windows Media Player does not support iPods automatically. However, through the use of a Windows Media plug-in (added application) available from another software publisher for a reasonable fee, Windows Media Player can see and sync to many iPod models. If you plan to get a plug-in to sync your music to your iPod, make sure you rip the music in an audio file format supported by iPods. Usually, the MP3 format is a safe bet.*

When the sync finishes, the List pane displays a message telling you that the sync is complete and you can now disconnect the device. At that point, you can power off and remove the device. Note that some devices also can sync through the Windows 8 sync feature. When you connect such a device, you can double-click its button on the Taskbar to open a window with options for the device. Double-click Set up sync in the window that appears, specify sync settings, and then click Sync now.

Figure 10.17 Place items to sync to the device in the List pane at the right.

 Downloadable podcasts are so named because they originally were developed for playback on Apple iPods. However, many podcasts are distributed in MP3 format, which means you can download and play them from Media Center and sync them from there with your non-iPod device.

Burning a Playlist to CD-R or DVD-R

Once you have created a playlist, you can burn it to a CD-R for your own personal use on other machines and audio devices. Again, copyright law applies, so burning song copies to give away to friends is not an appropriate use of this functionality. But if you have made your own original recordings, burning them to a disc can be a convenient way to back up your audio or share it with family and friends.

Here's How

To burn a playlist to a CD-R in Media Player:

1. Click the Burn tab.
2. Insert a blank CD-R in the drive. If a message about how to handle the blank media appears, ignore it.
3. Drag a playlist from the Navigation pane to the List pane at the right.

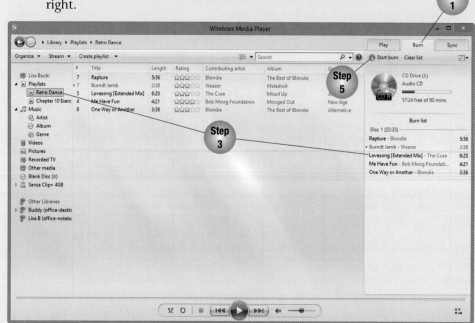

4. Add additional songs or playlists, checking to ensure that you have time (space on the disc) remaining before adding each.
5. Click Start burn in the List pane. After the burn finishes, Media Player automatically ejects the CD-R. You can insert another one and click the Start burn button to create another copy, if desired.
6. Click Burn to close the List pane.

Working with Media Streaming

stream To play back music from another computer or digital media receiver on your network

Windows Media Player can **stream** music over a network. This means that one computer can play back the music stored in another computer's Media Player Library. Network devices called digital media receivers also can play back the music from a computer's Player Library. To stream media from your system, media streaming must be turned on in Windows Media Player. This enables other computers and devices on the network to "see" or access your system's digital content. To stream music between computers, they must be using the Windows Vista operating system or later.

To turn on streaming, click the Stream button on the command bar, and then click *Turn on media streaming with HomeGroup*. Be sure to write down the homegroup password that is presented and then click Finish. If you previously set up a homegroup and made music sharing available, streaming may already be turned on, and that command will not appear. The next step is to determine which other computers and devices on your network can access your content for streaming. To allow all devices and users access, click Stream on the command bar and then click *Automatically allow devices to play my media*. Confirm this choice by clicking *Automatically allow all computers and media devices* in the Allow All Media Devices dialog box. Select the media to share, and then click Next. Record the homegroup password, if you have not done so previously, and then click Finish. To limit access to only select computers and devices, click Stream and then click *More streaming options*. In the *Show devices on* list, choose *Allowed* or *Blocked* as applicable for each choice or computer and then click Next. Choose media to share and then click Next. Record the homegroup password and then click Finish.

Once the media on another computer is shared for streaming, that computer appears in the Navigation pane in Windows Media Player, as shown in Figure 10.18. (If the libraries do not appear, click Organize and then click *Customize navigation pane*. Open the drop-down list at the top of the Customize Navigation Pane dialog box and then click *Other Libraries*. Click the *Show Other Libraries* check box to check it and then click OK.) Click the name of the library on another system to open it and then select and play music as you would on the library stored on your own computer.

Figure 10.18 Music can be streamed (played) from the library on another computer.

To stream content to another device, drag the content from your Music library to the Play tab. Click the Play to button (shown in Figure 10.19), point to Play To, and then click the device. Media Player connects to the device, as shown in Figure 10.20, and you can then use the controls in the Play To dialog box to control the playback.

Play to button

Note: *To change options for streaming, click the Stream button and then click* More streaming options *in the menu that appears. For example, you can specify a name for your media library and change what devices and programs can access shared media.*

Figure 10.19 Use the Play tab to stream music or other content to another network device, such as a digital media receiver or TV.

Figure 10.20 After the device is connected, use the controls to manage playback.

Exercise 6

Burning a Music CD-R

1. Click the Burn tab.
2. Insert a blank CD-R disc (one of your own or one provided by your instructor) in the system's CD-R or DVD-R drive.
3. Drag the Chapter 10 Exercise 05 List playlist that you created in Exercise 5 of this chapter from the Navigation pane to the List pane.
4. Click Start burn.
5. When the burn process finishes and the disc ejects, label the disc **C10E06** and then submit it to your instructor.
6. Close Windows Media Player.

CHAPTER SUMMARY

- You can import pictures from a digital camera or a storage card inserted in a media card reader. Attach the device, power it on, click or tap the first prompt, and select the *Import photos and videos* choice with *Photos* under it in the AutoPlay pop-up prompt that appears.
- Imported pictures are placed in a new subfolder of the My Pictures user folder, which is monitored by the Pictures library. This folder window has special features for working with picture files. You specify the folder name to use each time you import pictures.
- Click Slide show in the View group on the Picture Tools Manage tab in a Pictures library window to play the pictures in the current folder as a slide show. Right-click the slide show to see commands for controlling it.

- Use the Zip choice in the Send group on the Share tab of a Pictures library window to Zip (compress) multiple selected pictures together in a single zipped folder file. You can then email that file using the Mail app or an installed email client.
- Imported pictures are available for viewing, editing, and printing in Photo Gallery. Download the program from windows.microsoft.com/en-US/windows-live/essentials-home. To start this application, choose the Search charm and then click Photo Gallery under *Apps*. Or, if a Photo Gallery tile appears on the Start screen, you can click it there.
- To change how Photo Gallery lists images, right-click a blank area in the list of thumbnails, point to *Group by*, and then click a choice.
- Use the File tab's Include folder command in Photo Gallery to include pictures from other folders. Use the choices in the *Share* list in the Share group on the Home tab to share selected pictures to an online service such as Facebook or Flickr.
- Double-click a photo in Photo Gallery to edit the photo using choices on the Edit tab, and then click Close file to apply your changes.
- In the Pictures library, click an image and then click the Details pane to add a tag or rating. Or, right-click it, click *Properties*, and then click the Details tab. In Photo Gallery, click an image and then click the Tag and caption pane on the View tab to work with the file name, rating, tags, and other information.
- To prepare and send a print job, click Print in the Send group on the Share tab in the Pictures library, or click the File tab, point to *Print,* and then click *Print* in Photo Gallery.
- You can view pictures in the Pictures library using the Photos app. Click the Photos tile on the Start screen to get started.
- The Photos app enables you to connect to an online service, such as Facebook or Flickr, to view the photos stored there.
- Manage your digital music in Windows Media Player. Start this application by selecting the Search charm and then clicking Windows Media Player under *Windows Accessories*.
- Use the Navigation pane at the left to navigate in Media Player.
- Music in the Music folder of your user folder becomes a part of the Music library in Windows Media Player automatically. You also can insert an audio CD and then use the Rip CD command to rip it.
- To save a group of songs as a playlist that you can replay at any time, click the Play tab. Drag songs from the library to the List pane at the right, and then click Save list.
- To play a song or playlist, double-click it.
- You can take songs or other audio information with you by syncing from Media Player to a portable device.
- Click the Burn tab, insert a blank CD-R, drag songs or playlists to the List pane, and then click Start burn to burn a CD-R.
- Click Stream and then click *Automatically allow devices to play my media* to enable other systems and devices on your network to stream music from your Media Player library. Select a shared library from another computer in the Navigation pane to stream its music to your current system. Or, use the Play to button on the Play tab to send music or other media from your computer to another network device such as a digital music receiver or TV.

Working with Digital Photographs and Music

CONCEPTS CHECK

Completion: Answer the following questions in a Word document.

Part 1

Multiple Choice

1. The My Pictures folder in your personal folder is monitored by the _____.
   a. Pictures locker
   b. Digital drawer
   c. Pictures library
   d. Pictures finder

2. The free downloadable _____ application enables you to work with your digital photos.
   a. Windows Digital Photo Editor
   b. Photo Gallery
   c. Pictures Explorer
   d. Windows Pictures Finder

3. Adding a _____ assigns a category to a digital picture.
   a. rating
   b. label
   c. tag
   d. caption

4. Adding a _____ assigns stars to a digital picture.
   a. rating
   b. label
   c. tag
   d. caption

5. Playing a _____ show displays the images from a folder on the screen.
   a. photo
   b. desktop
   c. folder
   d. slide

6. The new _____ app enables you to view your online photo albums.
   a. Pictures
   b. Photos
   c. Camera
   d. Messaging

7. The _____ application enables you to play digital songs.
   a. Windows Song Player
   b. Windows CD Player
   c. Windows Media Player
   d. Windows Audio Player.

8. Importing a song from an audio CD is called _____ the song.
   a. importing
   b. playing
   c. converting
   d. ripping

9. Create a _____ to select songs that you want to hear together.
   a. playlist
   b. song list
   c. favorites list
   d. replay list

10. You can _____ songs or a playlist from Media Player to a portable device.
    a. copy
    b. trade
    c. sync
    d. push

Part 2

Short Answer

11. Explain how to start transferring images from a digital camera to your computer.

   _____

12. In what folder does Windows 8 place the imported pictures?

   _____

13. How do you navigate to and select a photo in the Photos app?

   _____

14. When you print digital photos, what do you select to control the size for the printed image(s)?

   _____

15. Explain one method for adding a tag to a digital photo.

   _____

16. Which pane in Windows Media Player do you use to display certain pictures or songs?

   _____

17. Explain how to start adding music from an audio CD to the Music library in Windows Media Player.

   _____

18. In what folder does Windows 8 place the imported songs?

   _____

19. Name one reason to create a playlist.

   _____

20. True or False: It is legal to share digital photos you have found online or digital songs copied from an audio CD with other users.

   _____

SKILLS CHECK

Save all solution files to the default Documents folder or any alternate folder specified by your instructor.

Note: *If the Notification bar appears at any point during these exercises, click the Close (X) button to close it.*

Guided Check

Assessment 1

Play a Slide Show of Sample Pictures
1. View the sample pictures in the Assessment 01 student data folder.
    a. Start Windows, display the desktop, and then click the File Explorer button on the Taskbar.
    b. Navigate to the folder that holds the Chapter 10 student data files.
    c. Double-click the *Assessment 02* folder.
2. View picture information.
    a. Click a picture thumbnail.
    b. Click the View tab, and in the Panes group, click the Details pane.
3. Start and pause a slide show.
    a. On the Picture Tools Manage tab, click Slide show in the View group.
    b. Right-click the second image that appears and then click *Pause*.
    c. Right-click again and then click *Play*.
4. Document and stop the slide show.
    a. Capture a screen shot of the desktop and then save it as **C10A01**.
    b. After viewing the show several moments longer press Esc.
5. Click the View tab, and in the Panes group, click Details pane to close that pane. Close the folder window.
6. Submit the screen shot to your instructor.

Assessment 2

Add a Folder of Pictures to Photo Gallery
1. With your instructor's permission, download and install Photo Gallery from windows.microsoft.com/en-US/windows-live/essentials-home, if it is not on your system. Start Photo Gallery.
    a. Select the Search charm.
    b. Click Photo Gallery under *Apps*.
2. Import the pictures.
    a. Click the File tab.
    b. Click Include folder.
    c. Use the folder tree in the Pictures Library Locations dialog box to select the folder that holds the data files for this assessment.
    d. Click OK.
    e. Capture a screen shot of the desktop and then save it as **C10A02**.
3. Leave Photo Gallery open for the next assessment.
4. Submit the screen shot to your instructor.

Edit Photo Info and Apply a Fix

1. Add your name as a photo caption.
   a. Drag to select the thumbnails of all three of the photos imported in Assessment 2.
   b. If the Tag and caption pane does not appear, click the View tab on the ribbon and then click Tag and caption pane.
   c. Click *Add caption* in the pane.
   d. Type your name and then press Enter.
2. Add a tag.
   a. Click *Add descriptive tags* in the Tag and caption pane.
   b. Type flowers and then press Enter.
3. Fix the color in a photo.
   a. Double-click the ***Rhododendron.jpg*** image thumbnail.
   b. Click the Color down-pointing arrow in the Adjustments group on the Edit tab, and then click the third preset on the third row: *High temperature, low tint*.
   c. Capture a screen shot and then save it as **C10A03**.
4. Exit Photo Gallery.
   a. Click Close file at the right end of the Edit tab and then click OK at the message that tells you that you can revert your changes to the file.
   b. Click the File tab and then click *Exit* to close the program.
5. Submit the screen shot to your instructor.

Rip and Rate Music

1. Start Windows Media Player.
   a. Select the Search charm.
   b. Click Windows Media Player under *Windows Accessories*.
2. Rip an audio CD.
   a. Insert the audio CD.
   b. Click Rip CD, if the rip does not start automatically.
   c. After the ripping concludes, click the Stop button, if necessary.
   d. Right-click the CD listed in the Navigation pane at left and then click *Eject*.
3. Rate songs.
   a. Double-click *Music* in the Navigation pane to expand it, if needed. Otherwise, click it.
   b. Click *Album* under *Music*.
   c. Double-click the album (CD) that you ripped in Step 2.
   d. In the *Rating* column, click to assign a star rating to at least three of the songs.
   e. Capture a screen shot and then save it as **C10A04S03**.
4. View the rated songs.
   a. Click *Music* in the Navigation pane.
   b. Click Organize, point to *Sort by*, and then click *Rating*.
   c. Capture a screen shot of the results and then save it as **C10A04S04**.
   d. Click Organize, point to *Sort by*, and then click *Album*.
5. Close Windows Media Player.
6. Submit the screen shots to your instructor.

On Your Own

Assessment

5

Import, Zip, and Email Pictures

1. Use a digital camera (your own or one provided by your instructor) to shoot at least three pictures for this assessment. (Ideally, you will not have any images stored on the camera when you start.)
2. Connect the camera to your computer, power it on, and then change to its Playback or Transfer mode, if required.
3. Click *Import photos and videos,* if the AutoPlay message box appears, and then use the Photos app to import the newly shot images to a folder named Chapter 10 Assessment 05.
4. In File Explorer, open the Pictures library and then navigate to the Chapter 10 Assessment 05 folder.
5. Select all of the picture files, and then use the Zip command to create a single zip file, naming it Chapter 10 Assessment 05. Close the Pictures library.
6. Go to the Start screen and then start the Mail app.
7. Select the desired email account and then click the New button.
8. Address the email to your instructor, enter Chapter 10 Assessment 05 as the message subject, and then attach the zip file that you created in Step 5.
9. Send the message and then close all open apps and folders.

Assessment

6

Print Pictures

1. Start Photo Gallery, and then select two of the three pictures you imported and emailed in Assessment 5.
2. Click the File tab, point to *Print,* and then click *Print.*
3. Select the printer specified by your instructor, leaving the *Paper size* and *Quality* settings as is.
4. Scroll down the list of layouts and then click the *3.5 x 5 in. (4)* choice.
5. Increase the *Copies of each picture* setting to 2.
6. Click Print.
7. Label the printout as **C10A06** and then submit it to your instructor.
8. Close the Photo Gallery app.

Assessment

7

View Pictures in the Photos App

1. Start the Photos app from the Start screen.
2. Navigate to the Chapter 10 Assessment 05 folder.
3. Capture a screen shot of the results and then save it as **C10A07.**
4. Return to and close the Photos app.
5. Submit the screen shot to your instructor.

Assessment

8

Download and Play Audio

1. Close Windows Media Player, if it is running.
2. From the desktop, start Internet Explorer and then go to www.nasa.gov/multimedia/podcasting/index.html.
3. Click one of the links under *Audio Podcasts.*
4. Right-click the Listen now link (located below each of the audio podcasts) for one of the podcasts and then click *Save target as.*
5. In the Save As dialog box, save the file in the Music library and then click Save. The podcast downloads to your computer.
6. Close the message at the bottom that tells you that the download is complete.
7. Close Internet Explorer.
8. Start Windows Media Player.

9. Navigate to the podcast file (click *Music* in the Navigation pane) in the library. The list should still be sorted by album as the result of a previous assessment, and the podcast is listed as an Unknown album. Double-click it, or click it and then click the Play button in the playback controls at the bottom of Media Player.
10. Capture a screen shot and then save it as **C10A08**.
11. Stop the playback and close Media Player.
12. Submit the screen shot to your instructor.

CHALLENGE PROJECT

You are organizing a client seminar to be held in meeting rooms at a local hotel. On the morning of the seminar, continental breakfast will be offered to participants. Your boss has asked you to provide some music to play during the breakfast to set a nice tone for the event. Use Windows Media Player to create a CD mix for the event. Rip several songs, arrange them in a playlist, and then burn the playlist to a CD-R. Label the CD-R as **C10A09** and then submit it to your instructor.

Part 3

Microsoft® Windows® 8

Basic Networking and System Maintenance

- Using Your System on a Network

- Maintaining Your System

- Adding Software and Hardware

CHAPTER

11

Using Your System on a Network

PERFORMANCE OBJECTIVES

Upon successful completion of Chapter 11, you will be able to:

- Connect to a network
- Create and use a VPN connection
- View network locations
- Map a network drive
- Share files and folders on the network
- Work with network printers
- Troubleshoot a network
- Set up an Internet connection
- Work with streaming media

Most computers do not stand alone—they are connected to one or more other computers via cables or wireless connections. When two or more computers connect, they form a network. In this chapter, you will learn how to use networks to share information between computers.

Networking Basics ■■■■■■■■■■■■■■■■■■■■■■■■■■■

A *network* is a group of connected computers. Networked computers can share files and printers with one another, and can share an Internet connection. When connected computers are in the same room or even the same building, they are part of a *local area network (LAN)*. When the computers are spread out over a greater distance, such as in different buildings or even different cities, they are part of a *wide area network (WAN)*.

Most business networks are *client/server* networks. They consist of one or more end-user computers, which are the *clients,* and one or more computers that handle the administration of the network, which are the *servers.* On a small network, a single server handles all of the administrative tasks; on larger networks, there are separate servers for tasks such as file storage (file servers) and printer sharing (print servers). A client/server network that is managed with Windows Server software is known as a *domain.*

Small networks (consisting of fewer than 20 computers) can be set up to be *peer-to-peer (P2P).* In a P2P network, there is no server; all of the clients share the administrative burden of maintaining the network. A P2P network is also known as a workgroup.

network A group of connected computers

local area network (LAN) A network in which the computers are near one another, such as in the same building

wide area network (WAN) A network in which the computers are physically separated, such as in different buildings or cities

client/server A type of network in which one or more servers administers the network, providing services to client computers

client An end-user computer in a network

server A computer dedicated to administering the network

domain A client/server network running Windows Server software on the server

peer-to-peer (P2P) A network consisting only of client computers

Using Your System on a Network

369

workgroup A peer-to-peer, Windows-based network

homegroup A connected group of Windows 8 (or Windows 7) computers in a home (P2P) network

Wi-Fi The popular name for the 802.11 wireless RF standard, encompassing variants including 802.11b, 802.11g, and 802.11n

RJ-45 connector A plug, like a telephone plug but slightly wider, used to connect a computer to a network

network interface card (NIC) A circuit board, or a built-in component on a motherboard, that provides network connectivity for a computer

Windows 8 computers in a *workgroup* also can be part of a homegroup. A *homegroup* consists of two or more computers in a P2P network. Homegroups make file and printer sharing especially easy between computers. Only Windows 7 and Windows 8 computers can be a part of a homegroup. However, you can still share files and printers in a workgroup between computers running different Windows versions—just not using the homegroup feature. Being part of a homegroup is optional and is a choice only for computers in workgroups, not domains. A computer can be a part of only one homegroup at a time.

Wired versus Wireless Networks

A computer can connect to a network either via a cable (wired) or a wireless connection. Different computers on the same network can connect in different ways. For example, your desktop computer might connect via a cable, and your notebook via wireless.

The most popular type of wireless network is a radio frequency (RF) type, conforming to a standard known as IEEE 802.11, or *Wi-Fi*. There have been several versions of the 802.11 standard, including 802.11b, 802.11g, and 802.11n. The latter is the most recently developed and the fastest, operating at up to 600 Mbps at a range of about 200 feet (more or less, depending on walls, floors, or other obstructions).

Wireless connections are more convenient than wired connections because there are no cables, but they are also slower and less robust. A typical wired connection runs at about 1 Gbps. A typical wireless one runs at about three-fifths of that (and that is best-case speed with 802.11n, which not all computers support). In addition, a wireless connection can sometimes temporarily lose the signal, especially when you are at the edge of the range.

Wireless networks are also more subject to security breaches than wired ones. With a wired network, an intruder must have access to your router or switch to plug a cable into it. With a wireless network, however, anyone within the vicinity can tap in. Therefore, wireless networks require security measures to ensure that only authorized computers can connect. There are several types of wireless security, including the following, listed here in order of oldest (and least secure) to newest (and most secure): Wired Equivalent Privacy (WEP), Wi-Fi Protected Access (WPA), and WPA2. Each of these is a different method of requiring a computer to provide an access code before it can connect.

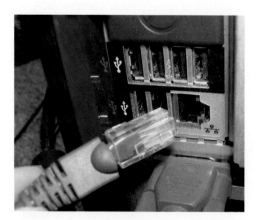

Figure 11.1 An RJ-45 jack connects a computer to a wired network.

What You Need to Connect to a Network

Most computers today have an *RJ-45 connector*, which allows them to plug into a wired network. This connector looks like a telephone plug except it is slightly wider (shown in Figure 11.1). To connect to an existing wired network, you run a cable from that plug to the router or switch. In many offices, wired ports are built into the wall, as telephone and electrical outlets are; if your office has one of these, you can connect a cable from your computer to the wall jack.

The RJ-45 connector is a part of the computer *network interface card* (NIC), which can be a separate add-on card inside the computer or can be built in on the motherboard itself. It works the same either way. (A computer with a wireless NIC does not have an RJ-45 jack; instead it has a small antenna.) If your computer does not have a NIC, you can add one yourself, or have a technician add one for you.

Note: *Your NIC appears in the Device Manager under the* Network Adapters *category. You will learn how to use the Device Manager in Chapter 13. If it does not appear there, you might not have a NIC installed.*

If you are setting up a new network, you also need a box that each computer's network cable plugs into, a central gathering point such as a *switch*. This box directs the traffic between the computers in the network, delivering packets of data to the correct location. (A more sophisticated form of a switch, called a *router,* is able to direct traffic between network segments on a larger network and to share an Internet connection on a home network.) For a wireless network, the connector box is called a *wireless access point (WAP)* or a wireless router.

Note: *If you are installing a new NIC, you must set it up to work in Windows by installing a device driver. In Chapter 13, you will learn how to install new hardware and make sure it has a working device driver.*

switch A box into which computers connect that directs network traffic among the computers

router A type of switch that directs traffic between different segments of a network

wireless access point (WAP) A switch for wireless networking

Connecting to a Network ▪▪▪▪▪▪▪▪▪▪▪▪▪▪▪▪▪▪

Windows 8 is adept at detecting network connections, so provided you have a NIC installed and a wired connection established, Windows simply starts using the network, making its resources available to your computer.

With a wireless connection, the first time you use Windows 8 you must set up the connection. After that, the connection reestablishes itself automatically each time you turn on the computer and the network becomes available.

Using the Network and Sharing Center

The Network and Sharing Center provides a central location for checking network connectivity and network sharing settings. Figure 11.2 shows the Network and Sharing Center for a computer with a wireless network connection.

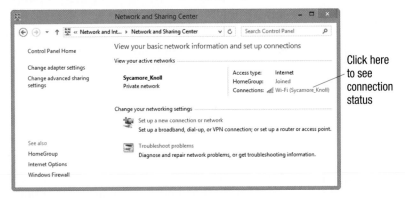

Click here to see connection status

Figure 11.2 The Network and Sharing Center shows network information.

To display the Network and Sharing Center (Control Panel Method): ◀ **Here's How**

1. Select the Settings charm and then click Control Panel.
2. Under the *Network and Internet* category, click *View network status and tasks*.

To display the Network and Sharing Center (File Explorer Method):

1. Open any File Explorer window. (For example, click the File Explorer icon on the Taskbar.)
2. In the Navigation pane at the left, click *Network*.
3. On the Network tab, click *Network and Sharing Center*.

To display the Network and Sharing Center (Desktop Method):

1. Right-click the Network icon in the notification area.
2. Click *Open Network and Sharing Center*.

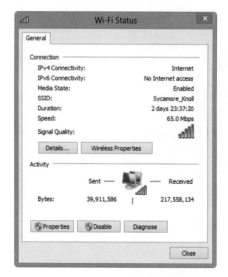

Figure 11.3 Details about the network connection appear in a Status window.

Viewing the Status of a Network Connection

From the Network and Sharing Center window, you can get information about a connection by clicking the hyperlink at the right of *Connections*. In Figure 11.2, for example, the link is Wi-Fi (Sycamore_Knoll).

Figure 11.3 shows the details for a wireless connection; wired connections do not have *SSID* or *Signal Quality*, nor do they have a Wireless Properties button.

The details displayed include:

- **IPv4 Connectivity.** This is the IP addressing type used for the Internet and for most LANs. If you are connected to the Internet, IPv4 shows Internet.

- **IPv6 Connectivity.** This is the IP addressing type used for newer LANs. If you are on a private local area network, this will show as Local; if you are on a public network, it will show as Limited. If the network you are on does not use IPv6, you will see No Internet access.

- **Media State.** Enabled should appear here if the connection is enabled.

T I P ▶ If you want to see the exact IP address in use for either IPv4 or IPv6, click Details.

- **SSID.** This identifier, used only in wireless networks, is the name specified by the wireless access point or wireless router. *SSID* is often, by default, the name of the manufacturer of the hardware, such as Linksys. In Figure 11.3 it is Sycamore_Knoll.

- **Duration.** This shows how long the connection has been up and running. When you restart the computer, it resets the counter.

- **Speed.** This states the speed of the network in megabytes per second (Mbps). For a wireless network, this is typically somewhere between 11 Mbps and 100 Mbps; for a wired network it is usually either 100 Mbps or 1000 Mbps.

- **Signal Quality.** These bars, shown only for wireless networks, indicate the signal strength between the computer and the wireless access point.

- **Details.** Click this button for more detailed information about the connection.

- **Wireless Properties.** Available only for wireless connections; click this button to open a Properties box in which you can determine whether the connection should be established automatically and whether security should be enabled.

SSID Stands for Service Set Identifier; the name of the wireless access point or router

A wireless network location can be classified as Private or Public. When you first connect to a wireless network, Windows prompts you to select Private, Public, or Guest. (Notice in Figure 11.2 that *Private network* appears under the network name.) The Public setting is appropriate when you are connecting to a network in a public place, such as when using a wireless Internet connection at a coffee shop or at a school. This setting prevents other computers from discovering your computer and browsing its shared content. The Public setting is appropriate when you are connecting to your home or business LAN; it allows you to see other computers and devices and allows others to see yours. Guest is the most restrictive choice; use it when you are skeptical of the safety of the router or wireless access point to which you are connecting.

Viewing and Changing the Workgroup or Domain Name

If connected to a network, your computer is either assigned to a domain or a workgroup. (If the value of *Homegroup* is Joined in the Network and Sharing Center window, as shown in Figure 11.2, you can assume you are part of a workgroup.) Within that domain or workgroup, each computer is assigned a unique network name.

In most cases, it is not important what these names are. However, for certain troubleshooting activities, you may need that information. You may occasionally need to change it, too, if directed by a system administrator or technical support representative.

To determine the workgroup or domain name:

1. Open the Control Panel.
2. Click *System and Security*.
3. Under the System heading, click *See the name of this computer*.
4. Scroll down to the *Computer name, domain, and workgroup settings* section and then examine the names there.

To change to a different workgroup or domain:

1. Perform Steps 1–4 of the preceding procedure.
2. Click the Change settings link. The System Properties dialog box opens.
3. Click the Change button.
4. Click the *Domain* or the *Workgroup* option.
5. Type the name of the domain or workgroup.
6. Click OK.
7. At the confirmation box, click OK.
8. Click Close.
9. At the prompt to restart, click Restart Now or Restart Later.

Network icon

Figure 11.4 Network icon in notification area.

Figure 11.5 Select the desired network with which to connect.

Connecting and Disconnecting a Wireless Network

The first time your computer connects to a particular wireless access point, you must confirm that connection, and if it is a secure network, you must enter the security information needed for it. Thereafter, when your computer comes into range of that access point, it automatically connects using those same settings (provided you have it set up for automatic connection).

When wireless networks are available, an icon that looks like stair steps (or cell phone signal bars, if you prefer) appears with a small starburst on it (shown in Figure 11.4). When you click that icon, a panel opens at the right side of the screen showing the available networks. Click the desired network, as shown in Figure 11.5, and then click Connect. You can optionally mark the *Connect automatically* check box to enable Windows 8 to establish this network connection automatically in the future, whenever your computer is within range. Some networks have security (discussed in the next section); if you are connecting to a security-enabled network for the first time, you are prompted to enter an access code or key. If you do not know what code to use, ask the person who set up the network.

To connect to a wireless network:

1. In the notification area, click the Network icon.
2. Click the name of the network with which to connect.
3. (Optional) Click the *Connect automatically* check box.
4. Click Connect.
5. If prompted for an access code or key, enter it.
6. Click away from the panel to close it.

To disconnect from a wireless network:

1. In the notification area, click the Network icon.
2. Click the network name.
3. Click Disconnect.

Configuring Wireless Network Security

In Figure 11.5, the network's icon shows a shield on it, indicating that it is not a secure network. Most wireless networks, however, do have security encryption enabled. When you connect to a wireless network for which the access point requires security, you are prompted to enter a network security key or access code. This code is generated by the configuration software for the access point. Depending on the brand and model of the access point, you can access that configuration software either via a utility you install on one of the attached computers or via a web browser interface (by entering the IP address of the access point).

As mentioned previously in this chapter, there are several types of wireless security encryption, and the computer must use whatever type the wireless access point uses. The setup involves selecting the encryption type and then entering a network security key, which is a string of characters that translates to a code.

To enable wireless network security:

1. Set up the desired security settings on the access point or router, following the directions provided with the device. Make a note of the security code you set up on the access point as well as the security type and the encryption type.
2. From the Network and Sharing Center, click the network name at the right of *Connections*. A Wi-Fi status box appears.
3. Click Wireless Properties.
4. Click the Security tab.
5. Open the *Security type* list and then click the type of security to use.
6. Open the *Encryption type* list and then choose the encryption type.
7. Type the security key code to use in the *Network security key* text box.
8. Click OK.

Exercise 1

Getting Information about Your Network Connection

1. Open a Word document and then save the file as **C11E01**.
2. Determine the domain or workgroup to which your computer belongs and record the name in your Word document:
   a. Open the Control Panel.
   b. Click *System and Security*.
   c. Under the *System* category, click See the name of this computer.
   d. View the information at the right of Workgroup or Domain and then record it in your Word document.
3. Determine your computer's IPv4 address and the duration of the connection:
   a. Open the Network and Sharing Center.
   b. Click the hyperlink for your connection, at the right of *Connections*.
   c. Record the value listed at the right of *Duration*.
   d. Click Details.
   e. Record the value listed at the right of *IPv4* address.
   f. Click Close.
   g. Click Close.
4. Submit your Word document to your instructor.

Creating and Using a VPN Connection ▪▪▪▪▪▪▪▪▪

The Internet, by default, is not a secure transfer medium for sensitive data. You can connect to another computer, but you cannot guarantee that someone will not snoop on that connection. Because of this, many companies do not allow Internet access to their most sensitive data resources, such as customer databases and financial data.

virtual private network (VPN) A secure software tunnel that runs from one computer to another using the Internet as its conduit

If you need to connect to your company's network but you are not physically near it, you might choose to create a *virtual private network (VPN)* connection. A VPN connection is a secure software tunnel that runs from one computer to another using the Internet as its conduit. When you are connected to your workplace's LAN via a VPN connection, it is as if your computer were in the building where the LAN resides, and your connection to it is as secure as if you were using the network there. VPN connectivity might be necessary to use certain resources that are restricted to only local LAN users and not available via the Web, such as customer databases.

After you initially set up the VPN connection, you can easily reestablish it at any time without having to reenter the settings.

Note: *If the connection fails, right-click the VPN connection name and choose* **Properties** *to configure its settings. Check with your VPN provider to find out what settings to use. If your VPN provider wants you to use a certain domain name, prefix your user ID with the domain name followed by a backslash, like this: ADS\ yourname.*

To set up a VPN connection:

1. Open the Network and Sharing Center.
2. Click *Set up a new connection or network*.
3. Click *Connect to a workplace*.
4. Click Next.
5. Click *Use my Internet connection (VPN)*.
6. Type the Internet address into the *Internet address* box and type a description in the *Destination name* box.
7. Mark any of the check boxes to enable special options for the connection.
8. Click Create.

To connect to a VPN connection:

1. Click the Network icon in the notification area.
2. Under Connections, click the VPN and then click Connect.
3. Type the user name and password needed to connect.
4. Click OK and then wait for the connection to be established.
5. Click away from the panel to hide it.

The connection runs in the background and remains established until you reboot, sign out, or disconnect manually.

To disconnect a VPN connection:

1. Click the Network icon in the notification area.
2. Click the VPN connection.
3. Click Disconnect.
4. Wait for the connection to terminate.

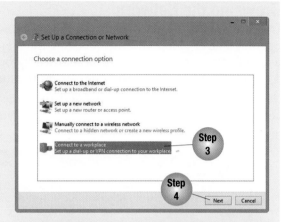

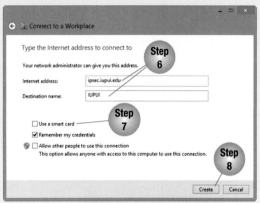

Viewing Network Locations ■■■■■■■■■■■■■■■■

When a network connection is established—whether via a wired or wireless network or a VPN connection—you can access network locations that have been made available to you. These can include folders on a dedicated file server and/or folders on individual client computers that the owners have chosen to share.

Browsing the Network

One way to access a network location is to browse for it. You can do this by opening File Explorer and then clicking the Network link in the Navigation pane; a list of computers that is part of your workgroup or domain appears. In Figure 11.6, the computers and other devices in the local workgroup appear.

The network locations available depend on the network connectivity of the computer. Depending on your network type, you may see computers, network storage devices, network-aware printers, media devices, and other resources.

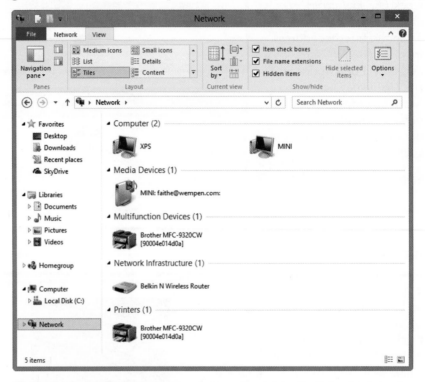

Figure 11.6 Browse the computers on your network from the Network window in File Explorer.

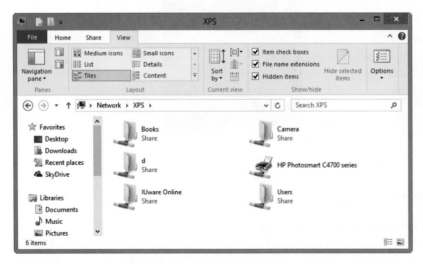

Figure 11.7 The shared resources from the chosen computer appear as icons; double-click an icon to access that resource.

Double-click one of the icons to browse the available drives and folders. For example, in Figure 11.7, you can see that the computer called XPS is sharing five folders and one printer driver. You can access any drive or folder by double-clicking it, as if it were an icon on your own local system. Double-clicking a folder icon opens that folder and displays its files; double-clicking a printer icon opens the print queue for that printer.

Mapping a Network Drive

If you frequently access the same network location, you might want an easier way than browsing to access it. You could map that location to a drive letter. The new drive letter appears in the Computer window, along with your other local drives, and you can double-click that drive letter to quickly access the referenced location (shown in Figure 11.8).

The mapped drive can be used in any program, even programs that do not ordinarily support reading/writing from network locations. Network drive mapping is also a good tool to use when setting up systems for less experienced computer users because it is much easier for them to remember a letter than a complete path to a network location.

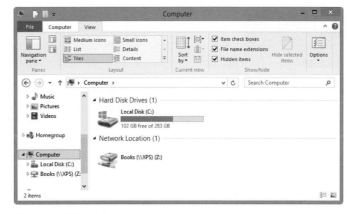

Figure 11.8 A mapped network drive letter appears under Computer, along with your other drives.

You can set up the mapping to reestablish itself automatically each time you sign in, if desired. That way you never have to think about the location being located on the network; as far as your system is concerned, the location is another hard drive on your own system.

TIP An alternative to mapping a network drive is to create a shortcut to the network location on the desktop or in the Navigation pane. The shortcut is as quick and easy to access as a drive letter.

To map a network location to a drive letter:

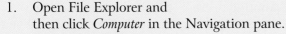

1. Open File Explorer and then click *Network* in the Navigation pane.
2. Browse to the location containing the folder to be mapped.
3. Right-click the folder and then choose *Map network drive.*
4. Select the drive letter to use.
5. Mark or clear the *Reconnect at sign-in* check box.
6. Click Finish.

To disconnect a mapped network drive:

1. Open File Explorer and then click *Computer* in the Navigation pane.
2. Right-click the mapped drive.
3. Click *Disconnect.*

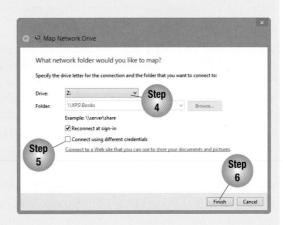

Accessing Files and Folders on the Network

1. Open a Word document and save the file as **C11E02S01**.
2. Open File Explorer and then click *Network* in the Navigation pane.
3. Record the names of the network resources that appear at this top level of network browsing (up to six items) and their types (computers, network drives, network printers, and so on).
4. Double-click one of the items you see and then record what icons appear within it (up to six items).
5. Select a network folder and then map drive letter Y to it:
   a. Right-click the folder and then choose *Map network drive*.
   b. Select *Y* as the drive letter.
   c. Clear the *Reconnect at sign-in* check box.
   d. Click Finish.
   e. Close the new File Explorer window.
6. Capture a screen shot of the Computer window, showing the mapped network drive, and then save the file as **C11E02S06**.
7. Disconnect the drive mapping:
   a. From the Computer window, right-click the mapped drive.
   b. Click *Disconnect*.
8. Submit your Word document and screen shot to your instructor.
9. Close all open windows.

Sharing a File or Folder on the Network ■■■■■■■■■

In addition to using resources provided by other computers on your network, you also can set up your own computer to make your drives or folders available. For example, suppose you are working on a project that several other people in your organization also need to contribute to. You could place the project files in a folder on your hard disk and then share that folder on the network.

Note: *Should you share a folder directly from your own computer or should you copy that folder to a network-accessible location such as your company's file server? There are pros and cons to each. If you copy the files to a location that is always available, such as a file server, others will be able to access them even if your own computer is turned off. On the other hand, if you keep the files on your own local hard disk, then you will always be able to access them even if the network goes down.*

Choosing Which Libraries to Share with Your Home Group

If your computer is part of a homegroup, you can specify which of your libraries you want to make available to others. You can control individual libraries by right-clicking a library's icon, pointing to *Share with*, and then choosing a sharing option. You also can control multiple libraries at once by modifying your homegroup sharing settings.

Note: *As you learned in Chapter 3, you can add other files and folders to a library. The Documents library, for example, can consist of not only the My Documents folder on your hard disk, but also any other folders that you have specified should be part of that library.*

To choose default libraries to share:

1. Open the Network and Sharing Center.
2. At the right of *Homegroup,* click the Joined hyperlink.
3. Click *Change what you're sharing with the homegroup.*
4. For each of the default libraries, open the *Permissions* drop-down list and then click *Shared* or *Not Shared.*
5. Click Next.
6. Click Finish.

To share other libraries:

1. Open File Explorer and then click *Libraries* in the Navigation pane.
2. Right-click the icon that represents the library you want to share.
3. Point to *Share with.*
4. Click *Homegroup (view)* or *Homegroup (view and edit).*

Configuring Network Sharing

On all networked computers, regardless of whether you use a homegroup, you can fine-tune the network sharing permissions. This includes options such as whether file and printer sharing is turned on, whether other computers should be able to see yours when browsing the network, and whether passwords are required for sharing.

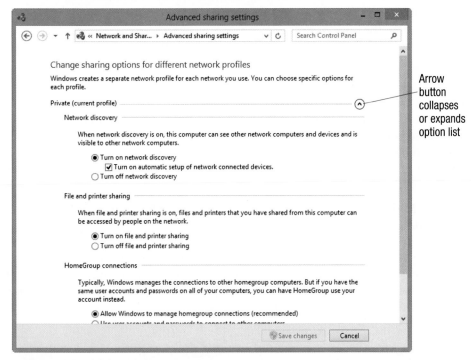

Figure 11.9 Fine-tune sharing settings.

There are three separate sets of properties for network settings: one used for Private networks, one used for Guest or Public networks, and one for All networks. The settings are different because you will probably want permissions for public networks to be strict and limited to prevent strangers from invading your privacy. Each set can be expanded (by clicking the down-pointing arrow) or collapsed (by clicking the up-pointing arrow) (shown in Figure 11.9). Here are the settings you can control:

For Private and Guest or Public Networks:

- **Network discovery**. Determines whether others browsing the network can see your computer.
- **File and printer sharing**. Determines whether file and printer sharing (in general) are enabled on your computer.
- **Homegroup connections**. Determines how homegroup connections are authenticated. Can be set only for Private networks.

For All Networks:

- **Public folder sharing**. Determines whether the folder named Public is available to others.
- **Media streaming**. Determines whether your music and video content is available for others to play on their computers by streaming it from yours.
- **File sharing connections**. Determines the level of encryption used to protect the connection when file sharing. A lower level of encryption is slightly less secure, but allows more, different devices to have access.
- **Password-protected sharing**. Determines whether passwords are required when others try to access your files, folders, or printers.

> **Here's How**
>
> **To change a network sharing setting:**
>
> 1. Open the Network and Sharing Center.
> 2. Click Change advanced sharing settings (if part of a homegroup) or Change advanced sharing options (if not part of a homegroup).
> 3. Choose the options desired.
> 4. Click Save changes.

Sharing with Public Folders

Each local user of a computer has a set of public folders. These folders exist for the specific purpose of file sharing. One way to share certain files, then, is to place the files to be shared in one of these public folders. These are not dependent on being part of a homegroup; they work on all network types, P2P or client/server.

Note: *Make sure Public folder sharing has been enabled so others can see your public folders. See the preceding section.*

To access your public folders, open File Explorer and navigate to the Users\Public folder. This opens a set of public folders, with names that reflect the suggested content for each one (shown in Figure 11.10). You can move or copy files from any location to one of these folders.

Note: *When you browse the content of someone else's computer via the network, as you learned to do previously in this chapter, that user's Public folder appears as one of the resources associated with his or her computer.*

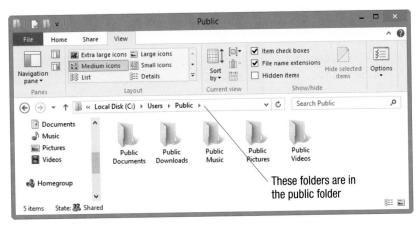

Figure 11.10 Place content in a public folder to share it with others on your network.

Sharing Individual Folders and Drives

There are several ways to share individual folders and drives. One way, as you just saw, is to place them in a Public folder and then make public sharing available.

If you are using a homegroup, you can easily share folders, with either view or view and edit access. Right-click the folder, point to *Share with*, and then click one of the homegroup sharing options.

If you are not using a homegroup, you can share the folder or drive via Windows' File Sharing interface.

To share a folder with your homegroup:

1. Right-click the folder.
2. Click *Share with*.
3. Click one of the homegroup options:
   a. *Homegroup (view)*
   b. *Homegroup (view and edit).*

Note: *You also can choose homegroup sharing options on the View tab.*

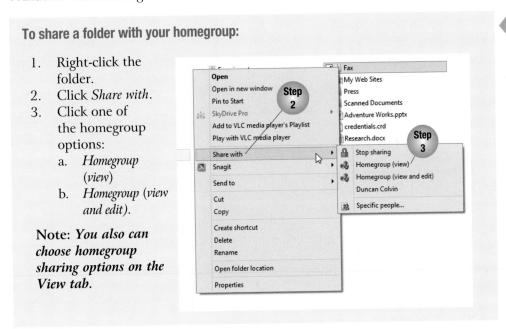

To share a folder (without a homegroup):

1. Right-click the folder.
2. Click *Share with*.
3. Click *Specific people*.
4. Type (or select) *Everyone* and then click Add.
5. In the *Permission Level* column, select a level (*Read* or *Read/Write*).
6. Click Share. A confirmation appears notifying you that your folder is shared.
7. Click Done.

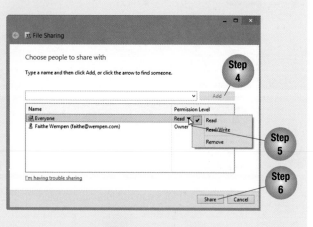

To share a drive:

1. Open File Explorer and then click *Computer* in the Navigation pane.
2. Right-click the drive and then choose *Share with, Advanced Sharing*.
3. Click the Advanced Sharing button.
4. Mark the *Share this folder* check box.
5. (Optional) Change the *Share name* to something more descriptive. (By default it is the drive letter.)
6. Click OK.
7. Click Close.

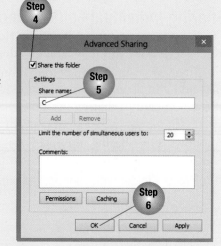

To unshare a folder:

1. Right-click the shared folder and then choose *Share with*.
2. Click *Stop sharing*.
   OR
1. Select the shared folder.
2. On the Share tab, click *Stop sharing*.

To unshare a drive:

1. From the Computer window, right-click the drive and then click *Share with, Advanced sharing*.
2. Click the Advanced Sharing button.
3. Clear *Share this folder*.
4. Click OK.
5. Click Close.

Setting Up User-Based Sharing Permission

By default, all network users can access shared folders with equal permissions. No user name or password is required. If you prefer to fine-tune permissions based on the individual user, you can enable password-protected sharing and then set up permissions for each allowed user.

Note: *The users to whom you assign permissions must be set up as local users of your computer. Therefore, you should set up their user accounts in advance. (To do so, see "Managing User Accounts and Passwords" in Chapter 15.)*

A user can have any of these permission levels assigned for accessing a particular folder:

- **Reader.** The person may read the files but not change them.
- **Contributor.** The person may read files, add files, and change or delete the files that they themselves add.
- **Co-owner.** The person may view, change, add, and delete files.

Here's How

To enable password-protected sharing:

1. Open the Network and Sharing Center.
2. Click Change advanced sharing settings.
3. In the *All Networks* section, click *Turn on password protected sharing*.
4. Click Save changes.

To assign a user permission to a shared folder:

1. Right-click the shared folder and then click *Share with, Specific people*.
2. Open the drop-down list at the left of the Add button and click the local user to whom you want to add permission.
3. Click Add.
4. Open the Permission Level drop-down list for the user and then select the desired level.
5. Click Share.

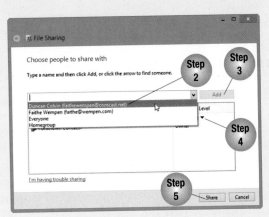

Exercise 3

Sharing Folders on the Network

1. Open a Word document and then save the file as **C11E03**.
2. Check the network sharing settings to make sure file sharing and public folder sharing are enabled and to make sure password protection is disabled:
   a. View the Network and Sharing Center.
   b. Click Change advanced sharing settings.
   c. In the *Private* section, if file and printer sharing is turned off, turn it on.
   d. In the *All Networks* section, if password protected sharing is turned on, turn it off.
   e. In the *All Networks* section, if public folder sharing is turned off, turn it on.
   f. Click Save changes.
3. Share the Chapter 11 Student Data Files folder on your hard disk:
   a. Browse to the folder containing the data files for this course.
   b. Right-click the Chapter 11 data folder and then click *Share with, Specific people*.

c. Type Everyone and then click Add.

d. Click Share.

e. Click Done.

4. Copy the Chapter 11 data folder to your Public Documents folder:

a. Select the Chapter 11 data folder and then press Ctrl + C to copy it.

b. Navigate to C:\Users\Public\Documents.

c. Press Ctrl + V to paste.

5. Go to another computer on your network and attempt to access the Chapter 11 data folder on your hard disk (the original, not the copy in the Public Documents folder). In your Word document, record the steps you took and whether they were successful.

6. From the other computer, attempt to open, make changes to, and then save **Memo.docx**. In your Word document, record the steps you took and whether they were successful.

7. From the other computer, repeat Steps 5 and 6 with the copy in the Public Documents folder. Record your results.

8. Return to your own computer and unshare the original Chapter 11 data folder:

a. Right-click the Chapter 11 data folder and then click *Share with*.

b. Click *Stop sharing*.

9. Submit your Word document to your instructor.

Working with Network Printers ■■■■■■■■■■■■■■■

network-aware printer A printer with a built-in network interface card, capable of connecting directly to the network without going through a computer

shared printer A locally installed printer on a computer that has been set up to be shared with others

Two types of printers can be available on a network: those that are truly network-aware (that is, they have their own network interface card and their own address), and those that are shared with an individual computer. A *network-aware printer* can be connected directly to the network so that it does not rely on any particular computer being active to be available. A *shared printer* is a locally installed printer on a computer that has been set up to be shared with others. When the shared computer is turned off or disconnected from the network, the printer becomes unavailable to network users.

Installing a Network Printer

Before you can print to a network printer, you must set up a driver for it on your computer. This is done using the Add Printer Wizard and is covered in "Adding a New Printer" in Chapter 13 in greater detail. Windows 8 can set up some printers automatically without any user intervention, so the printer you want may already be installed.

The Add Printer wizard enables you to select either local or network printers. If you choose to install a network printer, it scans the network and presents you with a list of the available printers, both network-aware ones and shared ones. You can tell the difference by looking at the address. A network-aware printer has an IP address (a numeric address) listed for it, whereas a shared printer has a network path containing the name of the computer to which it is attached. For example, in Figure 11.11, the last printer in the list is shared and the others are network-aware.

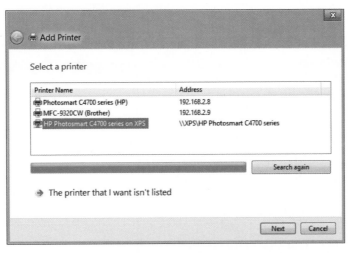

Figure 11.11 When browsing for network printers, both network-aware and shared printers are included in the list.

Here's How

To set up your computer to use a network printer:

1. Open the Control Panel.
2. Under *Hardware and Sound*, click *View devices and printers*.
3. Click Add a printer.
4. Wait for the wizard to search for available printers and then click the printer you want to use (shown in Figure 11.11).
5. Click Next.
6. If prompted to install a driver, select the printer's make and model from the list, or click Have Disk, and then follow the prompts to select a driver. If you are prompted to trust the printer, click Install driver. If the User Account Control prompts you to allow changes to your computer, click Yes. Click Next.
7. If needed, change the printer's name in the *Printer Name* box. (This is possible only for network-aware printers, not shared ones.) Then click Next.
8. For a network-aware printer only, you may be prompted to share the printer with others. Because other computers can access this printer directly, as you did, sharing the printer with others is not necessary. Click *Do not share this printer* and then click Next.
9. Clear the *Set as the default printer* check box if you do not want this printer to be the default.
10. (Optional) Click Print a test page if you want to test the connection.
11. Click Finish.

Sharing a Local Printer

You can make your own local printer available to other network users so that they can set it up on their computers as described in the previous section. A shared printer shows a sharing symbol on its icon, the same as with a shared folder (shown in Figure 11.11).

If the other network users also run the same version of Windows, the needed driver is copied to their computers automatically when they set up the printer. If there are people on the network who have other versions of Windows, however, you must make drivers available for those versions, or those users must supply their own drivers for the printer.

To share a local printer on the network:

1. Open the Control Panel.
2. Under *Hardware and Sound*, click *View devices and printers*.
3. Right-click the printer and then click *Printer properties*.
4. Click the Sharing tab.
5. Mark the *Share this printer* check box.
6. (Optional) Change the *Share name*, if desired, to more accurately describe the printer.
7. (Optional) To make other drivers available:
   a. Click Additional Drivers.
   b. Mark the check boxes for additional Windows versions to support.
   c. Click OK.
   d. If prompted, insert a disc containing the driver for each additional version and then click OK.
   e. Follow the prompts to finish installing the additional driver(s).
8. Click OK.

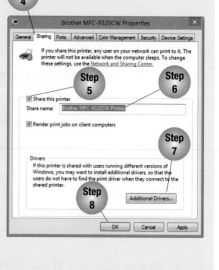

Exercise 4

Working with Network Printers

1. Share your local printer on the network, using your initials as the share name:
   a. Open the Control Panel.
   b. Under *Hardware and Sound*, click *View devices and printers*.
   c. Right-click your local printer (if you have more than one, use any) and then click *Printer properties*.
   d. Click the Sharing tab.
   e. Mark the *Share this printer* check box.
   f. In the *Share name* box, type your initials.
   g. Click OK.
2. Go to another computer on your network (or trade with another student) and then set up the shared printer from your original location as a network printer on that computer:
   a. Reopen the Printer window, if it is not still open.
      Hint: Control Panel, View Devices and printers.
   b. Click Add a printer.
   c. Click Add a network, wireless or Bluetooth printer.
   d. Wait for the wizard to search for the printers and then click the printer that has your initials as the name.
   e. Click Next.
   f. If prompted that a driver is already installed, click *Use the driver that is currently installed (recommended)* and then click Next.
   g. Click Next.
   h. Click Print a test page.
   i. Click Finish.

3. Delete the printer driver from the Printers window. Right-click its icon and then click Remove device. Click Yes.
4. Return to your original computer and then unshare the shared printer.
5. Write your name on the test page that prints and then submit it to your instructor

Troubleshooting the Network ■■■■■■■■■■■■■■■■■■

As an end user in a corporate network, you will seldom need to worry about troubleshooting because your network probably has a full-time network administrator or other IT expert who administers it. However, if you have a small peer-to-peer network in your home or business, you might not have professional help at your disposal, and you might need to troubleshoot any problems that occur yourself.

Diagnosing and Repairing a Network Connection Problem

When a network connection is not functioning correctly, Windows can help you determine why. The Windows Network Diagnostics utility can examine your network connection and suggest the probable causes for the current problem and possible solutions. It also can help you reset the network adapter, which can sometimes resolve an intermittent problem.

To diagnose a network problem:

1. Open the Network and Sharing Center.
2. At the right of *Connections*, click the name of the current connection. The Status box for the connection appears.
3. Click Diagnose.
4. Evaluate the options that appear and then click the option most suited to your situation. For example, you might choose to reset the network adapter.
5. Click OK.

Access type:	Internet
HomeGroup:	Joined
Connections:	ᴴᵗᵗ Wi-Fi (Sycamore_Knoll)

Step 2

Here's How

Determining the IP Address of a Computer

An *Internet Protocol (IP) address* is a numeric identifier of a computer on the network. IP addresses can be local (that is, apply only to your LAN) or can apply to the computer's address on the Internet at large. Windows 8 recognizes two types of IP addresses: IPv4 addresses (the older style, currently used on the Internet) and IPv6 addresses (a newer type, not widely used now, but made available for future implementation). You will mostly work with the IPv4 addresses, which consist of a set of four numbers, each between 0 and 254, separated by periods, like this: 192.168.0.1. An IPv6 address is more complex; it consists of a series of hexadecimal numbers (that is, numbers that use not only digits 0 through 9 but also letters a through f).

You do not usually need to know your computer's IP address; Windows 8 handles it behind the scenes. However, if you are working with a technician to diagnose a connectivity problem, the technician may ask you to look up the IP address assigned to the computer.

Internet Protocol (IP) address A numeric address that uniquely describes the address of a computer or other network-aware component on a network or on the Internet

You can find the IP address that your computer is using in two ways: look at the network connection details or use a command-line interface to run the Ipconfig command.

If you are working with an IT professional to troubleshoot a problem, he or she might also ask you for the **subnet mask**. This numeric code indicates what part of the IP address represents the subnet and what part represents the individual address of the computer. A **subnet** is a group of computers that shares a common top-level identifier, similar to the telephone numbers in a certain area code. A subnet mask with an IPv4 addressing scheme consists of four numbers separated by periods, such as 255.255.255.0. Subnet masks are necessary because different networks divide the available digits in the IP address differently.

A subnet mask is actually a long string of 1s and 0s with all of the 1s at the beginning, like this: 11111111.11111111.11111111.00000000. The subnet mask carries only one useful piece of information: the point at which 1 turns to 0. For example, in the above string, it does so after the 24th 1. Each set of eight digits is considered a separate binary number and is then converted to decimal. For example, 11111111 in binary is 255 in decimal. Because it is most common for a subnet mask to switch from 1 to 0 at one of the points where there is a decimal point, most subnet masks consist of only 255s and 0s. However, it is possible for a subnet mask to have a break point in other spots, like this: 11111111.11111 111.11110000.00000000, resulting in a subnet mask in decimal numbering of 255.255.240.0.

In addition to the computer's IP address, you also may find it helpful to determine its **default gateway**. This is the address of the device that takes the network connection out of its local subnet and into the larger network (your company's network, or the Internet). Later in this chapter you will learn how to ping an address to determine if a connection exists to it, and you might want to ping the default gateway's address.

subnet mask A numeric code that indicates what part of the IP address represents the subnet and what part represents the individual address of the computer

subnet A group of computers that shares a common top-level identifier, similar to the telephone numbers in an area code

default gateway The IP address of the port that leads out of your local subnet and into the larger network or the Internet

Here's How

To find the computer's IP address:

1. Open the Network and Sharing Center.
2. At the right of *Connections*, click the name of the current connection. The Status box for the connection appears.
3. Click Details. The Network Connection Details dialog box opens.
4. Note the IPv4 IP address.
5. Note the IPv4 subnet mask.
6. Note the IPv4 default gateway.
7. (Optional) If needed, note the Link-local IPv6 IP address.
8. Click Close.
9. Click Close.

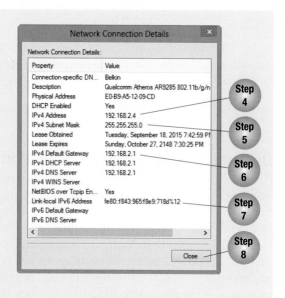

To find the computer's IP address via command-line interface:

1. From the Start screen, type cmd.
2. Click Command Prompt.
3. Type ipconfig and then press Enter.
4. Note the IP addresses, the subnet mask, and the default gateway.

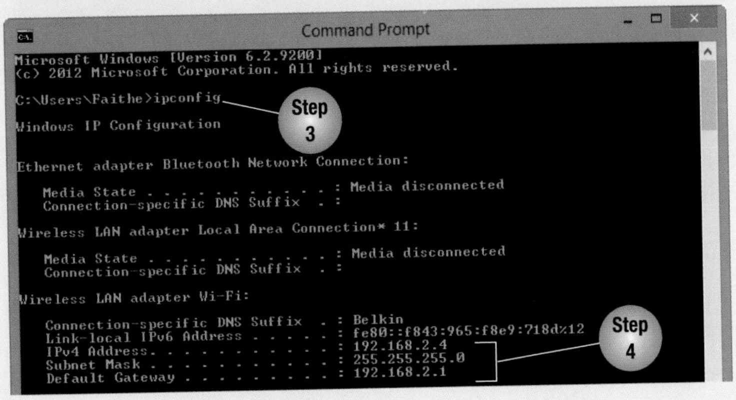

5. Close the command prompt window.

Using Ping to Check the Connection

Network problems often are not your computer's fault but instead are caused by a breakdown in the communication pipeline somewhere between your computer and the intended destination. That destination could be a website, a file server on your LAN, a shared printer on someone else's computer, or any other network-addressable location.

IT professionals use a command-line utility called PING to check the connectivity between a computer and another network location, and based on the results, they can narrow down where the breakdown in communication is occurring. For example, suppose your computer is connected to a router, which in turn is connected to a server, which in turn is connected to the Internet. If you cannot access the Internet, which component is at fault? To figure this out you check the connection between your computer and the router first. If that connection is working, then you check between your computer and the server. You keep working through the connection, from closest to farthest away, until you find the part that is not working.

You can "ping" a device based on its IP address (IPv4). Pinging sends an inquiry to that device, requesting a response. If the response comes back, you know the connection is working between your computer and that device.

If you see a reply, as shown in Figure 11.12, the connection is working. If a message appears indicating that the request timed out, as shown in Figure 11.13, either the connection is not working or the address you are pinging does not support ping requests (as is the case with www.microsoft.com, for example).

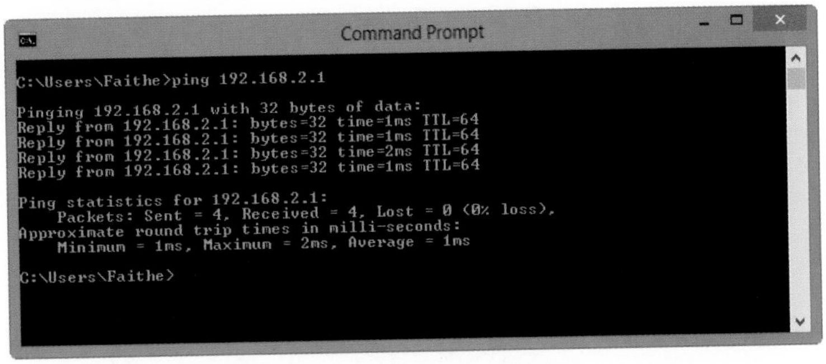

Figure 11.12 A successful ping results in replies.

Note: *You can ping either by IP address or by web address (for example, www.emcp.com). If you ping a web address, a Domain Name System (DNS) server on the Internet resolves (converts) the web address to the equivalent IP address.*

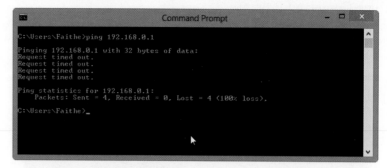

Figure 11.13 An unsuccessful ping times out.

What addresses should you ping? Start by pinging the loopback address: 127.0.0.1. If this works, then the computer's NIC is set up correctly. Then try pinging the computer's own IP address. If that works, ping the default gateway. From there, continue pinging addresses that are progressively farther away from your computer until you find the breakdown.

Here's How

To ping an IP address or web address:
1. Click Start.
2. Type cmd and then press Enter.
3. Type ping, a space, and then the IP address or web address to check.
4. Press Enter.
5. Wait for a reply or for the connection to time out.

Understanding Internet Connections ■■■■■■■■■■

The Internet is a big network of interconnected computers that communicate using the IPv4 addressing system that you learned about previously in this chapter. Using the Internet, you can exchange email with others, visit web pages, post your own web content, and much more.

To connect to the Internet, you need either an always-on Internet connection via your company's LAN, or an account with an Internet Service Provider (ISP), which then provides you with a means of connecting. Different ISPs offer different means of connecting; some of the options that might be available to you in your home or business, depending on its location, include:

- **Digital Subscriber Line (DSL).** A high-speed connection that uses unused portions of regular telephone lines; requires a DSL terminal adapter.
- **Cable.** A high-speed connection that uses digital cable TV wires to carry Internet service; requires a cable modem.
- **Satellite.** A medium-speed connection that uses a two-way satellite dish to carry Internet service; requires a satellite dish with receiver/transmitter and a satellite terminal adapter.
- **Dial-up.** The oldest, slowest type of connection, but sometimes the only available option in isolated areas or due to a tight budget; requires a modem.

Each type of service requires its own unique type of modem or terminal adapter. A *modem* (short for modulator/demodulator) converts between digital data from the computer and analog (sound) data that can be sent over a telephone line or cable TV line. When a connection is all-digital, as with DSL and cable, which requires no conversion between analog and digital, the device is referred to as a *terminal adapter*.

To set up any type of Internet connectivity except dial-up, get a startup kit from the ISP, or schedule professional installation (necessary for satellite service, for example, because of FCC regulations governing transmitters). The computer sees one of these always-on connections as a network connection and treats it accordingly, making Internet services automatically available to your computer. You do not need to connect or disconnect.

Note: *You can share an always-on Internet connection with multiple computers in your home or office by using a router. A router functions as a switch in the network, serving as a gathering point at which all of the computers in the network connect, but it also can manage an Internet connection. You connect the modem or terminal adapter to the router, and the router then shares that connection with all of the computers to which it is attached.*

Dial-up connectivity is different. With a dial-up connection, you must create a connection in Windows and then activate that connection whenever you want to use the Internet. You disconnect the connection when you are finished using the Internet. To create a dial-up connection, open the Network and Sharing Center, click Set up a new connection or network, click *Connect to the Internet*, and then follow the prompts.

Working with Streaming Media ▪▪▪▪▪▪▪▪▪▪▪▪▪▪

If you have pictures, videos, or other media stored on your computer, you may want to share it with other network users. You could copy all of the media to a DVD and then hand it to the person, but it may be more efficient to allow other users to access your media library from the network and then stream what they want to view or hear. For example, you could put all of your music on one computer in your household, and every computer in the house could access it.

Note: *Depending on your TV, DVR, or home theatre equipment, you may also be able to stream media from your computer to your TV. Check the manuals that came with your devices to find out how. You may discover additional devices to stream to via the Devices charm. If any eligible devices are detected on your network, a command will appear enabling you to set them up.*

The first step in sharing your media content with other computers and devices is to adjust your network settings to allow media streaming. You do this from the Network and Sharing Center, under Change Advanced Sharing Settings.

modem Short for modulator/demodulator; a device that converts between digital computer data and analog sound wave data that can be transmitted via telephone or cable TV lines

terminal adapter A communication device that sends and receives all-digital networking data, such as for a cable or DSL Internet connection

To configure Windows to stream media:

1. Open the Network and Sharing Center.
2. Click *Change advanced sharing settings.*
3. In the *All Networks* section, under *Media Streaming,* click *Choose media streaming options.*
4. Make sure the *Allowed* check box is marked next to Media programs on this PC and remote connections.
5. Click Next.
6. Make sure that Music is set to Shared, and click Next.
7. Make a note of the homegroup password if one is displayed.
8. Click Finish.

After enabling media server access, you can go to another computer on your network, browse the network to locate the media server on the remote computer, and then double-click the media server icon to browse the media content available (shown in Figure 11.14). In some cases, you also can access the network media server from applications as if it were a drive. For example, in Windows Media Player, you can include network locations when creating playlists and playing music or videos.

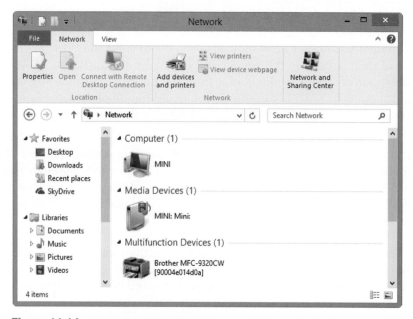

Figure 11.14 When a computer's media streaming is enabled, other computers see it as an available network location in File Explorer.

- A network is a group of connected computers. When in the same building, it is a local area network (LAN). When spread out over a greater distance, it is a wide area network (WAN).

- A client/server network consists of one or more end-user computers (clients) and one or more servers to handle the administration. A peer-to-peer network has no servers and is typically small.

- A wired network uses cables (typically with RJ-45 connectors, which are like wide telephone plugs) that plug into a computer's network interface card.

- A wireless network uses radio frequency (RF) or infrared signals. The most popular type of wireless is IEEE 802.11, also called Wi-Fi. It is a type of RF-based Ethernet.

- The computers of a network connect to a switch, router, or wireless access point.

- To display the Network and Sharing Center, open the Control Panel and then click *View Network Status and Tasks*.

- A network can be Public or Private. Security is higher on a public network.

- To connect to a wireless network, click the network icon in the notification area. Click the network with which to connect and then click the Connect button.

- Wireless networks typically employ security to keep unauthorized users out. From the Network and Sharing Center, click the network name at the right of *Connections*. Click Wireless Properties, click the Security tab, and then from the *Security Type* list, click the type of security you want to use.

- To change the workgroup or domain name for a computer, open the Control Panel, click *System and Security,* and then click System. Click *Change Settings* and then on the Computer Name tab, click Change.

- A Virtual Private Network (VPN) connection is a secure software tunnel that runs between computers using the Internet as its conduit.

- To set up a VPN connection, open the Network and Sharing Center, then click *Set up a new connection or network*, choose *Connect to a workplace*, and then follow the prompts.

- To browse a network for available files, open File Explorer and then click *Network* in the Navigation pane.

- Mapping a network drive assigns a drive letter to a network location. From File Explorer, right-click a network location and then click *Map Network Drive*.

- To share your own files on the network, the network must first be set up as a Private network (rather than Public). To share public folders, enable public folder sharing in the Network and Sharing Center (click Change Advanced sharing settings).

- To share folders other than the public ones, right-click the folder and then choose *Share with, Advanced Sharing* (for a drive) or *Share with, Specific People* (for a folder).

- To assign a user permission to a shared folder, right-click the folder, choose *Share with, Specific People*, and then add users and permission levels for them.

- To use a network-shared printer, set up the printer with the Add Devices and Printers utility, the same as any other printer (*Control Panel, Hardware and Sound, View Devices and Printers*), except specify a network location for it.

- To share your own printer, right-click the printer's icon in the Devices and Printers window, choose *Printer properties*, and then click the Sharing tab. Mark the *Share this printer* check box and then click OK.
- To diagnose a network problem, open the Network and Sharing Center, click the network name at the right of *Connections* to view its status and then click Diagnose.
- To determine a computer's IP address, open the Network Connection Details box (see previous item) or use the Ipconfig command at a command prompt.
- A subnet is a group of computers in a network segment. A subnet mask is a code that describes what part of an IP address refers to the subnet and what part refers to an individual computer.
- A default gateway is the IP address of the port that leads out of your local subnet.
- At a command prompt, use the Ping command to check connectivity between your computer and another one.
- You can make your Music and Video libraries available for streaming to other computers on your network. Others can browse your music and video the same way they would browse for other shared folders on your computer.

CONCEPTS CHECK

Completion: Answer the following questions in a Word document.

Part 1

Multiple Choice

1. When network computers are in the same room or building, they are part of a(n) _____ .
   a. wide area network (WAN)
   b. local area network (LAN)
   c. client/server network
   d. enterprise network

2. A network that includes one or more servers is a _____ .
   a. wide area network (WAN)
   b. local area network (LAN)
   c. client/server network
   d. P2P network

3. A network that consists only of clients is a _____ .
   a. wide-area network (WAN)
   b. local area network (LAN)
   c. client/server network
   d. P2P network

4. Another name for the IEEE 802.11 standard is _____ .
   a. Wi-Fi
   b. infrared
   c. USB
   d. parallel

5. What kind of connector is common on a NIC?
   a. RJ-11
   b. RJ-14
   c. RJ-35
   d. RJ-45

6. Which IP address type is used for the Internet today?
   a. IPv2
   b. IPv4
   c. IPv6
   d. IPv8

7. An SSID is applicable only to what type of connection?
   a. client/server
   b. cable
   c. wireless
   d. wired

8. When connecting to a wireless network that provides Internet access at a local coffee shop, you should set the connection to be a_____ network.
   a. Public
   b. Discoverable
   c. Private
   d. Work

9. Which of these is a valid IPv4 address?
   a. 192.168.0
   b. 192.168.0.1
   c. 192.266.851.22
   d. 192.168.0.1.1.6

10. What command checks the connectivity between your computer and another computer or network device based on the IP address?
    a. Ping
    b. Trace
    c. IpConfig
    d. WindowsIp

Part 2

Short Answer

11. What are three types of wireless network security?

    _____

12. What are the three permission levels you can set for sharing a folder with a particular user?

    _____

13. What error message will you see if Ping does not work?

    _____

14. What is the difference between a modem and a terminal adapter?

    _____

15. Which type of Internet connection is slowest and least preferable? Explain why.

_____

16. 255.0.255.0 is not a valid subnet mask. Explain why.

_____

17. Suppose a printer has both a USB connector and a NIC, so you can choose to connect it directly to the network or share it from an individual computer. What are the benefits of connecting it directly to the network?

_____

18. Would someone who runs a different version of Windows than you be able to use your shared printer? If not, why? If so, what would you need to provide, if anything?

_____

19. When you share a folder on your hard disk without specifying password-protected sharing, who will be able to access it?

_____

20. If you can successfully ping the computer's loopback address but not its default gateway, what does that tell you about where the connection problem lies?

_____

SKILLS CHECK

Save all solution files to the default Documents folder or any alternate folder specified by your instructor.

Guided Check

Assessment

1

Disconnecting and Connecting a Network

1. Open a Word document and then save the file as **C11A01**.
2. Disconnect all existing network connections.
   a. In the notification area of the Taskbar, click the network connection icon to display the Networks panel. If there is a wireless network listed, click the network name and then click the Disconnect button.
   b. On the back of your computer, unplug any RJ-45 connectors, disconnecting any wired connections.
3. Record in your Word document what you had to do to disconnect all of the network connections.
4. Try to access the Internet. Record in your Word document what error message(s) you see.
5. If you unplugged an RJ-45 connector in Step 2, reconnect it, and then record what happens on the screen. Look both in the notification area and in the Network and Sharing Center window.

6. If you disconnected from a wireless network in Step 2, reconnect to that network.
   a. Click the Network icon in the notification area.
   b. Click the wireless network with which to connect.
   c. Click the Connect button.
7. If applicable, record what messages appeared on the screen when you reconnected the wireless connection. Look both in the notification area and in the Network and Sharing Center window.
8. Try to access the Internet again. If it does not work, troubleshoot, and then record what steps you took.
9. Submit your Word document to your instructor.

Assessment 2

Collecting Information about Your Network Connection

1. Open a Word document and then save the file as **C11A02**.
2. Open the Network and Sharing Center.
   a. Open the Control Panel.
   b. Under Network and Internet, click *View network status and tasks*.
3. Click the network name at the right of *Connections*.
4. Collect the following information and then record it in your Word document.
   • Media state
   • Duration
   • Speed
5. Click Details.
6. Collect the following information and then record it in your Word document.
   • Physical address
   • IPv4 IP Address
   • IPv4 Subnet Mask
   • IPv4 Default Gateway
7. Click Close to close the Details box.
8. Click Properties to see the connection properties and then look at the installed items in the *This connection uses the following items* list.
9. Record the items in your Word document and then click OK.
10. Click Close to close the Properties box for the connection.
11. Submit your Word document to your instructor.
12. Close the Network and Sharing Center window if it is still open.

Assessment 3

Browsing the Network

1. Open a Word document and then save the file as **C11A03**.
2. Browse the network.
   a. Open File Explorer.
   b. In the Navigation pane at the left, click *Network*.
3. Notice which items are available for browsing in the Network window and then record their names in your Word document.
4. Double-click one of the items. Record what happens.
5. Click the Back button to return to the Network window's list of items and then repeat Step 4 for another item. Again, record what happens.

6. If you are able to view a shared folder on one of the computers on the network, try the following:
   a. Select any data file in the shared folder. (For example, choose a Word document, an Excel file, or a plain text file.)
   b. Press Ctrl + C to copy it and then press Ctrl + V to paste the copy.
   c. Rename the copy to your last name. (Keep the same file extension.)
   d. Open the copy by double-clicking it. Make a change to the file, save the changes, and then close the file.
   e. Delete the copy.
7. Note in your Word document which parts of Step 7 you were able to accomplish and which parts did not work. Based on this experiment, how do you think the folder-sharing security settings are configured on that computer?
8. Submit your Word document to your instructor.

Partner Exercise: Working with Public Folders

1. Open a Word document and then save the file as **C11A04S01**.
2. Create a new text file in your Public Documents folder with your last name as the file name.
   a. Open File Explorer.
   b. Navigate to C:\Users\Public.
   c. Double-click *Public Documents*.
   d. Right-click a blank area and then choose *New, Text Document*.
   e. Type your last name as the document's name and then press Enter.
3. Switch computers with a partner and then browse the network to find the text file you created in Step 2. When you find it, capture a screen shot of the window and then save it as **C11A04S03**.

   If you are unable to find the text file, troubleshoot, and then document your steps in your Word document.
4. Open the text file in Notepad (by double-clicking it) and then type your full name in it. Save your changes and then close the file.

   If you are unable to complete Step 4, troubleshoot and then document your steps in your Word document.
5. View the Properties for the file (right-click the file and then choose *Properties*).
6. Capture a screen shot of the Properties window and then save it as **C11A04S06**.
7. Submit your Word document and your screen shots to your instructor.

On Your Own

Examining the Security Settings of a Wireless Access Point

1. Open a Word document and then save the file as **C11A05**.
2. Using your web browser, access the setup utility for your wireless access point. In your Word document, write the address you used. Enter the address in the Address bar of your web browser preceded by http://, like this: http://192.168.0.254.

Note: You will need to know the IP address that the wireless access point uses for this purpose. It is usually an address in the 192.168.x.x range. Your instructor or the documentation that came with the device will tell you what to use.

3. In the web-based configuration utility, look at the settings available for the access point. What types of wireless security does this access point support? What options are available? Record the answer in your Word document.
4. Submit your Word document to your instructor.

Assessment

6

Changing the Workgroup Name

1. Open a Word document and then save the file as **C11A06**.
2. View the System Properties dialog box. *Hint: Control Panel, System and Security, System, Advanced system settings.* On the computer Name tab, make a note of the current workgroup or domain and then record it in your Word document.
3. Click the Change button, and if the *Workgroup* option button is not selected, select it. Type STUDENTS as the workgroup name.
4. Save the changes and then restart the Computer.
5. Try to browse the network via the Network window and then record the results in your Word document.
6. Change at least one other computer in your network over to this same STUDENTS workgroup.
7. Try again to browse the network and then record the results.
8. Change all of the computers back to their original network membership (workgroup or domain).
9. Try again to browse the network in the Network window and then record the results.
10. Submit your Word document to your instructor.

Assessment

7

Experimenting with a VPN Connection

1. Establish a VPN connection to your work or school.
2. Look in the Network and Sharing Center, in the Computer window, and in the Network window to see what differences you can observe when the VPN connection is established. You might need to disconnect and reconnect from the VPN connection several times to check for differences.
3. In a Word document, write a brief report explaining the differences you observed, save it as **C11A07**, and then submit it to your instructor.

Assessment

8

Exploring Network Printer Properties

1. Share a local printer on the network.
2. On another computer, set up the shared printer as a network printer.
3. On the computer to which the printer is directly connected, right-click the icon for the printer and then choose *Properties*. Examine the printer settings available there.
4. Repeat Step 3 on the computer that uses the printer via the network and then examine the printer settings available there.
5. In a Word document, write a brief report explaining the differences, save it as **C11A08**, and then submit it to your instructor.

CHALLENGE PROJECT

You work for a small business that has six computers, and you have been asked to set up a network for file and printer sharing and for Internet connectivity. Your boss purchased a commercial DSL package that comes with a single DSL terminal adapter.

He also purchased a router that has six RJ-45 jacks, a connector for the incoming DSL line, and a wireless networking antenna, so it can function both as a router and as a wireless access point. Two of the computers in the office are laptops with both wired and wireless capability; the other four have RJ-45 jacks for wired connections but have no wireless capability. You have plenty of cables available for connecting components to one another.

Draw a diagram showing how you would connect all of the computers, the router, and the DSL terminal adapter. Use dotted lines to represent wireless connections and solid lines to represent wired ones. Submit the diagram to your instructor.

Maintaining Your System

PERFORMANCE OBJECTIVES

Upon successful completion of Chapter 12, you will be able to:

- Use Windows Update to keep Windows current
- Add or remove a font
- Use Disk Cleanup to remove unneeded files

- Expand memory with Windows ReadyBoost
- Defragment a disk
- Configure power settings
- Use administrative tools

To keep Windows 8 running optimally, you can run system utilities that improve system performance, safeguard your data, and fine-tune system settings. These tasks are optional but can make Windows run better and more efficiently.

Using Windows Update to Keep Windows 8 Current

Windows Update is a free service from Microsoft that downloads the latest patches, fixes, and updates from Microsoft's servers for Windows and other Microsoft products. By default, Windows Update runs automatically behind the scenes, downloading updates as they become available. You also can trigger an update manually, review updates that are already installed, and, in some cases, remove previously installed updates (for example, if a recent update has caused a problem with your system).

Windows Update
A free service from Microsoft that downloads the latest patches, fixes, and updates from Microsoft's servers for Windows 8 and other Microsoft products

Displaying Windows Update

You can access Windows Update via the *System and Security* section of the Control Panel. From the Windows Update screen, you can see when the system last checked for updates, when the last update was installed, and more (shown in Figure 12.1). Along the left side are links to common activities for working with Windows Update.

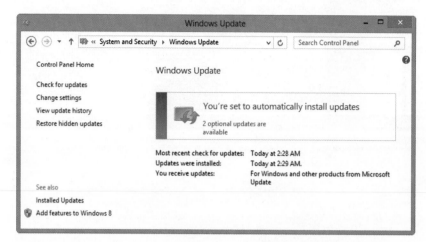

Figure 12.1 View and manage Windows update settings via the Control Panel.

Here's How

To display the Windows Update screen:

1. Open the Control Panel.
2. Click the *System and Security* category.
3. Click *Windows Update*.

T I P To open the Control Panel, select the Settings charm and then click Control Panel. Or, if you have the Show All Folders option enabled in File Explorer, click the Control Panel icon from the Navigation pane in File Explorer.

Changing Windows Update Settings

When a computer is connected full-time to the Internet, as with a broadband connection, updates occur automatically. However, some people choose to turn off automatic updates for a variety of reasons. For example, some people prefer to control when updates occur because some updates require the computer to be restarted, and they do not want the computer automatically restarting itself (and possibly causing them to lose unsaved work in applications) when they are not expecting it.

For important updates, you can choose one of these actions (shown in Figure 12.2):

- **Install updates automatically (recommended).** Updates are downloaded and installed at the specified time (unless the particular update requires user input or accepting a license agreement). If an update requires a restart, the restart occurs automatically. This is the default setting in Windows 8.

- **Download updates but let me choose whether to install them.** Updates are downloaded, but then they wait for the user to trigger their installation. This is useful for people who might not always want every update that is offered.

- **Check for updates but let me choose whether to download and install them.** An update notice appears, but the download does not occur until the user triggers it. This is useful for people on dial-up connections so that the download does not interfere with Internet performance at a critical time.

■ **Never check for updates (not recommended).** Windows Update does not run automatically. This is useful in some managed corporate environments where updates are controlled by an administrator or provided by a company server rather than downloaded directly from Microsoft.

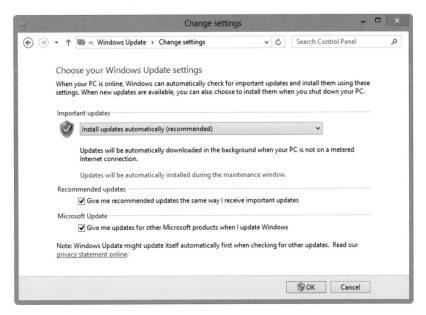

Figure 12.2 Choose how Windows Updates should occur.

Some updates are more important to the system's functionality than others. For example, an update that patches a security hole is more important than one that slightly improves the functioning of a specialized utility that few people use. Windows Update categorizes the updates in one of three levels of priority:

■ **Important.** Affects the system's stability and security. These updates are always included.

■ **Recommended.** Fixes a problem with or improves the performance of a nonessential Windows 8 component or add-on. These updates are included automatically only if the check box is marked under *Recommended Updates* (shown in Figure 12.2).

■ **Optional.** Updates or enhances parts of Windows 8 that not everyone uses, such as support add-ons or foreign language packs. These updates are not downloaded automatically; you must manually run Windows Update (as described later in this chapter) to acquire them.

Microsoft Update is a separate feature from Windows Update; it includes updates for Microsoft products other than Windows itself, such as Microsoft Office, Microsoft Visual Basic, and so on. If you would like to include updates for other products in the Windows Update process, make sure the check box under *Microsoft Update* is marked (shown in Figure 12.2).

Updates are installed according to the ***maintenance window*** set up for your computer. Maintenance activities include software updates, security scanning, and system diagnostics. By default, the maintenance window occurs daily at 3 a.m., but you can change it. If your computer is in use at the scheduled time, or if maintenance is behind schedule, automatic maintenance will run the next time the computer is not being used.

 Quick Fix

Not All Options Visible If you do not see the lower part of the settings window (shown in Figure 12.2), enlarge the window or scroll down.

maintenance window The specified time of day at which scheduled maintenance activities occur

To change Windows Update settings:

1. Open the Control Panel, click *System and Security*, and then click *Windows Update*.
2. Click Change settings.
3. Click to open the drop-down list under *Important Updates*.
4. Click the desired update option.
5. (Optional) Change the maintenance window if desired:

    a. Click the maintenance window hyperlink.

    b. Open the *Run maintenance tasks daily at* drop-down list.

    c. Select a different time.

    d. Click OK.

6. Mark or clear the check box in the *Recommended Updates* section.
7. Mark or clear the check box in the *Microsoft Update* section.
8. Click OK.
9. If prompted, click Yes to restart the computer.

Checking for and Installing an Update

If your settings do not specify that Windows 8 check automatically for updates, you must click the *Check for Updates* link in the Windows Update window to initiate a check. If any new updates are found, they appear in the Windows Update window. From there, click Install Updates to download the important updates (if not already downloaded) and install them. Even if Windows Update reports that no important updates are available, there still may be useful updates that you want. For example, you might want a device driver update for a piece of hardware on your system. Complete the following steps to select optional updates, in addition to installing the important ones.

To choose and install updates:

1. Open the Control Panel, click *System and Security*, and then click *Windows Update*.
2. Click the link for optional updates, if any are available. A list of available updates appears.

3. Mark the check boxes for the updates you want.
4. Click Install.

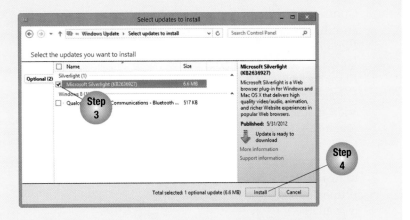

5. Respond to any prompts that appear, such as accepting a license agreement.
6. Wait for the updates to download and install, if necessary.

Reviewing the Update History

The *Update History* list displays the Windows 8 updates that have been installed on your system. To see it, click *View Update History* in the Windows Update window. You then can double-click any of the lines to open its details, as shown in Figure 12.3. If any of the updates does not have a Succeeded status, view its details and then click the link in the details under *Help and Support*.

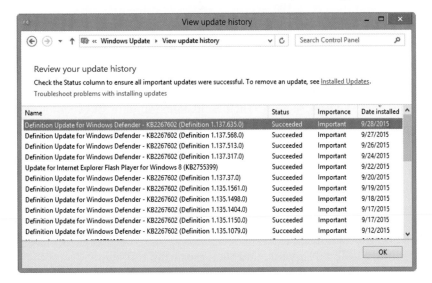

Figure 12.3 The update history lists the updates that have been installed.

Removing an Update

Not all updates can be removed; some of them, such as security patches, permanently affect Windows 8. Other updates, however, can be removed, and the files they affected rolled back to their previous versions. This might be useful, for example, if an update caused an unexpected problem with a device or application.

To remove a Windows 8 update:

1. Open the Control Panel and then click *Programs*.
2. Under *Programs and Features*, click View installed updates.
3. Click an update to uninstall. If uninstall is available, an Uninstall button appears.
4. Click Uninstall or double-click the update to uninstall.
5. If prompted for confirmation, click Yes.

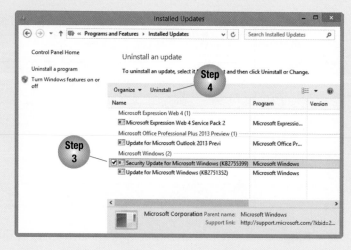

Exercise 1

Updating Windows

1. Open the Control Panel and then click the *System and Security* category.
2. Under *Windows Update*, click the *Turn automatic updating on or off* link.
3. Under *Important Updates*, open the drop-down list and then choose *Check for updates but let me choose whether to download and install them*.
4. Click OK.
5. Click Windows Update, and then click *Installed Updates* in the left pane.
6. Scroll down to the *Microsoft Windows* section. Click an installed update and then observe whether an Uninstall button appears above the list.
7. For one of the updates that has an Uninstall button available, click Uninstall.
8. Click Yes to confirm, if prompted. If prompted to restart your computer, click Restart Now and then wait for it to restart.
9. Open the Control Panel and then click the *System and Security* category.
10. Under *Windows Update*, click *Check for updates*.
    At least one update should appear available (the one you uninstalled). If no updates are available, click the Check for updates link in the left pane. If there are still no updates available, try uninstalling a different update, and then repeating this step.
11. Click the Install updates button and then follow any prompts to install it.
12. When a message appears notifying you that the updates were successfully installed, or that you must restart your computer to finish installing updates, capture a screen shot of this window and then save it as **C12E01**.
13. Check with your instructor, and, if needed, return the automatic updating setting to its previous state (probably *Install updates automatically*).
14. Submit the screen shot to your instructor.

Viewing, Installing, and Removing Fonts ▪▪▪▪▪▪

As a generic definition, a *font* is a typeface, a style of lettering. Windows 8 uses fonts for on-screen display of text and also in applications that produce documents that contain formatted text, such as word processors and spreadsheets.

Windows 8 manages the font collection itself and makes nearly all fonts available to all applications. For example, suppose you install Microsoft Office, which comes with dozens of fonts. All of those fonts can be used in other Windows programs, too, not just Office applications.

Each font is a file (or in some cases more than one file) installed on your hard disk. Since these fonts are "software," they are considered *soft fonts.* You can see a list of all of the soft fonts on your system via the Control Panel (*Appearance and Personalization, Fonts*), as shown in Figure 12.4.

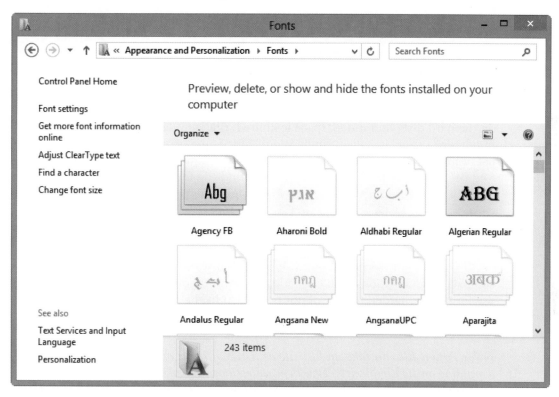

Figure 12.4 To display a list of fonts on your system, from the Control Panel choose *Appearance and Personalization* and then click Fonts.

Note: *Some printers have their own built-in (printer-resident) fonts that you can use in some applications. The printer's driver defines these fonts to Windows 8; they are separate from the fonts you are learning about in this section. For information about your printer's built-in fonts, consult its documentation.*

To see a sample of a font, double-click it to open a window containing sample text in that font at various sizes, as shown in Figure 12.5. Some font icons represent a group of fonts, so when you double-click them, more font icons appear; if that happens, double-click one of the font icons that appears to see a sample of it.

To install a new font in Windows 8, open a File Explorer window for the folder that contains the new font. Right-click the font file and then choose *Install.* Alternatively, drag and drop the font file to the Fonts window.

Maintaining Your System

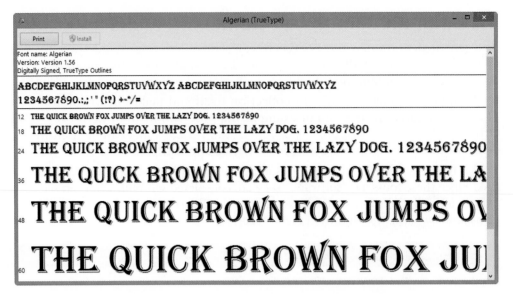

Figure 12.5 Double-click a font in the Fonts window to display a sample of it.

Many people like to have as many fonts as possible to choose from, but sometimes you might want to remove font files. Each font file takes up space on the hard disk, and if disk space is limited, the cumulative effect of having hundreds of fonts installed can be significant. Some people also prefer to keep the list of installed fonts small because it reduces the amount of scrolling through the font list they have to do in applications to find the font they want to apply.

The easiest way to remove a font is to delete its icon from the Fonts folder. Click it and then press the Delete key to do so. If you think you might want to reinstall that font again at some point, copy the font to a backup folder (by dragging and dropping it from the Fonts folder to another folder).

If you are not worried about disk space, but want to make the font list more compact in applications, you can hide one or more fonts from most programs that use fonts. The hidden fonts will not be hidden in the Fonts window itself, only in applications.

Note: *A font file can take up as little as 8 KB of space or many megabytes of space depending on its complexity. TrueType collections can take up as much as 35 MB in some cases, for example. To find out which fonts are taking up the most space, view the Fonts window in Details view and then sort the display by size. If Size is not one of the columns displayed, choose* View *and then choose* Details. *Mark the* Size *check box and then click* OK. *Next, click the* Size *column heading to sort by size. Scroll the display to the right if you do not see the* Size *column after adding it.*

Here's How

To view the Fonts window:

1. Open the Control Panel.
2. Click *Appearance and Personalization.*
3. Click *Fonts.*

To install a font:

1. From the Fonts window, right-click the font file.
2. Click *Install.*

To remove a font:

1. Click the font file in the Fonts window.
2. Press the Delete key.
3. Click Yes.

To show or hide fonts not in your language:

1. In the Fonts window, click *Font settings*.
2. Mark or clear the *Hide fonts based on language settings* check box.
3. Click OK

To hide an individual font from applications:

1. In the Fonts window, right-click the font to hide.
2. Click *Hide*.

To unhide a hidden font:

1. In the Fonts window, switch to Details view (View, *Details*).
2. Right-click a font that shows Hidden in the *Show/hide* column.
3. Click *Show*.

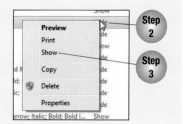

Exercise 2

Removing and Reinstalling a Font

1. Create a new folder on the C drive called FontBackup and open it.
2. Open the Control Panel's Fonts window (Control Panel, *Appearance and Personalization*, *Fonts*).
3. Select a font and then press Ctrl + C to copy it to the Clipboard.
   Different systems have different fonts; ask your instructor which font to use. Make sure you do not pick one that has a curved arrow on its icon; those are font shortcuts, not actual font files.
4. Display the FontBackup folder and then press Ctrl + V to paste the font into it. Depending on the font you chose in Step 3, you may find that several files appear when you choose paste.
5. Capture a screen shot of this window, save it as **C12E02**, and then submit it to your instructor.
6. Display the Fonts window and then delete the font you copied.
7. From the C:\FontBackup folder, right-click the font file(s) and choose *Install*.
8. Close the FontBackup folder.
9. Close the Fonts window.

Using Disk Cleanup to Remove Unneeded Files ■■■■■■■■■■■■■■■ ■■■■■■■■■■■■■■■

Hard disks over time accumulate files that you do not need to keep, such as temporary Internet files and leftover files from software installations. When a hard disk is almost full, system performance suffers. Therefore, it is good practice to run Disk Cleanup periodically to delete files that Windows 8 no longer needs.

You can choose to clean up only your own files (that is, files associated with your user account) or system files for all users on the computer. The latter removes more files, but you risk possibly cleaning up (that is, deleting) files that another user on the computer might have intended to keep.

Disk Cleanup identifies files in various categories that you can delete to save space. Mark or clear the check box of a category, or select it and then click View Files to see exactly what the category contains.

Here's How

To run Disk Cleanup:

1. From the Start screen, open the Computer window.
2. Right-click the desired hard drive to clean up and then choose *Properties*.
3. On the General tab, click Disk Cleanup.
4. Wait for Disk Cleanup to calculate the space to be freed up.
5. In the Disk Cleanup window, mark or clear check boxes for each category of file to clean up.
6. (Optional) To clean up system files, click the Clean up system files button and then wait for system files to be cleaned.
7. Click OK.
8. Click Delete Files to confirm and then wait for the files to be cleaned up. (It may take up to 30 minutes; you can use your computer for other tasks while you are waiting.)
9. Click OK to close the Properties dialog box for the hard drive.

Defragmenting a Disk ■■■■■■■■■■■■■■■■■■■■ ■■

fragmented file A file that is stored in multiple noncontiguous clusters on a hard disk

defragment To reorganize the file storage on a disk drive so that as many files as possible are stored contiguously

When a file is stored on a disk, it is placed in contiguous clusters on the drive surface if there is room. This makes the file easily accessible to the disk's read/write head, and disk access time is fast. Over time, as the file is modified, the additional pieces are written to nonadjacent areas, and the file becomes *fragmented*. The disk's read/write head must move around to pick up the pieces, so the disk access time suffers. *Defragmenting* a disk can improve its performance by rewriting files to contiguous clusters.

Windows 8 automatically defragments drives once a week, by default, based on the maintenance window defined for your computer. You can initiate a manual defragment operation at any time, or change the interval of the automatic activity.

To open the Disk Defragmenter utility:

1. Open the Computer window.
2. Right-click the drive to defragment and then click *Properties*.
3. On the Tools tab, click Optimize.

To run a manual disk defragmentation:

1. Start the Disk Defragmenter utility.
2. In the Disk Defragmenter dialog box, click the drive you wish to optimize (usually drive C), and then click Optimize.
3. Wait for the defragmentation to finish. (It can take a long time; you can use your computer for other tasks while you are waiting.)

To schedule automatic defragmentation:

1. Start the Disk Defragmenter utility.
2. Click Change settings.
3. Make sure the *Run on a schedule (recommended)* check box is marked.
4. Specify how often from the *Frequency* drop-down list.
5. Click OK.

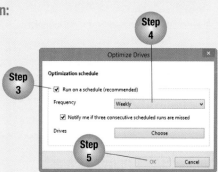

Cleaning up and Defragmenting a Hard Disk

1. Start Disk Cleanup for the C drive.
2. Mark the check boxes for all possible files to delete except Office Setup Files (if present), Setup Log Files, and Thumbnails, and then complete the Disk Cleanup process.
3. Start the Disk Defragmenter and start the defragmenting process now.
4. While you are waiting for the process to complete, capture a screen shot of this window, save it as **C12E03**, and then submit it to your instructor.
5. Click Close. The defragmentation continues in the background.

Expanding Memory with Windows ReadyBoost ■■

ReadyBoost enables you to use storage space from a removable media device, such as a USB flash drive, for additional RAM. When you connect a ReadyBoost-capable storage device, the AutoPlay dialog box includes an option to use the device to speed up your computer. You then can specify the amount of space that should be devoted to this purpose so that you can continue using the device for regular storage as well.

A system can benefit by having one to three times the amount of ReadyBoost storage as it has physical RAM. For example, if you have 1 GB of RAM in your system, a USB flash drive of 4 GB would be best allocated for 1 to 3 GB of storage for ReadyBoost and the remaining storage for regular file storage.

Note: *Not all USB flash drives work with ReadyBoost. Windows 8 determines whether yours is supported.*

Here's How

To expand memory with ReadyBoost:

1. Connect the USB flash drive.
2. If a message appears that prompts you to tap to choose what to do, tap that message box. If not, open the Computer window, right-click the USB flash drive, and then choose *Open AutoPlay*.

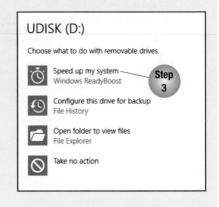

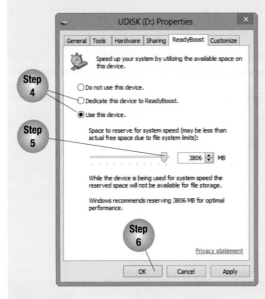

3. Click *Speed up my system Windows ReadyBoost*.
4. On the ReadyBoost tab, click *Dedicate this device to ReadyBoost*.
   OR
   Click *Use this device*.
5. If you chose *Use this device* in Step 4, drag the slider to specify the amount of disk space to allocate to ReadyBoost.
6. Click OK.

Configuring Power Settings ■■■■■■■■■■■■■■■■■

Many people leave their computers on most of the time to avoid spending time rebooting every time they want to use it. However, leaving a computer on consumes a significant amount of power. On a computer that is plugged in all of the time, this is merely a slight increase in the electric bill, but on a laptop computer running on batteries, full power-usage can quickly drain the battery and decrease the amount of time the computer can be used before needing to be recharged.

Creating a Power Plan

A power plan defines whether and how the system will partially shut itself down to save power after a specified period of inactivity. You can configure a computer in two ways to save power: turn off the display after a time, and put the computer to sleep after a certain amount of time.

When a computer sleeps, everything except RAM and the CPU is shut down to save power. When the user wakes up the computer, the system resumes quickly (compared to a full reboot) because Windows 8 is already in RAM and does not have to be reloaded. When the computer is running on batteries, eventually the battery does run down in this mode and the computer shuts off, but it takes a long time (up to several days) for that to happen.

The three default power plans predefined in Windows 8, as shown in Figure 12.6, include:

- **Balanced (recommended).** A balance of power savings versus performance.
- **Power saver.** Aggressive power savings at the expense of some performance.
- **High performance.** Consistently high performance at the expense of power savings.

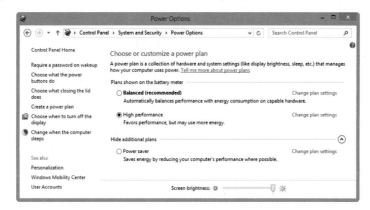

Figure 12.6 Windows 8 offers several power plan presets.

Depending on your computer, there may be one or more additional power plans available.

After selecting a plan, you can customize it by configuring advanced power settings. These power settings enable you to selectively set various pieces of hardware, such as the hard disk, wireless adapter, and so on, to turn off after a certain amount of time. These components do not use as much power as the monitor, so they save electricity less dramatically, but they do contribute to power usage.

To test your power settings, leave the computer idle for the amount of time specified in the power plan and then see what happens.

To select a power plan:

> **Here's How**

1. Open the Control Panel.
2. Click *System and Security*.
3. Click *Power Options*.
4. Click one of the power plans.

To customize a power plan (basic customization):

1. Open the Control Panel.
2. Click *System and Security*.
3. Click *Power Options*.
4. Click the *Change plan settings* link next to the power plan to customize.

Note: *Perform Steps 5–8 separately for* On battery *and* Plugged in *if you are on a laptop computer. On a desktop computer there is only one set of controls.*

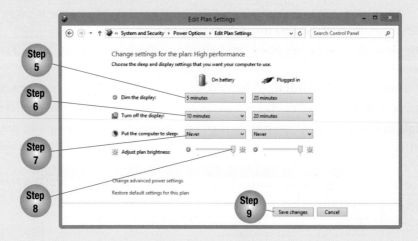

5. Open the *Dim the display* list and then select an amount of time (or choose *Never*).
6. Open the *Turn off the display* list and then select an amount of time (or choose *Never*).
7. Open the *Put the computer to sleep* list and then select an amount of time (or choose *Never*).
8. Drag the *Adjust plan brightness* slider to adjust the screen brightness level.
9. Click Save Changes if finished, or go on to the next section to do advanced customization.

To customize a power plan (advanced customization):

1. Perform all steps in "To customize a power plan (basic customization)" above.
2. Click the *Change advanced power settings* link.
3. In the Power Options dialog box, click the plus sign next to a category to expand it. Some categories may have subcategories and require clicking additional plus signs.
4. Change the setting(s) for the selected category as desired.
5. Repeat Steps 3–4, as needed.
6. Click OK.
7. Click Save Changes.

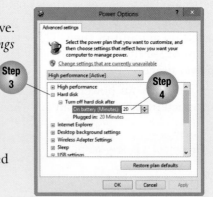

An even deeper Sleep mode called *Hibernate* uses no power at all and is useful when leaving a computer idle for longer periods of time. Hibernate is useful primarily for laptops running on batteries, and because there are sometimes incompatibilities between it and some systems, it is disabled by default. Hibernate copies the contents of RAM to a special region on the hard disk and then shuts down the computer. When you turn it back on, the data is copied back to RAM and the computer wakes up as if it were in Sleep mode.

Windows 8 also supports a mode called *Hybrid sleep*, which is a combination of sleep and hibernate. It is enabled, by default, on desktop systems, and disabled, by default, on laptops. Hybrid sleep saves the system state to the hard disk, just the way hibernate does, but, instead of shutting down, it puts the computer in Sleep mode afterward. That way, you can resume from Sleep mode quickly, but if something happens that causes the computer to shut down, your open files and settings are restored from hibernate.

You can enable hibernate and/or hybrid sleep from the Advanced Power Options under the *Sleep* category. Set the *Hibernate after* and/or *Allow hybrid sleep* settings to something other than *Never*.

Defining Power Buttons and Turning On Password Protection

As you saw in the preceding section, one way for sleep to be triggered is for the computer to sit idle for the amount of time specified in the power profile. Another way to trigger sleep is to configure the power button(s) to place the computer in Sleep or Hibernate mode.

Some computers have separate Sleep and Shut Down buttons; others have only a Power button. Sleep buttons are more common on notebook computers, but also can be found on some multifunction keyboards.

The Power button can be defined to trigger any of these states: Do Nothing, Shut Down, Sleep, or Hibernate. The Sleep button can be defined to trigger any of those except Shut Down.

When a computer wakes up from sleep or hibernate, anyone has full access to it unless you password-protect the wake-up. You can add some security to that by requiring the user's password to be reentered when the computer wakes up.

Note: *Password protection works only for user accounts that require a password to sign in to Windows 8 because the same password is used for wake-up.*

Here's How

To define power button settings and optionally require a password on wake-up:

1. Open the Control Panel.
2. Click *System and Security*.
3. Click *Power Options*.
4. Click *Require a password on wakeup* at the left side of the window.
5. Open the *When I press the power button* list and then select an action.
6. Open the *When I press the sleep button* list and then select an action.
7. Open the *When I close the lid* list and then select an action.
8. Click *Require a password (recommended)* or *Don't require a password*.
9. Click Save Changes.

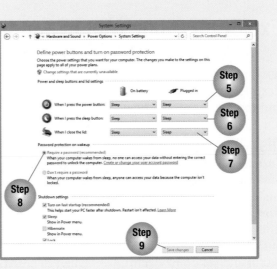

Quick Fix

Computer Goes into Hibernate Instead of Sleep
If your computer goes into Hibernate rather than Sleep mode, check the timing you have set for each mode. If the Sleep time is less than the Hibernate time, the computer switches from Sleep to Hibernate when the Hibernate time comes. Set the Hibernate time to less than Sleep time so that Hibernate is triggered first. The computer then remains in Hibernate and ignores the Sleep directive.

Quick Fix

Option to Require a Password Unavailable
If the *Require a password (recommended)* option button is unavailable, click the Change settings that are currently unavailable hyperlink near the top of the dialog box.

To reset a preferred plan to its default:

1. Click the *Change Plan Settings* link next to the power plan's name.
2. Click the *Restore default settings for this plan* link.
3. Click Yes.
4. Click Cancel.

Exercise 4

Managing Power Settings

1. Open the Power Options in the Control Panel.
2. Redefine the Power saver plan to the following basic settings:

   Note: *If you are using a laptop, make these changes for the On battery settings.*

   - Turn off the display in 3 minutes.
   - Put the computer to sleep in 5 minutes.
3. In the Advanced settings for the Power saver plan, under *USB settings*, set the *USB selective suspend setting* to Disabled when on battery power and then click OK.
4. Capture a screen shot of this window, save it as **C12E04**, and then submit it to your instructor.
5. Save the changes to the Power Saver plan.
6. Make sure the Power Saver plan is selected.
7. Wait three minutes to confirm that the display turns off.
8. Wait two more minutes to confirm that the computer goes into Sleep mode.
9. Press any key to wake up the computer.
10. Reset the Power Saver plan to its default settings.
11. Close all open windows.

Exploring Other Windows Administrative Tools ■■

The Windows 8 tools and features you have learned about so far in this chapter are all most users need to keep their systems running well. Windows 8 is a flexible operating system, though, and it includes many other powerful tools and features for large businesses, servers, and highly secure environments.

Disk Management

Disk Management is an administrative tool that provides information about the physical disks that are attached to your computer (shown in Figure 12.7) and enables you to set up new hard disks, change drive letters, and perform other storage configuration tasks. Most people do not often add or remove hard disks from their computers, so this utility is not for everyday use. People who manage business computers that hold large amounts of data use this feature to help them install and set up new hard disks when the existing disk drives get full. To change a drive's letter, right-click a drive and then choose *Change Drive Letter and Paths*. You also can format and partition drives, as well as view the contents of drives that are normally hidden from view in File Explorer, such as recovery partitions.

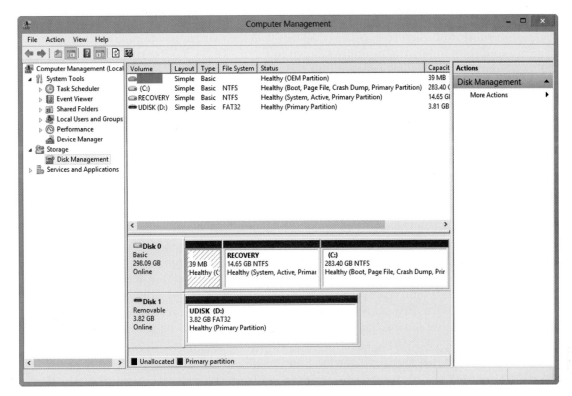

Figure 12.7 Disk Management shows the disks and their statuses.

Here's How

To browse disks with Disk Management:

1. Open the Control Panel.
2. Open the *View by* list and then click *Large icons* or *Small icons*.
3. Click Administrative Tools.
4. Double-click Computer Management.
5. Click Disk Management (under Storage in the left pane).

Storage Spaces

The Windows 8 Storage Spaces feature enables you to combine the storage space from multiple physical disk drives into a single pool of storage and segment that pool into whatever size chunks you like. Each chunk is assigned a drive letter and becomes a virtual drive. You can resize virtual drives on-the-fly and add more physical drives to increase the size of the pool as needed. You also can set up mirrored drives, in which two physical drives contain the same information at all times. Doing so provides extra data security because if one drive goes bad, the other one still has all of the data intact.

To access Storage Spaces, open the Control Panel (and change back to Category

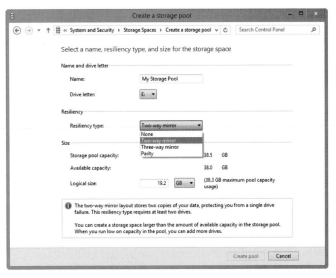

Figure 12.8 You can set up a storage pool with two or more physical drives.

view if you changed to some other view in the previous steps), click *System and Security*, and then click Storage Spaces. Click Create a new pool and storage space and then follow the prompts (shown in Figure 12.8). To use this feature, you must have at least two other physical drives in addition to your hard drive. The drives can be internal or external and can use any interface.

BitLocker Drive Encryption

Businesses that store sensitive data, such as important trade secrets or government data, must take every precaution to make sure that the data is not stolen. Data thieves use all kinds of sneaky, creative ways to operate, and one of these is to steal the physical hard disk of a computer. The computer itself may be locked down, but with a few turns of a screwdriver, the hard disk is out of there.

To prevent thieves from being able to read the data on a stolen hard disk, Windows 8 provides the BitLocker feature. BitLocker encrypts the entire hard disk so that it cannot be read when booted up in any computer other than the one for which it is authorized. The drawback of BitLocker is that it may make it more difficult for you to recover your files if there is a problem with your computer. When you use BitLocker, you are prompted to create a recovery key; this is a file that contains a "key" that allows the encrypted drive to be read.

To turn on BitLocker, open the Control Panel, click *System and Security*, and then click BitLocker Drive Encryption. Click the Turn on BitLocker hyperlink and follow the prompts to set it up. Before you do so, though, check with your company's IT department; when BitLocker is implemented, it is typically done so company-wide (or at least department-wide) rather than on an individual computer.

CHAPTER SUMMARY

- Windows Update works automatically to download and install the needed updates. You can configure it by way of the *System and Security* category of the Control Panel.
- Fonts are available throughout Windows 8, regardless of the program that originally supplied them. Many fonts are installed automatically with certain programs, such as Office.
- To install new fonts, drag and drop fonts to the Fonts folder or right-click a font file and then choose *Install*.
- To save hard disk space, Disk Cleanup partially automates the process of selecting and deleting files that you no longer need. Run it from the disk drive's Properties box, on the General tab.
- Defragmenting a disk rearranges file storage so that files can be accessed more quickly. It is done automatically at regular intervals. You also can manually initiate it from the drive's Properties box on the Tools tab.
- ReadyBoost enables you to connect a USB flash drive and then use part of it to boost system performance by providing an extra memory cache. When you insert the flash drive, the AutoPlay box presents ReadyBoost as one of the play options.

- Power plans define the power management settings for Windows 8. There are three default plans: Balanced, Power saver, and High Performance. Each of these can be fully customized.
- To set power options, open the Control Panel, go to *System and Security,* and then choose *Power Options*.
- Use Disk Management (via Computer Management) to partition and format disk drives and change drive letters.
- Storage pools, new in Windows 8, enable you to combine multiple physical storage devices into a single logical drive letter.

CONCEPTS CHECK

Completion: Answer the following questions in a Word document.

Part 1

Multiple Choice

1. What is the default setting for Windows Update?
   a. Do nothing
   b. Notify of updates but do not automatically download or install
   c. Download updates but do not automatically install
   d. Automatically install and download updates

2. What are the three levels of priority that a Windows 8 update can have?
   a. Important, Recommended, and Optional
   b. Critical, Important, and Recommended
   c. Important, Standard, and Extra
   d. High, Medium, and Low

3. From which screen do you remove Windows 8 updates?
   a. Uninstall Programs
   b. Installed Updates
   c. Device Manager
   d. Appearance and Personalization

4. To prevent a font from showing up in applications, but still leave it installed on your system, _____ it.
   a. mask
   b. hide
   c. restore
   d. clip

5. Where in the Control Panel is the Fonts folder located?
   a. System
   b. Appearance and Personalization
   c. Security
   d. Users

6. Which of these does Disk Cleanup do?
    a. Deletes unused icons from the desktop
    b. Deletes unneeded files from the hard disk
    c. Defragments the disk
    d. Repairs disk errors

7. Why is fragmentation a problem on a disk?
    a. Results in disk errors
    b. Makes the CPU run slower
    c. Degrades disk access time
    d. Clutters up desktop with unwanted icons

8. What do power plans control?
    a. Voltage generated by power supply
    b. Idle time before parts of the computer go into low power-usage mode
    c. Speed of the CD-ROM drive
    d. All of the above

9. Which two things can you specify for a preferred power plan without opening the advanced settings?
    a. Turning off monitor and putting computer to sleep
    b. Turning off monitor and turning off hard disk
    c. Putting the computer to sleep and putting the computer in Hibernate mode
    d. Putting the computer to sleep and turning off the monitor

10. Which password should be entered on wake-up?
    a. Administrator password
    b. User password for the signed-in user
    c. A separate screen saver password you specify
    d. None of the above

Part 2

Short Answer

11. What is the purpose of BitLocker encryption?

_____

12. What power-saving mode is a combination of Sleep and Hibernate modes?

_____

13. Why would you set up a power plan for a desktop computer, even though it never needs to run on batteries?

_____

14. List one benefit of using Storage Spaces.

_____

15. Why would someone want to *not* have Windows Update always download and install updates automatically?

_____

16. Explain the difference between a soft font and a printer-resident font.

_____

17. What does the ReadyBoost feature do?

_____

18. Why would you want to hide certain fonts from your applications?

_____

19. List four types of files that Disk Cleanup can remove.

_____

20. How does defragmenting improve system performance?

_____

SKILLS CHECK

Save all solution files to the default Documents folder or any alternative folder specified by your instructor.

Guided Check

Assessment 1

Removing and Reinstalling a Windows Update

1. On a blank sheet of paper, write your name and today's date.
2. Set Windows Update to not check for any updates automatically.
   a. Open the Control Panel and select *System and Security, Windows Update*.
   b. Click Change settings.
   c. Under *Important Updates*, choose *Never check for updates (not recommended)*.
   d. Click OK.
3. Remove one of the Windows 8 updates that has already installed and then write on your sheet of paper which one you removed.
   a. Click Installed Updates.
   b. Click an update to uninstall. Make sure you choose one for which an Uninstall button appears.
   c. Write down the name of the update on your paper.
   d. Click Uninstall, or double-click the update.
   e. If prompted to confirm, click Yes.
4. Check for and then install updates.
   a. Click the Back button to return to the main Windows Update window.
   b. Click Check for Updates.
   c. Click Install Updates.
5. Display your update history.
   • Click View Update History.
6. Capture a screen shot of this window and then save it as **C12A01**.
7. Turn on automatic updates.
   a. Click the Back button and then click Change Settings.
   b. Click *Install updates automatically (recommended)*.
   c. Click OK.
8. Submit the screen shot to your instructor.
9. Close all open windows.

Maintaining Your System

423

Installing a New Font

1. Check to see whether the font Tuffy is installed on your computer. If it is, remove it. If it is not installed, go on to Step 2.
   a. Open the Control Panel and then choose *Appearance and Personalization*, Fonts.
   b. Look for all font names that begin with "Tuffy" in the font list. If any appear, select them, press Delete, and then click Yes to confirm.

   Note: *To more easily browse for the Tuffy font, view the list in Details view and then sort by the* Name *column.*

2. Install the Tuffy font from the Chapter 12 Student Data Files folder.
   a. Open the Chapter 12 folder.
   b. Open the Fonts window.
   c. Drag and drop all four variations of the Tuffy font to the Fonts window.
3. From the Fonts window, refresh the display and then display a sample of Tuffy Medium Italic.
4. Capture a screen shot of this window and then save it as **C12A02**.
5. Close all remaining open windows.
6. Submit the screen shot to your instructor.

Improving System Performance

1. Run a Disk Cleanup operation on the C drive, cleaning up as much as possible.
   a. From the Computer window, right-click the C drive and then choose *Properties*.
   b. On the General tab, click Disk Cleanup.
   c. Mark the check boxes for all categories except *Office Setup files* (if present).
   d. Click OK.
2. Defragment all internal hard disks.
   a. From the Computer window, right-click the C drive and then choose *Properties*.
   b. On the Tools tab, click Optimize.
3. Set the defragmentation scheduling to once a month.
   a. Click Change settings.
   b. Open the *Frequency* list and then click *Monthly*.
   d. Capture a screen shot of this window and then save it as **C12A03**.
   e. Click OK.
4. Click Optimize and then close all remaining open windows. The defragmentation will continue in the background.
5. Submit the screen shot to your instructor.

Controlling Power Settings

1. Open the Power Options. (Open the Control Panel and choose *System and Security, Power Options*.)
2. Redefine the High Performance power plan to turn off the display after one hour.
   a. If necessary, click Show additional plans and then click *Change plan settings* at the right of *High performance*.
   b. Open the *Turn off the display* list and then choose *1 hour*.

   Note: *If working on a laptop, change the settings under* Plugged in *for this assessment.*

3. Customize the High Performance power plan to never turn off hard disks.
   a. Click *Change advanced power settings*.
   b. Click the plus sign next to *Hard disk*.
   c. Click the plus sign next to *Turn off hard disk after*.
   d. Change the setting value to *Never*. (Type the word Never in the box.)

   Note: *In Step 3d, working on a laptop, change the setting next to* Plugged in.

   e. Capture a screen shot of this window and then save it as **C12A04**.
   f. Click OK.
   g. Click Save Changes.
4. Submit the screen shot to your instructor.
5. Close the Power Options window.

On Your Own

Assessment 5

Changing a Drive Letter with Disk Management
1. Open Disk Management (*Administrative Tools, Computer Management, Disk Management*).
2. Connect a USB flash drive to the computer and then note the change to Disk management's list of drives. Note the drive letter assigned to it. Close the Removable Disk Properties dialog box if it pops up.
3. In the lower pane, right-click the area representing that drive letter and then click *Change Drive Letter and Paths*.
4. Click the Change button.
5. Change the drive letter to Q: and then click OK. Click yes to confirm.
6. Capture a screen shot of this window and then save it as **C12A05**.
7. Submit the screen shot to your instructor.
8. Change the drive letter back to its original letter and then close Disk Management.

Assessment 6

Exploring Other Sources of Fonts
1. Open a web browser window and then perform a web search for public domain fonts.
2. From a website that offers free public domain fonts, find a font that interests you.
3. Download that font and then install it on your computer.
4. Open a Word document and type your name and today's date in the new font. Save the file as **C12A06** and then submit it to your instructor.

Assessment 7

Exploring Disk Cleanup
1. Open a Word document and save it as **C12A07**. Record the information you gather in the following steps.
2. Open the Properties box for the C drive and note how much available space it reports that you have.
3. Start a Disk Cleanup operation, and choose to clean up only your own files. Mark all of the check boxes and then note how much space it reports that you will gain.
4. Run the Disk Cleanup operation.

5. Open the Properties box for the C drive and note how much available space you have.
6. Based on this experiment, write a paragraph explaining how the estimate of the amount of space in Step 3 was or was not accurate compared to the amount of space actually freed up. Submit the file to your instructor.

CHALLENGE PROJECT

Suppose you are in charge of writing the policies for the regular maintenance that should be done on all of the computers in your school. Which utilities should be run, and how often? Create a policy instructing users what to do and then write a paragraph explaining why you made the decisions you did. Save the paragraph as **C12A08** and then submit it to your instructor.

Adding Software and Hardware

PERFORMANCE OBJECTIVES

Upon successful completion of Chapter 13, you will be able to:

- Install a program
- Set default programs
- Control program startup
- Remove a program

- Install a program update
- Add a printer
- Work with hardware
- Configure a second monitor

To extend your computer's capabilities, you can install new software and hardware. New software enables you to perform different tasks with the computer, and new hardware makes the computer run better or faster or gives it additional storage or input/output functionality.

Installing and Removing Software ▪▪▪▪▪▪▪▪▪▪▪ ▪

Windows 8 comes with a few handy programs that you can use for basic operations, such as writing a letter with WordPad, adding numbers with Calculator, and drawing pictures with Paint. However, for most business tasks (and many personal ones as well), you will want to buy and install additional software.

New computers sometimes come with extra software in addition to the default applications that come with Windows 8. Some of this software might be useful, but not all of it is helpful for every user's situation; you will likely want to remove some of the preinstalled software to free up disk space. You might sometimes also want to remove software you have installed (for example, if you need to install a new version and the manufacturer recommends uninstalling old versions first, or if you decide you do not like the program and want to get rid of it).

As you learned in Chapter 5, there are two types of applications in Windows 8: the traditional desktop applications that have been a staple of Windows for many versions now, and the newer Windows 8 apps. Each type has a different process for installation and removal. The following sections explain how to install and remove both types.

Installing Software

Almost all programs have a setup utility that automates the installation and performs three functions:

■ Copies the needed files to your hard disk. In most cases, you do not need to have the program's CD inserted in the computer to use the program after it has been installed. However, some games do continue to require the CD, either because of the large size of its video clips or to prevent unauthorized duplication or sharing.

■ Makes needed changes to the Windows *registry*. The registry is a configuration database in which system settings are stored—everything from display settings to information about installed hardware and software.

■ Adds a shortcut to the Start screen. Depending on the program, it might also place a shortcut to the application on the Taskbar and/or the desktop.

When you buy software on a CD or DVD, the setup utility and all of the files to be copied to the hard disk are contained on the disc. The disc also typically contains an *Autorun.inf* file that tells Windows how to start the setup utility automatically when the disc is inserted. When you insert the CD or DVD, an AutoPlay box might appear, as shown in Figure 13.1. Click Run setup.exe (or whatever the name of the file is) to start the setup program. Follow the prompts that appear on the screen.

When you download a desktop application, it usually comes packaged in a single executable file that contains the setup program plus all of the files to be installed. When you run that file, the setup program unpacks and installs the needed files.

A setup program might ask if you want a Typical or Advanced installation. A typical installation uses a default location to store the files and installs a default set of options and settings. An advanced installation enables you to fine-tune the installation. In most cases, the default location is the best choice.

The most common way to acquire a Windows 8 app is to download it from the Windows Store. Some of the apps in the Windows Store are free; others you must pay for. Click the Windows Store tile on the Start screen, browse for and select the app you want, and then follow the prompts to download and install it, as shown in Figure 13.2. As the app downloads and installs, a message appears in the upper right corner of the Store app screen letting you know the status. When it finishes, a system sound plays, and the message closes.

Figure 13.1
By default, Windows prompts for an action when you insert a disc.

Figure 13.2 One of the Windows 8 apps available for download from the Windows Store.

To install a Windows 8 app:

1. From the Start screen, click Store.
2. Click the category to browse.
3. Click the app to install.
4. Click the Install button.

Here's How

Step 1

Adding a Program to the Start Screen or Taskbar

Some programs, such as some free ones you download from the Web, are simple, consisting of a single executable file. Because such programs do not need to change the registry or copy any files to your hard disk, they do not require a setup utility. Therefore, if you want a shortcut to such a program to appear on the Start screen or Taskbar, you must create it manually.

 TIP You can use this procedure to create a shortcut to any file on the Start screen or the Taskbar, not only for an executable program file. You might create a shortcut to a folder or a data file, for example.

To create a Start screen shortcut:

1. Open a File Explorer window and then navigate to the folder containing the executable file of the program.
2. Right-click the executable file.
3. Click *Pin to Start*.

Here's How

Step 3

Adding Software and Hardware

To create a Taskbar shortcut:

1. Open a File Explorer window and then navigate to the folder containing the executable file of the program.
2. Right-click the executable file.
3. Click *Pin to taskbar*.

Removing a Program

When you remove a program, Windows 8 does the following:

■ Removes references to that program from the registry

■ Deletes the program's files from the hard disk

■ Removes shortcuts to the program from the Start screen, Taskbar, and/or desktop

Windows knows how to do these things because most applications come with an uninstall file that provides advice about its removal. Windows reads that information and performs the steps that the uninstall file recommends.

Note: *In some cases an uninstall operation is performed imperfectly, either because the uninstall file's instructions are not clear or because Windows is unable to perform some of the functions because of security limitations or files being in use. After a program has been uninstalled, you might notice that a folder for it still exists on the hard disk, for example, or a shortcut to it (non-working) still appears on the desktop. You can delete such remnants manually, as you would delete any folder, file, or shortcut.*

You can access the uninstall information for all installed desktop-style programs via the Control Panel in Windows 8. From the Control Panel, under the *Programs* category, click Uninstall a program to see the list of installed programs that are eligible for removal. Figure 13.3 shows an example list, but your list will be different.

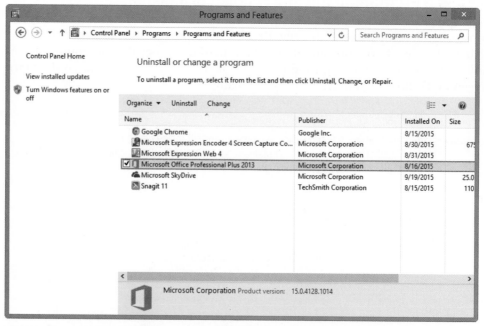

Figure 13.3 Windows 8 recognizes these programs as being installed. You can uninstall one by selecting it and then clicking Uninstall.

Different programs uninstall differently. Some have separate utilities for uninstalling and for changing the installation, for example. In Figure 13.3, the selected application, Microsoft Office Professional Plus 2013, has separate buttons. Other applications have a single utility (and a single button) for changing and for uninstalling.

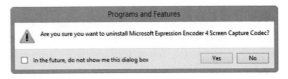

Figure 13.4 After selecting a program to uninstall and then clicking Uninstall, you are prompted to confirm.

Once you click the Uninstall button (or Uninstall/Change button), the uninstall instructions provided for that program launch an uninstall process that varies greatly among applications. Some involve only Yes/No prompts, as shown in Figure 13.4, with no user interaction required. In other cases, you must specify options for the uninstall process, such as whether to keep your configuration files for the program.

To uninstall a Windows 8 app, right-click the item on the Start screen and then click Uninstall.

Here's How

To uninstall a desktop application:

1. Open the Control Panel.
2. Under *Programs*, click Uninstall a program.
3. Click the program to uninstall.
4. Click the Uninstall button or the Uninstall/Change button, whichever appears.
5. Follow the prompts to uninstall the program.

To uninstall a Windows 8 app:

1. Open the Start screen.
2. Right-click the app to uninstall.
3. Click Uninstall.
4. Click Uninstall.

Quick Fix

Incomplete Uninstall
If the uninstall is not "clean," meaning there are some orphaned files and folders left on your hard disk after the uninstall, browse to the Program Files folder and then delete them. However, they are probably taking up little space and will not be harmful if left on your hard disk.

Exercise 1

Installing and Removing a Program

1. Open the folder containing the data files for this chapter, and then double-click *PureSudokuSetup.exe*.
2. If you see a User Account Control warning, click Yes.
3. Click Next.
4. Click I accept the agreement.
5. Click Next four times to move through the Install Wizard.
6. Click Install.
7. Click Finish.
8. Capture a screen shot of the Pure Sudoku application window that appears and then save the file as **C13E01S08**.
9. Close the Pure Sudoku application window. Leave the Sudoku application installed so that you can use it in Exercise 2.

10. Open the Start screen and then click Store.
11. Click the Top free tile.
12. Click a tile for one of the free apps.
13. Click Install.
14. After the app has installed, run the app and then capture a screen shot of it. Save it as **C13E01S14** and then submit both screen shots to your instructor.
15. Close the app.
16. On the Start screen, right-click the app and then click Uninstall.
17. Click Uninstall to confirm.

Quick Fix

No Store Tile
If the Store tile does not appear on the Start screen, type **Store**. When the Store icon appears, click it.

Using Compatibility Mode ■■■■■■■■■■■■■■■■■■■■■

Some older programs designed for previous versions of Windows do not install correctly and/or do not run correctly under Windows 8 using default settings. Such programs sometimes can be tricked into running by employing the Windows 8 Compatibility mode. You can use it on a setup utility and also on the executable that runs the program.

Windows 8 provides an easy way to assess a program's compatibility needs. Right-click the executable file for the program and then click *Troubleshoot compatibility*. A step-by-step troubleshooting process walks you through the steps needed. You also can manually configure compatibility settings by right-clicking the executable, choosing *Properties*, and then making compatibility settings changes on the Compatibility tab.

Compatibility mode in Windows 8 can emulate any of the following: Windows 95, Windows 98/Me, Windows XP, Windows Vista, or Windows 7. For XP and Vista, there are also separate settings for different service packs. Choose the highest-level service pack if you are not sure which to pick.

To set up Compatibility mode, you must be able to access either the executable file for the program in question or a shortcut to that executable.

Note: *Because running a setup program in Compatibility mode does not automatically set up the application itself to run in Compatibility mode, you must configure the application's executable file separately after the setup has completed.*

Here's How ▶

To open the folder where an executable file is stored:

1. On the Start screen, right-click and then choose All apps.
2. Right-click the desired application, and then click Open file location.

Step 2

Note: *The location that opens in Step 2 contains a shortcut to the executable, not the executable itself. (Step 4 opens the location of the executable.) However, you can set Compatibility mode for a shortcut if you like, rather than setting it for the original executable. If you do so, the program runs in Compatibility mode only when it is started from that shortcut.*

3. In File Explorer, right-click the shortcut to the application and then choose *Properties*.
4. Click Open File Location. The location containing the executable opens.

To automatically configure compatibility settings:

1. Open File Explorer and then navigate to the folder containing the executable file for which to set compatibility, as in the preceding steps.
2. Right-click the executable file and then click Troubleshoot compatibility.
3. Click Try recommended settings.
4. Click Test the program. If a User Access Control warning appears, click Yes.

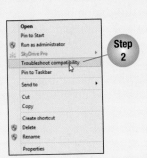

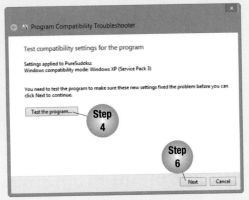

5. When the program opens, check it to make sure it is working correctly, then close it.
6. Click Next.
7. If the program worked, click Yes, save these settings for this program. Or, if the program did not work, click No, try again using different settings, and then follow the prompts.
8. When finished troubleshooting, click Close.

To manually configure compatibility settings:

1. Right-click the executable file and then click *Properties*.
2. Click the Compatibility tab.
3. Mark the *Run this program in compatibility mode for* check box if not already marked.
4. Open the drop-down list below the check box and then select the Windows version desired.
5. (Optional) Change any additional settings in the *Settings* section to further enhance compatibility.
6. Click OK.

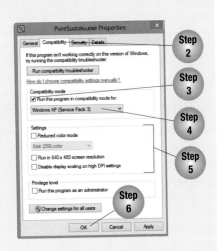

Adding Software and Hardware

Troubleshooting and Removing a Desktop App

1. Open File Explorer and then navigate to C:\Program Files\Pure Sudoku. This program was installed in Exercise 1.
2. Right-click *PureSudoku.exe* and then click *Troubleshoot compatibility*.
3. Click Try recommended settings.
4. Click Test the program. If a User Account Control window appears, click Yes.
5. When the program runs, close the program.
6. In the Program Compatibility Troubleshooter window, click Next.
7. Click Yes, save these settings for this program.
8. Click Close the troubleshooter.
9. Right-click *PureSudoku.exe* and then click *Properties*.
10. Click the Compatibility tab.
11. Capture a screen shot of the *PureSudoku.exe* Properties box, save the file as **C13E02**, and then submit it to your instructor. Close the PureSudoka Properties dialog box.
12. Open the Control Panel and then click Uninstall a program under Programs.
13. Click *Pure Sudoku 1.52*.
14. Click Uninstall and then click Yes.
15. Click OK.

▼ **Quick Fix**

Missing Folder
In Step 1, if the Pure Sudoku folder is not in C:\Program Files, look in C:\Program Files (x86).

Setting Default Programs ■■■■■■■■■■■■■■■■■■■■■■

Some tasks can be performed using your choice of programs. For example, you can open a hyperlink in any web browser you like, such as Internet Explorer, Chrome, or Opera, and you can play music files in Windows Media Player or in a third-party music application such as iTunes.

A file's extension indicates its type. For example, a .txt extension indicates a text file. Windows assigns each extension to an application; that application takes ownership of all files of that type so that when you double-click the file to open it, it opens in that application. By default, Notepad is the application associated with .txt files, so any .txt files you open appear in Notepad.

As you become proficient with your computer, you may develop preferences for one application over another. For example, you may prefer the Chrome browser and want any selected hyperlinks to open in that program rather than Internet Explorer.

There are two ways to examine and change the assignments of extensions to applications:

- You can browse a list of programs and tell a program that it should "own" (that is, be the default program for) all of the file types it supports, or you can tell it precisely which file types to own.

- You can browse a list of file extensions and then change the programs that are assigned to one or more of them.

To choose a program as the default for all file types it supports:

1. Open the Control Panel.
2. Click *Programs*.
3. Under Default Programs, click Set your default programs.
4. Click a program. Information about it appears.
5. Click Set this program as default.
6. Click OK.
7. Close the Control Panel window.

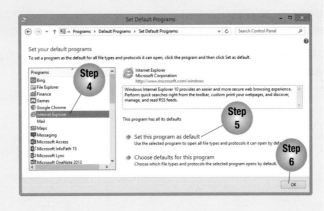

To choose a program as the default for individual file types it supports:

1. Open the Control Panel.
2. Click *Programs*.
3. Under Default Programs, click Set your default programs.
4. Click a program. Information about it appears.
5. Click Choose defaults for this program. A list of file types supported by this program appears.
6. Mark or clear the check boxes for the available file types.
7. Click Save.
8. Close the Control Panel window.

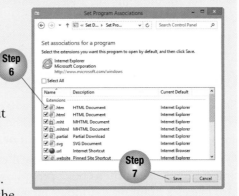

To set a file type to always open in a specific program:

1. Open the Control Panel.
2. Click Programs.
3. Under Default Programs, click Make a file type always open in a specific program.
4. Select a file extension.
5. Click Change program. A list of the installed programs that can handle this file type appears.
6. Click the program you want to use for this file type.
7. Click Close.
8. Close the Control Panel window.

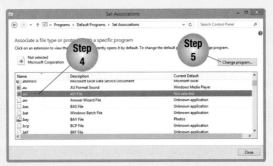

Changing the Default Program for a File Type

1. Click Start and then click Control Panel.
2. Click *Programs*.
3. Under Default Programs, click Make a file type always open in a specific program.
4. Select the .bmp file type.
5. Click Change program. Note the current default for that file type; at the top of the list, the default will begin with "Keep using...". It may be Photos, for example. (Photos is the Windows 8 app for photo viewing.)
6. Click Paint.
7. Click Close.
8. Navigate to the folder containing the data files for this chapter and then double-click **bowl.bmp**. The image opens in Paint.
9. Capture a screen shot of the Paint window with the **bowl.bmp** file open. Save it as **C13E03** and then submit it to your instructor.
10. Change the default for the .bmp file type back to the setting you noted in Step 5.
11. Close all open windows.

Controlling Automatic Program Startup ■■■■■■■■

Some programs start automatically when Windows starts. Such programs usually control a hardware device or keep some useful service running in the background, such as an updater for an application or an instant message delivery system.

Having programs load automatically at startup has both advantages and drawbacks. It is handy to have programs that you frequently use preloaded, but it also places a drain on Windows memory resources to have many programs loaded that are not actively being used. In addition, the more programs that load at startup, the longer it takes Windows to start.

Setting Up a Program to Start Automatically

You can set up a program to load automatically at Windows 8 startup by placing a shortcut for it in the Startup folder. Each user has his or her own folder located at C:\Users*username*\AppData\Roaming\Microsoft\Windows\Start Menu\Programs\Startup, where *username* is the user account name.

Note: *The AppData folder is hidden by default. If you do not see it, click the View tab and then mark the* Hidden Items *check box.*

To place a shortcut in the Startup folder, first create the shortcut. You can do this by pressing the Alt key and then dragging the executable file from any Explorer window to the desktop. Alternatively, if there is already a shortcut for that program elsewhere (such as on the desktop or pinned to the Taskbar), you can press the Ctrl key and then drag the shortcut to create a copy of it. Open File Explorer, navigate to the above-listed location, and then drag the shortcut to the Startup folder.

Here's How

To set a program to start automatically at Windows 8 startup:

1. Create a shortcut to the program on the desktop.
2. Open File Explorer and then navigate to C:\Users*username*\AppData\Roaming\Microsoft\Windows\Start Menu\Programs\Startup, where *username* is the user account name.
3. Drag the shortcut from the desktop to the Startup folder.

T I P You may notice that other programs load at startup automatically, in addition to those that have shortcuts in the Startup folder. Most programs that set themselves up for automatic startup do so by creating registry entries for themselves that trigger the loading. End users should not attempt to set up such registry entries themselves; the Startup folder method works fine and is much safer.

Preventing a Program from Starting Automatically

Some programs set themselves up to load automatically at startup when you install them. Sometimes this is necessary, or at least highly recommended, for the optimal performance of the software or its related device. For example, antivirus software should always be loaded automatically at startup to prevent against virus infection, and if you need certain activities to happen when the computer is unattended, such as fax receiving, the controller for those activities should be loaded. Other times, it is a waste of the computer's memory to keep software, such as an instant messaging program that you seldom use, loaded at all times.

You can prevent a program from loading automatically at startup in several ways. Depending on the situation, one of the easy methods might work, or you might have to resort to something more drastic.

First, check the Startup folder for a shortcut to that program (located at C:\Users*username*\AppData\Roaming\Microsoft\Windows\Start Menu\Programs\Startup, where *username* is the user account name). You worked with this folder in the previous section. If you find such a shortcut there, delete it (by right-clicking it and then choosing *Delete*).

If you do not find the shortcut in the Startup folder, next try looking in the program itself to see if there is a setting that controls the program's startup. If there is, turn that setting off; the program then makes the needed change to the registry automatically. For example, in Figure 13.5, notice that you can configure Yahoo! Messenger to load automatically at startup via the check box at the top of the window.

If neither of those methods works, you can use the Task Manager to disable the automatic startup. This utility's Startup tab lists most of the applications that load at startup, and you can selectively enable or disable each one. This method does not remove the entries from the registry; it only disables them.

You can set this program to load at startup.

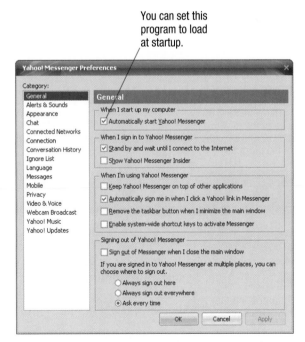

Figure 13.5 Some programs have a setting you can adjust that controls whether it loads at startup.

To prevent a program from loading at startup using the Task Manager:

1. From the desktop, right-click the Taskbar and then click *Task Manager*.
2. Click the Startup tab. If you do not see any tabs, click More details.
3. Click the entry you want to disable.
4. Click the Disable button.
5. Close the Task Manager window.

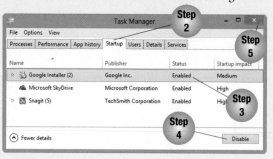

Exercise 4

Enabling and Disabling Automatic Startup

1. Create a shortcut on the desktop to the Calculator program:
   a. Open File Explorer and then navigate to C:\Windows\System32.
   b. Hold down Alt and drag **calc.exe** to the desktop.
2. Place the Calculator shortcut you created in the Startup folder:
   a. Navigate to C:\Users*username*\AppData\Roaming\Microsoft\Windows\Start Menu\Programs\Startup, where *username* is the user account name.
   b. Drag the shortcut to the Startup folder.
3. Capture a screen shot of the open Startup folder showing the Calculator shortcut, save the file as **C13E04**, and then submit it to your instructor.
4. Restart the computer and then confirm that Calculator starts automatically. You will have to display the desktop to confirm this.
5. Open File Explorer and then delete the Calculator shortcut from the Startup folder.
6. Restart the computer and then confirm that Calculator does not load.

Installing a Program Update ■■■■■■■■■■■■■■■■■■

patch A program update intended to fix a problem with the original version of the program

Manufacturers release updates for programs periodically to fix problems and to enhance capabilities. When an update is intended primarily to fix a problem, it is known as a ***patch***.

The process for acquiring updates for a program depends on the program and its manufacturer. Windows Update takes care of updating some Microsoft programs automatically, such as Microsoft Office. (See "Using Windows Update to Keep Windows 8 Current" in Chapter 12.)

Figure 13.6
A number on the Store tile indicates available updates for Windows 8 apps.

Windows 8 apps receive updates from the Windows Store. On the Store tile on the Start screen, you may see a number in the lower right corner, which indicates the number of updates that are available for your installed applications. To install any available updates, click the Store tile and then click the Updates hyperlink in the upper right corner of the Windows Store screen.

Some programs provide shortcuts to the company's website and to updates via a Help menu or the program's properties or options.

If none of the preceding options is available, you might want to check the manufacturer's website manually, using your web browser to search for downloads and updates. The company's website information is probably available on the box that the program came in, or in its documentation, or you can find it by doing a quick web search on the company's name.

Adding and Removing a Printer ▪▪▪▪▪▪▪▪▪▪▪▪▪

One of the most common pieces of hardware to add to a system is a printer. Printers enable you to generate hard-copy printouts of your work. Printers come in many varieties, including laser and inkjet. Some printers are *multifunction devices (MFD)*, which combine the features of a printer with that of a scanner, copier, and, in some cases, fax machine.

Most printers today use a USB interface, so they can easily be connected and disconnected at any time. USB devices are *hot-pluggable*, meaning you do not have to wait until the computer is turned off to connect or disconnect them. USB printers also fully support the *Plug and Play (PnP)* device-support standard. Windows therefore recognizes them automatically and either installs a driver or prompts you for a driver location. Given a compatible device and system BIOS and a compatible Windows version (Windows 95 and higher), Plug and Play allows a computer to see and configure a device without having to manually tell Windows what resources to assign to the device.

Note: *Some old printers use a parallel interface, also known as an LPT port. LPT stands for Line Printer. This type of interface consists of a 25-pin plug at the computer end and a 36-pin Centronics plug at the printer end. This interface is not hot-pluggable; you should connect this type of printer only when the computer's power is turned off. Printers connected via this interface might automatically be detected in Windows 8, or you might need to run the setup software that comes with the printer.*

Adding a New Printer

When you add a printer to Windows 8, you are adding a printer driver, not the printer itself. A driver is software that acts as a translator between a hardware device and Windows. You can have more than one driver installed for the same printer, each configured with different settings, and thereby make the printer behave differently depending on which driver you print with. For example, if a printer is able to print using two different modes, you could have a driver set up for each mode. Windows 8 calls printer drivers "printers," but keep in mind that this term refers to the driver, not the printer hardware.

The best procedure for setting up a printer in Windows depends on whether you have a setup disc for that printer. If a setup disc is available, you should use it. During the setup, you are prompted to turn on and connect your USB printer to the system. Most printers come with print management software that must be installed in Windows 8 to use the printer's full capabilities. If you allow Plug and Play to detect the printer, it installs a minimal set of drivers for the printer and sometimes does not install the extra software.

If you have a driver disc for the printer but it does not contain a setup program, connect the printer to the computer via USB interface and then allow Windows 8 to prompt you for the driver disc.

multifunction device (MFD) A printer that also has other functions, such as scanner, copier, and fax machine

hot-pluggable Able to be connected or disconnected while the computer is up and running

Plug and Play (PnP) A standard that enables Windows to recognize and configure hardware automatically

T I P Most printer manufacturers maintain a library of drivers for various models and operating systems on their websites, free for downloading.

If you do not have any type of driver for the printer, try connecting the printer anyway; Windows 8 comes with a small collection of printer drivers, and if your printer happens to be one of the included models, Windows 8 can set it up for basic printing functionality.

T I P Multifunction devices might work as printers without any setup software, but to enable the extra functions, such as copying, you need to install the software designed specifically for the device. You may be able to download it from the manufacturer's website if you do not have the disc.

local printer A printer attached directly to your computer

network printer A printer attached to your network or shared by another computer on your network

Bluetooth A type of short-range, wireless interface designed to allow computers and devices to communicate without cables

You can set up either a local or a network printer. A ***local printer*** is one that is attached directly to your computer. A ***network printer*** is one that is attached to your network (wired or wireless) or shared by another computer on your network. You also can set up a Bluetooth printer, provided both the computer and the printer have compatible Bluetooth interfaces. ***Bluetooth*** is a type of short-range wireless interface designed to allow computers and devices to communicate without cables.

To set up a new printer that Windows does not automatically detect, open the *Devices and Printers* section in the Control Panel and then click the Add devices and printers button to run a utility that sets up any new printers it finds. If that utility cannot see the new printer, click Cancel and then try the Advanced printer setup utility.

Here's How

To set up a printer:

1. Open the Control Panel.
2. Under *Hardware and Sound*, click View devices and printers.
3. Click Add a printer.
4. Wait for the utility to locate the printer. If it does, click it and then click Next, and continue to step 5.
   If the utility does not find your printer, click Stop and then click The printer that I want isn't listed.

5. If the utility finds the printer, click it and then click Next.

6. If prompted for the driver, select the printer manufacturer and model, or click Have Disk, browse for the driver, and then click Next.

7. Type a name for the printer, or accept the default name, and then click Next.

8. At the Printer Sharing screen, choose one of the following:
   - Do not share this printer
   - Share this printer so that others on your network can find and use it. Then change the share name, location, and/or comment, if you want.

9. Click Next.

10. Mark or clear the *Set as the default printer* check box as desired.

11. (Optional) Click Print a test page.

12. Click Finish.

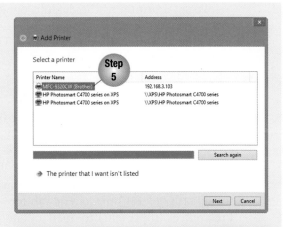

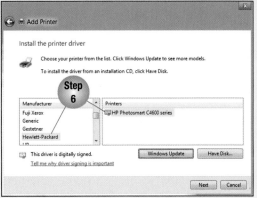

Quick Fix

Printer Not Found
If the utility cannot find the printer using Advanced printer setup, the printer is probably not connected to the computer correctly or the printer is not turned on. Or, if it is a network printer, perhaps the network is down or the printer has not successfully joined the network.

 T I P You can install a printer driver for a printer that you do not have, and you can even assign it to a port that does not exist on your computer. Although Windows 8 sees it as a valid printer, it does not produce output when you try to print to it. In situations where you need to set up someone's computer, but you do not have his or her printer physically present, this is a useful feature. You can install the printer's driver and prepare the system for it and then connect the printer later. You will practice doing that in Exercise 5.

Choosing the Default Printer

When you set up a printer, as in the preceding section, you can specify whether the printer should be the default one. (Only one printer at a time can be the default, so if you choose a new one as the default, the previous setting is cleared.) You can manually specify a different default printer at any time.

 Quick Fix

Wrong Dialog Box
If you see only two tabs, General and Hardware, you have opened the wrong dialog box. Right-click the printer's icon and then choose *Printer Properties* (not Properties).

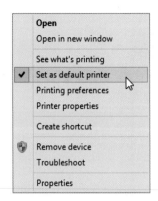

Open
Open in new window
See what's printing
✓ Set as default printer
Printing preferences
Printer properties
Create shortcut
Remove device
Troubleshoot
Properties

Figure 13.7 Choose the default printer by right-clicking a printer and then clicking *Set as default printer*.

To set a printer as the default, open the Devices and Printers window (from the Control Panel), right-click the printer, and then choose *Set as default printer* (shown in Figure 13.7). The current default printer appears with a green circle and check mark.

Working with Printer Settings

Each printer has its own Printer Properties box, which you can access by right-clicking its icon and then clicking *Printer Properties*. The tabs and settings in the Properties dialog box vary depending on the printer model, but generally include those listed in Table 13.1.

Depending on the printer, additional settings may also be available to adjust. Look on the General tab for a Preferences button. Click Preferences (if present) to open a dialog box where you can set a default page orientation, paper size/type, and print quality.

Table 13.1 Tabs in a Typical Printer's Properties Box

General	Specify the name to appear with the printer's icon and then print a test page. From here you also can click Printing Preferences to open a dialog box in which you can set paper type, resolution quality, and other appearance-based settings.
Sharing	Choose whether to share the printer with others on your network.
Ports	Choose the port to which the printer is connected.
Advanced	Specify when the printer will be available (useful if sharing it, for example) and whether to use the Windows 8 print spooler. There are also buttons here for setting printing defaults and using separator pages.
Color Management	If it is a color printer you can click a Color Management tab or button to open a dialog box to sync the printer's colors output to the colors on your display.
Security	You can set permissions here for who is allowed to use and control the printer.
Device Settings	A tree-style collection of many of the settings available for this individual printer. This list changes radically depending on the printer and its capabilities and can include paper handling, font substitutions, and installable options such as duplexing and flash memory cards. Figure 13.8 shows the settings for a typical printer.

Removing a Printer

Disconnecting a printer physically from the computer does not necessarily remove the printer's driver from Windows. For local USB printers, disconnecting the printer does make the printer disappear from the Devices and Printers window (in the Control Panel), but its driver remains installed, and if you reconnect the printer, it reappears automatically. For parallel and network interface printers, the printer's icon remains in the Printers window when the printer is disconnected.

To remove the printer's driver from Windows, uninstall it from the Devices and Printers window by right-clicking it and then choosing *Remove device*.

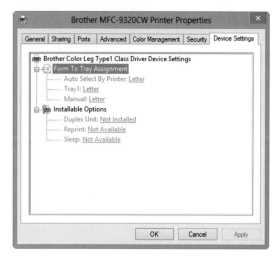

Figure 13.8 The Device Settings tab enables you to control miscellaneous settings specific to that printer.

To remove a printer from Windows 8:

Here's How

1. Open the Control Panel.
2. Under *Hardware and Sound*, click View devices and printers.
3. Right-click the printer's icon and then choose *Remove device*.
4. Click Yes.

Exercise 5

Installing and Removing a Printer Driver

1. Open the Devices and Printers window:
   a. Open the Control Panel.
   b. Under *Hardware and Sound*, click View devices and printers.
2. Add a LaserJet 4 driver as a local printer on LPT2:
   a. Click *Add a printer*.
   b. Click *The printer that I want isn't listed*.
   c. Click *Add a local printer or network printer with manual settings* and then click Next.
   d. Open the *Use an existing port* list, click *LPT2 (Printer Port)*, and then click Next.
   e. In the *Manufacturer* list, click *HP*.
   f. In the *Printers* list, click *HP LaserJet 4200 PCL6 Class Driver* and then click Next.
   g. Click Next when prompted to change the printer's name.
   h. Click Next when prompted to enable sharing or not.
   i. Clear the *Set as the default printer* check box.
   j. Click Finish.
3. Open the Printer Properties box for the new printer and then display its Device Settings tab:
   a. Right-click the HP LaserJet 4200 PCL6 Class Driver icon and then choose *Printer properties*.
   b. Click the Device Settings tab.
4. Capture a screen shot of the window, save it as **C13E05**, and then submit it to your instructor.

5. Click OK to close the Properties box.
6. Remove the HP LaserJet 4200 printer:
   a. Right-click the HP LaserJet 4200 PCL6 Class Driver icon and then choose *Remove device*.
   b. Click Yes.

Working with Hardware ■■■■■■■■■■■■■■■■■■■■

Hardware refers to the physical components of a computer, such as the keyboard, the mouse, the disk drives, the CPU, and so on. Windows 8 communicates with each piece of hardware and coordinates operations between devices. Windows 8 automatically detects and configures the essential pieces of hardware, such as the processor, memory, and motherboard, when you install Windows itself. End users can install, update, and remove less critical devices.

Understanding Device Drivers and System Resources

device driver Software that works with Windows to send and receive instructions for a particular hardware device

system resources Areas of memory, interrupts, and/or DMA channels that are assigned to devices so that they can communicate with the system

Each hardware device speaks its own language. To translate between it and Windows 8, a *device driver* is required. A device driver is software that works with Windows to send and receive instructions for a particular hardware device. In many cases, several files work together to form the device driver. To see what files a device is using, view the device properties.

Windows 8 comes with a large collection of device drivers for popular devices, including display adapters, sound cards, modems, and so on. In addition, when you buy a new device, it comes with drivers on disc for various operating systems. You also can download and install new device drivers for existing devices to add capabilities or fix problems.

Each device communicates with Windows 8 via a set of *system resources*. System resources are assigned to the device to provide conduits through which the device can communicate with Windows 8 and with the CPU. A device may use the following types of system resources:

■ **Memory range.** An area of RAM set aside for the device's use.

■ **I/O range.** An area of RAM set aside for transferring data to and from the device.

■ **Interrupt request (IRQ).** A signaling line that the device uses to get the CPU's attention.

■ **Direct memory access (DMA) channel.** A less commonly used channel that enables the device to bypass the CPU to write directly to memory.

Windows 8 automatically assigns system resources to devices via Plug and Play.

Note: *In previous Windows versions, resource assignments sometimes conflict and users need to manually change them. However, this is rarely necessary in Windows 8 because it handles resource assignments more smoothly.*

signed driver A device driver that has been certified to work under a certain Windows version

Windows 8 strongly prefers that drivers be signed drivers. A *signed driver* has been certified by Microsoft to work with Windows 8. Companies that make drivers must put their drivers through an approval process to receive certification. Signed drivers have a digital signature that also indicates that they have not been corrupted or altered since their signing. Driver-signing was invented to combat poorly written drivers that cause system problems that are difficult to troubleshoot.

You can display the Device Manager window by resource by choosing View, *Resources by Type*. Then you can see exactly what DMA channels, I/O addresses, IRQs, and memory addresses are in use.

Here's How

To display a device's Properties box:

1. Open the Control Panel and then click *System and Security*.
2. Under System, click Device Manager.
3. Click the arrow next to the device's category. The category expands.
4. Double-click the device to open its Properties box.

To view device driver details:

1. Display the device's Properties box, as in the preceding steps.
2. Click the Driver tab.
3. Click Driver Details.
4. Note the driver files listed.
5. Click OK.
6. Click OK.

To view device resource assignments:

1. Display the Properties box for the device, from Device Manager.
2. Click the Resources tab, if present.

   Note: *Not all devices have a Resources tab. Try a different device if it is not present. A display adapter is a good choice.*

3. Note the resources being used.
4. Click OK.

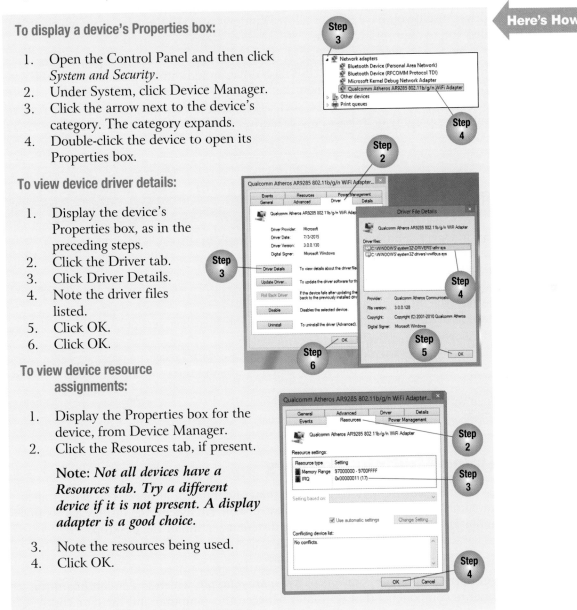

Adding a Plug and Play Device

As you learned previously in this chapter, devices that you can connect when the computer is running are referred to as hot-pluggable. The interface type determines whether a device is hot-pluggable; USB, FireWire (IEEE 1394), and Ethernet network connectors (RJ-45) are all hot-pluggable interfaces. On the other hand, most of the older interfaces, such as legacy parallel and serial ports and PS/2 ports, are not hot-pluggable; you must shut down the computer and power off the device (if applicable) before you make those connections. You also must shut down the computer to insert expansion boards inside the computer.

Regardless of the interface type, if the device is Plug and Play-compatible (and almost all devices are), Windows 8 recognizes it automatically. The device either automatically installs the driver, prompts you to insert a driver disc, or prompts you to point it toward a driver on your hard disk or other disk. You can insert a driver disc if you have one, or allow Windows to go online and/or search the hard disk for an appropriate driver.

The prompts vary depending on the native support Windows 8 provides for the device. For example, for a USB flash drive, an indicator appears briefly in the notification area letting you know that a driver is being installed for the drive, automatically. For other devices, such as sound or display adapters, you likely need to run a setup utility or at least provide a driver for the device to work properly.

Exercise 6

Viewing Device Driver Information

1. Open Device Manager and then view the properties for your display adapter:
    a. Open the Control Panel and then click *System and Security*.
    b. Under System, click Device Manager.
    c. Click the arrow next to *Display adapters*.
    d. Double-click the display adapter.
2. View the current driver information and make a note of the driver version:
    a. Click the Driver tab.
    b. Make a note of the *Driver Provider*, *Driver Date*, and *Driver Version*.
3. Capture a screen shot of the window, save it as **C13E06**, and then submit it to your instructor.
4. Close all open windows.

Using Multiple Monitors ■■■■■■■■■■ ■■■■■■■■ ■

Windows 8 enables you to use more than one monitor at once. You can set all monitors to duplicate the same display, or you can extend the display across the monitors so that each one displays a different section of the desktop.

Installing the Second Monitor

display adapter A circuit board or built-in component to which the monitor attaches and which translates between the computer and the monitor

A computer monitor connects to a *display adapter*, which is a circuit board (or built-in component) that translates between the computer and the monitor. A monitor can have two types of connections to a computer:

■ **Video Graphics Array (VGA).** A 15-pin, *D*-shaped connector

■ **Digital Video Interface (DVI).** A white, rectangular connector

Many display adapters have one connector of each type. On such cards, you can connect two separate monitors. If your display adapter has only one connector, you must install a second display adapter to use multiple monitors.

Note: *Many notebook computers have two separate connectors for external monitors: one VGA and one DVI. That does not necessarily mean, however, that you can have three separately configurable monitors (the built-in screen plus two others). The display adapter built into a notebook computer typically supports only one display at a time, so if you hook up an external monitor, the same image appears on both at once; you might not be able to extend the desktop onto a second monitor.*

To connect a second monitor, shut down the computer and the monitor. Connect the monitor through a cable to the computer, and then restart Windows 8. Windows should automatically detect the new display adapter.

Configuring the Second Monitor

When you initially install a second monitor, the same display appears on both monitors. You can change this by adjusting the display settings, as shown in Figure 13.9. Each monitor appears as a separate box.

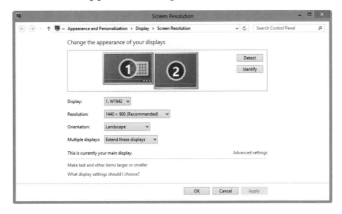

Figure 13.9 Each monitor's display can be configured separately if you have more than one.

To determine which monitor each box represents, click Identify. The number flashes briefly on each monitor screen. Drag the on-screen monitor boxes in the sample area so that they match the way they are physically oriented on your desk.

You can adjust each monitor's settings separately. Click the on-screen monitor box and then set the following for it:

- **Resolution.** The number of individual pixels (dots) that make up the display image. The higher the resolution, the smaller things will appear.

- **Orientation.** The direction of the display. The default is landscape, but you might choose to stand a monitor on its side and use Portrait, for example.

- **Multiple displays.** One monitor is your primary monitor; that is the one on which the Taskbar appears. Choose a primary monitor from the *Multiple displays* drop-down list.

Here's How

To configure a second monitor:

1. Right-click the desktop and then choose *Personalize*.
2. Click Display.
3. Click *Change display settings*.
4. Click Identify to figure out which monitor is which.
5. Drag the sample boxes in the dialog box to match the monitors' physical locations.
6. Click the box for the new monitor.
7. Open the *Multiple displays* list and then choose *Extend desktop to this display*.
8. If needed, click *Resolution* and then drag the slider to choose a different resolution.
9. If needed, click *Orientation* and then choose a different orientation.
10. Click OK.
11. Close all open windows.

CHAPTER SUMMARY

- Installing software copies files to the hard disk, makes changes to the registry, and adds a tile for the application to the Start screen.

- Software on CD typically contains an Autorun file that tells Windows how to start its setup utility automatically when the disc is inserted.

- To install a Windows 8 app, open the Store tile, find an app you want, and then click Install.

- To uninstall (remove) a desktop application, open the Control Panel and then, under *Programs*, click Uninstall a program. Choose the program, click its Uninstall button, and then follow the prompts.

- To uninstall a Windows 8 app, right-click its tile on the Start screen and then click Uninstall.

- To create a Start screen shortcut, find the file in File Explorer, right-click it, and then choose *Pin to Start*.

- Compatibility mode helps Windows 8 simulate previous versions of Windows to allow programs that were written for those previous versions to run. Right-click a program, choose *Properties*, click the Compatibility tab, and then set up compatibility options. Or, to automate the process, right-click the file and then click *Troubleshoot compatibility*.

- To specify the default programs to use for certain file types, from the Control Panel, choose *Programs*, Default Programs.

- To set a program to start automatically at Windows 8 startup, place a shortcut to it in the Startup folder, which is located in C:\Users*username*\\AppData\\Roaming\\Microsoft\\Windows\\Start Menu\\Programs\\Startup, where *username* is the user account name.

- To prevent a program from starting automatically, remove its shortcut from the Startup folder. If that does not work, open the Task Manager and then open the Startup tab. Click the entry to disable and then click the Disable button.

- Most printers use a USB device, so they are hot-pluggable. Connect them, and Windows 8 automatically installs a driver for them or prompts you for a disc containing the driver.

- If you have a setup disc for the printer, run the setup program to install the printer's software, which may include not only a driver, but also helper programs. This is important, especially for multifunction devices (printer/scanner/copier/fax).

- You can tell Windows to look for new printers. From the Control Panel, choose *Hardware and Sound*, View devices and printers, Advanced printer setup, and then follow the prompts.

- To set the default printer, right-click the printer's icon and then choose *Set as default printer*.

- To set a printer's properties, right-click the printer's icon and then choose *Printer Properties*.

- Each hardware device requires system resources and a device driver.

- Plug and Play enables devices to be automatically configured when connected to the computer (that is, set up with resources and drivers as needed).

- System resources include memory range, I/O range, an interrupt request (IRQ), and a direct memory access (DMA) channel. Not all devices require all types of resources.

- A driver is a translation utility that relays commands between Windows and the device. Windows 8 prefers signed drivers, which are drivers certified to work with Windows 8.

- A display adapter is a circuit board or built-in component to which a monitor connects. To configure the display adapter, right-click the desktop, choose *Personalize*, click *Display* and then click *Change Display Settings*.

CONCEPTS CHECK

Completion: Answer the following questions in a Word document.

Part 1

Multiple Choice

1. The _____ is a configuration database where system settings are stored.
   a. task list
   b. registry
   c. storage bank
   d. Windows 8 archive

2. Which of these operating systems does Compatibility mode not emulate?
   a. MS-DOS
   b. Windows XP
   c. Windows 95
   d. Windows 7

3. To make a program load automatically at Startup, place a shortcut to it _____ .
   a. in the root directory (C:\) of the hard disk
   b. in the C:\Windows\System folder
   c. on the desktop
   d. in the Startup folder for the current user

4. Which of these types of programs should not be disabled from loading automatically at startup?
   a. Antivirus software
   b. Word processing software
   c. Game software
   d. Accounting software

5. Older printers use a parallel interface, also known as a(n) _____ port.
   a. COM
   b. USB
   c. LPT
   d. Legacy serial

6. Which type of printer interface is hot-pluggable?
   a. USB
   b. LPT
   c. COM
   d. Legacy serial

7. A _____ printer is one that is directly connected to your computer.
   a. network
   b. remote
   c. local
   d. legacy

8. Which of these is NOT a type of system resource?
   a. USB port
   b. I/O range
   c. IRQ
   d. DMA channel

9. What is a signed driver for Windows 8?
   a. A driver written specifically for the device with which it is being used
   b. A driver certified to work with Windows 8
   c. A driver written and provided by Microsoft
   d. None of the above

10. To have two monitors on a system, what hardware do you need?
    a. A display adapter with two connectors on it
    b. Two separate display adapters
    c. A built-in display adapter
    d. Either a or b

Part 2

Short Answer

11. What three things does a setup program typically do?

    _____

12. When you remove a program, what three things are removed?

    _____

13. What is the purpose of Compatibility mode and what problems does it solve?

    _____

14. Describe the advantages and drawbacks of having programs load automatically at startup.

    _____

15. How is a hot-pluggable device different from one that is not hot-pluggable?

    _____

16. What is Plug and Play?

    _____

17. What is the purpose of a device driver?

    _____

18. Describe how to open the Devices and Printers window, from which you can add and remove printer drivers.

_____

19. What distinguishes hardware from software?

_____

20. Describe two ways to get a driver for a device.

_____

SKILLS CHECK

Save all solution files to the default Documents folder or any alternative folder specified by your instructor.

Guided Check

Assessment

1

Installing and Removing Software

Your instructor will provide software for you to install for this exercise. It may be a commercial product on a disc, or instructions to download a setup file from a website or a server on your LAN.

1. Install the software on your computer.
   a. Insert the disc containing the software. If an Autoplay window appears, close it (if it came on disc).
   b. In a File Explorer window, double-click the setup file for the software.
   c. Follow the prompts to install it.
2. Run the software, capture a screen shot of it, save it as **C13A01**, and then submit it to your instructor.
3. Uninstall the software.
   a. Open the Control Panel.
   b. Under *Programs*, click Uninstall a program.
   c. Click the program to uninstall.
   d. Click the Uninstall button or the Uninstall/Change button, whichever appears.
   e. Follow the prompts to uninstall the program.

Assessment

2

Running an Application in Compatibility Mode

1. Start a third-party program installed on your computer (not one that was supplied with Windows 8) and then exit it.
   a. Open the Start screen.
   b. Right-click and then choose All apps.
   c. Find a program that did not come with Windows 8 itself and then click it.
   d. Open a few menus in the program to confirm that it works, and then exit the program.

2. Display the Properties box of the tile for that program on the Start screen.
    a. Open the Start screen.
    b. Right-click and then choose All apps.
    c. Right-click the tile for the program and then choose *Open File Location*.
    d. Right-click the executable file (or the shortcut to it) and then choose *Properties*.
3. Set the program to operate in Compatibility mode for Windows 98/Windows Me and for 256 colors.
    a. Click the Compatibility tab.
    b. Mark the *Run this program in compatibility mode for* check box.
    c. Open the drop-down list and then click *Windows 98/Windows Me*.
    d. Mark the *Reduced color mode* check box.
    e. In the drop-down list, select *8-bit (256) color*, if necessary.
    f. Click OK.

4. Run the program from its shortcut.
    a. Open the Start screen.
    b. Right-click and then choose All Apps.
    c. Click the program's shortcut. If a Windows User Account Control dialog box appears, choose to allow the program to run.
    d. Capture a screen shot of the running application, save it as **C13A02**, and then submit it to your instructor.
5. Return to the Properties box and then turn off Compatibility mode for that program.
    a. Open the Start screen.
    b. Right-click and then choose All Apps.
    c. Right-click the shortcut to the program and then choose *Open File Location*.
    d. Right-click the executable or shortcut and then choose *Properties*.
    e. Click the Compatibility tab.
    f. Clear the *Run this program in compatibility mode for* check box.
    g. Clear the *Reduced color mode* check box.
    h. Click OK.

Assessment

3

Controlling Program Startup

1. Set up Notepad to run at startup.
    a. Open File Explorer and then navigate to C:\Windows\System32.
    b. Hold down the Alt key and drag notepad.exe to the desktop.
    c. Navigate to C:\Users*username*\AppData\Roaming\Microsoft\Windows\Start Menu\Programs\Startup, where *username* is the user account name.
    d. Drag the notepad.exe shortcut from the desktop to that folder.
2. Restart the computer, display the desktop, and confirm that Notepad loads automatically. Close Notepad.
3. Right-click the Taskbar and then choose *Task Manager* to open the Task Manager. If you do not see tabs, click More Details.
4. Capture a screen shot of the Startup tab showing the Notepad shortcut, save it as **C13A03**, and then submit it to your instructor.
5. In Task Manager, disable Notepad from starting automatically.
    a. Click the Startup tab and then select Notepad.
    b. Click Disable.
6. Restart the computer and confirm that Notepad does not start.
7. Open the Task Manager and reenable the Notepad item.
    a. Right-click the Taskbar and then click *Task Manager*.
    b. Click the Startup tab.
    c. Click Notepad.
    d. Click Enable.

8. Delete the Notepad shortcut from the Startup folder.
   a. Open File Explorer and then navigate to C:\Users*username*\AppData\\Roaming\Microsoft\Windows\Start Menu\Programs\Startup, where *username* is the user account name.
   b. Right-click the Notepad shortcut and then choose *Delete*.

Assessment 4

Getting Printer Information
1. Open the Devices and Printers window from the Control Panel.
   a. Open the Control Panel.
   b. Under *Hardware and Sound*, click View devices and printers.
2. Display the properties for the default printer and then display printing preferences.
   a. Right-click the default printer and then choose *Printer properties*.
   b. On the General tab, click *Preferences*.
3. Capture a screen shot of the Printing Preferences dialog box, save it as **C13A04**, and then submit it to your instructor.
4. Click OK to close the Printing Preferences dialog box.
5. Click the Print Test Page button on the General tab of the printer's Properties box.
6. Submit the printout to your instructor.
7. Close all open windows.

On Your Own

Assessment 5

Installing and Removing Software on Your Own
Your instructor will provide software for you to install for this exercise. It may be a commercial product on a disc, or instructions to download a setup file from a website or a server on your LAN.
1. Install the software on your computer and document the step-by-step actions you took.
2. Run the software, capture a screen shot of it, save it as **C13A05**, and then submit it to your instructor.
3. Uninstall the software.

Assessment 6

Finding a Printer Driver
Open a Word document and then save the file as **C13A06.** Record your answers to the following questions and then submit the file to your instructor:
1. What is your printer's make and model, and how did you determine this?
2. What is the printer's driver version, and how did you determine this?
3. What is the URL for the Support portion of the printer manufacturer's website?
4. What is the most recent driver version number available for this printer?

Assessment 7

Viewing Resource Assignments
1. Display Device Manager.
2. Display a list of resources by type. ***Hint: Use the Resources by type command on the View menu.***
3. Expand the *Direct memory access (DMA)* category by clicking its arrow.
4. Capture a screen shot of the Device Manager window, save it as **C13A07**, and then submit it to your instructor.
5. Close all open windows.

Assessment

8

Working with Multiple Monitors

For this exercise, you will need a computer that has two display adapters, or a single display adapter with multiple monitor ports on it, and you will need two monitors that can connect to those ports.

1. Shut down the computer, and then connect the second monitor, if it is not already connected.
2. Restart the computer.
3. In the Screen Resolution section of the Control Panel, set up the new monitor to extend the desktop.
4. Capture a screen shot of the Screen Resolution window showing both monitors, side by side. Save the file as **C13A08** and then submit it to your instructor.

CHALLENGE PROJECT

Suppose you need to add a printer and an additional monitor to your computer. Examine your computer to determine the following:

1. What types of printer interfaces can your computer accept? LPT (parallel)? USB? Bluetooth? Wireless?
2. How many more monitors (if any) can your computer support without having to add another display adapter? What type(s) of interface(s) are available: VGA or DVI?
3. Write a paragraph summarizing your findings, save it as **C13A09**, and then submit it to your instructor.

Part 4

Microsoft® Windows® 8

Power Computing Topics

- Troubleshooting and Repairing Your System

- Securing and Monitoring Your System

- Sharing Information On and Off the Road

Troubleshooting and Repairing Your System

PERFORMANCE OBJECTIVES

Upon successful completion of Chapter 14, you will be able to:

- Check a disk for errors
- Troubleshoot programs
- Fix system problems
- Troubleshoot printing
- Troubleshoot hardware problems
- Use Remote Assistance

Over time, Windows 8 can develop problems because of improper shutdowns, poorly written applications, file corruption, or other situations. You can troubleshoot and repair many common problems yourself, without the help of an IT professional.

Getting Troubleshooting Help ▪▪▪▪▪▪▪▪▪▪▪▪▪▪▪

Windows 8 includes a Troubleshooting utility in the Control Panel. This utility walks you step by step through common problems and solutions. The steps are different depending on the problem type you choose. For example, if you are having a problem with the sound on your computer not working, a hardware troubleshooter examines your system and either fixes the problem itself or suggests things for you to try.

Here's How

To get troubleshooting help:

1. Open the Control Panel.
2. Under *System and Security*, click Find and fix problems.
3. Click the category that most closely matches the problem.

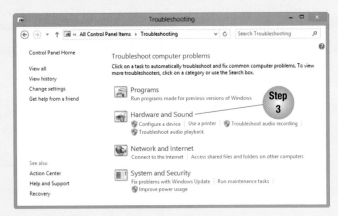

4. If a list of topics appears, click the topic you want.
5. Follow the prompts to run the Troubleshooting utility for the selected problem.

Checking a Disk for Errors ■■■■■■■■■■■■■■■■■■■■■

master file table (MFT) The table of contents for a disk formatted with the NTFS file system

file system error An error or discrepancy in the way the disk's file system keeps track of storage locations

Each disk has an internal table of contents that maps the physical locations on the disk to specific file and folder names. When Windows 8 needs to retrieve a file from the disk, it consults this table of contents to find where to look on the disk for that file. This table of contents is called the **master file table (MFT).**

When an event causes Windows to shut down abnormally, such as a power outage or crash, the abnormal shutdown may create a **file system error**. For example, if a file was in the process of being written to the hard drive when the power went out, the file's information may be improperly recorded in the hard drive's MFT. Such errors, if uncorrected, can potentially snowball. An error in the file system can cause a system crash, which can, in turn, cause more file information to be improperly recorded. File system errors also can cause the files themselves to become corrupted by writing their data to the wrong location on the disk.

Another type of error a disk can have is a ***bad sector*** error. Bad sectors are physically unreadable or unwritable spots on the surface of the disk. These errors are sometimes caused by physical trauma to the computer, such as falling off a table or being kicked, but bad sector errors also can develop spontaneously as a hard disk begins to fail.

The Check Disk utility runs a check of the file system and scans for bad sectors on the drive. It does not repair the bad sectors it finds; instead, it relocates the data (if possible) from a bad sector to a good one, and it updates the MFT or FAT to reflect the new location of the data.

To check a disk for errors:

1. Open File Explorer and then click *Computer*. The Computer window shows all available drives.
2. Right-click Local Disk (C:) and then click *Properties*. The Properties dialog box opens.
3. Click the Tools tab.
4. Click Check. If the user Account Control window displays a warning, click Yes.

Here's How

Open
Open in new window
Pin to Start
Turn on BitLocker

Share with ▶

Format...

Copy
Paste

Create shortcut
Rename   **Step 2**

Properties

Step 3

Local Disk (C:) Properties

General | Tools | Hardware | Sharing | Security | Quota

Error checking
This option will check the drive for file system errors.
⊘ Check   **Step 4**

Optimize and defragment drive
Optimizing your computer's drives can help it run more efficiently.
Optimize

OK   Cancel   Apply

Step 5

Error Checking (Local Disk (C:))

You don't need to scan this drive

We haven't found any errors on this drive. You can still scan the drive for errors if you want.

➞ **Scan drive**
You can keep using the drive during the scan. If errors are found, you can decide if you want to fix them.

Cancel

5. If the message You don't need to scan this drive appears, click Cancel, or, to scan the drive anyway, click Scan drive.
6. Wait for the scan to finish and then click Close.
7. Click Cancel to close the Properties dialog box.

Note: *Error checking is performed separately for each drive letter, so if you have multiple hard disk drives listed in the Computer window, you must repeat the process for each drive.*

Troubleshooting Application Problems ■■■■■■■■

An application can have either or both of two problems: it can fail to start, or it can crash while running. The term *crash* is somewhat generic, referring to the program ceasing to function normally. It can involve any of the following:

- Program becomes unresponsive to keyboard, mouse input, or both
- Program operation slows to a crawl
- Program shuts down unexpectedly, sometimes losing unsaved work
- Error messages appear
- Windows itself becomes unresponsive to keyboard, mouse input, or both

Program crashes can be caused by any of several problems, both hardware- and software-related. To troubleshoot such a problem, first shut down the malfunctioning software, if it did not terminate by itself. Then determine the root cause of the malfunction.

Shutting Down a Malfunctioning Program with the Task Manager

When a program crashes, it might terminate itself automatically, usually with an error message explaining what happened. However, in some cases, the program window stays open, and you must shut down the malfunctioning program manually.

When a program stops responding to keyboard and mouse input, Windows displays that program's window with a white haze over it, and a message box appears letting you know that the program has become unresponsive. You can choose either to restart the program or return to the program to wait for it to respond. (Some programs trigger false alarms when they take longer than normal to respond to certain commands.)

Note: *When a program crashes, you may be prompted to send more information about the crash to Microsoft. This is optional and sends no personal data about you or your usage habits. The information helps Microsoft track the problems that occur most frequently among users, so the development team can focus its efforts on correcting those problems in future updates.*

If Windows does not notice that the program has become unresponsive, you can display the Task Manager and shut down the program manually.

The Task Manager has two views: More Details and Fewer Details. The Fewer Details view shows only the running applications in a plain window, as shown in Figure 14.1. Click More Details (at the bottom) to switch to the More Details view, which has multiple tabs of information. The running apps appear in the *Apps* section on the Processes tab in this view (shown in Figure 14.2).

Figure 14.1 Task Manager in Fewer Details view.

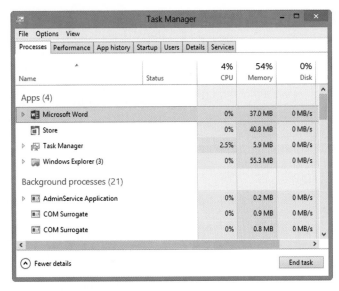

Figure 14.2 Task Manager in More Details view.

Here's How

To shut down a program with the Task Manager:

1. Right-click the Taskbar and then click *Task Manager*. If the User Account Control window appears, click Yes. The Task Manager opens.
2. Click the program you want to shut down.
3. Click End task.

Diagnosing the Root Cause of Program Crashes

Programs may crash for several reasons. Table 14.1 explains some of the possibilities. It can be difficult to know which problem is the root cause in a given instance, so you might need to try several fixes.

Table 14.1 Program Problems and Solutions

Problem	*Possible Fixes*
Setup not successfully completed OR Program files missing or corrupted	Repair or reinstall the program, as described in the next section. This is the most common fix.
Poorly written program	Download a program patch or update from the manufacturer's website.
Program not compatible with Windows 8	Run program in Compatibility mode, as described in Chapter 13.
File system errors OR Bad sectors	Run Check Disk, as described previously in this chapter. You might then need to repair or reinstall the program.
Compatibility problems between program and the display adapter	Update the device driver for the display adapter, as described later in this chapter. Download an update from the program's website.

Figure 14.3 If a program's setup program has a Repair function, you can use it to correct problems with the program installation without having to remove and reinstall it.

Repairing a Program

Repairing or reinstalling the program can fix problems that are caused by corrupted or missing files. Repairing is often better than reinstalling because it does not require removing the program first. (If you need to remove and reinstall a program, see Chapter 13.)

Not all programs can be repaired. If a program can be repaired, an option for repairing is available via the Uninstall a program subcategory of the Control Panel. In some cases, the Repair command silently does a repair in the background; in other cases, it reopens the application's setup utility to perform the repairs, as shown in Figure 14.3.

Exercise 2

Practice Correcting Program Problems

1. Open WordPad. (From the Start screen, type WordPad and then click the WordPad tile.)
2. Close WordPad using the Task Manager:
   a. Right-click the Taskbar and then click *Task Manager*.
   b. Locate and click the Windows WordPad Application in the list of running apps.
   c. Click End task.
   d. Close Task Manager.
3. Check the *C* drive for errors using Check Disk:
   a. Open File Explorer and then click *Computer*.
   b. Right-click the *C* drive and then click *Properties*.
   c. Click the Tools tab.
   d. Click Check.
   e. Click Scan Drive.
   f. Wait for the scan to finish, and when a message appears that the disk check is complete, capture a screen shot of the window showing that confirmation message. Save the file as **C14E02** and then submit it to your instructor.
   g. Click Close.
4. (Optional) Repair Microsoft Office, if installed:
   a. Open the Control Panel and under Programs, click Uninstall a program.
   b. Click Microsoft Office. (The exact name varies depending on your version.)
   c. Click *Change*.
   d. Click *Repair*.
   e. Click Continue.
   f. Follow the prompts to finish repairing Office.

Fixing System Problems ■■■■■■■■■■■■■■■■■■■

System problems are the big ones—the problems that prevent Windows from starting up correctly or from running at a decent performance level once started, regardless of the application being used. System problems can be caused by any of the following:

- Viruses or malware infections.
- Disk errors, either physical or logical (see the previous section).
- Corrupted Windows system files, caused either by disk errors or by bad or incomplete updates.
- Bad changes made to the registry (usually by an amateur techie or a poorly written driver or setup application).
- Files that are supposed to load at startup but are missing or corrupted.
- Bad updates to essential device drivers, such as the display adapter's driver. The driver update might have been corrupted, or it might have been the wrong driver for the device.
- Programs that are no longer installed but still try to load automatically at startup.
- Incompatibility between the computer's hardware and a driver.
- Incompatibility between the computer's hardware and a recent Windows update.
- Incompatibility between the computer's hardware and a recently installed application.

In the following sections you will learn about common actions you can take to solve these types of problems.

Booting to Safe Mode

If Windows does not boot normally, you might try booting to *Safe Mode*. Safe Mode works when regular booting will not in cases such as when a program or non-essential driver trying to load at startup is the problem.

> **Safe Mode** A startup mode that loads only the essential device drivers and does not load any of the programs that are scheduled to load at startup

Booting to Safe Mode does not fix anything by itself. It is a means to an end. After you boot to Safe Mode, you can use one of the utilities in the following sections to perform actions that may fix the problem. For example, you might run a virus removal tool after booting to Safe Mode, or replace a defective device driver.

When you boot to Safe Mode, Windows looks different in several ways. The display resolution is plain VGA, which is 640 × 480 resolution and 16 colors. The words "Safe Mode" appear in the four corners of the desktop (shown in Figure 14.4), and a Help window appears explaining the purpose of Safe Mode.

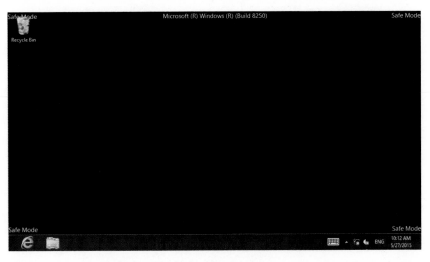

Figure 14.4 Safe Mode may allow you to make system changes or implement fixes that are not available when Windows is running normally.

To boot to Safe Mode:

1. From the desktop, select the Settings charm, and then click *Change PC settings*.
2. Click the *General* category.
3. In the right pane, scroll down to the *Advanced startup* section and then click Restart now.
4. Click Troubleshoot.

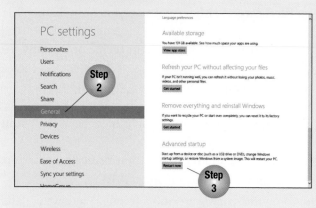

5. Click Advanced options.
6. Click Startup Settings.
7. Click Restart.
8. When you see a Startup Settings menu, press 4 to select Enable Safe Mode.
9. Wait for Windows to finish loading in Safe Mode.
10. When you are finished working in Safe Mode, reboot.

Once you are in Safe Mode, you can go about fixing the root cause of the problem. Think about what you did right before the problem started and then do one or more of the following:

- If you recently updated a device driver, roll back the update, as described later in this chapter in "Rolling Back a Driver."

- If you suspect a virus or malware infection, run a utility that detects and removes that type of threat.

- If you recently installed a new program, remove it, as described in Chapter 13 in "Removing a Program."

- If you think that a program that loads automatically at startup is causing the problem, disable that program from starting, as described in Chapter 13 in "Preventing a Program from Starting Automatically."

- If you are not sure what caused the problem, restore the system to a previous restore point, as described in "Restoring the System to an Earlier State," later in this chapter.

Note: *Some of your hardware may not work in Safe Mode. For example, sound may not play, and, unless you chose Safe Mode with Networking, you cannot access your local network or the Internet.*

Booting to Safe Mode with Networking

1. From the desktop, select the Settings charm and then click *Change PC settings*.
2. Click *General*, scroll down to *Advanced startup* in the right pane, and then click Restart now.
3. Click Troubleshoot.
4. Click Advanced options.
5. Click Startup Settings.
6. Click Restart. The Advanced Boot Options menu appears.
7. Press 5 to select Enable Safe Mode with Networking.
8. Sign in to Windows, typing your password if prompted.
9. Close the Windows Help and Support window.
10. Explore the menus, the File Explorer window, the network locations available, and so on. Make a list of the differences you observe between regular operating mode and Safe Mode. Record your list in a Word document, save it as **C14E03**, and then submit it to your instructor.
11. Reboot the computer normally.

Restoring the System to an Earlier State

Windows system files contain information about every aspect of your system's current state, including what hardware you have, what applications are installed, what users are authorized, and what those users' preferences are. These system files are a complex, frequently changing group of files, stored in multiple hidden locations on your hard drive. Whenever you install a new application, driver, or anything else, it affects your system files.

If Windows starts malfunctioning after you do something that affects system files, the easiest fix is often to use **System Restore**. This utility enables you to roll back the system files to previously saved versions, which can wipe away whatever error was recently introduced.

Windows 8 creates a **restore point** every day, provided the System Protection feature is turned on. (It is on by default, but someone may have turned it off, or it might have been turned off automatically if the hard disk was full at some point.) A restore point is a copy of all of the important system files that you need for a System Restore operation. You also can manually create additional restore points whenever you like. A good time to create a restore point, for example, is before you install an unknown program or driver that may not be compatible with Windows 8.

There are two different methods to restore from a restore point. One of them uses the Control Panel's interface, and the other uses the Windows 8 interface. Both accomplish the same end. If you are able to access Windows normally and open the Control Panel, use the quicker Control Panel method.

System Restore A utility that enables you to roll back the system files to previously saved versions

restore point A copy of the system files from a certain point in time

Here's How

To create a restore point:

1. From the Control Panel, click *System and Security* and then click *System*.
2. In the Navigation bar at the left, click *System protection*.
3. Click Create.
4. Type a name for the restore point.
5. Click Create.

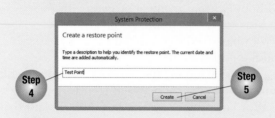

Step 4

Step 5

6. When a message appears that the point has been created, click Close.
7. Click OK to close the System Properties dialog box.

To enable or disable automatic restore point creation:

1. From the Control Panel, click *System and Security* and then click *System*.
2. In the Navigation bar at the left, click *System protection*.
3. Click Configure.
4. Click *Turn on system protection*, or click *Disable system protection*.
5. If you enabled system protection in Step 4, drag the Max Usage slider to the desired limit amount.
6. Click OK.
7. Click OK to close the System Properties dialog box.

Step 4

Step 5

Step 6

To restore from a restore point (Control Panel method):

1. From the Control Panel, click *System and Security* and then click *System*.
2. In the Navigation bar at the left, click *System protection*.
3. Click System Restore.
4. Click Next.
5. Click the restore point you want to restore to.
6. Click Next.
7. Click Finish.
8. Click Yes.
9. Wait for Windows to reboot and then click Close.

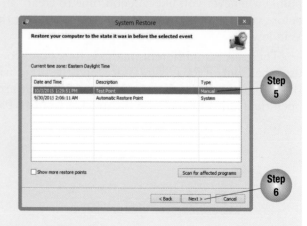

Step 5

Step 6

To restore from a restore point (PC settings method):

1. From the desktop, select the Settings charm and then click *Change PC settings*.
2. Click the *General* category, scroll down to the *Advanced startup* section in the right pane, and then click Restart now.
3. Click Troubleshoot.
4. Click Advanced options.
5. Click System Restore.
6. When prompted, click your user name, enter your password, and then click Continue.
7. At the System Restore box, click Next.
8. Click the restore point to return to and then click Next.
9. Click Finish.
10. If prompted to confirm, click Yes.
11. Wait for Windows to reboot and then click Close.

Exercise 4

Creating a Restore Point

1. From the Control Panel, click *System and Security* and then click *System*.
2. Click *System protection*.
3. Click Create.
4. Type Exercise 4 Test as the name of the restore point and then click Create.
5. At the confirmation box, click Close.
6. In the System Properties dialog box, click System Restore.
7. Click Next.
8. Capture a screen shot of the window showing the Exercise 4 Test restore point in the list, save it as **C14E04**, and then submit it to your instructor.
9. Click Cancel.
10. Click Cancel to close the System Properties dialog box.

Refreshing or Reinstalling Windows 8

Sometimes Windows becomes corrupted or broken beyond the point at which you can fix it yourself by making minor system adjustments. It may be slow to start up, or there may be long delays between clicking a command and something happening. Applications might crash, or Windows might spontaneously reboot or display a cryptic error message.

Windows 8 offers two options that make the repair process as foolproof and painless as possible:

- **Refresh.** Cleans up your Windows installation by replacing any missing or changed system files, while enabling you to keep your photos, music, videos, and other personal files.

- **Reinstall.** Wipes the slate clean on your computer and then completely reinstalls Windows in factory-fresh condition. You lose everything that was on your hard disk.

When problems occur, try Refresh first because it is less invasive and you have less work to do afterward to restore all of your files and applications. If that does not work, resort to Reinstall.

Note: If you have User Account Control (UAC) set to always notify you (the highest security setting), you cannot use Refresh or Reinstall until you lower that setting. Any of the settings lower than the highest one will work. To manage User Account Control settings, go to the Action Center in the Control Panel.

Here's How

To refresh Windows:

1. From the desktop, select the Settings charm and then click *Change PC settings*.
2. Click the *General* category, and then, in the right pane, under the section *Refresh your PC without affecting your files*, click Get started.
3. Click Next.
4. If prompted, insert the Windows DVD or plug in the other device from which you installed Windows.
5. Click Refresh.
6. Wait for Windows to refresh and restart.

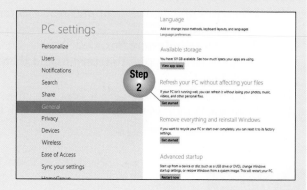

To reinstall Windows:

1. From the desktop, select the Settings charm and then click *Change PC settings*.
2. Click the *General* category and then, in the right pane, under the section *Remove everything and reinstall Windows*, click Get started.
3. Click Next.
4. If prompted, insert the Windows DVD or plug in the other device from which you installed Windows.
5. Click Reinstall.
6. Wait for Windows to reinstall and restart.

Note: If you proceed past Step 4 in either of these procedures, it will take a long time to complete. If you are just practicing, you may wish to cancel before Step 5.

Restoring Files from a Windows 7 Backup Set

Windows 7 came with a Backup program that enabled you to back up individual files and folders to another location, in case something happened to your computer that rendered the originals inaccessible. Windows 8 does not include that feature because it uses the File History feature instead (see Chapter 4). However, Windows 8 provides access to the Backup utility that came with Windows 7, in case you should need to restore files from a previously created backup set.

To access the Windows 7 backup program, open the Control Panel in Large Icons view. *Hint: **Change the View By setting in the upper right corner.*** Choose Windows 7 File Recovery and then click the *Select another backup to restore files from* hyperlink. Select the backup set you want (click Browse network location, if necessary, to find it) and then follow the prompts to select and restore the needed files.

Troubleshooting Printing Problems ■■■■■■■■■■■

Windows 8 manages the printing processes for all of the installed printers so that each application is relieved of that responsibility. You can print from several different applications to the same printer, and Windows sends each print job to the printer one by one.

Sometimes, however, problems occur and the print job does not emerge from the printer as expected. The problem can be with the printer itself, with the print queue, or with the individual print job.

Troubleshooting Physical Problems with a Printer

Often the root cause of a printer problem is the printer itself. Before assuming that Windows or the printer driver is at fault, check the following:

- Is the printer plugged in and turned on? Look for a power light or message on the printer that indicates it is receiving power.
- Is the printer online? Some printers have an Online button that toggles the printer online and offline. This is different from being powered on; it controls the connection to the computer.
- Is the printer connected to the computer? This connection can be via a cable (parallel or USB), Bluetooth, wireless, or LAN.
- Does the printer have sufficient paper and ink or toner?

 T I P If all of the physical aspects of the printer appear to be operational, try printing a test page from the printer's own controls. The instructions for doing this can be found in the printer's documentation; it usually involves pressing certain buttons on the printer in a prescribed sequence or choosing a test page from the printer's LED interface. If the printer successfully prints a test page, then you know the problem is with Windows or with the printer's connectivity.

Opening the Print Queue to View Printer Status

After you have confirmed that the problem is not with the printer itself, the next step is to open the printer's queue. Windows 8 maintains a separate queue for each printer driver installed.

To view a printer's status and queue:

1. From the Control Panel, under *Hardware and Sound*, click *View devices and printers*.
2. Double-click the printer for which you want to get information.

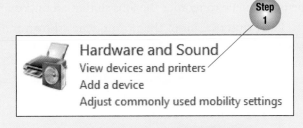

Here's How

Step 1

Hardware and Sound
View devices and printers
Add a device
Adjust commonly used mobility settings

3. Examine the information that appears, including the number of documents in the queue.

   Note: Depending on the printer's driver, you may see a screen as shown here, or you may be taken directly to the queue, as shown in Step 5.

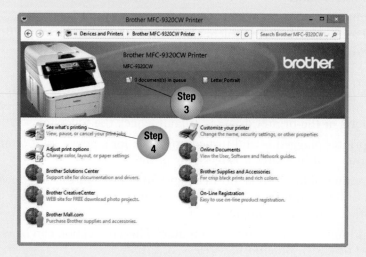

4. If the print queue does not appear, double-click the See what's printing icon. The queue for the printer appears.

5. Examine the queue. There is probably nothing in it (as shown here) because print jobs go through the queue and are completed fairly quickly unless there is a problem.

Controlling the Queue

Print jobs go through the queue automatically, without your help. However, at some point you might want to control the queue manually. For example, if a large print job was sent to the printer accidentally, you might want to pause the queue to prevent the job from completing, so as not to waste the paper. You also might pause the print queue to reorder the jobs so that an important one prints before the others.

The Printer menu in the print queue (shown in Figure 14.5) contains commands for controlling the entire queue at once:

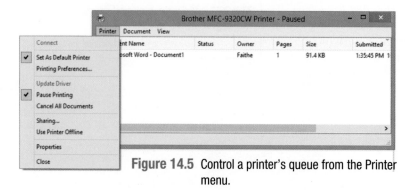

Figure 14.5 Control a printer's queue from the Printer menu.

- **Printer, Pause Printing.** Pauses the entire print queue. You can select this command again to toggle the queue back on.
- **Printer, Cancel All Documents.** Clears the entire print queue. Any unprinted print jobs are deleted.

▼ **Quick Fix**

Pause Is Unavailable
If the Pause Printing command is unavailable, choose Open as Administrator from the Printer menu.

Controlling an Individual Print Job

In addition to pausing, restarting, and clearing the entire queue, you also can pause, restart, and clear individual print jobs within it. For example, you could pause a print job to let other jobs move ahead of it in the queue, or to get more information about it before allowing it to print.

Another way to reorder the jobs in a print queue is to change a job's priority. By default, all print jobs have the lowest priority; you can make a job rise to the top of the queue by setting its priority higher than that of the other print jobs with which it is competing.

◀ **Here's How**

To pause a print job:

1. Click the print job in the queue.
2. Click Document, *Pause*, or right-click the print job and then click *Pause*.

To resume a paused print job:

1. Click the print job in the queue.
2. Click Document, *Resume*, or right-click the print job and then click *Resume*.

To delete a print job:

1. Click the print job in the queue.
2. Click Document, *Cancel*, or right-click the print job and then click *Cancel*.
3. Click Yes.

To reprioritize a print job:

1. Right-click the print job and then choose *Properties*.
2. On the General tab, drag the Priority slider.

   Note: *The priority numbers run from lowest (1) to highest (99).*

3. Click OK.

Controlling a Print Queue

1. Pause the queue for the default printer:
   a. In the Control Panel, under *Hardware and Sound*, click View devices and printers.
   b. Right-click the printer and then choose *See what's printing*.
   c. Open the Printer menu and then choose *Pause Printing*. If *Pause Printing* is unavailable, choose *Open as Administrator* and then try again.

   Note: *Pausing printing may not be possible if your default printer is a network printer that another computer controls. If so, try a different printer, if one is available, or ask your instructor for help.*

2. Open Notepad, type your name, and then print to the default printer. Close Notepad without saving your changes.
3. Open Paint, draw an oval, and then print to the default printer. Close Paint without saving your changes.
4. Open Internet Explorer and then browse to www.emcp.com. Print to the default printer and then close Internet Explorer.
5. Open the print queue. It contains three documents.
6. Delete the second print job (the print job from Paint):
   a. Select the second print job.
   b. Click Document, *Cancel*.
   c. Click Yes.
7. Set the priority for the web page print job to 99:
   a. Right-click the print job and then choose *Properties*.
   b. Drag the Priority slider to the highest setting.
   c. Click OK.
8. Pause the web page print job:
   a. Select the web page print job.
   b. Click Document, *Pause*.
9. Click Printer, *Pause Printing* to resume the print queue and allow the Notepad print job to print.
10. Resume the web page print job to allow it to print.
11. Submit the two printouts to your instructor.

Troubleshooting Hardware Problems ▪▪▪▪▪▪▪▪▪

Most hardware problems are not problems with the hardware itself, but with its configuration in Windows. As you learned in Chapter 13, each device needs a driver and some system resources to function. If either of these is set up incorrectly, the device will not function correctly.

When a device is not functioning properly, first check that Windows has correctly identified the device, assigned resources to it, and loaded its driver.

resource conflict A conflict between two devices that both try to claim the same resource, such as a certain IRQ or memory address

- ▪ **Is the device identified correctly?** If the device appears as Unknown Device, Windows was not able to identify it correctly. To solve this problem, run the setup utility for the software that came with the device.

- ▪ **Are there any resource conflicts?** A *resource conflict* occurs when two devices both try to claim the same resources (for example, the same IRQ or I/O address). When this happens, one (or both) of the devices involved in the conflict does not function correctly.

- **Does the driver load?** When a device driver cannot be loaded, the device cannot function. A driver might not load because of incompatibility between it and Windows 8 (especially if it is an older driver) or because it is corrupted.

All of these questions can be answered by examining the device in Device Manager. Device Manager shows a list of all installed hardware. When you double-click a device, a Properties box opens and displays its status (shown in Figure 14.6).

You can find the following information in the device's Properties box:

- **General tab.** Look for the message "This device is working properly," as shown in Figure 14.6. If the device is not working, a message explaining the problem appears here instead.

- **Resources tab.** Not all devices have a Resources tab, but if there is one, look for a "No conflicts" message, as shown in Figure 14.7. If there is a resource conflict, information about it will appear in that area instead.

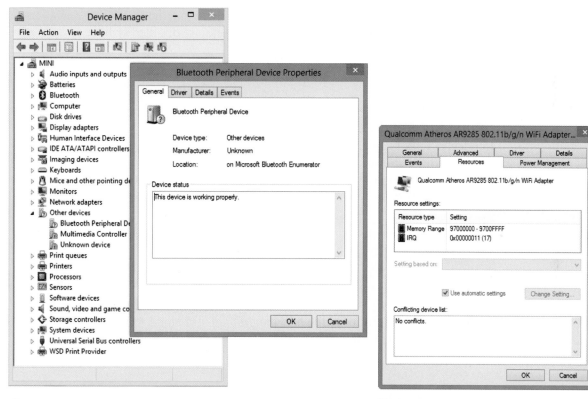

Figure 14.6 Use Device Manager to examine the properties of a device and determine its status.

Figure 14.7 Examine the device's resource usage on the Resources tab.

To check a device's status:

1. Open the Control Panel and then click *System and Security*.
2. Under System, click *Device Manager*.
3. If the device's category is not expanded, click the arrow next to the category to expand it.

   Note: *In most cases, if a device has a problem, its category automatically appears expanded so that the device is visible.*

4. Double-click the device to open its Properties box.
5. On the General tab, check the *Device status* section for a message. A common error is that the drivers are not installed, as shown here.

6. If the device has a Resources tab, click it, and then check the *Conflicting device list* section for a message. If there was an error on the General tab, there may not be any resource information available because devices that are disabled or have no drivers installed do not use resources.
7. Click OK.

Removing and Redetecting a Device

If a device reports an error, you can sometimes correct it by removing the device and allowing Windows 8 to redetect it. Removing the device releases the resources assigned to it so that Windows can reassign new resources when it redetects the device. This corrects most resource-related problems.

To remove and redetect a device:

1. From Device Manager, select the device.
2. Press the Delete key, or click the Uninstall icon on the toolbar.
3. Click OK.
4. Click the Scan for hardware changes icon on the toolbar.

Enabling and Disabling a Device

When you remove a device, as in the preceding section, the device is redetected automatically the next time Windows scans for hardware changes. In addition to scanning when you click the Scan for hardware changes icon, Windows also automatically scans at startup. Therefore, a device that has been removed in Windows but is still physically attached or installed is usually redetected.

If you want a device to be permanently disabled so that it does not use any resources or load any drivers, you must either physically remove it from the computer or set it to be disabled in Windows. (Motherboard devices, such as built-in sound or display adapters, must be disabled because they cannot be removed.)

Note: *One reason you might disable a device is that a duplicate device exists in the computer that is better than the original. For example, you might have built-in sound support on the motherboard, but also have a PCI expansion board that is an advanced sound card with better features. You could disable the onboard sound to free up its resources.*

Here's How

To disable a device:

1. From Device Manager, click the device.
2. Click *Disable* on the toolbar. A warning appears.
3. Click Yes.

Step 2

To enable a device:

1. From Device Manager, click the disabled device.
2. Click *Enable* on the toolbar.
   OR
1. From Device Manager, double-click the device.
2. On the General tab, click Enable Device.
3. Click Next.
4. Click Finish.
5. Click Close.

Installing or Updating a Device Driver

Device manufacturers periodically release updates to their drivers that either enhance the device's capabilities or correct problems with it. For example, if you install a new game and the game crashes frequently, sometimes an update to the display adapter's device driver will correct the problem. You may also need to install a device driver if Windows cannot detect a driver for that device automatically.

Drivers are typically available from the manufacturers' websites. Drivers usually come in an executable package (that is, a file with an .exe extension). You download the file and then double-click it to run it.

When you run the executable file, one of two things might happen:

- A setup program might run that automatically installs the update (most common).
- The driver files might extract themselves to a folder on your hard disk, and then you would need to install the driver update manually (less common).

Here's How

To manually install a driver update:

1. In Device Manager, click the arrow next to the device's category to expand the category
2. Double-click the device to open its Properties box.
3. Click the Driver tab.
4. Click Update Driver.
5. Click *Search automatically for updated driver software*. If software is found, follow the prompts to install it.
   OR
   Click *Browse my computer for driver software* and then continue to Step 6.

6. If you know the location of the driver, click Browse to locate it. Otherwise enter your hard disk's letter in the *Search for driver software in this location* box and make sure the *Include subfolders* check box is marked.
7. Click Next and then follow the prompts. If Windows is unable to locate a better driver, a message appears that the best driver is already installed.
8. Click Close.

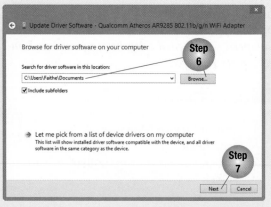

Rolling Back a Driver

Windows 8 retains the previously used driver when you install a new one, so you can return to it later if the new one proves to be a problem. To reverse an update, use the Roll Back Driver feature.

Here's How ▶ **To roll back a driver update:**

1. From Device Manager, double-click the device.
2. Click the Driver tab.
3. Click Roll Back Driver.
4. Follow the prompts to roll back the driver to the previous version.

Exercise 6

Working with Device Drivers

1. Open Device Manager and then view the properties of your sound card, or if your computer does not have sound, of a nonessential component such as a modem:
   a. Open the Control Panel, click *Hardware and Sound*, and under Devices and Printers, click Device Manager.
   b. Click the arrow next to the device category.
   c. Double-click the device.
2. View the current driver information and then make a note of the driver version:
   a. Click the Driver tab.
   b. Make a note of the *Driver Provider*, *Driver Date*, and *Driver Version*.
   c. Capture a screen shot of the window, save it as **C14E06S02**, and then submit it to your instructor.
   d. Click OK.
3. Use the Internet to find the device manufacturer's website or the website of the computer manufacturer. Look up your device by model number, and if a driver is available that is newer (by date and version number) than the current one, download it.

4. Check with your instructor and, if directed, install the driver update. Otherwise, make a note of the website where the driver could be downloaded.

   Note: *Depending on the update and its format, you might either run an executable setup program or use the Update Driver button in the display adapter's Properties box.*

5. Identify a nonessential device that has a Resources tab in its Properties box:
   a. Display the properties box for a device. (A wireless network adapter is a good choice. Ask your instructor to help identify a device to use, if needed.)
   b. If it does not have a Resources tab, click Close and then try another device.
6. Disable the device using Device Manager:
   a. Select the device.
   b. Click the Disable icon on the toolbar.
   c. Click Yes.
7. Display the Resources tab in the Properties dialog box for the device.
8. Capture a screen shot of the window, save it as **C14E06S08**, and then submit it to your instructor.
9. Reenable the device:
   a. Select the device.
   b. Click the Enable icon on the toolbar.
10. Close all open windows.

Using Remote Assistance ■■■■■■■■■■■■■■■■■■■■■

It can often be difficult for a technician to troubleshoot a computer problem over the phone or via email because he or she cannot see the computer's screen and must rely on the end user to try different fixes. Remote Assistance makes remote troubleshooting much easier by enabling someone to view and take control of a computer over the Internet or a LAN.

Note: *Do not confuse Remote Assistance with Remote Desktop. The latter enables you to sign in to another computer remotely, exactly as if you were physically sitting at that computer. Remote Desktop grants the connecting user more privileges and is less controllable than Remote Assistance, so it is not the preferred connection type for troubleshooting. Remote Desktop is covered in Chapter 16.*

Configuring Remote Assistance Settings

Because the person taking control of your computer via Remote Assistance has the power to make changes to your system that can help or harm it, Windows 8 has security measures in place to prevent unauthorized access to your system, using this tool.

You can enable or disable Remote Assistance as a whole in the System Properties dialog box (Remote tab). You also can configure its settings to allow only the access you prefer. For example, you can prevent the person connecting from taking control of your system, and you can specify the amount of time an invitation remains open. You also can restrict connections to allow access only to people using Windows 8.

To enable and configure Remote Assistance:

1. In the Control Panel, click *System and Security*.
2. Under the *System* section, click *Allow remote access*.

   Note: *The* **Allow Remote Assistance connections to this computer** *check box is checked by default.*

3. Click Advanced.
4. Mark or clear the *Allow this computer to be controlled remotely* check box. If you clear this check box, people connecting to your computer can watch what you are doing, but cannot do anything themselves.
5. Use the drop-down lists to set the maximum amount of time that an invitation can be open. The shorter the amount of time, the less likely an invitation will be intercepted by an unauthorized person, but the less time a legitimate helper has to respond as well.
6. Mark or clear the *Create invitations that can only be used from computers running Windows Vista or later* check box.
7. Click OK.

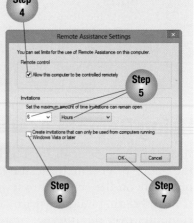

Requesting Remote Assistance

To request Remote Assistance, you send an invitation to someone from whom you want help. The easiest and most common way to send this invitation is via email. When you work through the invitation process, Windows prompts you for the email address to which to send the invitation and then generates the email to be sent via your default email program with the invitation as an attachment.

To request Remote Assistance:

1. From the Start screen, type assistance.
2. In the Search pane, click Settings.
3. Click *Invite someone to connect to your PC and help you, or offer to help someone else*.

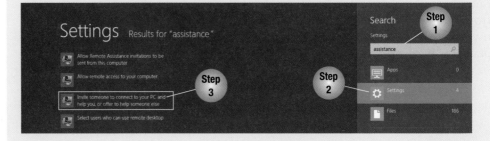

4. Click Invite someone you trust to help you.
5. Click Use email to send an invitation.
6. When Remote Assistance opens a new email in your default email program, enter the recipient's email address.

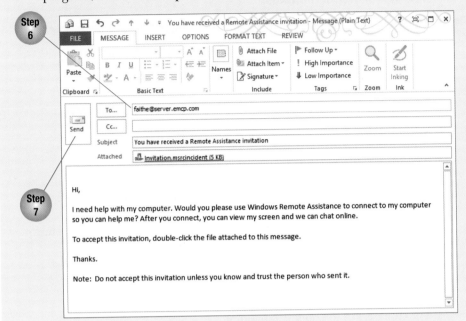

7. Click Send. A box appears with a string of letters and numbers; this is the connection password. Make a note of it.
8. Send another email to your helper (or contact him or her in some other way), to provide the connection password.

After you send a Remote Assistance request, a small Remote Assistance window appears, containing the connection password. Leave this window open while you wait for the person to respond.

Giving Remote Assistance

When you receive a Remote Assistance request via email, the file attachment contains an invitation, including all of the technical details needed for your computer to connect to the requestor's computer.

After the invitation has been accepted and the two computers are connected, you can share control of the remote computer (so that your keyboard and mouse work on it). Shared control does not take away that user's ability to continue using his or her own keyboard and mouse but adds yours as additional input devices.

You can choose to chat with the other user by opening a Chat window, and you can choose to send files to and receive files from the other user.

Here's How

To give Remote Assistance:

1. Double-click the attachment file in the email you received. When prompted to save or open it, click Open.
2. Type the connection password. If you do not know it, phone or email the person who sent the invitation to find out what it is.

3. Click OK.

   Note: *On the machine to which you are connecting, a prompt appears asking whether the requestor wants you to connect. The requestor must click Yes for you to continue.*

4. After the connection is established, a Helping window appears showing you the requestor's desktop.
5. (Optional) Click *Actual size* to display the requestor's screen at the same resolution he or she is using, or click *Fit to screen* to see his or her entire desktop at once. (A single button toggles between these two commands.)

To take control of the remote computer:

- Click *Request control*. On the machine to which you are connected, a prompt appears asking whether the user wants you to take control. The user must click Yes for you to continue. In the dialog box in which the user clicks Yes, there is a check box that will enable you to respond to User Account Control prompts. The user must mark this if he or she wants you to be able to do so (recommended).

To release control of the remote computer:

- Click *Stop sharing*.

To chat with the user of the remote computer:

1. Click *Chat*. A Chat panel appears.
2. Type a message in the bottom of the chat panel and then click Send or press Enter. On the machine to which you are connected, a chat window opens, and that user can chat with you using that interface.

To send a file to the user of the remote computer:

1. Click *Send file* on the toolbar.
2. In the Open dialog box, select the desired file and then click Open. On the machine to which you are connected, a prompt appears asking whether the user wants to accept the file. The user must click Yes to receive it. On the user's computer, a Save As dialog box opens; the user must specify a location for the file and then click Save to complete the transaction.

To disconnect from the remote computer:

1. Click *Disconnect* on the toolbar.
2. Click Yes.
3. In the Windows Remote Assistance window, click Cancel.

- To troubleshoot problems, open the Control Panel and then, under *System and Security*, click Find and fix problems.

- A disk can develop errors that cause programs and Windows to crash or have other problems. To fix them, click Check on the Tools tab of the drive's Properties box.

- To shut down a malfunctioning program, display the Task Manager by right-clicking the Taskbar and then choosing *Task Manager*. Select the program and then click End Task.

- The root cause of a program crash can include a problem with the program's setup utility, missing or corrupted program files, a bug in the program, incompatibility with Windows 8, errors on the disk, and incompatibility between the program and the display adapter.

- Some programs can be repaired via the Uninstall a Program link in the Control Panel. Select an installed program and then click the Change or Uninstall/Change button. If a Repair option appears, work through it. Not all programs have this feature.

- Safe Mode (with or without networking) boots Windows 8 in a mode with minimal driver support. This often enables you to start Windows to run repair utilities when Windows will otherwise not boot. To access Safe Mode from Windows 8, select the Settings charm and then click *Change PC settings*. In the *General* category, click Restart now. Click Troubleshoot, click Advanced options, click Startup Settings, and then click Restart. Press 4 to choose Enable Safe Mode, or press 5 to choose Enable Safe Mode with Networking.

- Printer problems are often a result of user error. Check that it is plugged in, online, connected to the computer, and stocked with ink and paper.

- To check a printer's status, open the Devices and Printers window from the Control Panel and then open the printer's queue by double-clicking the printer's icon, and, if the queue does not appear, by clicking See What's Printing.

- In the print queue window, use the Printer menu for operations involving the entire printer, such as pausing it or cancelling all pending print jobs.

- Use the Document menu for operations involving individual print jobs. For example, you can pause or resume a print job, delete it, or display its properties (from which you can adjust its priority).

- Most hardware problems involve the device's configuration in Windows. The most common problems are device driver issues and resource assignment issues.

- Use Device Manager to see a list of installed devices and to check the status of each device. To see a device's status, double-click it and then look on the General tab of its Properties box. Operational devices display "This device is working properly."

- Look on the Resources tab of a device's Properties box for information about its resource assignments. Operational devices display "No conflicts."

- To remove a device from Device Manager, select it and then press the Delete key or click Uninstall. The device will likely be redetected either the next time you start Windows, or when you refresh Device Manager's listing with Scan for hardware changes.

- To turn off a device in Windows so that it is not redetected later, disable it. Select it from Device Manager and then click the Disable icon.

- Updating a device driver sometimes corrects a problem with it. In most cases, driver updates are executable downloads, but you might occasionally need to install a driver update manually. To do so, from Device Manager, double-click the device, click the Driver tab, and then click Update Driver.

- If a driver update causes the device to malfunction, return to the previous driver by using Roll Back Driver. From the Device Manager, double-click the device, click the Driver tab, and then click Roll Back Driver.

- Remote Assistance enables one user to connect to another user's computer to provide troubleshooting help.

CONCEPTS CHECK

Completion: Answer the following questions in a Word document.

Part 1

Multiple Choice

1. To troubleshoot problems with your computer, open the Control Panel and, under _____, click Find and fix problems.
   a. System and Security
   b. Programs
   c. Network and Internet
   d. Hardware and Sound

2. On a disk formatted with NTFS, the table of contents for the disk is stored in a _____ .
   a. registry
   b. boot sector
   c. master file table
   d. boot record

3. In Windows 8, what utility finds and fixes file system errors?
   a. Disk Cleanup
   b. Disk Defragmenter
   c. Scan Drive
   d. Check Disk

4. How do you display the Task Manager?
   a. Right-click the desktop and then choose *Task Manager*.
   b. Right-click the Taskbar and then choose *Task Manager*.
   c. Triple-click the desktop.
   d. Point the mouse in the upper right corner of the screen.

5. How do you access Safe Mode?
   a. Open the PC Settings Windows 8 interface and then, in the *General* category, click Restart Now.
   b. Open the Control Panel, click *System and Security*, and then click *Device Manager*.
   c. Open the PC Settings Windows 8 interface, and then, in the *System* category, click Startup modes.
   d. Open the Control Panel, click *Hardware and Sound*, and then click Safety.

6. What utility lets you return to a previous version of your system files?
   a. Safe Mode
   b. Refresh
   c. Reinstall
   d. System Restore

7. If you want to return Windows to its default state, deleting all user files, installed applications, and settings, which troubleshooting option should you use?
   a. System Restore
   b. Refresh
   c. Reinstall
   d. Backup

8. From which menu in a printer's queue do you pause the printer (all print jobs at once)?
   a. Document
   b. Printer
   c. File
   d. Edit

9. If you want to turn off a device so that Windows does not redetect it next time it starts up, what should you do to the device in Device Manager?
   a. Uninstall
   b. Disable
   c. Remove
   d. Hibernate

10. Where in the Control Panel do you enable or disable Remote Assistance?
    a. System and Security
    b. Users
    c. Network and Internet
    d. Desktop

Part 2

Short Answer

11. Name three possible causes of a file system error.

_____

12. What is the difference between Refresh and Reinstall?

_____

13. How do you initiate a Check Disk operation on a hard disk?

_____

14. How can you tell that a program has crashed?

_____

15. List three causes of program crashes.

_____

16. List one reason you might boot to Safe Mode.

_____

17. Explain a type of problem that could be corrected with System Restore.

_____

18. What are three visual clues that would tell you that Windows was running in Safe Mode?

_____

19. List three things you can check on a printer to eliminate the printer itself as the cause of not being able to print.

_____

20. List three things to check in Device Manager for a device that is not working correctly.

_____

SKILLS CHECK

Save all solution files to the default Documents folder or any alternate folder specified by your instructor.

Guided Check

Troubleshooting a Network Problem
1. Open a Word document and then save the file as **C14A01**.
2. Disable your network adapter in Device Manager.
   a. Open the Control Pane, click *System and Security*, and then, under System, click Device Manager.
   b. Expand the *Network Adapters* category.
   c. Click your network adapter and then click *Disable* on the toolbar.
   d. Click Yes to confirm. If prompted to restart, do so.
3. Troubleshoot your network connection, allowing Windows to correct the problem.
   a. Open the Control Panel and then, under the *System and Security* category, click Find and fix problems.
   b. Click Hardware and Sound.
   c. Click Network Adapter.
   d. Click Next.
   e. If prompted to choose which adapter to troubleshoot, click All network adapters.
   f. Click Next.

g. Follow the prompts that appear to complete the repair. Record the exact prompts that appeared and the choices you made. If the repair failed, explain what happened and then make the repair manually by reenabling the device.

4. Close all open windows and then submit your results to your instructor.

Assessment 2

Checking a Disk for Errors

1. Display the Tools tab for your hard drive's properties.
   a. Open File Explorer and then click *Computer*.
   b. Right-click the *C* drive and then choose *Properties*.
   c. Click the Tools tab.
2. Check the *C* drive for file system errors.
   a. Click Check.
   b. Click Scan drive.
3. As the scan is running, take notes about what you see on the screen. Save the file as **C14A02** and then submit it to your instructor.

Assessment 3

Exploring Printer Error Messages

1. Open a Word document and then save the file as **C14A03**. Record the answers to the questions in the following steps.
2. Remove the paper from your printer.
3. Open Notepad, type your name, and then print to the default printer.
   a. Start Notepad.
   b. Type your name.
   c. Click File, *Print*.
   d. Click the Print button. What indicator or message appears in Windows, if any, alerting you that the printer is out of paper?
4. Open the printer's queue.
   a. Open the Control Panel.
   b. Under *Hardware and Sound*, click View Devices and Printers.
   c. Right-click the printer and then choose *See what's printing*.
   d. What indicator or message appears in the print queue window indicating that the printer is out of paper?
5. Turn off the printer's power. What indicator or message appears in the print queue window, if any?
6. Replace the paper in the printer.
7. Pause the print queue.
   • From the print queue window, click Printer, *Pause Printing*.
8. Turn the printer back on. What indicator or message appears in the print queue window?
9. Delete the print job without printing it.
   • Select the print job and then press Delete.
10. Resume the print queue.
    • From the print queue window, click Printer, *Pause Printing*.
11. Submit your file to your instructor.

Assessment 4

Removing and Reinstalling a Device.

1. Open Device Manager.
   • Open the Control Panel, click *System and Security*, and then, under System, click Device Manager.

2. Uninstall the driver for your keyboard.
   a. Click the arrow next to *Keyboards*.
   b. Select your keyboard and then press Delete.
   c. Click OK. If prompted to restart your computer, click No.
3. Reinstall the keyboard by clicking *Action, Scan for hardware changes*.
4. View the driver information for the keyboard.
   a. Click the arrow next to *Keyboards*.
   b. Double-click your keyboard.
   c. Click the Driver tab.
   d. Click Driver Details.
5. Capture a screen shot of this window, save it as **C14A04**, and then submit it to your instructor.
6. Close all open windows.

On Your Own

Assessment
5

Updating and Installing a Device Driver
1. Open Device Manager.
2. Identify a device that is made by some other manufacturer than the computer itself, such as a modem, sound card, display adapter, or network card.
3. Find that device manufacturer's website and then find the available driver downloads for the device.
4. View the device's current driver information in Device Manager and then compare its version number and date to that found on the website.
5. If the version on the Web is newer than the one currently installed on your computer, download and install it.
6. Write a one-page report detailing the version numbers you found, whether you installed the update, and if so, what steps you took to do so. Save the file as **C14A05** and then submit it to your instructor.

Assessment
6

Team Exercise: Using Remote Assistance
Work in pairs for this exercise, with each person on a different computer. One person is the Requestor and the other is the Helper.
1. Requestor: Make sure Remote Assistance is enabled on your computer.
2. Requestor: Send a Remote Assistance invitation to your partner's email address.
3. Helper: Receive the invitation and respond to it, connecting to the Requestor's computer.
4. Requestor: Respond to the prompt to enable the Helper to connect to your computer.
5. Helper: Open a Chat window and then have a short chat conversation.
6. Requestor: Send a file from your computer to the Helper's computer.
7. Helper: Receive the sent file and then store it in the Documents folder.
8. Helper: Capture a screen shot of the window showing the Requestor's computer on your screen, save the file as **C14A06**, and then submit it to your instructor.
9. Helper: Disconnect your connection to the Requestor's computer.

Assessment
7

Exploring System Restore
System Restore does not reverse all system changes; there are some settings that are not included. To test this, create a restore point and then make at least eight changes to user settings in the Control Panel (Personalization, mouse settings, keyboard settings, sound settings, and so on). Return to your restore point and see which changes reverted and which changes did not. Record your notes, save the file as **C14A07**, and then submit it to your instructor.

Exploring Advanced Boot Options

1. Open a Word document and then save the file as **C14A08**. Record the notes you take in the following steps.
2. Repeat Steps 1–6 from Exercise 3 to open the Advanced Boot Options menu.
3. Boot to the first mode listed and then take notes about what happens, including the appearance, performance, and functionality of Windows.
4. Repeat the process for each of the other boot modes on the menu, making notes of how each is unique. Submit your findings to your instructor.

CHALLENGE PROJECT

Suppose your friend Jennifer has asked you for help with troubleshooting a computer problem. She claims that ever since she installed a sound card last week, her favorite game crashes intermittently. Write a letter to her explaining the actions she can take to try to fix the problem and in what order you recommend she try the various possible fixes you propose. Save your letter as **C14A09** and then submit it to your instructor.

CHAPTER 15

Securing and Monitoring Your System

PERFORMANCE OBJECTIVES

Upon successful completion of Chapter 15, you will be able to:

- View system information
- Use the Task Manager to track system performance
- Evaluate system performance
- Manage user accounts and passwords
- Use encryption to secure files
- Secure a USB flash drive with BitLocker

$\blacksquare$ s you become more proficient with Windows 8, you may want to explore its tools and utilities for enhancing system performance and security. You can view system information, evaluate system performance, manage permissions to sign in and to perform certain activities, keep sensitive files secure between users, and more.

CPU Stands for Central Processing Unit; the main microchip that serves as the brain of the computer; also called the processor

Viewing System Information

When evaluating your system for compatibility with new software you want to purchase, or for possible upgrades, the first step is to gather a set of basic facts about the computer's hardware and software. This information is available via several utilities in Windows 8.

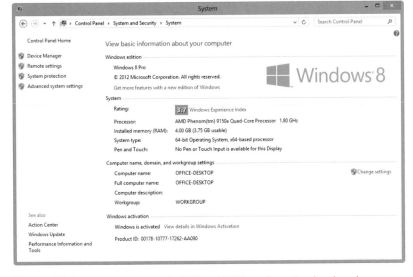

Viewing the Installed CPU and RAM

The **CPU** type/speed and the amount of RAM installed are the two most significant indicators of system performance. When you shop for new software, the system requirements listed on the box always include a minimum value for each of those specifications. To find out the CPU (processor) and the RAM amount, open System in the Control Panel, as shown in Figure 15.1.

Figure 15.1 Check the system's CPU and RAM configuration by choosing System in the Control Panel.

Note: *The System information does not include a Windows Experience Index rating until you have rated your system (shown in Figure 15.1). See the section "Rating System Performance" for the steps to do so. You can update the rating at any time.*

Here's How

To check CPU and RAM:

1. From the Windows desktop, select the Settings charm and then click *Control Panel*.
2. Click *System and Security*.
3. Click System, or click View amount of RAM and processor speed.

Alternate Methods:

1. On the Windows desktop, click the File Explorer button on the Taskbar.
2. Right-click *Computer* in the Navigation pane at the left side of the Libraries window.
3. Click *Properties*.
   OR
• From the Windows desktop, select the Settings charm, and then click *PC info*.

Viewing Detailed System Information

Sometimes you need detailed system information beyond the CPU and RAM specifications. For example, you might need a summary of all installed hardware, or you might need to know the exact version of Windows you have. To gather this information, use the System Information utility.

Note: *Windows 8 is available in many versions: the Windows 8 and Windows 8 Pro retail versions, the volume-licensed Enterprise Edition, and the RT edition for ARM-based portable devices. In addition, when Windows 8 is updated with service packs, there are minor feature and compatibility changes, too. That is why sometimes knowing only that you have Windows 8 is not enough, especially if you are gathering information for troubleshooting purposes.*

The System Information utility presents a system summary, as shown in Figure 15.2, which provides the most often needed facts about a system. This data appears when the top level of the *System Summary* tree is displayed. Beneath the top level are three sections: *Hardware Resources*, *Components*, and *Software Environment*. Select one of these to gather other, more specific information in the selected section.

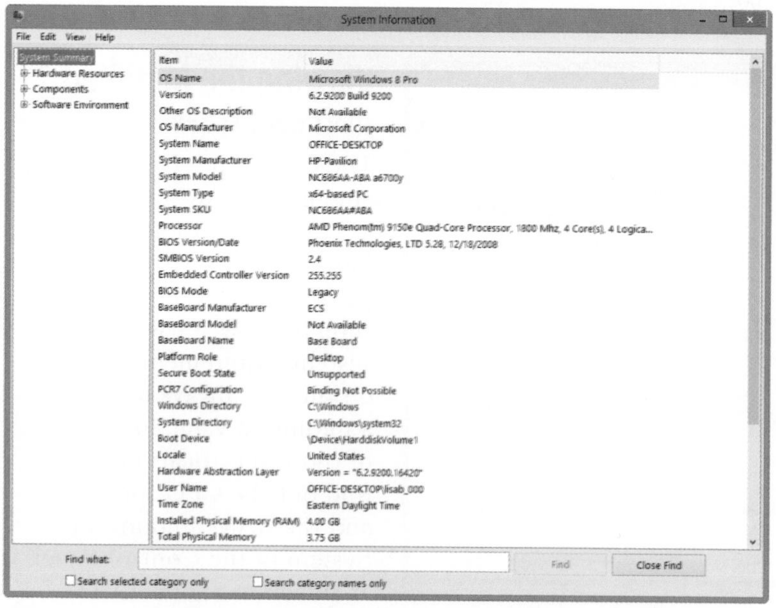

Figure 15.2 Gather more detailed information about the system from System Information.

As you learned in Chapter 13 in "Working with Hardware," you can use the Device Manager to see a list of all installed hardware. You can then view driver and resource information for each device.

Another way to get information about hardware is via the System Information utility's *Components* section, which breaks down hardware by type. Select a type to see detailed information about each item of that type. Figure 15.3, for example, shows detailed information about a hard disk.

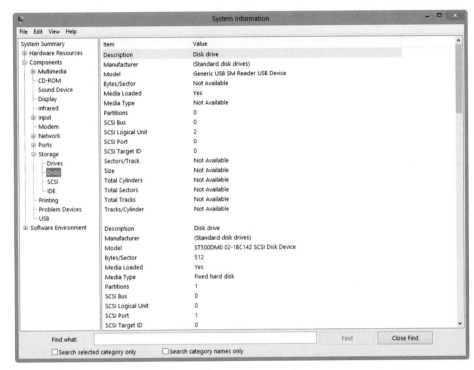

Figure 15.3 Detailed information about each hardware device is available in the *Components* section of System Information.

Here's How

To open System Information:

1. From the desktop select the Settings charm and then click *Control Panel*.
2. Click *System and Security*.
3. Scroll down and then click Administrative Tools.
4. In the list in the Administrative Tools window, double-click *System Information*.

To view detailed information about a hardware component:

1. Open System Information.
2. Click the plus sign next to *Components*.
3. Click a device category.
4. Click a device within the category.

Rating System Performance ■■■■■■■■■■■■■■■■■

Computer experts can quickly tell, by looking at the data in System Information, how well the computer will perform in Windows 8, but for the average user, the data can be difficult to interpret. To help simplify the process of evaluating system performance, Windows 8 provides a Performance Information and Tools utility, as shown in Figure 15.4. It reduces the complex matter of a system's performance level to a simple numeric value called the Windows Experience Index base score and suggests ways to improve that number.

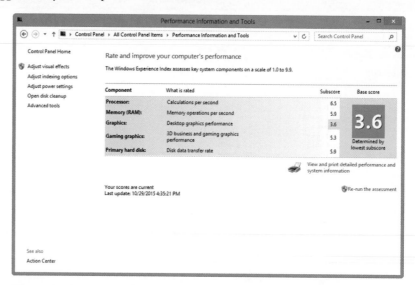

Figure 15.4 Rate your system with the Performance Information and Tools utility, available in the Control Panel.

The system is evaluated on five criteria: Processor, Memory (RAM), Graphics, Gaming graphics, and Primary hard disk. Each of these is assigned a numeric value, with higher being better. The computer's overall score is determined by the lowest score in these five areas. For example, in Figure 15.4, the computer's overall score is a 3.6 because of the graphics, even though it scores significantly higher in other areas. Based on the results in Figure 15.4, a reasonable recommendation for improving this system's performance would be to install a higher-quality display adapter.

Here's How

To rate system performance for the first time:

1. From the desktop, select the Settings charm and then click *Control Panel*.
2. Click *System and Security*.
3. Click System.
4. At the lower left, click Performance Information and Tools.
5. Click Rate this computer and then enter an administrator password, if prompted.
6. (Optional) Click View and print detailed performance and system information.

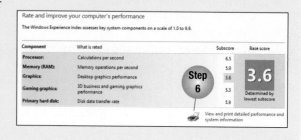

7. (Optional) Scroll to view the detailed information and then click Print this page to print the information.

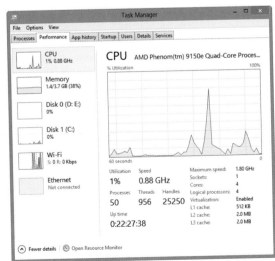

To update the system performance rating:

1. From the desktop, select the Settings charm and then click *Control Panel*.
2. Click *System and Security*.
3. Click System.
4. At the lower left, click Performance Information and Tools.
5. Click Re-run the assessment and then enter an administrator password, if prompted.
6. (Optional) View and print details as desired.

Tracking System Performance ▪▪▪▪▪▪▪▪▪▪▪ ▪▪

Whereas the Performance Information and Tools utility in the preceding section predicts system performance based on its configuration, the Task Manager describes actual performance at a given moment in time.

Note: *Task Manager is a multipurpose utility, and performance data analysis is only one aspect of its capability. It also provides information about running applications, processes, and servers; and lists the users who are connected to the computer.*

To view the Task Manager, right-click the Taskbar and then choose *Task Manager*. Click the More details arrow button in the lower left corner of the Task Manger window to display tabs, if needed, and then click the Performance tab to see information about CPU and memory usage, hard disk activity, and network activity (shown in Figure 15.5).

The CPU usage graph shows how much of the CPU's time is being occupied by running programs. If the CPU is running at 100 percent for more than a few seconds at a time, then a program is probably malfunctioning. This is by far the most common cause of sluggish system performance caused by high CPU usage. To shut down the malfunctioning program, click the Processes tab, click the program under Apps, and then click End task.

If the CPU is consistently running at higher than 50 percent most of the time, not just when a program is malfunctioning, then you could probably get improved performance from a computer with a better, faster CPU. It is normal for the CPU usage to spike and sag as the computer operates, so brief spikes to 100 percent CPU usage is not an indicator of an insufficient CPU.

Figure 15.5 Check out CPU and memory usage and more on the Performance tab of the Task Manager window.

Click *Memory* in the list at the left to display more detailed data about memory usage. The Memory usage graph shows how much of the physical memory is being used. The actual number (in megabytes) is less important than the percentage of usage. If the green Memory bar consistently runs high (that is, higher than 50 percent on an ongoing basis), your system could benefit from the addition of more RAM.

Likewise, click a disk at the left to view active time and disk transfer rate diagrams, as well as stats such as read speed and write speed. Click *Wi-Fi* or *Ethernet*, if active, to check network throughput and network connection information.

To get more detailed performance tracking information, click the Open Resource Monitor link at the bottom of the window. The Resource Monitor utility shows more detailed information about the programs and system processes currently using the CPU, Disk, Network, and Memory resources. Click a category bar to expand more information about that category. For example, in Figure 15.6, detailed CPU and Network usage data is shown.

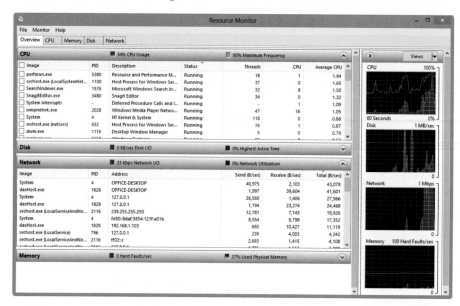

Figure 15.6 The Resource Monitor shows performance monitoring in more detail than the Task Manager can provide.

Exercise 1

Examining Your System Configuration

1. Open a Word document and save it as **C15E01**.
2. Using the System properties, determine your CPU (processor) type/speed and amount of RAM and then record it in the file.
3. Using System Information, determine the model and size of your primary hard disk and then record the information.
4. Using System Information, determine the driver version for your display adapter and then record it.
5. Using Performance Information and Tools, determine your computer's Windows Experience Index base score and then record it.
6. Determine which component is the limiting factor in the score and then record it.
7. Display Task Manager and then, on the Performance tab, click Open Resource Monitor.

8. In the Resource Monitor window, determine the percent used of physical memory and then record it.
9. Close all open windows.
10. Submit your file to your instructor.

Managing User Accounts and Passwords ▪▪▪▪▪▪

Security at the local computer level is handled via user accounts, which are secured by passwords. (Chapter 1 explains in detail how to create user accounts.) Depending on the signed-in user, certain activities are either allowed or disallowed, such as configuring system settings, adding and removing programs, and accessing certain files and folders. The feature that regulates these permissions is called User Account Control.

Understanding User Account Control (UAC)

User Account Control (UAC) is a security feature in Windows 8. It provides an easy way to restrict users from making system changes that will affect other users or the system itself.

Windows 8 users can be configured for either of two levels of permission:

- **Administrator.** Has full rights to do anything to the system, including changing security settings.
- **Standard.** Has full rights to do anything that affects only that user, such as changing screen colors, but cannot make changes that affect other users, and cannot change security settings.

If you are signed in as an Administrator (that is, if your user account is part of the Administrator group), then whenever you do something that requires UAC permission, a box appears asking you to confirm that it is really "you" doing it intentionally. This prevents applications from making such changes without your knowledge.

If you are signed in as a Standard user, Windows 8 prevents you from performing the operation altogether, or asks you to enter an Administrator-level user's name and password as an override.

Throughout the Windows 8 interface, activities that require Administrator-level UAC permission are shown with a multicolored shield symbol next to their links, as shown in Figure 15.7.

Figure 15.7 A shield icon means that Administrator-level permission is required.

Setting the UAC Notification Level

In Windows 8, you can customize the level of security that UAC provides by choosing one of four UAC notification levels:

- **Always notify.** The strongest setting. Provides UAC notification when a program installs software, makes changes to software, or changes your Windows 8 settings.

- **Notify me only when apps try to make changes to my computer (default).** UAC messages appear with program changes, but not with changes to Windows 8 settings.

- **Notify me only when apps try to make changes to my computer (do not dim my desktop).** This is the same as the above setting except the Windows 8 desktop does not become dimmed and unusable when the messages appear; you can respond to them at your leisure.

- **Never notify.** UAC notifications are turned off entirely.

Microsoft recommends leaving UAC set to its default and running Windows 8 as a Standard user most of the time to ensure the greatest security against unwanted system changes. However, on your home system, you might decide that UAC is too intrusive and a more lenient setting than the default is necessary.

Here's How

To adjust the User Account Control level:

1. From the Windows desktop, select the Settings charm and then click *Control Panel*.
2. Click *System and Security*.
3. Under Action Center, click Change User Account Control settings.
4. If you are signed in as a Standard user and are prompted for an administrator password, enter it and then click Yes.
5. Drag the slider to the desired setting.
6. Click OK.

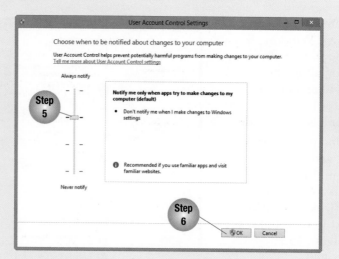

7. If a UAC box appears, click Yes.
8. If prompted to restart, click Restart Now.

You can fine-tune the behavior of User Account Control through the Local Security Policy utility. By default, for example, Standard users cannot perform any system activities, and you cannot override that by entering the credentials of an Administrator account. However, you can change that behavior and enable Windows 8 to prompt you for Administrator credentials when needed, by changing the security policy.

Note: *Some of the advanced features in this chapter require the Professional version of Windows 8. Your instructor can advise you on whether to complete any exercises involving these features, but you should learn about them in general to complete the chapter.*

To open the Security Policy configuration for User Account Control:

1. On the desktop, right-click the Taskbar, point to *Toolbars*, and then click *Address*.
2. Click in the *Address* text box on the Taskbar, type secpol.msc, and then press Enter. If prompted to confirm, click Continue.
3. Double-click Local Policies.
4. Double-click Security Options.
5. Scroll down to the User Account Control entries.
6. Repeat Step 1 to hide the Address toolbar when desired.

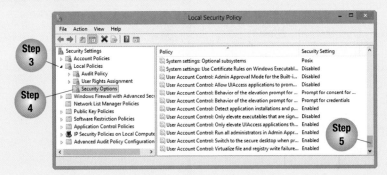

To enable Standard users to elevate to an Administrator account when needed:

1. Follow the preceding steps.
2. Double-click *User Account Control: Behavior of the elevation prompt for standard users*.
3. Select Prompt for credentials, if necessary.
4. Click OK.

Removing or Disabling a User Account

You can either delete or disable a user account that is no longer needed on the system. Deleting it removes it entirely. Disabling it prevents it from appearing on the Windows 8 Start screen as one of the choices, but retains its settings and documents in case you want to use them later. You can reenable the account later when you are ready to use it and access its files.

If you delete a user account, you are prompted to choose whether you want to keep its files or not. If you decide to keep its files, they are moved to a folder on your desktop.

To delete a user account:

1. Sign in using an Administrator account.
2. From the desktop, select the Settings charm and then click *Control Panel*.
3. Click *User Accounts and Family Safety*.
4. Under User Accounts, click Remove user accounts.
5. Click the account to delete.
6. Click Delete the account.

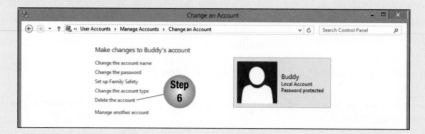

7. Click Delete Files to remove the account's files, or click Keep Files to retain them.
8. Click Delete Account.

To disable a user account without deleting it:

1. From the desktop, click the File Explorer icon to open the Libraries window.
2. Right-click *Computer* in the Navigation pane and then click *Manage*.
3. Double-click Local Users and Groups.
4. Double-click Users.
5. Double-click the user to disable.
6. Click the *Account is disabled* check box to check it.
7. Click OK.

To reenable a disabled user account:

1. From the desktop, click the File Explorer icon to open the Libraries window.
2. Right-click *Computer* in the Navigation pane and then click *Manage*.
3. Double-click Local Users and Groups.
4. Double-click Users.
5. Double-click the user to enable.
6. Click the *Account is disabled* check box to clear it.
7. Click OK.

All Windows 8 systems include a special account with the user name of Administrator, which is not used for standard operations, but only for administrative tasks, such as repairing a Windows 8 installation. By default, the Administrator account is disabled. You can access it from the Local Users and Groups window, though, and you can enable it the same way you enable any other disabled account.

Changing between Standard and Administrator Account Types

You can switch between Administrator and Standard account types as needed. For example, if a computer that was formerly used by one employee will now be shared, you may want to change the first employee's account type from Administrator to Standard and then set up the new user as a Standard account so that neither user can make system-level changes that affect the other person's work.

Here's How

To change an account type:

1. From the desktop, select the Settings charm and then click *Control Panel*.
2. Under *User Accounts and Family Safety*, click Change account type.
3. If you are signed in as a Standard user and are prompted for an administrator password, enter it and then click Yes.
4. Click the account to change.
5. Click Change the account type.
6. Click the option button for the desired account type: *Standard* or *Administrator*.
7. Click Change Account Type.

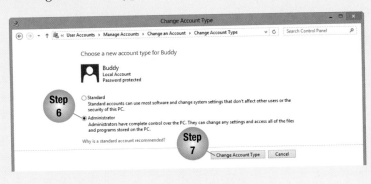

Changing the User Account Name

For local accounts (not Microsoft accounts), you can change the user's account name, if needed. This can be helpful if you need to make sign-in names more distinct, or to make a sign-in more anonymous.

Here's How

To change the user name of a Standard account:

1. From the desktop, select the Settings charm and then click *Control Panel*.
2. Click *User Accounts and Family Safety*.
3. Click User Accounts.
4. Click Manage another account.
5. If you are signed in as a Standard user and are prompted for an administrator password, enter it and then click Yes.
6. Click the account to change.
7. Click Change the account name.
8. Type the new name in the *New account name* text box.
9. Click Change Name.

Setting, Resetting, or Changing an Account Password

A local account can be set up with no password. Microsoft recommends, however, that you assign a password to each Administrator account to prevent unauthorized changes to the system settings. And because Microsoft accounts connect to your online account information, you can change only your own account password. Even when signed in as an administrator, you cannot change the password of another user's Microsoft account.

Use caution when changing passwords for local accounts. The user will lose encrypted files, certificates, stored website and network passwords, and other security information.

strong password A password that is difficult to guess; it must have at least six characters and use numbers, capital and lowercase letters, and special characters

 T I P For the best security, use strong passwords. A ***strong password*** is one that is difficult to guess. That means it has sufficient length (usually six characters or more), is not a word from the dictionary, uses both capital and lowercase letters, and includes numbers, letters, and special characters.

Here's How

To set a password for the currently signed-in user (Microsoft account):

1. From the Start screen, select the Settings charm and then click *Change PC settings*.
2. Click the *Users* category.
3. Click Change your password. Windows accesses your online account information.
4. Type your old password in the *Old password* text box.
5. Type the desired password in the *New password* text box.
6. Repeat the password in the *Reenter password* text box.
7. Click Next.
8. At the message that tells you the password has been changed, click Finish.

To change the password for the currently signed-in user (local account):

1. From the Start screen, select the Settings charm and then click *Change PC settings*.
2. Click the *Users* category.
3. Click Change your password. (If the account does not have a password, click Create a password.)
4. Type your password in the *Current password* text box and then click Next.
5. Type the new password in the *New password* text box.
6. Repeat the new password.
7. Type a password hint in the *Password hint* text box.
8. Click Next.
9. Click Finish.

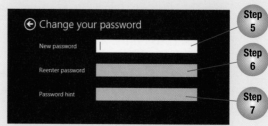

 T I P To remove the password of a local account, leave the text boxes blank in Steps 5 and 6 above.

To change the password of another local user's account:

1. Sign in as an Administrator.
2. From the desktop, select the Settings charm and then click *Control Panel*.
3. Click *User Accounts and Family Safety*.
4. Click User Accounts.
5. Click Manage another account.
6. Click the account to change.
7. Click Change the password.
8. Type the new password in the *New password* text box.
9. Repeat the new password in the *Confirm new password* text box.
10. Type a hint in the *Type a password hint* text box.
11. Click Change password.

 T I P To remove the password, leave the text boxes blank in Steps 8 and 9 above.

To force password change at next sign-in:

1. On the desktop, click the File Explorer button to open the Libraries window.
2. Right-click *Computer* in the Navigation pane and then click *Manage*.
3. Double-click Local Users and Groups.
4. Double-click Users.
5. Double-click the user who requires a password change.
6. If there is a check mark in the *Password never expires* check box, click to clear it. Click the *User must change password at next logon* check box to check it.
7. Click OK.

Saving Password Reset Data

When you sign in with a Microsoft account, you can always sign in to that account online to change the password, or use the lost password features there to retrieve your password. For a local account, however, you need to use another method for restoring password information.

You may have noticed the warning Control Panel presents when you change the password of a local user account: "If you do this, [User Name] will lose all EFS-encrypted files, personal certificates and stored passwords for websites or network resources." The same warning appears if an administrator tries to change a user's password. When a standard user account's password is added or changed by an administrator account, then the standard user can no longer access encrypted files or email messages. Stored website and network passwords are also lost. To avoid this potential data loss, every standard user should create a ***password reset disk*** for his or her account. "Disk" is a misnomer, because in addition to being able to save the password information to a floppy disk if your system is equipped with a floppy disk drive, you also can save the information to a USB flash drive or a flash drive in another format if your computer is equipped with the right reader (drive). You use Control Panel to create the password reset disk.

password reset disk Data stored on a USB or other flash drive that enables you to reset your user account password if you forget it

You need to save password reset data only once for the signed-in account. No matter how many times you change the password after that point, you can reset them as long as you have the flash drive or disk. That is because the password reset data does not store the passwords; it stores a code that grants permission to reset them.

Note: *The password reset data applies only to the currently signed-in account; if you want to be able to recover passwords for all accounts, you must repeat the process while signed in to each user account on your system.*

Here's How

To save password reset data for a local account:

1. Insert your media. (Plug the USB into the USB port, or insert another form of flash media into the appropriate slot.) If any AutoPlay messages open, ignore them.
2. From the desktop, select the Settings charm and then click *Control Panel*.
3. Click in the search text box at upper right and then type reset.
4. Under User Accounts, click Create a password reset disk. The Forgotten Password wizard opens.
5. Click Next.
6. From the drop-down list, choose the drive on which to create the password reset disk.

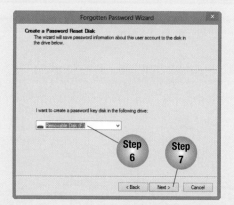

7. Click Next.
8. Type the current password for the signed-in account in the *Current user account password* text box, or leave the box blank if there is currently no password.
9. Click Next.
10. When the Forgotten Password wizard displays the message "Progress: 100% complete," click Next and then click Finish.
11. Remove your media from the drive and then store it in a safe location. Close the Control Panel.

T I P Your password reset disk enables you to reset passwords to restore access to accounts that you are locked out of because you do not know their passwords.

To use password reset data for a local account:

1. Restart Windows 8 and then swipe up from the bottom of the screen to display the sign-in screen that prompts you to select a user and enter a password. If needed, click the left-pointing arrow and then click the local user account for which you want to use the password reset data.
2. Connect the USB flash drive containing the password reset data.
3. Leave the *Password* box blank and then click the arrow button to attempt a sign-in. A message appears that the user name or password is incorrect.
4. Click OK. A Reset password link appears below the sign-in box.
5. Click Reset password. The Password Reset wizard runs.
6. Click Next.
7. Choose the drive on which the password reset data is stored and then click Next.
8. Type the new password and then type it again to confirm in the applicable text boxes.
9. Type a hint in the *Type a new password hint* text box.
10. Click Next.
11. Click Finish.
12. Sign in to the local account using the new password.

Turning the Guest Account On or Off

A *guest account* enables visitors to use your computer without knowing the password for any of the user accounts. It is by nature a limited account; users signed in as Guest cannot make system changes.

The guest account is disabled by default, meaning that it does not appear on the Welcome screen when the computer starts up.

guest account A limited-access user account designed to be used by anonymous users who do not have a regular account on the computer

To enable the Guest account:

1. From the desktop, select the Settings charm and then click *Control Panel*.
2. Click *User Accounts and Family Safety*.
3. Click User Accounts.
4. Click Manage another account.
5. Click Guest.
6. Click Turn On.

To disable the Guest account:

1. From the desktop, select the Settings charm and then click *Control Panel*.
2. Click *User Accounts and Family Safety*.
3. Click User Accounts.
4. Click Manage another account.
5. Click Guest.
6. Click Turn off the guest account.

Seeing How User Accounts Work

1. Sign in using an Administrator account.
2. Open a Word document and save it as **C15E02**.
3. Turn the Guest account on.
4. Create a new Standard user account called Test. Do not assign a password to it.
5. Set the Test account so that the user is forced to change the password at first sign-in.
6. Sign out and then sign in as the Test user. Set the account password to Test. Record the exact wording of the password prompt in your file.
7. Try making changes to any Control Panel option that has a shield icon on it. Record what happens.
8. Sign out and then sign in as Guest.
9. Note the key difference on the Start screen and then record it in your file.
10. Sign out and then sign in with the original account you used in Step 1 or the account you usually use (if different).
11. Submit your file to your instructor.

Using Encryption to Secure Files ■■■■■■■■■■■■■■

By default, Windows 8 uses **NTFS** as its *file system*. Windows 8 supports some older file systems for backward compatibility, such as **FAT16** and **FAT32**, but if you use NTFS you get additional benefits in file management. One of these benefits is the ability to encrypt files.

Understanding Encryption

When multiple users share a computer, each user account has its own private file storage areas, including its libraries. Users cannot browse each other's libraries. However, when a user stores a file in a folder that all users can access, that file is unprotected and anyone may work with it.

Encrypting provides security for a file that is stored in one of those public areas. When a user encrypts a file or folder, it becomes the private property of that user, and it can be accessed only when the user that created it is signed in. This is true regardless of its storage location, as long as it is stored on a drive that uses NTFS.

Encryption is based on the user account, not on a password (except in the sense that the user account itself has a password for signing in). As long as you are signed in as the user who encrypted the file, the encryption is invisible. The only indication that a file or folder is encrypted is that its name appears in green. You can encrypt either a folder or an individual file. When you encrypt a folder, everything inside that folder is also encrypted, but if you move any of those items outside the folder, they lose their encryption. On the other hand, when you encrypt an individual file, it remains encrypted as long as it is on an NTFS drive. (If you move it to a drive that uses some other file system, it becomes unencrypted.) Microsoft recommends encrypting folders rather than files whenever feasible because it is easier to keep track of what is encrypted that way.

NTFS Stands for New Technology File System; a 32-bit file system for Windows 2000, Windows XP, Windows Vista, Windows 7, and Windows 8 that offers improvements over older file systems

file system A set of rules for how the operating system stores and retrieves files on a disk

FAT16 A 16-bit file system, now mostly obsolete, used with MS-DOS and Windows 95

FAT32 A 32-bit file system, now mostly obsolete, used with Windows 98 and Windows Me

To encrypt a folder:

1. Right-click the folder in a File Explorer window and then click *Properties*.
2. On the General tab, click Advanced.
3. Mark the *Encrypt contents to secure data* check box.

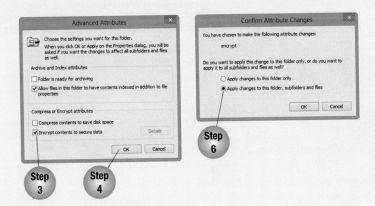

4. Click OK.
5. Click OK to close the Properties box.
6. If necessary, click *Apply changes to this folder, subfolders and files*.
7. Click OK.

To encrypt an individual file:

1. Right-click the file and then click *Properties*.
2. On the General tab, click Advanced.
3. Mark the *Encrypt contents to secure data* check box.
4. Click OK.
5. Click OK to close the Properties box.
6. Click *Encrypt the file only*.
7. Click OK.

To decrypt a folder or file:

1. Right-click the folder or file and then click *Properties*.
2. On the General tab, click Advanced.
3. Clear the *Encrypt contents to secure data* check box.
4. Click OK.
5. Click OK to close the Properties box and then respond to any warning messages that appear.

Understanding BitLocker

BitLocker Drive Encryption is an advanced Windows 8 feature that enables you to encrypt the contents of an entire disk drive. Although using BitLocker for a hard disk drive is an advanced feature that requires an administrator to change system policy settings, you can use BitLocker To Go to encrypt your USB flash drives for greater file security. This can be particularly useful if you have personal financial information or confidential business information that you need to protect, yet store on a portable drive.

To use BitLocker To Go on a USB Flash drive:

1. Insert your USB flash drive in a USB port.
2. From the desktop, select the Settings charm and then click *Control Panel*.
3. Click *System and Security*.
4. Click Bitlocker Drive Encryption.
5. Click the down-pointing arrow button at the right of your flash drive.
6. Click Turn on BitLocker.
7. In the dialog box, click the *Use a password to unlock the drive* check box.
8. Enter and confirm the password in the applicable text boxes.
9. Click Next.
10. At the next screen that asks how to back up your recovery key, click Save to a file. Select a save location, enter a file name in the Save BitLocker recovery key as dialog box, and then click Save.
11. Click Next.
12. Leave Encrypt used disk space only selected and then click Next.
13. Click Start encrypting.
14. At the message that encryption is complete, click Close.

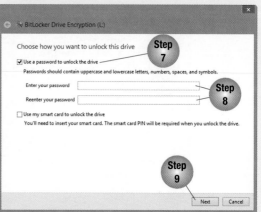

To remove BitLocker To Go protection from a USB Flash drive:

1. Insert your USB flash drive in a USB port.
2. From the desktop, select the Settings charm and then click *Control Panel*.
3. Click *System and Security*.
4. Click Bitlocker Drive Encryption.
5. Click the down-pointing arrow button at the right of your flash drive.
6. Click Unlock drive. At the BitLocker prompt, type in the password you assigned and press Enter.
7. If a confirmation dialog box appears, click Turn off BitLocker again.
8. At the message that decryption is complete, click Close.

Exercise 3

Encrypting and Decrypting Files

1. Open a Word document and save it as **C15E03**.
2. Open the Chapter 15 data folder.
3. Encrypt the file **EncryptMe.rtf**. Encrypt only the individual file, not the folder.

    Note: *If prompted to back up your encryption certificate and key, click Back Up later.*

4. Sign out and then sign in as a different user.

5. Try to open **EncryptMe.rtf**, entering an administrator password, if prompted. Record the error message that appears in your file.
6. Sign out and then sign in using your original user account.
7. Copy the file **EncryptMe.rtf** to the desktop. Is it still encrypted? Record the answer and explain how you determined this.
8. Decrypt the original **EncryptMe.rtf**.
9. Encrypt the Chapter 15 data folder and all of its contents.
10. Sign out and then sign in as a different user.
11. Open the Chapter 15 data folder. Record any error message that appears.
12. Copy **EncryptMe.rtf** from the Chapter 15 folder to the desktop and then record any prompts or messages that appear. Is it still encrypted? Record the answer and explain how you determined this.
13. Sign out and then sign in using your original user account.
14. Decrypt the Chapter 15 data folder.
15. Drag all copies you made on the desktop to the Recycle Bin.
16. Submit your file to your instructor.
17. Delete the user account named Test.
18. [Optional] Disable the Guest user account.

CHAPTER SUMMARY

- To view system information, open the Control Panel, click *System and Security*, and then click System. You also can click File Explorer from the desktop, right-click *Computer* in the Navigation pane, and then choose *Properties*. Or, select the Settings charm from the desktop and then click *PC info*.

- For more detailed information, select the Settings charm, click *Control Panel*, *System and Security*, Administrative Tools, and then double-click *System Information*.

- To rate your system's performance, open the Control Panel, choose *System and Security*, System, and then Performance Information and Tools. Click Re-run the assessment to update your computer's Windows Experience Index base score.

- To view CPU and memory usage, display the Task Manager by right-clicking the Taskbar on the desktop and choosing *Task Manager*. Click the Performance tab.

- Windows 8 security is handled via user accounts, which are secured by passwords.

- User Account Control (UAC) is a security feature that restricts certain activities based on the permission level of the signed-in user. Users can have either Administrator (full) or Standard (partial) permission level.

- To adjust the UAC level, open the Control Panel, choose *User Accounts and Family Safety*, User Accounts, Change User Account Control settings.

- To remove a user account, open the Control Panel and then, under *User Accounts and Family Safety*, click Remove user accounts. Click the account and then click Delete the account.

- A strong password is one that is difficult to guess.

- To change your Microsoft account's password, from the Start screen select the Settings charm and then click *Change PC settings*. Click the *Users* category, click Change your password, and then follow the prompts.

- To change a local account's password, from User Accounts and Family Safety, select the user, click Change the password, and then follow the prompts.

- To enable or disable the Guest account on the system, from User Accounts and Family Safety, click User Accounts, Manage another account, Guest. Click Turn on or Turn off the guest account.

- The Windows 8 file system, NTFS (New Technology File System), enables users to encrypt files so that other people signed in to the same computer cannot view them.

- To encrypt a file or folder, right-click it and then choose *Properties*. On the General tab, click Advanced, click *Encrypt contents to secure data*, and then click OK.

- Use BitLocker To Go to encrypt a USB flash drive.

CONCEPTS CHECK

Completion: Answer the following questions in a Word document.

Part 1

Multiple Choice

1. Which piece of information is *not* available when you select System in the Control Panel?
   a. CPU speed
   b. CPU type
   c. Amount of RAM
   d. Display adapter

2. How do you find out the computer's Windows Experience Index score?
   a. Open the Control Panel, click *System and Security*, System, Performance Information and Tools
   b. Right-click Computer and then click *Manage*
   c. Open the Control Panel and then click *System and Security*
   d. Open the Control Panel and then click *Advanced Tools*

3. Suppose a system has different subscores for each of the five performance areas. What is the computer's overall Windows Experience Index base score?
   a. The average of those numbers
   b. The lowest of those numbers
   c. The highest of those numbers
   d. None of the above

4. What are the primary two factors measured on the Performance tab of the Task Manager?
   a. Hard disk access and CPU usage
   b. CPU usage and display adapter frames per second
   c. CPU usage and memory usage
   d. Number of applications running and number of services

5. If your system suddenly starts running sluggishly and your CPU usage is at 100 percent, what is probably the problem?
   a. Inadequate CPU
   b. Not enough RAM
   c. Malfunctioning application
   d. Bad device driver

6. The primary purpose of User Access Control (UAC) is to _____ .
   a. prevent users from reading each other's documents
   c. prevent virus infection
   b. enhance the effectiveness of the Windows Firewall
   d. prevent one user from making system changes that will affect other users

7. Which type of user is blocked from performing certain system activities via UAC?
   a. Remote
   b. Standard
   c. Administrator
   d. Roaming

8. What is the name of the built-in user account that is designed to allow people who do not have their own individual user accounts to use the computer?
   a. Standard
   b. Open
   c. Visitor
   d. Guest

9. When a file is encrypted, in what color does its file name appear?
   a. Black
   b. Red
   c. Green
   d. Blue

10. What happens when you copy a file (not individually encrypted) from an encrypted folder to an unencrypted one?
    a. The file stays encrypted.
    b. The file becomes unencrypted.
    c. An error message appears and the file does not copy.
    d. A shortcut rather than a true copy is created.

Part 2

Short Answer

11. What can you find out from System Information that you cannot glean from the System area in the Control Panel? List at least three things.

    _____

12. How is the Windows Experience Index base score determined?

    _____

13. What is the primary difference between the Windows Experience Index score and the performance information you can gather from the Task Manager's Performance tab?

    _____

14. What four factors can you monitor from the Resource Monitor?

_____

15. What does a shield icon mean when it appears next to a link in the Control Panel?

_____

16. Why does Microsoft recommend that you run Windows 8 as a Standard user rather than as an Administrator on a day-to-day basis?

_____

17. Describe how to change the password for a Microsoft account.

_____

18. Why would you disable a user account rather than remove it?

_____

19. Describe the qualities of a strong password and give an example.

_____

20. Why would you typically need to encrypt a folder located outside a protected location such as your Documents folder?

_____

SKILLS | CHECK

Save all solution files to the default Documents folder or any alternate folder specified by your instructor.

Guided Check

Assessment 1

Collecting System Information

1. Determine the model and speed of your computer's CPU and the amount of RAM it has.
   a. From the desktop, click the File Explorer button on the Taskbar.
   b. Right-click *Computer* in the Navigation pane and then click *Properties*.
   c. View the Processor and Memory (RAM) information in the System area of the Control Panel.
   Processor model: _____
   RAM installed: _____
2. Determine the exact version of Windows 8 you have from System Information.
   a. With the Control Panel window still open, click Control Panel Home in the upper left corner. Click *System and Security*, click Administrative Tools, and then double-click *System Information* in the list.
   b. Record the Version number listed in the System Summary.
   Windows version: _____

3. Determine the display adapter model from System Information.
   a. Double-click *Components*.
   b. Click *Display*.
   c. Record the display Name listed in the top line of the right pane.
      Display adapter model: _____
4. Close the System Information, Administrative Tools, and Control Panel windows.
5. Record the information you gathered in a Word document, save it as **C15A01**, and then submit it to your instructor.

Assessment

2

Rating System Performance
1. View your system's Windows Experience Index base score and then determine which subsystem has the lowest score.
   a. From the desktop, select the Settings charm and then click *Control Panel*.
   b. Click *System and Security*.
   c. Click System.
   d. Click Performance Information and Tools at lower right.
   e. Click Re-run the assessment. (If the computer has not previously been assessed, click Rate this computer.)
   f. Examine the scores of each subsystem, and then record the following information.
      Your system's overall score: _____
      Subsystem with lowest score: _____
2. Open the Resource Monitor.
   a. Right-click the Taskbar.
   b. Click *Task Manager*.
   c. If needed, click the More details button and then click the Performance tab.
   d. Click Open Resource Monitor at the bottom.
3. In the Resource Monitor window, be sure to click the CPU choice in the list at the left and then record the following information as you open and close several applications.
   Average usage level when using a small application such as Calculator:
   _____
   Average usage level when using a large application:
   Application: _____
   CPU usage: _____
   Highest usage percentage observed at any point: _____
4. Close the Task Manager and Control Panel windows.
5. Record the information you gathered in a Word document, save it as **C15A02**, and then submit it to your instructor.

Assessment

3

Creating and Deleting User Accounts
1. Create a local, standard user account.
   a. Sign in using an Administrator account.
   b. From the Start screen, select the Settings charm and then click *Change PC settings*.
   c. Click the *Users* category.
   d. Under *Other users*, click Add a user.
   e. Click Sign in without a Microsoft account and then click Local account.
   f. Type Standard Student in the *User name* text box.

2. Set a password for Standard Student.
   a. Type **student** in the *Password* box.
   b. Type **student** in the *Reenter password* box.
   c. Type **Not a teacher** in the *Password hint* box.
   d. Click Next and then click Finish.
3. Capture a screen shot of the PC settings screen showing icons for each user account on the system at this point (scroll down, if needed). Save the file as **C15A03S03** and then submit it to your instructor. Return to the PC settings screen.
4. Sign out and then sign in as Standard Student.
   a. Drag down from the top of the screen to close PC settings.
   b. Click your user name at upper right.
   c. Click Sign out.
   d. Swipe up from the bottom of the lock screen and then click Standard Student.
   e. Type **student** in the *Password* box and then press Enter.
5. Open PC settings and then attempt to create another user account.
   a. From the Start screen, select the Settings charm, and then click *Change PC settings*.
   b. Click the *Users* category.
   c. Note, under *Other users*, the message that you must sign in as an administrator to add users.
6. Remove the password from the Standard Student account.
   a. Under *Sign-in options* on the PC settings screen, click Change your password.
   b. Type **student** in the *Current password* box and then click Next.
   c. Leave all of the text boxes blank on the next screen, click Next, and then click Finish.
   d. Close the PC settings screen by dragging down from the top.
7. Sign out and then sign in as the user you were originally signed in as.
   a. Click the Standard Student user name at the upper right of the Start screen.
   b. Click Sign out.
   c. Drag up from the bottom of the screen to display the users.
   d. Click your user account.
   e. Type your password in the *Password* box and then press Enter.
8. Delete the Standard Student account.
   a. Sign in using an Administrator account.
   b. Click the Desktop tile on the Start screen, select the Settings charm, and then click *Control Panel*.
   c. Click *User Accounts and Family Safety*.
   d. Under User Accounts, click Remove user accounts.
   e. Click Standard Student.
   f. Click Delete the account.
   g. Click Delete Files.
   h. Click Delete Account.
9. Enable the Guest account.
   a. Back at the list of accounts, click Guest.
   b. Click Turn On.
10. Capture a screen shot of the Manage Accounts window at this point, showing that the Standard Student account has been deleted and the Guest account enabled. Save the file as **C15A03S10** and then submit it to your instructor.

11. Disable the Guest account.
    a. Click Guest.
    b. Click Turn off the guest account.
12. Close the Control Panel window.

Assessment

Encrypting Files

4

1. Encrypt the entire Paradigm Windows 8 folder on your hard disk.
   a. Open a File Explorer window on the desktop and then navigate to the location that holds the Paradigm Windows 8 folder.
   b. Right-click the *Paradigm Windows 8* folder and then click *Properties*.
   c. On the General tab, click Advanced.
   d. Click *Encrypt contents to secure data*.
   e. Click OK.
   f. Click OK to close the Properties box.
   g. If necessary, click *Apply changes to this folder, subfolders and files*.
   h. Click OK.
2. Copy the Chapter 15 data folder to a USB flash drive.
   a. Double-click the *Paradigm Windows 8* folder.
   b. Select the Chapter 15 data folder and then press Ctrl + C.
   c. Insert the USB flash drive and then display its contents.
   d. Press Ctrl + V.
3. Sign in as a different user. Create a new user account, if needed.
   a. Go to the Start screen.
   b. Click your user name at upper right.
   c. Click Sign out.
   d. Swipe up from the bottom of the screen, and then click a different user account than you used previously.
   e. Type the password and then press Enter.
4. Attempt to access the Chapter 15 data folder both on the hard disk and on the USB flash drive.
5. In a Word document, write a brief explanation of what happened when you tried each. Save it as **C15A04** and then submit it to your instructor.
6. Sign in using the original user account you started with and then display the desktop.
7. Remove encryption from the Paradigm Windows 8 folder.
   a. Open a File Explorer window and then navigate to the location that holds the *Paradigm Windows 8* folder.
   b. Right-click the Paradigm Windows 8 folder and then click *Properties*.
   c. On the General tab, click Advanced.
   d. Clear the *Encrypt contents to secure data* check box.
   e. Click OK.
   f. Click OK to close the Properties box.
   g. With the *Apply changes to this folder, subfolders and files* check box checked, click OK.
8. Close the File Explorer window.

On Your Own

Assessment

Comparing Information from Different Utilities

5

1. Open the System Information utility. From the desktop, click Settings charm, *Control Panel*, *System and Security*, Administrative Tools, and double-click *System Information*.

2. Open Device Manager. (Device Manager was covered in Chapter 14.) From the *System and Security* category in the Control Panel, click Device Manager under System.

3. In Device Manager, choose View, *Resources by type*.

4. Compare the information presented in the *Hardware Resources* section of System Information to the information shown in Device Manager.

5. In a Word document, write a report summarizing the major differences and similarities, and describe situations in which one or the other might be more useful. Save it as **C15A05S05**.

6. Close Device Manager and then open the System Configuration utility (MSCONFIG). From the Administrative Tools window, double-click *System Configuration*.

7. In the System Configuration window, click the Startup tab.

8. On the Startup tab, click Open Task Manager.

9. Compare the information presented in the two windows.

10. In a Word document, write a report summarizing the major differences and similarities, and describe situations in which one or the other might be more useful. Save it as **C15A05S10**.

11. Submit your reports to your instructor.

12. Close all open windows.

Assessment 6

Planning System Improvements

1. Complete Assessment 1 to get a snapshot of your system's performance and bottleneck areas.

2. Formulate a plan for improving the system's Windows Experience Index base score, which might include buying new hardware, finding new drivers, or other activities.

3. Research online the prices and availability of the solution you propose.

4. In a Word document, write a report explaining your plan, its benefits, and its estimated cost. Save it as **C15A06** and then submit it to your instructor.

Assessment 7

Experimenting with User Access Control

1. Open a command prompt window, type secpol.msc, and then press Enter. Or, open Control Panel, click *System and Security*, click Administrative Tools, and then double-click *Local Security Policy*.

2. Open Local Policies > Security Options.

3. Make sure that *User Account Control: Behavior of the elevation prompt for standard users* is set to *Prompt for credentials*.

4. Sign out and then sign in as a Standard user. (Create a standard account first if none exists.)

5. Try to access an item in the Control Panel that a standard user would not normally be able to access. Record the exact wording of the message or prompt that appears in a Word document and then save it as **C15A07**.

6. Sign out and then sign in with an Administrator-level user account.

7. Open the Local Security Policy utility (**secpol.msc**), as described in Step 1.

8. Open Local Policies > Security Options.

9. Set *User Account Control: Behavior of the elevation prompt for standard users* to *Automatically deny elevation requests*.

10. Sign out and then sign in as a Standard user.

11. Try to access an item in the Control Panel that a standard user would not normally be able to access. Record in your file the exact wording of the message or prompt that appears.

12. Sign out and then sign in with an Administrator-level user account.

13. Turn User Access Control off altogether and then restart the computer.

14. When the computer reboots, sign in as a Standard user.
15. Try to access an item in the Control Panel that a standard user would not normally be able to access. Observe what happens.
16. Write a report explaining what happened at Steps 5, 11, and 15 in your file and then submit it to your instructor.
17. Reset *Behavior of the elevation prompt for standard users* to *Prompt for credentials* in the Local Security Policy utility, and reset User Access Control to its default (restart your computer afterward, if necessary).

Assessment

8

Experimenting with Encryption
1. Encrypt an individual file (any file from the Paradigm Windows 8 folder).
2. Make copies of that file in as many of these locations as you have access to:
   • In a different folder on the same hard disk
   • On a different hard disk that also uses the NTFS file system
   • On a hard disk that uses the FAT16 or FAT32 file system
   • On the Windows 8 desktop
   • On a USB flash drive
   • On a writable CD or DVD disc
3. Sign out and then sign in as a different user.
4. Try to access each of those copies. In a Word document, write a report listing which ones you could access and which ones you could not. Try to determine on what basis some copies were available and others were not, and include your hypothesis in your report. Save the report as **C15A08** and then submit it to your instructor.

CHALLENGE PROJECT

Your company is considering purchasing a new 3-D graphics application. The product has the following minimum requirements:
   • Windows 7 or higher
   • 2 GHz or faster CPU
   • 4 GB of RAM
   • CD or DVD drive
   • Display adapter with at least 128 MB video RAM
   • Hard disk drive with at least 2 GB of free space

1. Gather information about your system and determine whether it meets these requirements.
2. In a Word document, write a brief report explaining how you gathered the needed information, and compare the system's actual specifications to the required ones.
3. Because the minimum specifications for a program are just that—minimums—and often insufficient for that program's top performance, how likely is it that this program will run at its top performance on your current computer? Explain your answer.
4. Save your report as **C15A09** and then submit it to your instructor.

Sharing Information On and Off the Road

PERFORMANCE OBJECTIVES

Upon successful completion of Chapter 16, you will be able to:

- Synchronize folders and computers
- Fix syncing problems
- Set up your system to use offline folders
- View web content offline
- Enable Remote Desktop connections and specify allowed users

- Make a Remote Desktop connection
- Use Windows Mobility Center to manage battery power and more
- Use Presentation features
- Conserve battery power on a mobile computer

Today's mobile computers and devices facilitate a "work anywhere" environment like never before. Windows 8 includes a number of features to help you work more effectively with mobile computers in the business environment. This chapter shows you how to use the mobile computing and networking functions offered in Windows 8.

Syncing Files between Devices ■■■■■■■■■■■■■■■■

Synchronization (a.k.a. sync) is the process of keeping multiple copies of the same file matched with each other. For example, if you have the same document on your desktop computer and your notebook computer, the Sync feature can make sure that every time the two computers connect with one another, they compare notes about which has the more recent version, and the computer containing the older copy updates itself from the newer copy. You also can sync files between your computer and a network file server, or, in some cases, between your computer and a portable music player or smartphone. Windows 8 syncing is handled via the Sync Center. Figure 16.1 shows the Sync Center window. In Figure 16.1, Offline Files, a feature that you will learn about later in this chapter, has already been set up. This feature may not yet be enabled on your computer.

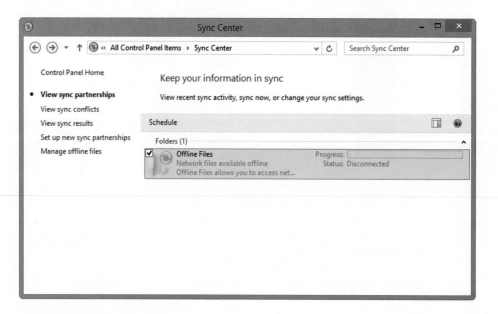

Figure 16.1 The Sync Center window.

Here's How **To open the Sync Center:**

1. Open the Control Panel.
2. Click the *View by* down-pointing arrow and then click *Large icons*.
3. Click Sync Center.

When you issue a command to perform synchronization, the Sync Center compares the versions in each location. If they are identical, it does nothing. If they are different, it determines which version to keep and which to replace. If it finds a new file in one place, it copies it to the other; if it finds that you have deleted a file in one location, it deletes it from the other. (You set up rules to tell it which location should be the ruling one when locations differ in their content.)

Before you can use the Sync Center, you must have something to synchronize. The next section explains how to set up offline files for this purpose.

Making Network Files Available Offline

Offline Files Network files that are locally cached (saved) on your hard disk so that copies are available even when the network is not functioning; also refers generically to the copies of the network files stored on your local computer

When important files are stored on a network, if the network becomes unavailable for a period of time, anyone who needs to use those files is out of luck. Depending on the nature of the files, this can be a significant inconvenience. *Offline Files* is a feature that alleviates this problem by storing copies of those network files locally on your own hard disk. If the network files are unavailable, you can still use the local copies.

You can set an individual file or an entire folder to be available offline. The only criteria are that the location must exist on a computer other than your own and that both locations are on the same network. You can synchronize between a desktop computer and a notebook, between two notebooks, or any other combination.

Offline Files must be enabled before you can use this feature, and it may be disabled, by default, on your computer. See the following steps to learn how to enable it and how to choose which files to make available offline.

To enable Offline Files:

1. From the Sync Center, click *Manage offline files*.
2. If the Enable offline files button appears, click it. (If Disable offline files appears, Offline Files is already enabled.)

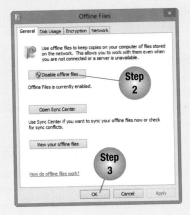

3. Click OK.
4. If a message appears that you must restart your computer, click Yes.

To set a file or folder for offline use:

1. Open File Explorer and then browse your network to locate the folder or file you want to make available offline.
2. Right-click the folder or file.
3. Click *Always available offline*.

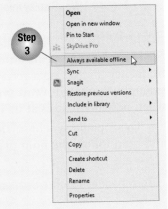

Viewing Synchronization Status

Once you have set up at least one file or folder to be available offline, synchronization occurs automatically in the background. A Sync Center icon appears in the notification area (shown in Figure 16.2); you can click this icon to display the Sync Center.

Figure 16.2 The Sync Center icon appears in the notification area after the first synchronization.

In the Sync Center, you can check the synchronization status by clicking the *View sync results* choice in the list at the left. If any errors occurred, they appear in the Sync Results; otherwise, messages appear here showing when the sync started and completed, as shown in Figure 16.3. When a sync runs, a progress bar appears. After the sync finishes, if any errors occurred, a link identifying the number of errors appears. Clicking that link is another method to view errors. Click *View sync partnerships* in the pane at the left to return to the starting point for syncing.

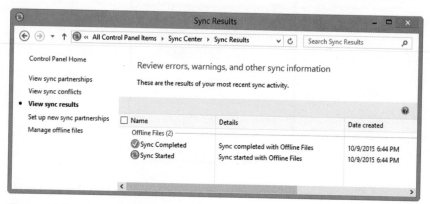

Figure 16.3 Display information about the most recent sync activity.

Scheduling Synchronization

Synchronization occurs automatically, by default, but you may want to adjust its frequency and set up a certain time at which files should be synchronized. For example, you might want synchronization to occur in the middle of the night when network load is at its lowest point.

To schedule synchronization, click the Schedule button in the Sync Center and then follow the prompts to set up a specific time and interval.

Here's How

To schedule synchronization:

1. Open the Sync Center.
2. Select the item to sync, such as Offline Files or a specific folder within Offline Files.
3. Click Schedule.

Note: *If there is already an existing schedule, a prompt appears after Step 3 asking whether you want to create a new schedule, modify an existing one, or delete an existing one.*

4. Mark or clear check boxes for the items to sync. The items listed here are the remote folders/files you have previously set up to be available offline.
5. Click Next.

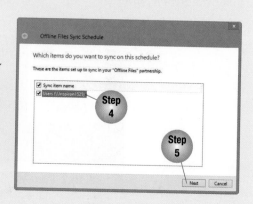

6. Select the way the sync will be triggered:
    *   At a scheduled time
    *   When an event occurs
7. If you chose *At a scheduled time* in Step 6, specify a start date and time and how often the sync should repeat. If you chose *When an event occurs* in Step 6, mark the check boxes for the events that should trigger the sync.

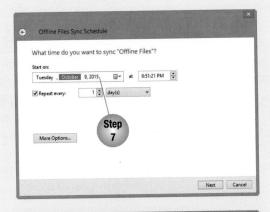

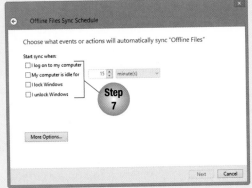

8. (Optional) Set additional options as follows:
    a. Click More Options.
    b. Mark or clear check boxes as desired to fine-tune the scheduling.
    c. Click OK.
9. Click Next.
10. Type a name for the sync schedule.
11. Click Save schedule.

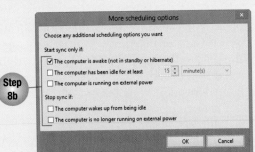

To edit an existing sync schedule:

1. Open the Sync Center.
2. Select the item with the sync schedule, such as Offline Files.
3. Click the Schedule button.
4. Click *View or edit an existing sync schedule*.
5. Click the sync schedule you want to change.
6. Click Next.
7. Complete Steps 4–11 of the preceding procedure.

To delete a sync schedule:

1. Open the Sync Center.
2. Select the item with the sync schedule, such as Offline Files.
3. Click the Schedule button.
4. Click *Delete an existing sync schedule*.
5. Click the sync schedule to delete.
6. Click Delete.
7. Click OK.

Performing a Manual Synchronization and Resolving Conflicts

In addition to following a synchronization schedule, Windows 8 can perform manual synchronization any time you request it. To initiate a manual sync, click the item to sync in the Sync Center and then click the Sync button.

When a network connection is temporarily unavailable and both copies are edited in the interim, the next time you try to synchronize, a conflict occurs. Because both the local and the network version changed, Windows 8 is not sure which changes should prevail.

To resolve a sync conflict:

1. Open the Sync Center, if needed.
2. Click *View sync conflicts* in the list at the left.
3. Click a conflict in the list.
4. Click Resolve.
5. Select the version you want to keep or choose to keep both versions.

Exercise 1

Synchronizing Offline Files

1. Open File Explorer and then browse to a network location that contains one or more documents. Your instructor may provide a path to a network location to use for this exercise. If not, you can use any folder on any shared drive, either on a file server or on another user's computer. To keep it simple, use a document in plain text or RTF format.
2. Make one or more network documents or folders always available offline from your computer:
   a. Right-click the document.
   b. Click *Always available offline*.
3. Allow the sync to complete and then close the window.
4. Disconnect your network connection. Open the Network and Sharing Center and then disable the wireless connection. If it is a wired connection, unplug the network cable from the back of your computer.
5. Open the Sync Center.
6. Click *Manage offline files* in the list at the left.
7. Click the View your offline files button.
8. In the window that appears, browse again to the network file you chose in Step 1. (You may have to start from the Computer icon.) Ordinarily you would not be able to do this without a connection, but because Offline Files is active by default, you can browse the local copies of the files in that location.

9. Capture a screen shot of the file window showing the offline files, and then save the file as **C16E01**.
10. Open an offline document file in that location, make a minor change to it, and then save and close it.
11. Reconnect the network connection.
12. Sync the files:
    a. Open the Sync Center.
    b. Click Offline Files.
    c. Click the Sync button.
13. If any conflicts occurred (which may happen if other students also opened and modified the same file and then synchronized their changes), choose to keep the copy on your own local hard disk.
14. Submit the screen shot to your instructor.

Note that you can sync offline files manually at any time by clicking the Sync button that appears in the Windows Mobility Center (shown in Figure 16.6 later in this chapter) and then clicking *Sync offline files in this folder if it appears* when you browse to the location marked for offline use. You also can use the Sync Center to sync offline files, as previously discussed in this chapter.

Viewing Web Content Offline

Switching to offline viewing when browsing the Web in Internet Explorer (IE) is useful if you have an insecure or pricey Internet connection, as when you are browsing via a "free" dialup plan in which your usage minutes are limited. You can browse to a page, wait until it fully loads, go offline, read the contents, and then go back online when you are ready to move to the next page.

To go offline after a Web page loads, open the File menu in Internet Explorer (press Alt, if needed, to access the menu system) and then click *Work Offline*, as shown in Figure 16.4. To resume working online, open the File menu and choose *Work Offline* again to remove the check beside it.

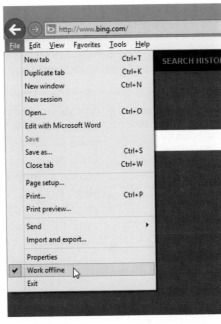

Figure 16.4 You can go offline and back online in Internet Explorer.

1. Click the Internet Explorer button on the Taskbar to launch Internet Explorer.
2. Go to www.emcp.com.
3. Click the Mission Statement link near the top of the page.
4. After the page loads, open the File menu (Alt + F) and then click *Work offline*.

5. Click the Careers link. A message appears telling you that Internet Explorer went online to open the requested web page.
6. Capture a screen shot of the message and then save the file as **C16E02S07**.
7. Click Go back offline.
8. Disable your Internet connection temporarily.
9. Click the Contact link. A message appears notifying you that you are not connected to a network.
10. Capture a screen shot of the message and then save the file as **C16E02S11**.
11. Close the Webpage unavailable while offline message, and then click Back. The prior EMC Publishing web page appears.
12. Reenable your Internet connection.
13. Close Internet Explorer.
14. Submit the screen shots to your instructor.

Connecting to a System with Remote Desktop ▪▪

The Remote Desktop capability goes beyond giving you the simple ability to work with copies of files offline. With a Remote Desktop connection, you can connect to another computer over the local network or the Internet. Not only can you access files on the computer, but you also can use the programs installed on that computer and possibly other resources, such as printers, if the network permits.

Making a Remote Desktop connection works like this:

host The computer that holds the files, programs, and resources to be used during a Remote Desktop connection

- The computer that holds the files, programs, and other resources to access is called the *host*. This computer must use a Windows version that enables it to serve as a Remote Desktop host. Window XP Professional, and the Business, Enterprise, and Ultimate Editions of Windows Vista and Windows 7 and 8 enable a computer to serve as a host. The host computer must be set up to allow Remote Desktop connections, and the host computer must be turned on. The host computer might be your desktop computer at work that has the working files and programs you need to complete a project.

- The computer that you will use to access the host from a remote location is called the client. This computer can be running any version of Windows 8, 7, or Vista, as well as either version of Windows XP, as long as the Remote Desktop client software has been downloaded from Microsoft and installed, if needed. The client computer might be your mobile computer for work, with which you are accessing the Internet wirelessly or over the company network, for example.

- Both computers must be connected directly to the company network or connected remotely to the company network via the Internet and on the same workgroup. The network must allow permission for this type of connection. Windows Firewall has to be set on both computers to allow Remote Desktop as an Exception. Also, if authentication is not required, then that security feature must be turned off on the host computer.

If your office desktop computer is set up to serve as the host and is connected to the company network, you could connect to your desktop over the company's network with your mobile computer while in a colleague's office to demonstrate a new piece of software, for example. Or, if you live a distance from work and need to work from home, you could leave the office system on and connected to the Internet in case you need to sign in and transfer files or access a program not installed on your mobile computer, such as a corporate accounting program.

Enabling Your Computer for Remote Desktop Connections

Enabling your Windows 8 computer to serve as the host for Remote Desktop connections may sound intimidating, but you turn the feature on easily through the Control Panel.

To enable Remote Desktop connections to your computer (the host):

Here's How

1. Open the Control Panel and then click *System and Security*.
2. Under *System*, click Allow remote access. If a User Account Control dialog box appears, enter the administrator password and then click Yes. The System Properties dialog box appears with the Remote tab selected.
3. Mark the Allow remote connections to this computer check box, if it is not already selected.
4. If a Remote Desktop message box warns you about the system being set for sleep and hibernate, click OK.
5. Click OK.

Specifying Who Can Connect via Remote Desktop

For security reasons, the ability to connect to a host system via Remote Desktop works by inclusion. On the host system, you must identify each user who is allowed to connect. Generally speaking, you should add yourself (because you might be signing in to your own system from another system to fix it) or any other users who have a user account on the host system.

To add yourself or another user to the list of users who can sign in to the host system:

Here's How

1. Open the Control Panel and then click *System and Security*.
2. Under *System*, click Allow remote access. If a User Account Control dialog box appears, enter the administrator password and then click Yes. The System Properties dialog box appears with the Remote tab selected.
3. Click Select Users.
4. Click Add in the Remote Desktop Users dialog box.
5. Type the user's name in the *Enter the object names to select* box of the Select Users dialog box.
6. Click OK. The user's name (or email address) appears in the list of users.
7. Click OK to close the Remote Desktop Users dialog box.
8. Click OK to close the System Properties dialog box.
9. Close the Control Panel.

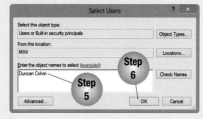

Making a Remote Desktop Connection

To connect remotely to another computer, your computer and the remote one must both be connected to a common network and must both be powered up. You can then start Remote Desktop and make the connection.

Here's How

To connect to a host computer via Remote Desktop:

1. On the client computer, from the Start screen, type Remote, and then click Remote Desktop Connection.
2. In the Remote Desktop Connection dialog box, type the name of the computer to connect to on the network in the *Computer* text box. (Or, click the drop-down list arrow, and then click a listed computer or browse for another, depending on the version of Windows that you are using and how the network is set up.) For some networks, you may need to type the host system's IP address. For connecting over the Internet, you need to include both the domain name and computer name.

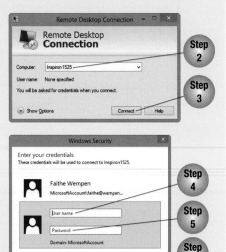

3. Click Connect.
4. Type your user name (the one you added to the host system) in the top *User name* text box. Or, if your email address appears in the dialog box, click it to select it to use for sign in.
5. Type your password in the *Password* text box.
6. Click OK.
7. If a message informs you that Remote Desktop cannot verify the host computer's identity, click Yes.
8. If your remote system is on a network that requires authentication, you are prompted to enter that information. Do so at the prompt and then click OK or Connect to continue.

   The remote computer's desktop (or Start screen) appears on your screen with a title bar across the top that displays the name of the remote computer.

Note: *Some Remote Desktop connections require a Remote Desktop (RD) Gateway for connecting to a corporate network and may require the assistance of your network administrator. You can click Show Options in the Remote Desktop Connection dialog box, click the Advanced tab, and then click the Settings button to change RD Gateway settings as advised by your system administrator.*

When the remote desktop initially appears, it may be maximized on the desktop. If so, a title bar appears at the top of the screen that displays the name of the remote computer and contains Minimize, Restore, and Close buttons (shown in Figure 16.5). Click the Restore Down button at the top to reduce it to a window. Within the window, you can start programs, view folders and files, and perform other needed activities using the resources of the host computer. To close the connection, close the window. In the Remote Desktop Connection dialog box that prompts you to confirm the disconnect, click OK.

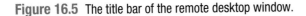

Figure 16.5 The title bar of the remote desktop window.

Exercise 3

Establish a Remote Desktop Connection

Note: This exercise requires that you have access to two computers that are both running Windows 8 and are on the same network. One person can do this with two computers, or two people can do the exercise together each on his or her own computer. One computer will be arbitrarily designated "A" and the other "B." Your instructor will provide an administrator password. Both users should sign in to an account with a password.

1. Enable Remote Desktop Connection on both computers:
   a. Open the Control Panel and click *System and Security*.
   b. Under the *System* heading, click the Allow remote access link. If a User Account Control dialog box appears, enter the administrator password and then click Yes. The System Properties dialog box appears with the Remote tab selected.
   c. Click *Allow remote connections to this coputer*.
   d. If a Remote Desktop message box warns you about the system being set for sleep and hibernate, click OK.
   e. Click OK.
2. On computer A, start Remote Desktop Connection: (If the connection is unsuccessful, specify users who can connect using the steps shown previously in this chapter.)
   a. From the Start screen, begin typing and then click Remote Desktop Connection.
   b. Enter the name of computer B in the *Computer* text box.

Note: If you do not know the computer's name, open the System item in the Control Panel; the computer's name appears in the Computer name, domain, and workgroup settings area.

   c. Click Connect.
   d. Enter or select the user name.
   e. Enter the password.
   f. Click OK. Click Yes if prompted that the identity of the remote system cannot be verified.
3. On computer A, open the Control Panel in the Remote Desktop session:
   a. Open File Explorer and then click Control Panel in the Navigation pane.
   b. If the Remote Desktop Connection window appears maximized, click the Restore Down button at the top middle area of the screen.
   c. On computer A, capture a screen shot of the desktop and then save the file as **C16E03**.
4. On computer A, stop the Remote Desktop Connection:
   a. Click the connection window Close (X) button.
   b. Click OK when prompted to finish disconnecting.
5. Reverse roles and then repeat Steps 2–4 to connect to computer A from computer B. The user of computer B should capture a screen shot from his or her own computer so that each user has a screen shot of the connection that he or she made.
6. Submit the screen shots to your instructor.

Improving Notebook Performance ■■■■■■■■■■■■

Windows 8 collects a variety of system settings useful to road warriors in an item of the Control Panel called Windows Mobility Center. Mobility Center provides the settings you need for activities such as choosing another power management method, syncing, and working with settings for presentations.

Using the Windows Mobility Center
Open Windows Mobility Center via the Control Panel.

Here's How

To start Windows Mobility Center:

1. Open the Control Panel.
2. Click *Hardware and Sound*.
3. Click Windows Mobility Center.

As shown in Figure 16.6, Windows Mobility Center provides a centralized location to adjust settings for Brightness, Volume, Battery Status, Screen Orientation, External Display, Sync Center, and Presentation Settings.

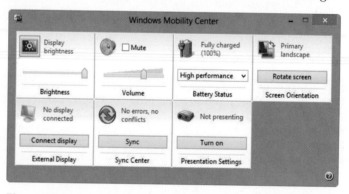

Figure 16.6 Use Windows Mobility Center to access settings you work with often on your mobile computer.

If you have not yet set up sync partnerships, click Sync Settings to do so. If sync partnerships are in place, a Sync button appears; click the button to sync files immediately. Click the button in the *Wireless Network* section to turn wireless networking on and off, a feature you might use for security reasons. You also can adjust the display brightness here and connect to an external display. When you finish using Windows Mobility Center, click its window Close (X) button to close it and then close the Control Panel.

Viewing and Managing Battery Power
One important factor to manage for a mobile computer is its power consumption when it is not plugged in to a power outlet. Battery charge life has not improved by leaps and bounds in recent years as have other aspects of computer efficiency, so it pays to make sure the system has the right power settings if you know you will be away from a power source for some time.

When you use your mobile computer on battery power alone, get in the habit of moving the mouse pointer over the Battery Meter icon in the system notification area. When you do so, information about the current battery level (or battery levels, if your mobile computer has two batteries) pops up, as shown in Figure 16.7. If the battery gets low, a battery alarm appears prompting you to plug in quickly.

You can choose another power plan to help conserve battery power or not, depending on what you are currently doing with your mobile computer. Windows 8 offers the following default power plans, which generally work by adjusting system (CPU) performance.

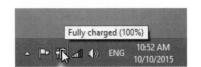

Figure 16.7 Check your mobile computer's battery level frequently in the notification area.

- **Balanced.** Adjusts the CPU speed based on the programs you are using. This setting works in general-purpose circumstances.

- **Power saver.** Reduces system performance to conserve power. You might use this setting if you are away from power for some time and are performing less intense activities, such as typing a letter or working on a spreadsheet. This setting is not available on the Battery Meter icon's menu.

- **High performance.** Consumes the most power but allows maximum system performance in situations when you need it. For example, you might use this setting if you are delivering a presentation that includes animations and video, which consume a lot of power. This setting may not be available on some portable computers.

Windows 8 enables you to use one of a couple of methods to change to another power plan on your mobile computer.

Here's How

To change power plans on a mobile computer:

1a. Click the Battery Meter icon, click the desired power level, and then click the desktop.
OR

1b. Open the Windows Mobility Center, open the drop-down list in the *Battery Status* section, and then click the desired plan.
OR

1c. Open the Control Panel, click *Hardware and Sound*, and then click Power Options. Click the desired power plan.

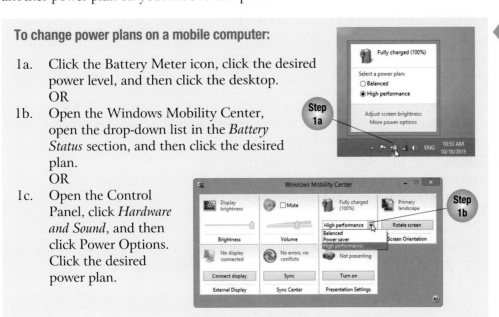

Certain parts of the mobile computer hardware can be power hogs. For example, on many mobile computers, the display consumes more power than other parts such as the hard disk or CPU. You can edit plan settings and create custom power plans that manage how long the system can be idle before the display shuts off or the computer goes to sleep. (Chapter 12 presented the details about creating and managing power plans.) As a reminder, you can find power plan settings by opening the Control Panel, choosing either *System and Security* or *Hardware and Sound,* and then clicking Power Options.

Note: *The exercises in the remainder of the chapter assume that you have access to a mobile computer, either your own or one provided by your instructor for class use.*

Managing Mobile Computer Battery Life

1. Unplug the mobile computer so that it is running on battery power.
2. Wait a few minutes and then move the mouse pointer over the Battery Meter icon in the notification area.
3. Capture a screen shot of the battery level and then save the file as **C16E04S03**.
4. Click the Battery Meter icon in the notification area.
5. Click *High performance*. If that is not one of the choices, click *More power options*. In the Power Options dialog box, click Show additional plans and then click High performance.
6. Capture a screen shot showing the power plan selections and then save the file as **C16E04S06**.
7. Click the desktop.
8. Change back to the prior power plan.
9. Submit the screen shots to your instructor. If you plan to continue using the computer, plug it back in.

Conducting a Presentation ▬▬▬▬▬▬▬▬▬▬▬▬▬▬

Sharing information over a network or the Internet works for many purposes. But sometimes, you need to deliver your message in person. Mobile computers enable you to carry your on-screen presentation with you and deliver it to the people who need to see it, whether you are trying to land a new client, report results at the home office, or train a group of colleagues about a new procedure. This section presents the mobile computing features that help you present more effectively on the road.

Setting Up the System to Present

As noted previously, a key time when you do not want the monitor powering down or other such interruptions is when you are delivering a live presentation. Windows 8 enables you to tell the system that you are delivering a presentation. When you do so, the system does not sleep or shut down, and no pop-up notifications appear in the notification area. You also can turn off any screen saver in use, change volume, and display an alternate background for the desktop.

Here's How ➤

To turn on presentation settings:

1. Open the Windows Mobility Center.
2. In the *Presentation Settings* section, click Turn on.

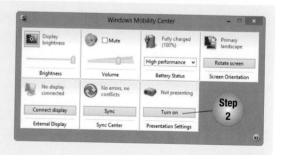

To turn on and adjust presentation settings:

1. Open the Control Panel, click *Hardware and Sound*, and under the Windows Mobility Center heading, click Adjust settings before giving a presentation.
2. Mark the *I am currently giving a presentation* check box.
3. Adjust other settings as desired.
4. Click OK.

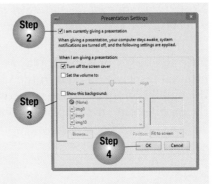

After you turn on presentation settings, an icon for presentation settings appears in the notification area. Double-click the icon to reopen the Presentation Settings dialog box to make changes. You also can right-click the icon and then click *Stop Presentation* to turn off presentation settings.

The Windows Mobility Center also includes settings you might want to use when presenting, and using it is a good option because you can minimize and maximize it easily to change settings. You can drag the Volume slider to change system volume. If you already made changes in the Presentation Settings dialog box and merely want to turn those presentation settings on and off, you can click the Turn on/Turn off button in the *Presentation Settings* section.

Displaying a Presentation on a Projector or Other External Device

When you deliver a presentation, it is increasingly common to connect to a larger external monitor or projector to deliver the presentation at a size that is more visible to audience members. Windows 8 offers functionality to ensure that an external display is connected and functioning in the manner that you need.

To work with an external display:

Here's How

1. Connect the display to the external display port on the mobile computer and then power on the display, if needed.
2. Open the Control Panel, click *Appearance and Personalization*, and then click Display.
3. In the pane at the left, click *Project to a second screen*.
4. In the panel that appears at the right, select one of the options provided.

Note: *Depending on the nature of the display you connect, Windows 8 may automatically change the color scheme or other display settings.*

If you choose to show the presentation on the second screen only, you can press the fn key plus the display key (one of the function or F keys with an external display icon on it in the same color as the label on the fn key button) on the mobile computer to toggle between showing the presentation externally, on the mobile computer display, or both.

Exercise 5

Working with Presentation Settings

1. Open the Control Panel, click *Hardware and Sound*, and then click Adjust settings before giving a presentation (under Windows Mobility Center).
2. Mark the *I am currently giving a presentation* check box, if it is not already marked.
3. Click the *Set the volume to* check box and then drag the slider to the right to set the volume to 70 or so, according to the pop-up tip that appears.
4. Capture a screen shot and then save the file as **C16E05S04**.
5. Click OK.
6. Close the Control Panel window.
7. Right-click the presentation settings icon in the notification area.
8. Capture a screen shot with the icon menu choices open and then save the file as **C16E05S08**.
9. Right-click the presentation settings icon in the notification area again, if needed, and then click *Stop Presentation*.
10. Submit the screen shots to your instructor.

Working with Power Conservation Options on a Mobile Computer ▪■▪▪▪▪▪▪▪▪▪▪▪▪▪▪▪▪▪▪▪▪▪▪

Chapter 1 explained that the sleep and hibernate modes help conserve power while preserving information for when you are ready to resume work. These features are worth a second mention for mobile computer users because power conservation becomes critical when using the system on the road. These modes reduce the mobile system's power consumption to 1–2 percent of the norm.

Using Sleep Mode

When you put the system to sleep, Windows 8 saves your files and information about which programs are open both in system memory and on the computer's hard disk (or just system memory for a mobile computer); then it puts the computer in a lower-power state. (It does not shut the computer down.) When you wake up the system, your programs and files reappear on the desktop after a brief time, as little as several seconds.

Your work remains secure when the system is asleep because if your account is password-protected, you must enter the password when you wake up the system. Unauthorized users therefore cannot wake up your computer and pry. You also can set up the system to go to sleep after a particular timeframe. If you then leave the computer unattended, it saves and secures your work automatically, plus saves power.

To put a computer to sleep, display the Settings charm, click the Power icon, and then click Sleep.

On many mobile computer models, you can use the hardware power button to put the system to sleep, as well. In the Control Panel's Power Options, you can specify what the power button on the computer does; you can configure it to make the computer power down, sleep, or hibernate, for example.

When the computer goes to sleep, the computer's power and disk lights may remain on, and the hardware power button might blink slowly. To wake up the computer, press the hardware power button quickly. If a sign-in screen prompts you to enter your account password, type your password in the *Password* text box, and then press Enter or click the arrow button at the right of the *Password* text box.

Adjusting Sleep Settings

By default on a mobile computer, if you leave the system in sleep mode for three hours and the battery power gets too low, sleep mode makes sure all of your work is saved to the hard disk and then shuts down the system. Also, by default you can put the system to sleep by shutting the computer's lid. Open the lid to wake it back up as usual.

You can change this functionality to suit how you use your mobile computer. You can change how the power button and lid work with sleep in the Control Panel.

One of the options you can choose for what happens when you press the power button or close the lid is Hibernate. As you may recall from Chapter 1, Hibernate copies the contents of RAM to the hard disk and then shuts down, for quicker wake-up than when booting from scratch.

To change power button and lid behaviors on a mobile computer: ◄ **Here's How**

1. Open the Control Panel, click *Hardware and Sound*, and then, under Power Options, click Change what the power buttons do.
2. Choose the desired mode from each drop-down list as needed.
3. Click Save changes.
4. Close the Control Panel window.

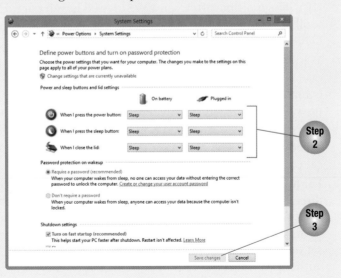

- Synchronization (or sync) is the process of keeping multiple copies of the same file (on different computers) matched with each other. In Windows 8, syncing is handled via the Sync Center.

- Open the Control Panel, click the *View by* down-pointing arrow, click *Large Icons*, and then click Sync Center to start the Sync Center.

- To sync, a folder or file must be marked as available for offline use. To mark a folder or file as such, right-click the folder or file and then click *Always available offline*. (If the command is unavailable, the Offline Files feature needs to be enabled, as described in the section "Making Network Files Available Offline.")

- You can sync a portable device such as a digital music player, PDA, or compatible mobile phone with the Sync Center. With the Sync Center open, attach the device to your system and then power it on. In the Tasks list at the left side of the Sync Center, click *Set up new sync partnerships*, click the device to add in the list that appears, and then click Set up above the list. This establishes the sync partnership and performs the first sync.

- To schedule synchronization, select the item to schedule, click the Schedule button in the Sync Center, and then follow the prompts to set up a specific time and interval.

- To initiate a manual sync, select the item to sync and then click the Sync button in the Sync Center.

- To resolve a sync conflict, open the Sync Center, click *View sync conflicts* in the Tasks list, click a conflict on the list, and then click Resolve. Select the version you want to keep or choose to keep both versions.

- You can switch to offline viewing when browsing the Web in Internet Explorer (IE). To go offline after you have viewed a web page, click File on the IE toolbar and then click *Work Offline*. To resume working online, click File, *Work Offline* again.

- With a Remote Desktop connection, you can connect to another computer over the local network or the Internet. Not only can you access files on the computer, but you also can use the programs installed on that computer and possibly other resources, such as printers, if the network permits.

- The computer that stores the files, programs, and other resources to access is called the *host*. The computer that accesses the host from a remote location is called the *client*.

- For a Remote Desktop connection to work, both computers must be connected directly to the company network or connected remotely to the company network, the Internet, and on the same workgroup. The network must allow permission for this type of connection. Windows Firewall also has to be set on both computers to allow Remote Desktop as an Exception. Also, if authentication is not required, then that security feature must be turned off on the host computer.

- Open the Control Panel, click *System and Security*, and then click Allow remote access (under System) to set up your computer to enable Remote Desktop connections.

- You can specify which users are allowed to connect to your system remotely.

- To connect to the host via Remote Desktop Connection, run *Remote Desktop Connection* from the All apps list on the Start screen. In the Remote Desktop Connection dialog box, type the name of the computer to connect to on the network. Click Connect and then enter your user name and password when prompted.

- Windows Mobility Center provides the settings you need for mobile computer activities, such as choosing another power management method, syncing, and working with settings for presentations.

- To start Windows Mobility Center, open the Control Panel, click *Hardware and Sound*, and then click Windows Mobility Center.

- When you use your mobile computer on battery power alone, get in the habit of moving the mouse pointer over the Battery Meter icon in the system notification area to monitor remaining battery power.

- You can choose another power plan to help conserve battery power or not, depending on what you are currently doing with your mobile computer. To change power plans, click the Battery Meter icon, click the desired power level, and then click the desktop.

- Windows 8 enables you to tell the system that you are delivering a presentation so that the system does not sleep or shut down and pop-up notifications do not appear in the notifications area. You also can turn off any screen saver in use, change volume, and display an alternate background for the desktop.

- To turn on presentation settings, open the Control Panel, click *Hardware and Sound*, and then click Adjust settings before giving a presentation (under Windows Mobility Center). Mark the *I am currently giving a presentation* check box. Adjust other settings, as desired, and then click OK.

- When Windows 8 does not automatically detect an external display, or after you have set one up with the New Display Detected dialog box, you can choose *Connect to a Projector* (from the Start screen, from All apps) and then make a choice to connect to the monitor.

- The sleep and hibernate modes help conserve power while preserving information for when you are ready to resume work.

- To put a computer to sleep, display the charms, click the Power icon, and then, in the menu that appears, click *Sleep*. To wake up the computer, press the hardware power button. If a sign-in screen prompts you to enter your account password, type your password in the *password* text box, and then press Enter.

CONCEPTS CHECK

Completion: Answer the following questions in a Word document.

Part 1

Multiple Choice

1. How do you access the Sync Center?
   a. from the Control Panel
   b. from Device Manager
   c. from your Documents library
   d. any of the above will work

2. Where do you go to enable offline files?
   a. Network and Sharing Center
   b. Sync Center
   c. Start screen
   d. Devices and Printers

3. You are prompted to _____ the system after you disable offline files.
   a. sleep
   b. hibernate
   c. backup
   d. restart

4. What do you have to create when you want to use the Sync Center to sync a portable device?
   a. Bluetooth connection
   b. Outlook file
   c. Sync partnership
   d. Network share

5. When you want to sync a location automatically at a later time, what can you do?
   a. Create a synchronization schedule
   b. Open Device Manager
   c. Start Windows in Safe Mode
   d. Adjust the Power Options

6. The _____ enables you to change common mobile computer settings.
   a. Sync Center
   b. Network and Sharing Center
   c. Add Device Wizard
   d. Windows Mobility Center

7. Changing the _____ adjusts the rate at which the mobile computer depletes the battery.
   a. display resolution
   b. power plan
   c. power button behavior
   d. screen saver

8. Enable _____ to reduce on-screen interruptions during a presentation.
   a. ratings
   b. captions
   c. presentation settings
   d. presentation pointers

9. Attach a(n) _____ to a mobile computer to give a presentation.
   a. external monitor
   b. digital camera
   c. projector
   d. Either a or c

10. Use the _____ to wake a sleeping system.
    a. Start screen
    b. computer's power button
    c. charms' power command
    d. Close (X) button

Part 2

Short Answer

11. Explain briefly how Offline Files works.

    _____

12. Explain how to make a file always available offline.

    _____

13. Suppose you have a file set up to be always available offline, and the network is down. Where can you go to see your files?

    _____

14. What causes a synchronization conflict to occur?

    _____

15. What is Remote Desktop Connection for?

    _____

16. How do you un-maximize (restore) a remote desktop connection window?

    _____

17. Explain one way to check battery power status.

    _____

18. Explain how to display Windows Mobility Center.

    _____

19. Explain the benefit of enabling presentation settings.

    _____

20. Why would you want to sleep a mobile computer?

    _____

SKILLS CHECK

Save all solution files to the default Documents folder or any alternate folder specified by your instructor.

Guided Check

Setting Up Offline Folders and Sync

1. Set up a folder for viewing offline.
   a. Open File Explorer.
   b. Click *Network*.
   c. Navigate to the folder on the network.
   d. Right-click the folder.
   e. Click *Always available offline*.
2. Capture a screen shot.
   a. Right-click the synced folder again.
   b. Capture a screen shot of the window and then save it as **C16A01**.
3. Close the window.
4. Submit the screen shot to your instructor.

Managing the Synchronization Schedule

Note: *This assessment assumes that Offline Files is set up (see Exercise 1), and a sync is scheduled.*

1. Start the Sync Center.
   a. Open the Control Panel.
   b. Click the *View by* down-pointing arrow and then click *Large icons*.
   c. Double-click Sync Center.
2. Click Offline Files.
3. Click Schedule and then click View or edit an existing sync schedule.
4. Click the schedule name and then click Next.
5. Mark all of the check boxes, if they are not already marked, and then click Next.
6. Select today's date and then select a time 15 minutes from now.
7. Clear the *Repeat every* check box.
8. Capture a screen shot of the window and then save it as **C16A02S08**.
9. Click More Options.
10. Mark the *The computer is no longer running on external power* check box.
11. Click OK.
12. Click Next.
13. Capture a screen shot of the window and then save it as **C16A02S13**.
14. Click Save schedule.
15. Submit the screen shots to your instructor.
16. Wait for 15 minutes and then watch for sync activity on the system.
17. Delete the sync schedule.

Disabling and Enabling Offline Files
   1. Start the Sync Center.
      a. Open the Control Panel.
      b. Click the *View by* down-pointing arrow and then click *Large icons*.
      c. Double-click Sync Center.
   2. Click *Manage offline files*.
   3. Click Disable offline files.
   4. Enter an administrator password in the User Account Control dialog box, if it appears, and then click Yes.
   5. Capture a screen shot of the Offline Files dialog box and then save it as **C16A03S05**.
   6. Click OK.
   7. Click Yes to restart the system.
   8. Reopen the Sync Center and then click *Manage offline files*.
   9. Click Enable Offline Files.
  10. Enter an administrator password in the User Account Control dialog box, and then click Yes.
  11. Capture a screen shot and then save it as **C16A03S11**.
  12. Click Yes to restart the system.
  13. Submit the screen shots to your instructor.

Choosing Another Power Scheme in Mobility Center
   1. Start Windows Mobility Center.
      a. Open the Control Panel.
      c. Click *Hardware and Sound*.
      d. Click Windows Mobility Center.
   2. Change to the Power saver power plan.
      a. Open the drop-down list in the *Battery Status* area.
      b. Click *Power saver*.
      c. Capture a screen shot and then save it as **C16A04**.
   3. Close the Windows Mobility Center.
   4. Close the Control Panel window.
   5. Submit the screen shot to your instructor.

On Your Own

Synchronizing Files for a Trip
Suppose you are going on a trip and taking your notebook computer with you. You need to make sure that all the data files for this course have up-to-date copies on the notebook computer's hard disk. Describe step by step how you would do the following:
   • Make the data files from the desktop computer available offline to the notebook computer.
   • Manually synchronize the files before you leave on your trip.
Record the detailed steps to make these things happen, save the file as **C16A05**, and then submit it to your instructor.

Viewing Offline Files
Suppose you are on your trip and need to look at the files you synced in Assessment 5. Record the detailed steps to do so, save the file as **C16A06**, and then submit it to your instructor.

Showing Mobile Computer Content on Another Display

This exercise requires a mobile computer and an external monitor or projector. If you do not have access to a mobile computer and external monitor, your instructor may provide them, and you can work in teams to complete this assessment.

1. Start Windows Mobility Center on the mobile computer.
2. Power on the external monitor or projector.
3. Connect the monitor or projector to the display port on the mobile computer.
4. Open the Control Panel, click *Appearance and Personalization*, and then click Display.
5. In the pane at the left, click Project to a second screen.
6. Caputre a screen shot and then save it as **C16A07**.
7. Reopen the panel by repeating Step 5 and then click Extend. Note how the display changes between the two monitors.
8. Reopen the panel again and then choose Duplicate. Note how the display changes between the two monitors.
9. Reopen the panel again and then choose PC screen only.
10. Disconnect the external display and then turn it off.
11. Submit the screen shot to your instructor.

Change Sleep Settings, Sleep, and Restart

This assessment requires a mobile computer.

1. Open the Control Panel, choose *Hardware and Sound*, and then, under Power Options, click Change battery settings.
2. Click *Choose what closing the lid does*.
3. In both the *On battery* and *Plugged in* columns, open the *When I close the lid* drop-down list and then click *Sleep*.
4. Capture a screen shot and then save it as **C16A08**.
5. Click Save changes, but leave the Control Panel window open.
6. Close the lid of the mobile computer.
7. After a few moments, open the lid and then press the hardware power button to turn the system back on.
8. If prompted, type your password and then press Enter.
9. Submit the screen shot to your instructor.
10. Change the *When I close the lid* setting back to its original setting (if it was not *Sleep*) and then close the window.

CHALLENGE PROJECT

You are working at home and have the ability to connect to your office computer with a Remote Desktop connection. In a Word document, describe the overall process for setting up and making a Remote Desktop connection, and list at least two reasons why you would do so. Save the file as **C16A09S01** and then submit it to your instructor.

If possible, you and a classmate connect over a network and make a Remote Desktop connection to each other's computer. Capture a screen shot, save it as **C16A09S02**, and then submit it to your instructor.

Glossary

accelerators A feature in IE that enables you to perform tasks with selected content, such as mapping a selected location or performing a search for a selected term

active content Online content that is interactive or animated; also loosely refers to pop-ups and certain downloads that may be required to run such content

active (current) window The working window on the screen, in which you can make selections and perform other actions

adware A type of malware that pops up ads or redirects your web browser

Align icons to grid A feature that snaps an icon into alignment with a desktop grid when you move the icon

app bar The bar that displays available command choices at the top or bottom of an app when you display commands

application or program A set of instructions for performing a particular task or set of tasks, such as word processing or drawing a picture

apps Short for applications; a program that performs a useful task for the user

arranging Summarizing the items in a library into stacks based on a property

attributes On/off flags set for a file, such as read-only

Auto arrange icons A feature that arranges desktop icons to fill the desktop grid slots in order

auto-hide A feature that hides the Taskbar unless the mouse pointer is over the Taskbar location

Autorun.inf An instruction file that tells Windows what to do (for example, run a setup utility) when the disc is inserted

bad sector A sector on a disk surface from which the drive cannot read, write, or read and write data

binary A numbering system consisting of only 1 and 0

Bing The latest Internet search engine from Microsoft

Bing suggestions A feature that enables Bing to suggest searches that are more specific based on the search term you enter

bit A single binary digit

Blu-ray A high-capacity type of DVD that stores 5 GB of data per layer

Bluetooth A type of short-range, wireless interface designed to allow computers and devices to communicate without cables

browse Displaying and reading web pages in whatever order suits you

byte A group of eight bits forming a single character of information

CD Stands for compact disc; a removable, optical disc that stores about 700 MB of data

charm A new type of hidden icon that enables you to access Search, programs, system settings, and more

Check Disk A Windows-based utility for finding and fixing physical and logical errors on a disk

client An end-user computer in a network

client/server A type of network in which one or more servers administers the network, providing services to client computers

close To remove a file from the program window and working memory

cloud computing Working via various services and data storage locations online, so that you can access those tools and information from any Internet-connected computer or device

command An action that you tell a program to perform

command prompt A line of text displayed by an operating system to indicate that it is prepared for you to type in commands

Compatibility View A view in Internet Explorer that enables it to better display sites and pages designed for older browser versions

compression Using an algorithm that reduces file size

compression algorithm A mathematical formula used to remove wasted space in a file so that it takes up less space on the disk

contact A listing including the email address and other contact information of a person entered in the People app

contextual tab A tab that appears to offer additional commands and choices for a selected object

control A type of selection mechanism in a dialog box

Control Panel The central location where you can change system preferences and settings

cookie A small, plain text file that stores your settings for a specific website

CPU Stands for Central Processing Unit; the main microchip that serves as the brain of the computer; also called the processor

crash A situation in which a program ceases to operate normally

default gateway The IP address of the port that leads out of your local subnet and into the larger network or the Internet

defragment To reorganize the file storage on a disk drive so that as many files as possible are stored contiguously

desktop The starting point for file-management activities in Windows 8, where you can view and organize information

device driver Software that works with Windows to send and receive instructions for a particular hardware device

Dialog box launcher A button found at the lower right corner of a group on a ribbon tab that you click to open a dialog box

digital camera A device that captures pictures and stores them on digital storage media

digital picture An image or picture saved in digital format for use in computer documents and web pages

disk compression A means of decreasing the amount of space that files occupy on a disk by storing them more compactly

disk drive A mechanical device that reads and writes disks

display adapter A circuit board or built-in component to which the monitor attaches and which translates between the computer and the monitor

domain A client/server network running Windows Server software on the server

dual-layer disc A type of DVD that stores data in two layers, enabling it to approximately double its capacity

DVD Stands for digital versatile disc (or digital video disc); a removable, optical disc that stores about 4.7 GB of data per layer

email Short for electronic mail; provides the ability to send and receive digital messages via a wired or wireless network, or more broadly, the Internet

email account In the Mail app, a collection of settings that enables the program to send and receive email for a variety of different email account types, including Gmail (Google), Yahoo!, Hotmail, and Outlook (including Exchange)

email address The identifier that specifies where an email address should be delivered, including a user name, the @ symbol, and the domain. For example, janet22@emcp.com (pronounced "janet 22 at emcp dot com") is the email address for user janet22 on the emcp.com domain

emoticon A small graphic inserted into a message to convey tone or emotion, such as a smiley face icon

event A time period for which you have scheduled a particular activity in Calendar

exiting or shutting down Closing a program to remove its instructions and open files from RAM

extended partition A secondary partition, in addition to the primary partition(s)

FAT16 A 16-bit file system, now mostly obsolete, used with MS-DOS and Windows 95

FAT32 A 32-bit file system, now mostly obsolete, used with Windows 98 and Windows Me

favorite page A frequently visited website or page that is saved in the list in the Favorites Center for easy access

file Digital information that you create and save with a name for later retrieval; a file may include programming instructions, an image, text, or any other type of content; also called a document

file attachment A file created in a program other than your email software that you designate to be sent with an email message

File Explorer The file management interface in Windows 8

file list The area in a folder or library window that shows the files and folders in the folder or library

file name extension A period and additional letters appended to the file name to identify the file format

file property Information about a file or information attached to a file

file system A set of rules for how the operating system stores and retrieves files on a disk

file system error An error or discrepancy in the way the disk's file system keeps track of storage locations

filtering Displaying only certain items based on a property

firewall Software or hardware that prevents unauthorized access to ports

first-party cookie A cookie placed on your hard disk by the website you are visiting

flash card reader An internal or USB drive that reads and writes removable flash RAM cards

flash RAM A static type of memory used as an alternative to disk storage

floppy disk A flexible, plastic disk encased in a hard, square, plastic shell that holds 1.44 MB of data

folder An organizing unit for storing related files together in groups; also called a location

font A typeface—a style of lettering—appearing either on the screen or in print

fragmented file A file that is stored in multiple noncontiguous clusters on a hard disk

gestures Windows 8 actions that enable you to manipulate items on touch-enabled devices, with equivalent mouse actions for traditional computers

graphics tablet An external input device that generally connects to the computer via a USB port and with which you can select commands, give user input, and draw images using a stylus (pen)

group A named set of individual users to which the same permissions are assigned

grouping Arranging items into grouped sections of a list based on a property

guest account A limited-access user account designed to be used by anonymous users who do not have a regular account on the computer

hang When the computer appears to freeze up and stop working during a particular operation

hard disk drive A sealed drive unit that contains a set of metal disks

hard reboot or restart Restarting the system by powering it off and back on

hardware Physical computer parts

hibernate A more advanced shutdown state that saves your work and shuts the system down; your in-process work reappears on the desktop when you restart your system

history An IE feature that tracks websites and pages you have visited within a recent time period—by default, the previous 20 days

homegroup A connected group of Windows 8 (or Windows 7) computers in a home (P2P) network

host The computer that holds the files, programs, and resources to be used during a Remote Desktop connection

hot-pluggable Able to be connected or disconnected while the computer is up and running

hyperlink An item on a web page that you click to display another web page or to download information

hypertext A document format or system in which the document contains links to other content

icon A small picture that represents an item (object) or choice in Windows 8 and Windows programs

Inbox The Mail account folder that holds email messages you have received

indexing A process that creates an index, an internal information set about a location, used to enable faster searching

Internet Protocol (IP) address A numeric address that uniquely describes the address of a computer or other network-aware component on a network or on the Internet

Internet time server A website that provides highly precise times

intranet A private network, usually within a company or organization, that uses the same types of content and the same protocols as the Internet

Jump List A menu of frequently used documents and commands that you can access for a program via the Taskbar

junk email Like paper junk mail, these are commercial email messages sent to you without request; also called spam

junk email filter A Hotmail and Gmail feature that automatically moves likely junk email messages to the Junk email folder

library A location for working with a particular type of file; each library may monitor a number of storage locations to identify and track a particular type of file such as a digital picture

Live File System A type of CD and DVD file system that enables discs to be written to multiple times

local account A type of Windows 8 user account that does not connect automatically to the cloud or sync settings between the different systems you use

local area network (LAN) A network in which the computers are near one another, such as in the same building

local file permission The permission to access a file belonging to another user on the same computer

local printer A printer attached directly to your computer

lock A state that hides the desktop without shutting down the system or changing its power consumption

Lock screen The screen that appears when you lock your system or wake it from sleep or hibernate

magnetic disk A disk platter that stores data in patterns of magnetic polarity

mail server A computer with software that enables it to manage email sending, receiving, and storage

maintenance window The specified time of day at which scheduled maintenance activities occur

malware A generic term for software that is designed to harm your computer

master file table (MFT) The table of contents for a disk formatted with the NTFS file system

Mastered A type of CD and DVD file system that requires files to be written to the disc all at once

MathML An XML-based standard for describing mathematical expressions in programs, published by the W3C Math Working Group (www.w3.org/Math)

maximize To increase a window to full-screen size

menu A list of commands, usually appearing along the top of a window or as a list when you click a button or icon

message body The text of an email message, entered or viewed in the message screen

message header The key message information, including date sent, sender, recipient(s), and subject; also called the email header

Message list pane The pane that lists the email messages in the currently selected folder in the Accounts and folders pane

message screen The area where you compose and address an email message in the Windows 8 Mail app; also called a composition screen

metadata Information attached to a file that provides descriptive data such as the author's name

Microsoft account A type of Windows 8 user account that automatically connects to the cloud to take advantage of online storage, apps, and syncing features

minimize To reduce a window to a Taskbar icon to temporarily clear it from the desktop

modem Short for modulator/demodulator; a device that converts between digital computer data and analog sound wave data that can be transmitted via telephone and cable TV lines

mouse A device on which you roll and then press buttons to control a desktop or notebook computer

mouse pointer The on-screen graphical indicator whose movement corresponds with your movement of the mouse so that you can select objects

multifunction device (MFD) A printer that also has other functions, such as scanner, copier, and fax machine

multitask The ability of Windows 8 to have multiple activities processing at the same time, such as having multiple programs running and multiple windows open simultaneously

network A group of connected computers

network attached storage (NAS) An external hard disk that is accessed through a network interface

network-aware printer A printer with a built-in network interface card, capable of connecting directly to the network without going through a computer

network Interface card (NIC) A circuit board, or a built-in component on a motherboard, that provides network connectivity for a computer

network printer A printer attached to your network or shared by another computer on your network

network sharing permission The permission to access a file stored on a different computer

nonvolatile A type of storage that does not lose its data when not powered

notification A message that pops up in the notification area to warn you about a situation that may require action or a settings change

NTFS Stands for New Technology File System; a 32-bit file system for Windows 2000, Windows XP, Windows Vista, Windows 7, and Windows 8 that offers improvements over older file systems

Offline Files Network files that are locally cached (saved) on your hard disk so that copies are available even when the network is not functioning; also refers generically to the copies of the network files stored on your local computer

open To load a file into the program window and working memory

OpenXPS A portable document format from Microsoft that enables you to create an OpenXPS (.oxps) document from any program by printing to the Microsoft XPS Document Writer

operating system (OS) The interface software that enables a user to work with system hardware and other software installed on the computer system

operating system files Files that the operating system (Windows 8) needs to start the system and keep it running

optical disc A disc platter that stores data in patterns of reflectivity

Outbox The Mail account folder that holds email messages that you have composed but not sent

parent The location immediately above the current one in the drive hierarchy

partition To logically divide the space on a physical hard disk into one or more logical drives

password A secret series of characters that must be entered to access an account or make changes

patch A program update intended to fix a problem with the original version of the program

path The complete location of a file, including its disk letter and the folders in which it is located

Peek thumbnail A thumbnail image of a file that pops up when you point to the minimized file's Taskbar button

peer-to-peer (P2P) A network consisting only of client computers

persistent cookie A cookie that remains on your hard disk indefinitely; also called a saved cookie

personal folder The parent folder holding folders for a user's account

pin Designating an item such as a program or file to appear as a tile on the Start screen or as a button on the Taskbar for easy access

plain text (.txt) A file format for document files that does not allow for or save any text formatting information

playlist A list that specifies a group of songs for Media Player to play and the order in which to play them

Plug and Play (PnP) A standard that enables Windows to recognize and configure hardware automatically

pop-up An extra window that appears automatically as a result of a certain web page being displayed

port A numbered software channel that directs network input and output

primary partition A bootable partition; a disk drive must have at least one primary partition

print to a file A method of converting a file to a more easily shared format

printer driver The printer control file that interprets print information from an application

private network A network in which you know and trust all of the other computer users in the network

public network A network in which you do not know or trust all of the other computer users in the network

RAM Stands for Random Access Memory; the working menu that holds programs and unsaved work

rating Assigning a certain number of stars to a file to identify how much you like it or how important it is

recipient A person to whom you are sending an email message

refresh rate The rate at which the display redraws the image on the screen

registry The configuration database that contains the settings that Windows needs to recognize your installed hardware and software and to recall your user interface preferences

resolution The dimensions of the current display size setting, expressed in pixels (dots) wide by pixels tall

resource conflict A conflict between two devices that both try to claim the same resource, such as a certain IRQ or memory address

restore To return a window to its size before it was maximized

restore point A copy of the system files from a certain point in time

ribbon An enhanced tabbed toolbar in which each tab offers commands for a particular overall activity and groups commands for more specific activities

Rich Text Format (.rtf) A basic document file format that preserves some text formatting

rip Copy music from an audio CD and convert the songs to digital format

RJ-45 connector A plug, like a telephone plug but slightly wider, used to connect a computer to a network

root directory The top level of a disk, outside of any of its folders

router A type of switch that directs traffic between different segments of a network

RSS (Really Simple Syndication) feed Regularly updated website information, such as news or pictures, which a user can visit or subscribe to; also called XML feeds, syndicated content, and web feeds

Safe Mode A startup mode that loads only the essential device drivers and does not load any of the programs that are scheduled to load at startup

save To preserve a file's information on disk

save location The folder where a library will physically store any file or folder created or copied to the library

search engine A website/service that uses an index method to track and retrieve web documents that match specified terms

secure site A website that uses a secure protocol, https://, rather than the usual http:// to ensure that the communication is not intercepted or hacked

server A computer dedicated to administering the network

session cookie A cookie that is automatically deleted when the browser window is closed; also called a temporary cookie

Shake A feature that enables you to minimize several open windows at once by dragging the title bar for the window you want to keep open side to side at a rapid pace

Share contract The Windows 8 app contract that enables apps to share (exchange) information

shared printer A locally installed printer on a computer that has been set up to be shared with others

shortcut A pointer icon to the original file that it represents

sign out To exit your user account and desktop without shutting down the system

signed driver A device driver that has been certified to work under a certain Windows version

sleep A power-saving state that preserves your work in memory and on the hard disk so that you can resume working quickly

slide show A feature that automatically displays on the screen each picture from a folder in sequence

snail mail Slang term for postal mail; derived from the fact that postal mail is slow relative to email

Snap A feature that enables you to maximize or resize a window automatically by dragging the window to the edges of the screen

soft reboot or restart Using a menu command, keyboard combination, or reset button to restart the system

software A computer program that typically performs a specific activity

solid state drive (SSD) A high-capacity flash RAM storage device that acts as a hard disk drive in a system

sorting Arranging items in a particular order based on a property

spyware A type of malware that spies on your computer usage

SSID Stands for Service Set Identifier; the name of the wireless access point or router

Start screen The Windows 8 screen that enables you to access your apps and cloud-based features; also the starting point for app and system activities in Windows 8

stream To play back music from another computer or digital media receiver on your network

strong password A password that is difficult to guess; it must have at least six characters and use numbers, capital and lowercase letters, and special characters

subnet A group of computers that shares a common top-level identifier, similar to the telephone numbers in an area code

subnet mask A numeric code that indicates what part of the IP address represents the subnet and what part represents the individual address of the computer

switch A box into which computers connect that directs network traffic among the computers

switch A forward slash and a letter or phrase code that specify a further aspect of how a command line command should run

sync To make sure a connected device or mobile computer has the same up-to-date files as your main computer

system resources Areas of memory, interrupts, and/or DMA channels that are assigned to devices so that they can communicate with the system

System Restore A utility that enables you to roll back the system files to previously saved versions

tablet PC A type of laptop computer on which you can select commands and give other user input using a stylus (tablet pen) or sometimes a finger

Taskbar A bar at the bottom of the desktop that you use to manage active tasks

template A file with formatting and possible starter content that becomes the basis for a new file

terminal adapter A communication device that sends and receives all digital networking data, such as for a cable or DSL Internet connection

theme A named collection of appearance settings you can apply to the Windows 8 desktop

third-party cookie A cookie placed on your hard disk by an advertisement on a website you are visiting

tile The box representing an app on the Windows 8 Start screen

title bar The bar at the top of a windowed application that lists the program name, as well as the name of any open file, and has controls for working with the window

toggle A command or feature that can remain in an "on" (toggled on) or "off" (toggled off) state

touchpad A built-in control device on a mobile computer or notebook computer that you can use instead of a mouse

URL (Uniform Resource Locator) The address of a web page

USB flash drive A USB drive with a flash RAM chip permanently embedded

user account The user name, password, settings, permissions, and restrictions that govern how Windows 8 allows a particular user to work with the system

User Account Control (UAC) The overall Windows 8 security component that works with user accounts to prevent unauthorized system changes

user input device A device, such as the mouse and keyboard, that enables you to give commands to and enter information into a computer

User Switching Changing between user accounts without shutting down files or programs for any signed-in user

viewer application An application that can read files printed or converted to a particular type of file format

virtual folder A temporary logical grouping of files, such as the files resulting from filtering or searching

virtual private network (VPN) A secure software tunnel that runs from one computer to another using the Internet as its conduit

virus A self-replicating, malicious program that spreads from one executable file to another

visual suggestions Enhanced search functionality provided by a search partner that enables the search suggestions list to include images and information

volume label A text description stored on the disk and displayed in the disk properties in Windows

web browser A program that enables you to view and retrieve information from the World Wide Web

web mail A service that enables you to access your email through a web browser rather than a standalone email program

web page An HTML file (web document) stored in a particular location

Wi-Fi The popular name for the 802.11 wireless RF standard, encompassing variants including 802.11b, 802.11g, and 802.11n

wide area network (WAN) A network in which the computers are physically separated, such as in different buildings or cities

window An independent frame that holds a program, document, or folder contents

Windows 8 apps Apps designed specifically for Windows 8, optimized for use on touchscreen devices and for a cleaner look and feel

Windows Media Audio (WMA) The default file format to which Windows Media Player converts and saves song files

Windows Update A free service from Microsoft that downloads the latest patches, fixes, and updates from Microsoft's servers for Windows 8 and other Microsoft products

wireless access point (WAP) A switch for wireless networking

workgroup A peer-to-peer, Windows-based network

World Wide Web A structure of linked documents stored on Web server computers connected to the Internet

worm A self-replicating, malicious program that spreads from one computer to another, infecting the computer itself rather than any individual file

Index

optical disc, 58
optical media, 68. *See also* CDs (Compact Discs); DVDs (Digital Video Discs)
Option buttons, **22,** 23
Organize tools, copying/moving using, 102–103
orientation (monitor), 447
Outbox, defined, 307
Outlook
    accessing with home.live. com, 300
    changing spam settings, 314
    contact syncing, 316
    icon, 318, **318**
    managing messages, 312, 314
    using Mail app, 300

P

Paint, creating basic pictures, 170–181, **181**
palettes, drop-down, 22, **22**
panes
    Details, 85, **85**
    Navigation, 84, **84,** 86, **86**
    Preview, 85, **85**
    resizing, 143
parallel interfaces, 439
parent, 88, **88**
partitioning, 75–76, **76**
password reset disk, 501–502
passwords
    case-sensitivity, 8
    changing account, **500,** 500–501
    clearing, 282–283, **282–283**
    picture, 37
    saving reset data, 501–503, **502**
    strong, 35, 500
pasting
    after error message, 184
    digital pictures, 333
    in email messages, 304
patch, defined, 438
paths, 87, 241
Peek, using to preview desktop, 225
peeking, 17, **17**
Peek thumbnails, 24, **24**
peer-to-peer (P2P) networks, 369–370. *See also* workgroups
pen, adjusting, 206
People app
    addressing email, 302, **303**
    working with contacts, **316,** 316–319
PerfLogs, 87
Performance Information and Tools utility, 492–493, **492–493**
permissions, 152–154, **153, 154**
persistent cookies, 279
personal folder, 91–93, **92**
personal information, removing, **149,** 149–150
personalization, customizing

from Control Panel, 202, **202**
Photo Gallery
    adding folders using, 340, **340**
    applying information, 344–345, **344–345**
    closing, 339
    correcting images, 342–343, **343**
    deleting images, 341
    downloading, 338, **339**
    emailing images, 344
    importing images, 339–340, **339–340**
    opening, 338
    organizing images, 341, **341, 342**
    printing images, 346, **346**
    viewing images, 341, **341**
Photos app, 332, 334, 347–349, **348, 349**
picture passwords, 37
pictures. *See also* digital pictures
    creating with Paint, 170–181, **181**
    user accounts, 39
Pictures library
    adding folders, 340, **340**
    applying information, 344–345, **344–345**
    playing contents on TV, 337–338, **338**
    printing images, 346, **346**
    as screen savers, 336
    slide shows, 336
    viewing pictures, 333–335, **334**
    zipping pictures, **336,** 336–337
pin, defined, 218
pinching, described, 6
PING, 391–392, **391–392**
pinned items, 15
pinning
    apps to Start screen, 217–219, **218**
    programs to Taskbar, **221,** 221–222, **222**
    web pages to Start screen, 262, **262**
    websites to Taskbar, 257, **257**
PINs
    creating longon, 38, **38**
    managing, 39
plain text (.txt) format, 173, **173**
Player Library
    adding files, **350,** 350–351
    redisplaying, 354
playlists
    building, 353, **353**
    burning to CD-R or DVD-R, 356
    playing, 354
Play tab, 351
Plug and Play (PnP)
    adding devices, 445–446
    defined, 439
podcasts, 355
pointer devices, described, 4
pointers (mouse), changing

appearance, 205
pointing, described, 4
pop-up, defined, 274
pop-up blockers, configuring, 274–275, **275**
ports, 284
Power button, 417
power-conserving features, signing in, 7
power settings plans, 414–415, **415, 416**
presentations, conducting, **530–531,** 530–532
pressing and holding, described, 6
Preview pane, 85, **85**
    displaying, 141–142, **142**
primary partition, 75
Print command, 20
printer driver
    defined, 167
    installing, 439–441, **440–441**
    removing, 443, **443**
printers
    choosing default, 441–442, **442**
    controlling queue, 470–471, **470–472**
    installing, 167, 439–441, **440–441**
    interfaces, 439
    Microsoft XPS Document Writer, 169, **169**
    multifunction, 439
    network, 386–388, **387–388**
    removing, 443, **443**
    settings, 442
    shared, 386
    troubleshooting, 168, 469–472, **469–472**
    viewing queue and status, 469–470, **470**
printing
    digital pictures, 346, **346**
    email messages, 316, **316**
    files, 167–169
    single page, 14
Print Preview, 168
print to a file, defined, 167
privacy
    blocking and allowing cookies, 279–281, **280–281**
    configuring preferences, 278–284, **279–283**
    configuring tracking protection, 278–279, **278–279**
private networks, 285, 373, 382
processor, **489,** 489–490
Program Files, 87
programs. *See also* apps; software; Windows 8 apps
    changing file name extension assignments, 434–435, **435**
    closing, 163, **163**
    controlling automatic startup, 436–438, **437–438**
    copying data from files in different, 183–185, **184**
    defined, 161

incomplete uninstalls, 430, 431
installing, 428, **428, 429**
installing updates, 438–439
notification area to work with, 16
opening from Control Panel, 202, **202**
opening from Start screen, 12
opening with Search charm, 13, 162
pinning to Taskbar, **221,** 221–222, **222**
removing, 430–431, **430–431**
searching for, **12–13,** 13, 162, **162**
setting default, 434–435, **435**
troubleshooting problems, 428, 432–433, **432–433,** 460–462, **460–462**
using Compatibility mode, 432–433, **432–433**
protocols, 241
public folders, 382, **383**
public networks, 285, 373, 382

Q

Quick Access Toolbar, 84, **84**

R

RAM (random access memory)
    additional with ReadyBoost, 413–414, **414**
    defined, 162, 489
    flash RAM, 58, 59, **59**
    tracking usage, 494, **494**
ratings, applying, 344, **344**
read-only files, 148
ReadyBoost, 413–414, **414**
Recent locations button, 88, **89**
recipients, 301–302, **302**
Recordable (R) discs, 70
recording speed, 72
Recycle Bin, 121
    bypassing, 122
    configuring, **124,** 124–125
    emptying, 124
    permanently deleting from, 123
red eye (images), 343
redisplaying
    Player Library, 354
    windows, 24
Refresh button, 240, **240,** 246, **246**
refreshing Windows 8, 467–468, **468**
refresh rate, defined, 209
region, opening from Control Panel, 202, **202**
registry
    defined, 428, 463
    entries for automatic startup, 437
reinstalling Windows 8, 467, 468
Remote Assistance, using, 477–480, **478–479**
Remote Desktop, 524–526, **525–527**

web pages
    adding to Favorites Center list,
        254–255, **254–255**
    browsing, 244–246, **244–246**
    defined, 241
    delivering to IE, 258–259, **259**
    going to, 242–243, **242–243**
    going to favorite, 256, **256**
    loading finicky, 240
    opening in new tabs, **247,**
        247–248
    pinning to Start Screen, 262,
        262
    secure, 272
    viewing offline, 523, **523**
websites. *See* web pages
wheel (mouse), changing scroll,
    205
wide area network (WAN), 369
Wi-Fi vs. wired networks, 370
wildcards, using in searching,
    114
windows
    changing color and appear-
        ance, 208–209, **209**
    closing, 29, **29**
    defined, 23
    maximizing, 25, **25,** 26
    minimizing, 23–24, **24,** 25, 26
    moving, 27–28
    moving between, 28, **28**
    opening more than one, 95

redisplaying, 24
resizing, 26, **26,** 27
restoring, 25, **25**
Windows 7 backup set, using,
    468
Windows 8 apps
    about, 9, **10**
    closing, 31, 189
    commands, 29–30, **30,** 189
    installing, 428–429, **429**
    installing updates, 438–439,
        439
    interface, 29–31, **30**
    snapping, 31, **31**
    starting, 189
    switching between, 30, **30**
    uninstalling, 431, **431**
    viewing all open, 189–191,
        190, 191
Windows 8 interface. *See also*
    File Explorer
    apps, 29–31, **30**
    buttons, 18
    charms, 11–12
    desktop, 11
    dialog boxes, 22–23
    icons, 17–18
    opening a program, 12–13
    other menus, 19–20
    ribbons, 20–21
    Start screen, 9, 11
    Taskbar, 14–17

windows, 23–29
Windows 8 personal folder,
    91–93, **92**
Windows 8 versions, 490
Windows Defender, 286–289,
    287–288
Windows Firewall, 284–286,
    284–286
Windows Journal, using, 176,
    176, 177
Windows Media Audio (WMA),
    350
Windows Media Player
    adding files, **350,** 350–351
    browsing songs, 351
    building playlists, 353, **353**
    burning playlists to CD-R/
        DVD-R, 356
    Music app, 349
    opening and exiting, 350
    playing playlists, 354
    rating songs, 351, **351**
    ripping songs, 351–353, **352**
    syncing to portable device,
        354–355, **355**
Windows Mobility Center, 528–
    529, **528–529,** 531
Windows Update
    changing settings, 404–406,
        405–406
    defined, 403
    installing updates, 406–407,

    406–407
    opening, 403–404, **404**
    removing update, 407–408,
        408
    reviewing history, 407, **407**
wired networks, 370
wireless access point (WAP), 371
wireless networks
    connecting and disconnecting,
        374, 374–375
    security, 270, 375
WordPad, formatting text files,
    174, 174–175
workgroups, 369–370, 373–374
Working with People address
    autocompletion, 302
World Wide Web. *See also* Bing;
    Internet Explorer (IE)
    defined, 239
    searching, **249–250,** 249–
        253, **252–253**
worms, 287–289
writable CD drive, 58, 60
writable DVD drive, 58, 60

X
Xbox LIVE accounts, 349

Z
zipped files, 306